# Private Property Loss in the War of 1812

## Also by Greg H. Williams and from McFarland

*The U.S. Navy at Normandy: Fleet Organization and Operations in the D-Day Invasion* (2020)

*The Last Days of the United States Asiatic Fleet: The Fates of the Ships and Those Aboard, December 8, 1941–February 5, 1942* (2018)

*The United States Merchant Marine in World War I: Ships, Crews, Shipbuilders and Operators* (2017)

*The Liberty Ships of World War II: A Record of the 2,710 Vessels and Their Builders, Operators and Namesakes, with a History of the* Jeremiah O'Brien (2014)

*World War II U.S. Navy Vessels in Private Hands: The Boats and Ships Sold and Registered for Commercial and Recreational Purposes Under the American Flag* (2013)

*The French Assault on American Shipping, 1793–1813: A History and Comprehensive Record of Merchant Marine Losses* (2009)

*Civil War Suits in the U.S. Court of Claims: Cases Involving Compensation to Northerners and Southerners for Wartime Losses* (2006)

*World War II Naval and Maritime Claims Against the United States: Cases in the Federal Court of Claims, 1937–1948* (2006)

*Civil and Merchant Vessel Encounters with United States Navy Ships, 1800–2000* (2002)

# Private Property Loss in the War of 1812

*A Catalog of Compensation Claims*

GREG H. WILLIAMS

McFarland & Company, Inc., Publishers
*Jefferson, North Carolina*

**ISBN (print) 978-1-4766-5859-9**
**ISBN (ebook) 979-8-3686-0105-2**

LIBRARY OF CONGRESS CATALOGING DATA ARE AVAILABLE

Library of Congress Control Number 2026014671



Printed in the United States of America

*McFarland & Company, Inc., Publishers*
*Box 611, Jefferson, North Carolina 28640*
*www.mcfarlandpub.com*

The United States are bound by the Constitution to repel and protect each State from invasion. This being the duty of the United States, the right to occupy necessary stations, and to call to their aid all necessary means for the protection of the army and property of the Government, in cases of emergency, must be admitted. This right is believed to extend, when necessary, to the forcible taking of ships, boats, teams, provisions, &c., always paying a reasonable compensation for the use of property, and the value for what is not returned; but no collateral damage can, in any case, be allowed.

These are some of the necessary inconveniences under which individuals hold their property in the several States of this Union; and if their interests are sometimes prejudiced by reason of the necessary exercise of it by the Government, it is their misfortune, and one for which Government does not hold itself accountable.

The Committee of Claims, February 29, 1840

# Table of Contents

*Preface* 1

*Introduction* 3

The First Congress 7

The Northern Frontier 11

Vermont 44

Connecticut 50

The District of Maine 54

The Michigan Territory 63

Illinois 102

Indiana 110

Ohio 115

The Niagara Frontier 132

Pennsylvania 209

The Chesapeake Campaign 213

Missouri 307

Kentucky 310

Tennessee 315

The Mississippi Territory 317

Georgia 329

Louisiana 331

*Appendices* 361

The Lost, Captured, or Destroyed Property Act of April 9, 1816 361

Amending the Act of April 9, 1816 362

War of 1812 Restitution for Slaves 362

Claims Filed for Vessels at the Treasury Department Under the Act of March 2, 1827 368

The Court of Claims 369

*Bibliography* 371

*Index* 373

# Preface

Historians have devoted little attention to the property losses of the civilian populations who were caught in the middle of the wars on American soil, or who might even have been the actual targets of the enemy, or whose property was sacrificed for the exigencies of war.

The claims by owners of private property for reimbursement for property that was captured, damaged, destroyed, or taken for public use during the Revolutionary War were initially considered by the Board of Treasury, but while Congress had genuine sympathy for the sufferers, there was no legislation to guide payments and no money was available for compensation in any case, so very few were ever settled.

The records of claims appear in the Board of Treasury reports of the Continental Congress, the Statutes at Large, the American State Papers, and the Congressional Serial Sets.

Under the auspices of Congress, Richard Peters, Esq., collected all the Public Acts, Private Acts, Resolutions, and Treaties that were passed by Congress and arranged them chronologically into the Statutes at Large, first published in 1789. Money allocated or expended by Congress for public purposes was passed as a Public Act and for the benefit of persons as a Private Act, as in the case of satisfying a claim.

The American State Papers, edited and compiled by Walter Lowrie, Secretary of the Senate, and Walter S. Franklin, Clerk of the House of Representatives, likewise by authority of Congress, include a volume of Claims, with an index, published in 1834 for the years 1789 to 1809.

During the 15th Congress in 1817, a number of books, serially numbered on the spine, were published to document the work of each session of Congress and include House and Senate Committee Reports on claims with an index of names. As the claims became more numerous, they were published in separate volumes. The actual Serial Set volumes, which include many maps and foldout pages, will be found only in federal depository libraries. Most volumes have been reproduced digitally for online use, but generally only the texts themselves are available.

The claims for this book were found by a page-by-page search of the Statutes at Large and the Congressional Serial Set from volume No. 1 to volume No. 512, the 1st session of the 30th Congress, convened on December 7, 1847. No new claims from the War of 1812 were found after the 29th Congress. It is believed that all, or most, of the paid claims have been found. Most of the claims that were disallowed and reported are included for historical interest and statutory aspects.

Claims filed by active duty military for real property lost or damaged and merchandise belonging to Army sutlers and Navy pursers are also included since the courts recognized their stock as personal property and, in the case of pursers, not associated with their military service. Sutlers were civilians who obtained permission from Army commanders to sell merchandise to soldiers on or near a post or a station or within the confines of a fort. Pursers in the Navy aboard ship were commissioned officers who, in addition to their official duties, sold goods they purchased with their own money to crew members at a small profit.

Most of the original Private Acts and Committee reports are very sketchy in detail so an effort has been made to provide more information about them and the people involved. In that regard, thanks are due to Katy Sternberger, Research Librarian and Archivist at the Portsmouth Athenaeum in Portsmouth, New Hampshire; Jean London at the Hampden, Maine, Historical Society; Nam Jin Yoon at the Columbia Law School library for help in sorting out old legal and text problems; Scout Noffke, Reference & Special Administrative Specialist, Dartmouth College, Rauner Special Collections Library; Justin Kline, Access Services Assistant at Louisiana State University; and the Naval Academy's Nimitz Library.

Recorded history is a combination of fact, fiction, speculation, and opinion created by participants, observers, researchers, or those with an agenda. It is intended that the myriad events related in this book are reasonably accurate and that no person or situation is misrepresented in any way.

# Introduction

In the earliest days, whenever possible as circumstances allowed, American commanders gave certificates or vouchers to the owners of private property taken for government use, often with an estimated value, in case a future claim was presented.

On February 20, 1782, a commissioner was appointed for each State to examine claims and a somewhat complicated schedule involving depreciation and other burdensome factors was published to settle accounts. The Confederation of Congress had no money to pay claims for damages and resolved on June 3, 1784,

> that it be referred to the several States, at their own expense, to grant such relief to their citizens, who may have been injured, as they may think requisite; and if it shall hereafter appear reasonable that the United States should make any allowance to any particular States, which may be burdened much beyond others, that the allowance ought to be determined by Congress, but that no allowance be made by the commissioners for settling accounts for any charges of that kind against the United States.

Alexander Hamilton directed the commissioners to "make reasonable allowance for the use of stores and other buildings hired for the use of the United States, by persons having the authority to contract for the same, but that rent not be allowed for buildings which, being abandoned by the owners, were occupied by troops of the United States."

Apparently, residents who fled in terror from their homes on the approach of the enemy were considered to have "abandoned" their buildings. As he further stated:

> According to the laws and usages of nations, a State is not obliged to make compensation for damages done to its citizens by an enemy, or wantonly or unauthorized by its own troops; yet, humanity requires that some relief should be granted to persons who, by such losses, are reduced to indigence and want; and, as the circumstances of such sufferers are best known to the States to which they belong, that it be referred to the several States (at their own expense) to grant such relief, to their citizens, who have been injured, as they may think requisite; and if it shall hereafter appear reasonable that the United States should make any allowance to any particular States who may be burdened much beyond others, that the allowance ought to be determined by Congress; but that no allowance be made by the commissioners for settling accounts, for and charges of that kind against the United States.

Reasonable compensation was to be allowed for wood, forage, or other property used "upon producing satisfactory evidence thereof, by the testimony of one or more disinterested witnesses." Eventually, property impressed or occupied for the use of the government by order of a military officer or government agent came under the Fifth Amendment.

On November 13, 1794, the House of Representatives established a formal Committee of Claims and a Committee on Military Affairs to review petitions from citizens and recommend action by Congress. The Committees were very jealous of the public purse and full documentation and evidence were required, as would be in a fact-finding court of law. In time, several other Committees were added.

To deal with the very numerous claims for specific classes of losses of a similar nature from civilians, active duty military, militia in the service of the United States, and widows and orphans, Congress wrote laws as Public Acts outlining the requirements under which relief could be granted within a specified period of time.

Attorneys became aware of the new laws. They were published in newspapers to inform the public, but not everyone got the news and some were minor children when the loss occurred.

The process for filing a claim could be simple and quick or very complicated and time consuming. Claimants either sent their petition and supporting documents to their representative in Congress or hired an attorney. All petitions and statements of witnesses and officers or agents of the government had to be taken under oath, generally by a justice of the peace. The claimant's representative introduced a bill for relief in the House, which was then referred to the appropriate Committee. The Committee often requested additional information which meant finding and deposing witnesses or obtaining documents from the Treasury, War, or Navy Department.

Most claims from the War of 1812 with strong evidence were resolved soon after the war and through the 1820s. After that, the children of the principals contested claims into the 1830s and then, infrequently, the grandchildren into the 1840s. Claims at that late date were rarely approved due to a statute of limitation or lack of evidence. To complicate matters, the British burned the Treasury Building in 1814, and in 1833 an arson fire destroyed more records.

After all the evidence was presented, the Committee wrote a report and a recommendation to Congress. The report was published and Congress debated the matter and voted as a Committee of the Whole to approve or reject the recommendation of the Committee. In some cases a rejected claim was approved many years later.

In approving the allocation of money for a Private Act, Congress either specified the amount to be paid out of the Treasury or directed the appropriate accounting officers to investigate the actual loss and determine the amount due. The money came from the Treasury, War, or Navy Department and was generally made available during the current or the next fiscal year, and the claimant or their legal representative had to go to Washington to collect the money.

## *A Note on Language and Text*

In dealing with handwritten and printed material from this time period, different spellings of the names of the same people or geographical locations often occur in documents that might have been transcribed, revised, or printed several times. In most cases, names and places have been corrected from the original text when necessary for convenience.

The written language at the time was very different from the structured grammar we use today. For easier reading, common spellings of the day like defence, connexion, and enterprize have been converted to modern spellings, and capitalization has also been added where it would normally be used today. Text was often composed in large blocks without any breaks, so this material has been edited to be more readable to modern eyes.

The language in public documents was notoriously and unnecessarily superfluous. All dates and monetary values were often spelled out in full, which increased the volume of text enormously, and there are often enough commas in one document to fill a lake. Much of this original text has been edited to eliminate unnecessary verbiage, while retaining all of the relevant and factual information.

At the time of the Revolution, very few people had a middle name, but by the War of 1812 the practice had become fairly common. This helps in identifying people, but even so, in written and published documents people were almost always referred to by their last name only, or sometimes their initials, which often makes it difficult to identify persons. In order to minimize confusion and to reconcile names more easily, first names have been inserted into the original text where none appeared originally, but still, some identities remain uncertain.

In the interest of simplicity and convenience, the claims are arranged by geographical region, more or less in accordance with the flow of the war, but this arrangement is somewhat arbitrary as events were occurring at the same time in different regions of the nation.

# The First Congress

The first Congress was scheduled to meet at the City Hall in New York City at present-day 26 Wall St. on Wednesday, March 4, 1789, and not all members showed up, but there were enough to conduct business.

The first session began in New York City as scheduled on March 4, 1789, and continued to Tuesday, September 29, 1789. George Washington was President, John Adams, Vice President, and Gen. Henry Knox, Secretary of War.

## *The War Department Established*

As stated on August 7, 1789:

> There shall be an executive department to be denominated the Department of War and that there shall be a principal officer therein, to be called the Secretary for the Department of War, who shall perform and execute such duties as shall from time to time be enjoined on, or entrusted to him by the President of the United States, agreeably to the Constitution, relative to military commissions, or to the land or naval forces, ships, or warlike stores of the United States, or to such other matters respecting military or naval affairs, as the President of the United States shall assign to the said department, or relative to the granting of lands to persons entitled thereto, for military services rendered to the United States, or relative to Indian affairs; and furthermore, that the said principal officer shall conduct the business of the said department in such manner, as the President of the United States shall from time to time order or instruct.

Section 4 authorized the Secretary of War to take custody of all records, books, and papers of the War Department.

## *The Treasury Department Established*

Congress created the Treasury Department September 2, 1789. All public documents, and copies of public documents, made their way to the Treasury Department, or were supposed to be there. The act of March 3, 1817, authorized four Auditors who provided the Committee of Claims with copies of receipts, vouchers, and certificates issued by officers in the field for services provided or merchandise or property impressed for public service. As stated, in part:

> It shall be the duty of the First Auditor to receive all accounts accruing in the Treasury Department, and, after examination, to certify the balance and transmit the accounts, with the vouchers and certificates, to the First Comptroller, for his decision thereon.
>
> It shall be the duty of the Second Auditor to receive all accounts relative to the pay and clothing of the army, the subsistence of officers, bounties and premiums, military and hospital stores, and the contingent expenses of the War Department.
>
> It shall be the duty of the Third Auditor to receive all accounts relative to the subsistence of the army, the quartermaster's department, and, generally, all accounts of the War Department other than those provided for, and to examine the accounts which he shall receive, and certify the balance, and transmit

> the accounts, with the vouchers and certificates, to the Second Comptroller, for his decision thereon.
>
> It shall be the duty of the Fourth Auditor to receive all accounts accruing in the Navy Department, or relative thereto.

Most property losses came to the attention of the Third Auditor. Peter Hagner, 45, who started as a clerk in 1793, was appointed to that position and served until 1849.

## *West Point*

On July 31, 1786, Gen. Henry Knox, head of the War Department, reported to Congress that a parcel of land in New York called West Point was of such strategic importance that it should be retained as a permanent military post, "in case of an invasion of any of the Middle or Eastern States by a marine Power."

The land belonged to Stephen Moore. Secretary of the Treasury Alexander Hamilton responded to say that "so much of the tract of land called West Point, as shall be judged requisite for the purpose of such fortifications and garrisons as may be necessary for the defense of the same" should be purchased.

Moore had to file a claim to get his money, and in 1790, after he had moved to North Carolina, he was paid $11,085 for the property actually occupied by the Army.

## *The Militia*

On May 8, 1792, Congress passed an act, "to provide for the National Defense by establishing a Uniform Militia throughout the United States." Their organization was to be in conformity with regular Army divisions, brigades, regiments, battalions, and companies, and "every free able-bodied white male citizen of the respective states resident therein, who is or shall be of the age of 18 years, and under the age of 45 years (except as herein excepted) shall severally and respectively be enrolled in the militia by the captain or commanding officer of the company, within whose bounds such citizen shall reside, and that within 12 months after the passing this act."

## *Fort Pontchartrain du Détroit*

The British failed to vacate fortified positions in North America as required under the terms of the Jay Treaty on the pretext of protecting their fur trade from French competitors. On July 11, 1796, Capt. Moses Porter and 65 soldiers of the 1st Artillerists & Engineers removed the British from Fort Pontchartrain du Détroit, which they were supposed to have evacuated.

## *The Navy Department Established*

Congress created the Navy Department on April 30, 1798. Benjamin Stoddert, a merchant from Maryland who had served on the Board of War during the Revolution, was appointed secretary.

## *British Import Bans*

On April 18, 1805, in response to British depredations on neutral American maritime commerce and the impressment of American sailors, Congress banned the importation from England after November 10 of all leather, silk, hemp, flax, tin (except in sheets), brass, woolen hosiery, window and other glass products, silver and plated ware, all paper goods, nails and spikes, hats, ready-to-wear clothing, playing cards, beer, ale, porter, pictures and prints. Bans were lifted and reinstated several times in response to various conditions.

## *The* Chesapeake-Leopard *Incident*

On June 22, 1807, a number of French ships were at Annapolis, Maryland, under siege by a British squadron just offshore. When Master Commandant Charles Gordon's 42-gun American frigate *Chesapeake* came out to join Commodore James Barron's squadron for a Mediterranean cruise, Capt. Salusbury Pryce Humphreys, the commander of the 52-gun frigate *Leopard,* was waiting for him. The crew of the *Chesapeake* was still in the process of securing for sea and stowing gear for an extended cruise and they weren't in any shape for a fight.

Humphreys sent a message over saying he was looking for five British deserters he was told had enlisted for the *Chesapeake* at the rendezvous at Norfolk and most likely had changed their names. He identified them as John Strachan, Daniel Martin, William Ware, Jenkin Radford, and George Tincombe, and said he had orders to remove them.

John Straughan (Strachan), a native of Queen Anne's County, Maryland, had enlisted for a term of one year and was from Captain Gordon's area, the Eastern Shore of Maryland. Daniel Martin was a free black man from Philadelphia, and William Ware was from Massachusetts. All three told Captain Gordon they had been pressed from American merchant ships and were forced to serve aboard the *Melampus.*

Refusing the demands of a British commander at that time always brought some form of gunfire, and when the *Leopard* opened fire, John Lawrence, James Arnold, and John Sheckley were mortally wounded and eight were variously wounded, including Captain Gordon.

The incident inflamed American passions and on July 2, President Jefferson ordered all British ships out of American waters.

The British, never ones to respect international law or custom, responded on October 17 to say they would continue kidnapping anyone they pleased. The practice had been fully endorsed by Lord Nelson as a necessary measure to man the ever-expanding British fleet as they built an empire, "upon which the sun never set."

## *Tecumseh*

On November 7, 1811, American forces under Indiana Territory Gov. William Harrison attacked Indians led by Tecumseh at a river near present-day Battle Ground, Indiana, in retaliation for depredations against settlers. What became known as Tippecanoe prevented Tecumseh from consolidating tribes against American expansion, but also resulted in driving many Indians into Canada where they later joined the British. Tecumseh was righteously angered over the Treaty of Fort Wayne where he asserted the Indian participants were plied with alcohol to induce them to relinquish millions of acres of land. He later stated, "Eleven debt-ridden, whiskey-soaked 'treaty chiefs' do not have the authority to sign agreements for lands they do not own or have authority over."

## *The War Hawks*

Political intrigue, French deception, British efforts to foment Indian rebellions on the frontiers, and continued impressment of American sailors created the "War Hawks" in Congress and a spirit of righteous indignation emerged throughout the country, except in New England, where secession was threatened if war came. They believed their maritime trade would be totally devastated by war with England.

As tensions with the United States increased, British fur traders in Upper Canada began recruiting Indians to assist them in defeating the United States should war come, using the promise of spoils, and all which that entails, and the return of their lands to them. When it was revealed that British agents were trying to get New England and Louisiana to secede, President Madison made an appeal to Congress for a declaration of war.

## *War Again*

Congress declared war on June 18, 1812, with a vote of 79 to 49 in the House and 19 to 13 in the Senate even though the Army and Navy were in no condition to fight a protracted war. The public was generally as divided as Congress, but most everyone supported revenge for the *Chesapeake*, an end to British depredations, and the impressment of sailors.

In response to "Mr. Madison's war," riots broke out in Baltimore, residents of the District of Maine east of the Penobscot declared their loyalty to King George III, and New England states refused to call out their militias and began smuggling and selling large lots of provisions to British forces in Canada.

The British ambassador, Sir Augustus Foster, brought the news home along with conditions for peace and diplomatic efforts to resolve the conflicts began.

Most of England's army was occupied in Europe at the time so if diplomatic efforts failed, "chastising Brother Jonathan" would primarily be up to the Royal Navy. Most of the British army and naval officers who arrived in North America were sent from other campaigns around the world, and when they left North America after the war ended, they went to other wars and battles on other fronts.

The initial American plan was to stop an attack from Canada, and it wasn't going well. In August 1812, Adm. John B. Warren was appointed commander in North America and sailed for Halifax on the 14th in his 74-gun flagship *San Domingo* with some expectation that diplomatic efforts might avoid an all-out war.

The American garrison at Fort Detroit surrendered two days later without a fight. Warren sailed for Bermuda for the winter, which was the usual practice, but diplomatic efforts by the admiral failed. On November 11 the New Jersey legislature expressed their opposition.

Parliament's preferred tactic with limited resources was a strict blockade of the entire East Coast, Adm. Warren having only the *San Domingo*, 7 frigates, 9 brigs and sloops, and 5 schooners for the entire station. He was to avoid battles if possible and no occupation or possession of territory was contemplated. On April 20, 1813, Warren arrived off Annapolis.

On April 27, 1813, American army and naval forces defeated British regulars, militia, and Ojibwe Indians at York, present-day Toronto, and in the process a number of unfortunate incidents of arson and looting occurred. Public ordnance and private supplies and provisions were seized and carried away when the Americans left some weeks later. The success at York did not contribute materially to America's ultimate victory in the war, but the looting and arson did have a substantial effect on British conduct later.

On May 26, 1813, Adm. Warren proclaimed the major ports from New York to Mississippi under blockade. He then complained to the Admiralty that he didn't have enough ships to effectively blockade even one port, and his lack of aggressiveness was arousing criticism in Parliament.

# The Northern Frontier

The Northern Frontier was commanded by Gen. Henry Dearborn at Greenbush, New York, until July 6, 1813, when he was succeeded by Gen. James Wilkinson.

In 1807, Jacob Brown was commissioned a captain in the 108th Regiment of New York Militia, and in 1809 made colonel. In 1811 he was appointed brigadier general in the New York Militia and commanded the Army of the Niagara.

New York governor Daniel D. Tompkins ordered Gen. Brown's Lewis, Jefferson, and St. Lawrence County militias to guard the 50-mile local frontier from St. Regis to Ogdensburgh on the St. Lawrence River, and Col. Christopher P. Bellinger's 27th Regiment of New York Militia from the Mohawk Valley was sent to Sackets Harbor.

## *Sackets Harbor (Town)*

A piece of property in a sheltered cove at Black River Bay on Lake Ontario was in foreclosure and was to be sold at auction at the Tontine Coffee House in New York. A New York lawyer and investor named Augustus Sacket became interested in the property and after inspecting the area he concluded it would be a suitable location for a harbor. He purchased the property on June 20, 1801, and began attracting settlers and by the fall of 1802 about 30 families had settled there to farm and fish. In 1803, the first physician, Dr. William Baker arrived and in 1805, several English families arrived.

The harbor was declared a port of entry in 1805 and Sacket became the first Collector of Customs. The town surrounding the actual harbor became known as Houndsville and the next year Sacket became supervisor of the town.

In 1805, Jefferson County was created out of Oneida County and he became known as "Judge Sacket" and a captain of a militia company. In 1809 he moved back to New York, then to Pennsylvania and on April 22, 1827, he died while traveling back to his harbor from Newburgh, New York.

In 1808, Lt. Melancthon Taylor Woolsey was appointed commander of the naval station at Sackets Harbor and commanded the 16-gun brig *Oneida*.

When war came, Woolsey was relieved as commander at Sackets Harbor by Capt. Isaac Chauncey, but retained command of the *Oneida*.

### The *Salina*

In 1809, Attorney Rufus Reed and shipmaster Daniel Dobbins decided to get into the salt trade. The main commodities traded and transported were furs, salt, hemp, and mocock—a type of food container made out of tree bark. They purchased the schooner *Catherine*, which they renamed *Salina*, after the village of Salina, New York, the heart of salt production, and now a suburb of northwestern Syracuse. The salt was put up in barrels and transported to domestic markets or sometimes brought to Mackinac Island and traded for furs, which were then sold at Montreal.

In July 1812, a month after the war started, Dobbins, Rufus Reed, and William Reed happened to be at Fort Mackinac under the command of Lt. Porter Hanks.

After considerable deliberation, Maj. Gen. Isaac Brock, commander of British forces in Upper Canada at Fort Malden, ordered Capt. Charles Roberts, at St. Joseph Island, to seize the fort and on July 17 Lt. Hanks surrendered and the *Salina* was captured and used by the British to haul supplies.

Capt. Roberts paroled the entire garrison and ordered Dobbins and the master of one other vessel to transport his prisoners to Cleveland, about 300 miles to the south, which Dobbins agreed to, and while en route, he put in at Detroit.

Lt. Hanks also left for Detroit, and when arrived he was charged with surrendering Fort Mackinac and in August he was put on trial. When Detroit was attacked on the 16th during his trial, a cannon ball fired from across the river crashed into the room and mortally wounded him.

Gen. William Hull surrendered Detroit that day, August 16, and Dobbins was taken prisoner. He was then in some danger of being prosecuted for violating his parole agreement by not proceeding directly to Cleveland, even if he needed stores or water at Detroit.

As it happened, a British friend Dobbins had known before the war, Col. Robert Nichols, was put in charge of taking the paroled prisoners from Detroit to Cleveland by boat and Nichols made sure Dobbins was aboard one of them, and they arrived after a perilous three-day journey.

At Cleveland, Dobbins managed to find a small sloop and sailed to his home at Presqu'Ile—present-day Erie, Pennsylvania—about 90 miles east, where he arrived on August 24. He related all of these events to his family and after a few days met with Gen. David Mead, the regional militia commander, and made a formal report. Mead then sent him to Washington City to report the situation.

He arrived in early September and a cabinet meeting was called where Dobbins gave a full account of the perilous situation on the Northern Frontier and was asked for his advice on shipbuilding in the area.

Parole was a pledge by a person who accepted it not to bear arms against the captor until formally exchanged, but could engage in recruiting, guarding supplies, and other "internal" duties. Parole had to be voluntary on both sides and could only be offered by a commissioned officer.

## *Shipbuilding*

It was obvious the Great Lakes would be a theater of naval operations and when Daniel Dobbins was in Washington, he was asked if he thought Presqu'Ile would be suitable for a shipyard. He said it would be for building shallow-draft vessels. There were extensive stands of oak and pine, a sawmill, blacksmiths, tradesmen, farms, and stores, and the town of around 400 was protected by an island just offshore, which formed a bay whose only entrance was through a shallow channel across a sand bar, limiting the draft of vessels to six feet.

After some discussion of other locales, President Madison and Secretary of the Navy Paul Hamilton agreed on Presqu'Ile and also believed Pittsburgh, three days away, would answer for a sufficient supply base.

On September 15, 1812, Dobbins was given $2,000 to build four gunboats and the next day he accepted the rank of Sailing Master in the Navy.

Around the same time, Capt. Chauncey was appointed commander of naval forces on Lake Ontario and Lake Erie, with headquarters at Sackets Harbor along with a shipyard. He sent Master Commandant Jesse D. Elliott and Lt. Samuel Angus to set up a naval station at Black Rock, near Buffalo, New York, and take control of Lake Erie.

Chauncey and Elliott were initially opposed to building ships at Presqu'Ile and others thought Black Rock was a better site. Even though Dobbins was already given funds for his operation by Washington, he got no formal authority from Commodore Chauncey to start. Dobbins employed all the skilled workers he could, bought materials with the money he had, and in November hired master shipwright Ebenezer Crosby.

On January 1, 1813, Chauncey and the famous shipbuilder Henry Eckford visited Presqu'Ile. Both approved of the site and Chauncey authorized Dobbins to purchase timber and build two sloops-of-war. Shortly after, around March 10, Noah Brown, a master shipbuilder arrived from New York with 25 carpenters.

For local defense, Capt. Thomas Forster had about 60 local citizens, but when Capt. Oliver Hazard Perry arrived on March 27 from Black Rock he became alarmed at the security situation and immediately sent for Gen. David Mead, the regional militia commander, and in short order 1,000 militia were encamped and later reinforced with several hundred Pennsylvania Volunteers.

In April 1813, the 4-gun *Ariel* was launched; the 20-gun *Lawrence* on May 21; the 2-gun *Scorpion* and 3-gun *Porcupine* that spring; and the 20-gun *Niagara* that summer. Owing to the exigency of the situation, the shipwrights were forced to build with green, unseasoned lumber, but that doesn't seem to have affected their performance, although the crews probably carried an extra supply of caulking material. The 16-gun *Oneida*, 24-gun *General Pike*, 20-gun *Madison*, and 16-gun *Sylph* were built at Sackets Harbor.

The harbor was attacked again on May 29, 1813, and resisted by the 1st Regiment of Light Dragoons.

In June 1813, Perry gave Dobbins command of the 1-gun storeship *Ohio*, a schooner the Navy purchased and converted at Black Rock.

The Sackets Harbor Battlefield State Historic Site, 504 W. Main St. in Sackets Harbor features costumed interpreters, demonstrations, a picnic area, and tours.

## Charles Douglass

As reported by the Committee of Claims on December 21, 1821:

> The petitioner represents that some time previously to the declaration of the late war against Great Britain, he had a considerable quantity of goods, then purchased and lying in the province of Upper Canada. That, as a citizen of the United States, he wished to secure his property by transporting it within the American lines, as was usual to be done by those placed in situations similar to his. For this purpose, application was made to Cornelius P. Van Ness, collector at Burlington, Vermont, to know whether the goods would be admitted to an entry by bringing them to Burlington. The collector's reply was, he "would permit them to be entered at the custom-house in the usual mode by giving a penal bond and bond for double duties," which was agreed to by the petitioner, and which, he says, was the universal custom by which citizens of the United States secured their property that appeared to be in jeopardy from the enemy, unless they would take the oath of allegiance, which, as an American citizen, he could not do.
>
> His goods, amounting at invoice cost to $12,679, he ordered to be brought to Missisquoi Bay, with an intention of having them transported to Burlington, but while preparations were making, Colonel Isaac Clarke, commanding a corps of riflemen then in the service of the United States, crossed with his men to Missisquoi Bay, seized the whole of the goods, and, without the formality of judicial investigation, divided them among his officers and soldiers. For the loss thus sustained he asks reimbursement of Congress.
>
> The committee have had no evidence that the goods in question were *bona fide* the property of the petitioner. It seems, indeed, a

little surprising that a merchant of the city of New York should, some time previously to the war, have imported goods through the province of Lower Canada, and suffered them to remain there so long as the year 1812. Mr. Van Ness, who has favored this claim with his certificate, seems careful to remark that he knew nothing of the manner in which Mr. Douglass became possessed of the goods.

On the supposition, however, that he was *bona fide* the owner, it does not follow that Colonel Clarke was bound to know the fact in an enemy's country, or that it could reasonably be presumed he would know it. If, therefore, it was lawful for him to take enemy property in the country of the enemy, the committee think it would be equally so for him to take the property of our own citizens found in the country of the enemy, and situated as it appears the property was at that time. On the other hand, if it was not lawful to take, when it was thus situated, the property either of the enemy or our own citizens, the committee think the taking of the goods in this instance by Colonel Clarke was an act performed on his own personal responsibility, for which he alone, not the government is liable to the petitioner.

The prayer of the petitioner ought not to be granted.

Baie Missisquoi is the part of Lake Champlain north of the border with Québec, Canada.

## The *Lord Nelson*

British subject James Crooks was a merchant at Fort Niagara and in 1792 was joined there by his brother, William. In 1795 they moved to New Ark, present-day Niagara-on-the Lake, where they operated a gristmill and distillery and owned the trading schooner *Lord Nelson*, built in 1811.

On June 5, 1812, the *Lord Nelson* was proceeding peacefully on a lawful voyage from Prescot, on the St. Lawrence River, to New Ark. The *Oneida* was on patrol when lookouts spotted them, and Lt. Melancthon Woolsey decided to seize the vessel, "for a pretended violation of the laws of the United States," and escorted them into the harbor.

Sackets Harbor was very vulnerable to attack and Woolsey kept a lookout at his masthead. On July 19, five British sloops-of-war were spotted, "beating up the bay." The alarm was sounded and Gen. Brown's militia was sent to reinforce the 27th Regiment.

The same day, 127 members of the 21st Regiment of Infantry "marching down the Northern lakes to Sackett's Harbor" were captured by the British and sent to Québec.

Capt. Woolsey stated the ships were under the command of Commodore Hugh Earl, "a provincial officer," on the Provincial Marine ship *Royal George*, 20 [guns]. The other ships were the *Earl of Moira*, 18, schooner *Prince Regent*, 10, and *Seneca*, 1.

The British seized a small sloop loaded with flour and the crew was sent ashore with a message from the commander demanding the *Lord Nelson* and the *Oneida*. It said he did not wish to attack, but if a shot was fired he would burn the town. Earl was unaware of a 32-pounder mounted on shore under the charge of Sailing Master William Vaughn. The demand was refused and the squadron soon felt the effects of 24-pound shot, the largest available. After two hours, the *Royal George* was hit with the loss of eight sailors, and they decided to shove off.

William Vaughn is credited with firing the first shot of the war.

The *Lord Nelson* and cargo were libeled in a prize court on August 26. The cargo of glass, gunpowder, oil, canvas, scythes, 100 iron bars, 7 barrels of flour, and other general merchandise was sold by the marshal for $1,972.10. The schooner was sold to Capt. Woolsey on behalf of the United States for $2,999.25, and "annexed to his squadron, armed, and was used against the British during the war." The schooner was reported lost some time later.

William and James Crooks both served in Canadian militia units during the war and then filed a claim for the loss of their schooner.

James and William sued the United States in district court and were awarded all the funds from the sale, but on July 11, 1817, Theron Rudd, the clerk of the court, "absconded with all the funds of the court, and no part thereof was paid to the owners of the *Lord Nelson*." The amount embezzled was around $80,000.

On February 11, 1819, the Committee on Finance awarded the owners $4,243.32, but apparently no money was paid, and the case dragged on for decades. A commission appointed by Secretary of the Navy Mahlon Dickerson found the vessel was worth $5,000 and the cargo $2,943.76. The United States finally refused to accept liability for the unlawful act of Lt. Woolsey.

## William Cogswell

As reported by the Committee of Claims on February 18, 1820:

> The petitioner states that he was an inhabitant of Upper Canada at the commencement of the late war, served the British two months, took protection under the American forces, gave information where some British public property was secreted, which was taken by the American troops, had to fly from Canada and lost his property and papers. He afterwards remained on the lines and served with American parties.
>
> Your committee are of opinion that the rewards of such persons for such services should be secret, and that it does not become the Legislature of a great, just, and honorable nation, by its acts, to reward any kind of treachery. The prayer of the petitioner ought not to be granted.

## Israel Ellsworth

As reported by the Committee of Claims on February 14, 1834:

> The petitioner states he moved into Canada from the State of Vermont in 1810 and purchased a farm of 125 acres, and remained in Canada until after the declaration of war in 1812, when he was enrolled in the militia and draughted into the service, but refusing to take the oath of allegiance, and also refusing to take up arms against the United States, a prosecution was commenced against him, which was carried to final judgment, and his property was confiscated and sold, whereby he lost all he had, amounting to $1,200.
>
> He returned to the State of Vermont where he has since resided. He prays, in consideration of his sacrifices, that Congress will grant him relief.
>
> Several persons who are acquainted with the petitioner have signed a certificate stating he is a person of good moral character, and that they have no doubt his statement is true. The deposition of Robert Lawrence supports the allegations of the petition. Joseph Hartcutt, a justice of the peace in the province of Canada, and lieutenant colonel 2nd Regiment of Leeds Militia, certifies that the petitioner left the province in 1813 under arms and that in consequence of it his land was confiscated and sold, worth £175 currency.
>
> The Hon. Mr. Joel Turrill, who presented the petition, mentioned in a memorandum made by him on the papers that additional testimony might be expected.
>
> The committee think it useless to put the party to the trouble or expense to obtain testimony to prove a case which ought not, in their opinion, to be favorably considered if all the facts stated are admitted to be true.
>
> The United States have not made provisions to pay her own citizens who have remained in the country for their property which was destroyed by the enemy during the late war, unless their property was in the military service and lost or destroyed in consequence of being so used. A grant of land was made to the Canadian volunteers, and two or three cases exist where Congress has made donations of lands to those who were residents in Canada and left there and came to the United States, and their property was destroyed. But other circumstances existed than a refusal to take up arms and a confiscation of property. Dr. Eliakim Creasley left valuable mills, which were destroyed by the order of General Duncan McArthur to prevent the enemy from obtaining a supply of flour from thence. Several claims of character similar to the one under consideration have been presented and rejected.
>
> If a citizen of the United States abandons his country for a residence in a foreign country, he must hazard the chances of war. The

committee do not think it necessary to go more fully into the reasons why it is inexpedient to recommend relief; but they rely on the concurrent opinion of all previous Congresses to sustain them that the prayer of the petitioner ought not to be granted.

In 1809, Joel Stone was appointed colonel of the 2nd Regiment Leeds Militia in Leeds County, Ontario, Canada, on the St. Lawrence River.

## Moses Ally

As reported by the Committee of Claims on October 29, 1814:

> At the declaration of war against Great Britain, and for some time previous thereto, the petitioner was an inhabitant of Upper Canada. In the summer or autumn of the year 1812, he came to the United States and reported himself to Gen. Henry Dearborn, who then commanded on the Northern Frontier. Being considered of suspicious character, he was arrested by military authority and sent to Greenbush, in New York, for examination.
>
> At the time of his arrest he had in his possession a sorrel stud-horse, which was, by direction of the officer who arrested him, placed in the possession of Mr. Benjamin Van Vleek, for safe-keeping, at the expense of the United States, until he should receive further orders how to dispose of him. He kept the horse until the 16th of April, 1813, when, having had his house and property consumed by fire, he delivered the horse over for safe-keeping to a Mr. Norton, of Lewis county. He kept him until September, 1813, when he sold him, at the price of $20, to pay for his keeping.
>
> It does not appear to the committee who was the purchaser, but from the manner in which the account for keeping the horse is credited, it is presumed that Norton himself was the purchaser. It appears, also, to the committee from the certificate of Gens. Wilkinson and Dearborn, that the charge against the petitioner was not well founded. He then received an order from Gen. Wilkinson for his horse to be delivered to him clear of the expense of keeping, but upon application, found that he had been sold to pay that expense.
>
> The petitioner asks of Congress the value of the horse.
>
> The committee are of the opinion that the United States are under no legal obligation to pay for the horse. If the petitioner had a good title to the property, it is presumed he would be entitled to recover his value of the man in whose possession he was placed by the officer. Having been put in his possession upon conditions, and with instructions to keep him at public expense, it is believed he was not liable to be sold for that expense; they, therefore, recommend the prayer of the petitioner ought not to be granted.

## David Kilbourn

As reported by the Committee on Military Affairs on February 12, 1830:

> The petitioner sets forth that he is a native citizen of the United States, within which he remained until after the termination of the Revolutionary war, when he removed into Upper Canada. Although residing in that Province, his attachment to his country was undiminished, and he was always desirous of promoting its interests.
>
> In the year 1813, at the solicitation and by the authority of General James Wilkinson, then commanding officer of the American army upon the Northern Frontier, he engaged to examine, secretly, the British posts in Canada, to procure accurate information in their numbers and position, and to communicate the result to the American commander.
>
> He executed this commission to the entire satisfaction of General Wilkinson, by whose agent he was promised ample compensation for his services, and indemnity against any loss which he might suffer for having undertaken them.
>
> The enemy, having been informed of the petitioner's employment and acts, apprehended him, confined him to prison, treated him harshly, and purported putting him to death, when he made his escape. He was again taken, again subjected to similar treatment, and again threatened with death, which would inevitably have been his portion had he not a second time effected his escape.
>
> After his escape he repaired to General Wilkinson's camp at French Mills, who renewed to him his former promises, furnished

him with money to defray his expenses to Sackett's Harbor, and recommended him to the Quartermaster at that post, who employed the petitioner in his office. From ill health he was obliged to relinquish this situation, since when he has resided in the State of New York, where he is now living under the complicated burthens of old age, infirmity, and indigence, and that, since his compulsory abandonment of Canada, his property there, which he valued at $10,000, has been confiscated, and its proceeds paid into the Provincial Treasury.

Under these circumstances he prays that he may be compensated for his services and indemnified for the loss of his property.

That such services as were performed by the petitioner would, if discovered, expose him to the penalty of death, no other testimony is requisite to establish, than the universal and well known practice of nations in similar cases. That he did perform these services faithfully, and that they were highly useful and important, is proved most fully and satisfactorily, and that justice and policy would dictate that he should be liberally remunerated for them is unquestionable.

It must be recollected that the petitioner was not a traitor to his country when he penetrated into the British encampments, but an American citizen. Had he been a traitor, whatever odium might have been attached to his conduct, our government would have been bound to reward his treason. The committee feel no hesitation in awarding to him what they consider to be a compensation for his services and the personal peril to which they exposed him, and for that purpose they report a bill. They entertain as little doubt as to the justice and policy of indemnifying the petitioner for any property which he lost by the execution of his dangerous commission, but, as the testimony submitted to them is defective, both as to the value of the property which he alleges to have been confiscated, and its confiscation, they recommend that no further allowances be made to him, until he produces stronger evidence to substantiate these facts than the committee have been furnished with.

David Kilbourn was paid $1,000 in 1832. On March 3, 1837, after further review, the Secretary of the Treasury was directed to pay Kilbourn $2,500, "for loss of property he sustained in consequence of services rendered by him on the northern frontier during the late war with Great Britain."

## *Sackets Harbor (Claims)*

### William Baker

As reported by the Committee of Claims on December 21, 1835:

The petitioner represents that he was the owner of a new and extensive two story wooden dwelling house at Sackett's Harbor, in the State of New York, and that in the month of February, 1812, it was taken possession of by the troops in the service of the United States, and used as barracks or quarters for four companies of militia for some time; and after they were discharged, the commanding officers retained the possession of the house, and used it as accommodations for the general's guard, it being contiguous to his quarters, and it was thus occupied until the 20th of April of the same year.

The petitioner made application to General Pike, the commanding officer, for the rent, and damages done to the house by the troops, and two commissioned officers were appointed by him for the purpose of being associated with one appointed by the citizens to ascertain and liquidate the damages. The commissioners so appointed did assess the damage sustained at $252.32, according to his belief.

The petitioner has presented his claim to the War Department for adjustment and was informed that there was no law authorizing the payment of such damages.

It further appears that the testimony of Elisha Camp, the appraiser appointed on behalf of the citizens, that he, in company with an officer designated for that purpose, as he understood, did appraise the use and damages at $225.30 as appears from a certified memorandum now in possession of the deponent, and he also states that the house of Baker was a large two story building and much injured by the occupation of the troops.

This case was examined by the Committee of Claims at the first session of the 23rd Congress and a report favorable to the petitioner's claim was then made, which is adopted as a part of this report, and a bill is herewith reported for his relief.

## Whitford Gill

As reported by the Committee of Claims on April 15, 1830:

It appears from the testimony of John Bliss that he was Assistant Deputy Quartermaster General in 1814 at Sackett's Harbor in the month of May. He employed the petitioner to transport in his boat from Salmon River to Sackett's Harbor a quantity of cannon shot, gun carriages, and various other articles, and that while the boat was thus employed, it was captured by the enemy, as he understood, without any fault of the owner, master, or crew, and that he made to the owner no compensation for the loss.

Robert Gardner testifies that he was on board the boat at the time she was captured. The boat sailed from Sackett's Harbor on the 14th of May, 1814, and went to Salmon River, took on board a cargo of gun carriages, cannon ball, and shells, and on the 17th of May, on their return off Stony Point, a British barge armed with ten men having been concealed in the bushes on the Point, put off and fired into the transport boat, and captured her with the cargo and crew, which were taken to Kingston in Upper Canada. He says the capture was without the fault of the master or crew, and that the boat was worth $750.

Elisha Jones testifies that about two hours before the capture of this transport, he was captured. He states that after he was taken, the enemy hauled his barge into the bushes and lay concealed until the transport barge of the petitioner appeared off the Point, when he put the barge into the water, armed and manned, and having fired into, captured the boat, which he estimates to be of the value of $750.

Jesse Hopkins testifies that the boat was worth $600.

The claim was filed with the Commissioner of Claims but all the testimony was not filed until after the expiration of the law of April 9, 1816, so that the Third Auditor had no right or authority to finally adjudicate and settle the claim.

Whitford Gill was paid $750 in 1834.

## Thomas L. Ogden

As reported by the Committee of Claims on March 7, 1820:

The petitioners were the proprietors of the village of Sackett's Harbor, in the state of New York, during the late war, and allege they have sustained damages in consequence of its having been held as a naval and military station on behalf of the United States. The amount of the claim was rendered on oath, 1st December, 1817, at $6,450 and on the 10th of December, 1818, Mr. Ogden makes an exhibit increasing the claim to $7,175. It is represented that 371 acres of woodland was consumed by troops for fuel and other public purposes, which is charged at $10 per acre, making $3,710. For fences destroyed for fuel and the rental of 119 acres for work, parade, and burial grounds, and for turf to construct forts, $3,170 are charged, making together $6,880.

The general occupancy and consumption of the property is very abundantly proved, both by several of the officers in command and others.

It is admitted in the evidence that the inhabitants of the village participated in the use of fuel without the privity or consent of the agent. Gen. William McComb thinks the proprietors were much benefitted by his removing the wood from a swamp contiguous to his station. The value of the petitioner's estate must have been greatly increased from this place having become a military and naval station and that value must be of continuance. In the removal of turf, the converting it into a manure, and the fertility communicated to a soil from the residence of an army leaves little room for a claim of damage from that circumstance.

The committee cannot judge the actual effects of the occupation of the petitioner's property on its value, but from the circumstances belonging to the case, unaided by a view of the premises, or the opinions of those who have viewed them. They are led to doubt, however, whether the petitioners have not been, upon the whole, gainers, as they now stand. It must be remarked also the Madison Barracks have since been erected on part of the encampment ground, the site for which has been purchased by the United States of the petitioners. In this purchase it may be fairly supposed so much of the charge for

> rent as applies to that ground has been fairly merged.
>
> On full consideration the committee are inclined to believe the claim allowable so far as it is connected with the consumption of wood from 371 acres of ground, to wit: $3,710. The wood used in the cantonment must have remained to the proprietors and the residue of the claim, for reasons above stated, is deemed not equitable. They submit to the Senate a bill embracing these principles.

Ogden was from New York. His petition was presented on behalf of himself and William Bayard, Henry B. Brevoort, Duncan P. Campbell, James Lenox, Robert Lenox, Herman Le Roy, Cornelius Ray, Benjamin W. Rogers, Joshua Waddington.

Ogden was paid $3,710 by the War Department in 1825. Henry B. Brevoort filed a claim for $320, the value of 8,000 feet of boards, which was denied on December 12, 1822.

## John B. Gaynor

In July 1813, the British squadron on Lake Ontario was planning an expedition against American forces. John B. Gaynor, a sailor on board one of the vessels, had some conflict with a lieutenant and claimed physical abuse. Apparently having no recourse, he decided to desert, which he did, and reported to Comm. Chauncey at Sackets Harbor. He divulged what information he knew and was then confined. After some time he was released, but had suffered permanent injury to an arm and petitioned Congress for money to support "a wife and six helpless children." Lt. Col. Richard Smith of the Marines and 15 others vouched for his veracity and character but there was no law under which he could be compensated.

## Eber Hubbard

Brig. Gen. Richard Dodge, commander of the 4th Brigade, New York Militia at Sackets Harbor, directed his agent, Albert Anderson, to purchase supplies from local merchants Jabez Foster and Orville Hungerford for delivery to Ogdensburg. Foster hired boat owner Eber Hubbard to deliver the goods, which he did without incident, but on the return trip his boat was seized.

Gen. Dodge's contract with Foster & Hungersford stipulated their company would be compensated for any losses and since Hubbard had been "ordered" to carry the supplies he felt the same provision should apply to him.

His petition was presented on December 20, 1820, and on December 22 the Committee of Claims rejected the claim. They were subsequently overruled by the Committee of the Whole. As reported by the Committee of Claims on March 12, 1830:

> The committee made a detailed report in this case on the 11th of January, 1830, and not being fully satisfied on several points, a resolution was submitted that the petitioner had not furnished such evidence in support of his claim as would justify granting relief. Some of the witnesses testified that the boat was laden with provisions, one or more of them said that she was laden with munitions of war, and others that she was laden with munitions of war and provisions.
>
> Albert Anderson was the contractor, and it became important to know who chartered the vessel. This has been explained by General Dodge, who commanded at Sackett's Harbor, and by whose direction the boat was obtained. He says that by the term "munitions," he intended to include whatever was for the use of the troops, and that, although the cargo was principally provisions for the sustenance of the troops at Ogdensburg, still that there were a few quarter casks of powder on board of her. The evidence was not explicit as to the time the boat lay at Ogdensburg, after discharging her cargo, nor as to her employment.
>
> It is now proven to the satisfaction of the committee that she was not employed there after her cargo was discharged, and that she left as soon as General Jacob Brown believed it to be safe for her to depart. The committee

wished further information as to the casks and boxes that were on board of the boat when she was captured, whose they were, and by what authority they were put on board.

Timothy Burr states that the casks belonged to the contractor, and that having been emptied at Ogdensburg, and being wanted at Sackett's Harbor, for further use, the contractor directed that they be put on board of the boat when she returned. The casks having a connection with the execution of the contract for supplying the army, the committee do not think that the employment of the boat was changed by having them on board. Whether the case is examined with reference to the 6th article of the contract made with Mr. Anderson, wherein the United States became bound to pay for all losses the contractor might sustain by the capture of the vessel in which the provisions were transported, or whether it be considered in reference to the order of General Dodge to employ the boat for transporting munitions of war, the committee does not perceive that the result will be different, as, in either case, did the owner of the boat agree to run the risk; but, on the contrary, he was expressly told that he should be compensated the loss if any was sustained. The boat seems to have been under the direction of the officers of the army, as to her sailing or remaining in port.

Henry Lewis was on board of the boat at the time of the capture, and he says that every attempt was used to run from the enemy, after he was discovered, that could have been used, without being able to effect an escape. The captain or master of the boat soon after left this section of the country, and his residence (if living) is not known. Two witnesses, one of whom built the boat, say she was worth $700. She is represented to have been a boat of two masts, and strong.

The committee think, with the additional and explanatory testimony, that the petitioner is entitled to relief, and report a bill.

## Samuel F. Hooker

As reported by the Committee of Claims on April 1, 1818:

The petitioner was owner of a garden and certain lots in the village of Sackett's Harbor, which were occupied by the troops of General Zebulon Pike in January, 1813, for a parade ground and the erection of fortifications. The petitioner states the death of General Pike has prevented the obtainment of his certificate of the fact. Evidence, taken under commission by authority of the Commissioner of Claims, establishes the occupancy in manner and for the purposes alleged to the satisfaction of the committee.

On April 20, 1818, Congress authorized the accounting officers of the Treasury Department to settle his claim for property taken and occupied for public use, and for a house and barn destroyed by the enemy at Cape St. Vincent, or Gravelly Point, which had been rented by authority of the United States for barracks. The sum allowed was not to exceed $3,867.06.

In June 1813, Hooker was involved in another incident resulting in a claim for $8,000. As reported by the Committee of Claims on December 1, 1818:

In the month of June, 1813, Mr. Samuel F. Hooker, of New York, chartered a schooner-rigged boat called the *Lady Washington*, belonging to William Dolway and Capt. Ishmael D. Hill, citizens of said State, to take a freight from the port of Oswego, on Lake Ontario, to Niagara. After lading the vessel with Hooker's goods, application was made to him by Mr. Smith, acting in the Quartermaster's Department, and Alvin Bronson, Esq., the United States army and naval storekeeper, to take on board a quantity of public property for the use of the American army.

To this Hooker objected on the grounds that in the event of capture of the vessel his property would be subjected to condemnation if found on board with the property of the United States. But at length, upon the earnest solicitations of these officers, and a representation of the urgency of the case, together with their assurances that the United States would indemnify Hooker in case of the condemnation of his property, he yielded and part of his property was taken out of the vessel and the public property put on board.

The *Lady Washington* was captured on her voyage to Niagara, and the property of Hooker, amounting to $8,130.20 was condemned as public property.

The committee believe the facts stated to be

> true, and that the consent of Mr. Hooker to receive the public property on board with his own was rather a compromise with power, than the thing desirable to him, as, in case of absolute refusal on his part, the vessel might have been pressed into the public service, and thus all hopes of his expected commercial profit lost.
>
> It appears, too, that Mr. Hooker was much influenced by the assurance of indemnity, which he had great reason to expect; and the opinion that Mr. Hooker's property was condemned in consequence of its association with public property is much strengthened by the consideration that private property had always been respected and given up by the enemy, both before and after the capture of the *Lady Washington*; and it is in evidence to the committee that the condemnation did take place because the whole cargo of the *Lady Washington* was believed by the enemy to be public stores.
>
> With this view, the committee report a bill for the relief of Samuel F. Hooker.

Capt. Hill stated that on June 15, they "fell in with the British fleet at day break in the morning, and that after myself and crew had made every possible exertion to escape, the schooner and cargo was captured and carried away."

Elbert Anderson, Jr., was the contractor supplying provisions for the Army at Fort George. On June 1, 1813, he purchased 35 boxes of candles weighing 2,819 lbs., 26 boxes of soap weighing 4,633 lbs., and 11 tierces of whiskey, equaling 627¾ gallons from James Thorn of Townsend, Bronson & Co. in the amount of $1,789.62. These goods were put aboard the schooner on the 11th. Anderson was paid for his loss.

Alvin Bronson, owner of the schooner *Penelope* and a partner in Townsend, Bronson & Co. was appointed military storekeeper at Oswego by the quartermaster general.

Ezra Housefield, of Sheffield, England, was in the hardware business and came to New York in 1800 and established a settlement. He apparently was a close friend of Augustus Sacket, who named his settlement after his friend.

Samuel Hooker opened the first major mercantile establishment in Housefield in 1808 and stocked $20,000 worth of merchandise. He reportedly sold $17,500 of that within 50 days.

Hooker tried three times to collect $8,000 for goods he alleged were lost "from the compulsory commixture of public property" but did not succeed as there was insufficient evidence to prove the goods put aboard in place of his own were actually public property at the time of their seizure.

## Cornelius Huson

As stated by the Committee on Pensions and Revolutionary Claims on March 5, 1822:

> The petitioner states that while he was at Sackett's Harbor in the year 1813, he, with his horses and sleigh, was impressed into the service of the United States by Jacob Tuckerman, then forage master in the said service, "to carry troops and loading for the use of the army from Sackett's Harbor to Gravelly Point." That while in this service thus imposed upon him, "his horses and sleigh were utterly lost while passing over the ice on the lake, and himself desperately wounded by the breaking of his breastbone and several of his ribs."
>
> The fact of impressment is satisfactorily proved. The alleged fact of the petitioner's wounds rests on his own affidavit, and that of John Amringe. The petitioner swears on its plunging over the cakes of ice, which broke his breastbone and ribs on the right side, and occasioned the loss of the use of his right arm, which would for a short time totally disabled him, and deprived him of all sense and recollection.
>
> John Amringe swears that he went from Albany to Sackett's Harbor in company with Huson, that while at the latter place both were pressed with their teams to carry loading to Gravelly Point. That Huson, "in performing this tour of duty, was wounded in his body by the operation of a sleigh, the ice being very bad and dangerous."
>
> That the third day after the wound he (Amringe) "left Huson in such situation that

he supposed he would not live to see the next morning."

It also appears by the affidavit of Sebastian Visscher, who was appointed a commissioner by the district judge of New York to take the testimony of witnesses in relation to this subject, that the facts necessary to support the petitioner's claim have been once proved, and the testimony forwarded to the War Office, and there lost or mislaid.

It is also proved to the satisfaction of the committee that the petitioner's wounds render him totally incapable of manual labor. The committee therefore recommend that Huson be allowed a pension at the rate of $8 per month, to commence from the 3rd day of December, 1821.

Cornelius Huson was paid $250 in 1822. Gravelly Point in the U.S. is in Arlington County, Virginia, on the west side of the Potomac River, across from Washington City. It is now part of the George Washington Memorial Parkway.

## Edward Lee

As stated by the Committee of Claims on February 22, 1830:

It appears to the committee that it is proven by the testimony of General Jacob Brown, then commanding at that station, and by the testimony of several other witnesses, that in the year 1813, the militia were called out in great numbers to oppose a meditated attack on Sackett's Harbor; that the United States had not yet furnished provisions sufficient for sustaining the troops collected there, and particularly that there was a great deficiency in the article of bread.

Edward Lee was a baker at Sackett's Harbor and had on hand a large quantity of hard bread to fulfill a contract made with the Navy Department for supplying the Navy on Lake Ontario. The soldiers, having ascertained where this bread was, broke open the house where it was deposited, and consumed about 5,000 pounds of it.

General Brown was not acquainted with the design to take this property prior to the time of breaking open the house; but that he was so well satisfied of the necessity that existed of having the bread for the use of the troops, that he took no measures to prevent the soldiers from consuming it. The quantity consumed was ascertained at the time, as near as could be under the circumstances of the case, by persons designated by General Brown, and one of them testifies he thinks the quantity was 5,000 pounds, and that that kind of bread under the contract to supply the Navy was fixed at 7 cents per pound.

The rule heretofore established by the committee, and which has been repeatedly sustained by the House, is this: that in cases of wanton trespass committed by the soldiers of our army on the property of a citizen, no relief is granted because the government is not responsible for the trespass of her soldiers, but, in order to determine the wantonness of the act, the attendant circumstances must be examined and considered. Soldiers are entitled to fuel, but if none is furnished, and they have taken it from an individual to preserve them from the inclemency of the season, or for the purpose of cooking, the individual has been compensated. So also when articles of food have been taken to prevent the soldiers from starving or suffering. In all of the exigencies that may exist, the best course would be for the Commanding Officer to take the articles, if the owner will not dispose of them at a fair price, and have judicious and disinterested men to appraise them. Although he would not, by so doing, exempt himself from being liable to the owner, yet he might safely rely on the justice and magnanimity of his government to afford him relief, and there would be a greater certainty of the true value of the articles taken than otherwise can be obtained. The committee is not disposed to relax the rule. The article taken was that which the government was bound to furnish. The committee is satisfied that it was not furnished, that the troops were in want of it, and took it from the petitioner.

A bill is herewith presented.

Edward Lee was paid $350 in 1832.

## William Tryon

As reported by the Committee of Claims on January 4, 1839:

The petitioner states that on the 9th day of October, 1814, he was carrying on the shoe business at Sackett's harbor and had on hand an extensive assortment of boots, shoes, leather, &c. His dwelling-house, store, and work-shop were seized and occupied by troops of the United States by order of General Oliver Collins, then commanding at that station. The troops, when taking possession of the buildings, threw into the street boots, shoes, and leather, a great proportion of which was destroyed or carried off and wholly lost to the petitioner, whereby he sustained damage exceeding $500, although the petitioner earnestly requested the property might be suffered to remain where it then was until he could carry it away.

The only evidence in support of the petition is the deposition of William Vaughan. He states that in 1814, ,when the petitioner's shop was taken possession of by the orders of Major Samuel Brown, then quartermaster, for the use of the troops, they threw his leather, shoes, &c. into the streets. It was impossible for Tryon to have saved more of his property than he did. He and others assisted in securing the property, but it impossible to prevent the soldiers from plundering and destroying a great quantity of the property.

April 29th, 1830, the Committee of Claims reported unfavorably upon the petition. January 24th, 1832, the Committee of Claims also reported against the petition, and another unfavorable report was made on the 11th day of last May, and it does not appear that a favorable report has ever been made upon it.

The prayer of the petitioner ought not to be granted.

## Lemuel Arms

As stated by the Committee of Claims on February 2, 1824:

The petitioner states that on the 12th day of October, 1814, at Sackett's Harbor, in the state of New York, he was the owner of a building, which, on the aforesaid day, by order of Brigadier General Oliver Collins, commanding the United States' forces at Sackett's Harbor, issued to the Deputy Quartermaster General, forcibly impressed and taken possession of, for quarters for the United States' forces. That the building was occupied for quarters, and for stabling, until January, 1815, when the building was pulled down by the order of the Assistant Quartermaster General to make room for enlarging the cantonment, and that the building was of the value of $150, including the rent, from the 12th day of October to the time of its destruction.

The petitioner produces testimony of Silas Pierson, barrack-master. He states that, agreeably to the order of Brigadier General Collins, and the order of Major Samuel Brown, he went to the houses of such of the inhabitants as were required for quarters, and among others, to a building belonging to Lemuel Arms, which was taken possession of, and occupied for quarters for the militia for about one month and a half, and then occupied as a stable until January, 1815, when it was pulled down, and that the value of the building was $150 and the rent $12 per month, appears from the testimony of Jna. Buts and Daniel Sandford. The destruction of the building appears from the testimony of Henry W. Sergeant; the ownership of the building appears from the testimony of Joseph D. Beal, Asa Pool, Elisha Camp, and Lemuel Arms.

From the testimony accompanying this case, the committee are satisfied that the facts are fully proved and therefore report a bill for his relief.

# *Utica*

## Michael Hogan

As reported by the Committee of Claims on March 12, 1818:

The petitioner's house in the village of Utica, in the state of New York, was forcibly occupied in February, 1813, for about 15 days by Capt. Samuel Moore, commanding a detachment of volunteers then in United States' service for quarters for his men. Considerable damage appears to have been done to the house by the detachment, for which the petitioner has not been compensated.

In July following the occupancy, an appraisement was had by certain persons agreed on by Quartermaster General Robert Swartout and the petitioner, who adjudged the damage at $1,225. This appraisement was not approved by the Quartermaster General, he being advised from the War Department the claim could only be allowed by act of Congress. The committee believe the claim is reasonable to a certain extent, and report a bill for its allowance.

Hogan was awarded $1,100.

## *North Bay*

### Marinus W. Gilbert

Marinus Gilbert had extensive dealings with the military as a merchant, paymaster, and sutler. Gilbert filed a claim for $90 for a horse, "taken and killed in going express from Sackett's Harbor to North Bay, by order of Commodore Chauncey."

Willys F. Pease was deposed on January 29, 1817:

> Willys F. Pease, of Brockville, Upper Canada merchant, being duly sworn on the Holy Evangelist, doth depose and say that in the month of May, 1814, he was employed by Marinus W. Gilbert as chief clerk. While Marinus was in the employ of Commodore Chauncey in forwarding the naval stores from Oswego Falls to North Bay, on Oneida Lake, and from thence to Sackett's Harbor, this deponent was ordered by Commodore Chauncey to carry a letter to Gilbert with all possible dispatch and to provide a horse for the purpose, which this deponent did. The distance from Sackett's Harbor to North Bay is about 54 miles, and the horse died near North Bay, immediately on his arrival and the cause was by excessive hard and fast travelling. The value of the horse was $90. The pay for the horse was requested from Commodore Chauncey, who declined paying stating that he would refer the case to the Navy Department, and at the same time saying that there could be no doubt but that Mr. Gilbert would be paid for the horse by the United States. This deponent further says that he has no interest in the claim whatever, and further saith not.

Gilbert was paid $90.

## *Ogdensburg*

The 700-mile St. Lawrence River flows from Lake Ontario to the Gulf of St. Lawrence. The 13-mile Oswegatchie River flows into the St. Lawrence about 110 miles southwest of Montreal.

In 1749, the Abbé François Piquet built Fort de la Présentation at the mouth of the Oswegatchie River to enlist the aid of the Iroquois Indians against the British. The fort came under British control in 1760, but they refused to relinquish it after the Revolutionary War. The Jay Treaty of November 19, 1794, required evacuation of all frontier forts on or before June 1, 1796, which Parliament assented to.

On August 11, 1796, Nathan Ford, Samuel Ogden, and a small number of others arrived from Morristown, New Jersey, and settled on the east side of the Oswegatchie. In 1810 the population was around, 1,245.

In 1812, Capt. Benjamin Forsyth's company of riflemen was garrisoned in one of the buildings at the old fort. On February 7, 1813, Forsyth led 300 troops to Brockville, Ontario, to rescue some American prisoners and confiscate stores. On February 22, 1813, Lt.-Col. George Richard John "Red George" Macdonnell's regulars and militia crossed the frozen St. Lawrence from Fort Wellington at Prescott and captured the village.

### Marinus W. Gilbert

Gilbert claimed $80.60 for hospital stores taken at Ogdensburg, "by order of General Thomas Benedict, of the New York militia, and Capt. Benjamin Forsyth, of the United States' Rifle Corps, for the use of the army," taken by Lt. William G. Shade, for the use of Capt. Reuben Gilder's 14th Regiment company.

On November 25, 1816, Richard Bland Lee appointed commissioners Perley Keyes, Hart Massey, John M. Canfield, Joseph Clark, and Calvin McKnight to assess Gilbert's losses pursuant to the Act of April 9, 1816, and they reported a settlement of $80.60 for hospital stores and $140 for the bateau and tools.

## Nathan Ford

As reported by the Committee of Claims on March 25, 1822:

The petitioner, of Ogdensburg, New York, submits a claim for the sum of $9,095, the items of which are thus stated:

The Garrison, or Old French Barracks, occupied by Capt. Benjamin Forsyth and his riflemen, $5,220; a 36 by 28 foot distillery adjoining, and also occupied by the troops, $500; a large boat taken by the troops, $20; damage to four of his houses in the village, $700; interest for five years, $2,355.

It is testified that a building called "the old French Barracks," contained 16 habitable rooms and 23 that were occupied by the troops from some time in the fall of 1812 till the 22nd of February, 1813, under a contract for a rent of $1 per day.

On the latter day, Ogdensburg was captured by the enemy and the building, including the adjoining distillery, were destroyed by burning, and the boat then lying on the shore near the barracks had been occasionally used by Major Forsyth for military purposes, and was, by fire and otherwise, much injured by the enemy. Other buildings, situate in the village of Ogdensburg were occupied by the troops for the deposit of stores and clothing, and military quarters, and were much injured by the enemy.

The manner of the injury alleged to have been done to the latter buildings is not stated, and until it be shown to have been such as an enemy might rightfully do, that part of the claim must be rejected. It is not perceived by the committee that the circumstances of the boat having been "occasionally used for military purposes" the preceding fall, can give to the owner a claim upon the government for the injuries which might have been done to it while lying upon the land, at a season when the waters are enclosed by the ice.

Whether payment shall be made for the house called the old French Barracks, and adjoining distillery, ought to depend upon the rules which shall be definitely adopted relative to other like cases. Under these circumstances the prayer of the petitioner ought not to be granted.

Capt. Forsyth, of North Carolina, was commissioned 2nd Lieutenant in the 6th Infantry on April 24, 1800, and made captain on July 1, 1808. He was promoted to major on January 20, 1813, and mortally wounded at Odelltown, New York, on June 28, 1814. Capt. John Lytle, of the 4th Rifle Regiment; Capt. Forsyth's second in command; Daniel W. Church, Adjutant to the 23rd Regiment of New York Militia; and Gen. Jacob Brown, certified the loss of the Barracks and distillery to the amount of $6,020. John Eaton testified that the Ford residence was known as the Thorp House.

## Jonathan Hall

As reported by the Committee of Claims on February 25, 1846:

The only material allegation in the petition is, "that in the year 1813, and during the last war between the United States and Great Britain, the petitioner resided at Ogdensburgh, in the State of New York, with his family. At the battle of Ogdensburgh, which took place on the 22nd of February, 1813, and in which the British succeeded in taking possession of the village, they did, on that and several successive days, plunder the inhabitants of considerable property," and the petitioner was so plundered of property of the value of $528.

As a recommendation to the favorable consideration of Congress, he states that he had charge of a 12-pounder cannon, and served faithfully as a volunteer. These facts, if proved, plainly furnish no ground for relief. The committee therefore recommend that the petition ought not to be granted.

## Samuel Fuller

As reported by the Committee of Claims on January 11, 1844:

The petitioner represents that at the commencement of the last war with Great Britain he resided with his family in Canada. When the war was declared, he was ordered by the commanding officer of militia there to take up arms in defense of that country, and on refusing to do so, he was imprisoned in a guard-house, from which he made his escape after a confinement without rations of 20 days

> and crossed the river on two raft-oars to the United States. His wife and children followed him under a flag of truce, leaving behind a sleigh, harness, and horses, with some other property, which, it is alleged, were promised to be sent after them, but which have never been received.
>
> His family were afterwards settled at Ogdensburg, and when that place was attacked by the British forces, his wife and children, in his absence, exerted themselves in saving to the United States a quantity of beef and pork, of the value of $1,000 and upwards, besides several articles belonging to a Captain Kelick of the army.
>
> For these services and loss of property the petitioner claims compensation of the United States.

The facts were certified by John Lytle, a captain at Ogdensburg, but the committee rejected the claim for lack of evidence as to dates and value of losses.

The officer cited is probably Capt. Giles Kellogg, whose company of artillery from Schoharie County, enlisted in the winter of 1812 for one year. They left on Monday, December 28, with orders to report to Maj. Benjamin Forsyth at Ogdensburgh as relief troops. Capt. Kellogg was giver $250 for expenses. The company lost all of their property in the attack at Ogdensburgh, and on November 16, 1813, the company was discharged at French Mills. On December 10, 1813, Capt. Kellogg was honorably discharged at Utica, New York, by Maj. John Herkimer.

## Thomas B. Benedict

Jane Benedict filed a claim, as stated by the Committee of Claims on March 28, 1834:

> The petitioner claims of the United States $3,009.89, the estimated value of property destroyed and captured by the enemy during the late war, which belonged to her late husband.
>
> The grounds of relief appear to be, first, that Thomas B. Benedict was in the military service of the United States with the command of a lieutenant colonel, and his military character was well known to the enemy, and second, that his house at Ogdensburg had been occupied by General Brown and his staff, and military books and papers were in the house at the time Ogdensburg was captured and this house was destroyed.
>
> Neither of these grounds has been considered as sufficient for granting relief in similar cases. If the first were established, the United States would be the warrantee, insurer, and guarantor of all the personal property of those who should be in the military service of the United States, and as such, liable to remunerate for any loss sustained by the destruction or capture of such property by the enemy.
>
> The petitioner says Thomas B. Benedict applied several times to obtain compensation for the losses, but failed for reasons not known to the petitioner. Much is stated of the services of Thomas B. Benedict, and of his devotion to the public cause, and of the confidence reposed in him by the authorities of the State of New York, and of the indigence and poverty of the petitioner, no part of which are the committee disposed to controvert. The committee, however, cannot, for any or all of these causes, depart from well established and settled principles. The petitioner is not entitled to relief.

## Joseph York

A claim filed by Lavinia York, as stated by the Committee of Claims on January 16, 1841:

> The petitioner claims compensation for property destroyed at Ogdensburg by the British army during the late war. The petitioner sets forth that her late husband, Joseph York, Esq., being sheriff of the county of St. Lawrence, and jailer, occupied the building erected in the village of Ogdensburg as a court house and jail. He was himself an officer and commanded one of the guns manned by volunteers at the time the village was taken.
>
> Joseph York was taken prisoner, and some of the volunteers he commanded by him were taken, and others wounded, and others killed, while the personal property in the house, amounting to near $400 in value was destroyed by the British forces. For the loss of the property thus destroyed the petitioner asks compensation.

Taking all the facts set forth in the memorial as established, the committee entertain the opinion that by the rules which have heretofore governed the legislation of Congress, they cannot afford the relief sought. The only instance in which our Congress have paid for buildings destroyed by an enemy is when such buildings have been in the military occupation of our troops. In the present instance, the compensation is not for buildings but for personal property wantonly destroyed by the enemy contrary to the usages of civilized warfare, and such as Congress have uniformly refused to grant indemnity for. The committee are of opinion that the memorialist is not entitled to relief.

## Andrew McCollum

Dr. McCollum filed a claim for $1,850 for damages done to his home in Ogdensburgh on February 22, 1813, destroyed by the British, "in consequence of its having been occupied by the army of the United States," and $4,440 interest at 7 percent to February 22, 1833, the date of his claim.

Depositions from David Jones and John Scott were taken in December 1816, but they failed to "prove the occupation of the building down to the time of destruction, by the officer who ordered its occupation."

Thomas B. Benedict, the commander at Ogdensburg, provided a sworn statement on December 22, 1816:

> I certify that, in the fall and winter of 1812 and '13, the house of Andrew McCollum, in the village of Ogdensburg, in the county of St. Lawrence, was occupied by my authority as quarters, for myself and officers of the staff, &c., and as a deposite for public stores, such as equipments, arms, and ammunition, &c.; that on the 22d day of February, 1813, on the capture of this place by the enemy, as I am advised, and verily believe to be true, the house was captured and partly destroyed by the enemy, and I have no doubt but the destruction was in consequence of such occupation; and I further certify it was a large and valuable house well furnished.

Peter Hagner, the Third Auditor, was asked to confirm all the details and replied that the home was actually rented on October 1, 1812, to Gen. Jacob Brown at $25 a month along with an adjoining office at $5 a month until January 1, 1813. The rent of $90 was paid until December 25, 1812, and received by Maj. Henry Seymour, Brigade Quartermaster, 5th Brigade of detached militia. It was also learned that Col. Benedict left the service on December 26, 1812, so could have no firsthand knowledge of the loss.

Capt. John Polly testified that he heard the commander of the British forces say the house was marked for destruction owing to its occupation. Samuel Gordon and Nathan Goff appraised the damages at $1,850. The claim was denied.

## William Russell

William Russell was an attorney and a merchant in Ogdensburgh who filed a claim for 8 barrels of mess pork at $20 per barrel; 450 pounds of cheese at 9 cents per pound; and 96 barrels of flour at $8.50 per barrel, total $1016.50. He also claimed $1,280.79 in interest for 24 years.

As stated by the Committee of Claims on June 21, 1836, in part:

> Mr. Russell, in his petition, represents that in the spring of 1812 he opened a public house in Ogdensburg. After the declaration of war in June following, he also engaged in trade in the various articles of provisions, such as beef, pork, flour, butter, cheese, &c., with which he, from time to time, furnished the troops stationed at that place. His house, being the largest public house in the village, became the resort for the officers of the army, and the supporters of our country's liberties during the season and until the 22d February, 1813, when the place was taken by the enemy.
>
> Of the troops stationed there, Captain Benjamin Forsyth, of the riflemen was first in command, but was at that time across the Little River in the old French fort, and Captain John Lytle was in the village with his troops,

with the exception of 5 or 6, made good their retreat, and the enemy made prisoners of all the citizens they could find. The petitioner was one of the number.

After burning all the public buildings and water craft, they plundered his house, set fire to the bridge, and through fear that the Americans might return with a reinforcement, made a precipitate return to Canada. The prisoners were first placed in the picket at Prescott, opposite to Ogdensburg, where they could see the movements on the American side. They saw our troops return to the village and carry away what property they could find, which was done to prevent its falling into the hands of the enemy in case they should again cross over.

When he was taken prisoner, he had on hand 1,000 pounds of cheese, 20 barrels of mess pork, 100 barrels of flour, and considerable other property which was, all of the principal part of it, taken by order of the officers of the United States and converted to the use of our army, and for which he had never received any remuneration or compensation whatever.

He was released from imprisonment and permitted to return home on parole of honor on the 24th February, 1813. When he returned he found he had been completely stripped of all his property, his house had been pillaged, the door of his shed where his flour had been taken had been broken open, and the whole of the flour had been taken, his 20 barrels of mess pork, and 450 pounds of cheese had been carried away, and a great variety of other articles of property. On inquiry, he found 96 barrels of flour, 8 barrels of pork, and 450 pounds of cheese had been carried away by order of the officer at the time commanding the American forces at that post, but was unable to learn who took the other property.

The officers, boarders, and other persons against whom he had bills, and who owed him to a considerable amount, had gone, some to Sackett's Harbor, some to the Niagara frontier, and others to parts unknown, so that he not only lost his goods, but his debts which were due to him, and which he should doubtless have secured, had he not been taken prisoner. These losses reduced him at once to a state of abject poverty, in which situation he had always remained from that day to this. He first made his accounts against the State of New York, but they were rejected on the ground that it belonged to the United States to pay them.

He contracted to sell them to one John W. Bulkeley, for which he was to pay a certain sum or return them. He utterly failed to fulfill his contract, and several years elapsed before the petitioner again obtained possession of the papers. Soon after he obtained them, a fire occurred in the building he then occupied and in the hurry of removing his effects, the papers were misplaced, and as he supposed till recently were forever lost. On emptying an old trunk of rubbish a few months ago, he unexpectedly found them in the shape in which they are presented for allowance and adjustment. It will under these circumstances be seen that the delay in presenting them had been wholly unintentional on his part, and that he trusted he should be allowed both principal and interest.

William W. Bowen, Samuel Gray, and Matthew Gray testified under oath that they saw the goods being removed on order of Capt. Lytle.

One local civilian resident, Elias Hyde, offered his services to Capt. Lytle "in removing the property that belonged to the United States in the arsenal, and a ball from the enemy passed through his hips." He languished in pain until he died on March 17, leaving a son and a pregnant wife, Hannah, who gave birth to a daughter.

On March 1, 1813, Gen. Brown wrote from Brownville to Gen. Dearborn and Gov. Tompkins he was leaving immediately for Ogdensburg, as he stated:

> I then proceeded to Ogdensburg with a view of destroying in the course of the ensuing night, every species of provision the enemy had not got off. On my arrival I found much remaining, and a disposition amongst the people to give me every assistance. Believing then that those provisions might be saved for our own use, every sleigh that could be commanded was put in requisition, and I flatter myself that it will all be saved. A person was also sent to Hamilton, and I trust what remained there will be got back and saved.

No records of a claim could be found in New York or Washington and no vouchers for hire of the sleighs or teams could be found. No record of Russell ever furnishing provisions to the troops could be found, and discrepancies over where exactly the flour was stored were noted—in the cellar or in a shed.

He also claimed $522.89, $28.80 for rations, and $221.88 interest as power of attorney for Harvey Church, whose 20-ton boat was hired on July 7, 1812, by Lt. Col. Thomas B. Benedict to transport troops to Toussaint Island, and which was captured and lost there during a battle on September 16. Col. Church issued a certificate for $350 to Harvey Church on September 24, 1812, and stating its loss. No record for other expenses could be found and the petition was dismissed.

## *Antwerp*

### Peter Vroman

The claim was filed by Gabriel Vroman, as reported by the Committee of Claims on May 17, 1838, in part:

> The petitioner states that his father, Peter Vroman, kept a tavern at Antwerp, in the State of New York during the last war with Great Britain. In February, 1813, after the capture of Ogdensburg by the British, the American troops, in their retreat under the command of Major Benjamin Forsyth, to the number of 400 or 500, including two companies of dragoons, were destitute of provisions, forage, fuel, &c., and were furnished by his father, with the following articles: 8 barrels of pork, about 500 bushels of oats, a large quantity of hay, wood, and many other articles. He states at that time his father was sick, and on his recovery, he found his property was gone, and that he always claimed there was due to him $500, no part of which was ever paid.
>
> Ephraim Taylor testifies he was at Peter Vroman's house in February, and saw a multitude of soldiers. This was a day or two after the battle at Ogdensburg. In a short time he hired to Mr. Vroman as a laborer, and he heard the family say they furnished soldiers with provisions. Mr. Vroman said he never received his pay, and that he intended to apply to the government.
>
> John Lytle testifies that he was captain of a company of volunteers attached to the rifle regiment. On their return from Ogdensburg on the 24th or 25th of February, the troops stopped at the house of Peter Vroman. Vroman furnished them with provisions one night and part of two days to the number of 400 or 500 and that some of the officers paid their bills.
>
> In the summer of 1815, he says Mr. Vroman came to Fort George and requested Major Forsyth to pay the bills of his troops. Major Forsyth agreed to pay the bills, or have them arranged when he could see the commanding officer.
>
> Mary Edwards testifies she lived at Peter Vroman's at the time, and knows that several hundred soldiers were provided with provisions and that Mr. Vroman furnished pork, flour, and oats to the troops, and that several cords of wood were taken and consumed by the troops for cooking and for other purposes. She understands pork was $20 per barrel and flour $10.
>
> Francis McAlliston testifies he lived 7 miles south of Mr. Vroman's and heard the soldiers say they were entertained by Mr. Vroman and understood he was kind to them.
>
> Daniel Heald testifies that Major Forsyth and other officers said their bills were not paid at Vroman's, but they should be, and he heard Mr. Vroman say he had not been paid, and, as Major Forsyth was dead, he had no hope.
>
> Lucas Gillet testifies that Mr. Vroman said he intended to apply to the government for his pay.
>
> Abram Lewis testifies that Mr. Vroman was an illiterate man and depended on the honesty of those with whom he dealt.
>
> Mr. Hagner has not been able to find that the claim was ever presented to his office for settlement. He, however, finds that a payment was made on the 31st of March, 1813, by a quartermaster at Sackett's Harbor, to the order of Roland Hall on his account, dated February 25, 1813, for "a house-room and entertainment for 70 men of Major Forsyth's rifle battalion after the fall of Ogdensburg, $18.16." The certificate is signed by "John Lytle, captain; Benjamin Forsyth, major

commanding," with a certificate from Brigadier General Jacob Brown that the refreshments were furnished by his order.

Mr. Hagner says such evidence was usually given by officers in command when supplies were not paid for when furnished, and, being done in the case of Mr. Hall, he infers that the same officers would give their certificates to Mr. Vroman for any supplies he furnished to the same troops.

The battle at Ogdensburg was fought on the morning of the 22nd of February, 1813. There is no account or specifications of items, except as to the pork, beef, and oats. After this lapse of time, the committee would require the most satisfactory evidence to sustain a claim that has lain dormant for a quarter of a century. The petitioner is not entitled to relief.

## *Peru*

### Elisha I. Winter

Elisha Winter, of Peru, New York, was a Federalist member of the 13th Congress from March 1813 until 1815. He was paid $143, "for a pair of horses with a sleigh and harness, taken from him for the use of the army of the United States, in the month of March, 1813."

He later became involved in railroading and was president of the Lexington & Ohio Railroad.

## *Sodus Point*

Sodus is on the south shore of Lake Ontario.

### William Eadus

William Eadus filed a claim for $4,259.50 for 1 two-story house, $2,500; 3 feather beds, $60; bed clothes, $80; 6 bedsteads, $60; 5 underbeds, $35; 1 carpet, $25; 1 mahogany dining table, $30; 1 cherry dining table, $10; 1 bureau, $16; 1 breakfast table, $10; 1 stand, $3; 1 dozen chairs, $12; 1 six-plate stove and pipe, $25; 2 sets of bed curtains, $32; 2 bedspreads and one quilt, $30; 6 bed cords, $6; earthen, and 2 full sets of china, $100; kitchen furniture, $200; 1 pair of plated candlesticks, $4; 2 pair of brass candlesticks, $4; 3 pair of snuffers and trays, $6; 6 table cloths and 12 towels, $40; 1 side board, $30; 1 woman's beaver hat, $10; wearing apparel for self, wife, and eight children, estimated at $500; looking glass, $12; family pictures, $10; books, $60; 1 spy glass, $25; soap and tallow, $8.

1 barrel of mess pork, $25; tea and sugar, $10; 1 barrel of vinegar, $15; 2½ barrels of flour, $23.75; medicine and vials, $5;

3 hair trunks, $24; 15 stone pots, $7; paints for house and vessel, $60; black lead, $2; fringe, $15; $15; 1 box of window glass, $8; 3 tea boards, $10; horse tackling (silver plated) $30; leech tub, $3; 1 garden rake, $3; pick axe, $2; 2 hoes, $2; 1 brace of pistols, $12; gun, $12; 1 dirk bought of Alexander P. Darragh, purser of the brig *Oneida*, $12; fruit trees and poultry, $10.

On June 26, 1813, Brig. Gen. William Burnett, commander of the 24th Brigade, New York Militia, wrote to Gov. Daniel D. Tomkins from his headquarters at Phelps, Ontario County, New York:

> On the evening of the 15th instant, I received information by express that the enemy had landed at Genesee river and committed some depredations, and were steering for Sodus bay, where considerable public property was stored. I ordered out Lieutenant Colonel Swift's regiment and Major Granger's rifle battalion, who marched on Wednesday. Captain Dorsey's company of exempts marched at the same time, and under my directions removed the public property to the safest place which time and the country afforded, and dismissed the troops on Saturday morning.
>
> On the evening of the same day, an express arrived that the enemy's fleet had anchored off Sodus bay, and were preparing to land. I immediately ordered those who had not proceeded with me to return, and detach an officer for the remainder, but the enemy had effected a landing before more than 40 or

50 arrived, and who, though provided with only a few cartridges, engaged with them; but, owing to the darkness of the night and the superior force of the enemy, were obliged to fall back to where the stores were secured, and had four men wounded, and one since dead. The enemy, as I am informed by the officer of the flag the next day, had seven men killed. In the mean time, I had ordered out Lieutenant Colonel Howell's regiment, Major Rogers' battalion, and Captain Ree's company of artillery, who arrived on the two following days. A number of volunteers arrived at the same time, part from Colonel Dobbin's regiment, Seneca county.

On Sunday morning, the enemy set fire to, and destroyed six buildings, and soon after embarked and left the shore, taking with them, as informed by Mr. Merrill, about 230 barrels of flour, a few barrels of whiskey and pork, principally private property, and then demanded the surrender of the public property, and a deserter, whom they would exchange for one they had taken along the shore, which was immediately refused.

I ordered Lieutenant Colonel Howell's regiment, Major Rogers' battalion, to Putneyville, where the enemy had steered their course, and had previously ordered part of Lieutenant Colonel Colt's regiment to Sodus, and dismissed Colonel Swift's, they having been on duty for some time. The property saved to the public consists of about 800 barrels of flour and pork, and is now sufficiently secured from the enemy, having ordered a guard to remain and protect it.

The returns of the number of men have not yet been made out, but will be immediately attended to, and sent to your excellency. The season of the year is now so important to farmers, who compose the greater part of our country, has proved to be such a loss to those ordered out, by leaving their business, that some provisions in this case will be necessary to be made, and for the teams that removed the public property.

The alacrity with which the citizen soldiers obeyed the call of their country in its defense, cannot be too highly commended. The enemy, too well aware of the patriotism of our citizens, left their situation without effecting their greatest purpose (the taking and destroying of our stores) before 150 men had assembled.

William Eadus was paid $2,000, in 1838.

Lt. Col. Philetus Swift commanded the 71st Regiment from Phelps, Ontario County.

Maj. Granger is possibly Pierce or Elihu Granger, of the Ontario County militia. Regular and militia units were known to operate together, sometimes with militia officers in command, to the annoyance of the regular officers.

The "Exempts" were a group of Revolutionary War veterans who were exempt from military service by virtue of their age but who volunteered for service in the New York militia.

Lt. Col. Gilbert Howell commanded the 39th Regiment from Ontario County.

Maj. William Rogers commanded a battalion of New York Militia.

Lt. Col. Hugh W. Dobbin commanded the 102nd Regiment from Junius, Seneca County.

Lt. Col. Samuel Colt commanded the 42nd Regiment from Geneva, Ontario County.

A report by the investigating Commissioner, Robert W. Stoddard in December, 1817:

> William Burnett, brigadier general of the 24th Brigade of New York Militia, states that on the 16th June, 1813, intelligence was received that the British had landed at Genesee River, and were coming to Sodus where was deposited large quantities of provisions and stores destined for the American army then in service against Canada. He thereupon ordered into the service of the United States the regiment of militia commanded by Lieutenant Colonel Swift, and ordered it to repair to Sodus for the protection of the public property. Such militia did assemble here and removed a considerable part of the provisions to a place of safety. Elias Hull was a captain then in the service of the regiment and Col. Asahel Bannister was a quartermaster to it.
>
> On the morning of the 19th of June, 1813, the enemy not then appearing, the greater part of the militia was dismissed, and only a guard retained for the property so removed.

In the night of that day the British fleet put into Sodus bay, landed a party of men, carried away or destroyed the provisions remaining in the storehouse of Nathaniel Merrill, and burnt that storehouse and several other buildings, among which was the house of the claimant, and that it is his opinion that the depositing the provisions at Sodus induced the enemy to come there, and was the cause of the destruction of the claimant's house and the houses of other private citizens.

Col. Asahel Bannister states that in the attack made by the British on the village of Sodus, he acted as quartermaster to Colonel Swift's regiment of militia, then in the service of the United States, and was the bearer of a flag of truce to the enemy, and met by the flag from them. The officer who bore the British flag proposed to him to spare the village and not to burn or destroy private property upon condition that the public stores and provisions which had been removed were given up to them. Quartermaster Bannister replied that he was not authorized to make such stipulation, but would report to his officers, and in 3 or 4 hours would return them an answer.

He reported to his officers what had happened and again bore a flag to the enemy and informed them that the public property would not be given up to them. The British officer distinctly stated that their intention was only to obtain the public provisions and if they were given up peaceably, would engage not to come again to Sodus during the war, unless it should again be made a deposit for public stores or become a military post.

For want of proper camp equipage, he, as quartermaster, was obliged to make use of private dwellings for barracks for soldiers then in service, and that he ordered a commandant of a company to take possession of the claimant's house and that he believes in consequence of the orders given by him, the house was occupied by the soldiers for barracks. On the first landing of the enemy, a smart conflict ensued between the British and a party of militia a little west of the claimant's house in which several of the enemy were killed and wounded, and that he is of the opinion that the depositing the public stores and provisions at Sodus, and assembling and stationing a party of militia in the claimant's house were the causes of the destruction of it.

Elias Hull states that a large quantity of provisions, destined for the American army were deposited at Sodus and on or about the 16th June, 1813, an alarm was spread that the enemy were coming to seize these provisions. A large number of militia, under command of General Burnett marched to the defense of Sodus. He was a captain and commanded a company in Colonel Swift's regiment, and with his company went to Sodus by command of General Burnett. By the exertions of the militia, a considerable part of the provisions were removed to a place of safety. A breastwork or fortification was thrown up on the lot, and very near the house of the claimant for defense and to prevent the enemy from landing and was occupied by the soldiers for that purpose. A part of his company were, by his express and positive orders and direction, quartered in, and made barracks of the house of the claimant for the want of tents and other necessary camp equipage. The commanding general ordered that the private houses in the village should be used for quarters and barracks. In the night of the 19th June, the British fleet put in to Sodus bay and landed a party of men. At this time, a considerable part of the militia had been dismissed, but on receiving intelligence of the arrival of the enemy, he repaired to the scene of action and collected as many soldiers as he could, and placed an outguard at the breastwork and stationed the main body at no great distance from the battery in the road between the house of William Wickham and the house of the claimant.

The enemy first attacked the guard in the breastwork and drove them from it, and then came along the road to where he and his party were stationed. The party under his command fired upon the enemy and retreated. The enemy then commenced plundering the provisions and stores which had not been removed. The enemy's ships on the lake and gun-boats in the bay, commenced a cannonade in such direction that the claimant's house was nearly shot to pieces and it was afterwards set fire to and consumed. It is his opinion that the depositing of the provisions at Sodus induced the enemy to come there, and that on their arrival, finding the claimant's house had been occupied for barracks and a breastwork thrown up on his lot, and then occupied by an armed force, and making resistance, were the causes of destruction of the claimant's house and effects by the enemy.

John Holcomb, Esq., states that in June, 1813, he resided at Sodus, and was a captain of militia, and was ordered out to rendezvous there with his company. It was deemed advisable to throw up a breastwork to prevent the enemy from landing and that the duty was assigned to him. He did throw up a breastwork on the lot, and very near the house of the claimant. The claimant's family were obliged to leave.

Amos Hull, Esq., late a major-general in the militia of the State of New York, states that, prior to the destruction of the house and property of Mr. Merrill by the enemy, it was represented to him that large quantities of provisions and public stores destined for the American army were deposited along the shores of Lake Ontario, and particularly at Sodus, and that the places were totally defenseless, and the provisions and stores holding out an inducement to the enemy to seize them and commit depredations on the inhabitants, he ordered, for the protection of the citizens, a quantity of public arms to be distributed at the several points along the shores of the lake, and particularly at Sodus, to be put into the hands of the neighboring militia in case of any sudden attack. There being no arsenal or other safe and convenient public buildings at the places wherein the arms could be deposited, he uniformly directed them to be deposited with some respectable private person whom he held responsible for the same, and that the arms to be placed at Sodus were receipted by and received by Mr. Merrill, and to be by him put into the hands of the militia.

Nathaniel Merrill states that his storehouse at Sodus was, by the express order and direction of the agents of the United States, occupied as a place of deposit for the provisions and stores of the United States destined for the American army. The village of Sodus was a place of inconsiderable trade, and until the depositing the public stores, held out to the enemy no inducement to destroy the village. After those stores were deposited, fears for the safety of the village were excited in the inhabitants, and representations were made of its defenseless situation to Major General Hall, who ordered a quantity of arms and ammunition to be kept at Sodus for the purpose of defense in case of an attack.

As reported by the Committee of Claims on February 17, 1818, in part:

To prove the occupancy of the house as barracks at the time of its capture and destruction, the deposition of Elias Hull is adduced. In June, 1813, he had command of a company of men in the United States' service and took possession of the petitioner's house, by order of General William Burnett, commander of the 24th Brigade, New York Militia. Asahel Bannister, the quartermaster, converted it into barracks. The petitioner was absent, being on board Commodore Isaac Chauncey's fleet on Lake Ontario as a pilot, and the petitioner's family was obliged to leave the house to make room for the soldiers.

On the 16th of June, 1813, intelligence was received that the British had landed at Genesee River, and were coming to Sodus, where were deposited large quantities of provisions and stores destined for the American army, then in service against Canada.

The militia were ordered out under General Burnett, and accordingly assembled at Sodus for its defense. While at Sodus, the militia were employed in removing the public property from the storehouse of Nathaniel Merrill, in which it had been deposited, to a place of safety, perhaps in the woods, some distance from Sodus.

On the morning of the 19th of June, the enemy not having come to Sodus as was expected, the militia were discharged, except a guard of about 49 men under the command of Elias Hull, and in the occupancy of the house, which he continued to occupy till the enemy's troops landed on the point in the evening of the 19th of June when a skirmish took place, when several men were killed and wounded on both sides.

The British troops retired in the night and were gone awhile, but early on Sunday morning of the 20th relanded, marched to Sodus, set fire to the place, and captured or destroyed what property was in Merrill's storehouse, burnt the storehouses and several other houses, among which was the house of the present claimant, William Eadus. For this loss, sustained under such circumstances, he asks Congress to pay him for his house, valued at $2,500, and for the furniture therein, valued at $1,759.75.

The committee do not find that this case comes within the provisions of the act of April, 1816. It does not satisfactorily appear that the claimant's house was ever in the military occupation of the United States. General Burnett, under whose authority the house must have been occupied, if it was occupied at all, is silent on this head. Some of the other witnesses do state that between the 16th and the morning of the 19th, the house was occupied, but the evidence is so vague and indistinct as greatly to diminish the confidence to be placed in it.

An adverse report was made by the Committee of Claims on January 16, 1832, and again on March 26, 1832, with testimony from Asahel Bannister, Dudley Marvin, Thomas Wafer, Alexander Lyall, John Holcomb, George Chapin, Ismael D. Hill, Jesse Brown, Thomas Lewis, Nathaniel Merrill, Elizabeth C. Fitzhugh, Bennet Farr, John Fellows, Elisha Sisson, and Nathaniel Kellogg, Jr.

The committee stated, in part:

> All testify, in general, without going into particulars, that the guard of about 40 men under Captain Elias Hull, retained by order of General Burnett, to guard the provisions and stores removed, were quartered, and continued to be quartered, in the house of the petitioner till the evening when the enemy landed and set fire to the village, and burnt the house.
>
> It does not appear what opportunity these witnesses had of knowing the facts to which they in general terms testify unless it might be inferred from some expression in the affidavit of Farr, that he belonged to Captain Hull's company. Every person, the least familiar with legal proceedings, knows the deceptiveness of depositions taken ex parte, unless made full and particular, showing the means the witness has of being acquainted with the facts he relates, so that it may be seen what he knows as coming under his own observation, and what he knows, or thinks he knows, from the relations of others. This case will illustrate this remark.
>
> The committee are not satisfied that the destruction of the petitioner's house was occasioned by its occupancy by the troops in the service of the United States as barracks, and they adhere to their opinion, heretofore expressed, that he is not entitled to relief.

As reported by the Committee of Claims on May 17, 1836, in part:

> Whether the house of the petitioner, which, it is acknowledged on all hands, was, for some time, occupied as barracks for part of the militia stationed in the village of Sodus, was so occupied after the morning of the 19th of June, in the evening of which day, or during the night following, the house was burnt; and whether it was destroyed in consequence of such occupancy, appear to be questions not satisfactorily explained by the testimony adduced to the former committees.
>
> Upon a revision of all the evidence heretofore submitted, as well as the report of the commissioner made in December, 1817, obtained by the Third Auditor, and on file in his office—explained and confirmed, as this evidence is, by the additional testimony, now first furnished of two British officers, John Harris and James Richardson—this committee are convinced that the United States cannot justly refuse payment for the house of the petitioner.
>
> The good character of the two witnesses last mentioned is sustained by vouchers that do not leave a reasonable doubt of the credibility of Harris and Richardson. They state upon oath that they were among those who landed at Sodus at the time mentioned for the purpose of taking the provisions known to be there and in that neighborhood. Their orders from Sir James Yeo, their commander, were not to destroy private property. The house of the petitioner was burnt because they were fired upon by the American troops from its doors, as well as from a breastwork on the same lot, and near the house; and because, from the additional circumstance of finding arms in said house, they concluded it was occupied by the American troops as quarters, as well as for defense, and that it was, therefore, proper and right it should be destroyed.
>
> The value of the house seems to have been set by some of the witnesses whose depositions were furnished to the commissioner in 1817, at $2,500, and by others, among whom is Alexander Lyall, a carpenter by trade, and who aided in building the house, at $2,000. The weight of testimony would seem to be for the lesser sum.
>
> The claim for personal property, consisting of furniture and clothing, amounting to $1,759.75, cannot, consistently with the usages of Congress, be allowed. The committee therefore report a bill for $2,000.

Elias Hull was in Lt. Col. Philetus Swift's 71st Regiment of New York Militia. His company was ordered into the service of the United States by Gen. Burnett from June 16 to 24, 1813, inclusive.

Capt. John T. Ree's 4-pounder fired a salute at Geneva, New York, on November 4, 1813, in honor of Comm. Oliver H. Perry's arrival alone on horseback. He left the next morning for his home at Newport, Rhode Island, for the winter.

## David M. Lewis

As stated by the Committee of Claims on December 28, 1829, in part:

> The petitioner claims of the United States to be compensated for the loss of 200 barrels of flour, which he says was destroyed at Sodus Bay in the State of New York by the British in consequence of its being stored in the store house of Nathaniel Merrill, which was occupied by the United States' troops for barracks in 1813.
>
> It was the duty of the petitioner to have removed his flour, and that the officers could not have done it without the consent of the owner.
>
> The country was new, the means of conveyance limited, and employed by the officers in removing the public property. If this point was material, the committee would still consider that he was guilty of great negligence. The witnesses state that it was known, or at least feared, as early as the 16th of June that the enemy would probably land at Sodus. Between that period and the night of the 19th, when the enemy took possession of the place, there was surely time for him to have brought to his aid from the surrounding country the means of transporting his flour to a place of safety.
>
> If the petitioner has commingled his property with that of the government, he must abide the loss, unless the government has prevented him, by impressing his means of transportation, from securing his property. The witnesses, several of them, state that it was occupied by our troops, leaving the inference to be drawn that the flour was destroyed by fire communicated to the store house.
>
> Thomas Lewis, who was on board of the British fleet, and who commanded a party that landed, states that the British were in great want of provisions, that they took from this store house of Merrill's a quantity of flour. Jesse Brown says he saw the British in the act of plundering and carrying away the flour.
>
> The government does not pay for the loss of personal property under such circumstances.

## William Wickham

William Wickham filed a claim with the Treasury Department, which was denied by Peter Hagner, the Third Auditor. He replied on July 19, 1825:

> Sir: I have received yours of the 2d July, and am truly sorry that you cannot make any award in my favor. Perhaps, if the original papers were found, you might be of a different opinion. That my house was not occupied at a second call, is very true; for the militia did not get here until the damage was done, although they had plenty of time, for they were within three miles of the place all night.
>
> There was at the time in the store-houses at this place about 1,000 barrels of flour, which was removed by the citizens of the village, and which, had the citizens agreed to have given up, the houses would have been saved. This offer was made by a flag of truce from the enemy's fleet.
>
> But, sir, I think my claim to be among the strongest, for, at the time my house was burnt, it was occupied as the post office, and it was a positive command of the British commander, when the boats left the ships, to destroy the post office and all the papers. Of this fact there is proof, among my papers, in an affidavit from the boatswain of Sir James Yeo's ship, who resided here at this place about a year since the war, and heard the order given after the boats had left the ship.
>
> I could say much of my own case, but it is unnecessary. But I have always been of opinion that had the public stores been kept away, or had there been a force here to protect us, our property would have been saved. I had been but about one year in this part of the country when my house was burnt, and had bought it only about six months when it was burnt, and with it all I possessed.
>
> The grand canal has now taken all business from our place, and left me without any possible

means of paying debts, which the destruction of my property has brought upon me. I have been threatened with prosecution, and have kept it off only in the expectation that the late appropriation of Congress might supply me funds.

Yours respectfully,
William Wickham

As reported by the Committee of Claims on December 30, 1836, in part:

The petitioner asks remuneration for the destruction of his buildings at Sodus Bay, in the State of New York, but the enemy during the war, and for the destruction of his furniture and other articles consumed in his house.

His buildings are described as follows, viz: One two-story house, $5,000; kitchen adjoining, $800; wood-house, $150; furniture and other articles, $910. Total $6,800.

When the troops were at Sodus Bay, William Wickham owned and occupied the buildings mentioned. Some of the soldiers cooked their victuals in his kitchen; one officer is said to have had a room in his house; and one witness says he thinks some of the soldiers occupied some of the rooms in the house as sleeping rooms.

It is not stated where the guard was stationed, but it is not pretended that they occupied any of Mr. Wickham's buildings, and the presumption is, inasmuch as the guard was detailed to protect the property that they were with the property, which had been removed to what was considered a place of safety.

In the evening of the 19th the enemy landed and burnt Mr. Merrill's store-house, with the dwelling house of Mr. Wickham and others. Some of the witnesses say there was a smart engagement when the enemy landed near Mr. Wickham's house, when several of the enemy were killed. The enemy sent a flag of truce, which was met by a similar one from the Americans, and the bearer of the British flag proposed to spare private property if the public property was delivered up.

The value of the buildings is proven by several witnesses. Major Perrin Willis wrote to the Secretary of War on the 4th of June, 1817, giving some account of the landing of the enemy and the burning of Trupeville (Sodus Bay) which was afterwards communicated to the House of Representatives.

It will appear from Mr. Wickham's letter to Mr. Hagner, dated July 19, 1825, that the writer did not pretend that his house was occupied by the troops of the United States, or as a place of deposit, at the time it was destroyed, but he thought the occupation was so recently before the buildings were destroyed that his claim was within the spirit and meaning of the acts mentioned.

In the opinion of the committee, the testimony does not prove that the buildings were at any time so occupied as to bring the case within the intention or meaning of the acts heretofore mentioned.

The occupation must be that which, for the time being, makes the buildings public property, and, therefore the legitimate subjects of destruction by the enemy.

Soldiers called out on a sudden emergency do not change the ownership of a house by cooking a few meals of victuals in a kitchen; nor is such change made by an officer occupying a room in a house, nor by soldiers sleeping in it where the owner remains in possession and controls his property. But when these buildings were destroyed, the militia that had occupied them were dismissed and it does not appear by any legal testimony that the enemy ever knew that soldiers were in them at any time. The witnesses concur in saying that the public stores attracted the attention of the enemy, and the fact that he offered to spare private property if the public property was surrendered, is conclusive that he did not consider the dwelling-house as public property; and that the destruction was wanton and revengeful.

The committee cannot, without departing from long-settled principles allow the claim.

## *Chateaugay*

Chateaugay, in Franklin County, on the Adirondack Frontier, was settled in 1796. Troops were stationed there and a skirmish or battle was reportedly fought just north of the town.

### Ichabod Peck

The petition was submitted by Mary Peck, as reported by the Committee of Claims on February 13, 1839:

The petitioner states that Ichabod was a sutler to the 29th Regiment United States Army, acting in that capacity during the years 1813 and 1814, and that he furnished the officers and soldiers from his shop, by orders of Colonel Guilford D. Young. Young took from his shop at Chateaugay, Four-Corners, New York, a large amount of property in groceries and provisions.

He brought an action against Young in Chittenden County, Vermont, and recovered judgment against him for the sum of $1,783.56 in 1815. A new trial having been granted, Peck was unable to prosecute the claim whereby he lost all benefit therefrom. The petitioner further states that she is poor and prays for relief in the premises.

Among the papers is an account in which the United States is made debtor to Peck as follows:

"To sundry articles, clothing, provisions, and other necessary articles for the use of the army, made use of and destroyed at Chateaugay, October 10th, 1813, consisting of rum, brandy, tobacco, and other groceries, amounting in all to the sum of $2,239.51."

Ichabod Peck, then residing in Lower Canada, deposes that on or about October 10th, 1813, all the articles were taken by the United States troops and "were made use of by the troops and were destroyed and wholly lost to him."

Nathan Smith, of Burlington, Vermont, says he saw some soldiers of the 29th Regiment forcibly enter the shop under the direction of an officer, take what was in the shop, and set fire to the building, and he states this was done by direction of Colonel Young, who was present.

Benjamin Fellows deposes that the property was forcibly taken by the troops from Peck.

Malachi Lovering deposes that on or about the 10th October, 1813, he was a lieutenant in the 11th Regiment of Infantry and was personally knowing to Lt. Col. Guilford D. Young ordering a detachment under the command of Captain James B. Spencer, "to go and take the provisions, groceries, &c. of Ichabod Peck, who was a sutler at Chateaugay, and that he knows of no payment having been made for the articles destroyed."

It will be noted that Nathan Smith alone states that any property in the shop was destroyed by fire.

The papers are accompanied by a power of attorney from Ichabod Peck to Joseph Potter, of Burlington, Vermont, dated in 1816, authorizing him to collect debts, &c.

The cause of this order on the part of Colonel Young does not appear satisfactorily. One deponent says it was said at the time to be because Peck sold a gill of rum to a soldier.

It appears by a certificate of the clerk that a suit was commenced at the September term of Chittenden County Court by Peck, against Guilford Young and that in September, 1815, Peck recovered judgment by verdict for $1,733 damages and also costs of suit. A new trial was granted at the term, and at the February term, 1816, a second verdict was rendered for the plaintiff for $758.34, and, on motion, a new trial was granted, and that, in September, 1816, the following entry was made: "Nonsuit for want of bail; defendant's cost, $29.09."

If, through poverty, Peck was unable to prosecute his suit further as stated in the petition, it is certainly to be regretted.

It does not appear upon what ground new trials were twice granted, but there is reason to believe, from the circumstances that, while the transaction was recent, two juries found verdicts for Peck against Colonel Young, that he had sustained damage for which Colonel Young was personally responsible.

The committee can see no ground whatever to support a claim against the United States. It is not proved that any property was taken from Peck for the use of the United States army by orders of Colonel Young, or any other officer, and the United States are not responsible for the unauthorized acts of military officers, much less for their trespasses.

They therefore recommend that the petitioner is not entitled to relief.

Ichabod Peck was a Revolutionary War veteran from Massachusetts and served at Dorchester Heights, Trenton, Long Island, and in Sullivan's retreat from Rhode Island. He applied for a pension in 1818 due to his "reduced circumstances."

Guilford Dudley Young, of Connecticut, was honorably discharged on June 15, 1815, from the 29th Infantry and was mortally wounded on August 18, 1818, during Miranda's Mexican expedition.

## Philip Bryant

As stated by the Committee of Claims on February 24, 1818:

In 1813, the petitioner volunteered as a lieutenant under Captain David Erwin of the militia and continued in service till discharged by Major General Wade Hampton. In the winter of 1814 he was employed by Colonel Daniel Bissel to reconnoiter the enemy's lines and to watch their movements.

A part of his house was occupied as a guard-house during the time the army remained there, which was about three months. About the time of the evacuation of the American army, there were stored at his house 30 barrels of beef and pork, which belonged to the United States.

Immediately after the removal of the American army, the enemy approached them, and because they found public property at his house; because they had performed this service, and because a part of his of his house had been occupied by a guard, they became much exasperated and plundered or destroyed whatever of furniture and other personal property they could find. At the same time they also injured the house itself as much as they could, without entirely demolishing it, destroying the doors, floors, and windows. He therefore prays Congress to indemnify him to the amount of $600.

The petitioner himself assigns to the enemy a plurality of motives for the destruction: to wit, "that he had rendered service to his country; that a guard had occupied a part of his house some time previously to the destruction; that beef and pork were in it."

To say that an enemy is at liberty to destroy the property of citizens because they serve their country, saps at once the foundation of patriotism, and overthrows the whole system of honorable warfare among nations. Such a principle would prepare the way for every terrible ill attending a war, not of victory, but of extermination.

The committee are unable to determine the quantum of injury done to the petitioner on account of each of these distinct, if not contradictory, motives which have been imputed to the enemy. It appears to them that, taking into view all the circumstances of the case, the more rational conclusion will be that the destruction of the property is only another instance of outrage committed by the enemy during the late war. The prayer of the petitioner ought not to be granted.

Lt. Bryant lived in Chateauguay with his wife Sophia and was in Capt. Erwin's company from March to November 1813. In the battle there on October 26, 1813, the British repelled the American advance into Lower Canada and eventually to Montreal. At some point the Bryant's moved to Erie, Pennsylvania.

# *Franklin County*

## William G. and Benjamin Roberts

As reported by the Committee of Claims on March 4, 1822:

The petitioners ask remuneration for sundry losses alleged to have resulted from the taking of their property by the troops of the United States in the fall of 1813, to wit:

200 rods of good rail fence, at 40 cents—$80; 7 tons of hay taken from the barn, $70; 40 shocks of rye and oats, $40; 20 shocks of wheat, $40; 150 bushels of turnips taken from the field, $37.50; 25 bushels of potatoes taken from the field, $12.50; 6 bushels of onions taken from the garden, $9, for a total of $289.

The property is alleged to have been taken while the troops under the command of General Wade Hampton were passing and repassing from the borders of Lake Champlain to the county of Franklin, in the state of New York. It is not shown, nor is it even alleged, that the property was taken by order of any officer of the United States, or that any necessity existed for the taking, and, in the opinion of the committee, the claim be rejected.

# *New York City*

## Eleanor Lawrence

As reported to the Senate by Secretary of War Calhoun on December 19, 1820:

It appears that in 1813 a volunteer corps in the service of the United States took possession of

> a part of the petitioner's farm and that in 1814 General Swift, by order of the government, erected certain defenses, which, with the farm and its buildings, continued to be occupied by the troops of the United States until August, 1816, when it was evacuated.
>
> After the evacuation a person was employed to take charge of the property of the United States left on the premises, who has continued to perform that duty to the present time, without, however, considering it as excluding the occupancy of the buildings and farm by the proprietor.
>
> Upon a full consideration of the facts, Mrs. Lawrence appears to have a well founded claim against the government for damages which she may have sustained in consequence of the occupation of her farm by the troops of the United States, or from injuries resulting therefrom.
>
> It appears by the petition she proposes two modes of redress, either to convey the farm to the United States, at what it originally cost, with interest thereon, or to retain it and to be remunerated for the damages which she has sustained. It may be proper to remark that it would not appear to be advisable to accede to the former mode as it appears by the report of the board of engineers charged with preparing a plan for the defense of the coast that the position will not be required for the defense of New York and that it is not necessary for military purposes.
>
> This Department has no information as to the amount of damages which the petitioner may have sustained, but should the Senate believe the claim to be well founded, I would respectfully suggest the propriety of the passing of an act of the claim on equitable principles under which measures would be taken to ascertain the exact amount of damages.

Eleanor Lawrence was paid $1,070 in 1823.

Joseph Gardener Swift was in the first graduating class of West Point and joined the engineers. He supervised construction of Fort Johnston in North Carolina in 1804, the Governor's Island Batteries at Boston in 1808, and then coastal defenses. During the war, he was chief engineer of the Department of New York and commanded a brigade on Staten Island under Gen. Wilkinson. He was in the Battle of Crysler's Field and continued engineering and survey work after the war.

## David Griffing

David Griffing lived in Brooklyn. As reported by the Committee of Commerce on January 22, 1839:

> It appears that the petitioner on the 28th of April, 1813, during the war with Great Britain, was part owner of the sloop *Maria Anne*, of Riverhead, and while the petitioner was engaged in transporting wood through Long Island Sound for the New York market, on account of the owners of the sloop, she was captured and burnt by barges attached to and fitted out by the British frigate *Acasta* and sloop-of-war *Atalanta*.
>
> The committee are unanimously of opinion that the petitioner is not entitled to relief from Congress, and ask to be discharged from the further consideration of the petition.

The *Atalanta* was probably Capt. Frederick Hickey's 18-gun sloop *Atalante*, which was wrecked off Halifax on November 10, 1813.

## Robert Brady

As stated by Peter Hagner, the Third Auditor, on April 13, 1844, in part:

> The petition of Robert Brady represents that in 1813 he was the owner of the schooner *Eagle*, then lying in the port of New York. In June she was taken possession of for the benefit of the government and loaded with combustible materials for the purpose of sending her amongst the British fleet then blockading New London, with a view to its destruction. The contemplated object was so far successful that a boat belonging to the *Ramilies*, 74, which was sent to take possession of the schooner, together with a crew estimated at 100 men, were utterly destroyed. His vessel at the time she was taken of was worth $2,500 to $3,000 and was so valued at the time.
>
> He was so circumstanced pecuniarily, as to render an application to his government for indemnification unnecessary, but now, having

been brought by adverse circumstances, to a state of comparative poverty, he presents his claim, relying fully upon its sense of justice to indemnify him for the loss then sustained.

The papers accompanying his petition consist of a certified copy of the register of the vessel issued at Philadelphia on the 30th July, 1811, and a testimonial of the good character of the petitioner dated Philadelphia Feb. 23, 1844, having 12 signatures thereto, expressed to be of merchants and other citizens of Philadelphia.

The vessel, according to the register, was a schooner of 77–27/95 tons, built at Plymouth, Massachusetts, in 1798, and it shows the petitioner was only a joint owner with John Wood, the master of it.

With reference to the blockade of Commodore Decatur's squadron in the harbor of New London in the summer of 1813, there is found a description of an attempt to blow up some of the English vessels by a fire-ship, containing as follows: "The fire-ship was called the *Eagle*, and fitted out for the purpose by John Scudder. It was supposed that on her being captured, she would be taken alongside one of the vessels of war, when, in attempting to unload her, a considerable quantity of powder and other combustibles would have been set on fire. The attempt was made in the month of June. She was taken possession of by the British but blew up before she got alongside of any of their large vessels. At the time of explosion four boats were alongside, which were all, with the men on board them, destroyed. It is supposed that upwards of 100 of the British perished."

I am not aware of any means accessible to me, whereby to ascertain who John Scudder was or by whom he was employed. If by a naval officer, the account as to his transactions, would more probably have been rendered to the Navy Department than to the War Department.

No documents were found at the Navy Department, and, as stated by the Committee of Claims on January 15, 1846: "That for the reasons set forth by the Third Auditor, the committee recommend the rejection of the prayer of the petitioner."

## The *Catherine Eliza*

As reported by the Committee of Claims on February 28, 1844:

The petitioner, Cornelius V.C. Ludlow, represents that in 1814 he was joint owner with John Whitman of the schooner *Catherine Eliza*, of 42 tons burden, of which Whitman was master, and engaged in carrying firewood from South Bay of Long Island to the port of New York, and while so engaged, on or about the last of July, 1814, and while under way from Fire Island inlet to Sandy Hook, she was intercepted by the British squadron under command of Admiral George Cockburn, driven ashore near Rockaway or Cochran's inlet, where she was pursued by the enemy's boats, set fire to, and destroyed with her cargo of wood, alleged to be worth, in all $2,500, or upwards, for which indemnity is claimed of the United States.

These facts are established by the depositions of Morris Covert, Andrew Nostrand, and Hendrick Lott, but are not sufficient to form the basis of a claim on government. The United States have never been known to respond to damages to the individual owners of vessels captured or destroyed by the enemy in time of war.

If the owner of any vessel chooses to expose it to the risk of capture, in the pursuit of a profitable trade in the face of an enemy during the continuance of war, no liability can attach to the government under which he may live, on account of its capture or destruction.

The committee think the petitioner is not entitled to relief.

## Rulif Van Brunt

Rulif rented about 30 acres in Brooklyn "to the north of the lane of Samuel Bouten, meeting the south lane of William Cornwell's land," and was to "plough the stalk ground and sow it with oats or barley, and seed it with clover, and plough one other lot for corn or market truck."

Van Brunt's petition, in part:

Your petitioner, Rulif Van Brunt, respectfully represents that he is a citizen of Schenectady county, in the State of New York, and in the year 1814 was a resident of Brooklyn, in the county of Kings and State of New York, and was the lessee of a certain lot of land in Brooklyn from one John Jackson, of the same place, for the term of one year from the 1st day of April, 1814, to the 1st day of April, 1815, at a rent of $325 per annum, which rent was duly paid to John Jackson.

Your petitioner entered upon the premises on the 1st day of April, 1814, and cultivated the same by putting in a crop of grain and vegetables.

On the 9th day of August, 1814, the premises were entered upon by the military authorities of the county, and, as he is informed, by the military raised under the charge of the committee called the Committee of Defense of the city of New York, and the premises were occupied from and after the 9th day of August, 1814, until about the 3rd day of December, 1814, and a fort called Fort Green was erected thereon, which was occupied by the military of the United States, and the whole premises and the crops grown and growing were taken, appropriated, and destroyed by the committee, or by the military, or by those acting under their authority, and your petitioner thereby lost his entire crop, his labor, and the rent paid by him for the premises, and was damaged thereby in the sum of $1,050.

Van Brunt filed a claim in December 1844, for $960 that was referred to the Committee on Claims, and then, on January 7, 1850, to the Committee on Military Affairs, who issued an adverse report. On April 29, 1852, it went back to the Committee on Claims and on May 3, 1854, a bill passed authorizing the Treasury Department to audit and adjust the claim and to pay an amount not exceeding $750, but on June 10, 1854, the bill went back to the Committee on Claims on, and on February 22, 1855, another adverse report was issued. On March 3, 1855, the matter went to the newly-formed Court of Claims.

Jeremiah Johnson, of Brooklyn, who knew Jackson, stated the signature on Van Brunt's lease was John Jackson's, and he testified on October 8, 1844:

I certify that the 22nd Brigade of New York Infantry, under my command, was ordered into the service of the United States and encamped at Fort Greene, in the county of Kings, on 2nd day of September, 1814, on land owned by John Jackson, which, with a house and barn, he had rented to Rulif Van Brunt. About half of the land whereon the fort was built, and the land whereon the brigade encamped, is included in the lease of Mr. Van Brunt. All the fence was removed from the land, and the produce of his labor destroyed before the 2nd of September. The dwelling-house was in the possession of a man named Turney, and the barn was occupied as a guard-house by my order, on the consent of John Jackson.

I further certify that John B. Coles and John Morse, of the city of New York, and myself, appraised the damages sustained by John Jackson and several other persons, occasioned by the occupation of their land for the public service and defense, and that the damage sustained by Mr. Van Brunt was not appraised by us.

Samuel Doxsey, "superintendent of the poor of Kings County," knew John Jackson and Van Brunt and testified that he was a member of the 64th Regiment of New York Militia in Gen. Jeremiah Johnson's command and that all the straw, hay, and grain was used for bedding, and that "Van Brunt was compelled to abandon the farm and procure a house for his family and stabling for his stock elsewhere."

As reported by the Committee on Military Affairs on January 22, 1850:

The petitioner sets forth that in 1814 he was a resident of Brooklyn, New York, the lessee of 30 acres of land at a rent charge of $300 a year. That his premises in September were occupied by a military party, ordered out by the Committee of Defense of the city of New York. In occupying, they destroyed his crops, &c., to the amount of $1,000.

As evidence of the lease, the article of agreement is presented, well authenticated. As evidence of the payment of rent to the lessor, the petitioner presents two receipts for $81; each satisfying a half year's rent, terminating in July preceding the fall of the military occupation.

The petitioner presents no vouchers showing the payment of rent for the last half year within which period the damage accrued. The petitioner shows, by proof, that some period soon after the damage accrued—as the committee are left to conclude from the certificate of one of the witnesses—the damage was appraised, and for some mysterious reason the petitioner, although a severe sufferer, was overlooked.

All of the facts have brought the committee to the conclusion, that if a claim ever did exist, it was a claim against the city or State of New York, and should have been then presented for liquidation.

From the fact that there is no evidence of the payment of rent for the last half year, and the fact that the lessor received assessment of damage for an injury done at the same place, at the same time, and by the same means, it is quite probable that the lessor and lessee adjusted the matter between them.

The claim, as presented to the committee, shows upon its face evident dishonesty.

On June 6, 1859, the Court of Claims rejected the claim for want of evidence. This is one of the very last claims from the War of 1812.

## John J. Johnson

The petitions of John J. Johnson, Samuel Plumb, Ralph Patchen, Samuel Bouton, Hannah Debois, and Margaret Duffield, all of Brooklyn, were addressed together. Fort Greene was in Brooklyn. As stated by the Committee of Claims on January 5, 1819:

John J. Johnson describes his claim for $995, thus: "To use and occupation of land for entrenchments, redoubts, parade ground, &c., from the 1st of December, 1814, to the 1st of June, 1815, near Fort Greene." In support of which John Jackson, Ralph Patchen, and Jacob Pearsall, under date of June, 1815, certify that they "are acquainted with the damages and injuries done by the United States and its agents by the occupation of his land, and are of opinion that the charge is correct."

Robert Bogardus, who signs "late Col. 41st Regiment Militia, and commanding Fort Greene," certifies under date of the 30th of September, 1815, "that the land of John J. Johnson was necessarily continued in use for public purposes from the 1st of December, 1814, till the removal of the ordnance, &c. from Fort Greene and its dependencies, which took place in August and September, 1815. The amount of injury done to, or what would be a fair compensation for the use of the land, he will not undertake to say, not being a competent judge," and further certifies, "that the persons who have signed the annexed certificate are respectable freeholders."

To the above certificate is annexed that of J.G. Swift, in the following words: "The land mentioned was to my knowledge occupied by lines, &c."

John Jackson in an affidavit made on oath the 6th January, 1817, states, "that he is acquainted with the property of John J. Jackson, that he has examined the land, and that Johnson has sustained damages to the amount of $750, according to the best of his knowledge and belief."

Jacob Pearsall and Ralph Patchen made their affidavits on the 6th of January, in which nearly the same words are used, except in lieu of $750, they estimate the damage at the exact sum claimed by the petitioner.

Philip Reed testifies that, "he is well acquainted with the value of property in Brooklyn, that he is of opinion the annexed account is a reasonable charge for damages sustained by him during the period therein charged."

The committee feel no difficulty in admitting that the petitioner may have sustained damage for which he has a fair claim to compensation, but they cannot admit that he has made out a case which will authorize an allowance to any amount whatever; there being nothing of legal certainty in the case presented. They are far from feeling a disposition to question the correctness of the statements and opinions of the witnesses, and trust they shall not be understood as intending to question them, when they express a belief that there is not sufficient certainty in any of the affidavits to support an indictment for perjury, in case their whole contents were false. The affidavits furnish no data by which to test their truth.

The petitioner ought surely to have furnished the committee the name of the officer or "agent" who took possession of and occupied his land. If his claim consisted in rent for the use of his land, he ought to have shown the quantity of the land occupied, and what was a fair price for the rent of the like lands in the vicinity. If for damages in digging up the land, he ought to have shown the extent of the digging.

Independent of the objections already stated, there are others, which, in the opinion of the committee, must be deemed fatal to the claim, until removed by clear and unequivocal testimony. It is understood to have been a rule of the Department of War, "that when private lands and buildings are occupied by troops of the United States, a reasonable compensation shall be made to the proprietor by the quartermaster of the district or post, and when a rate of compensation cannot be satisfactorily agreed on, discreet and disinterested persons shall be appointed by the quartermaster and proprietor to appraise the rent, which shall be settled by the quartermaster, and the damages paid."

After an attentive examination of the case, the committee have been unable to discover any proper grounds for allowing any part of the claim; and as those of Samuel Plumb, Ralph Patchen, Samuel Bouton, Hannah Debois, and Margaretta Duffield are of the same nature, and supported by no better testimony, they recommend that the prayer of the petitioners ought not to be granted.

Col. Joseph Gardner Swift, of Massachusetts, was appointed chief engineer in the regular Army on July 31, 1812.

## *New Utrecht*

### Thomas D. Smith

Catherine M. Smith, of New York, filed a claim as reported by the Committee of Claims on June 15, 1836:

The petitioner states the guard of the 42nd Regiment of the United States Infantry, stationed at New Utrecht, on discharging their pieces, on the 26th of September, 1814, killed a horse, the property of her husband, Thomas D. Smith. She says the animal was in a field where he was usually kept. The guard fired across the road into the field without warning, and that they had always previously discharged their pieces on the river.

She requests compensation to be made with interest thereon from the 20th of September, 1814. She says vouchers were sent to Congress many years ago, of which copies are now furnished.

The copies referred to are an appraisement made on the 31st of October, 1814, signed by Peter Cortelyon, said to have been appointed by Col. Bogardus, and also signed by George Van Brunt, said to have been chosen mediator and also signed by William A. Bayley, said to have been appointed by Mr. Smith; also the copy of a certificate said to have been signed by Robert Bogardus, colonel commanding at New Utrecht at that time, which states, "that the guard of the 42d regiment United States infantry, stationed at New Utrecht, in the act of discharging their pieces, after relief, on the 26th of September, 1814, shot a horse, the property of Thomas D. Smith; that the horse died a few hours thereafter."

Also, the copy of a certificate, purporting to have been signed by Robert Bogardus, as follows:

"The within is a copy of a certificate given by me at the time it bears date; I well remember the circumstances to which the certificate refers. Robert Bogardus, October 2, 1832."

The original papers are not before the committee. The committee applied at the clerk's office and examined its own books without being able to find that the claim was ever presented before.

The copies are greatly deficient. Col. Bogardus does not state how he has any knowledge of the things about which he certifies. Was he present, and did he see the guard fire? Did he give the command? Why did the guard fire in that direction, or at the time when they had uniformly before fired on the river? How did Col. Bogardus know the horse was shot at that time by the guard? If Col. Bogardus cannot answer these inquiries from his personal knowledge, the testimony of the officer who commanded the guard should be taken.

The committee would desire to know whether complaint was made at that time by Mr. Smith, and whether any suit was commenced by him, and if so, against whom, and with what result?

The claim as now presented should not be admitted because the testimony is greatly defective; but the United States have not paid for trespasses that have been wantonly committed by her military or naval forces, nor under civil authority.

The whole facts in the case should be presented, that the committee might judge, whether they took this case out of the general rule. The petitioner is not entitled to relief.

# Vermont

## *Vermont Claims*

### Oliver and Mary Wiley

In 1812, Oliver and Mary Wiley lived in Alburgh, Vermont, just below the present Canadian line.

When the war started in June, Lt. Col. Zebulon Pike was a deputy quartermaster general. He was promoted to colonel of the 15th Regiment of Infantry on July 6, "for the command of the land forces in an expedition against York, the capital of Upper Canada"—present-day Toronto. The plan was to embark troops at Sackets Harbor aboard Comm. Isaac Chauncey's schooners for the trip north.

Philip B. Robert was in charge of building barracks at Plattsburgh, and in January 1813, Pike ordered the troops stationed at Alburgh to join his army at Plattsburgh, about 20 miles south of Rouse's Point across Lake Champlain from Alburgh. The officers were directed to impress horses and sleighs in the area to transport the men and their baggage.

In the meantime, Oliver was drafted into the militia, and while in service, on or about January 1, 1813, his "two-horse team, sleigh, and harness were pressed by the United States troops under command of General Pike into the service of the United States." Being then in militia duty, he was obliged to hire Thomas Clark, a reliable man he knew, to drive his team and lookout for them while in service.

When his horses were returned two months later, "they were entirely used up and died immediately, and the harness broken in pieces, the sleigh broken and tied up with withes, and both sleigh and harness valueless." He claimed at the time Clark's labor was worth $2 a day, his horses were worth $200, the sleigh and harness $50, but he was never paid, was never given or demanded a receipt, and the matter was apparently forgotten.

Why he never filed a timely claim after that was not stated, but on February 28, 1854, he was deposed under oath for the purpose of claiming $1,280 from 1813: $200 for two horses, one sleigh and one harness valued at $60 and the Army's use of the team and a driver for 60 days at $3 a day, the total being $430, plus $910 in interest at 6 percent from 1813. Stephen and James Wiley, of Chazy, were deposed as witnesses before Anthony Trombly, Justice of the Peace, at the same time.

On March 23, 1855, Oliver and Mary assigned their claim to their son, Albert, and Albert subsequently sold all rights to the claim to James Valentine, of Champlain, for $100 and Valentine petitioned the Court of Claims.

On November 25, 1858, George Weeks, 67, of Rouse's Point, testified that on March 8, 1813, he was a farmer in Champlain County, New York, when a lieutenant and eight soldiers came to his house and ordered him to take them to Alburgh with his team and sleigh, which he did. He said other teams and sleighs were seized at Alburgh when he was ordered to the army camp at Plattsburgh.

After Thomas Clark arrived at Plattsburgh, he waited nine days for a squad to get ready to depart, and he was ordered to Sackets Harbor, 95 miles to the southwest. George Weeks went along with the group and reported:

> He was in company with claimant's team all the way from Plattsburgh to Sackett's Harbor. The sleighing was poor, some of the time bare ground; some of the teams were loaded heavier than others. Claimant's team was heavily loaded, and obliged to keep up with those that were lighter loaded. They were not suffered to lag behind, and were urged forward, whether able to go or not. I noticed that claimant's team was urged beyond its strength, not by the driver, but those in the sleigh and the officers in command. When they got to Sackett's Harbor, claimant's harness was all drawn to pieces, and his sleigh broken, and horses jaded out. In returning, the horses gave out at Canton, and were unable to draw the broken, empty sleigh. The driver was obliged to lead the horses home.

Richard Steanburgh, 71, of Duane, New York, said his team was also pressed into service and that he knew Oliver Wiley's team was gone 60 days and that both horses died soon after returning home owing to, "loading them so heavily, and compelling them to proceed and keep up with the army." He stated the horses were worth $200, the sleigh and harness $50, and that neither Oliver Wiley nor Thomas Clark were ever paid.

He stated that on March 1, 1813, the United States pressed his own driver and team to transport troops and military stores from Alburgh, Vermont, to Plattsburgh, New York, and from Plattsburgh to Sackets Harbor. As a result of very hard service and poor and limited forage, the horses died and the harness and sleigh were ruined.

James Valentine, of Chazy, was married to Richard Steanburgh's sister.

The Court found there was no hard evidence as to how long Oliver Wiley's team and sleigh were gone, he never filed a claim, and the statute of limitations—two years—had expired long before, and the claim was denied on February 11, 1860.

## Libeus Forbes and Orange Hoisington

On June 9, 1836, the Committee of Claims reported that in 1813 General John Chandler, gave orders "to impress the means of transporting his command."

Commissioners were afterwards appointed to settle and adjust the claims. Libeus Forbes' sleigh, two horses and harness were impressed and lost. Orange Hoisington's sleigh was impressed and lost.

On June 1, 1814, the commissioners awarded Forbes $139 and Hoisington $17.50 plus $20 for going to Burlington to get the accounts.

On November 20, 1816, the money was paid to Abishai Hoisington, attorney for Forbes and Hoisington at Plattsburg. Abishai was also from Windsor.

Forbes and Hoisington lived in Windsor, Vermont. Libeus married Chloe Hoisington on December 6, 1804, in Windsor. He also owned property in Richland, Ohio.

## Aaron Bellamy

As reported by the Committee of Claims on February 13, 1838:

> It appears that General Dearborn ordered Col. Clarke, in April, 1813, to remove a quantity of provisions on Lake Champlain to a place of safety beyond the reach of the enemy. Col. Clarke directed Major Justus Bellamy to procure a vessel, and to remove the provisions accordingly.
>
> The vessel of Aaron Bellamy, of Vermont, was employed for that purpose. Some time in July, Judge Ezra Meech informed Col. Clarke a quantity of flour that belonged to the United States was at his landing, and exposed to be captured. Col. Clarke immediately ordered Major Justus Bellamy to attend to its removal.

> There were no vessels in sight, and he proceeded down the lake for the purpose of procuring one, and, discovering the vessel of Aaron Bellamy standing for Crown Point, where the master, Thomas Babcock, had been directed to take a quantity of iron ore and transport to White Hall, a part of which had already been freighted and was employed with the vessel in conveying the residue, Major Bellamy directed Babcock to proceed to the landing of Meech at Shelburne Bay, and remove the flour. He refused, and assigned as a reason that he was obliged by a contract to remove the iron ore and that he was fearful if he went north he would fall in with the enemy, who was known to be in that part of the lake.
>
> Major Bellamy then told him he would impress him and his boat into the service. Mr. Babcock still refused. Major Bellamy then showed him Col. Clarke's order and threatened him with a prosecution and imprisonment if he did not go, supposing he had that power vested in him. Capt. Babcock then went with the vessel, and while loading at Shelburne Bay, the enemy surprised and captured the vessel with the flour.
>
> It is stated by Major Bellamy that no contract was made for the hires and use of the vessel; that no risk was incurred by the owner, and that it was seized and captured without any fault of the owner or master. Several witnesses say the value of the vessel was $1,500, and that the loss to the owner was much more. The vessel was about the burthen of 50 tons as stated by one witness, and if it were not for the remark of the commissioners, the committee would be inclined to estimate the value of the vessel higher, from the testimony, than it was put at by Mr. Bradbury. But, as they were on the spot, and knew the weight to be given to the evidence, the committee will take the highest value as estimated by Capt. Francis Bradbury.
>
> They think the claimant is entitled to relief, and report a bill.

Aaron Bellamy, of Vergennes, was paid $900 in 1834. Justus Bellamy was Aaron's father. Col. Clarke was probably Col. Isaac Clark of the 11th Infantry Regiment.

## Gideon King and Ezra Thurber

Ezra Thurber, a tide waiter (customs inspector) and spy from Point au Roche, New York, and Gideon King, of Burlington, Vermont, were shipowners. By 1800 "Admiral King" owned about 40 percent of the merchant fleet on Lake Champlain, including the sloops *Essex*, *Dolphin* and *Lady Washington*. When war came in 1812, he obtained letters of marque.

In October 1812, Master Commandant Thomas Macdonough was sent to Lake Champlain to stop the British advance from Canada and set up his headquarters at Burlington. He then acquired three merchant sloops, the *Growler*, *Eagle*, and *President* and put 11 guns on each.

*Growler*, purchased at White Hall, New York, at the very southern end of the lake was commissioned under Lt. Sidney Smith and captured on June 3, 1813, near Île aux Noix in the Richelieu River and taken into service by the British.

*Eagle*, purchased at White Hall and commissioned under Sailing Master Jarius Loomis, was also captured on June 3, 1813, near Île aux Noix. The boat entered British service as the *Finch*.

*President* was purchased by the War Department, transferred to the Navy, but was soon sold out of service as unserviceable.

With the loss of these vessels, the British were able to control the lake so Macdonough began building a fleet on Otter Creek at Vergennes, Vermont.

On July 31, 1813, Archibald Ferris, master of the *Essex*, was at White Hall waiting to take a cargo of salt and nails to merchants along the shore as far as Plattsburg, New York, about 80 miles to the north. He planned to leave when word arrived that the coast was clear of British ships.

That day, Navy Sailing Master Samuel Kettletas, in charge of 18 bluejackets, arrived at White Hall with orders from Capt. James Renshaw to proceed to Burlington, about 65 miles north, to join Macdonough's command. Kettletas saw the *Essex* and requested Capt. Ferris to take them to their destination as an urgent matter and said if he refused he would seize his vessel. After Capt. Ferris explained the nature of the risk, Kettletas agreed to go only as far as Capt. Ferris thought it was safe without risk of capture, and the sailors came aboard. They got underway and stopped at Essex, about 12 miles south of Burlington, to obtain information about British ship movements, and when they learned the British were near Plattsburg, Ferris refused to go any farther. Kettletas then took charge and left Ferris ashore. Ferris then became anxious that he might incur the wrath of the owners and at some point got a boat, came up to his ship, and at Burlington ordered the Navy men off.

It was deemed unsafe to stay there so Ferris headed back to White Hall in very light winds and a short time later, after about 15 miles, they were captured, possibly by Cdr. Daniel Pring's British sloop *Linnet*. Pring referred to the Americans as "Jonathans" and burned the *Essex*, possibly because he had no sailors to spare for a prize crew. Since the Americans had no other ship to report to, he released them, and Kettletas and Loomis were both present during the battle on September 11, 1814.

Thurber and King's heirs filed a claim on December 27, 1821. Capt. Ferris testified that if he had been allowed to return to White Hall from Essex his vessel would not have been lost. In addition none of the cargo was consigned to anyone at Essex or Burlington so could not be discharged there. Joseph F. Finney, who was on board the *Essex* testified on Capt. Ferris' behalf along with Uriah Higgins, Charles McNiel, and William Martin. All testified the value of the vessel was at least $1,200.

The claim was last filed on January 13, 1826. There was considerable discussion as to whether or not a contract existed between Kettletas and Ferris and what the true nature of the danger was at the time. The Committee held the loss was covered by Sec. 3 in the Act of April 1816.

During the battle on Lake Champlain on September 11, 1814, *Linnet* was severely damaged by Macdonough's flagship *Saratoga* and the two sloops of Macdonough's original little fleet were recaptured.

Ezra Thurber and the legal representatives of Gideon King were paid $1,200 in 1830. For prize money for captures on Lake Champlain, Comm. Macdonough was paid $22,807; Sailing Master Samuel Kettletas $2,012.17; and Jarius Loomis $2,012.75 as reported by the Secretary of the Navy John C. Calhoun on December 17, 1818.

## Loudon Case

That there be paid to Loudon Case, of the state of Vermont, the sum of $92, the value of a yoke of oxen impressed into the military service of the United States in the fall of 1813.

January 7, 1824. (6 Stat. L. 291)

In 1810 Case lived in Salisbury, Vermont, and, until 1812, operated a tavern in Middlebury with Artemas Nixon. His oxen were never returned. He was paid the $92 by the War Department in 1827.

## Joseph C. Doxey

Doxey's petition, dated September 10, 1845:

I, Joseph C. Doxey, of Burlington, county of Chittenden, in the State of Vermont, aged 56 and six months, do, on my oath, testify and declare, that at the time of the last war with Great Britain, in the months of August and September, 1813, General Wade Hampton, then commander of the American army in the north, did take possession of my farm on the east part of Burlington while my crops were ripening for harvest.

That, as well as other lands adjoining, he occupied my farm for camp ground and parade ground for his whole army consisting of some thousands of troops, the number I cannot distinctly remember. He kept possession of my farm as near as I can remember about five or six weeks. His troops drained my well of all the water it contained; they burnt up some of my fence for fuel; they laid waste to my fields common, which put me to the expense of watching my crops to keep them from being all destroyed; they destroyed much of my grass and grain, and the rest of my growing produce; they damaged my fruit orchard and destroyed my fruit; they damaged my garden and much of it they destroyed.

I was promised by the officers at the time that I should be paid for all damage. The army marched off in the night time, unbeknownst to me, and never paid my damage, nor any part thereof. At that time I was not aware that I could claim any redress. Very soon afterwards I was informed that the government was bound to make good my damage. I attempted to make out my claim, and obtain evidence to support it. Papers were sent to Washington, which were intended to exhibit my claim and the evidence to prove the claim. The papers were sent back to me and I gave up all hopes of ever obtaining back any part of my loss.

My present attorney, after examining the subject, informs me that the papers were not made up nor presented to any proper form, so to be received in any department in the United States government.

I further testify and declare that my damage at that time was appraised by two disinterested freeholders of sound judgment and good integrity, viz: Abel Owen and John Vansicklin, Jr., who gave it as their opinion under oath that my crops and fence at the like, were damaged to the amount of $75, which was considered by them to be my net loss, without taking from the appraisal my time and trouble of watching my fields.

I have not sold or transferred, nor in any manner disposed of my claim, nor any part thereof, to any person whatever, and that there is no person authorized to sell or in any way dispose of the same. I have never received any part of the sum awarded me by the appraisers, nor has any other person received any part thereof for me.

Malachi Corning, 69, was a lieutenant in Hampton's army and testified on September 10, 1845, to the extent of the damages. On April 6, 1846, the Committee of Claims awarded Doxey the $75.

## Sylvester Phelps and Charles Landon

As reported by the Committee of Claims on January 20, 1838:

From the statements of the petitioners and the evidence produced in the case, it appears that on the 28th day of January, 1815, a detachment of the 10th Regiment of United States Infantry under the command of Captain Philip Brittain, a commissioned officer, while on their march from Burlington, Vermont, to Plattsburg, New York, arrived in the evening of an extremely cold day in the town of South Hero in the State of Vermont and by the order of Captain Brittain and of Daniel Standiford, an assistant deputy quartermaster, took possession of a part of the house of Phelps & Landon as quarters for the troops, and that a part of the house was so occupied as quarters, particularly a large chamber therein through the night, and until about 10 o'clock the next day when the troops removed from the town.

The weather being very cold, unusually large fires were kept burning in the large chamber occupied by the troops through the night and a part of the next day. When the troops left the house, their fires were reduced to a heap of coals, and no fire was afterwards made in the room. In consequence of the great heat caused by the fires, the fire communicated through the hearth and back of the fire-place to the wooden parts of the building and at about 10'oclock the following night, and 10 or 12 hours after the troops had removed, a fire broke out on the outside of the end of the house, directly opposite to the fire-place, and the house with its contents, and an adjacent barn, were destroyed.

The following is a schedule of the property consumed, with its appraised value: 1 tavern or dwelling-house, $2,100; 1 barn $100; 100 bushels of corn, $100; 4 tons of hay, $32; 200 bushels of potatoes, $100; 2 beds and bedding, $100; 4 barrels of cider, $24; 1 man's saddle, $14; 1 woman's saddle, $18; 1 bridle, $2; total $2,590.

This case has been before the Commissioner of Claims for examination, and rejected.

It has also been heretofore presented to Congress, referred to the Committee of Claims, and reported against. The ground upon which the claim appears to have been rejected, in both instances, was that it did not at the time appear whether the house was taken possession of by the troops or without the consent of the owners of it, and also that it did not, when before examined, appear certain that the fire which destroyed the property was caused by the occupation.

Since this case was examined by the commissioner and the former committee, much additional evidence has been taken, and now accompanies the case, which, from the character and credibility of the witnesses, is entitled to credit.

Upon a careful examination of the case, the committee arrive at the conclusion that the house, and particularly the large chamber, was taken possession of and occupied by and under the order and direction of a United States officer for the use and accommodation of soldiers in the service of the United States without the consent of the owners, or of either of them, but contrary to their express wish and that no pay or compensation was ever made for the occupation or the damage sustained, and that the fire which consumed the property was caused by and originated from the fires kept burning while occupied by the troops and under their control.

Although the fire did not break out until 10 or 12 hours after the troops had removed from the house, yet, as it was communicated through the hearth or back of the fire-place to the wood-work adjoining, the committee do not find any such negligence on the part of the owners in discovering the fire in time to arrest its progress, as should defeat a claim for relief.

The committee are therefore of opinion that relief should be granted for the loss of the house, and report a bill for that part of the claim.

That part of the claim which embraces the personal property and the barn, which stood detached from the house, not coming within the rules under which relief is granted in such cases, is rejected.

Sylvester Phelps and the heirs or legal representatives of Charles Landon were paid $2,100 in 1842.

Isle La Motte is a 2×6-mile island in Lake Champlain opposite Chazy, New York, across a 1-mile wide channel. The border between New York and Vermont bisects the channel. To the southeast is North Hero Island and below that, the 3×-14-mile Grand Isle. The area and town of South Hero occupies the southern part of Grand Isle. The area was granted by the Vermont legislature to Ethan Allen, Samuel Herrick, and 363 other veterans of the Revolutionary War in appreciation for their services. The town of South Hero was chartered by the Vermont legislature on October 27, 1779. The first arrivals were Ebenezer Allen and Alexander Gordon in 1783, right after the war ended.

# Connecticut

## *Connecticut Claims*

### Gurdon Robbins

Gurdon Robbins lived in Hartford. As reported by the Committee of Claims on January 28, 1837:

> The petitioner states that in early 1813 he associated with others in constructing a vessel of war at Middletown, in the State of Connecticut, of about 250 tons burthen. The vessel was launched in September, 1813, and was designed for the service of the United States. The company was prompted to this enterprise by the inducement held out by an act passed the 3d March, 1813, entitled, "An act supplementary to the act for increasing the navy."
>
> The model and size of the vessel were advised by the officers and agents of the government, and special care was taken to have the vessel so constructed as to meet the views of the government, or its agents, as indicated in the aforesaid act.
>
> After the vessel was launched, but before she could be finished, to prevent destruction by the ice in the Connecticut River, she was taken down the stream to the bay and harbor of Pettepaug, 8 miles above the mouth of the river. Here the vessel was found to be exposed from a quarter, and to an extent of which the petitioner and his associates were not apprised until, from the obstructions by ice, she could not be removed to a more secure place further up the stream. At this time the fears and views of the petitioner and his associates were expressed to the proper authorities of the government solicited, but without effect.
>
> The vessel was completely rigged and finished at an expense of $17,000. Her ballast and provisions were all on board, and she awaited only a favorable wind to proceed to the city of New York. In the night of the 8th of April, 1814, a detachment of marines in barges was sent by Commodore Hardy from the fleet off New London, which took possession of the vessel and, after a vain attempt to get her out of the river, set her on fire and she was entirely consumed.
>
> Assuming the facts alleged to be true, the committee apprehend that the relief prayed for cannot be granted. These effects to individual citizens are the consequences of a state of war and present some of the various reasons why war should not be resorted to by any government without the most controlling necessity. It may well be inquired upon what principle this claim can be made upon the government? It cannot be urged upon the ground that the vessel was, or ever had been, in the occupation or under the control of the government. Neither is it pretended that there was any contract, express or implied, binding the petitioner and his associates to construct this vessel for the government, nor binding the government to receive her after she was constructed. And it is believed that no one will hazard the opinion that if the owners could have obtained for the vessel after she was completed a better price from an individual than the government would have given, she never would have gone into the service of the United States.
>
> That the owners intended to sell her to the government is more than probable, but the committee apprehend this can furnish no sufficient reason for the claim, before that intention was consummated by contract. It is believed that reasonable and prudent precaution would have enabled the owners to have avoided the loss.
>
> The prayer of the petitioner ought not to be granted.

In the summer of 1813, Comm. Sir Thomas Hardy's British fleet entered Long Island Sound and began seizing fishing and merchant vessels and bombarding shoreside communities. In January 1814, they anchored off New London, Connecticut. A landing force under Capt. Richard Coote went up the river and went ashore a 3 a.m. A historical marker states:

> On April 7–8, 1814, a British raiding force of 136 sailors and marines rowed six miles up the Connecticut River from warships anchored in Long Island Sound to attack American shipping in Essex, then known as Pettipaug. By the time it was over 27 vessels had been burned including six newly built privateers. Despite the efforts of 500 American militia, soldiers, sailors, and marines to prevent their escape the British made it back to their ships with minimal casualties. It was the largest single loss of American shipping of the War of 1812.

## John J. Avery

As reported by the Committee of Claims on January 31, 1834:

> The petitioner says he contracted to sell to the United States, acting for himself on the one part and the United States, represented by Major Hezekiah Goddard, acting quartermaster general, on the other part, two acres of land in Groton, in the State of Connecticut, for the consideration of $400. The contract was made on the 24th day of August, 1814, and the land was purchased for the purpose of occupying it by a fortification and battery to defend the harbor of New London.
>
> He says the land was taken possession of by the officers of the United States and suitable defenses were erected, in doing of which the soil was removed and the land greatly damaged in value. He says he has not received any compensation either for the use and occupation of the land, or for the damages done to it.
>
> Hezekiah Goddard says he contracted with Mr. Avery for the land and agreed to give $400 for the two acres; that he made the contract by directions received from General Thomas Cushing, and took possession of it, and erected a breastwork and a furnace for hot shot, and that in the construction, the land was dug over and much injured. He says Mr. Avery never gave a deed, but he understood he was willing to do it. The land was occupied until peace took place and was no longer wanted by the United States. He does not know of any compensation having been paid either for the land or for its use and occupation.
>
> The chairman of the committee addressed a letter to Mr. Goddard, and, among other things, an inquiring was made whether there was any written agreement, or any memorandum in writing, made at or about the time of making the contract. Mr. Goddard enclosed a deed of the land, made by Mr. Avery on the 24th day of August, 1814, but which was not acknowledged, because General Cushing's letters on the subject were not answered.
>
> Mr. Barber, a member of the committee, confirms a statement made in the petition, and, living in the immediate neighborhood, and having assisted in the construction of the works, his statements are entitled to the highest credit.
>
> Ralph Hurlbutt testifies the land was much injured by the erection of said works. Large and deep holes were dug, and the surface rendered very uneven, unfit for cultivation, and otherwise much injured. He says the land before was valuable on account of its soil and location, and that other land, near to this land, was sold by Mr. Avery, about the same time at $200 per acre.
>
> John L. Smith testifies to the same, except he does not set any value upon the land.
>
> Stephen Lay and Samuel B. Wheeler testify they were well acquainted with the land at the time, and they particularly describe its situation, locality, and quality, and the injury done to it, and they say the damage the land suffered by the erection of the works was $300.
>
> The committee have ascertained from other sources, to their satisfaction, that the damages to the petitioner were $200, and as he has always been ready and willing to convey the land, and as the United States do not want it for the purposes of defense, the committee think the petitioner should be paid the damages, and for that purpose they report a bill.

Hezekiah Goddard was on the staff of the Connecticut Militia.

## Nathaniel Canada

Nathaniel Canada died in 1834. The petition was filed by John Howard, his administrator, as reported by the Committee of Claims on March 2, 1836:

The petitioner represents that Nathaniel Canada, in the year 1814, was the owner of a toll-bridge erected over the Niantic River in the state of Connecticut under grant from the state.

The bridge, together with a toll-house erected upon it, was used as a military post by troops in the service of the United States, sometime during that year. While so occupied, the boats from the British squadron chased a sloop and burnt her near the bridge, and burnt the toll-house and partly destroyed the bridge in consequence of its military occupation.

Stephen Prentiss, Samuel Gorton, Alden Latham, and several others prove that the bridge and toll-house were occupied as a military post, but do not state by whose orders they were so occupied, or that they were so occupied at the time of their destruction.

Asa Comstock swears that he was a colonel in the Connecticut militia in the year 1814, and, with his regiment, was called into the service of the United States. He, with a part of his regiment, were detached by order of General Thomas H. Cushing, then the commanding officer at New London, and posted at Niantic bridge, owned by Nathaniel Canada, and that the bridge and toll-house were occupied by his men, "that in the summer of the said year, while said bridge and building were so occupied by me, in the service of my country, as a military post, the British squadron, then lying a short distance in Long Island Sound, sent their boats with a detachment of men in pursuit of a sloop which had taken refuge at the bridge, and burnt the sloop, and set fire to the bridge, and greatly injured the bridge, and that the injury to the bridge was in consequence of its being so occupied as a military post."

John French testifies: "I was a captain of military during the last war with England. In the year 1814, I was called into the service of my country, with my company. I was personally knowing to a military post being established on Niantic Bridge by General Cushing, having often business at said post, and a station kept up by men bearing arms, living in the house on the bridge, by the order of General Cushing. Our men were in the house held as a military post when the British made their attack on the bridge, and when they drove the men from their post, an express was sent to New London for help. I, with my men and cannon, went immediately to the scene of battle, found the troops driven from their post on the bridge, the bridge burnt, and greatly damaged."

There is no satisfactory testimony before the committee as to the amount of damage done by burning the toll-house and bridge. There is a valuation of damages made by C. Griffing, Griswold Avery, and David French, under oath, in which they say the damage sustained by Nathaniel Canada, "must be between $3,500 and $4,000."

The committee are unable to ascertain from the certificate of valuation whether this estimate is only of the actual loss suffered by the burning, or whether it includes, also, consequential damages from the loss of the tolls of the bridge for a time. If the latter, the committee cannot sanction that part of the claim which may be for consequential damage, for reasons too obvious to need any argument.

But the committee believe that compensation should be made for the actual loss sustained by the burning of the toll-house and bridge in consequence of its military occupation by the troops of the United States; and for this purpose, they report a bill to authorize the proper accounting officer of the Treasury to ascertain the actual loss, and when ascertained, that the amount be paid to the legal representative of Nathaniel Canada.

Nathaniel Canada served in Col. Jeremiah Mason's Regiment of Connecticut Militia during the Revolution and married Sally Brown on November 6, 1796, at New London. They had a daughter Caroline who died on September 12, 1805, at age 1, and a daughter Augusta C., who died on November 26, 1814, at 4 months. Daughter Phebe lived to 71.

Lt. Col. Comstock's 33rd Regiment of Connecticut Militia was inducted into the service of the United States from June 21 to the 25th, 1813, and from August 15 to the 25th, 1814. The colonel died on December 16, 1835, at Lyme, Connecticut.

Pvt. Alden Latham was in Capt. Josiah Manwaring's company in the 33rd Regiment; Pvt. Stephen Prentiss was in Capt. Thomas Dow's company in Lt Col. Freeman Tracy's 20th Regiment of Connecticut Militia; Capt. John French was in Col. William Moore's 3rd Regiment of Connecticut Militia, and Sgt. Samuel Gorton was in Capt. Asa Wightman's company in the 3rd Regiment.

## Phineas Meigs

As reported by the Committee of Claims on March 20, 1818:

> In May, 1814, a detachment from the enemy's ships then stationed off New London landed and set fire to a dwelling house owned by the petitioner, which was entirely consumed. The property is estimated at $600.
>
> Jonathan Swanton and Billy Dadd testify the house was uninhabited at the time; that paroles had frequently used it when on duty; that they had fired on the enemy from the point of land near the house; that there was straw on the floor to accommodate the militia when on duty, and that there was a large spar standing near the house which the fishermen used to climb to look out for schools of fish, which had the appearance of a flag staff, and which the enemy cut down; and that they have not the least doubt the enemy thought the house public property.
>
> In the two acts of Congress passed with especial reference to indemnity for property destroyed by the enemy, relief is confined to the two cases of occupation as places of military deposit, or as barracks by an order of an officer of the United States. Admitting the evidence given in this case in all its extent, it falls very far short of the rule laid down, and which the committee apprehend there is now no disposition to extend. Therefore, the prayer of the petitioner ought not to be granted.

Phineas was a private in the 6th Connecticut Regiment during the Revolutionary War.

# The District of Maine

On September 1, 1814, a British fleet entered Penobscot Bay. The small garrison at Fort Madison at Castine under 2nd Lt. Andrew Lewis of the 40th Regiment fired all four cannons, blew up their magazine, and fled for the hills. The British were generally welcomed at Castine, which became their headquarters of "New Ireland," all territory east of the Penobscot River, until the end of the war.

A statement by Jones Shaw, of Northport, regarding property:

> On the morning of the 23rd of September, 1814, and while the British were in possession of Castine, three of the barges that belonged to the English fleet, then lying at Castine, were seen approaching the harbor where I now reside, and two of the barges soon effected a landing of their crews, which consisted of about 25 or 30 marines, headed by an officer of the commodore's ship, all armed with guns, swords, &c. They soon arrived at my house and store and the officer, with some of the marines, with a gun presented to me, demanded of me in a very insolent manner the opening of the store-door, which I said I would do as soon as I could go into the basement story and open it, the door being fastened on the inside. But before I had time to open the door, several of the marines made a forcible entry through one of the windows, and commenced plundering several articles of clothing such as trowsers, shirts, stockings and hats, &c., being articles that I had not time to secure.
>
> They made a prisoner of me and kept me with them during their stay on shore, marching me around with them through the neighborhood, plundering several houses, during which time there was a constant fire kept up by the third barge that laid off the harbor, and by the militia and townsmen who had assembled. Two of my neighbors were slightly wounded by the enemy, and two of their shot were lodged in my house, viz: a pound-ball and a musket ball.
>
> It was supposed there were several killed on board of the barges while they were rowing in and out of the harbor. Several of my neighbors that belonged to the militia took a conspicuous part in the skirmish, viz: Zachariah Lawrence and West Drinkwater.

## *The District of Maine Claims*

### Isaac Snow

As reported by the Committee of Claims on June 7, 1844:

> The petition represents that Isaac Snow, of Thomaston, in the county of Lincoln, State of Maine, in the year 1813 commanded the schooner *Success*. He took on board stores for the American troops at Eastport, and on the 19th day of June, 1813, the schooner, while on its way to deliver the stores, was captured by the British schooner *Fly*, a privateer. Isaac Snow rose upon the captors and retook the schooner, pursued his voyage, and delivered the stores.
>
> During his next voyage the *Success* was again captured by the same privateer and burnt. The petitioner asks for relief, but does not specify whether it is sought as compensation for the schooner alleged to have been burnt, or for the gallant conduct said to have been exhibited.
>
> There is no proof that the schooner was the property of Captain Snow, that it was in the

public employ, or that it was lost, as alleged, or indeed, that there ever was such a schooner afloat. The committee, therefore, submit that the prayer of the petitioner ought not to be granted.

## Zachariah Lawrence

In the fall of 1813, Zachariah Lawrence and his crew of six fishermen claimed Capt. John Beyea's British trading sloop *Venture* as a prize of war at Eastport, but Captain Sherman Leland, of the 34th Infantry Regiment headquartered at Portland, commander of the military post at Eastport, and Lemuel Trescott, collector of customs for Passamaquoddy Bay, refused the claim on the ground that their fishing boat had no letter of marque. Capt. Lawrence petitioned Congress and the Committee of Claims during the 1st session of the 28th Congress approved the claim, then the Committee during the 29th Congress rejected it, "as altogether insufficient, and of a somewhat suspicious character."

Noah Edgecomb, captain of the privateer *Mary*, filed a prize claim on November 16, 1813, for the *Venture* and cargo. Silas Lee, the U.S. Attorney for the District of Maine, and Lemuel Trescott represented the government.

As stated in part by Judge David Sewall on December 14, 1813:

> The libel of Noah Edgecomb, commander of the private armed schooner called the *Mary*, did, on the high seas on the 1st day of November, 1813, subdue, seize, capture, and take the sloop *Venture* commanded by John Beyea with a cargo on board into the port of Eastport where the sloop and cargo now remain for adjudication.
>
> Silas Lee and Lemuel Trescott come before the court and claiming the sloop *Venture* and her cargo onboard, as forfeited the State, do say that prior to the pretended capture on the 20th day of August, 1813, at St. John's, in the province of New Brunswick, being a colony and dependency of Great Britain, the cargo of the sloop *Venture* consisting of the growth, produce, and manufacture of Great Britain, and articles the importation from Great Britain, or any colony or dependency thereof, into the United States, then was, and for a long time before had been, and still is, prohibited by the statutes of the same States, put on board of the sloop *Venture* with the intention to import into the United States, and with the knowledge of the master of the *Venture* with intention of importing cargo into the United States and with the wicked and fraudulent view and design of evading the statutes on all goods and merchandise brought into the United States, other than by capture, were then and there collusively aiding, assisting, counseling, contriving, and directing.
>
> The attorney doth further aver that afterwards on the day alleged in the libel, the same goods and merchandise and with the wicked and fraudulent views and designs aforesaid, were imported at Eastport, and that after the pretended capture, and while the sloop *Venture* was lying within the harbor of the King, was taken to and under the protection of a ship or sloop-of-war called the *Martin*, being a 20-gun ship, belonging to the King, and then and there lying at Friar's bay—viz:, at Campobello, and within a short distance of Eastport, and on the 7th day of November the sloop *Venture* having removed under the guns of the *Martin*, she, by and with the permission of the *Martin* departed therefrom and voluntarily proceeded to and arrived at Eastport and within reach of the guns of the fort at Eastport and having so arrived, was brought to and captured by Sherman Leland, captain and commanding officer of the United States fort at Eastport, and by him and by the collector of the district of Passamaquoddy was then and there seized and forfeited to the United States.
>
> Wherefore the attorney prays the advisement of the court here, and that the sloop *Venture* and her cargo, with her tackle, apparel, and furniture, may not be condemned to the libellant as good and lawful prize or war, but that the same may be decreed forfeited to the United States and disposed of according to law, and that the libellant may be condemned in costs touching the premises.
>
> Upon a hearing, it appears the capture, as originally pretended to be made, was collusive. That very soon afterwards the sloop *Venture* and cargo were taken into the custody of an armed British vessel, and remained under

> the care and protection of the British vessel several days and until she was taken possession of by the collector with the aid of Sherman Leland, without any compulsion of the commander of the privateer *Mary*, or any of her officers or crew.
>
> It is therefore considered, adjudged, and decreed that the sloop *Venture* and cargo are not liable to forfeiture and condemnation as lawful prize of war to the owners, officers, and crew of the privateer *Mary*, but are hereby adjudged and decreed to be by law forfeited to the United States; that the same be sold at public auction; that the moneys arising from the sale thereof be appropriated according to law, and that a precept issue, directed to the marshal or his deputy, to carry his decree into effect.

The sales were thus: hardware, crates of crockery ware, and casks of spelter and copperas to Henry Smith for $13,679.50; 5 casks of wine to Mr. Morse for $852.39; 40 casks of hardware to Sherman Leland for $6,492.35; 1 trunk of dry goods to Allen Armstrong for $115; 1 mattress and carpeting to Allen Armstrong for $106; coffee, bread, and sugar to Daniel Swett for $43; and the sloop, tackle, and apparel to Mr. Buckman for $510.

Spelter is zinc and copperas is ferrous sulfate, used in making dyes and ink.

Zachariah Lawrence then came forward and claimed to be the real captor, along with six crew, as reported by the Committee of Claims on June 14, 1844:

> The petitioner sets forth that in the autumn of 1813, he and six others under his command captured and brought into the port of Passamaquoddy, in the State of Maine, a British sloop named the *Venture* having on board a valuable cargo. This capture was made in a fishing boat for which he had no commission.
>
> The vessel and cargo came into the possession of Captain Sherman Leland, the commanding officer of the military post at Eastport, who reported the vessel and cargo to the custom-house officer, after which they were libeled, condemned, and sold. The proceeds amounting to $21,163.31, after paying all costs, were paid by John G. Thornton, the marshal, to the collector. This sum was distributed according to law—one half going to the United States, and the other half to Sherman Leland, he being considered the informer, and drawing the informer's share.
>
> He states that the reason urged at the time by the government officers for not allowing pay to the petitioner and assistants was that they had no commission to cruise on the high seas and make captures.
>
> Shortly after the capture, Zachariah Lawrence went home, a distance of 160 miles, and within a few months thereafter went west and settled in Ohio and has there resided ever since.
>
> In support of his claim the petitioner has furnished the depositions of Lewis Pitcher, John McLain, Reuben Branard, and Joshua Pendleton who testify they were at Eastport at the time and knew Lawrence with six men under his command did capture and bring into Passamaquoddy a large British sloop, that they ran her in alongside of the wharf at Eastport and gave her into the possession of Captain Leland, who reported the sloop and cargo to the custom-house officer whose name was Lemuel Trescott, and that Lawrence and his men did not receive any compensation and that Branard and Pendleton helped unload the vessel, and that $175.91 was paid to sundry witnesses, laborers, &c.
>
> The committee are of opinion that, although the proceeds may have been distributed in accordance with law, yet, as the persons who performed the service, and, are in justice, entitled to at least the informer's share, have been deprived of that, in consequence of their ignorance of the law, and the management of the government officers who were interested in getting possession of this vessel and cargo, that the petitioner is entitled to relief, and have reported a bill for that purpose.
>
> In fixing the sum, the committee have been governed by the following rule: Taking the $21,163.31 as the net proceeds, one-half of which, $10,581.31 has been paid into the Treasury, one-fourth $5,290.82 the informer's share, they propose to divide as follows: Seven persons were engaged in the capture; give each man one share, and the commander two shares, would make eight shares. By this division, the sum due the petitioner would be $1,322.70, the amount placed in the bill.

After the June 14, 1844, report was

published, some questions arose as to what actually occurred because none of the crew of the fishing boat ever testified as to the exact circumstances of the alleged capture.

Their search revealed that the *Venture* was libeled by Capt. Noah Edgecomb and his crew of the private armed vessel *Mary*, and the question arose, "Was it a falsehood concocted to make the sloop and cargo lawful prize, or to defraud the United States?"

As stated by the Committee of Claims on February 21, 1846, in part:

> Congress has not the power to interfere with the decree, and the rights of the parties under it, and the committee doubt the propriety of interfering to disturb the judgment of the court and the vested rights of individuals. The committee have come to the conclusion that the petitioner is not entitled to relief, and offer the following resolution: That the claim be rejected.

On July 23, 1850, the Court of Claims rejected Zachariah Lawrence's claim.

## Eastport Bond Holders

> That upon payment by Jabez Maury, John W.C. Baxter, Samuel Wheeler, Jonathan Bartlett, Josiah Dana, and Aaron Hayden, citizens of the United States, of certain bonds now in suit in the District Court in Maine, given by them to the United States, for duties on goods imported into the district of Passamaquoddy, amounting to the sum of $65,508.17, which bonds, on the capture of Eastport, on the 11th day of July 1814, fell into the hands of the enemy, and were afterwards, by the Vice Admiralty Court of Nova Scotia, decreed good and lawful prize, and the amount thereof ordered to be distributed among the captors, and attachments issued against the principals and sureties in said bonds, to compel the payment thereof, the United States will indemnify the principals and sureties in said bonds, and save them harmless against the loss thereof, and for the expenses already incurred by them in consequence of said loss; which expenses shall be ascertained by the accounting officers of the treasury.
>
> April 29, 1816. (6 Stat. L. 175)

John Baxter, who was bonded for $16,303.48, was arrested and jailed for 90 days at Halifax, while the others were the subject of "hot pursuit" in the United States.

Importers provided, and are still required to provide, a surety bond to cover the cost of import duties, taxes, or any fines and penalties that might arise during the process of landing imported goods. Having the necessary funds up front allows merchandise to be landed expeditiously for all concerned without having to wait for administrative or legal proceedings to conclude if a problem does arise. Bonds could be carried over to subsequent shipments, usually for up to a year. Today, bonds are posted to Customs and Border Protection on shipments valued at $2,500 or more.

## James Caze and John Richaud

Caze and Richaud were from New York. As reported by the Committee of Claims on January 6, 1817:

> At the sale of a prize-ship called the *Victory*, by the marshal of the District of Maine on the 25th of May, in the year 1814, the petitioners became the purchasers; and for the purpose of keeping safely the sails of the vessel, they were deposited in the store-house of John Crosby, of Hampden, in the county of Hancock.
>
> In the month of September, when the British forces invaded Castine, it was deemed prudent by Captain Charles Morris, who commanded the United States ship *Adams*, to set her on fire to prevent her falling into the hands of the enemy, and from the ship the fire communicated itself to the store of Mr. Crosby, and burnt it, together with the sails of the ship *Victory*.
>
> At the same time the British naval force took possession of the ship and, after the

peace, carried her off. The petitioners request of Congress such relief as they may think just and proper.

The committee are of opinion that, so far as regards the destruction of the sails of the vessel, the petitioners are entitled to relief, and therefore report a bill to that effect.

The British took the *Victory* to Castine and after the peace treaty was signed sailed it away. Caze and Richaud filed a claim for the loss, and on February 10, 1818, Secretary of State John Quincy Adams reported that the situation, as well as with all the slaves taken by the British, "it is yet a subject of negotiation between them, and the claim of the petitioners, it is believed, must abide the issue of that negotiation." On January 13, 1819, the Committee denied the claim for the *Victory*.

As stated by George Wheeler regarding Castine:

When the fleet sailed up the harbor, the whole population turned out to witness the sight, though not without feelings of dismay. The inhabitants on the Brooksville side ascended the high hill in the northern part of the town and waited, with intense anxiety, to obtain a view of the expected conflict. Making this place the head-quarters of their forces, the British soon began to send out foraging parties through the region round about and even across the bay. In a very short time also, they sent detachments up the river and succeeded in capturing the towns of Hampden, Bangor, Frankfort, and Bucksport.

They brought back from their incursion, some 18 or 20 horses, a large number of oxen, sheep, etc., and six vessels. These vessels were the *Bangor Packet*, the schooner *Oliver Spear*, the *Hancock*—which was taken—the *Lucy*—which was lost—the *Polly*—which was ransomed—and the "beautiful boat" *Cato*.

The *Liverpool Trader*, belonging to Mr. Joseph Perkins, was burned. They burned and destroyed many other vessels, and required bonds from the several towns to deliver up to Castine, within about a month, all the remainder that were uninjured.

Upon the 1st and 5th of September, General Sir John Sherbrooke and Rear Admiral Edward Griffith issued proclamations to the effect that, if the people would remain quietly at their homes and continue to pursue their usual avocations, would surrender all their arms, and would refrain from communicating intelligence to the Americans, they should have protection and safety ensured to them. Also, that the municipal laws and civil magistrates would be supported, and that all citizens who would furnish the troops with provisions, should receive pay for the same.

There were frequent changes of the British forces and vessels, occurring during the year, but there were seldom less than 14 or 15 sail of this squadron in the harbor. The English repaired Fort George, occupied it with a garrison, and mounted some 60 cannon there. They also enlarged the trench, said to have been made by Mowatt in 1779, so as to form a canal 10 or 12 feet in width and 80 rods in length. This canal was dug fully as much to prevent desertions as to guard against a surprise. Desertions were becoming of daily occurrence, and still took place after this canal was dug.

The English about this time made Castine a port of entry, and appointed William Newton, Collector of the Customs. The property of Josiah Hooke, the former Collector—who had succeeded in escaping with all the public papers—was confiscated. All the vessels belonging here previous to the surrender of the place were, however, returned to their owners, and were allowed a clearance and free intercourse with New Brunswick, and other British Provinces.

Ebenezer Perkins was master of his father's ship. Perkins also owned the ship *Camden*, captured by pirates near Cuba.

The town's militia offered no resistance and 2nd Lt. Andrew Lewis, of the 40th U.S. Infantry, spiked the guns at the fort and fled north with two small cannons.

Fort George was built by the British in 1779 on the Bagaduce Peninsula at Castine, Maine, to aid in establishing New Ireland. It was also known as Fort Majabigwaduce. Fort George is on the National Register of Historic Places and offers living history exhibits.

## John Crosby

In late 1812, Capt. Charles Morris was given command of the newly-rebuilt sloop-of-war *Adams* at the Washington Navy Yard. Chesapeake Bay was blockaded at that time and he couldn't leave until January 18, 1814.

A cruise to the African coast was followed in May to Newfoundland and was cruising in the Bay of Fundy between New Brunswick and Nova Scotia, managed to evade a large British warship on the way home, possibly by fleeing into the Bay of Fundy, but on August 17 they somehow managed to go aground on Isle Haute in the upper Bay. Some damage control and a rising tide enabled them to get underway, although further repairs were still needed. At this point they might have spotted or encountered the British fleet from Halifax, Nova Scotia, sent to occupy Maine and establish the colony of New Ireland.

Morris went past Castine about 50 miles up the Penobscot River to Hampden, and tied up at John Crosby's wharf, which was adjacent to his storehouse. On September 3, the British arrived in the 900-foot wide river where Morris was confronted, "by a large and powerful British squadron." Morris and his crew fought for as long as they could, but seeing the situation hopeless, he decided to destroy his ship to keep it out of the enemy's hands. Unfortunately, and predictably, the fire spread to the wharf and storehouse, destroying both. John Crosby and John Crosby, Jr., filed claims for their loss, which were approved on April 1, 1816.

## William Rice

As stated by the Committee of Claims on January 5, 1820:

> The petitioner, of Bangor, District of Maine, represents that during the late war and previous to the 4th day of September, 1814, he was owner of three-fourth parts of the hull of a new ship of about 256 tons burden lying in the Penobscot River near the town of Bangor. He, being liable to do militia duty, was ordered into service on the 1st day of the month to assist in repelling the invading enemy who were approaching up the river. He continued in service until the militia retreated on the 3rd day of the month when the enemy advanced and took possession of Bangor and of all the vessels lying near that town.
>
> On the morning of the 4th of the month, the enemy burnt and wholly destroyed the vessel. He further represents that if he had been at liberty to attend to his property on the 2nd and 3rd days of the month, he could have saved the vessel by taking her to a place of safety or have her sunk in deep water in the river. He asks Congress to make remuneration for his loss.
>
> Several witnesses testify as to the fact of Mr. Rice being in the service of his country, some of whom state that they understood at the time that the enemy gave as a reason for burning the vessel that she belonged to persons lying on the west side of the river and who were fighting against them, and that this was the only vessel burnt on the east side of the river at that time.
>
> The committee recollect of no case where Congress have made remuneration for property lost under such circumstances and they therefore recommend that the prayer of the petitioner be rejected.

## Josiah Hook, Jr.

As reported by the Committee on the Judiciary on January 10, 1822:

> The petitioner states that he was collector of the port of Penobscot, and on the 20th of September, 1814, in the execution of his office, he seized 21 oxen, one heifer, and one steer, as forfeited to the United States, for an attempt to transport them from the town of Penobscot to Castine, to supply the enemies of the United States with provisions, which cattle were afterwards duly libeled in the district court of the United States for the district of Maine, and an interlocutory decree was obtained that the cattle should be sold at public auction and the proceeds deposited in the Cumberland Bank for the benefit of whomsoever it might concern.
>
> Afterwards a final decree passed that the proceeds should be paid to Josiah Hoit, the claimant, but the judge of the district court certified there was reasonable cause for seizure.

The petitioner further states that afterwards Josiah Hoit commenced an action of trespass against him in the court of common pleas of Hancock county and on the third Tuesday of June, 1817, Josiah Hoit recovered judgment against him for the sum of $897.82 and $60.73 for his cost of suit. Upon which the petitioner took out a writ of review against Josiah Hoit and proceedings were had thereon. At the supreme court held at Castine on the third Tuesday of June, 1818, upon a special verdict rendered, the former judgment was affirmed, with costs taxed at $6.46, which judgment he was compelled to pay. He also states that he had expended $200 in defending himself in those suits and prays to have several sums repaid him.

Your committee are of opinion that the prayer of the petitioner ought to be granted.

Josiah Hook, Jr., was paid $1,165 in 1824.

## Noah Miller

Noah Miller was a major in Lt. Col. Jacob Ulmer's Regiment of Maine Militia. In October 1814, he hired a fishing boat belonging to Charles Thomas and enlisted Privates West Drinkwater, Kingsbury Duncan, John Duncan, Jr., Samuel Duncan, and Jonathan Clark, Jr., all from Capt. Jonathan Frye's company, as volunteers to seek out British vessels with the promise of potential monetary reward—or, failing that, being hung as pirates.

Charles Thomas was deposed on December 9, 1837:

> I, Charles Thomas, of Lincolnville, State of Maine, testify that some time in the month of October, 1814, Major Noah Miller, of Northport, came to me and wished to hire a boat which I owned for the purpose of cruising in Penobscot Bay in order to intercept and capture such English vessels as might be bound to Castine with supplies for the British troops which were in possession of Castine.
>
> I declined hiring my boat to him unless I could go with the boat. Major Miller said he wanted to hire men to go with him, and he would hire me. Major Miller said he would give me $2.00 per day for my services and $1.00 per day for the use of my boat. I agreed to go with him for that sum. I accordingly took my boat and went cruising with Major Miller a number of days in Belfast and Penobscot Bays.
>
> Not falling in with any English vessels after cruising a number of days, I returned home to Lincolnville and left my boat in charge of Major Miller, who was the captain of our crew. In a few days after I returned home, Major Miller took my boat and went out in the bay off against Northport and captured an English sloop bound to Castine with supplies for the troops. After Major Miller captured the sloop he returned my boat to me and paid me for the use of it, and also for my services.
>
> I always thought that Major Miller acted as a private citizen in all his privateering expeditions against the British during the war, and that he acted in that capacity when he captured the English sloop *Mary*. I never heard a word said about Major Miller being a revenue officer at that time.

Capt. Thomas Darling's sloop *Mary* was bound from Halifax to Castine with a cargo of munitions, dry goods, and clothing and was seized about 5 or 6 miles from Castine. Miller and his prize were "pursued by an armed force" but managed to reach Camden.

David Alden, of Camden, testified that he saw the capture take place, and that M.C. Waters, the supercargo on the *Mary*, offered him $1,000, "if he would persuade Miller to permit him to ransom her." Alden told Miller not to do it.

A 74-gun British ship of the line soon appeared off Camden, as stated by Maj. Miller:

> An armed vessel of the enemy, a 74, was at Camden threatening to burn that village unless the *Mary* and her cargo should be given up, and the whole seaboard, which at that time was almost entirely commanded by them, was threatened with devastation.
>
> A reward of $10,000 was offered for my capture. The excitement was, of course, very high, and so great were the fears of the people lest these threats should be carried into effect, that some of my own countrymen thought the only way of propitiating the enemy would be

to surrender me to their mercies, and spies were actually on the alert for the purpose of seizing me at some unguarded moment.

Under these circumstances I was strongly importuned by the collector, Mr. Hook, to put the property into the possession of the United States. During the whole week he was dinning this advice in my ears, telling me I could not possibly reap any benefit from the prize, and that my duty as a good citizen required me to pursue such a course as would be of the greatest advantage to the country.

The "town authorities" along with the collector of the District of Waldoborough, "represented to the commander of this ship that the capture was wholly the private enterprise of Major Miller. Being hardly pressed, he was at a loss what to do, as he did neither know nor understand his rights."

Major Miller, then "fearing the cargo would not be safe, he, at great exertions, caused it to be unladed, placed in a secure situation, and afterwards to be carried to Portland."

The prize crew of the *Mary* were then ordered to sail for Lincolnville while M.C. Waters and Miller went there by land.

At Lincolnville, supercargo Waters offered Philip Ulmer and John Wilson $1,000 each to ransom the vessel and cargo, and Ulmer stated that Maj. Miller was offered £10,000 as a ransom and Ulmer £1,000, "not to interfere with and prevent it."

At that point, Josiah Hook, the collector of the customs for the District of Penobscot, in whose jurisdiction the capture took place, told Miller to surrender his prize to him, "and have her condemned, as he could not take any other course with the property. Being over-persuaded, and ignorant of his rights, he yielded to these representations."

Hook then took possession of vessel and cargo and sold both at auction for an amount in excess of $66,000, after deducting court costs and charges. One half was paid into the Treasury of the United States and, "the other half distributed according to law." Hook gave Maj. Miller $90, "and he now prays that he may be allowed to take what was so paid into the public treasury, being himself very poor, infirm, and needy."

Noah Miller was awarded $10,000, and each crew member $1,000. By 1856, West Drinkwater and Kingsbury Duncan were the only militia crew still alive and they sued on behalf of themselves and the legal representatives of the deceased for their share on the grounds that Maj. Miller promised them equal shares of the $69,790.64 from the sale and the $33,213.17 that went into the Treasury.

On June 4, 1852, Kingsbury Duncan was deposed:

In the year 1814 I went with Noah Miller, of Northport, who said he was authorized by Josiah Hook, collector of the port of Castine, to capture smugglers employed in carrying provisions to the British at Castine. Our crew consisted of Noah Miller, Jonathan Clark, West Drinkwater, Ingraham Duncan, and myself.

We cruised in the night time between Belfast and Castine, and succeeded in capturing a number of boats laden with provisions bound to Castine, carried them into Ducktrap, and stored them and kept guard over them for some 15 days, Miller having left us for that length of time.

After the provisions were taken to Miller's house and salted and otherwise disposed of by Miller, we started again on the night of November 13th. John and Samuel Duncan joined us, and Ingraham was left on shore sick. We cruised about 6 miles from Castine, captured the British sloop *Mary*, laden with munitions of war and dry goods, and carried her into Camden harbor where we discharged her and the goods were taken to Portland the same day.

Jonathan Clark, Samuel Duncan, and myself then took her round to St. George's River and was paid $15 by the town of Camden for the job.

After the capture Miller wished to ransom the vessel and cargo, but the crew would not consent. He then left the vessel about 3 miles from the place of capture, and took with him the king's agent and supercargo and let them go, and they proceeded direct to Castine where a frigate started in pursuit. I was informed on my return that she appeared off Camden in about five hours after we left the sloop. Miller behaved more like a crazy man than a sane one, and turned traitor to the crew, and tried his best to deprive us of a dollar of the prize. Miller agreed with me to go equal shares. I was loath to go again as we were much exposed on the bay where we resided, 12 miles from Castine. Miller lived back in the country 7 miles, and consequently was not exposed as we were. Miller was a man of no learning and not fit to take charge; knew nothing about a vessel or boat. The crew were all good pilots and always used to the water.

Philip Ulmer came on board at Ducktrap and went with us to Camden. He was tidewaiter at Ducktrap and he received $1,000 out of the prize. I have understood that testimony going to show that the sloop was re-captured is being produced. I positively say that no attempt was made to re-capture, and that no one boarded the vessel except Ulmer, as above stated, until Miller came on board after we arrived in Camden harbor. He was sent on board by two men, strangers to me. In twelve hours after the capture she was discharged and the cargo on its way to Portland. And I further say that I consider Ingraham Duncan as one of the crew, and equally entitled to a share with the rest of the crew.

The case presented interesting and unique legal issues, being that neither Charles Thomas, his boat, or Major Miller held a letter of marque. The court found the claimants were entitled to additional money because they believed Major Miller, as a commissioned militia officer, "was authorized to capture the enemy's land or sea forces, or any who might be rendering the enemy 'aid and comfort' by furnishing supplies."

## Joseph Dixon

In the early 1700s Robert Eliot, of Newcastle, New Hampshire, settled on Gerrish Island, in Kittery, District of Maine. His descendants formed the Second Parish in the town of Kittery, which they referred to as Eliot. The residents of the Northerly Parish in Kittery, Maine, incorporated the town of Eliot in 1809 after many years of dissatisfaction and long travel distances to meetings, long travel being seven miles.

Joseph Dixon, of Eliot, had property on the Piscataqua River just above Portsmouth known as Dixon's Point.

On December 13, 1813, the frigate *Congress* returned to Portsmouth for repairs after an extended cruise to Brazil. Since the ship was probably moved out of the shipyard for security reasons or to free up space for other vessels while more of the minor work was being done, Dixon's Point was seen as a good site to build a small fort to protect the ship. The structure was known as Fort Eliot. *Congress* remained there without incident for the duration of the war.

Dixon filed a claim for damage done to his land, but did not have any evidence to support his claim until Samuel Leighton was deposed and swore that he was well acquainted with the property, "on whereon a small fort was erected in the Summer of 1814; that in the building of the fort, about half an acre of land was rendered useless for his improvement, by carrying off all the soil, and that Dixon gave about $100 per acre for the land, and that the deponent considers the damage done to the land to be about $30 and the use of it since the year 1814, had not the soil been removed, to have been worth at least $3.00 per annum."

Joseph Dixon was paid $30 in 1830.

# The Michigan Territory

The French and their Algonquin allies built Fort Pontchartrain du Détroit in 1701 to protect French fur traders from the English and their Iroquois allies.

During the American revolt, British forces built Fort Michilimackinac at present-day Mackinaw City, Michigan, but relocated it in 1780 to Mackinac Island in upper Lake Huron just east of Mackinac Strait between upper and lower Michigan. Lake Michigan was to the west. American forces seized the island in 1796.

The Northwest Territory was created in 1787 out of which the states of Michigan, Ohio, Indiana, Illinois, Wisconsin, and part of Minnesota were created. The Indiana Territory was created on May 7, 1800, with William Henry Harrison as governor.

Harrison was commissioned an ensign in 1791—then an Army rank—in the 1st Infantry Regiment and was sent to the Northwest Territory as aid-de-camp to Gen. Anthony Wayne. He resigned his commission in 1798 and in 1801 became governor of the Indiana Territory. When war was declared in 1812, he was promoted to brigadier general to command the Army of the Northwest.

Anthony Wayne was born in Pennsylvania in 1745 and became a surveyor. He joined the Continental Army in 1776 as an officer and was advanced over more experienced officers, apparently due to his bravado and impulsiveness—some said recklessness—which earned him the nickname "Mad Anthony."

Wayne participated in the failed Canadian expedition, but prevailed at Stony Point and helped prevent Benedict Arnold from surrendering West Point. He also advocated strongly for the economic welfare of his unpaid troops.

On June 30, 1805, the Michigan Territory was created out of land in the Indiana Territory. William Hull, a respected and admired Revolutionary War veteran living in Massachusetts was appointed governor on March 1, 1811, to serve a term of three years. Gen. Henry Dearborn, Commanding General of the Army, reportedly resisted Gov. Hull's desire for a naval fleet on Lake Erie.

In early 1812, the Territory's population was around 5,000, with 800 in the capital city of Detroit. Farms and homesteads were all around the Detroit, Rouge, and Raisin Rivers, and as far south as the Maumee River. Most of the residents were French Canadian with considerable intermingling with the Indians in language and trade. Mackinac Island had a fort, general store, and fur trading post. Apart from Detroit, Mackinac Island, and Hickory Island, the area was Indian territory.

An Army garrison of 120 soldiers was stationed at Fort Detroit. Fort Mackinac's 60 artillerists was commanded by Capt. Lewis Howard. On January 13, 1811, Howard died unexpectedly and was succeeded by 1st Lt. Porter Hanks.

Maj. Gen. Isaac Brock commanded British forces in Upper Canada at Fort Malden, across from the Detroit River from Detroit, and 260 miles south of Fort Mackinac.

Fort Mackinac was surrendered on July 17, 1812, and Capt. Richard Bullock's 41st Regiment of Foot garrisoned the Island.

On August 4, 1813, American naval forces arrived and landed Lt. Col. George Croghan's troops on Mackinac Island to retake the island. In an unsuccessful battle lasting just over an hour, 13 Americans were lost, 55 were reported wounded, seven later succumbing to their injuries. Among those lost was Maj. Andrew Holmes. The wounded were put aboard the Navy's 20-gun brig *Niagara* and on the 11th they sailed for Detroit, which had been retaken from British control.

In February 1814, Lt. Col. Robert McDougall, commander of the Glengarry Light Infantry, was ordered to reinforce the post on Mackinac Island in anticipation of an attack, and in 1815 the island reverted to American control.

The island eventually became a tourist destination and is now the Mackinac State Historic Park. Fort Mackinac has original buildings, exhibits, and living history demonstrations. The park is open year-round with ferry service to the island provided from Mackinaw City.

## *The Michigan Territory Claims*

### William Forsythe

Capt. Joel Collins gave Dr. Forsythe a certificate on March 26, 1814:

> The United States to William Forsythe, Dr.
>
> To one stable, 26 feet long, and 22 feet wide, 12 feet high, covered with boards, floored with oak plank, containing 1,152 feet of fluted timber, estimated at $281.
>
> To which is affixed the following certificate, to wit:
>
> I certify that the above amount is correct, and that a stable of the size and description therein contained, was taken from William Forsythe, for the use of the United States' military post at Sandwich.
>
> Joel Collins.
> Captain Com'd.

On January 23, 1815, he presented his claim to Col. Charles Gratiot at Detroit, which was approved for settlement. Dr. Forsythe contacted Capt. James McCloskey several times to request payment, but McCloskey had no money.

Forsythe sent the account to Washington, got no answer, and in 1830 took it directly to the Third Auditor's office, "who returned it as inadmissible."

With help from his representative in Congress, he was paid $281 in 1832 for "the value of a stable purchased by Captain Joel Collins to erect quarters for the United States troops at Sandwich in 1814."

Joel Collins was a veteran of the Indian wars and lived in Oxford, Ohio, in Butler County. Before the war, two companies of militia were ordered formed in Butler County, one on the east side of the Miami River and one on the west side. John Robinson, on Dick's Creek in Lemon Township, was elected captain of the Eastside company. William Robeson was elected captain of the Westside company and Collins enlisted as a private in his rifle company of volunteers. John Taylor was lieutenant. Robeson was soon promoted and Taylor was elected captain. When Taylor died in 1811, Collins was elected captain and he was commissioned on May 16, 1812, as captain of a company.

His company was assigned to the 1st Battalion, 2nd Regiment, 3rd Brigade, 1st Division of the Ohio Militia.

In the spring of 1812, Gen. James Findlay, commander of the 3rd Brigade, was preparing to join Gen. Hull's command and needed one rifle company. He ordered the two rifle companies from Butler County to muster at Hamilton on a certain day and the company with the largest members present would join Findlay's regiment. Findlay would have the rank of colonel in Hull's army.

The weather had been extremely wet and high water prevented many of Collins' men from getting to Hamilton and he was outnumbered by Robinson's company. Thus was Collins and his company, though sore at the time, saved from the calamity at Detroit.

That summer it was decided to reinforce the troops on the Northern Frontier and to secure troops from Butler, Clermont, Hamilton, and Warren Counties to comprise one battalion. Other counties would form a second battalion under Maj. James Galloway, of Xenia, and both battalions would form a regiment.

In August, Collins received his marching orders—to Lebanon in Warren County, where the general rendezvous would take place. Ephraim Gard was lieutenant, John Hall ensign, and there were four sergeants, four corporals, two musicians, and 79 privates.

At Lebanon they joined three other rifle companies, a company of light infantry, and an artillery company under Capt. Joseph Jenkinson, who was elected major. The next day they set out for Urbana via Dayton, but prior to reaching Dayton they received the news of Hull's surrender, the capture of the troops, and the advancement of British and Indians in the frontier. At Urbana they were joined by Maj. James Galloway's troops and the officers then elected David Sutton, of Warren County, as commander of the regiment.

A large number of volunteers enlisted at Urbana, but there was some delay in getting them organized. Generals Montgomery Meigs and Benjamin Tupper arrived and announced that William Henry Harrison, governor of the Indiana Territory and major general of the Kentucky militia, would assume command.

Collins then engaged in a variety of tasks on the frontier and in 1813 returned home. Soon after, he was commissioned a captain in the regular Army and ordered to recruiting duty at Cincinnati. After he had signed up 23 recruits he was ordered to a rendezvous at Franklinton and from there to Sandusky. Detroit was retaken during the Battle of Lake Erie in September 1813, and he was stationed there for some time.

On March 4, 1814, he was appointed commander of the garrison at Sandwich, Canada, where he built a fort. He also commanded the captured Fort Malden before being ordered back to Detroit where he commanded forces there until the end of the war.

## Henry Disbrow

The petition of Henry Disbrow:

> The petitioner in the month of June, 1812, procured, at great expense, a large quantity of pork, hams, white fish, and tar, which he had secured in a store-house upon Hickory Island opposite Fort Malden, in the Detroit River, and that in the first part of July following, the news of war having reached your petitioner, he procured a large and commodious boat for the express purpose of transporting the property to Detroit where it might be in safety, but that, when about removing the property, your petitioner's boat was forcibly taken from him by an officer acting under the immediate orders of General William Hull for the purpose of crossing the troops in the service of the United States under the command of General Hull, over the Detroit to Sandwich, in Upper Canada, in consequence of which your petitioner was deprived of the means, and the only means left him of getting away to a place of safety for his property.
>
> On the 9th day of July, 1812, the British and Indians came to the island and took and destroyed 118 barrels of pork, 2 barrels of hams, 2 barrels of white fish, and 1 barrel of tar, and for which your petitioner had been offered $2,206, had he not been deprived of taking it to market. Your petitioner has not been, neither is he now, able to procure the proper certificates and affidavits of the taking of the boat from either the commanding general or the officer, whose name your petitioner does not recollect, who took the boat, the one dying in disgrace, and the other having fallen in battle.

As stated by the Committee of Claims on February 10, 1846, in part:

This petition was presented to Congress in 1830 and reported on adversely. In 1832 it was again referred to the Committee of Claims, but it does not appear that any action was had upon it. In 1842 it was again referred to the Committee of Claims and reported upon adversely, and in 1843 there was another adverse report upon it. The petitioner asks compensation for the pork, &., taken by the British and Indians, not for the boat, or the use of it. But from a paper filed, a claim for the use of the boat 40 days, at $2.50 a day is also urged.

The committee are of opinion that the claim for the use of the boat comes in too questionable a shape to be allowed.

If the boat was not paid for at the time, it is a little remarkable that the petitioner should not only not have taken a certificate at the time from the officer taking the boat, but should not even recollect the name of the officer. The petitioner assigns as a reason for not taking afterwards the affidavit of General Hull that he died in disgrace, and for not taking that of the officer, that he was killed in battle. As the petitioner did not know the name of the officer when his petition was drawn, it is probable he never did know it, for, if so, he would not likely have forgotten it. And if he never knew it, it is strange how he should know that he fell in battle.

The affidavit of James Chittenden states that the boat of the petitioner "was forcibly taken from Disbrow by an officer," but is silent as to the name of the officer. The affiant states that he "likewise knows that all the water craft of every description then on the Detroit River fit for the service, was taken possession of and pressed into the service of the United States by the orders of the commanding General Hull for the purpose of crossing the river. On or about the 9th day of July, 1812, the British and Indians crossed over from Malden to the island and took 118 barrels of pork, 2 barrels of hams, 2 barrels of white fish, and 1 barrel of tar." The witness does not inform us how it was that he possessed such minute detail and accurate information as to the taking of the pork, &., and the craft, of which he speaks so positively, and thereby greatly impairs the weight of his testimony.

There are on file two affidavits purporting to be signed by G. Godfroy, who says that he took into possession by order of Gen. Hull, all the "water craft" within the "space of 10 miles, bordering on the Detroit River, and that he understood that one of the boats seized belonged to Henry Disbrow." That this deponent seized the petitioner's boat is not reconcilable with the statement of the petitioner himself, who says he does not recollect the name of the officer who seized it, and that he fell in battle.

The affidavit of Richard Smyth states the general taking of boats, &c., for transporting the troops to Canada and that he recollects that petitioner owned a flat-bottomed boat in 1812, but does not say whether it was seized or not.

The above comprises all the evidence in this case, which is deemed insufficient to establish the fact. The committee therefore recommend that the prayer of the petitioner ought to be rejected.

"G. Godfroy" is probably Maj. Gabriel Godfroy of the 1st Regiment of Infantry, Michigan Territory Militia, commanded by Col. Augustus B. Woodward at Detroit. Gov. William Hull was commander-in-chief.

## DeGarmo Jones

As reported by the Committee of Claims on February 9, 1831:

The petitioner presents, as the assignee of several land claims, nine receipts or certificates signed by Duncan Reed, a quartermaster in the service of the United States, and attached to an expedition commanded by Gen. McArthur, which passed from Detroit through Canada to Burlington, Vermont, in the fall of 1814. The aggregate amount of the receipts is $825.25, and were given for horses, corn, oats, hay, beef, pork, and some other articles, such as accoutrements for horses, &. The receipts express on their face that the property they contain was taken for the use of the detachment. The price of the provisions and forage is ascertained from a statement made out by Mr. Reed, wherein he gives the value of like articles as he purchased them on the expedition.

The petitioner has made an oath that he never received any compensation, and his clerks testify the receipts or certificates were purchased for valuable consideration. These were presented to the accounting officers in January, 1816, and were rejected on the ground that Captain Reed was supplied with funds more than adequate for defraying the expenses of the expedition in the quartermaster's department. They were again presented in 1830, and rejected, as not admissible without legislation.

Several inquiries were made of General McArthur, by order of the committee, the answers to which are contained in his letter of the 31st of January, 1830. He states that the certificates are genuine, that Duncan Reed was the quartermaster of his expedition, that he ordered the horses to be taken to remount his men, whose horses were unfit for service; that a part of the horses were given up to the quartermaster at Detroit, and, as he believes, sold. Others were rode home by those who were destitute of horses, and were placed under the care of commandants of companies, who were instructed to deliver them to the nearest quartermasters, and that the provisions and forage were absolutely necessary for the sustenance of the men and their horses.

General McArthur says his object in directing the certificates to be given was to enable the persons whose property had been taken to obtain the amount from the British government, unless an arrangement should be made by treaty, whereby it should become the duty of this government to pay. It is manifestly the policy of this government to adhere to and observe the principle that private property is to be respected in time of war. It is on this principle that this government has refused to pay for private property destroyed or taken by the enemy. It is on this principle that the British government stipulated by the treaty of peace to pay for property which should be taken away by her troops. Although the treaty did not provide for all the depredations committed on private property, still the principle is recognized.

It would be inconsistent with this principle that we should refuse to remunerate the losses of our own citizens, and also refuse to pay for property our own troops have necessarily taken from the citizens of Canada, and which has not only been used for the benefit of the service, but sold, and the proceeds applied to the public use.

Gen. McArthur states what objects he had in view in ordering the certificates to be given, but he has not stated that the owners of the property were informed of it; and the fact that they have afterwards sold the certificates to one of our own citizens is presumptive evidence that they supposed their claims were good on this government. Believing that the petitioner has a valid claim on the government, the committee report a bill.

DeGarmo Jones was paid $825.25 in 1832. The documents do not state who the supplies were taken from. It is probable that the owners sold the certificates for a lesser amount of their face value in exchange for being paid immediately. Jones was born in Albany, New York, in 1787, and moved to Detroit where he became a sutler to Reed's troops during the war. He became a wealthy merchant and politician. His petition was presented on March 29, 1830.

Col. Duncan McArthur's command of Ohio Militia was included in Brig. Gen. Hull's surrender of Fort Detroit on August 16, 1812.

## *Fort Detroit*

Antoine de la Mothe Cadillac wanted the center of fur trade at Michilimackinac moved further south. His request was approved by Count Jerome de Pontchartrain, the Minister of Marine, and in 1701 Fort Pontchartrain was built on the north side of today's Detroit River. The area was known as "le Detroit" (the strait) and by 1751 the post was known as Fort Detroit.

After the French and Indian War in 1760, the British controlled Detroit, the Great Lakes area, and all French land east of the Mississippi.

In 1778, during the American Revolution, the British built Fort Lernoult nearby and moved there. Fort Lernoult, Fort Detroit, Michilimackinac, Niagara, and other posts were supposed to be transferred to the United States pursuant to the

Treaty of Paris in 1783, but the British were reluctant to leave, wishing to preserve their lucrative fur trade, but were finally forced out in 1796 under the Jay Treaty.

With another conflict on the horizon, President Madison wanted William Hull, governor of the Michigan Territory, to assume command of an army. He was in Washington when Secretary of War William Eustis informed him of that desire, but, at age 60, he declined the assignment. Col. Jacob Kingsbury was then appointed but when he became seriously ill, Hull reluctantly accepted the position. He was then sent to Ohio to organize and command the 4th Infantry Regiment, along with 1,200 Ohio militia, and to plan a march to Detroit from Vincennes, Indiana.

Hull left for Dayton, Ohio, and on May 25, 1812, took command of three Ohio regiments under Colonels Lewis Cass, Duncan McArthur, and James Findlay. The volunteers were poorly equipped so he secured supplies from southern Ohio and left on June 1 for Urbana.

In June 1812, Congress authorized the formation of 18 additional regiments, from seven to 25. The 17th Regiment of Infantry was the second from Kentucky, organized at Georgetown by Col. Samuel Wells and commanded by Col. John Miller for the occupation of Detroit.

On June 10 they set out from Vincennes in company with 400 members of the 4th Infantry Regiment under Lt. Col. James Miller.

Hull did not follow an earlier route established by Anthony Wayne, but instead forged a trail through the swamps and marshes of northwest Ohio, which became known as Hull's Road. Unknown to the marchers, war was declared on June 18, and they reached the Maumee Rapids at present-day Perrysburg, Ohio, on the 28th crossed the river.

The troops still able to march arrived at Detroit on July 5 and were met by Michigan militia and 140 Michigan Legionary Corps members. Hull then ordered a road constructed from the settlement on the River Raisin, known as Frenchtown, to Detroit, approximately 34 miles north.

On July 12, 1812, Hull and his troops crossed the quarter-mile wide Detroit River into Canadian territory near present-day Sandwich, Canada, and occupied a farm house and prepared to assault Fort Amherstburg while waiting for supplies to arrive on the *Cuyahoga Packet*. When Hull appealed to the 300 or so Canadian militia to go home, they apparently had no interest in the war and left.

Remaining were 100 British soldiers and 150 Indians under Tecumseh. The British commander, Major-General Isaac Brock, was having trouble with morale among his troops, who were anticipating defeat, and he had to compel the reluctant militia to return to duty, and also convinced the Indians to join in.

On August 5, Tecumseh's Indians attacked 200 members of Maj. Thomas Van Horne's 2nd Ohio Regiment at Brownstown, south of Detroit, where half were lost. Word of this reached Hull and his troops and apparently the notion of being scalped or worse caused him great tribulation. At this point Gen. Brock created a ruse that caused Hull to believe he was greatly outnumbered and also used the Indians' presence and threats of uncontrolled atrocity as psychological warfare.

Hull was then informed the British had captured Fort Mackinac after the garrison surrendered. Lt. Col. Miller with 600 troops remained in Canada to guard the supply route around Sandwich while Hull returned to Detroit on August 7 and Gen. Brock with 100 British regulars, 300 militia, and 150 Shawnee Indians under Tecumseh prepared to attack.

Brock then decided to tell Hull on August 15 that if he refused to surrender he would not be able to control the Indians and Hull surrendered the fort on August 16 without a shot. All of the Americans and about 25 artillery pieces were seized.

It worked, and he decided the British force was too strong to attack and retreated back across the river to protect his supply route. On August 16, 1812, Hull surrendered Fort Detroit and 2,500 troops, shocking his officers and soldiers.

Henry Procter was born in Ireland in 1763 and joined the British army in 1781 as an ensign in the 43rd Regiment of Foot. He was in New York at the close of the Revolutionary War. He rose to lieutenant colonel in the 41st Regiment of Foot and was in Canada when war came in 1812, being then responsible for defending British positions in the Michigan Territory. He stopped the American advance toward Detroit, but failed to take Fort Meigs in 1813, and was present at the Battle of the Thames. He returned to England in 1815.

## General Hull's Capitulation Agreement

It is with pain and anxiety that Brigadier General Hull announces to the Northwestern Army that he has been compelled, from a sense of duty, to agree to the following articles of capitulation:

Art. 1. Fort Detroit, with all the troops, regulars as well as militia, will be immediately surrendered to the British forces under the command of Major General Brock, and will be considered as prisoners of war, with the exception of such of the militia of the Michigan Territory who have not yet joined the army.

2. All public stores, arms, and all public documents, including everything else of a public nature, will be immediately given up.

3. His Excellency Brigadier General Hull having expressed a desire that a detachment from the State of Ohio, on its way to join this army, as well as from Fort Detroit, under the command of Colonel Duncan McArthur, shall be included in the above capitulation, it is accordingly agreed to; it is, however, to be understood that such part of the Ohio militia as have not yet joined the army will be permitted to return to their homes, on condition that they not serve during the war. Their arms, however, will be delivered up, if belonging to the public.

4. The Garrison will march out at the hour of 12 o'clock this day, and the British forces will take immediate possession of the fort.

The army, at 12 o'clock this day, will march out of the east gate, where they will stack their arms, and then be subject to the articles of capitulation.

The handwritten Articles were signed on August 16 by Gen. Hull; Lt. Col. James Miller, 5th U.S. Infantry; Lt. Col. John McDonald, Ohio Militia; Capt. Elijah Brush, 1st Regiment Michigan Militia; British Capt. John B. Glegg, Gen. Brock's aid-de-camp; and Maj. Gen. Brock, 49th Regiment.

The loss of Detroit was a humiliating defeat and caused great alarm that a British and Indian invasion of the frontiers would begin. Detroit was considered such a strategic position for the Upper Canada campaign it was felt if it could not be held, the war itself could not be won.

Hull's forces returned to Cincinnati, and as commander of the Northwest Army, he was court-martialed and actually sentenced to death for surrendering the fort, but was pardoned and dismissed from the service in consideration of his Revolutionary War service.

The quartermaster estimated the loss at $23,000.09 based on upwards of 30 wagons and teams that were captured or destroyed, but the property had never been formally appraised. Prior to the signing of the Articles of Capitulation, the owners had been advised they would be reimbursed for any losses.

Colonel James Findlay, of the Ohio Volunteers, and James Taylor, acting quartermaster general to the Northwestern Army, both protested against the detention of private property as provided for in the articles.

As reported by the Committee of Claims on July 16, 1813:

It appears from the documents that the property taken at Detroit by the enemy consisted principally of wagons and teams hired by the deputy quartermaster to the army under the command of General Hull for the purpose of transporting the army and the necessary baggage of the army to the place of its destination. By the estimation of the quartermaster, the private property taken and detained amounted in value to the sum of $23,000.09. It is, however, evident that this estimation is merely conjectural because upwards of 30 wagons and teams which had been hired, and which were captured or destroyed were never appraised. The owners of this property voluntarily entered into the public service, for an equivalent in money.

Orders for the impressment of wagons and teams had been made out, but were never issued or executed in consequence of the owners voluntarily entering it for the hire into the public service. It is stated by the quartermaster that intimations were given by him, as well as by other agents of the government, to the proprietors that in the event of its being captured by the enemy, or destroyed in the service, they would be reimbursed, but no positive engagements to that effect were entered into.

It further appears that Colonel James Findlay, of the Ohio Volunteers, and James Taylor, acting quartermaster general to the Northwestern Army, did protest against the detention of all the property, for the loss of which this bill offers a remuneration, inasmuch as it was private property, and under the Articles of Capitulation signed at Detroit on the 16th of August, 1812, was to be respected.

The committee, therefore, according to the best views which they are enabled to take of the subject, cannot forbear expressing the opinion that the bill above alluded to ought not to pass.

On August 2, 1813, Congress authorized payment the loss of wagons and teams, "while actually employed in the transportation of baggage or supplies for the army under the command of Brigadier-General William Hull, during the summer of 1812, and which were captured or destroyed by the enemy on the surrender at Detroit," with the proper evidence, "as the President of the United States shall direct."

On December 17, 1817, Secretary of State John Quincy Adams reported with respect to the status of the claims:

The petitioners allege that they have suffered great losses in property by the violation, on the part of the British, and especially by the Indian savages, then acting as auxiliaries under them, of the capitulation by which, on the 16th of August, 1812, the Territory of Michigan was surrendered to the British General Brock; one article of which capitulation stipulated that private persons and property of every description should be respected.

That, by this violation of the capitulation, the petitioners acquired a just claim upon the British Government for indemnity and satisfaction, which they expected the Government of the United States would have prevailed upon that of Great Britain to make, by paying the petitioners for all the losses and damages sustained by them in consequence thereof.

The United States having concluded a treaty of peace, and subsequently a commercial treaty, with Great Britain, without mention being made of the Territory of Michigan, or of these claims of the petitioners, they have thereby lost their claim of redress and indemnity upon the British Government; but that the obligation of making it has thereby devolved upon the United States, to whose justice and liberality they appeal accordingly for restitution and payment.

Extracts from the documents upon the records of the Department of State are herewith annexed, serving to show the liberal principles upon which the Government of the United States were desirous of proceeding in terminating the war, and, at the same time the anxious care with which they urged a provision for indemnity for the citizens of the United States who had suffered loss or damages such as those complained of by the petitioners. This provision was insisted on until it was distinctly known that the only alternative to its abandonment was the inevitable continuance of the war.

How far the United States themselves are answerable to their individual citizens for losses and damages occasioned by the enemy, and unhappily incident to the condition of war, it is for the wisdom of Congress alone to determine.

In 1813, Fort Lernoult was renamed Fort Shelby after the governor of Kentucky, but was often referred to as Fort Detroit. A historical marker was placed at the corner of Washington Blvd. and Jefferson Ave. in downtown Detroit to mark the location of Fort Detroit.

Fort Dearborn was built on the south side of the mouth of the Chicago River in 1803 by Capt. John Whistler's 1st Infantry company. It was the furthest post to the west with a few homes and John Kinzie's fur trading store. The location is now the intersection of Michigan Ave. and Wacker Dr. in Chicago.

## Luther Chapin

Gen, Hull chartered Luther Chapin's schooner *Cuyahoga Packet* to transport tools, supplies, officers' baggage, the band, and those too sick to march the remaining 47-mile passage across Lake Erie and up the Detroit River to Detroit.

The British commander at Fort Amherstburg had received notice of war and the *Cuyahoga Packet* was captured by the Canadian brig *General Hunter* off Amherstburg, about four miles up the Detroit River. On board were all of Hull's papers, including plans for an attack on Fort Amherstburg, home to 300 regulars of Col. Henry Proctor's 41st Regiment of Foot, 400 Indians, and Canadian Essex militia units.

Luther Chapin, of Danbury, Ohio, submitted a claim that had been disallowed over technical issues regarding a "boat" as opposed to a "vessel" in the act of April 9, 1816.

On February 26, 1824, James Taylor, "late Quartermaster General N.W. Army," was deposed in Campbell County, Kentucky:

> The Northwestern Army, commanded by General Hull, halted a day on the east side of the Miami of the Lake. During that day, which I think was the latter end of June, 1812, on our march to Detroit, General Hull introduced me to Captain Chapin, as the owner of a packet, and stated to me that he, Chapin, understanding that the army would be at the Rapids of Miami about that time, had come there, expecting to get freight, and General Hull stated that he wished him employed. I suggested to General Hull that I thought there would be danger in passing by the British fort at Malden; that if the British had heard of the declaration of war, the commanding officer would certainly, in my opinion, seize or detain the vessel, as she was to be loaded with most of our military and hospital stores, and even officers and soldiers. I also suggested my fears that Captain Chapin might have been employed by the British with a view to capture the vessel, and advised him by no means to charter the vessel. He, General Hull, replied that he had no fears on any of these points, that he was well acquainted with Captain Chapin, and he did employ him, and, I think, engaged to pay him $50 for the trip, and the vessel was captured.
>
> I have no recollection that anything passed between General Hull and Captain Chapin, in my presence, as to the risk of either vessel or cargo. Indeed, General Hull seemed to have no idea of risk, for, to some of my objections as to the danger of capture, he assured me there was sufficient water on the American side of Gross Isle, and that the vessel need not pass by Fort Malden or in sight of it. This I found not the fact.
>
> To this assertion I cannot say, at this distant time, whether Captain Chapin assented or not, or whether he heard it, as I took General Hull aside and urged him not to send the stores and baggage of the army by water, but he persisted, saying he wanted to discharge as many of the wagons as he could, and I think he issued his order, that every officer should put on board of this vessel all his heavy baggage, and directed me to discharge all the wagons which could be spared, and I did discharge, I think, upwards of 20 wagons at that place.
>
> I think it my duty here to state that on my arrival at Detroit, I made considerable inquiry and since, as to the character of Captain Chapin, fearing that my suspicions had been well founded, that his object was more to serve our enemy than the United States, and the results of my inquiries have been favorable

to Captain Chapin's character, and I am now of opinion that Captain Chapin was not actuated by any improper motives in applying for the freight of the Army. I consider the sum, which I think was $50 was for the freight of the vessel. Under all the circumstances I am of opinion Captain Chapin ought to be paid for his vessel.

As reported by the Committee of Claims on February 13, 1826:

> The petitioner claims compensation for his schooner, the *Cuyahoga Packet*, captured by the enemy while in the military service of the United States at the commencement of the last war. The facts in the case, which seem to admit of no doubt, because abundantly proved, and some of them notorious, are briefly these:
>
> General William Hull, with the command of the Northwestern Army, arrived with a detachment of United States' troops at the Lower Rapids of the Miami of the Lake on or about the 1st day of July, 1812.
>
> The petitioner, having repaired to that place with his vessel, for the purpose of obtaining freight, was engaged by General Hull to transport a quantity of baggage, hospital stores, sick soldiers, and some officers from that place to Detroit for the compensation of $50.
>
> At this time neither General Hull nor the petitioner was made acquainted with the declaration of war, though such declaration was generally expected about this time. The danger of capture by the British was the subject of conversation between General Hull and the petitioner at the time of the contract, but formed no part of the consideration for which the $50 were agreed to be paid. On the contrary, the petitioner expressed his apprehension that the British, under some pretense, might be induced, in the expectation of immediate war, to capture the vessel, and demanded $75 for the service to be performed. In conclusion, General Hull declared that if the petitioner would accept $50 he would risk the vessel, protesting that if the British did capture her, he would consider it a declaration of war and conduct himself accordingly. The petitioner acceded to the amount of compensation proposed, took the freight on board, and proceeded on his voyage.
>
> Having arrived opposite Malden about the middle of the next day, his vessel was boarded by an armed boat from the British shore and captured—vessel, cargo, soldiers, and officers—and the petitioner himself detained as a prisoner some time. The petitioner's vessel was worth at the time of its capture, $2,000.
>
> General Hull fortified his confidence in the safety of the vessel from capture, in answer to remonstrances against risking so fatal a catastrophe, by stating that the petitioner might avoid the danger of capture by sailing between the American shore and Gross Isle—a channel out of the sight and reach of Malden. No such channel existed. The petitioner pursued the only practicable channel. There is no evidence to warrant the suspicion that the capture and loss of the vessel were sought by the petitioner, or could have been avoided by him.
>
> The committee are of opinion that this case comes within the principle and reason of the act to authorize the payment for property lost, captured, or destroyed by the enemy while in the military service of the United States, approved 9th April, 1816.
>
> It does not appear that the capture was "without any fault or negligence on the part of the owner." It was a vessel worth $2,000. By its capture the owner lost $2,000. The vessel, too, was occupied by order of an officer of the United States, and, for a time, was "a place of deposit for military stores" and served the purpose of "a barrack" for a portion of the military forces of the United States; and there is little room to doubt that its capture was occasioned by such military occupation.
>
> The committee are therefore of the opinion that the petitioner ought to be paid the value of his vessel, and for that purpose ask leave to report a bill.

Luther Chapin was paid $2,000 in 1830.

## Andrew Clark

Nancy McPherson filed a claim, as stated by the Committee of Claims on February 7, 1834:

> The petitioner was the wife of Andrew Clark, and resided with her husband on the river Huron where he cultivated a farm during the last war. Her husband was killed by the

Indians in an incursion made from Fort Malden for the purpose of intercepting the American troops on the route from Ohio to Detroit, and all their property taken away or destroyed, amounting in value to $1,078.75, and composed of a log house valued at $40, improvements upon the farm, but not specified, and personal property.

She also declares that General Hull encouraged her husband to continue on his farm, and to keep an amount of whatever property he might lose in consequence of the war, and that the loss should be made good by the United States, assigning as a reason for this, that he was situated near the route by which the troops of the United States were accustomed to pass and repass.

The petitioner seems to rely on this encouragement, given by General Hull to her husband, as a sufficient reason for the claim she now makes upon the government.

The committee sincerely regret that they cannot concur with the petitioner in this opinion. Her case is a hard one, but is in no wise distinguishable from many more instances of individual suffering and hardship.

There is no pretense that any portion of this property was impressed or taken by public authority for the use or subsistence of the army, nor was it occupied as a military deposit under the authority of an officer or agent of the United States. There is, therefore, no known regulation under which such a claim can be allowed.

## David Beard

The petition was filed by Parthenia Beard, as reported by the Committee of Claims on May 31, 1836:

David Beard, the father of the present claimant, presented his petition at the first session of the 19th Congress. The Committee of Claims reported against allowing the claim on the 20th day of April, 1826.

The claim is for 11 kegs of gunpowder, which was deposited in the United States magazine at Detroit in 1812.

When the papers were formerly presented there was a receipt signed by William McComb, Deputy Quartermaster General, stating the conditions on which the powder was taken. The receipt was as follows: "I do hereby certify that on this day, 14th of August, I have received in the public magazine of Detroit for safekeeping, 11 kegs of gunpowder marked 'Richmond I F Warranted,' and powder to be returned to them on demand."

This receipt is not now among the papers. It appears from the journal that leave was given to the petitioner to withdraw his papers on the 22d of May, 1826. The present petitioner says that there was a mistake in drawing the receipt and that it has been corrected by a deposition given by William McComb on the 6th of July, 1823.

That deposition is among the papers but does not in any particular disprove the receipt. It was first drawn so as to embrace the name of David Beard and Company, but was erased as to them and the deposition now speaks of an order on the merchants of Detroit, generally, to deposit what powder they had in their possession in the magazine for the public service, should the same be wanted. He then states that the merchants did deposit a number of kegs, but there is no designation of persons or companies.

Philip L'Ecuyer, under date of the 5th of March, 1836, testifies he was an inhabitant of Detroit in August, 1812, and that the powder of David Beard was deposited in the old banking-house in a fire-proof vault, and that General Hull, on the 14th or 15th of August, 1812, directed the powder to be removed to the United States magazine, and was received by William McComb, then acting artillery quartermaster. To the best of his knowledge and recollection, he is enabled to state the kegs were marked with the letters I F.

After so great a length of time, and when this testimony is brought forward to confront a writing, the committee wish to know how this witness is enabled to state what took place with so much accuracy and minuteness. What was his connection with the parties, or with the transaction? Was the order a general one, as testified to by Mr. McComb in 1823, or was it a special one directed to Mr. Beard?

We have, first, a copy of the receipt given by Mr. McComb to Mr. Beard, which remained in his possession until 1831 when he presented his claim to Congress; and second, the deposition of the same Mr. McComb taken in 1823 to prove that an order was given to the merchants, generally, to deposit their powder in the magazine for the public service, should the same be wanted. Neither of these papers sustain the deposition of Mr. L'Ecuyer.

It is singular that there should have been a mistake made in drawing the receipt so as to have it appear that the powder was received on deposit and to be returned when demanded if it was removed there by order of General Hull. And if such mistake was made, it is singular that Mr. Beard, having the receipt in his possession, should not have discovered it, and that it should not have been corrected by Mr. McComb, when he gave his deposition in 1823. The erasing of the name of "Beard and Company" from that deposition shows that the witness would not testify that the powder was delivered at the magazine under any order from General Hull, and the phraseology of the receipt shows that the agreement was a special one, and that the powder was delivered for safe keeping and not for use.

However safe the vaults of the bank might have been against fire, it is not improbable that two days before the surrender of Detroit, it was supposed the magazine, defended by the troops of the United States, would be still safer, so far as danger was apprehended from the enemy. If the United States used the powder they are liable to pay for it; but without such proof and where a special agreement has been produced by David Beard and now remains unexplained, the committee do not think they are holden to make any compensation. The petitioner is not entitled to relief.

The claim was rejected again on January 2, 1839.

## Isaac Ricker

Sgt. Ricker was from Montpelier, Vermont. He said he bought a horse at the end of April or the first of May 1812, and presented his claim on December 15, 1824. It was rejected on January 3, 1825, as reported by the Committee of Claims on May 9, 1826:

In the spring of 1812, the petitioner was a sergeant in Capt. Nathaniel F. Adam's company of the 4th Regiment of Infantry commanded by Col. James Miller, then stationed at Vincennes, in the State of Indiana. He had there in his possession, and was the owner of a horse, saddle, and bridle, worth, according to the certificate of Gen. Miller, $100.

Upon being ordered to march to Detroit, the petitioner took his property with him and on the march many of the troops falling sick, and transportation short, Col. Miller, in the month of June, 1812, impressed the horse, saddle, and bridle into the service of the detachment and so continued him until its arrival at Detroit. After their arrival the property was still retained in the service of the United States and used sundry times on expresses and so remained until the surrender of Hull, when they were captured by the British and wholly lost to the petitioner.

The horse was used on expresses after the detachment arrived at Detroit, the Committee think is now sufficiently proved by the affidavits of Curtis Phipps and Rowland Edwards, and the affidavit also of Gen. Miller himself, recently obtained, additional documents, produced since the last report of the Committee, and for the consideration of which the petition was again re-examined to them. This evidence, the Committee believe, now makes out the claim of the petitioner and they report a bill for his relief.

Sgt. Ricker stated later:

The horse never ate a mouthful of the Government's forage before taken into the service of the army; I bought and procured my own forage, to keep the horse on. I had application and opportunities on the march to sell her, and was anxious to sell her, but could not, as she was in the service of the army. I had particular application at Cincinnati and was calculating to sell her before we went in the wilderness, but was prevented by Colonel Miller's taking her. I bought her before we knew of the war, or of marching to Detroit, expecting the army to remain, sometime, where we then were—and was calculating to get a furlough to visit my friends.

Isaac Ricker was paid $100 in 1827.

Nathaniel Adams' company was under the command of Lt. George P. Peters. Sgt. Ricker stated he became sick at the Rapids and knew his horse had been used on an express to Malden by Lt. Peters and again by Lt. Paul Peckham and was then seized by the British.

In 1819, Capt. Peters, then of the Artillery, stated he had known Ricker for 4 or 5 years and that he was a tailor by trade and was, "distinguished for his bravery in the battle of Tippecanoe." Ricker later became a captain of an Independent Company of militia in Montpelier, as attested to by Samuel Prentiss and Timothy Merrill, both in the same company.

In May 1826, James Miller, then at Salem, Massachusetts, said that after about three days on the march the soldiers "became very sickly" and he took the horse, "for the purpose of getting on the sick soldiers to Detroit."

Ricker apparently entered the 34th Infantry, raised in Maine in 1813 from various militia units, and was discharged from Capt. William Sweet's company in the 3rd Sub Legion. He was paid $100 by the War Department in 1827.

The "old Fourth Regiment" was recruited in 1808, 1809, 1810, and 1811 for five-year enlistments and fought on the Wabash and at Tippecanoe. Recruits who enlisted got a $12 bounty but the 300-acre bounty land law had not been passed for enlisted veterans so they did not qualify for that benefit, while others who might have served as little as 30 days got the land bounty.

In 1812 the cash bonus was increased along with a quarter-section of land and before the war ended was increased to $100, and the monthly pay from $5 to $8.

Marshall S. Durkee enlisted at Springfield, Massachusetts, in the fall of 1808 and joined Capt. David Byers' company under Lt. Josiah Snelling with "48 non-commissioned officers and privates." His deposition was submitted to a Select Congress in 1837 and his harrowing tales of service and captivity in the 4th was, "well calculated to awaken a proper sympathy of the patriotic and suffering soldier" along with letters of support from former commanders, Generals William H. Harrison and James Miller urged Congress to act. (26th Congress, 1st session, Report No. 232)

Lt. Peckham could either be Lewis or Paul, of Rhode Island, and both in the 4th Infantry Regiment.

## Whitmore Knaggs

Whitmore Knaggs owned a farm at Spring Wells about 3 miles from Detroit and was an Indian agent, interpreter, and captain of a company in the 1st Regiment, Michigan Militia. When war came, his house, outbuildings, storehouses, barns, and stables were ordered to be occupied as barracks and a military station.

When the British and Indians attacked on the day before Gen. Hull's surrender, "the buildings were seriously damaged and mutilated, and personal property of great value taken or destroyed by the enemy," and which included livestock.

Knaggs presented a claim for $8,964.68¼, which was referred to Commissioner Richard Bland Lee. Evidence was provided by Maj. James Witherell, commander of four companies of Territory Militia; Duncan Reid, a captain in Hubert Lacroix's command; David Cooper, a member of Knaggs' company; James May, an acquaintance; Dr. William Brown, a neighbor; Theresa and Elizabeth des Compes Labadie; Pierre Solo; James Henry, William Brown, Robert Smith, Jacques Demari, Isabella Macomb, and Jean Baptiste Campeau, some of whom also filed similar claims.

Theophilus Mettez was orderly sergeant of Whitmore's company. Captain Abraham F. Hull, was Gen. Hull's aid-de-camp and was also in the home. Clothing, a mare, and colt worth $88.00 was reportedly taken by Pottawatomi, Delaware, Ottawa, Wyandot, and Chippewa Indians along with $2,310 worth of household goods.

On October 21, 1816, it was determined the claim did not fall under the law of 1816 because "it did not provide for the payment of partial and consequential damages, the destruction must be total to entitle the claimant." Lee filed a report on February 17, 1818.

Whitmore died, his wife Josette died, and the claim was taken up by his son, James Knaggs, and on December 13, 1856, it was referred to the Court of Claims and again denied for lack of evidence.

On January 4, 1830, Peter W. Knaggs, 34, who was a member of his father's company, was deposed:

> In the month of August, in the year 1812, the militia under my father's command were often stationed at or near my father's house, and also the troops in the regular service. Previous to the 16th of August, by order of the commanding officer, General Hull, my father with his company were stationed at my father's house, on the Detroit River, near where the enemy landed. During the night of the 15th and until in the morning of the 16th they remained at this station and before daylight on the 16th I well remember that my father received orders from the commanding officer at Detroit to march with his company, which orders were conveyed to him by Abraham F. Hull, son of General Hull. As soon as my father's house was left by his company and a detachment, I think under the command of Captain Josiah Snelling, the Indians began to plunder the house of its contents. Every article of clothing and household furniture of every kind was destroyed. Trunks were broken open and destroyed, the windows and doors demolished, the cattle of every description on my father's farm and about his house were wantonly killed.
>
> My father was sought for by the Indians after the capitulation of Detroit, who were determined to destroy him, and that we only escaped the vengeance of the savages by secreting ourselves amongst our friends. We were advised by our friends to depart from the city of Detroit in great secrecy. We went and landed at Erie, in Pennsylvania, and thence went to Washington. From Washington, in the winter of 1813, went to Sandusky, in Ohio, and from Sandusky, at the request of General Harrison, we joined General James Winchester at Fort Meigs, and we were taken at the battle of the Raisin. On the day of the battle we were separated. My father was taken to Malden and thence to Montreal. We were saved at the battle by two Indians. I was taken to Detroit where I was concealed for some months in the Rev. Gabriel Richard's house, and during the occupancy of this place by the British I and the rest of my father's family were imminently in danger of losing their lives. The Indians constantly sought to destroy us. My father returned about one year after the battle to his family at Detroit, where we were residing with their friends in a destitute situation, and in consequence of the total loss of all the property and of a large sum of money, my father and his family have been in embarrassed circumstances ever since. During the time that General Harrison remained at Detroit, we received rations from the United States commissary, according to the orders of General Harrison.

The family was sheltered in the home of James May.

## James Pierce

James Pierce, of Ohio, filed a claim for a wagon and four horses "employed in the service of the United States in the late war, and captured by the enemy at the surrender of Detroit."

The value of Pierce's wagon and four-horse team was appraised at $480 by James Foley and Edward S. Boteler at Urbana and he was paid $3.00 a day for the use of the team and wagon at the time it was attached to Gen. Hull's command under wagon master Presley Kemper. The driver was N. Thrasher. The term of service was from May 31 to August 16, 1812, and Pierce was paid $284 for the 78 days of use, but never for the loss of the property.

He was paid the $430 in 1822. Kemper was taken prisoner, but there's no record of Thrasher being seized.

## John R. Williams

John Williams had resided for many years in the Territory of Michigan and in

1811 purchased a 267-acre farm at Spring Wells near Detroit at auction from the United States. The farm was described as, "enclosed in part with a fence of cedar picketing, of a very costly character, a commodious frame dwelling-house, two spacious frame barns, a stable, carriage-house, ice-house, and other necessary out-houses, a well of excellent water, with a large well-enclosed garden containing a great variety of rare and valuable shrubbery, and two valuable orchards of fruit."

On June 27, 1812, he executed bonds and a mortgage to the United States in the amount of $3,200 and was to make four annual payments.

After the surrender of Detroit, Williams and his family were compelled to leave by the British for Fort Erie, across from Buffalo, New York, taking only what they could pack. They moved to Albany where John opened a store. The farm was subsequently occupied through 1814 by Ohio militia and Lt. Col. George Croghan's Rangers, and he lost a considerable amount of goods when Buffalo was attacked.

John, his wife Mary, and children were in New York when Capt. James McCloskey, assistant deputy quartermaster general, took possession of the farm and all the buildings, "for the purpose of quartering the troops of the United States, then stationed on that exposed frontier, the barracks at Detroit having been destroyed by the enemy when they evacuated that place a few days previous to the battle of the Thames."

As stated:

> During this period the dwelling-house became greatly injured and dilapidated; fences were taken down and used by the troops for fuel—that article being scarce and difficult to obtain, owing to the almost impassable state of the roads—the out-houses were destroyed, and the weatherboarding used for temporary sheds, fuel, and for making coffins for the soldiers, very many of whom died on the place; the orchards and shrubbery were extensively injured, or totally destroyed, and all the buildings rendered irreparable or literally destroyed at the time the place was evacuated by the United States troops.

John presented a claim in 1817 to Richard Bland Lee, the Commissioner of Claims: $4,000 for the use of and damage to Spring Wells farm; $180 for 3,600 rails and stakes taken by Col. George Croghan in 1813; $86 for oats, potatoes, and hay for Col. Richard M. Johnson's horse; and $19 for gunpowder and buckshot; $1,461.81 for bars of silver, silverplated ware, china, table and other lines, clothing, and jewelry valued at, which was not allowed.

On October 22, 1817, Henry J. Hunt, Richard Smyth, and Antoine Dequindre were appointed commissioners to take testimony. They deposed Robert Smart, François Cicot, Jean Baptiste Cicot, Col. Gabriel Godfroy, and Jacques Bourgea dit Provençal, all local residents. The appraisers concluded the damages could not be less than $4,000.

His claim was rejected on February 14, 1837. Another claim was presented by deposition dated March 9, 1844:

> During the last war with Great Britain, and upon the surrender of Detroit by General Hull to the enemy, he was compelled, in order to find security for his family, to leave Detroit, where he was born, and intended to return so soon as the circumstances of the country and the safety of his family would permit. At the time of his leaving Detroit and going to Albany, where he established himself and family until the close of the war, he was the owner of two houses in the city of Detroit, and two farmhouses, together with a valuable barn and other outhouses at Spring Wells, on the Detroit River. The farm at Spring Wells was in a high state of improvement as to the fence and buildings. When he left after the surrender of one of his houses at Detroit and those at Spring Wells were by him put in the keeping and possession of Dennis Campau, a citizen of the United States, and who continued in the possession and agency until the affiant's return to Detroit at the close of the war.

The other of his houses in Detroit was in the occupancy of his sister during that time. During the war his house in the care of Campau, and especially his houses and premises at Spring Wells, were taken possession of by the troops of the United States and used as quarters. A large number of troops were quartered at Spring Wells and in the houses and other buildings there and were broke to pieces and greatly injured; the fence, consisting of much cedar picketing and other valuable fences were used and burnt up for fuel. From the exposures and sufferings of the soldiers during the campaign previous and subsequent to their being quartered in his premises, many of them died while quartered on the premises. The boards and covering of the outhouses and barn were pulled of to make coffins or were there brought to be interred, in which way and by consuming the same for fuel, the outhouses were entirely destroyed, and barn nearly stripped of covering.

On the return of the affiant after the war, he found Spring Wells almost literally stripped and torn to pieces. He applied to Colonel Richard M. Johnson to certify the correctness of his claim for damages in the spoliation of Spring Wells, but was informed that he was on his return to Detroit from the pursuit of the enemy in Canada after its being retaken so wounded and cut to pieces and sick that he did not recollect what occurred being wholly unable from his condition at that time to observe the character and extent of the spoliations committed by the American troops, therefore he would not certify as to the status.

Springwells is included in the Historic Fort Wayne National Park at 6325 W. Jefferson Ave., Detroit.

## James Abbott

James Abbott owned a house and large stable that Assistant Quartermaster Duncan Reid seized and occupied for a barracks and military stores. On August 20, 1812, "the goods and furniture were destroyed and carried away, by the British and Indians, and the buildings burned." The value of lost property was estimated at $9,000.

His other property would not have been destroyed but for the military occupation of the United States. As stated by the Committee of Claims on December 12, 1822:

The Committee understand the rule to have been settled, that the government will not remunerate for property destroyed by an enemy, unless the destruction is such, as is authorized by the usages of civilized warfare; and that, agreeably to such usage, the destruction of private dwellings would not be lawful, except when necessary to effect the destruction of military supplies. Such does not appear to have been the fact in the present case. Nor was the property destroyed till after it had been some time in the possession of the British, subsequent to the surrender of Detroit.

As stated by the Committee of Claims on January 6, 1830:

It appears from the certificate of James McCloskey, given on the 12th of October, 1816, that on the arrival of the Army at Detroit in the fall of the year 1813, the soldiers necessarily made use of the rails of the petitioner for fuel, there being none furnished by the United States, and that the same could not be procured or purchased by the United States.

At the time the rails were taken, James McCloskey was Assistant Deputy Quartermaster General, but was out of service at the time the certificate was given, and the certificate not having been given under oath, it would have been rejected by the committee, if it was not supported by the certificate of Colonel Croghan, made on the 1st July, 1828, he says he was in the service at the time specified, and has a perfect recollection of the statement of loss by Mr. Abbott. And that, from the best of his impressions, the certificate of Mr. McCloskey is correct. Mr. McCloskey is dead.

Robert Smart testifies that he has a perfect recollection that the rails were taken and used by the troops of the United States stationed at Detroit, in 1813, under the command of Colonel Croghan.

Lambert Lafoy testifies that at the time the rails were purchased by Mr. Abbot of Daniel Robinson in the year 1812, he was a clerk to Mr. Abbott, and that he gave for the rails $70.

No fuel was furnished the troops stationed

at Detroit. There were no teams to convey it from the forest, which was some distance from the garrison. The soldiers were in a suffering condition, and that the consumption of the fences was necessary to prevent the soldiers from perishing, are facts established by the testimony of Governor Cass, in the case of Solomon Sibley, to which reference was made in the case of the representatives of Elijah Brush.

The committee thinks the testimony brings the case within the principles which have been frequently sanctioned by the House and report a bill.

James Abbott was paid $70 in 1830 for his fences.

## Catherine McNiff

As reported by the Committee of Claims on December 4, 1818:

The petitioner, of Detroit, Michigan Territory, represents that during the campaigns of 1813 and 1814, her house was occupied by the troops of the United States under the command of Major General Harrison. The house was taken or given to the troops without any contract having been made either for its use or for any injury it might sustain while so used, and that the rent which she subsequently received was no more than the reasonable and usual charge for such a house, and by no means sufficient to cover the extraordinary loss she has incurred from the great injury it received while in the occupation of the United States.

It appears to the committee that no usage, either of law or equity, could require more of the government than a compliance with its contracts. A contract may precede or follow the act or thing which is the subject of the contract. In this case the petitioner says, "no contract was made previously to the occupation of the house"; but the reception afterwards of a sum of money for the rent is as much a contract for the use of the house as if it had preceded the occupation.

It appears to the committee that the petitioner is careful not to disclose the amount which has been received, for nothing of the kind is to be found either in her own statements or in the other evidence adduced. Nor has anything been said as to the character of the injury, whether it necessarily resulted from the occupation of the house or from the wantonness of the troops. If, however, any injury was sustained beyond that for which she has been compensated, it must have been the latter character, for which the government has never been held responsible. The prayer of the petitioner ought not to be granted.

## David Cooper

Cooper was building a house in Detroit, as reported by the Committee of Claims on January 20, 1821:

Capt. Caleb H. Holder of the 17th Regiment of Infantry of the United States' army, issued an order to the troops under his command to take possession of a quantity of plank, and a chimney for the use of Fort Shelby, in the territory of Michigan. The plank and chimney were appraised at $80.

The committee are of opinion that the claim of David Cooper comes within the usual rule of allowance, and therefore report a bill.

Cooper was paid $80 in 1824.

## Robert Smart

As reported by the Committee of Claims on April 15, 1830:

The petitioner claims compensation for a quantity of lumber taken from him against his will by order of the Quartermaster General of General Harrison's army at Detroit in October, 1813, for the use of the United States, which he values at least $160. He also asks compensation for a horse forcibly taken from him for the use of the army, valued by him at $100. He claims further compensation for another quantity of boards taken from his fences and buildings in Detroit for the use of the army, and by order of Col. James McCloskey, the Quartermaster General, appraised by two men at $90. An account extends the first item to $375 for plank.

The committee is of opinion that considering the state of the country at the time, both sides of the strait having but recently been in possession of the enemy, and then in possession of the United States, no objection could be made to pay the petitioner, one of our own citizens, for the lumber taken for the necessary use of the army, merely from the circumstances that it happened to lie on the Canada side.

The depositions originally accompanying the petition did not very distinctly show what was included in each item, which, with other circumstances, raised several queries whether the whole lumber was taken in Canada? Whether the account presented in 1815, embraced both items in his petition, and if not, why not? Whether Ignace Morass, who took the lumber by order of the Quartermaster General, did not furnish as his own, and receive pay for it?

On the 30th of March, 1820, the petitioner had his claim presented to Congress by resolution, on which an unfavorable report was made April 5, 1820.

On recurrence to the files, two papers are found: one in relation to the horse, and the other to the boards and plank taken from his garden fence, and some shed or building charged in his account, and sworn to as consisting of 3,000 feet of boards at $30 per M. With this last account, is the deposition of Mr. William Watson, himself as late an Ensign in the 26th Regiment of Infantry, that he was present when Lt. Robert B. Crook of the 28th Regiment and some soldiers took from the petitioner's fence and building in Detroit, a large quantity of boards and planks which he says Lt. Crook afterwards informed him were made use of for coffins for deceased soldiers of the 28th Regiment.

On the charge for the horse are four depositions to prove the loss and value of the horse and that the horse was in the possession of a soldier in the army under General Duncan McArthur. It is in the deposition of John Cramer who represents himself to have been a private soldier in Captain Elias Murray's company of mounted militia in Gen. McArthur's command, in an expedition to Burlington Heights in 1814. About 10 miles above Detroit, one Frank Monroe, a soldier in the same company, brought into camp a horse he knew to be the petitioner's, that he rode him in that expedition, and that he verily believes Monroe took the horse with him to Ohio.

This evidence corroborated as it is by others, shows that the horse was unlawfully taken by a militia private soldier. The United States are not bound to indemnify the petitioner for a depredation of this character.

Accompanying the petition are the depositions of William B. Torrence, Peter J. Desnoyes, Ignace Morass, Oliver W. Miller, and James Conner. Miller and Conner were called on by James McCloskey, acting Quartermaster General of Gen. Harrison's army at Detroit, in the Fall of 1814, to appraise the value of the boards that had been taken from a shop and fence for the use of the army, and that they appraised the same as $90.

Ignace Morass testifies that he was employed by the Quartermaster General of Gen. Harrison's army to repair the public buildings for the use of the army at Detroit, in October, 1813, and was ordered to take all the lumber he could find for that purpose by force if he could not get it by purchase, and that in pursuance of that order he did take a quantity of lumber namely, plank, boards, and shingles, the property of the petitioner, and without his consent, and did use the same in construction of barracks and repairs of public buildings and for coffins for deceased soldiers. The quantity he does not recollect, but believes it to have been worth from $150 to $200. In his explanatory deposition, he says this lumber was taken from Sandwich and not from any building or fence, and that he never received of the United States any pay thereof himself, nor ever paid, or agreed to pay the petitioner therefore, or any part thereof.

It is satisfactorily proved that the petitioner's lumber was taken from Sandwich, and used in the reparation and building of barracks and public buildings necessary for the use and comfort of the army, or for coffins for deceased soldiers, and that his fence and boards from his shop in Detroit was also taken to supply the necessities of the army. What the value of all this lumber was is not so easily to ascertain.

In 1815, all that the petitioner claimed amounted to $123 only, and this claim had relation to lumber taken in Sandwich, and was proved by James Conner. In 1820 a claim was made for boards to the value of $90, intending evidently to leave out those taken from Sandwich, and this proven by William Watson. In 1829 and 1830 that portion taken at Detroit from fence and shop is proved by Conner and Miller, and Conner says nothing about that taken at Sandwich, and which must have been named in his first deposition. To render it still more embarrassing as to value and amount, the petitioner's account extends that taken at Sandwich to $375 certain, and indefinitely for boards and shingles beyond that sum.

The committee would not be too captious, but it does not perceive any satisfactory reason why the whole claim was not exhibited in 1815, and to the full extent of it. The value of the lumber must then have been better known than it can be now. No reason is offered why the appraisement of Miller and Conner was not resorted to in 1820, the show the value of the lumber taken in Detroit.

Under all these circumstances, the committee cannot come to any other conclusion, that the whole lumber of the petitioner used for the benefit of the United States, wherever the lumber might have been found, and for which he considered the United States bound to pay, was not of greater value than the amount of his first claim in 1815. The committee, therefore, report a bill for $123, as a full satisfaction for the petitioner's whole claim for his lumber taken for public use.

## James May and William Macomb

James May, of Detroit, was marshal of the Territory of Michigan and on April 26, 1826, was awarded $487.62 for his services as marshal.

William Macomb's widow, Sarah Macomb, of Detroit, also petitioned Congress on January 26, 1820, that her husband's legal representatives, "may be confirmed in their title to the Island of Grape Isle."

As reported by the Committee of Claims on January 2, 1822:

The petitioner states that in the year 1813 he occupied, under a lease, at the annual rent of $500, a farm, seven acres in front and 40 in depth belonging to the heirs of the late William Macomb near the city of Detroit and was the owner of another called the Cawisa farm adjoining the former of the same depth and two acres in front.

The quantity of land cleared and enclosed on those two farms was about 180 acres under good fence of which a large proportion consisted of post and rail, the posts being red cedar and the rails oak, and that about 65 acres were enclosed with white cedar pickets from 10 to twelve feet long.

In the month of October the American army, commanded by General Harrison, arrived at Detroit together with the Indians in the service of the United States, and that a part of the army and Indians commanded by General McArthur, encamped upon and near the premises of the petitioner. He further states that on the 9th or 10th of October a storm commenced and continued many days, which, rendering it impracticable to procure fuel in the existing state of the surrounding country, the troops destroyed his fences and pickets to supply themselves with fuel and carried away his out-buildings, either for fuel of for the erection of huts.

He applied to General Harrison, General McArthur, General Cass, and Colonel Butler, successive commanders at that post, during the following months, imploring them to restrain those depredations, but without any other effect than to receive assurances of indemnity for all the damage he should sustain.

About the month of April, he says, the whole of the fences, pickets, and out-buildings, on the premises had been made use of by the army; shortly after which time, Colonel George Croghan, having succeeded to the command of Detroit, issued an order to value the damage sustained by the petitioner.

Among the documents in this case is a copy of the order of Colonel Croghan dated April 28, 1814, addressed to Captain James McCloskey, then Acting District Quartermaster General, directing him to appoint two respectable citizens of the town to act cojointly with two others to be chosen by the petitioner for the purpose of determining the amount of damage sustained in the destruction of his property by the troops of the United States.

Conformably to this order, Henry J. Hunt and James Conner were appointed on behalf of the United States and James H. Audrain and Antoine Dequindre, chosen by the petitioner. A copy of the order from Captain McCloskey addressed to the valuers is also among the documents before the committee, by which it appears that they were directed to, "be particular in estimating the value of such property, viz. houses, barns, rails, &c. as were actually destroyed, burnt, and carried away by the troops, estimating such property at its real value, taking into consideration the defective state it was in at the time it was destroyed or used, because the property, viz. houses, barns, and rails, wanted repairs and the proprietor would have been under the necessity of repairing and replacing them in a short time."

Pursuant to this order, the valuers proceeded to determine the damages and have certified the amount on the Macomb farm to be $4,348.10 and on the Cawisa farm $880.55.

It appears that under the provisions of the Act of April, 1816, usually called the Claims Law, the above valuation was recognized and confirmed by the deposition of the valuers, taken before commissioners appointed for that purpose, by the Commissioner of Claims, who, thereupon, decided in favor of the claimant. This decision was disapproved by the Secretary of War, as the petitioner states, on the following exceptions: that the proof was defective, the damage done to houses and fences not distinguished, the estimate in gross, and apparently extravagant.

For the amount of damages ascertained as above, the petitioner, under the aforesaid circumstances, and with the aid of some additional evidence, asks to be remunerated by Congress. The proofs adduced to the Committee in support of this claim are substantially as follows:

General Cass, under date of November 19, 1817, at Detroit, certifies that in October, 1813, he was left by General Harrison in command of the troops at Detroit and continued until the latter part of December, during which time he boarded with James May, Esq., the petitioner. The quarters he occupied commanded a view of the Macomb farm; that he often saw soldiers carrying away the rails and pickets and sometimes portions of small buildings for fuel, "The situation of the country was such that no human exertions could procure an adequate supply of fuel for the troops," the weather being cold and stormy, many of the men in tents, and others scattered about in open and exposed quarters.

There was not, when the enemy evacuated the country, any quantity of fuel in store, as in ordinary years, procured while the weather was good and the roads passable. The country in the immediate vicinity of Detroit is impassable for teams after the fall rains commence. The timber for about three miles had been destroyed and it was impossible after the arrival of the troops to procure fuel from thence; and the procuring it by water at that tempestuous season was impossible.

In this situation it became absolutely necessary to burn such fuel as could be procured and, therefore, although the men were not authorized to take this fuel, they were not punished for doing so. It was used to preserve the lives of the troops in the severity of a northern winter in the most tempestuous weather, at an exhausted and important post, where no other means of supply could be adopted.

General McArthur, under date of May 20, 1820, at Chillicothe, certifies that in the autumn of 1813, when the army of General Harrison took possession of Detroit, there was little or no firewood to be procured; that it was impracticable to procure it through the Quartermaster's Department, and that the troops were compelled to make use of fencing, and that when the fact was represented to the General by the petitioner and others as an extreme grievance, his reply was that the troops must have firewood and that the government must pay the damages.

Major Charles Gratiot, under date of November 19, 1817, certifies to the fact of the fences, pickets, and out-buildings being used for fuel and for the erection of huts for the men on account of the dilapidated condition in which the country was left by the enemy, the exposed accommodations of the troops, and the badness of the roads, which made hauling from the woods impracticable.

Captain James McCloskey, late A.D.Q.M. General, on oath, declares under date of November 4, 1817, that he arrived at Detroit about the 1st of October, 1813, that the troops were encamped on and about the premises of the petitioner, that in the months of October, November, and December, or until the snow fell, fuel could not be procured sufficient for the troops; that from their exposed situation they were under the necessity of committing depredations on private property by pulling down pickets, fences, and all old buildings in the vicinity which were not occupied; that both farms were almost entirely stripped of their fences; that he often heard the petitioner complain to the officers who informed him it was not in their power to prevent it; that of the men stationed at Detroit about 1,500 were sick and unable at times to aid in procuring fuel, and that this witness at sundry times directed the soldiers to use any fences or timber they could find to supply the messes of those who were sick when a sufficient quantity of fuel was not furnished.

Peter Audrain, a citizen of Detroit, under date of November 5, 1817, states that on the arrival of General Harrison with the North Western army at that post in 1813, there being no barracks, part of the army with a band of Indians in the service of the United States, encamped on the premises of the petitioner; that there was no possibility of procuring fuel from the woods before January.

On a careful consideration of the foregoing evidence, the committee feel justified in the conclusion that the depredations resulted from the inclement and tempestuous character of the season and the exigencies of a suffering army thrown suddenly upon a position destitute of accommodations, and exhausted of supplies by the recent occupation of the enemy.

The damage done to the Cawisa farm was set at 79 panels post fence, $77.70; 10,130 rails, $254.50; 2,164 stakes, $53.60; a barn and horse-mill pulled down and taken to burn or erect barracks, $49.75.

The total award to the Macomb farm was $2,900 and the Cawisa farm $800, both paid in 1822.

## John Anderson

Colonel Anderson was the commander of the 2nd Regiment of the Michigan Territorial Militia. As reported by the Committee of Claims on December 31, 1817:

The petitioner states that after the surrender of Detroit and its dependencies, the only part of his property which did not fall a sacrifice to Indian barbarism and the other violations of the articles of capitulation which guaranteed the safety of private property, was a house at Detroit.

That on the arrival at Detroit of the army commanded by General Harrison, this house was taken possession of for the use of the army in October, 1813, and was subsequently, on the 14th of December in the same year, destroyed whilst in the use and occupied by the officers of the 28th Regiment United States infantry. He estimates his loss at $1,200, and, therefore asks that amount of indemnification from Congress.

The committee have examined with some care the evidence adduced in support of this claim. Their attention was first called to the deposition of Brigadier General Cass, at that time commanding the forces of the United States at Detroit. This officer states that when the troops reached Detroit they were generally destitute of the facilities necessary for encamping in the field; that it became indispensable they should occupy such houses of the citizens as could be procured by contract, and, in many instances, by impressment.

A company of the 28th Regiment of the United States was quartered in a house near the town, which he then understood, and yet believes, was the property of Colonel John Anderson; that this house while thus occupied, was burnt, and on inquiry made by him at the time, he had no doubt its destruction was owing to the carelessness of some of the individuals quartered in it; that of its value he knew nothing.

It is proved by the deposition of James McClosky, late assistant deputy quartermaster, that the house was occupied by a party of soldiers of the 28th Regiment United States infantry, and that during the occupancy it was consumed by fire, which he supposes to have been in consequence of the neglect of the soldiers; that possession of the house was taken without the knowledge of the owner; that from the dimensions of it, and the manner in which it was finished, he thinks $1,300 a reasonable compensation.

Jean Baptiste Comparet proves that the house was occupied as quarters by the troops under the command of General Harrison; that it was consumed while thus occupied, and was, in his opinion, worth $1,300.

Carlisle Harrison, quartermaster, verifies that the house claimed as the property of Colonel John Anderson, in the town of Detroit, was taken by officers of the 28th Regiment United States infantry for the purpose of quartering troops in it, and that on the 14th of December, 1813, it was consumed by fire.

> John McGawen, captain, certifies that a house said to belong to Colonel John Anderson, was, in the month of December, 1813, entirely consumed by fire, except a few window shutters and sashes, which were afterwards used in repairing quarters for the officers of the United States.

Anderson had another claims pending on his property at the River Raisin and on January 6, 1818, wrote a letter to Lewis Williams of the Committee of Claims from Washington City which he presented in person to Lewis, with "thanks for the attention I received on my claim to pass so soon" and containing a $500 bribe. As he stated, "Mr. Lee will hand some claims from the River Raisin, which will pass through your honourable committee, and I have a wish that the conduct of the British in that country may be related in full on the floor of Congress, which will give you some trouble in making out the report, and supporting the same." Williams was outraged and ordered Anderson out saying there would be no such favors granted!

The next day, Wednesday, January 7, 1818, Williams reported the entire to the House and Anderson was arrested. He was paid $1,300 in 1822.

Third Lieutenant Carlisle Harrison, of Kentucky, was 28th Regiment Quartermaster from August 1813 to June 1814. He was promoted to 2nd lieutenant on March 17, 1814, and was, "killed 16 July 1814 in action with Canadians disguised as Indians at mouth of Sturgeon's Creek, Upper Canada."

John Anderson was paid $1,300 in 1822.

## Solomon Sibley

Sibley's petition was presented on December 10, 1822. As reported by the Committee of Claims on March 16, 1824:

> The petitioner states that in the Summer of 1812, when the Territory of Michigan was possessed by the British, he was the owner of about 30 acres of ground near the city of Detroit, which was enclosed by a good fence, and that the fence remained in a good state of preservation until after the territory was re-occupied by our troops under the command of General Harrison. Owing to the great scarcity of fuel in the Fall and Winter of 1813, and the Winter of 1814, the soldiers from necessity were obliged to make use of the fence to secure them from the inclemency of the season, with the exception of so much of it as was taken by the commanding officer to strengthen the defenses of Fort Shelby.
>
> In 1816, he contracted with Julius Eldred to rebuild the fence for which he gave the sum of $303.60, and for which he prays remuneration, with interest.
>
> The petitioner further states that the troops erected a circular work of defense of earth surrounded by a deep ditch on his land and left the same standing to his great injury and annoyance for the leveling of which he also prays a compensation.
>
> The testimony proves the destruction of the petitioner's fence, and the amount for replacing it and for that amount, without the interest, the committee report a bill for his relief.
>
> The committee do not think the injury done to his land by the erection of the work mentioned is of that kind or extent that will justify them in recommending a compensation to be given.

Sibley was an attorney in Detroit, wrote the city's first charter in 1806, commanded a company of militia during the war, and on January 8, 1816, was nominated by President Madison to be the U.S. Attorney for the Michigan Territory. On May 10, 1820, he and Lewis Cass were appointed to be commissioners, "to hold treaties with the Indians of that Territory, for the extinguishment of their titles to lands within the same." On November 20, 1820, he "took his seat as the Delegate from the Territory of Michigan."

Solomon Sibley was paid $303.60, in 1824.

## Elijah Brush

As stated by the Committee of Claims on January 26, 1824:

The petitioner asks to be remunerated for the destruction of a quantity of fence taken by the troops of the United States in the fall of 1813 and winter of 1814 from the farm of the late Elijah Brush, situate near Detroit, and by them necessarily used for fuel.

The destitute situation of the territory of Michigan, after the disastrous and unfortunate campaigns of 1812, and at the time our troops regained possession of Detroit in the fall of 1813; the inclemency of the season; the prevalence of an epidemic among our troops; that they were destitute of fuel; the necessity that existed of using fences to prevent them from perishing by the frosts of the winter, are mentioned by Governor Cass in his testimony in the case of Solomon Sibley, to which he has, and this committee do refer.

That the fences of Elijah Brush were taken, appears from the testimony of Stephen Mack and Henry T. Hunt, to have been $500, as estimated by them in the spring of 1814, under the immediate orders of Quartermaster McCloskey and Col. Croghan, then commanding at Detroit.

The facts in support of this case are in every important particular similar to those that existed in the case of McCombs.

Adelaide was Elijah's widow. He was an Attorney at Law in Detroit who died on December 14, 1814, at age 34. Her petition for the destruction of "pickets, rails, and fencing, burned and destroyed by a detachment of the army of the United States" was presented on December 9, 1822, and the representatives were paid $500 in 1825.

James Abbott filed a similar claim for rails taken for fuel. He never received a certificate as James McCloskey, the assistant deputy quartermaster, was "out of service" in the fall of 1813 under Col. George Croghan. He was given one on October 12, 1816. His claim was verified by Lambert Lafoy, Abbott's clerk, who said the rails were purchased in 1812 from Daniel Robinson for $70.

Adelaide Brush, executrix of Elijah Brush, was paid $500, in 1824.

## *The Settlement of Detroit Claims*

As stated by a select committee on March 17, 1832:

The articles of capitulation by which the town and garrison of Detroit were surrendered to the British forces were signed August 16, 1812. By this unfortunate surrender, the property and lives of the inhabitants of Detroit were exposed to the cruelty and rapacity of the savage tribes, who, if not excited, were not restrained in their depredations and hostilities. The only security provided by the terms of the capitulation is embraced in the 3d article, viz. "That private persons, and property of every description, will be respected." This article was violated. In the evening of the same day on which it was executed, within one mile of the fort, a family was murdered by the Indian allies of the British forces, and the buildings and property on the farm plundered and destroyed.

On the 13th of February, 1813, a protest was forwarded to the Department of State, signed by thirty inhabitants of Detroit, French and American, complaining of an order of General Henry Procter, commanding them to depart from the territory forthwith, and thus to abandon their nearest relatives to all the cruelties and evils incident to a state of war, and their property to the mercy of marauding savages.

The testimony of General Harrison, confirming the fact of the violation of the capitulation, is explicitly given in a letter by him, November 3, 1813, to General John Vincent, in reply to one from General Procter, in which the latter had "entreated him to show every consideration for private families of the army, and facilitate the retreat of any families that may unfortunately have been interrupted in the attempt."

General Harrison, after assuring General Vincent that all possible kindness had been and will be extended to captives, adds, that this humanity could not be claimed "upon the score of reciprocity of treatment towards the American prisoners who have fallen into the hands of General Procter. The unhappy description of persons who have escaped the tomahawk of the savages in the employment of the British Government, who fought under the immediate orders of that officer, have suffered all the indignities and deprivations which human nature is capable of supporting. There is no single instance I have heard of, in which the property of officers has been respected. Some of the most atrocious depredations upon peaceable inhabitants have occurred under the eye of the British commander."

Within the last year, the community of Detroit, in which many of the sufferers at that gloomy period still live, sanctioned the following statement, since published by the order and with the special approval of the Historical Society of Michigan.

"The Indians, who were numerous and claimed large rewards for their co-operation, and who were but slightly, if at all, restrained by the garrison, carried plunder and devastation into almost every house, and through almost every farm in the territory. The miserable inhabitants had no alternative but to submit, or incur the hazard or more aggravated outrage. Most of the citizens of Detroit were sent into exile, and distress and ruin appeared inevitable."

In his message of December 7, 1813, President Madison alluded to the violation of the capitulation as a well authenticated fact. "The effect of these successes (he said, referring to later events of the war), has been, to rescue the inhabitants of Michigan from their oppressions, aggravated by gross infractions of the capitulation which subjected them to a foreign power."

Of the magnitude of the losses and injuries sustained by the inhabitants of Detroit by this well proven breach of national faith, contrary to the express stipulations of the capitulation, and in gross violation of the rules of civilized warfare, the committee are not in possession of any precise information.

The government of the United States is bound, by the sacred principles of equity, by the binding considerations of a reasonable protection, and by the law of nations, to make a just remuneration for these losses, sacrifices, and sufferings; and preparatory to a final decision of the subject, a bill is proposed to ascertain the nature and amount of each loss. In no respect can these losses and sacrifices be attributed to the citizens of Michigan. At all times, and on all occasions, they offered themselves freely to the call of their country. As citizens, they liberally and patriotically sustained their government. As soldiers they were gallant and brave. The government cannot refuse the compensation required.

The committee ask leave to report a bill.

General John Vincent commanded British forces on the Niagara Peninsula during the American attack in early 1813.

## *Frenchtown*

In 1780, settlers of French descent from Detroit and Canada who were loyal to the United States began farming alongside a river on the eastern shore of Lake Erie near present-day Monroe, Michigan. The river bank in that area was overgrown with wild grapes so the river became Riviere aux Raisin. The community became known as Frenchtown. In 1796 the area was seized from Great Britain by American forces.

In 1812, the main British base was at Fort Malden, Canada, only 18 miles north. Detroit, 35 miles to the south, was captured on August 16, 1812, and the British seized Frenchtown shortly thereafter. Frenchtown then had 33 families, mostly on the north side of the river.

At this time, Kentucky had the largest number of volunteers ready for service, and a contingent arrived, along with Michigan Territory volunteers, on January 18, 1813. The militia routed the small British detachment and their Indians allies and took possession of six houses on the north side of the river for their wounded, and occupied out houses, barns, stables, and took anything else of use.

Two days later, on the 20th, Brig. Gen. James Winchester arrived, and two days later, on the morning of the 22nd, substantial British forces under Col. Henry Proctor arrived forcing the Americans to surrender. The British generally left the population alone, but the Indians proved troublesome and the next day, the 23rd, they broke into the homes and murdered 47 wounded prisoners.

Some in-house seniority conflicts ensued and Maj. Gen. William Harrison assumed command of the Army of the Northwest to defend the Michigan Territory, and Brig. Gen James Winchester, who was formerly in command, was named second in command.

In response to these events, about 3,000 Kentucky militia were rapidly mobilized and rendezvoused at Cleveland, but they had insufficient arms, ammunition, equipment, and provisions for an extended campaign. Gen. Harrison then led a detachment to Upper Sandusky to establish his headquarters while Winchester took about 2,000 "untrained regulars" and Kentucky militia to the Rapids of the Maumee, near present-day Perrysburg, Ohio, about 30 miles south of Frenchtown, and built Fort Meigs.

Upper Sandusky, elevation 855 feet, is at the headwaters of the Sandusky River. Lower Sandusky, present-day Fremont, Ohio, elevation 575 feet, is 37 miles north as the crow flies from Upper Sandusky and 10 miles from Sandusky Bay.

Harrison wanted 10,000 troops but estimated 1,500 to 2,000 troops would suffice until the "residue of the army could arrive" as reinforcements and garrison forces. He planned to occupy Upper Sandusky as a major stores depot and use Fort Winchester (Defiance), Fort Jennings, and St. Marys to ready boats and sleds to carry provisions.

Planning for a winter campaign began immediately, but the actual march to Detroit would have to wait until the rivers and lakes froze over, "to bear the army, artillery, and its baggage," so no particular date could be fixed for the advance. All of the necessary forces would have to travel over 200 miles with all of their provisions since none could be procured in the Michigan Territory. Blockhouses to store supplies, pork, flour, corn, munitions, and supplies had to be built along the way, "and a vigilant watch kept upon the savages who might prowl upon flanks and rear." Several battles were fought with Indians, including forces under Tecumseh during this process.

Harrison had some reservations about the quality of the troops, including what he considered undisciplined volunteers from Kentucky. Gen. Simon Perkins would command brigades from Virginia, Pennsylvania, and Ohio and Col. Edward W. Tupper's force of 400 was at Fort McArthur, about 3 miles west of present-day Kenton, Ohio, along the route of Gen. Hull's road.

In mid–January, the term of enlistment for Tupper's troops was about to expire and on the 19th Harrison expressed in a letter to Tupper the wish that they would extend their service for an additional 15 or 20 days and apparently they did.

Winchester had six regiments of Kentucky volunteers, a battalion of Ohio Infantry, and a detachment of regular Army under Col. Samuel Wells to form the left wing as reinforcements for the main force. They would camp near the Rapids of the Maumee.

After the Army moved against Wabash and Lake Michigan Indians, Gen. Harrison directed Winchester to take three Kentucky regiments and the regular Army troops, about 1,300 in all from his camp, to about 5 miles below the mouth of the Auglaise River on December 31. The next day, January 1, 1813, Winchester sent a message to Gen. Harrison saying he was going to march the next day, but it took until the 9th to arrive at Gen. Tupper's camp owing to "a violent snow storm," and it finally reached Harrison at Upper Sandusky on the 11th. Harrison then immediately sent a shipment of hogs and ordered the artillery to set off for the Rapids as soon as Winchester sent word he had arrived, which he did on the 10th, but no word was sent to Harrison for several days.

When reports were first received at

Winchester's camp on January 13, 1813, that a British expedition was forming at Fort Malden, he wrote to Gen. Perkins on the 15th that he intended to "advance against the enemy," and to send one battalion of reinforcements to the Rapids. The letter was forwarded to Harrison, who became alarmed, and he set out for Lower Sandusky on the evening of January 17th and arrived the next morning.

Another report reached Winchester on the 16th, and he notified Harrison, which was received at 2 a.m. on January 19. Gen. Harrison immediately dispatched two regiments of Perkins' brigade for the Rapids and he accompanied them.

Winchester consulted his officers and all agreed an immediate response was warranted. On the morning of the 17th he sent 550 Kentucky volunteers and 100 Michigan Territory militia under Lt. Col. William Lewis to seize and hold Frenchtown. Shortly after, 110 members of Col. John Allen's 1st Regiment of Kentucky Militia met up with Lewis at Presque Isle. Lewis was then informed that there were about 400 Indians at the River Raisin.

The British forces consisted of 1st Regiment of Essex Militia, under Capt. William Elliot, and 2nd Regiment of Essex Militia, under Capt. Alexis Maisonville, about 200 civilians in all with one howitzer. They were from Essex County, Ontario.

The early morning of January 18 was bitterly cold when Lewis' and Allen's troops, armed only with muskets, set out through several inches of snow to cross Maumee Bay. They got to within six miles of Frenchtown when they were discovered by enemy scouts. Lewis left 300 Kentucky troops with Gen. John Payne's Kentucky Light Dragoons.

On arriving within 3 miles, Lewis was told the enemy was in position for defense and the British commenced an ineffective howitzer fire. Lewis' men navigated the slippery ice of the river and up the bank toward the town. The British and Indians fled into the forest where a battle commenced from about 3 p.m. until dark. The enemy was pushed back about 2 miles when the British and Indian survivors took their howitzer and removed to Brownstown to the north about halfway to Fort Detroit.

Lewis' Kentucky forces lost 13 with 54 wounded and then returned and occupied Frenchtown, having set to rest their reputation as undisciplined characters. That night the Indians came back for their dead and wounded and on the way back to Malden broke into some homes and murdered some residents.

The messenger Lewis sent with a report of the action to Gen. Winchester arrived the next morning before dawn and Winchester immediately sent word to Gen. Harrison, which he received on January 19 "informing me of the success of Col. Lewis" and he arrived at the Rapids on the morning of the 20th.

Col. Lewis called another conference and, although their situation was precarious so close to Malden, it was decided to remain at Frenchtown until reinforcements arrived. The news of the victory caused wild celebrations and visions of easily retaking Detroit. On the evening of the 19th, Gen. Winchester and Col. Samuel Wells left Maumee with around 300 troops, arrived at Frenchtown at 3 p.m. on the 20th, and camped in a field to the right of Lewis' troops under Col. Wells. Capt. Morris stayed behind with a rear guard and the stores and baggage. After looking over the situation, Gen. Winchester and his staff recrossed the Raisin and removed to a home owned by Col. Francis Navarre, over a mile from the troops on the north side.

Word had also been sent to British Col. Henry Proctor at Fort Malden and he immediately repaired to Brownstown, arriving on the evening of the 20th with about 500 regulars, militia, and sailors and about 600 Indians to plan a counter attack.

Col. Wells was very unhappy that a store of ammunition was not being distributed, no lookouts or sentries were posted, and the reinforcements had only ten cartridges each. He also felt the officers should be with the troops. He expressed his discontent, but his admonitions went unheeded.

On the morning of January 21, Winchester asked Peter Navarre and four of his brothers to go on a scouting mission to the mouth of the Detroit River and shortly after they met up with Joseph Bordeau, who was coming toward them. He had escaped from Fort Malden and informed them that a force of British and many Indians were en route and would be at the Raisin that night. The news was brought back to Winchester, but a resident and British loyalist, Jacques La Salle, said that wasn't true and Winchester dismissed the report. Col. Wells, however, had not doubted the scouts and he and Capt. William Lanham left immediately for the Maumee Rapids to get reinforcements. Maj. Elijah McClanahan then took command.

Later that afternoon, another scout confirmed the report but Winchester again dismissed it. Late that evening, Col. Lewis received word that a very large British force with artillery was at Stoney Creek, a few miles away, and they planned to arrive at Frenchtown the next morning. Again Winchester denied the report. Sentries were posted but no scouts were sent out along the roads owing to the weather.

That same day, the 21st, the 2nd Regiment of Gen. Perkins' brigade arrived and Harrison, who was "uneasy" about Winchester's situation, immediately dispatched Brig. Gen. John Payne's remaining Kentucky Light Dragoons to the River Raisin.

Around 5 a.m. the next morning alarm shots fired by the sentinels were heard. British Col. Proctor had arrived and shortly after bombs, artillery, and a charge commenced and thus began a horrific slaughter that cost close to 397 Americans, including 100 Kentuckian lives. Scores were wounded and Gen. Winchester and Col. Lewis were taken prisoner and directed his remaining forces to surrender. Major George Madison knew that would mean slaughter by the Indians and flatly refused Proctor's demand. Proctor then assured Madison that his men would be treated humanely and Madison agreed to surrender, but the Indians began plundering. The troops resisted so fiercely that when Col. Proctor left for Fort Malden with 547 prisoners they were not bothered. Proctor left many wounded behind who could not make the march, mostly the Kentucky volunteers.

The next day, the Wyandots returned to take whatever useful items they could find and in the process murdered dozens of the wounded in various ways and places, including on the march to Canada. This was the greatest loss of life in a single engagement during the war and the "River Raisin Massacre" inflamed the American public, especially in Kentucky. Of about 1,000 Americans, 197 were lost and missing, 737 were taken prisoner, and 33 reportedly escaped. The battle affected almost every family in Kentucky.

The prisoners arrived at Amherstburg on the 23rd and on the 26th proceeded on to Sandwich, Detroit, or Fort George where most were paroled. Gen. Winchester, Col. Lewis, and Maj. Madison were sent to Québec and confined at nearby Beauport until the spring of 1814 when they were exchanged for British prisoners of equal rank.

Like all engagements in populated areas, the conflict produced numerous claims for damages.

## Joseph Dozet and Antoine Bourgoud

As stated by the Committee of Claims on February 3, 1819:

On the 15th day of August, 1812, a part of the army commanded by Brigadier General Hull in the Michigan Territory was stationed at the garrison on the River Raisin commanded by Col. John Anderson and Capt. Henry Brush. Information was received from the spies that a large body of Indians was approaching the garrison to commence an attack. Orders were immediately issued to pull down the stockading and fencing enclosing the farms and lots adjoining the garrison within the range of the shot, and also to destroy the apple trees and the fences enclosing the garden and meadows adjacent thereto, that no place of security might be left for the savages, all which was done in conformity with the orders.

The property belonged to the petitioners and the damage is estimated to amount to $400. The committee are of opinion that as the property was destroyed by the order of an officer for the preservation and safety of the garrison, that it is a case entitled to allowance.

Dozet and Bourgoud were paid $400 by the Secretary of War in 1825.

## Isaac Ruland

As reported by the Committee of Claims on February 29, 1840:

The petitioner claims indemnity for property which he states to have been lost at the River Raisin in 1813 during the captivity of the petitioner.

For two horses, which he states were lost in the service of the United States; for moneys said to have been paid by the petitioner for the benefit of Government; for a boat taken by order of Colonel James Miller; for property which he alleges to have saved for the use of the United States at the mouth of the Detroit River.

The committee would remark that the affidavit of the claimant cannot be received to establish a distinct and substantive fact. The design of the present affidavit of the claimant being to establish the fact that the boat was either impressed or purchased by an officer of the United States, the committee are of opinion that no effect can be given to it.

The deposition of John Ruland does not establish any fact material in the case, and the committee are now left with the same proof as at the time of the former report.

The petitioner is not entitled to relief.

## Gabriel Godfroy

As reported by the Committee of Claims on January 28, 1819:

The petitioner was the owner of a large barn principally filled with wheat, and also a stable containing a considerable quantity of hay and other materials situated on the River Raisin in the Michigan Territory.

On the 18th day of January, 1813, the troops under the command of General Winchester arrived at the River Raisin and encamped on the premises of Godfroy about the barn and stable and remained thereon for four days, during which time the soldiers made use of the wheat and hay for their horses, and of the timber, boards, and plank lying in and adjacent to the barn and stable for their encampments. The fences and rails were destroyed for fuel.

On the 22nd of January, the enemy made their appearance in rear of the barn and stable; in consequence of which General Winchester, with his army, retreated a short distance when a heavy fire commenced on both sides. The enemy occupied the rear of the barn and stable as a place of security from the fire of the Americans. During the action a soldier advanced from the American lines with a torch and set the buildings on fire, which were consumed in a short time.

The value of the barn, stable, grain, hay, boards, timber, rails, &c. are estimated at $1,800.

Believing from the circumstances that these buildings were burned by order or the American commander for the purpose of aiding his engagement with the enemy, the committee report a bill to indemnify the petitioner for the loss.

Apparently no action was taken and on May 31, 1830, the Third Auditor of the Treasury was directed "to ascertain the value of a certain barn, the property of Godfroy, which was destroyed by order of an American officer to prevent its use by the British and Indians as a cover in the battle of the 22nd of January, 1813, at Frenchtown on the River Raisin; and also to ascertain the value of the personal property belonging to Godfroy and destroyed in about said barn, in consequence of the burning of the same." (6 Stat. L. 450)

Gabriel Godfroy and Jean Baptiste Beaugrand's claim of $7,256 for "one dwelling house, one barn, one storehouse, and three stables in consequence of the occupation as a military deposite under the authority of a United States' officer." They were able to prove $6,960 in losses.

As reported by the Committee of Claims on January 12, 1831:

> The petitioners were the owners of four buildings, namely, a dwelling-house, barn, stable, and store-house at Frenchtown on the River Raisin in the Territory of Michigan, which was destroyed by the British and Indians on the 23rd January, 1813, at the time of the massacre of their prisoners there. By the evidence filed in the cases of Gabriel Godfroy, Jean Baptiste Couture, Jean Baptiste Jerome, and others, whose buildings were burnt at the same time, and since paid for by the United States, it appears the petitioners' buildings were burnt under the same circumstances and for the same reasons should be paid for.
>
> A dwelling-house has been paid for by an award under the act of March 3, 1825; the evidence relative to the others was then deemed insufficient to bring them under the provisions of that act.
>
> The evidence of the value of the other three buildings makes the stable worth $20; the barn, $800; and the store, $800 to $1,000. Laurent Durocher testifies that he built the barn and that it cost full $800, and that he was acquainted with the cost of erecting the store-house, which was built in 1811, and had one part prepared for a bake-house, and estimates the value at $1,000.
>
> The committee estimate the value of all three buildings at $1,020, and being of the opinion that the petitioners are entitled to relief, report a bill for that sum.

## John Anderson

John Anderson claimed $9,000, "the alleged value of a large dwelling house, and all his furniture, a large store of goods, and a large stable, situate on the River Raisin, in the territory of Michigan, and said to have been destroyed by the enemy in consequence of a military occupation by the troops of the United States."

As he stated under oath to Commissioner Isaac Lee, appointed by Richard Bland Lee on November 15, 1817:

> On the 20th day of August, 1812, at a place called River Raisin, in the Territory of Michigan, I sustained damage to the amount of $9,000, by the destruction of my house and property, by the enemy, at which time my house was occupied as a military deposite, under the authority of an officer of the United States, as will appear by the certificates of Major James Witherell, Quartermaster James Abbott, and Duncan Reid; that said property was destroyed without any fault or negligence of mine; as I was informed by several British officers to secrete myself or I would lose my life by the Indians, which I did, and made my escape as soon as possible, to the interior of the United States, and did not see my family for about thirteen months.

Francis Navarre later stated:

> On the 23rd of January, 1813, being the day after the defeat of General Winchester, I sustained damage to the amount of $1,800; that I verily believe, in consequence of General Winchester and suite being at my house, on the morning of the action, the enemy came to take the property of the American troops, but in so doing, they took my property to the amount above stated, which thus came into the military service of the United States.

Francis Robert declared:

> On the 18th day of January, 1813, Colonel William Lewis, of the Kentucky troops, took possession of my house, at the River Raisin, in the territory of Michigan, and deposited knapsacks, pack-saddles, and other military equipments. The third day after the battle that was fought on that day, the Indians took possession of my house, while it was yet in the voluntary service of the United States, and took every article of furniture, excepting one bed, that was of little or no value; and every other species of property that was in the house, except three or four knapsacks that were empty: that no one of my neighbors, who lived near by, were plundered at that time. I therefore verily believe that the military deposit in my house caused the destruction of my property; that the property that was then and there taken, which belonged to me, was worth $400.

The Committee of Claims disallowed the claims of John Anderson, Francis Navarre, and Francis Robert.

Remuneration for these losses was not stipulated for at the treaty of Ghent, and the obligation fell upon the government. Claims were submitted in a timely manner to Richard Bland Lee's committee and an investigation showed all were just claims, but before any compensation could be made, Lee's term of service expired, and were referred to Congress, but no action was taken.

On January 25, 1822, the Committee of Claims considered the petitions of Jean Baptiste Jerome, James May, William Macomb, Gabriel Godfroy and Jean Baptiste Beaugrand, George McDougall, and Jean B. Couture, "of the town of Frenchtown, in the county of Monroe, in the Territory of Michigan." Petitions were executed on December 12, 1819, at Frenchtown. All were rejected at the time and one by Benjamin Lanfant was rejected: "evidence not being taken in the manner prescribed by law, it is passed over."

## Jean Baptiste Jerome

As stated by the petitioner on December 12, 1819:

> Your petitioner, for many years prior to the war, was a resident of Frenchtown.
>
> On the arrival of General Winchester with the troops under his command on the 18th day of January, 1813, your petitioner, by the order of General Winchester, furnished hay, wheat, and oats for the cavalry, his barn and stable for their use. His store and out-buildings were converted into barracks for the use of the troops, and the house was taken possession of by officers, together with all his furniture.
>
> Your petitioner had many barrels of flour, pork, whiskey, and lard, the exact quantity of each, or the number of barrels in the wholes, your petitioners does not recollect, which, by the order of Gen. Winchester, was furnished the troops, for all of which your petitioner was assured by Gen. Winchester a reasonable compensation would be made by the United States.
>
> On the surrender of General Winchester to the British and Indian forces, the 22nd day of January, 1813, while the American troops were in possession (though prisoner by the surrender) the house, barn, stable, store, and outbuildings, with all the furniture, personal property, and clothing of your petitioner and family, were burned and destroyed by the British troops and their auxiliaries, the Indians, your petitioner and family reduced to a destitute and wretched situation.
>
> Your petitioner further represents, that he could not, during the time General Winchester remained at Frenchtown after the surrender, obtain from him the necessary vouchers for the supplies furnished, or of the losses sustained owing to the impossibility of transacting business in such a scene of tumult, barbarity, and conflagration, as ensued the 22nd day of January, 1815.
>
> Your petitioner presented the before recited losses to the commission appointed pursuant to an act of Congress for the examination of claims, and they were estimated at $4,500, and the estimation or report of the commissioners were forwarded to Washington, but, for reasons unknown, your petitioner has not received any compensation or remuneration for his losses, or for supplies furnished the army under the command of General Winchester.
>
> Your petitioner humbly prays, if he is entitled to remuneration, that such measures may be adopted for his relief as your honorable body may think proper. As your petitioner in duty bound will ever pray.

Jerome claimed $5,064 in losses, but was able to prove only $3,112.50. Jean subsequently died, "in the service of the United States."

## George McDougall

McDougall claimed $2,000, but was able to prove only $1,000. As he stated:

> Prior to, and at the commencement of the late war, he was possessed of a valuable dwelling house and other buildings at the settlement of the River aux Raisins, in the district of Erie (now county of Monroe).

On or about the 18th of January, 1815, a detachment of American troops under the command of Col. Lewis moved on in advance of the main body of the American army then within the state of Ohio, and, by the order of Col. Lewis occupied your petitioner's premises as barracks and a place of deposite. Subsequently, on the 22nd of the month, Gen. Winchester being then in command, were attacked by the public enemy and notwithstanding its gallant effort to sustain itself, was defeated, and the enemy became possessed of the American fortifications and encampment.

In consequence, your petitioner's house and buildings were, by the public enemy, totally destroyed to the very great and distressing injury to your petitioner.

## Jean-Baptiste Couture

Jean, his wife Catherine, and son Medare, 28, were home at the time. James Garrard, of Bourbon, Kentucky, was deposed on December 11, 1828:

I was ordered by General Winchester on the 17th of January, 1813, to accompany Col. William Lewis, who was ordered by Winchester with a detachment of the American Army to the relief of Frenchtown on the river Raisin. We arrived at the town bout 2 or 3 o'clock on the 18th when an action immediately took place between our troops and the British and Indians, which continued until dark, or nearly so, when we retreated with our wounded into the town and took possession of the buildings by order of Col. Lewis for the accommodation of the wounded and the troops generally.

I was engaged until 8 or 9 o'clock at night before I had posted the guard and all the sentinels with their instructions for the night. I was a Major of Brigade and on that detachment attending to the duty of Brigade Quartermaster. After this, I attended to the wounded and then went to see where Col. Lewis was stationed as I quartered with him. I found him in the dwelling-house of Mr. J.B. Couture with Cols. Allen, Madison, and some others.

The orders of Col. Lewis were verbal and all of them given through me to the other officers and by them to the troops. I was ordered the next morning by Col. Lewis to get as many of our men sheltered in the buildings as possible and to examine for supplies for the troops. In consequence of which order I did take possession of every building marked on the map, from No. 1 to No. 16, either in part or altogether, and that from absolute necessity, having no wish to discommode the inhabitants. The buildings of J.B. Couture were occupied as follows: No. 11, as marked on the map was a stable in which my horse and others were kept; No. 12 was a store or lumber-house in which we kept our baggage, saddles, &c. No. 13, the dwelling where we quartered, and which was considered as headquarters; No. 14 was, I believe, a bake-house, or, probably a wash-house, which was occupied by Capt. McCracken and his company, it being on the right. There was also another building which formed a small avenue between the back of that and the front of No. 13 about three or four feet in width through which many of the enemy passed, and in which Capt. Hart was wounded.

On the 19th I made engagements for some flour with the inhabitants and found some that had been left by the enemy, which I distributed to the troops. I met with great difficulty in procuring fuel to prevent the men from being frost bitten, which was the principal cause of being compelled to take possession of and occupying the buildings.

After the battle of the 22nd January, that is to say, on the 23rd January, when on our march to Malden, we were overtaken by Dr. John Todd, who had been left with our wounded at Frenchtown, who gave us the information of the massacre of our wounded, and the destruction by the enemy of the buildings which we had occupied and within our lines; and it was then considered and believed and I then and do now believe, that the burning of the buildings was in consequence of their occupation by us, joined to a belief on the part of the enemy that the inhabitants were friendly disposed towards us.

The foregoing contains a true statement of facts, from the best of my recollection of the position of the town and of the circumstances that occurred in relation to Conture's property.

A claim for $3,000 was filed but only $2,500 was proved. Catherine and Medare continued to prosecute the claim, as she stated:

On the arrival of General Winchester at Frenchtown on the 18th day of January, 18 American officers of the army quartered at the house of the husband of your petitioners. In the battle of the 22nd day of January, 1813, between the American troops and the British and Indians, your petitioner's husband, in the service of the United States, was killed.

On the evening of the 22nd, the house, barn, stable, bake house, 30 sheep, 4 four cows, a number of hogs, a quantity of wheat, corn, oats, hay, all the clothing of your petitioner and family was burnt and destroyed by the Indians and British troops, and your petitioner, with several small children, left in a deplorable state of wretchedness and want.

Col. Lewis and other officers who quartered with your petitioner frequently assured that all supplies furnished, as well as for all losses, by reason, or in consequence of the army of General Winchester, would be paid by the United States.

Your petitioner is advanced in years, her husband and oldest son killed in the cause of their country, she left with numerous family without the means of support.

As reported by the Committee of Claims on December 30, 1829:

The committee, at the last session of Congress, reported a bill for the relief of the petitioners; but inasmuch as there was no evidence before the committee as to the value of the buildings destroyed, the bill provided that such value should be ascertained by the Third Auditor. That bill not having been reached on the list of bills, the petitioners have been enabled, during the recess of Congress, to obtain testimony which enables the committee at this time to report a bill for a specific sum. Three witnesses, who were well acquainted with the buildings, estimate them to be worth, at the time they were destroyed, the sum of $2,000.

The heirs of Jean-Baptiste Couture were paid $2,000 in 1830. Col. Lewis commanded the 5th Regiment Kentucky Militia. Medare was a private in Maj. James Witherell's Legionary Corps.

## Hubert Lacroix

Hubert Lacroix and his wife Archange farmed some distance west of the River Raisin settlement of Frenchtown. He also served as commander of the local militia, and when his company joined Major James Witherell's Legionary Corps in May 1812, the major wished him to move closer to the members of his company so he began building a new home along the river.

When Detroit was surrendered in August, Lacroix was captured, imprisoned at Fort Malden, and later paroled. He then returned home to continue working on his home.

The successful counterattack on January 18, 1813, against the British and Indians drove them out and the Kentucky militia used his partially-completed home for living quarters and a hospital, with the necessity of using much of the un-used building materials for firewood.

On January 22, the British and Indians returned and all of Lacroix's property and livestock were destroyed. Lacroix was taken prisoner and charged with violating his parole. After the war he was released and returned to start over again. He built a brick home, became colonel of the militia, and the sheriff of the newly-formed Monroe County in 1817.

Lacroix claimed $4,560, but proved $4,100. As he stated:

Your petitioner has been a resident of Frenchtown from 1799. On the declaration of the late war, your petitioner was chosen captain of a volunteer company, in which capacity acted until the capitulation of General Hull, from which time, until the 18th of January, 1813, he remained a prisoner of war.

After the battle on the 18th of January, 1813, between the forces of Gen. Winchester and the British and Indians at Frenchtown, your petitioner's house, situate near where the battle took place, being large and commodious, was, by the orders of Gen. Winchester, used and occupied as a hospital for the sick and wounded of the American troops. All the buildings and furniture was immediately put in requisition for their use. Your petitioner, by the order of Gen. Winchester, furnished butter, flour, lard, and other indispensables.

The cavalry were furnished large quantities of oats, hay, and corn. Your petitioner furnished for the troops flour, pork, whiskey, and other necessaries, and was assured by Gen. Winchester that a reasonable compensation would be made by the United States.

On the 22nd of January, 1813, Gen. Winchester surrendered to the British and the Indians in their service. Your petitioner was taken prisoner and on the evening of that day, savage barbarity commenced, by the butchery of the American sick and wounded, then being in your petitioner's house, and house, furniture, notes, accounts, and some money, were burned and destroyed by the British and Indians.

Owing to the scene of carnage and conflagration which ensued, and the confined situation of your petitioner, he was unable to procure from General Winchester the necessary vouchers for the supplies furnished, and for the losses sustained.

Your petitioner was immediately taken to Malden a prisoner where he remained confined for several months, and was conveyed from Malden on board of a vessel to be transported with others to Québec, from which he was released by the order of Gen. Proctor and returned to the River Raisin.

He owned in Frenchtown seven farms, 6 or 8 miles from the house, destroyed as above represented. On these farms there were small farm houses, barns, and other buildings. On one, a commodious dwelling, 50 feet long by 30 feet wide, furnished. In the several barns there were not less than 1,500 bushels of wheat, large quantities of hay, oats, and other produce. Large fields of corn, 60 head of meat cattle, 18 horses, and a large number of hogs, all of which, together with all other personal property, was burned, killed, and destroyed by the Indians, eight or ten days before the arrival of General Harrison on the River Raisin and your petitioner reduced to a miserable and wretched situation without necessary clothing for himself and family.

As reported by the Committee of Claims on January 14, 1829:

The petitioner claims compensation for the destruction of a house by the British and Indians on the morning of the 23rd of January, 1813, at Frenchtown, on the River Raisin, while in the military occupancy of the United States.

This claim, together with the other River Raisin claims, was before the Commissioner, Mr. Lee, under the act of the 9th April, 1816, for adjustment, and subsequently before the Third Auditor. They were before Congress in 1822. The Committee of Claims, on the 25th January, in that year, made a report adverse to the claim.

Since making that report, additional testimony has been submitted. The objection to the allowance of this claim heretofore has been that it did not appear the house was in the military occupation of the United States, by "order of an agent or officer of government." Another objection is now raised, that, admitting such an occupation, it does not appear that it was so occupied "at the time of its destruction."

It appears from the testimony of Col. Lewis, commander of the detachment, that three buildings, belonging to J.B. Jerome and others were occupied by his order for the use of the wounded men, and that the town was taken possession of by the troops under his command, it being necessary after dislodging the enemy. These three houses were burnt in the general conflagration of the place on the morning of the 23rd and have been paid for by the United States. At the time of their destruction they were occupied by American prisoners who had been put therein immediately after the battle of the 22nd, and who were inhumanly butchered by the Indians and burnt with the buildings. This was deemed a sufficient military occupation at the time of their destruction to authorize payment for their loss.

It appears from the reports of Gov. Cass, Messrs. Peter Audrain and George B. Larned, Commissioners appointed to take the examinations of witnesses in relation to these claims, "that on the morning of the 23rd January, 1813, the prisoners who were in the houses, including that of the petitioner, were massacred and the buildings themselves burnt in consequence of their previous occupation by the American troops."

To obviate the objection as to the occupation by order of an agent or officer of the government, the petitioner has procured the deposition of Major James Garrard who testifies that he acted as Brigade Quartermaster in Col. William Lewis's detachment. On the evening, and the next morning after the battle of the 18th, he was ordered by Col. Lewis to take possession of the buildings for the accommodation of the wounded and to shelter the men from the inclemency of the weather, and in consequence of such order the buildings were taken possession of by our troops and were occupied by them until after the battle of the 22nd January. It is further proved by the testimony of John M. McCalla, Adjutant in Col. Lewis's regiment, that the house of the petitioner was occupied by order of Col. Lewis.

In the opinion of the committee these depositions establish the fact of military occupation by order of the United States. There appears to be no discrepancy between the statements of Colonel Lewis and that of Garrard and McCalla. The former says that, "three of the houses were occupied by his order for the use of the wounded men; that as many as six houses were occupied by our troops, and that the whole town was taken possession of by our troops." Only three houses might have been occupied by Colonel Lewis's order for the use of the wounded, and yet, if what Messrs. Garrard and McCalla testify, be true, "that they did, by the order of Colonel Lewis, take possession of the buildings for the accommodation of the wounded, and also for the shelter of the men."

Then enemy continued in possession for some 24 hours and then reduced the buildings to ashes, the petitioner's house amongst the number. The whole constituted one transaction; it was a continuous act.

By a reference to the printed report, it will be seen that the value of the house, as sworn to by one witness, was $1,100, and by another $1,200. Another witness estimates the petitioner's whole loss, including his furniture (burnt in the house of Mr. Jerome) at $4,000.

As it has not been the practice of government to pay for the loss of personal property under such circumstances, the committee report a bill for $1,150.

On April 7, 1830, Lacroix was awarded $1,150 "in full satisfaction for the destruction of a dwelling-house by the British and Indians, at Frenchtown, on the River Raisin, on the 23rd of January, 1813, and at the time of its destruction in the military occupation of the United States."

There is a National Park Service marker on E. Elm Ave. in Monroe, Michigan, to mark the location of his home in town.

## Pascal Hickman

Claims for personal arms, horses, and accoutrements lost by soldiers in service of the United States are not included in this work, but this claim presents unusual circumstances, as reported by Third Auditor Peter Hagner on July 11, 1832:

Captain Paschal Hickman's widow seeks payment for eight rifles which he is alleged to have had in the hands of soldiers belonging to his company at the battle of the River Raisin on the 22nd January, 1813, and lost or taken by the enemy.

Of these soldiers the names of only five appear, viz. Francis Slaughter, Overton Brown, George T. Johnson, Simon Kenton, and Lapsley McBride.

On reference to the records of the late commissioner of claims, he has been found to have awarded $87 to Mrs. Hickman and Mr. John Smith, as administratrix of the estate of Captain Hickman, for the rifles and accoutrements he had lent to them, and for a sword lost by himself, and the official copy of the award on which the amount was payable at the Treasury appears to have been delivered to the attorney of Mrs. Hickman and Mr. Smith. The commissioner is also found to have made an award for $19 in favor of Lapsley McBride for a rifle, &c., lost in that battle, the official copy of which is now on file in this office. The return of arms and accoutrements lost in the battle, made out and certified by Lt. Peter Dudley, who commanded the company after Capt. Hickman's death, affords no evidence that either George T. Johnson or Simon Kenton sustained any loss. With the papers on which the award in favor of Captain Hickman's representatives was made, there is a deposition of Lt. Dudley, wherein he has declared that "he was frequently told by Capt. Hickman, and some of the private soldiers in his company that he had lent to his soldiers four or five rifles."

As reported by the Committee on Military Affairs on February 11, 1834:

The Committee on Military Affairs, to which

> was referred the petition of Eliza P. Hickman, widow and administratrix of Capt. Pascal Hickman, of Kentucky, who was killed at the battle of the River Raisin, report:
>
> The papers prove to the satisfaction of the committee that Hickman furnished five, at least, of his men with valuable and first rate rifles during their service, which terminated with the massacre at the River Raisin; that he was security for others of his men, and strong circumstantial evidence that he furnished eight instead of five; that the rifles cost about $40 each. The committee feel justified in making a report in favor of the administratrix for at least $200, and therefore report a bill for this object.

As reported by the Committee of Claims on April 20, 1834, in part:

> This case has been examined before, when it was discovered that the same claim had been presented to the Treasury Department, and paid, not the amount of $200 contained in the bill, as being the value of the rifles, but the sum of $87, which was the value of the rifles as proved by the commissioner of claims. The Military Committee of the House of Representatives have reported a bill for the relief of the petitioner, since the information was obtained that the claim had been paid without taking any notice of the facts disclosed in the letters of Mr. Hagner attached to the report made by the chairman of the Military Committee on the 12th of February, 1832.
>
> Admitting the claim was not paid, $40 for a rifle in the Western country is, within the knowledge of one member of the committee, a very extravagant price, and it is not believed it is at all possible that five rifles were ever collected together and owned by one man of the value of $40 each. It is startling that a claim should increase from $87 to $200; but it is alarming that it should be pressed when it has been paid about 14 years, and that it should pass one branch of the Legislature, and be favorably reported on in the other branch.
>
> The committee hope to attract so much attention to this claim, as to prevent its future success. The bill of the Senate should be rejected.

Pascal, Paskal, Paschal, or Paschall Hickman was born in 1778 in Virginia, and in 1793 is shown enlisting as a private in Lt. Col. Horatio Hall's Regiment, Cavalry, Kentucky Volunteers. In 1794 he was a private in the Scouts and Spies. He married Betsey Hall on March 11, 1797, in Frankfort, Kentucky, and in 1812 was a captain in Lt. Col. John Allen's 1st Rifle Regiment, Kentucky Volunteers. Col. Allen was also lost at Frenchtown.

The battle occurred in the vicinity of present day Monroe, Michigan, and is commemorated by the River Raisin National Battlefield Park, the only such site from the War of 1812. The only surviving relic of Frenchtown is apparently the Frenchtown Charter Township Hall at 2744 Vivian Rd., Monroe, Michigan.

## Française Suzare

As reported by the Committee of Claims on January 8, 1834:

> The petitioner states that Colonel Richard M. Johnson, with the regiment under his command, encamped on land in her possession at Frenchtown, on the River Raisin in the year 1813 on his march to Canada, and remained there one night and part of two days, and that 600 bundles of wheat, which she supposes to have contained 96 bushels of wheat, which she values at $96, and 280 bundles of oats, which she supposes to have contained 70 bushels of oats, which she values at $35, were taken by the order of Col. Johnson for the use of the regiment for foraging the horses. They took her fences for fuel, of which she says there were about 5,200 rails of the value of $104, which destruction of her fences was also by the orders of the commander. And as she has not received any compensation for the destruction and consumption of her property, she asks to be remunerated the several sums mentioned.
>
> Antoine Sergeant testifies he resided at the River Raisin at the time referred to and was a spy for Colonel Johnson's regiment and that he knows the petitioner had the wheat and the oats as she has stated, and that it was taken for the use of the regiment, and by Colonel Johnson's orders. There was a considerable quantity of rails taken for cooking and for warming the soldiers. The wheat he estimates

to be the quantity set forth in the petition and to have been of the value of $1.25 per bushel, and that the oats were worth 50 cents per bushel. He makes no appraisal of the value of the fence taken.

The chairman of the committee addressed a letter to the Hon. R.M. Johnson for information, and he has no doubt the property was taken, and says neither forage nor fuel were furnished to the troops under his command, which consisted of a corps of mounted volunteers, 1,200 strong.

From the situation of the residence of the petitioner, and the nature of the expedition, and the impossibility of furnishing forage and fuel at that place, and to a corps of mounted men whose march was more rapid than baggage or forage wagons could move in that new country, the committee think an allowance should be made to the petitioner. But as the testimony is not satisfactory as to the amount, the committee propose to refer the liquidation of the claim to the Third Auditor and for that report a bill.

Française Suzare was paid $214, in 1834. Col. Johnson was commander of Kentucky Mounted Volunteers in 1812 and 1813.

## George Agnew

Nancy, widow of George and sole heir, filed a claim for $2766.50 for crops and residential and farm property destroyed by the British and Indians at the River Raisin but could not prove the property was in the military service of the United States. Her claim was denied on January 15, 1833.

As stated by the Committee of Claims on March 23, 1844:

The petitioner is the widow of George Agnew, deceased. During the late war with Great Britain she resided with her husband at the River Raisin, and possessed good property at that time, and their house was a rendezvous for the United States troops. After the surrender of Detroit by General Hull, the enraged savages made a descent upon their house and premises, destroyed and carried away every vestige of property, except the clothes on their bodies, estimated to be worth $3,500, and consisting of neat cattle, hogs, one horse, and a large quantity of grain, all their household furniture, and wearing apparel—being their all.

The facts presented are confirmed by Joseph Reeland, but do not present a state of facts that would bring the claim within the provisions of any law or rule which has heretofore governed this committee or Congress in granting relief for losses of property during the operations of war.

The prayer of the petitioner ought not to be granted.

## Benjamin Lenfant

As reported by the Committee of Claims on February 14, 1824:

The petitioner asks Congress to remunerate him for the destruction of his mill-house at the River Raisin during the engagement that eventuated in the defeat of General Winchester during the late war, with its contents of wheat and hay, and for a quantity of nails, which he says General Duncan McArthur took on his march with a force under his command, destined to invade Canada, for the use of his command while it remained at River Raisin.

He states in his petition that a number of persons who had been members of Captain Hubert Lacroix's company, and were surrendered prisoners at Detroit, on hearing of the arrival of General Harrison at the Miami of Lake Erie, joined him, and proceeded with General Winchester to the River Raisin, acting as spies, but were advised by Winchester not to join the army in its encampment as they would be recognized if taken prisoners. In consequence of this advice, they took possession of the mill in question and fired from it upon the enemy, when, finding they were annoyed, the enemy fired one or more bomb-shells at the mill and set it on fire.

The mill is proven by several witnesses to have been worth $400 and its contents to have been worth $200.

The destruction of the mill and its occupation by eight or ten persons said to be spies, is said to have taken place by several witnesses and by one who says he was in the mill and was one of the persons who were denominated spies.

Without recurring to official reports and

to the history of that period, it is believed the petitioner has fallen into a gross error in supposing or asserting that General Harrison arrived at the Miami of the Lake before General Winchester occupied the River Raisin, or that General Winchester was at any time with General Harrison, about the period referred to. It is according to the recollection of one of the committee who was with General Harrison, that General Winchester occupied the post at the River Raisin while General Harrison was at Lower Sandusky, and that the latter did not march to the Miami until he was informed that General Winchester was at the River Raisin and was apprehensive of being attacked, when General Harrison marched to the Miami, with the hope he would be able to succor General Winchester if he should be attacked; and that General Harrison was between the Miami and the River Raisin, with a part of General Simon Perkins's brigade, when the news of Winchester's defeat reached him.

This error, if it be one, is noticed, principally to show how treacherous the recollection is, and to guard against placing too implicit confidence upon testimony taken 20 years after a transaction has taken place.

An omission to present any claim for this length of time is a strong circumstance against its validity. Were all other objections removed, it is an insuperable one, that there is no testimony from an officer that the building was occupied by his order. If General Winchester employed this corps of spies as stated by the petitioner and testified to by the witnesses, this employment might have been proven by him many years after the transaction took place. If they took possession of the building by order of an officer, such order most likely might have been proven by the officer giving it, if any claim had been set up within a reasonable time thereafter.

The committee are not disposed in these cases to relax the rules of evidence most wisely adopted in putting a construction upon the act of April 9, 1816. It must be proven that the occupation of the building was by the order of an officer, and the officer, if living, is the person to prove such an order was given, unless it was in writing, and if it was, the order must be produced, or its absence accounted for. The name of the officer in this case is not even mentioned.

The prayer of the petitioner ought not to be granted.

"Miami of the Lake," and versions thereof, was a name for present-day Toledo, Ohio.

## *Ste. Marie*

Les Saults de Sainte-Marie—the falls or rapids of St. Mary—was established as a Jesuit mission in 1668 by Claude Dablon and Jacques Marquette and became important in the fur trade when John Johnston arrived in 1790.

### John Johnston

John Johnston died in 1828 leaving a wife, Susan, and seven children. She filed a claim for £9,035 14*s*, Halifax currency, for goods seized by Maj. Andrew H. Holmes on July 23, 1814, as stated on March 2, 1830:

> The petitioner states her late husband, John Johnston, was a resident of St. Marie, in the county of Chippewa, in the Territory of Michigan, in the year 1814, and carrying on a trade in such goods as found a market there. The place was visited by Major Holmes in that year at the head of a detachment of American troops, and the dwelling-house and store-house was, by the detachment and by the order of Holmes, sacked, and the goods and property, not excepting small articles of household furniture and family clothing, carried off or destroyed, under a pretence that Johnston was an agent for the Northwest Company.

Her initial claim was rejected, as reported again by the Committee of Claims on March 25, 1836:

> In the summer of 1814, an expedition of American troops, under the command of Major Holmes, came to the residence of Mr. Johnston, who was then absent. The soldiers seized and took away the goods in the store and property in the house, and conveyed the same on board a boat. Mr. John Holliday, who was the clerk of Mr. Johnston, was present when this was done.

Major Holmes makes an official report of this transaction to Lieutenant Colonel George Croghan, under date of 27th July, 1814. He states that about two hours before he arrived there with his men, the Northwest agent had received notice of their approach, and had succeeded in escaping with a considerable amount of goods, after setting fire to the vessel at the falls. The design of this measure was frustrated by the intrepid exertions of Mr. Turner, with his own men and a few of Captain Saunder's company. The vessel was brought down the falls on the 25th, but having bilged, was destroyed by Mr. Turner. That much of the goods which they took was found in the woods on the American side, and were claimed by the agent of John Johnston, an Indian trader.

That he secured his property, 1st. Because it was lawful prize, according to the law of nations; 2d. Because Johnston had acted the infamous part of a traitor; having been a citizen and magistrate of the Michigan Territory before the war, and at its commencement; and at the time of said seizure discharged the functions of a magistrate under the British government; 3d. Because his agents armed the Indians from the store-house at his approach; and 4th. Because these goods, or a considerable portion of them, were designed to be taken to Michillimackinac, where Johnston had gone.

Commodore Arthur Sinclair, in his report, dated the 6th of August, 1814, states that Major Holmes, who commanded the troops at St. Marys, brought some goods, which he officially reported to Colonel Croghan to be good prize; that as neither of them could determine or judge of that matter, and as it was officially reported, he gave assurance that the strictest justice should be done the individuals, if it should appear to be such property; that an accurate inventory had been taken of the goods; and that a just and proper representation should be made to the court which should adjudge the case, and an immediate return be made accordingly.

It does not appear that any judicial proceeding was ever had in regard to these goods. The committee believe that no such proceeding was ever had in relation to them.

It does not appear that any part of the avails of these goods ever went into the treasury of the United States; nor is there any proof of what ultimately became of them.

The petitioner has exhibited proof to us that Mr. Johnston was not, at the time of this transaction, nor at any other time, the agent of the "North-west Company."

The testimony of John Holliday, who was the clerk of Mr. Johnston, has been taken by the petitioner, and laid before the committee. He states that he was present and saw the whole transaction.

The seizure, removal, and destruction of the goods took place on the 23d of July, 1814. The goods had been brought from Montréal the week before. He showed the invoice of the purchase to the officers. The goods were intended for the interior trade. The provisions were taken and eaten by the men; the clothes, shoes and hats, were taken and worn by both officers and men.

The testimony of William Keith was also submitted to the committee. He states that the goods were brought on board the United States ship *Niagara*, on which he then was, that great liberality of appropriations was exercised by all respecting the articles brought on board; pieces of cloths, and other articles, were individually appropriated; that a considerable part of the goods was thus appropriated, or otherwise made way with, before the squadron reached Detroit, that the residue of the goods was sold.

The committee believe there is no proof which tends to establish the fact that this property was, by an order of an officer of the army of the United States, in any way applied in aid of the expedition against the enemy in the Michigan country, commanded by Colonel Groghan; nor do they believe that property was sold, and the avails applied to the use of the government, or paid into the Treasury of the United States.

Nor does the property appear to have been taken by public authority, for the use or subsistence of the army. The property was taken by the order o an officer, but not for the use or subsistence of the army. This appears evident from the reports of the officer who ordered the goods to be taken. This report is official handmade at the time, and is therefore entitled to credit. He states the reasons which induced him to make the seizure, and the purpose for which it was made. His entire report negatives all and every pretence that the goods were taken by his order for the use or subsistence of the army.

That the goods were afterwards, in part, consumed or used by the men, does not vary the case. This consumption was not by the order of an officer, for the use and subsistence of the army, nor was the cloth and clothing taken in lieu of clothing to be furnished by the government to the soldiers, and a credit given to it by them for that which was used.

This appropriation and use was improper and probably illegal, but it was not such a use or application of the goods as brings the government under any obligation to pay their price.

If the goods were the property of an enemy, the government would not be bound to pay for them. From the report of the officer it would appear that this was his opinion at the time he took them into his possession.

The petitioner has furnished us with a letter from the Hon. Lewis Cass, in which he states that he found Mr. Johnston the active and ardent friend of this country, and that he rendered him valuable services in that quarter of the country.

Under this aspect of the case, and for the reasons cited in this report, the committee believe that the petitioner has not made out a case entitling her to relief.

Andrew Hunter Holmes, of Mississippi, was appointed captain in the 24th Infantry on March 12, 1812, and major in the 32nd Infantry on April 18, 1814. He was lost during the attack on Fort Mackinac on August 4, 1814.

The North West Company traces its roots to explorers Pierre-Espirit Radisson and Médard des Groseilliers who convinced London investors to mount a fur trading expedition to Hudson Bay. The 54-foot *Nonsuch* and smaller *Eaglet* left on June 2, 1668, but the *Eaglet* had to turn back due to storm damage. Capt. Zachariah Gillman continued on and made a landing. The crew built Fort Charles to winter in, and with help from friendly Cree Indians, they brought back a very valuable cargo of furs. The venture led to the formation of the Hudson's Bay Company in 1670, which became the North West Company in 1779, headquartered at Montreal. The company continues today in Winnipeg, Manitoba, Canada, and has operations in Western Canada, Alaska, the South Pacific, and the Caribbean.

# Illinois

## Chicago

### John Kinzie and Thomas Forsyth

After the fall of Fort Mackinac, Gen. William Hull decided Capt. Nathan Heald's 4th Infantry garrison at Fort Dearborn near Chicago should evacuate the post. His dispatch arrived on August 9 and ordered all arms and ammunition destroyed and all other goods distributed to the Indians prior to leaving. Around $6,000 worth of merchandise was given to the Pottawatomi Indians, but apparently he destroyed some of the supplies they wanted and they became upset.

Capt. Heald hired Kinzie & Forsyth to provide mules and horses to transport provisions and supplies to Capt. James Rhea at Fort Wayne. Kinzie and his family would accompany the evacuees.

On August 13 Capt. William Wells arrived from Fort Wayne with 30 Miami Indians as escort for the march, along with 50 regular soldiers and 12 Chicago militia. Departure was scheduled for the 15th, but there was some suspicion of trouble on the journey since Indians had apparently been observed organizing and taking up positions. Shortly after the party set out, about 500 Indians attacked. It was reported that 26 soldiers, all 12 militia, Capt. Wells, two women, and 12 children were killed. Twenty-nine soldiers, 7 women, and 6 children survived and were taken prisoner. Capt. Heald was also wounded and taken prisoner.

As reported by the Committee of Claims on December 31, 1813:

> The petitioners were traders at Chicago at the time of its evacuation by the American forces, and were in possession of a quantity of gunpowder and whiskey, which they had brought there for the purpose of selling. As the longer possession of that post, daily surrounded with hostile Indians, became dangerous, the commanding officer resolved to evacuate the fort and to destroy the public property; and, as the Indians were expected to take immediate possession of the place, Major Nathan Heald advised the petitioners to permit their property to be also destroyed, in order to prevent it from falling into the hands of the enemy, which was accordingly done.
>
> The fort was evacuated and taken possession of by the Indians immediately. In order to assist the party to make their escape, a number of horses and mules were furnished by the petitioners, which were captured about two miles from the fort.
>
> For the destruction of the whiskey and gunpowder, and for the loss of the horses and mules, the petitioners claim compensation.
>
> The committee believe that the horses and mules should be paid for by the Government, inasmuch as they were in the service of the United States and were captured by the enemy and have reported to the House a bill, which, if passed, will extend relief to them. But they cannot conceive that the petitioners can have any claim for a compensation on account of the destruction of their property because it had been brought by the petitioners, who were traders, to that place for the purposes of speculation. Nor do their pretensions to remunerate appear to receive any strength from the circumstances of the destruction of this property by an officer of the Government,

> because it would otherwise have fallen into the hands of the Indians where it would have been lost to the claimants.

Capt. Heald was promoted to major on August 26 and transferred to the 19th Regiment on April 18, 1814. He honorably discharged on June 1, 1814, due to his wounds.

Kinzie & Forsyth reported a total loss of $13,074.47. They managed to send $5,000 worth of pelts to Mackinac, but all were seized by the British. All of the rest of their hatters' furs, shaved deer skins, and merchandise was seized by the British and distributed to the Indians.

Forsyth claimed $60 for each horse and $90 for each mule. They also lost a large amount in horn cattle, hogs, whiskey, and merchandise they did not include in their claim.

Kinzie & Forsyth began on January 22, 1758, when Maj. William Haliburton, a British army chaplain in the 1st Regiment of Foot, and his wife Emily Anne, welcomed a daughter, Alice, in British-occupied Québec. William died the next year and Emily Anne married a British surgeon, Dr. John Mackenzie, and on December 23, 1763, she gave birth to a boy they named John. The family moved to Detroit, and shortly after that, Dr. MacKenzie died. In 1764, Emily Anne married William Forsyth, of New York, a widowed fur trader with four sons: William, Jr., Philip, Robert, and George.

This arrangement apparently did not suit young John and age 11 he ran away from home and made his way to Montreal where he apprenticed to a silversmith making Indian trade silver items—bracelets, cups, jewelry, necklace ornaments, trinkets—a market he would cater to for many years.

In 1768, John's family moved to Detroit and William Sr. purchased a tavern and a store to serve the 100 or so British troops. In 1771, a son they named Thomas arrived.

At some point, the wayward John was located and persuaded to return to the family. Once back in Detroit he met Angus Mackintosh who became a distributor of his silver products to the British and the Indians and at some point he and his half-brother Thomas went into the fur-trading business, capitalizing on William Sr.'s knowledge.

The Indians were allied with the British and in the fall of 1793 John came under some suspicion of being a British trader and his shop and business were reportedly burned by American forces. In 1797, he opened shops at Sandusky and Maumee to trade with the Indians.

One day, John and a friend of his discovered two sisters from Virginia—Margaret and Elizabeth McKenzie—who had been kidnapped by Indians in 1775 when Margaret, the oldest, was 10. John married Margaret and they had three children, James, William, and Elizabeth. Margaret's father subsequently learned of her whereabouts and convinced her to come home with her children.

On March 24, 1798, John married Eleanor Lytle McKillip, the widow of a British officer and daughter of Col. John Lytle, of Pennsylvania, and sometime around 1804, they moved to Chicago. Between 1803 and 1810 they had four children. John ran the Chicago operation while Thomas ran an office in Peoria.

Kinzie and his family were regarded as neutrals and were released and returned to Chicago. Thomas Forsyth, hearing of the massacre, joined them in Chicago three days later. In his reports, Forsyth spelled his partner's name as Kinsie.

From 1819 to 1822 John made silver for Angus Mackintosh at Sandwich, Upper Canada. John Kinzie died on December 23, 1828, in Chicago. Thomas Forsyth became an Indian agent, negotiated treaties, and ransomed prisoners.

As amended to the Potawatomie Indian treaty of September 20, 1828, Jean

B. Comparet was awarded $500, "for goods heretofore sold to the Indians." Eleanor and her four children were awarded $3,500, "in consideration of the attachment of the Indians to her deceased husband, who was long an Indian trader, and who lost a large sum in the trade by the credits given to them, and also by the destruction of his property. The money is in lieu of a tract of land which the Indians gave the late John Kinzie long since, and upon which he lived."

R.A. Forsyth was awarded $200 "for goods heretofore sold to the Indians," and $1,200, "in consideration of the debts due from the Indians to his late father, Robert A. Forsyth, who was long a trader among them, and who was assisted by his son, the present R.A. Forsyth. The money is in lieu of a tract of land which the Indians gave to the late R.A. Forsyth, since renewed to the present R.A. Forsyth, upon which both of them heretofore lived."

## *Peoria*

Pursuant to the act of May 15, 1820, for restitution as reported by Edward Coles, Register of the Land Office at Edwardsville, to Secretary of the Treasury William Crawford on February 1, 1821, in part:

> The old village of Peoria was situated on the northwest shore of Lake Peoria, about one mile and a half above the lower extremity or outlet of the lake. This village had been inhabited by the French previous to the recollection of any of the previous generation.
>
> About the year 1778 or 1779, the first house was built in what was then called La Ville de Mailett, afterwards, the New Village of Peoria, and of late the place has been known by the name of Fort Clark, situated about one mile and half below the old village, immediately at the lower point or outlet of Lake Peoria. The situation being preferred in consequence of the water being better, and, its being thought more healthy, the inhabitants gradually deserted the old village, and by the year 1796 or 1797 had entirely abandoned it and removed to the new village.
>
> The inhabitants of Peoria consisted generally of Indian traders, hunters, and voyagers, and had long formed a link of connection between the French, residing on the waters of the Great Lakes and the Mississippi River. From that happy facility of adapting themselves to their situation and associates, for which the French are so remarkable, the inhabitants of Peoria lived generally in harmony with their savage neighbors. It would seem, however, that about the year 1781 they were induced to abandon the village from the apprehension of Indian hostility, but soon after the peace of 1783, they again returned, and continued to reside there until the autumn of the year 1812, when they were forcibly removed from it, and the place destroyed by Captain Thomas Craig of the Illinois militia, on the ground, it was said, that him and his company of militia were fired on in the night while at anchor in their boats before the village by Indians, with whom the inhabitants were suspected by Craig to be too intimate and friendly.
>
> The inhabitants of Peoria, it would appear from all I can learn, settled there without any grant or permission from the authority of any government. The only title they had to their land was derived from possession, and the only value attached to it grew out of the improvements placed upon it. Each person took to himself such portion of unoccupied land as he wished to occupy and cultivate, and made it his by incorporating his labor with it, but as soon as he abandoned it, his title was understood to cease, with his possessions and improvements, and it reverted to its natural state, and was liable again to be improved, and possessed by anyone who should think proper.
>
> This, together with the itinerant character of the inhabitants, will account for the number of persons who will frequently be found, from the testimony in the report, to have occupied the same lot, many of whom it will be seen present conflicting claims.
>
> As is usual in French villages, the possessions in Peoria consisted generally of village lots on which they erected buildings and made their gardens, and of out-lots, or fields, in which they cultivated grain, &c. The village lots contained, in general, about one half of

an arpent of land; the out-lots, or fields, were of various sizes, depending upon the industry or means of the owner to cultivate more or less land.

As neither the old or new village of Peoria were ever formally laid out, nor had defined limits assigned them, it is impossible to have of them an accurate map. I have, however, sketched off one, founded on the testimony received in support of the claims, and from the information obtained from the most intelligent of the former inhabitants of the place; and though I am aware of its inaccuracy, yet I am induced to forward it along with the report, as it will tend to show the claims, and elucidate the testimony in support of them. I have not been able to ascertain with precision on what particular quarter sections of the military survey these claims are situated. It is believed, however, that the greater part of the land covered, both by the old and new villages, are in fractional quarter sections, and that the out-lots, or fields, are included in quarter sections, which have been granted as bounty lands to the soldiers of the late wars.

Local residents, often the children of the owners, were deposed and testified under oath as to their knowledge of the history of ownership, and a map was drawn showing each lot. Each claim was given a number.

The old French measurements often depended on geographic location, but generally a French pied du roi equaled 1.066 of an English foot of 12 inches. An arpent de Paris, commonly used in Québec and Louisiana, was equal to .84 of an acre.

Lot 1—Ettienne Bernard claimed one arpent he occupied, "about the year 1778 and continued to cultivate for about ten years, when he was driven off by the depredations of the Indians." Tousant Soulard and Joseph Graveline testified in support.

Lot 2—Augustine Roque built a house on about one arpent, "the year before the conquest of the country by Colonel Clark," and 10 or 12 years late "was driven from it by the depredations of the Indians." The lot was claimed by Augustine Roque, Jr., but was believed to have occupied parts of Lots 7 and 14. Ettienne Bernard testified in support.

Lot 3—Antoine St. Francis improved, "about two arpents situated about two miles above Fort Clark, and near the old Fort of Peoria," and lived on it for about 12 years until driven off by the Indians. Antoine's daughter, Charlotte, married Pierre Troge, who died, and Charlotte subsequently, "lost her reason." Her claim was filed by her guardian, Gabriel Latreille. Baptiste Graza and Charlotte Louige testified in support.

Lot 4—Louis Chatellereau built a house in 1778 on a 160 × 300 foot double lot in the old village of Peoria, and lived there until 1781, "when he and all the inhabitants of Peoria were induced to leave the place from fear of Indian hostility." Louis returned soon after the peace in 1783 until stayed until he died there in 1795. The lot was then occupied in 1795 by Mr. Chorette and his wife, Marie Josephe Tieriereau, until sold at auction to Gabriel Cerré by the heirs of Louis Chatellereau. The claimants were the heirs of Gabriel Cerré, represented by Pascal L. Cerré. Louis Chatellereau, Jr., also filed a claim. No. 5 was adjacent to Lot 4. Hyacinthe Saint Cyr testified in support.

Lot 5—The claimants were the heirs of Gabriel Cerré, represented by Pascal L. Cerré as per Lot 4. The claim was for 30 or 40 arpents, but the original size was not stated by Marie Josephe Tieriereau or the claimants. Hyacinthe Saint Cyr testified in support.

Lot 6—Louis Chatellereau occupied two arpents in the old village in 1790. Claimed by Louis Chatellereau, Jr., and by the heirs of Gabriel Cerré. Pascal L. Cerré testified that Chatellereau died on the lot in 1795.

Lot 7—John Baptiste Maillet had cultivated the 300 × 300 foot lot since at least 1790. Hypolite Maillet testified that he was born, "in a stockaded fort which stood on the lot in the new village of Peoria, and that his father lived on the lot for a long time." John was killed in 1801 and the lot was sold to John M. Coursoll, who sold it to Thomas Forsyth, until he was expelled by Capt. Craig.

Lot 8—A 300 × 300 foot lot adjoined to Lot 7 owned by John Baptiste Maillet and disposed of under the same circumstances. Pierre Lavassieur testified in support.

Lot 9—Thomas Forsyth cultivated about 20 arpents 2 miles southwest of Peoria in 1806, "at the river Gatinan, now called Kickapoo Creek," for about two years. Jacques Metté and Felix Fountain testified in support.

Lot 10—Thomas Forsyth commenced improvements on about seven arpents in 1807, "in the little Prairie about two miles from Peoria." Jacques Metté and Felix Fountain testified in support.

Lot 11—Francis Wilette built a house on half an arpent in 1788 and lived there until he died in 1804, leaving a wife and daughter Angelica. His wife died about two years later and the heirs sold it to Antoine Deschamps, who sold it to Felix Fontaine in 1811. Angelica married Louis Pilette, the claimant. It was also claimed by Felix Fontaine, who contended it was sold. The same circumstances apply to Lot 41. Drezy Blondeau and Simon Roi testified in support of Wilette. A survey error was found by the Court.

Lots 12—Francis Wilette built stables and out-buildings in 1788 on one half arpent. He died in 1806, leaving a wife and daughter Angelica, who married Louis Pilette, the claimant. Drezy Blondeau testified in support of Willete.

Lot 13–15 or 20 arpents on which Francis Wilette grew grain. "Louis Pillette, in right of Angelica, the daughter of the late Francis Wilette." Drezy Blondeau testified in support of Willete.

Lot 14—John Baptiste Maillet cultivated an 80 × 300 foot lot in 1790, "bounded on the east by a street separating it from the Illinois River, on the north by a lot claimed by Thomas Forsyth, on the west by a back street, and on the south by a lot of Francis Bucké." Mailett died around 1800, after which it was purchased by Jacques Metté, the claimant, who occupied it until the spring of 1812. Possibly infringed on land owned by Augustine Roque. Hypolite Maillet testified in support of his father.

Lot 15—John Baptiste Mailett cultivated an 80 × 300 foot lot adjacent to Lot 14. It was purchased by Jacques Metté, the claimant, who occupied it until the spring of 1812. Hypolite Maillet and Pierre Lavassieur dit Chamberlain testified in support.

Lot 16—Augustine Fiailteau, "in the year 1789, established himself on four lots of 80 × 300 feet each." In 1794 he sold the lots, about two arpents, to Pierre Lavassieur dit Chamberlain, the claimant. Also claimed by Augustine Fiailteau. Joseph Lapattré and Hypolite Maillet testified in support of Chamberlain.

Lot 17—Augustine Fiailteau occupied about 12 arpents in 1789 and sold it in 1794 to Pierre Lavassieur dit Chamberlain, the claimant. Joseph Lapattré and Hypolite Maillet testified in support of Chamberlain.

Lot 18—Pierre Lavassieur dit Chamberlain, the claimant, fenced and built a house on about half an arpent in Peoria in 1798. Hypolite Maillet and Michael La Claire testified in support of Chamberlain.

Lot 19—Francis Jourdan occupied an 80 × 300-foot lot in 1800 and around 1801 sold it to Pierre Lavassieur dit Chamberlain, the claimant, "who was forced from it by Captain Craig, who destroyed the village of Peoria in the fall of the year 1812." Hypolite Maillet and Michael La Claire testified in support of Chamberlain.

Lot 20—Pierre Lavassieur dit Chamberlain, the claimant, cultivated seven arpents a half mile southwest of Peoria, until forced to leave. Hypolite Maillet and Antoine Lapancé testified in support of Chamberlain.

Lot 21—Augustine Fiailteau, deceased, occupied half an arpent around 1791 and had a blacksmith shop. Tousant Souliere testified that he was there "at least ten years, when he was driven off by savage depredations." Claimed by Augustine's administrator, Gabriel Lattraille, but Pierre Lavassieur dit Chamberlain stated that he purchased the property in 1794. Ettenne Bernard testified that Fiailteau abandoned the lot. Tousant Souliere testified that Fiailteau lived there for at least 10 years and was "driven off by savage depredations."

Lot 22—Thomas Lusby, the claimant, purchased four arpents in 1795 from "Saint John" who had resided there for about 15 years. Lusby abandoned the property within two years. Joseph Lapatré, Michael La Croix, and Louis Coinoi testified for Lusby lived there for one or two years then abandoned it.

Lot 23—Thomas Lusby, the claimant, purchased half an arpent from "Laroach" who had lived there seven years. Joseph Lapatré and Louis Coinoi testified in support.

Lot 24—Thomas Lusby, the claimant, purchased half an arpent from Joseph Castion in 1794. Also claimed by Antoine La Claire, who stated he purchased it from Lusby. Simon Roi, Louis Coinoi, and Joseph Lapatré testified Lusby purchased the lot in 1798 or '99.

Lot 25—An 80 × 300-foot lot occupied by several persons since 1798, including Joseph Castion and Thomas Lusby, who sold it to Francis Racine in 1805, who sold it to Joseph

Dejeney, who sold it to Antoine La Claire in 1809. Jacques Metté testified La Claire was driven off in 1812.

Lot 26—John Baptiste Champlaine occupied an 80 × 300 foot lot in 1801 and sold it in 1810 to Antoine La Claire, the claimant, who stated he "cultivated it as a garden until the year 1812." Francis Racine and Joseph Metté testified for La Claire.

Lot 27—Louis La Bossieur occupied the 80 × 300 foot lot in 1794. He sold it to Michael Coursoll, who sold it to John M. Coursoll, who sold it to Michael La Croix in 1809, who "very soon after he purchased the lot, built a large two-story dwelling house, a large store-house, and other out dwellings, and cultivated a garden, and continued to occupy the same until 1812, when the village of Peoria was destroyed by Captain Craig." Antoine Deschamps and Jacques Metté testified for La Croix.

Lot 28—Simon Roi, the claimant, went to Peoria around 1793 and occupied, "one half of an arpent of land, and bounded northwardly by the lot of John Coursoll and southwardly by the lot of Louis Bisson." He built a house, "in which he lived near two years, when he abandoned it." Drezy and John Baptiste Blondeau testified for Roi.

Lot 29—Charles Le Doux and his wife occupied one half arpent in 1793, "bounded on the south by a lot of Antoine Roi; on the north by the lot of Francis Dupré, and on the east and west by streets." Charles died and in 1799 the wife married Simon Roi, the claimant, until they left Peoria around 1808. Drezy and John Baptiste Blondeau testified for Roi.

Lot 30—Charles Le Doux and wife occupied a one half arpent lot adjacent to Lot 29 in 1793 and built a stable and other outbuildings. Drezy and John Baptiste Blondeau testified for claimant Simon Roi.

Lot 31—Charles Le Doux and wife occupied six arpents adjacent to Lot 30 in 1793. Drezy and John Baptiste Blondeau testified for claimant Simon Roi.

Lot 32—Simon Roi, the claimant, and his brother Antoine Roi and Francis Racine cultivated 30 arpents, "situated on the east bank of the river Gatinau, near one league southwesterly from the village of Peoria." Antoine Cicare and Antoine Roi testified in support.

Lot 33—Antoine Roi claimed one half arpent he occupied in 1793 and built a house and lived there 5 or 6 years, "when he abandoned it and removed from Peoria." Michael La Claire and Simon Roi testified in support.

Lot 34—Antoine Roi claimed one half arpent he occupied in 1793 and built stables and other out-houses until he abandoned it and removed from Peoria. Michael La Claire and Simon Roi testified in support.

Lot 35—Antoine Roi claimed one-third of about 30 arpents, he, his brother Antoine Roi, and Francis Racine cultivated, "situated on the east bank of the river Gatinau, near one league southwesterly from the village of Peoria." Antoine Cicare and Simon Roi testified in support.

Lot 36—John Baptiste Maillet gave one-half arpent to claimant Francis Racine, Sr., in 1796 who built a home and lived there until it was destroyed by Capt. Craig. Simon Roi and Antoine Burbonne testified in support.

Lot 37—Francis Racine, Sr., claimed 20 arpents he occupied in 1807 "between the fields of Simon Roi and Antoine Burbonne" until 1812. Antoine Burbonne and Francis Racine, Jr., testified in support.

Lot 38—Francis Racine, Sr., claimed 18 arpents, "situated about 2 miles below the village of Peoria, and bounded to the north by the out-lot of Simon Roi, to the south and west by the river Gatinau, to the east by the prairie," out of 30 arpents cultivated in 1802 with Simon and Antoine Roi on equal shares. Hypolite Maillet and Antoine Roi testified in support.

Lot 39—Mr. Chorette sold one-half arpent to John Baptiste Defond, who died and his widow married Francis Racine, Jr., the claimant. Destroyed by Capt. Craig. Antoine Burbonne and Francis Racine, Sr., testified in support.

Lot 40—John Baptiste Defond, improved 3 or 4 arpents in 1805 and '06; destroyed by Capt. Craig. Defond died and his widow married Francis Racine, Jr., the claimant. Antoine Burbonne and Francis Racine, Sr., testified in support.

Lot 41—John Baptiste Maillet cultivated an 80 × 300-foot lot in 1792 until given to Francis Wilette. Acquired by Antoine Deschamps when Wilette died in 1804. Sold to Felix Fontaine in 1811, "until the village of Peoria was destroyed, and the inhabitants driven off by Captain Craig, in the year 1812." Claimed by Louis Pilette, husband of Francis Wilette's daughter Angelica, under the same circumstances as Lot 11. Antoine Deschamps, Hypolite Maillet, Pierre Lavassieur dit Chamberlain testified for Fontaine.

Lot 42—Francis Wilette cultivated an 80 × 300-foot lot in 1797 and gave it to Josette Carsereau around 1800. She married Felix Fontaine and they lived there until driven off in 1812 by Capt. Craig. Same as Lot 41.

Lot 43—Antoine Deschamps cultivated 9 arpents in 1807 and sold it in 1810 to Felix Fontaine until driven off in 1812. Felix was the claimant. Same witnesses.

Lot 44—Felix Fontaine, claimant, made improvements to 2½ arpents in the spring of 1810. Driven off in 1812. Jacques Metté and Antoine La Claire testified for Fontaine.

Lot 45—Louis Acaré sold one-half arpent to Francis Jourdan, who sold it to Pierre Lavassieur dit Chamberlain, who sold it to Simon Roi, who sold it to Baptiste Raboin in 1803, who abandoned it around 1810. Occupied by Louis Binet until driven off in 1812. Claimed by Baptiste Raboin and Louis Pencenneau, assignee of Louis Binet. Jacques Metté and Antoine St. Dennis testified that Raboin's rotten house was torn down, "the lot went to ruin," and in 1810 was improved by Louis Binet until run off by Capt. Craig.

Lot 46—Joseph Coudier, Sr., improved an 80 × 300-foot lot in 1796 and abandoned it shortly after and left Peoria. Claimed by Joseph Coudier, Jr. Simon Roi, Pierre Lavassieur, and Hypolite Maillet testified that Coudire, Sr., abandoned the lot and left Peoria.

Lot 47—Louis Le Boushier built a house in 1796 on one-half arpent and died around 1802. His widow, Josette Demouchelle, remained there about one year then left and subsequently married Hypolite Maillet, the claimant. Pierre Lavassieur dit Chamberlain and Michael Le Claire testified in support.

Lot 48—Louis Le Boushier cultivated 4 arpents in 1796 and died around 1802. His widow, Josette Demouchelle, worked the land for one year and then abandoned it. She subsequently married Hypolite Maillet, the claimant. Pierre Lavassieur dit Chamberlain and Michael Le Claire testified in support.

Lot 49—Hypolite Maillet claimed one-half arpent he cultivated and resided on between 1809 and 1812, until run off by Capt. Craig. Jacques Metté and Antoine Lapancé testified in support.

Lot 50—Hypolite Maillet claimed one-half arpent he cultivated between 1809 and 1812, until run off by Capt. Craig. Jacques Metté and Antoine Lapancé testified in support.

Lot 51—Hypolite Maillet claimed six arpents he cultivated between 1809 and 1812, until run off by Capt. Craig. Jacques Metté and Antoine Lapancé testified in support.

Lot 52—John Baptiste Maillet improved 15 arpents in 1797. His son, Hypolite Maillet, was the claimant. Francis Racine, Sr., Francis Jourdon, and Antoine Curbonné testified in support.

Lot 53—Hypolite Maillet, the claimant, improved 37 arpents between and 1812, until run off by Capt. Craig. Francis Racine, Sr., Francis Jourdon, and Antoine Curbonné testified in support.

Lot 54—Antoine Grand Bois built a house in 1801 on an 80 by 300-foot lot. He died in 1806 and his widow abandoned it about 2 years later. She died leaving several children. Antoine Lapancé was agent for the claimant heirs. Pierre Lavassieur dit Chamberlain and Hypolite Mailett testified in support.

Lot 55—Mr. Whitby built a house on 1 arpent in 1801 and sold it to Francis Racine, who sold it to Michael Le Claire, the claimant, in the spring of 1803; he then abandoned the property and left Peoria in 1806. Pierre Lavassieur dit Chamberlain and Hypolite Mailett testified in support.

Lot 56—Francis Buché, the claimant, improved 10 arpents, "situated at the foot of the bluff, about half a mile west of the village of Peoria," in 1809 until run off by Capt. Craig. Jacques Metté and Felix Fontaine testified in support.

Lots 57—Francis Boucher built a house on one-half arpent in 1795, "bounded northwardly by a lot of Francis Belhumer, eastwardly by Lake Peoris, southwardly by a lot of Joseph Laframboise, and westwardly by a street." The house fell into decay and ruin. Claimed by Joseph Boucher. Joseph Lapottué and Pierre La Vassieur testified in support.

Lot 58—Francis Boucher occupied in 1795, "an out-lot, or field, at the hill near the old village of Peoria, containing about six or seven arpents." Claimed by Joseph Boucher. Joseph Lapottué and Pierre La Vassieur testified in support.

Lot 59—John Baptiste Blondeau, the claimant, improved one-half arpent in 1799 and lived there about 5 years. Drezy Blondeau and Simon Roi testified in support. Some dispute over the boundaries arose.

Lots 60—Charles La Belle built a house on 10 arpents in 1809; run off in 1812 by Capt. Craig. Claim filed by Antoine Le Claire, agent for the heirs. Jacques Metté and Antoine Burbonné testified in support.

Lot 61—Charles La Belle cultivated 10 arpents in 1809; run off in 1812 by Capt. Craig. Claim filed by Antoine Le Claire, agent for the heirs. Jacques Metté and Antoine Burbonné testified in support.

Lot 62—Francis Dupré built a house on one-half arpent in 1799 and around 1801 sold it to John Demouchelle, who then abandoned it 2 or 3 years later and left Peoria. The home deteriorated and in 1810, Antoine Lapancé, the claimant, moved in. The land was also claimed by Simon Bertrand, husband of John Demouchelle's widow Mary. Jacques Metté and Simon Roi testified for Antoine Lapancé.

Lot 63—Antoine Lapancé, the claimant, built a house on an 80 × 300 foot lot in 1810 and was run off by Capt. Craig. The land was also claimed by Simon Bertrand. Pierre Lavassieur dit Chamberlain and Hypolite Maillet testified for Antoine Lapancé.

Lot 64—Antoine Lapancé, the claimant, improved 9 arpents in the spring of 1811 until run off in 1812. Pierre Lavassieur dit Chamberlain and Hypolite Maillet testified in support.

Lot 65—Louis Binet improved one-half arpent in 1801 who sold it to Mr. Parquette, who sold it to Antoine Burbonné, the claimant, who was run off in 1812 by Capt. Craig. The property was also claimed by Louis Penceneau, assignee of Louis Binet. Jacques Metté and Francis Racine, Sr., testified for Antoine Burbonné.

Lot 66—Antoine Burbonné, the claimant, occupied one-fourth arpent, "bounded northwardly by a street; southwardly by a lot occupied by Louis La Boushier; eastwardly by a street separating it from the last described lot, and westwardly by a street. Burbonne used it as 'an out-lot for stables,' until run off by Capt. Craig. Antoinne Le Claire and Jacques Metté testified for Antoine Burbonné."

Lot 67—Antoine Burbonné claimed four or five arpents, "situated near Peoria, and adjoining on the north the field of Francis Racine" he cultivated for about one year before being run off by Capt. Craig. Francis Racine, Sr., and Francis Racine, Jr., testified for Antoine Burbonné.

Lot 68—Louis Binet built a house in 1796 and in 1806 or 1807 sold it to Mr. Parquette, who sold it to Antoine Burbonné, who cultivated it until run off by Capt. Craig. The lot was claimed by Louis Penceneau and Antoine Burbonné. Simon Roi testified for Antoine Burbonné.

Lot 69—Francis Jourdan built a house on one-half arpent. He was succeeded by Baptiste Raboin, who left in 1807 or 1808 and the home went to ruin. In the fall of 1810, Louis Binet moved in, tore down the old house and built a new one until run off by Capt. Craig. Louis Penceneau and Baptiste Raboin both claimed the lot. Jacques Metté and Antoine St. Dennis testified for Louis Binet.

Lot 70—Augustine Laroche built a house on one-half arpent and was run off by Capt. Craig and the home was destroyed. Louis Penceneau, Jr., claimed that Laroche gave the lot to his father, Louis Penceneau, Sr., who built a house on it "soon after the peace in 1815 and lived there until the autumn of 1817." Louis Penceneau, Jr., claimed the property. Jacques Metté and Antoine St. Dennis testified for Augustine Laroche.

Thomas E. Craig was appointed captain in the 2nd Regiment of Volunteer Riflemen on September 5, 1812, in Maj. John Moredock's 1st Battalion from St. Clair County. He lived in Gallatin County then moved to Muhlenberg County, Kentucky.

# Indiana

## *Indiana Claims*

### James Leamaster

As reported by the Committee of Claims on March 3, 1836:

> It appears that in the month of September, 1812, after the massacre at the Pigeon Roost settlement in the then Territory of Indiana, by the hostile Indians, about 500 mounted volunteer militia from the state of Kentucky and Indiana Territory encamped near the cornfield of James Leamaster, and being destitute of forage and provisions, used whatever was necessary for them out of the cornfield by the permission of their officers.
>
> The value of the forage and provisions thus taken and used by the troops is sworn to by two witnesses, as in their judgement, not less than $100. In this estimate, General John Tipton, now a Senator from the State of Indiana, who commanded a company in the expedition, concurs.
>
> The committee report a bill to pay the petitioner $100.

Capt. Tipton commanded a mounted company in Lt. Col. Joseph Paddock's 5th Regiment of Indiana Territory Militia. The Pigeon Roost was in Scott County, Indiana, about 80 southeast of Indianapolis. The area was named for the large number of pigeons that inhabited the area when settlers arrived in 1809.

On the afternoon of September 3, 1812, 10 or 12 Indians murdered Jeremiah Payne and Isaac Coffman who were hunting about 2 miles north of the settlement and that evening they attacked and killed another 9 men and women and 15 children. Jane Biggs escaped with her three children to the home of her brother, Zebulon Collings, about 6 miles away the next morning. William Collings and Capt. John W. Norris, of the Indiana militia, fought the Indians for near an hour from the elderly Collings residence, and then escaped after dark with little children John and Lydia. The massacre caused extreme fear and anxiety throughout the area until the end of the war.

James married Nancy Donahoo on September 7, 1827, in Scott, Indiana. James subsequently died and Nancy was paid $100 in 1836.

The Pigeon Roost State Historic Site is located on Edrington Blvd., about 5 miles south of Scottsburg, Indiana.

### James B. McCutchen

The petition of James McCutcheon:

> The memorialist would respectfully represent that in or about the month of October, 1812, your memorialist resided on or near to Busseron Creek, in what now forms Sullivan County and State of Indiana, and in the year 1812 formed a part of what was then called the Indiana Territory.
>
> In or about the month of October, 1812, General Samuel Hopkins, who commanded a portion of the then forces of the United States, was passing up the river Wabash to encounter the Indians to the north. In his marches up the Wabash, stopped and encamped with the forces under his command near where your memorialist then resided, in and about the space of two weeks.
>
> General Hopkins had his headquarters,

with the main body of the army, at the upper end of Shaker Prairie, about 4 miles distant from where your memorialist was attending to a gristmill upon Busseron Creek, and that General Hopkins despatched from the main encampment on Shaker Prairie, two companies of dragoons, commanded by Joseph Allen and William Kellar, captains, up to where the memorialist resided. These two companies encamped for about two weeks upon the farm of the memorialist, at and near to the mill he was attending to. Captains Allen and Kellar pressed for themselves and their two companies of dragoons all the wheat, corn, hogs, chickens, and turnips, and burnt a great many of the fence rails of your memorialist.

Your memorialist avers that all of the property was taken at the order of the commanding officer; that it was used for the benefit, and behoof of the two companies of dragoons. The army needed them, provisions being exceedingly scarce in the then Indiana Territory; and further that the property was duly appraised by Captains Allen and Kellar at $175.

The evening before the army decamped, whilst they were in much bustle and confusion in preparing to move, your memorialist called upon the commissary for an order for his money, having previously thereto handed the appraisement of the property to the commissary. It being late in the evening, the commissary made an error in the order—giving it for 75 cents instead of $175. The next morning, finding the error in the order, proceeded immediately back to the army. They were about getting on to march and would not stop to give any satisfaction.

Your memorialist therefore prays that your honors may allow him compensation for his loss.

His claim was presented in 1832, presumably with the original certificate, but was rejected. As stated by the Committee of Claims on February 29, 1840:

The petitioner claims indemnity for corn, wheat, hogs, and cattle which he alleges were used and destroyed by the troops of the United States under General Samuel Hopkins in the month of October, 1812 at his residence on or near to Busseron Creek, in the Territory of Indiana.

The depositions of James D. Dawson, James B. McCutchen, and Thomas Holden state that the claimant suffered loss of property was taken from him by the troops under General Hopkins in the late war. There is no proof that the property was taken by the order of any officer in the service of the United States, or for the use of the troops of the United States. Without such proof, it has been the general practice of the committee to reject claims of this nature.

The committee are unwilling to depart from such practice in the present case and therefore recommend that the petitioner is not entitled to relief.

William Ledgerwood was deposed on March 25, 1846, and the claim was again rejected.

In September, 1812, mounted troops from Kentucky mustered at Vincennes, Indiana, under Gen. Samuel Hopkins, "to go against the northwestern Indians." There was no forage provided for their horses on the march to Fort Harrison. Some of those who were detailed as sentries at the encampments, returned to their tents in the morning to find their horses gone, presumably to look for food. Lacking an impressed horse, the owners were obliged to abandon their equipment and weapons and return home, some up to 150 miles away.

The 3,950-acre Busseron Creek Fish & Wildlife Area in Sullivan County offers fishing, hunting, trapping, foraging, hiking, water recreation, and bird and wildlife viewing. The area is managed by the Goose Pond Fish & Wildlife Area in the Indiana Department of Natural Resources.

## William Oliver

Around 1704, Jean-Baptiste Bissot de Vinsenne began trading with the Miami Indians around present-day Fort Wayne, Indiana. In due time structures were built, but the city traces its founding to October, 22, 1794, when Gen. Anthony Wayne's troops finished building a fortification. In 1800, a more substantial fort was built about 100 yards from the original structure.

On July 29, 1807, James Rhea, of New Jersey, was appointed a captain in the 1st Regiment of Infantry and in 1810 was sent with his company of about 70 troops to relieve Capt. Nathan Heald at Fort Wayne. Heald then went to Fort Dearborn near Chicago. When war came, William Oliver, 25, was the sutler at Fort Wayne.

Trouble with the Indians in the surrounding villages began almost immediately, causing Capt. Rhea to issue an order on July 12 to be in readiness to respond to any hostile activity.

Brig. Gen. James Winchester commanded the Army of the North West at Cincinnati, 150 miles to the south. Oliver was probably there on business when the garrison at Fort Dearborn was attacked on August 15.

On August 25, Gen. Thomas Worthington requested Col. Samuel Wells, commander of the 17th Regiment, to take a detachment of Kentucky militia for the defense of Fort Wayne, which was considered an important outpost. On August 22, 1812, William Henry Harrison, of Virginia, was appointed brigadier general in the Army and because of the exigency of the situation took control of Gen. Winchester's forces for the relief of Fort Wayne.

Word of the massacre at Fort Dearborn reached Fort Wayne on the 26th. On that day and the 27th of August, Worthington recruited seven companies of mounted volunteers of 40 men each while Gen. Harrison was organizing four Kentucky regiments and word was sent to Fort Wayne that relief was being organized.

William Oliver learned of these developments and his concern for his store and merchandise was possibly heightened by the lack of discipline, excessive alcohol consumption, and deterioration of defense works he knew existed at the fort. When he learned that a relief expedition was being organized, he approached Gen. Harrison for permission to assemble an armed scouting force to go along with Gen. Worthington and assess the situation and if possible secure his property. Gen. Harrison told him he would never see him again if he confronted the Indians, but granted his request, and 68 citizen and 16 Shawnee volunteers agreed to go. The expedition planned to leave on September 1.

On August 28, Stephen Johnston, an Indian trader with a message, was murdered near the fort while en route to Piqua, Ohio, about 100 miles south of Fort Wayne. The next day, Chiefs Winimac and Five Medals of the Pottawatomi and Miami tribes arrived with several hundred warriors who began milling around the fort and stealing garden produce, but Rhea held his fire.

Rhea sent word to Ohio governor Return J. Meigs for help, and on September 1, a detachment of Kentucky militia arrived at Piqua, as tensions flared, causing Capt. Rhea to post a note on September 3:

> It is earnestly hoped by the Commanding Officer that for this night every man will be at his post; relief is at hand but means may be taken to cut us off from that relief. Should any man be found inattentive to his duty, punishment ensues; For on this night our fame, our honor and every thing that is near & dear depends; be therefore Cautious and brave.

On September 4, the chiefs approached with a flag of truce and requested a meeting with Capt. Rhea and Indian agent Benjamin Stickney, and informed them of the loss of Forts Mackinac, Detroit, and Dearborn and apparently said they were next.

On approaching the fort from camp around 20 miles away, Oliver's scouts found the Indian's combined strength was much greater than anticipated, and the idea of an assault was abandoned.

Oliver was still determined to do something, and with three citizens and three Shawnees set out for the fort to further assess the situation. Chief Winimac had been conducting parleys under a flag of truce and apparently were in some disarray and Oliver was able to get inside the fort. He told the defenders that help was on the way and wrote a note about the situation to Gen. Worthington. The three messengers were chased as they left but were able to escape along the Maumee River on their mission. Gen. Worthington sent the note on to Gen. Harrison.

The escape of the messengers infuriated the Indians and the attack on the fort was renewed with great vigor. Capt. Rhea was reportedly in a drunken stupor when he met with the Indian chiefs on September 4 and who apparently demanded his surrender. That failing, the Indians assaulted two soldiers the next day, September 5, burned some homes in the village around the fort, and attacked the east side of the fort, which was repulsed.

With Capt. Rhea incapacitated in bed, Benjamin Stickney, and Lts. Daniel Curtis and Philip Ostrander of the 1st Infantry took over. Oliver's storehouses were apparently burned to keep the supplies out of the hands of the enemy.

On September 5, Gen. Harrison wrote to Secretary of War Eustis to say he had been informed that a British force had left Detroit on August 13 to attack Fort Wayne and he had dispatched 900 soldiers to reinforce the Ohio mounted volunteers. That evening, Chief Winimac was let into the fort for a meeting, probably to demand surrender, and later that evening the attacks were renewed with an unsuccessful attempt to set fire to the fort, after which they retired from the fort until later that night.

On September 12, around 2,200 Kentucky troops arrived and Gen. Harrison was able to drive off the attackers. Harrison arrested Capt. Rhea, but instead of a court martial he was allowed to resign, which he did on December 31.

On September 17, Gen. Harrison was formally appointed commander of the Army of the North West, but the dispute between Harrison and Winchester and the supporters of each festered for some time. William Oliver was subsequently paid for his losses, "on account of the destruction of his houses by order of the officer who commanded at Fort Wayne" but no amount has been found.

The details of the Siege of Fort Wayne, like so many others of a military nature, vary with almost every account. Very few even mention William Oliver, but based on his known location during the siege, it is reasonable to assume that he made an attempt to protect his property, as recorded. The actual military status of Thomas Worthington remains unsettled. His name does not appear in regular Army or Ohio Militia lists, but on September 13, 1812, Gen. Harrison at Franklinton wrote to "Gen. Worthington" at Chilicothe requesting a favor.

Soldiers in Maj. John Whistler's 1st Infantry command built a new fort in 1814–15. Whistler was a British soldier who was taken prisoner at Saratoga on October 17, 1777, and settled in Maryland. An exact replica of that fort was built at Fort Wayne and managed by the Parks & Recreation Department. The fort offers extensive historic exhibits and reenactments year-round at 1201 Spy Run Ave.

## William Wells

In 1784, at around age 14, William Wells was an orphan when he and two other boys were captured by Indians and taken to a settlement just north of present-day Logansport, Indiana. He was named Apekonit ("carrot top"), married a Miami Indian girl, and they had a daughter. A few years later, his brother Cary found him and persuaded him to return to visit family in Louisville, Kentucky, which he did, but then he returned to the Indian village. At some time in 1791, his wife and daughter were captured by troops under Gen. James

Wilkinson and sent to Cincinnati, and early that November, William led a Miami war party to defeat Gen. Arthur St. Clair on the Wabash.

After that, he visited Louisville again and then went to Cincinnati. In 1792 he accepted a position as a spy from Brig. Gen. Rufus Putnam. This commenced a flurry of activity in his life, but he found time to marry another Indian lass named Sweet Breeze. In 1793 he entered the U.S. Army and was wounded just before the Battle of Fallen Timbers. He and Sweet Breeze had four kids before she died in 1805. In 1809 he married Col. Frederick Geiger's daughter, Mary, during a time he was engaged in numerous military and Indian activities as an agent. They owned a farm at Fort Wayne from which a quantity of corn was taken "by order of General William H. Harrison, for the use of the army of the United States."

William died on August 15, 1812, while escorting survivors from Fort Dearborn to Fort Wayne. No date is specified for the loss. Fort Wayne was under siege from September 5 to September 12, 1812, so it's possible the corn was taken at that time by Harrison's troops. Mary filed a claim for the value of the corn taken and in 1817 she was paid $2,000, and also married Robert Turner.

# Ohio

## *Ohio Claims*

### Meshach Browning

As reported by the Committee of Claims on February 5, 1830:

> The petitioner asks to be compensated the value of two horses lost while he was in the military service of the United States in the year 1812 for the want of forage. The claim was presented to the Third Auditor in 1824 and rejected for want of proof.
>
> The petitioner, since that period, has obtained the testimony of James Taylor, Quartermaster General of the Northern Army, who proves that the petitioner's wagon and horses were in the service, and, as he thinks, by impressment, that they were discharged and paid for to the 16th July, 1812. The route of the Army was through the wilderness where no forage could be obtained, except at the Rapids of the Miami and at the River Raisin, and that the risk was incurred by the United States.
>
> John Davidson testifies that in the month of June, and between the 15th and 16th, he was called on, together with Joseph Haw, to appraise the horses of Mesheck Browning, and that they appraised them to be worth $100.
>
> Peter Deltz testifies that the horses of the petitioner died for the want of forage before they got back to Urbana. The particular day on which the horses died is not mentioned. The petitioner states that he was obliged to leave his wagon and was put to considerable expense in obtaining it, and that it was much damaged, and he asks to be remunerated for this damage, and the incidental expenses incurred in going after his wagon.
>
> As the horses died before the day the service expired, and to which he was paid, if the day the horses died was known, there would be a deduction made from the value of his horses to the amount paid for their services after the loss happened. The committee think the subject cannot be more equitably adjusted than to pay the petitioner the value of his horse, and let the damages his wagon sustained, and the incidental expenses he incurred in going after it, be set off against each other.
>
> A bill is reported for the value of the horses.

Meshach Browning was paid $100 in 1830. Browning was a celebrated hunter, trapper, frontiersman, merchant, and grain and sawmill owner in Garrett County, Maryland. In May 1812, he was hired to carry camp equipage to Dayton, Ohio, for the Ohio troops and on May 18 was paid $18.00 for six days' service by James Taylor, the military agent. Taylor was a banker and Army paymaster, and when war came he was appointed quartermaster general for Gen. Hull. In September 1812, Browning served briefly as a captain, in the 50th Regiment of Maryland Volunteers.

### John Core

As stated by the Committee of Claims on April 1, 1842:

> This claim is for the value of a horse, which the petitioner alleges was killed while in the military service of the United States in 1812.
>
> The material facts as established by the evidence are that the petitioner was an adjutant of militia in the military service of the United States. In that capacity in Ohio in 1812 he had the horse with him in the service. The horse

was taken without his consent by order of the quartermaster general of the corps to which the petitioner belongs for the use of a guide to a foraging party. While in this service, the guide of the foraging party being upon him with a loaded gun, the horse stumbled, fell, threw the rider, whose gun went off and killed the horse.

These facts are proved by the testimony of Richard Boyce and George Bare whose depositions were taken in 1816. This claim was presented to the proper accounting officer of the Treasury Department and by him disallowed on account of the construction put upon the 3rd section of the act of April 9, 1816.

January 17, 1817, the petition appears to have been first referred to the Committee of Claims of the House; it was again referred to the same committee on the 21st of February, 1831, and again February 9, 1842. It does not appear what, if any, disposition has been made of it in any way. The 5th section of the act of April 9, 1816, provides that where property has been impressed or taken by public authority for the use or subsistence of the army during that last war between the United States and Great Britain and the same shall have been destroyed the owner of such property shall be paid the value thereof. The committee think the taking of this horse is proved to have been taken by public authority for the use of the Army. It is true that the horse was in the military service of the United States, but the use for which he was taken was not to the use to which he was appropriated by the owner; and any taking and any use of the horse without the owner's assent be, the committee think, a taking and use within the meaning of the act. It did not follow that the United States had the consent of the petitioner to control and direct the use of this horse, because he, as adjutant, took it into the service for his own use. It is certified by Colonel Hindman and John Teeters.

Col. John Hindman commanded the 2nd Regiment of Ohio Militia. Richard Boyce and John Core were adjutants. John Teeters was a lieutenant in Capt. Jacob Gilbert's company in Col. David Sutton's 1st Regiment. George Bare was a private in Capt. James Wimp's company in Col. Robert Bay's 3rd Regiment. John Core was paid $80 in 1843.

## Ira Carpenter

As reported by the Committee of Claims on January 12, 1838:

The petitioner states that in 1812 and 1813, while United States troops were stationed at Delaware in the State of Ohio, he furnished a house for their use which was worth $100 a year. While it was in their occupation it was greatly injured and the fences on the premises and about the house used for fuel and entirely destroyed.

Upon the farm he had two and a half acres of corn which would have produced not less than 100 bushels, which was then worth $1.50 per bushel, all of which was used and destroyed by the troops.

At this time he was preparing to build a new house on the farm and had procured his boards, shingles, window frames, and sleepers worth not less than $100, all of which were used for fuel by the troops.

Edward Long, who was in the employment of the government as wagoner, took a mare and used her in his team until she was so injured as to be useless, and that she was worth not less than $65.

In 1812 he was a member of a light company ordered into service and put under the command of General Hull. He was employed in building Fort Stevenson, and had clothing to the value of $50 among the stores belonging to the United States, which, at Hull's surrender, were lost or destroyed, himself being on furlough.

Leonard H. Cowles states that in 1812 and 1813 he resided in Delaware. The United States troops were encamped in or near there. Sickness prevailed among the troops to a very great extent, and they had permission to live in the town whenever they could find accommodations. The town then being small, almost every house was occupied by them. The house, out-houses, and fences were much damaged. The fences, building materials, and whatever fell in their way were used for fuel. He cannot estimate in particular the petitioner's loss, but it was large. He passed the house frequently when it was occupied and observed that the premises were stripped and the house almost entirely. The deposition of Moses Byxbe substantially agrees with Cowles.

The following particulars embrace the petitioner's claim: Use of the house, $100; corn destroyed, $150; timber, boards, shingles destroyed, $100; injuries by Long, $65; clothing lost at Hull's surrender, $50. Total, $465.

It is evident that the use of the house was a voluntary courtesy to the sick and destitute soldiers, and is an evidence of that spirit of liberal philanthropy which so peculiarly characterized the pioneers of the West, and while the committee would be willing messengers of their country's gratitude for the patriotism and kindness displayed by the petitioner, they cannot without violating previously established regulations yield to him the desired reward.

To entitle the petitioner to a compensation for the use of the house, it should be made to appear to its occupation by the troops was by the order of the commanding officer of the station or corps.

The claim for corn is not sustained by evidence. It was used without authority from the proper officer, and without any apparent necessity therefore, and that part which was destroyed was the result of lawless aggression of the soldiers, for which the government rarely, if ever, respond in damages to the sufferer. The remedy is against the authors of the injury, and, if none is sought for there, none can be obtained elsewhere. The same objection exists to the claim for timber, boards, &c., destroyed.

The wagoner Long had no power to claim the use of his mare, or to impress her into the service of the United States, and if she was forcibly taken, the petitioner's remedy was against Long for the wrong done.

The claim for clothing lost at the surrender of Hull is equally untenable. The soldier, when entering into the service of his country, embarks in an enterprise peculiarly perilous, and yet he exacts no ensurance from his country upon his life; and his devotion to the interests should not be less conspicuous in repelling the miserly temptations of avarice, by rejecting an ensurance upon his clothes.

Why were these clothes left in camp when the soldier to whom they belonged was absent on furlough? And the inquiry would not be irrelevant why a private soldier in an army, which was daily expected to invade an enemy's country, should be encumbered with $50 worth of clothing. Why has not this claim been presented before?

With these views, the committee have come to the conclusion that the relief prayed for ought not to be granted.

Carpenter enlisted as a private in Col. James Renick's 2nd Regiment of Ohio Mounted Volunteers and Militia, and a sergeant in Lewis Cass's 3rd Regiment of Ohio Volunteers and Militia.

Moses Byxbe came from Berkshire County, Massachusetts, and used Revolutionary War bounty land grants to acquire land and platt the town of Delaware on May, 9, 1808.

## Paul D. Butler

Maj. Gen. Elijah Wadsworth commanded the 4th Division of Ohio Militia at the Battle of the Peninsula at the mouth of the Huron River on September 10, 1812. Immediately after this, Gen. William Harrison ordered Wadsworth's 800 troops and about 500 of Brig. Gen. Reasin Beall's 4th Division brigade of Ohio Militia to report to Gen. Simon Perkins, whose orders were to "proceed to Lower Sandusky and open a road thence to the Rapids of the Maumee." This was done after great difficulty in building 15 miles of causeway.

Paul Butler owned a farm in Ohio on which Gen. Perkins' troops camped. He was paid $3,285 on May 1, 1817, for corn, potatoes and hay, and $3,612.75 on June 14 for "various articles."

The Indian village of Wyandot on the Sandusky River was called Lower Sandusky and is now Fremont, Ohio.

## John Menary

Col. John Hindman, commander of the 2nd Regiment, 2nd Brigade, 4th Division of Ohio Militia, gave John Menary a receipt:

> September 6, 1812. Received one bay horse, appraised at eighty five dollars, for the use of the detachment ordered out by General Wadsworth, and the property of John Menary.

Maj. Gen. Elijah Wadsworth commanded the 4th Division of Ohio Militia at the Battle of the Peninsula at the mouth of the Huron River on September 10, 1812.

Menary apparently filed a claim some time previous, but became, "extensively engaged in business for some years; and more recently, because he has been confined by a paralytical shock, which has rendered useless his left side." His petition was presented on January 7, 1831. The Committee of Claims reported on January 14, 1831, that John Thompson and Peter Musser of the Committee certified the authenticity of Menary's receipt and approved his claim. John Menary was paid $85 in 1832.

## David Hull

As reported by the Committee of Claims on January 13, 1831:

> He asks to be remunerated for the loss of the following property, which was destroyed by the British and Indians in the fall of 1812 at the Rapids of the Miami of the Lake, to wit:
>
> 1 house, $500; 1 barn, $100; 1 store, $100; 1 warehouse and outhouse, $150; 1 bed and appurtenances, $50; household furniture, $500; 12 barrels of whiskey, 420 gallons at $1.50 per gallon, $630; 30 tons of hay at $5.00 per ton, $150; garden destroyed, $50; fences and other improvements destroyed, $100, 2 two-year-old neat cattle, $20; 5 yearlings, $37.50; 30 hogs, $150; 5 barrels of pork, $100; 3 barrels of flour, $24; 4 barrels of salt, $40; 4 cwt. of sugar, $50; 300 pounds of bacon, $37.50; merchandise, $1,400; one month's services for the protection of Fort Meigs during the spring of 1814, $30. Total $4,459.
>
> It appears the claimant was captain of a company of Michigan militia in the year 1812, and that he drew some arms at Detroit, which were deposited in his house or in his store when his company were not on duty. He was taken prisoner in August, 1812, and while so held in captivity, his property was destroyed by the British and Indians, in part, and in part was taken away.
>
> Pierre Menard is the only witness who has testified he was present when the British and Indians plundered the property. He says there were in the house United States' arms, musket and cartridges, or fixed ammunition. The buildings were burnt, he says, a few days after, by the British, on their return from Fort Wayne. It does not appear from his testimony whether he was present when the houses were burned or not.
>
> The laws on the subject of remunerating the owners of houses and buildings for their destruction by the enemy during the late war require that the buildings should be occupied as barracks or as a place of military deposit at the time of the destruction, and that destruction should have been in consequence of such occupation.
>
> It appears to the committee that the arms were left at the house or store of the claimant when the company was not on duty. It appears that it must have been in service at the time of Gen. Hull's surrender, and it is not easily perceived how the arms or ammunition of the company should have been deposited in the claimant's buildings after that event took place. It appears that no claim was made under the law of 1816 or any subsequent law.
>
> James Wilkinson testifies the store was made the place of deposit while Pierre Menard says the arms and ammunition were in the house.
>
> The committee, in deciding on these losses, have felt themselves bound to be governed by the principles and rules contained in the laws of April 9, 1816, and March 3, 1825, and they think the testimony in this case does not sustain the claim for the destruction of the buildings.
>
> As to the other property contained in the schedule, there has been no law, rule, or precedent which would authorize the committee to give this part of the claim a favorable consideration.
>
> Andrew Race and William Peters testify that the claimant, in the fall of 1814, raised a corps of men and took care of and protected Fort Meigs and the public property it contained after it was abandoned by a detachment of militia whose services had expired, until he was relieved by another detachment. They are, however, silent as to the time he was thus in the service. The committee think his conduct on this occasion was highly meritorious and that, on making proof of the time he was protecting the property of the United States, he ought to be compensated; but the

committee cannot, with the present testimony, ascertain the amount that should be allowed to him.

As reported on June 15, 1836:

The claim is for the destruction of buildings and their contents, in August, 1812, at the Maumee River. The amount of his loss is estimated at $4,459. It was presented at the 2d session of the 21st Congress and an unfavorable report was made.

It was stated that the petitioner was captain of a company and that arms were deposited at his house or store, and a military deposit was attempted thus to be made out.

The deposition of Cyrus Hunter was taken on the 30th of November, 1833, since the report of the Committee mentioned above. His testimony is taken to prove a military occupation of the house and store by reason of the arms being deposited at, or in one of them. This witness lived at the time at the River Raisin. He testifies he was at Fort Meigs in July and August, 1812, before and after the surrender of General Hull, where he saw David Hull drilling his company and knows the arms were deposited in his buildings. After General Hull surrendered, he says, he was at Fort Meigs when Capt. Hull tried to prevail on him (the witness) to remain with him (Capt. Hull) at Fort Meigs, but he left immediately for Urbana.

The committee will merely remark on this testimony that Fort Meigs was not commenced until after General Harrison's return from the Portage, the latter part of January or fore part of February, 1813, nor was the site a military station until so occupied by Gen. Harrison.

In a deposition given by Jacob Wilkinson on the 10th of November, 1830, he stated when speaking of David Hull, and of his property, "that Hull was taken prisoner by the enemy in the month of August, 1812, and that during the time he was detained as a prisoner, the British forces plundered his premises." From this testimony the committee was led to believe, when examining this case in 1834, that David Hull was with Gen. William Hull and was taken prisoner at the capitulation of Detroit.

From the testimony of Cyrus Hunter, it appears after General Hull's surrender that David Hull was in command of his company on the Maumee.

It may have been the case, but if so, it has escaped the recollection of the committee, that any prisoners were taken at the Maumee after Hull's surrender. In the articles of capitulation, all the inhabitants of the Territory of Michigan were surrendered as were all the military forces in the service on the march to aid General Hull. But it appears from Mr. Hagner's letter that Capt. Hull's company was not mustered into the service or in any way known or recognized.

Jacob Wilkinson and Andrew Race have given explanatory depositions since the former report was made. Gabriel La Paint's deposition has also been taken. These do not, in the opinion of the committee, establish a military occupation of the claimant's buildings, either as barracks or as a place for depositing military stores.

The company was not in the military service of the State of Ohio or of the United States. The ground on which allowances have been made for buildings destroyed by the enemy is that they were, for the time, public property. The fact that militia, at the time of mustering, placed their arms in a house or store or that the owner, for the protection of his property, had borrowed a number of muskets from the United States does not constitute a military occupation.

Some of the witnesses speak of United States property being in the buildings, to wit: "pork, flour, whiskey, &c." At the time referred to, the United States had no commissariat department. The army was supplied by contractors who not only furnished provisions, but dealt them out in rations to the troops. It is not perceived how the United States should have provisions there. Who deposited it, and for what purpose, are questions of importance. There is great looseness about the testimony.

If Captain Hull had officers they must better know what was done than a witness residing at the river Raisin, or than others who have given their depositions. The committee think, with the present testimony, the claimant is not entitled to relief.

Cyrus Hunter and Gabriel Lapoint were privates in Major James Witherell's detachment of Michigan Militia.

## Amos Miller

Mary Miller was the administratrix of Amos Miller, as reported on December 27, 1824:

> It appears that Amos Miller, in the year 1812, was the owner of a keel boat, with which he navigated on the Ohio River and its branches. Being at Portsmouth, at the junction of the Scioto with the Ohio, in the fall of 1812, he was taken sick and died. His boat was taken possession of by an officer in the service of the United States, by the advice of Return J. Meigs, then Governor of the state of Ohio, to transport the munitions of war from Portsmouth in a direction to the North Western army.
>
> The boat was not returned, but was destroyed by the ice in the winter of 1813; and its value was $450. The petitioner accounts for the delay in not presenting her claim to have arisen from not knowing where the witnesses resided, and prays relief.
>
> The facts stated in her petition are proven by the depositions of Governor Meigs, John H. Thornton, Elijah Glover, and Nathan K. Clough, to which the committee refer and consider that the petitioner is entitled to relief, which they report a bill.

Pvt. Elijah Glover served in Capt. William Kendall's Troop of Horse, of Scioto County, and Nathan Clough was a surgeon's mate in Col. Jacob Noel's 1st Regiment, Ohio Militia. John H. Thornton, of Scioto County, married Sarah Glover on September 18, 1809.

## Peter Lionberger

Peter Lionberger was a private in the 2nd Battalion of Lt. Col. Mills Stephenson's 2nd Regiment Ohio Militia. Anthony Pitzer was a major in Col. Stephenson's regiment. Pitzer was deposed on November 10, 1841:

> Major Anthony Pitzer, a resident of Licking County, deposed that he was the commandant of militia in Licking County. After the surrender of General Hull, he received orders from General Lynch for a draft of militia from his regiment. The draft was made, and, amongst others, Peter Lionberger, then and still a resident of Licking County, was drafted.
>
> Captain Joseph Sutton commanded the company of drafted men, and it being necessary that the company should be furnished with a baggage wagon, he called upon Lionberger, who was the owner of an excellent team, and induced him to let it go, assuring him that if any of his horses died in the service he would be paid for them.
>
> Lionberger did let his team go, which consisted of four very large, stout horses, which were in excellent order when they started. One of them was an iron gray.
>
> Major Pitzer ordered the horses, wagon, and all the apparatus to be appraised and directed Lionberger to report his team when he reached the place of rendezvous. He was present at Newark from which point the company marched, he thinks, some time in the month of September, 1812. He observed the team particularly when it started; the horses were in fine plight.
>
> In the month of February following, he was called upon to take command of a battalion of Ohio militia which had been drafted to join the Northwestern Army. He left Newark about the 27th of February, 1813, and near Columbus he met Peter Lionberger coming back with his team. The horses looked most miserable, poor, and jaded, and worn out—the team which, a few months before, was in such beautiful plight, appeared to be all gone to wreck.
>
> Major Pitzer did not return to Licking County until the fall of 1813, and when he did return he learned that two of the horses died shortly after their return, and one of them had died in the army. He has no knowledge of Peter Lionberger ever receiving from the government any compensation for the horses. He has lived a neighbor to Lionberger for the last 30 years, and he has made repeated applications to assist him in obtaining a compensation for the loss of the horses.

As stated by the Committee of Claims on May 25, 1842, in part:

> The petitioner represents that in the fall of 1812 he was a farmer residing in the county of Licking in the State of Ohio. After the surrender of Detroit by General Hull, there was a draft of Ohio militiamen, as petitioner

understood at the time, by order of an officer by the name of Lynch. Major Anthony Pitzer, of the county, commanded the regiment to which the petitioner belonged. A company was drafted from the regiment to perform a tour of six months, and, amongst others, the petitioner. After the draft was made and the petitioner was about to repair to Newark, the place of rendezvous, Major Pitzer called upon the petitioner and stated that a baggage wagon must be had for the company, and requested petitioner to furnish his team and wagon. Petitioner absolutely refused to do so. His team was a first rate one, and he could not spare it from his farm, whereupon Major Pitzer informed him that he was authorized by law to press the team into the service, and must do so, it being the stoutest and best team in the neighborhood. He, at the same time, assured the petitioner that he would be paid by the government for any damage which the team might sustain whilst in the service.

Finding that he would be compelled to let his team go, he yielded to the urgent entreaties of Major Pitzer, and, although greatly to his disadvantage, he geared up and drove into Newark, the place of rendezvous. His team was appraised at Newark, and he started from there early in October, 1812.

Before the company to which he was attached joined the main army, the winter had broken up, and the black swamp was almost impassable—his team was again and again mired down and had to be prised out. This hard usage and scarcity of feed soon destroyed the petitioner's fine team. A few weeks after he joined the army, his best horse, which had been appraised at $120, dropped dead in his gears. He represents that his other horses were much reduced before he got home, and two of his three remaining horses died shortly after he got home. He sought compensation at an early day and for that purpose obtained a copy of the record of appraisement of his team from the book of the quartermaster. This he lost before obtaining relief, and did not find it until recently.

The deposition of Major Pitzer, taken in 1841, confirms the material allegations of the petitioner. Henry Alexander, who says he was four months with petitioner in the service, testifies that one of the horses died while in the service—and that he took good care of his horses. He says the team was considered the second best in the regiment, and when the petitioner got home, the witness considered it not worth $10.

Joseph Beard knew the team. He says the petitioner returned home with three of his horses in March, 1813. One of the horses was not brought back. Two of them died shortly after his return, and the witness thinks their death was caused by the hardships they endured in the service.

From the Third Auditor we learn that one Peter Lionberger was paid as a private in a company commanded by Captain Joseph Sutton, of a regiment of which Charles Miller, first as major and afterwards as lieutenant colonel, was commanding officer, at the rate of $6.66 per month from 30th September, 1812, to 7th April, 1813. Opposite his name, this remark appears, "On duty as wagoner." It further appears that Peter Lionberger was paid for 58 days' hauling for the Northwestern Army from 3rd October to 3rd November. Six days, the receipt for which is dated. December 9, 1812, to February 25, 1813, the price paid was $3.00 per day—total $429.

The records of the commissioner who administered the law of April 9, 1816, show that on the 23rd of February, 1818, he awarded $100 to Peter Lionberger for the loss of a horse.

The committee are satisfied that the petitioner lost a horse by death while it was engaged in the military service of the United States, without fault or negligence on his part, and in consequence of the failure of the United States to furnish sufficient forage.

A bill appropriating $100 for the relief of the petitioner is hereby reported.

Capt. Joseph Sutton was in Col. Charles Miller's 3rd Regiment, Drafted Ohio Militia. Henry Alexander was a private in the same regiment.

Joseph Beard was a private in Capt. Nicholas Shaver's Rifle Company, Ohio Militia, from Licking County.

## Jacob L. Vance

As reported by the Committee of Claims on January 28, 1845:

The petitioner prays for compensation for a horse valued at $50, lost in 1813, whilst in public service, and for the services of his four-horse team at $3 per day for 18 days, commencing on the 17th of January, and ending on the 5th of February, 1813.

The petitioner was engaged in hauling flour for the use of the army from Urbana, in the State of Ohio, to McArthur's block-house, and while so employed he lost one of his horses, valued at $50.

From a letter from the Third Auditor, under date of April 15, 1814, it appears for hauling flour during the same year, the petitioner was allowed and paid $3 per day. When teams are thus employed by government officers, unless otherwise expressly stipulated in a written contract, made to induce an entrance into service upon occasions of great peril or of unusual difficulty, such teams are not insured by the United States against either injury or loss; the risk is upon the owner, and he is supposed to take into consideration the cost of the insurance, as well as the value of the labor of his team, when stipulating the price he will take for the use of his team per day. Hence, his claim for the value of the horse lost while in the service of the United States cannot be recognized as valid or obligatory. For the services of his team at $3 per day seems to be a reasonable compensation, and the one fixed upon at the time; and therefore, a bill allowing the petitioner $54 for the use of his team 18 days is herewith reported, and its passage recommended.

Fort McArthur was built in June 1812, on the Scioto River crossing site by troops under Col. Duncan McArthur as one of the forts along Gen. Hull's "trace" to Detroit. According to records, it was located, "in the northwest corner of Buck Township, about 3 miles west of Kenton in Hardin County, Ohio." A roadside historical marker was put up to identify the actual location a short distance from the river.

Jacob Vance was paid $50 for a horse and $54 for the use of his team of four horses and a wagon for 18 days in 1813 in 1847.

## Peter Ford

As reported by the Committee of Claims on May 22, 1828:

An order was given by Brigadier General Simon Perkins, commanding a brigade of Ohio militia in the service of the United States on the 21st day of January, 1813, to Luman Beach, a quartermaster in his brigade, to impress a sufficient number of teams to transport the baggage of a detachment, ordered from the Miami of the Lake, to reinforce General Winchester at River Raisin, and also to transport a supply of flour for the troops. In obedience to the order, Beach did impress a team of four oxen, a sled, and two chains belonging to Peter Ford.

The detachment proceeded on the ice towards the River Raisin and the teams proceeded by land. The teams were escorted by a guard and a driver was detailed for Ford's team and he was not with them.

On the 22nd day of January, the day on which the troops under the command of General Winchester were attacked and defeated, the team, with others, had proceeded to about midway from the Miami to the River Raisin, when information was given to the party by two men who were in the battle, but had made their escape, that General Winchester was defeated, and that the enemy was pressing towards the Miami, and but a short distance from where the party then was. After a short consultation, it was the conclusion of the party that it could not retreat safely with the teams, which were much fatigued, and that the oxen were unyoked, and the sled and chains left on the road. One of the oxen was afterwards found by Mr. Miller and driven to Erie, in the State of Pennsylvania, where Ford resided, and that Miller charged for his trouble and expense, $10.

The testimony establishes the value of the property not recovered to be $127.50. The Committee deduct from Mr. Ford's account one sled, which was lost on the retreat of our army from Miami to Portage River, of the value of $4.50, leaving $123; to which add $10, paid for the drift of the ox to Erie, distance of about 200 miles, making $133. The Committee think the petitioner is entitled to this sum, and report a bill.

## Joel Abbott, Jr.

As reported by the Committee of Claims on January 13, 1825:

In the month of November, 1812, Joel Abbott, Jr., entered his team, consisting of a wagon and four horses, into the service of the United States, during the late war, with Arthur O'Harra, wagon master, at Franklinton, in the state of Ohio, for the purpose of transporting provisions to the Northwestern Army.

That on the 1st day of February, 1813, Abbott was placed, with his team, under the command of Andrew Dill, wagon master to a brigade of wagons, attached to Col. John B. Campbell's Regiment of United States' Infantry and on the next day thereafter, one of the horses, of the value of $80, was impressed out of his team by the order of Campbell, in order to pursue one John Smith, a wagon master, who was deserting from the army of the United States, with his brigade of wagons; and while the horse of Abbott was performing service for the United States, he received a wound by a dislocation of one of his postern joints, which entirely disabled said horse for further service, and of which wound he soon thereafter died. It also appears from the evidence that Abbott entered his team at the risk of the United States. A bill is therefore reported for his relief.

Abbott was paid $80 by the War Department. Lt. Col. John Campbell, of Kentucky, commanded the 19th Regiment of Infantry, and in April 1814, transferred to the 11th Infantry. On July 5, 1814, he was wounded at Chippewa and died on August 28.

## Isadore Navarre

As stated by the Committee of Claims on March 28, 1832:

The memorialist claims compensation for a barge or bateaux of the value of $55 which was seized by the order of General Harrison for the use of the American troops at the Miami River in the spring of 1813. The petitioner declares that his boat was taken to Detroit with the army, that he has never heard of it since, nor received any compensation from any source for it, and that all the boats on the river were taken at the same time.

He also states, that about five years since, he procured his claim to be made out, and with the affidavits in its support, transmitted it to Washington to the then delegate from Michigan, but which, for reasons unknown to him, never were received. He also declares he made repeated efforts to obtain the testimony of General Harrison, but has never received any reply.

Medard Labadie testifies that in the latter end of April or the beginning of May, 1813, General Harrison ordered him, with some others attached to his army, to proceed down the Miami and collect all the boats, bateaux and canoes, and bring them to Fort Meigs, and to destroy such as they could not bring. They took possession of a large bateaux, the property of Isadore Navarre, shortly after which his company had a skirmish with the Indians, which was fought by them while in the bateaux, which they subsequently brought to Fort Meigs, where it was left in possession of the United States' troops and where he saw it last.

Antoine Sergeant corroborated the testimony of Labadie and states that he travelled on foot from Fort Meigs to Detroit and did not afterwards see this boat. It was a new boat, worth at that time at least $50, and thinks it never again came into the possession of the petitioner.

The claimant having referred to General Charles Gratiot in his memorial, in his reply states that he has a perfect recollection of the expedition sent down the Miami bay to destroy some property at Turkey Point, which had been abandoned by the owners; also of the skirmish spoken of between a party of refugees from Michigan, in General Harrison's camp, and a party of British Indians, and that they, the refugees, fought in a boat of the description stated by the petitioner, but whether or not it was the property of Mr. Navarre, he is unable to say.

One fact stated in the memorial the committee do not consider as being sustained by the evidence, viz. that this boat was impressed for the use of the American army and taken to Detroit. From the silence on this point, the committee conclude that the boat was left at the Miami when the army marched for Detroit.

General Gratiot states that the party was sent to destroy some property at Turkey Point, which had been abandoned by the owners, and it is quite reasonable to conclude that this was done to prevent its falling into the hands of the enemy. If so, this claim cannot be sustained against the United States. If the boat had remained, it would in all probability have fallen into the hands of the enemy, and of course lost to the petitioner. It was received, however, and brought in safely to Fort Meigs, and there is no evidence that it was used by the American troops subsequent to that period, but was left there, and with ordinary diligence on the part of the owner, might have been again recovered. Why this was not done the committee cannot tell.

The claimant has not satisfactorily accounted for the lapse of time between the date of these occurrences and the presentation of his petition, nor has he assigned any reason wherefore he did not present his case to the commission appointed under the act. Under all these circumstances, the committee think this claim should not be allowed.

## Daniel Fielding

As reported by the Committee of Claims on March 3, 1826:

> It appears from the evidence that Fielding entered himself, a wagon, gear, and four horses, into the service of the United States at Piqua, in the State of Ohio, on the 28th of August, 1813, at $3 per day, to serve for three months. The team was attached to a brigade of wagons under command of Andrew D. Brier, wagon-master. At Fort Meigs the horses of Fielding, and those of others, were ordered to be taken from their wagons and placed before some pieces of ordnance to transport them to Detroit at which latter place the team was discharged on the 15th day of October with an allowance of 12 days to return home, making in all 61 days.
>
> On the return of the team to Fort Meigs where Fielding's wagon had been left, the body of the wagon was missing and gone from the wagon. On his return from Fort Meigs with the running gear of the wagon, the horses were so reduced that they were not able to haul the running gear farther than Fort Findlay where the remains of the wagon were left, which Fielding had afterwards to be at the expense of sending for.
>
> On the 28th of October, being the next day after the expiration of the 12 days allowed to return home, and near to Fort McArthur, two of the horses were left, being so far reduced that they were unable to travel and were lost to the owner because the United States failed to supply them with sufficient forage, as is now unhesitatingly sworn to by the wagon-master, Andrew D. Brier.
>
> Heretofore the wagon-master only gave it as his opinion that the horses were lost for want of forage being furnished by the United States, but in a late deposition he leaves no room for doubting. It further appears from the account of Fielding as receipted to the Quartermaster after the expiration of the service, that he has received for the 61 days $183, and has also received $39 in lieu of that many days forage for his horses.

Fielding's claim was presented on February 4, 1823, and on January 23, 1824, the Committee of Claims reported unfavorably on his petition. With new evidence from Brier he was paid $120.50 by the War Department on March 17, 1827.

In 1812, Gen. Hull and his troops passed through Findlay toward enemy camps near Detroit. Fort Findlay was left garrisoned, Capt. Arthur Thomas in command, until abandoned at the end of the war. After 1815, the fort was occupied by a few Wyandot Indian families. Pioneers laid out the village of Findlay in 1821 near the site of the fort here on the Blanchard River. The river was named after Jean Jacques Blanchard, a French tailor, who settled in this area in the 1770s.

In 1802, James Findlay was the U.S. Marshal for the Northwest Territory and in 1812 commanded the 2nd Regiment of Ohio Volunteers.

Arthur John Thomas was born 1772 in Charles, Virginia, and married Mary Haynes on April 10, 1792. Son John was their firstborn.

In 1812, the Thomases lived on King's Creek about 3 miles from Urbana. His company was ordered to guard the public stores at Fort Findlay and on return in August 1813, father and son lost their horses when they apparently ran away and they became separated from the company.

On the 8th they camped at the Big Spring near Solomon's Town about 5 miles north of Bellefontaine. They were reported missing and the next morning searchers found their bodies murdered and scalped.

Prairie du Chien is the county seat of Crawford County, Wisconsin, and is considered the state's second oldest city after Green Bay. French explorers Jacques Marquette and Louis Joliet arrived on June 16, 1673, at the confluence of the Wisconsin and Mississippi Rivers, which gave explorers and fur traders access to the Mississippi.

## William Mendenhall

As reported by the Committee of Claims on March 3, 1826:

> The petitioner entered a wagon and a team of four horses in the service of the United States under wagon-master Andrew D. Brier on the 28th of August, 1813, at $3.00 per day. Two of the horses were taken by order of Major Wood to pursue the enemy from Detroit to the Moravian Towns, and were not returned.
>
> On the return of the other two horses to Fort Meigs they were put to the running part of the wagon to haul it home and the body was burned by order of the wagon-master. They proceeded as far as Fort Findlay on their return when they were too much reduced to haul the wagon farther and the same was left and the driver proceeded towards home with his horses and at Fort McArthur the wagon-master left them in charge of the driver, they being too weak to travel. Afterwards the driver endeavored to proceed with them when one of them became too weak to walk and was left in the wilderness between Fort Findlay and Madison and the other he drove to within about 15 miles of Dayton when he gave out and was left and the driver states that he understood that he died in a few days thereafter.
>
> The wagon-master states that the horses were furnished but one pack of oats each and two or three rations of hay from the time they left Fort Amanda on their way Northward until their return to Urbana.

Mendenhall was from Ohio and in 1813 might have been in Baltimore when his team and wagon were pressed into service. After the horses were lost he sold the wagon to the government. He was paid $133 for the use of the team from August 28 to October 27, forage for 44 days at $1.00 per day. He later filed a claim for $265 for the four horses and $60 for the wagon, and was allowed $140 by the commissioner. He was paid $85.50 by the War Department in 1827.

Capt. Eleazer Derby Wood, of New York, was brevetted major on May 6, 1813, for gallantry in the defense of Fort Meigs, and brevetted Lt. Col. on July 25, 1814, for gallantry at Niagara, Upper Canada. He was mortally wounded on September 17, 1814, "in the sortie from Fort Erie, Upper Canada."

Moraviantown, Ontario, Canada, was the scene of a battle on October 5, 1813, also referred to as the Battle of the Thames.

Fort Findlay was built at present-day Findlay, Ohio. Fort Findlay was 83 miles from Fort Meigs. A historical marker states:

> Early in the War of 1812, Gen. William Hull, commander of Ohio troops, ordered Col. James Findlay to open a road from Fort McArthur on the Scioto River to Blanchard's Fork. Under Findlay, a stockade 50 yards square, with a blockhouse at each corner, was erected here and named in his honor. The fort was used as a supply depot.

Fort Amanda was a supply depot for Fort Meigs built by Kentucky militia under Lt. Col. Robert Pogue in the fall of 1812 and enlarged the next spring by Ohio militia under Capt. Daniel Hosbrook.

Fort Amanda is commemorated by a granite monument in the Fort Amanda Memorial Park on the bank of the Auglaize River and offers hiking trails.

The Blanchard River is a fork of the Auglaize River, which is a tributary of the Maumee River, which runs into Lake Erie. Blanchard's Fork was an Ottawa Indian area in the Great Black Swamp wetland. The Indian village of Lower Tawa Town is present-day Ottawa, Ohio.

## Enos Terry

Terry filed a claim for $750 on September 27, 1821, as reported by the Committee of Claims on March 27, 1822:

> The petitioner represents that he was, in the fall of the year 1813, the owner of a Grist and Saw Mill on Greenville Creek, about one quarter of a mile below Greenville town, in the county of Darke in the state of Ohio.
>
> For the defense of the frontier settlements, a body of militia was stationed at Greenville under the command of General Edmund Munger. The troops were sickly, owing, it was said, to the stagnant water in the mill pond of the petitioner. General Munger ordered the dam to be destroyed by his troops, and the petitioner prays a compensation for his loss.
>
> The principal facts alleged in the petition are satisfactorily proven. There exists a doubt, however whether the sickness of the troops arose from the stagnant water or whether it was occasioned by the various causes incident to a camp, which generally generates diseases, and it appears from the testimony of one of the witnesses that it has been as sickly in the town of Greenville since the destruction of the dam, as at any time preceding.
>
> The committee are of opinion that if the position occupied by the troops was unhealthy in consequence of the petitioner's mill pond, that it would have been much more proper to remove the troops to a better situation than to enter upon the destruction of private property for their accommodation at the place they occupied. They see no necessity, or any reasonable excuse for this destruction, and consider this as one of those unwarrantable acts for which the individual acting is alone responsible.
>
> The committee, however, do not consider the question of much importance, as in either they do not consider the nation liable to make good the petitioner's loss. If the obstruction of the water occasioned the sickness, Gen. Munger, in common with every other member of the community injured thereby, had a right to remove that obstruction. If, however, the sickness was not occasioned by the erection and continuance of the dam, the demolishing of the dam was a wanton unauthorized act for which General Munger is personally responsible, and a court is the proper tribunal to give relief.
>
> They therefore recommend the petitioner is not entitled to compensation from the United States.

Gen. Munger stated on February 28, 1822:

> I ordered a company of men to be stationed at Greenville under orders from Governor Meigs and to protect the frontiers, and also ordered a mill dam to be torn down and put away as it was considered injurious to the people and soldiers health in Fort Greenville, which was then owned by Enos Terry, and that the water of the dam backed up to the garrison, and that almost all the soldiers were sick on account of the stagnation of the water, as was supposed to be the cause of the sickness.

Enos Terry conceded that the water could have been the source of the illness. One witness testified that he heard Maj. Henry Price, the commanding officer of Fort Greenville, order the soldiers to destroy the dam, as ordered by Gen. Munger.

Aaron Dean, a millwright who had built a number of mills, and Samuel Loring testified the destruction to the works was at least $1,000.

On October 20, 1821, Darke County sheriff, William Scott, testified "that the greatest part of the time within a few rods of the Fort, it has been as sickly in and about the Fort and town as it was before the dam was torn down."

Brig. Gen. Munger commanded the 2nd Brigade, 1st Division of Ohio Militia.

Fort Greene-Ville was built in 1793 on 55 acres as winter quarters for Gen. Anthony Wayne's army. The post was named after Nathanael Greene and had a 10-foot fence and blockhouses but was actually more of a military town than a fort. The Treaty of Greenville with the Delaware and Wyandot Indians was concluded there in August 1795. The site of the fort is now occupied by Greenville, Ohio. Excavations have revealed parts of the blockhouses.

## John H. Robinson

As reported by the Committee of Claims on January 8, 1834:

The petitioner claims the United States should pay him for three horses, whose value as $230, which were stolen from him in October, 1813, while he was transporting a load of flour from Upper Sandusky to Lower Sandusky in the State of Ohio.

He states that he went to Upper Sandusky with a load of oats for sale, when Quartermaster Hughes impressed him with his wagon and horses into the service of the United States to go to Lower Sandusky with a load of flour. On the second night, three of his horses were stolen by the Indians and never recovered. They were carefully tied to his wagon and were lost without any neglect on his part, and he says he never received any pay for the use of his wagon, although the flour was taken by the United States team to Lower Sandusky. He says he attempted to present his claim to the commissioner of claims, but was not able to do so until after the law expired, and that he has not been enabled to ascertain where the quartermaster resides.

The claim was presented to Congress on the 20th of January, 1820, and adverse report was made on the 11th of February, 1820.

In the affidavit made by the petitioner for the commissioner of claims, he states that his team was impressed by Sims, who was a quartermaster. He refers to the depositions of Joseph Cunningham, George Wilshorn, and John Edgar.

Joseph Cunningham, George Wilshorn testify that they were at Upper Sandusky in October, 1813, on their way to Lower Sandusky with their own private property and on being informed Robinson was about to take a load of United States property, they assisted in helping him to load his wagon with flour, and on their way to Lower Sandusky three of Robinson's horses were stolen or captured, and supposed to be by the Indians. The reason why Robinson's horses were stolen in preference to theirs, in their opinion, is that they were considerably farther from the fire than theirs.

John Edgar was acquainted with the horses and thinks they were worth $230.

Richard Thompson testifies that the petitioner, being in Upper Sandusky with a load of oats of his own property, was told by one Johnson, who was the principal wagon-master, that he must go to Lower Sandusky with a load of flour for the United States army and if he would not go willingly, he would make him go, upon which Robinson agreed to go. He says Hughes was quartermaster at Upper Sandusky.

In about two days Robinson came back and stated that three of his horses were lost, upon which Hughes requested he would take the United States horses and take his load on, but he does not know whether he went or not.

Isaac Painter testifies he was at Upper Sandusky at the time, and that Mr. Hughes employed John H. Robinson to haul a load of flour to Lower Sandusky and some days after he came back and said he had lost his horses, and while he stayed there he drew his rations as being in the United States service.

There is considerable discrepancy in the testimony relative to who was the officer who impressed or employed the team. The testimony of that officer is essentially necessary, if he is in existence, and if he is alive, it has been in the power of the petitioner to ascertain to what corps he belonged and very likely he might easily ascertain his residence, even at this period.

The committee cannot come to any other rational conclusion from this evidence than that the team and wagon were taken into the service by contract and not by impressment. There is not one of the witnesses who speaks of impressment. The horses were in the service by contract, the United States did not become the guarantors against thefts and accidents.

The committee think it is very likely the petitioner is entitled to compensation for the hire of himself and wagon until the horses were stolen, and for the use of his wagon and for his own services afterwards, but there is no evidence of the time for which an allowance should be made, nor is there any evidence relative to the price to be paid.

The committee submit that the prayer of the petitioner ought not to be granted.

Sgt. Isaac Painter and Musician Richard Thompson were in Capt. William Sumner's company of Ohio Militia during that time.

## John Thomas & Company

As reported by Third Auditor, Peter Hagner, on February 9, 1822, to Representative William McCoy:

I have the honor to acknowledge the receipt of your letter of the 4th instant, enclosing the petition of John Thomas and its accompanying documents, and expressing it to be the desire of the Committee of Claims to obtain information as to the justice of the claim and inquiring, in case it should be devested of certain suspicious appearances, pointed out by you, and the evidence in its favor should be considered the truth, whether John H. Piatt ought not to pay it, and whether he had not an account against the United States adjudicated in his favor, and whereon the United States would have to pay him money.

The petitioner represents that in the spring of 1814, he and his partners contracted with William Oliver, special commissary, to transport from Urbana to Fort Meigs 1,000 barrels of flour at $11.50 per barrel. That the boats whereon the flour was laden while going down the Auglaise River were stopped at Fort Jennings by Lieut. John Burget and 10 barrels of the flour impressed by his order, and at Fort Winchester, at the mouth of that that river, 11 barrels more were impressed by Capt. Samuel Aston.

The flour thus impressed were issued to the troops under the command of those officers and the abstracts of the issues returned to John H. Piatt and George Wallace, who had to supply the posts mentioned by contract.

The special commissary, William Oliver, on settlement of the account of the petitioner and his partners, not only refused to pay for the transportation of the impressed flour, but charged them for it at $9.50 a barrel, and informed them they must resort to the contractors for remuneration. That the contractors having refused payment on the ground that the officers were not justified in impressing the flour, the petitioner instituted suits against the officers, and subsequently against John H. Piatt, and having failed in both cases, the petitioner now asks for the passage of a law authorizing payment to him for the 21 barrels of flour charged to him and his partners, as before asked, and also for the transportation thereof.

By the account of William Oliver, the special commissary, it appears that in June, 1814, he paid to the petitioner and his partners $11,350.50 for the transportation from Urbana to Fort Meigs during the preceding months of March, April, and May, of 987 barrels of flour at $11.50 per barrel, and that he has credited as charged to them $342 for 36 barrels of flour, "which they lost transporting."

On reference to the accounts of Piatt & Wallace, it is found that, in consequence of the failure of Orr & Greely, a contract was entered into in February, 1814, by the special commissary, William Oliver, with Piatt & Wallace for the supplying, until the end of May, 1814, of the troops stationed at certain posts, of which Forts Jennings and Winchester were two. During and previous to the last mentioned month, (being that in which the flour is stated to have been impressed) part of Captain Aston's company was stationed at the former and the residue at the latter of those forts, and that Piatt & Wallace, on the settlement of their account by the Accountant of the War Department, on the 31st August, 1816, were credited for all the complete rations to which the company was entitled, to the end of May, on regular returns made out in their favor.

Nothing was then known at the Department as to any flour having been impressed by Captain Aston or Lieutenant Burget, and issued to the troops at the forts last mentioned, consequently, no deduction could be made from the account of Piatt & Wallace, or debit raised against them in respect thereof. It follows, therefore, that the United States have already fully paid for the subsistence of those troops, up to the time at which the contract of the gentlemen terminated.

It appears by the account of Orr & Greely that they were debited with the cost of considerable quantities of provisions, which, in consequence of their failure, had been purchased by the special commissary and delivered to their agents, and with the expenses of transporting the same. The 987 barrels of flour, for the transportation whereof the petitioner and his partners were paid by William Oliver, as before mentioned, were receipted for at Fort Meigs, by the agent of Orr & Greely, and were, with the expenses of transportation, included in the debits against them.

The United States derived no benefit from the stoppage made by William Oliver of $342 for the 36 barrels of flour lost by the petitioner and his partners, but were merely re-paid the cost thereof. If the whole quantity of flour received by the petitioner and his partners had been delivered to the agent of Orr & Greely, according to the contract, the amount of the debits against the latter would have been proportionably increased, both for the flour and its transportation. As it is, Orr & Greely have been charged for the quantity delivered to them, and the petitioner and his partners made good the deficiency. If the $342 thus paid by the latter, and the whole amount of expenses they incurred in the transportation of the flour to Fort Meigs, as stated in the deposition of Enos Thomas, their clerk, be deducted from the $11,250.50 them received of William Oliver, $741.71 will still be left for profit in the transaction.

Under all the circumstances, therefore, it does not appear to me that the petitioner is, on any principle, entitled to an allowance from the public either for the impressed flour or its transportation.

Piatt & Wallace having received credit for all the rations issued to the troops at Forts Jennings and Winchester during the continuance of their contract, and the balance found due them on the settlement of their account having been subsequently transferred to the credit of J.H. Piatt, they, in justice, doubtless ought to pay for the flour impressed, unless, independent thereof, the rations issued were complete, and in that case, the officers who impressed it were the only persons liable, their acts not appearing to have been authorized. The causes of the failure in the suits stated to have been instituted by the petitioner against the officers and J.H. Piatt are not explained.

According to a decision of the Second Comptroller on accounts of J.H. Piatt, there is a considerable balance in his favor, and which remains unpaid, but the documents in support of the present claim are not such as would now warrant a debit against him on the books of this office.

In the petition and the testimony, the quantity of flour agreed to be transported is stated to have been 1,000 barrels; the number receipted for at Fort Meigs by the agent of Orr & Greely, is only 13 barrels less, and yet 21 appear to have been impressed, and 15 others lost. These differences cannot be reconciled but by considering more than 1,000 barrels to have been originally received, and which, as the special commissary retained the cost of 36 barrels, was doubtless the case.

With regard to the suspicious appearances to which you called my attention, I have to state that the signatures of Captain Aston on his certificate and deposition have been compared with his signature on the rolls of his company, and are thought to be genuine. Lieutenant Burget belonged to that company, and to the receipts for his pay he has made marks; it is probable that when he impressed the flour a certificate was required of him, and being unable to write, that he directed the one filed to be given. The testimony as to the flour having been impressed as stated, is satisfactory to my mind, and the circumstance of upwards of 340 barrels of flour having been (as appears by the accounts of Piatt & Wallace) condemned by a board of officers at Fort Winchester on the 10th May, 1814, as unfit for issue, tends to render the fact of impressment the more likely.

John Thomas was paid $441 in 1825. John Burget and Samuel Aston were in Col. William W. Cotgreave's 2nd Regiment of Ohio Militia.

Fort St. Marys, at St. Marys, Ohio, was originally built by Gen. Anthony Wayne in 1794. In 1812, Gen. William Henry Harrison ordered Col. Joshua Barbee's 7th Regiment of Kentucky Militia to rebuild the fort, which then became Fort Barbee. At the same time, Gen. Harrison built a fort at present-day Defiance, Ohio, 50 miles to the north, which he named after Brig. Gen. James Winchester.

On September 21, 1812, Gen. Harrison ordered Lt. Col. Robert Pogue's Kentucky troops to make a road from Fort Barbee to Defiance and directed Col. William Jennings, commander of the 2nd Kentucky Militia, to establish a post midway between the two places. That was Fort Jennings, completed in October on the Auglaize River at present-day Fort Jennings, Ohio. These forts were also used as protected supply depots. The town was founded on the site in 1847. The fort was abandoned in 1815 and is now marked by a stone monument.

Fort Winchester is marked with a stone monument at W. 2nd St. and Washington Ave., and the site of Fort St. Marys is marked by a stone monument at 381 W. Spring St. in St. Marys, Ohio.

## Hosea Neal

Elizabeth Neal filed a claim for bounty land, as reported by the Committee on Military Affairs on January 12, 1838:

> It appears from the depositions of Lieutenant John Weaver and the applicant, that Hosea Neal, the husband of the applicant, was a private in Captain Thornton Posey's company of the 7th Regiment of Infantry and enlisted on the 7th of March, 1810, for five years.
>
> On the 21st day of July, 1814, whilst under the command of Lieutenant John Weaver of the 7th Regiment of Infantry, he was killed by Indians a few miles above the mouth of the Rock River on the Mississippi and it appears the widow of the deceased, herself received four wounds from the fire of the enemy, and that their child, about three years old, was killed, and their property, to the amount of $636.50, then on board of a boat, was lost.
>
> It also appears that a posthumous child, a daughter of the deceased, born on the 28th day of January, 1815, is now living.
>
> After due consideration of all the facts on which this application is made, your committee are of opinion that so much of the case as relates to the claim for compensation for property destroyed ought to be referred to the Committee of Claims.

Hosea married Elizabeth Pugsley on March 6, 1806, at Athens, Ohio. He did not qualify for bounty land since he enlisted prior to the act of December 24, 1811, which granted land to enlisted men who joined after that date. It appears that Elizabeth married John Fulton at Athens on February 16, 1817.

The 300-mile long Rock River flows into the Mississippi River at the "Quad Cities" of Moline and Rock Island, Illinois, and Davenport and Bettendorf, Iowa.

## George Jackson

As reported by Third Auditor Peter Hagner, on April 19, 1820, in part:

> It appears that on the 26th August, 1812, he furnished a wagon and four horses, appraised at $360, for the transportation of the baggage of a detachment of Ohio militia, commanded by Major Charles Miller. On the 30th of the same month, one of the horses, valued at $70, foundered and became unfit for service and was withdrawn by the claimant, and another substituted, valued at $20, which died a few days after, the cause of its death not stated. The horse so withdrawn was, by the claimant, taken to the house of David Vandenburgh and put under his care, where, after lingering a few days, it died.
>
> About the 1st of February, 1813, another horse died near Solomon's town in consequence, as is to be inferred from the language of the deposition, of not being supplied with sufficient forage, value not mentioned.
>
> On 14th February, 1813, the team was discharged at Miami Rapids by Captain William Piatt. In the spring of 1813, John Raney, the driver, returned home with one horse and informed the claimant that he had left the wagon and another horse 8 miles on that side [of] Urbana. Thereupon, the claimant sent his son and Raney with two horses to fetch home the wagon and the horse. They got the horse home, and the wagon and gear as far as Darby creek, within 13 or 14 miles of Franklinton, where the latter were again abandoned on account of badness of the roads. One of the horses which reached home died within about a month afterward in consequence, as is stated, of hard usage and want of food.
>
> In September, 1814, Benjamin Gardner, deputy quartermaster general, having been informed that a wagon and three sets of gear, understood to belong to the claimant, were at Mr. Blair's on Big Darby creek, he wrote to the claimant acquainting him of the fact, and of which no notice having been taken, he concluded the wagon and gear were public property, and caused them to be sold in the fall of 1815 for $32, which he subsequently offered to pay to the claimant, who refused to accept it on the ground that the wagon, &c. were worth more when taken into service.
>
> There is no proof that the team was in the

United States' service even at the time of the first abandonment of the wagon. As to the horses, no allowance could be made under the claims law, for the one which was withdrawn from the service on the 30th August, 1812, nor for that which died after its return home. No other could be paid for under that law, than the horse valued at $20, which was taken into service instead of the one withdrawn and died soon after, and the horse which died about the 1st February, 1813, if the evidence of their being in service at the time of their loss, and of the losses having happened without any fault or neglect of the owner, were satisfactory. If payment of full hire has been made for the services of the team, the necessary deductions for the hire of the two horses last mentioned would exceed the amount of their stated value, and of the sum for which the wagon was sold.

Jackson's claim was rejected on January 29, 1821. As a colonel, Charles Miller commanded the 3rd Regiment of Drafted Ohio Militia.

Sgt. Benjamin Gardner was with Lt. Col. John Mansfield's Lexington Alarm in April 1775, and in May was appointed 2nd lieutenant in the Colonel's Massachusetts Regiment. On January 1, 1776, he joined the Continental Infantry as a 2nd lt., and one year later he was a captain-lieutenant in the 5th Massachusetts. He made captain on November 1, 1778, and resigned on October 18, 1780. On May 19, 1813, he was appointed assistant deputy quartermaster general at the rank of captain and was honorably discharged on June 15, 1815. He returned to service in June 1816, and retired that October.

It was reported that John D. Raney died in Army service as a soldier two or three years later.

# The Niagara Frontier

The Niagara Frontier was commanded by Gen. Stephen van Rensaeler at Lewiston, New York.

The Niagara River runs 36 river miles north from Lake Erie at Buffalo to the south shore of Lake Ontario. Grand Island in the river creates the Canadian Channel on the western Canadian side and the American Channel to the east over the border. The elevation at Buffalo is around 575 feet. Niagara Falls is 7 miles downstream from Buffalo. The elevation on Lake Ontario at Newark, the downstream terminal on the Canadian side, and Fort Niagara on the American side, is 200 feet.

In 1781 a settlement in Ontario, Canada, was named Butlersburg to honor American loyalist Col. John Butler, leader of Butler's Rangers in the Revolutionary War. Under post-war British control the town was renamed West Niagara.

In 1792, West Niagara, on the southern shore of Lake Ontario and the west side of the mouth of the Niagara River, was renamed New Ark by Lieutenant Governor John G. Simcoe as the capital of Upper Canada. Fort George was just outside of town and was the westernmost British outpost in Upper Canada.

In 1791, Parliament granted Canadians the right to establish their own government with elected representatives. The English-speaking colonists formed Upper Canada, today's province of Ontario, with the capital at Newark, present-day Niagara-on-the-Lake on the west side of the mouth of the Niagara River. The French-speaking colonists formed Lower Canada, today's province of Québec, with the capital at Québec City on the St. Lawrence River.

In 1798, New Ark, or Newark, was renamed Niagara. The town is now Niagara-on-the-Lake.

When war came, American incursions into Canada spurred a response and on February 16, 1813, 20 officers and 550 soldiers, the first six companies of Col. Martin Hunter's newly-formed 104th New Brunswick Regiment of Foot, set out from Fredericton, New Brunswick, on snowshoes and pulling toboggans. They headed northwest, apparently along existing roads around 190 miles to Rivièr-des-Caps on the St. Lawrence River and then south 100 miles to Québec City, where they arrived on March 15. It was another 150 miles to Montreal at the mouth of the St. Lawrence on the northeast shore of Lake Ontario and then 168 miles south around to the southern shore, arriving at Kingston in April, just north of Sackets Harbor on Lake Ontario. They had marched 700 miles over 52 days.

One company of the 49th Foot under Lt. James Fitzgibbon was at Beaverdams, a small peninsula on Lake Gibson near Thorold around 7 miles northwest of Niagara Falls from which they conducted raids.

On May 27, 1813, the Americans captured Fort George, but the loss at Stoney Creek on June 6 apparently instilled some reluctance in Maj. Gen. Henry Dearborn's mind to venture much further north, and he was fired by Secretary of War John Armstrong.

Brig. Gen. John Parker Boyd, the commander at Fort George, decided to remedy the situation by attacking Thorold and on June 24, 1813, about 600 14th Infantry and Cavalry under Col. Charles G. Boerstler and Col. Cyrenius Chapin's detachment of 40 Mounted New York Volunteers set out from Fort George for a surprise attack on the lightly-garrisoned post.

When they stopped at Queenston, 6 miles due south of Fort George, for food and rest some of the men had trouble keeping their mouths shut, and a local resident, Laura Secord, the wife of James Secord, a Queenston merchant who had been seriously wounded at Queenston Heights on October 13, 1812, overheard talk and set out on foot with an Iroquois scout, about 9 miles west southwest as the crow flies, to warn Fitzgibbon of the attack. She reported what news she had, but Fitzgibbon was reluctant to act without confirmation, a peculiar, but probably necessary, aspect of military operations.

On the 24th, Iroquois Indian scouts confirmed the report to Capitaine Dominique Ducharme and Capt. William Kerr. Word was sent to Fitzgibbon and an attack was made on the Americans at Beaverdams that day.

Around 300 Mohawk Indians attacked the Americans, along with 100 more commanded by Capt. Kerr, until Fitzgibbon arrived with 50 soldiers. After about three hours the Americans were inclined to surrender, but would not give in to the Indians, fearing the reasonable prospect of atrocities. Fitzgibbon fibbed and said he had a much larger force en route and surrender to him presently would prevent what the Indians would most surely do. A deal was reached when flank companies of Col. Martin Hunter's 104th Regiment arrived. American fatalities were 25 and 50 wounded, including Boerstler. Indian casualties were five lost and around 25 wounded.

The 104th's winter march is celebrated in British military history as a singular event and the battle cemented British control of the Niagara Frontier through 1813.

Maj. Gen. Amos Hall and Brig. Gen. Peter B. Porter commanded New York Militia. As Gen. Hall stated on January 20, 1817, at Washington:

> During the fall of 1812, the attention of the American commanders was engaged in operations against the enemy, and at the close of that campaign on the 1st of December, an army of near 5,000 men was found, in an inhospitable climate, an inclement season, without quarters, and assailed by a deadly disease. It became indispensable, therefore, to the preservation of the lives of the men that the buildings of the citizens should be occupied for sheltering the troops, and during that winter, the whole Niagara frontier assumed the appearance of a military cantonment. This occupation continued very generally until about the 1st of the succeeding May, when the troops left their winter quarters and proceeded to the attack of Fort George.
>
> During the summer of 1813, the villages of Buffalo and Black Rock on the southern part of the frontier, were considerably relieved, having comparatively but few troops quartered in them, but most of the buildings on the northern part of the frontier, from the falls to Fort Niagara, still continued in public occupation. The army was principally at Fort George, but the sick and wounded, with their attendants, several guards of infantry, and a considerable part of the cavalry, were still quartered on the American side, and were distributed among the houses, barns, and other buildings from Lake Ontario to the falls. I frequently passed up and down the river in the course of that summer and fall and there was scarcely a building that had not the appearance of being occupied by the military. I left the frontier about the middle of December, 1813, and therefore cannot speak from my own knowledge of the extent of the military occupation at the time of the invasion by the enemy.

Capt. Isaac Swayze commanded His Majesty's Royal Artillery Drivers from

June 1812, until September 1813. He was deposed, as transcribed, on November 27, 1816:

During the summer season of 1812 the deponent, for the purpose of drill, passed to and from Niagara to Queenston, the road leading along the bank of the Niagara River, several times each week with from 8 to 10 pieces of artillery.

Most of the buildings on the American side were occupied by American troops, from which buildings the artillery were, when passing, continually annoyed by fire of the troops so stationed at the buildings. One time in particular, the artillery were fired at by platoons from the American side. The deponent ordered one of the pieces to be prepared for firing on the Americans, but, on reflection, desisted.

The deponent left the Upper for the Lower province of Canada in September, 1813, and attended the session of Parliament in the winter of 1813 and 1814 in the Upper Province.

He again returned to Montreal where he had a conversation with Col. John Murray who commanded the British forces that took Fort Niagara in December, 1813. Col. Murray said that the American frontier was not burned on the ground of retaliation, but was destroyed expressly for the purpose of depriving the United States army of quarters or barracks and as places for military deposit.

In 1814 the deponent had a conversation with Lt. Gen. Sir Gordon Drummond, who said in substance that the American Niagara frontier was destroyed to prevent its being occupied hereafter. The frontier was not destroyed from a principle of retaliation, that it was beneath the British government to have destroyed the frontier from such motives. He was convinced Gen. George McClure destroyed Newark without the order of the government, but that the only motive in destroying the frontier was because buildings had been occupied by the United States and to prevent the same from again occupying the same.

The deponent on the 18th of December, 1813, had a conversation with Sir George Prevost at Québec in the province of Lower Canada. He observed that he had received information that Newark, in Upper Canada, had been burned by the American force. The deponent suggested the plan of destroying the American frontier in retaliation, to which Sir George promptly replied, "No, Capt. Swayze, no retaliation shall take place while I am in command." The deponent, as well as most other officers in His Majesty's service, had, for a long time previous to December, 1813, intended to burn the buildings on the American side of the river to prevent their having a harbor or barrack so near the British army, from which they experienced a continual annoyance.

The orders given by the British generals commanding on the Niagara frontier were generally verbal. The deponent was in service about one year and a half year, and in that time only received two written orders, that there was no written order for destroying the American frontier, but believes the order was verbal.

Lt. Col. Thomas Dickson of the Upper Canada Militia at Queenston stated at Lewiston on November 30, 1816:

It was generally supposed on the Canadian frontier that both the villages of Lewiston and Buffalo were occupied as military posts previous to and during the month of December, 1813.

On the 19th December, the day on which Fort Niagara was taken by the British, two cannon shot were fired from Lewiston battery into the village of Queenston which lodged in the bank near my house where Captain Alexander Cameron of the Provincial Artillery and myself were at the time. A few hours afterward, I saw the Indians and British troops in Lewiston and most of the houses in flames.

After the destruction of Buffalo and Black Rock, about the end of December or beginning of January, I was informed by the officers of the 1st Regiment of Royal Scots, under command of Lt. Col. John Gordon, that they had marched down with orders to scour the American frontier from Buffalo to Fort Niagara via Manchester and Lewiston and at the time understood the orders given were to scour the lines to prevent them from being again occupied by the American troops. I was in Queenston on the 10th of December when Niagara, commonly called Newark, was burned by the Americans and had no suspicion that anything of the kind was to take place though I had been a prisoner with the Americans in Fort Niagara and was allowed by Gen. McClure to go home to see my family, and Commodore Robert H. Barclay, who was at my house on the 6th December.

The British army advanced on the 11th and 12th December to Queenston and Fort George. On the 19th December, Fort Niagara was taken and Lewiston burned, and as the commander in chief was at that time in Lower Canada, I believe Fort Niagara was taken and Lewiston burned by order of the general commanding Upper Canada.

Gen. George McClure, commander at Fort George, stated:

The council deemed it necessary that Newark should be destroyed, not only for the defense of Fort George, but also that of Niagara, and the other military posts on the American side of the straits. In pursuance of the authority contained in the letter, the town was set on fire and burnt after the inhabitants had been duly apprised and requested to remove themselves and property. About the time of the execution of this order, it was the unanimous opinion of the council of war that the American force could not stand a siege in Fort George because the time of service of the draughted militia had expired and no advices of reinforcement or others to supply their places, and, accordingly the Fort was evacuated on or about the first week in December, 1813, and the American troops crossed the river Niagara.

On their arrival on the American side, I ordered the few troops that remained to quarter themselves at Lewiston, Manchester, and Buffalo. Many of the houses in Youngstown were then, and had previously been, occupied by our troops as a hospital, and I knew the troops did quarter themselves in different private buildings in Lewiston and Buffalo. A large quantity of arms, ammunition, provisions, &c., destined for the use of the army were more or less deposited in private buildings in Lewiston and Buffalo.

A deputation of the inhabitants of Buffalo expressed an apprehension that the town would be destroyed by the enemy in consequence of such occupation. I told the inhabitants that the troops must be accommodated and expressed a belief that government would indemnify them for any losses, and that during a good part of the fall of 1813, the private buildings in the towns on the Niagara River were occupied by the American troops in the service of the United States.

I believe the consequence of destroying the towns on the Niagara River was to show the station of the American troops a considerable distance from the river, and it is my belief that the enemy would have destroyed the American towns on the river long previous to the destruction of Newark if they had them in their power, with a view of protecting their own frontier. Necessity compelled me to quarter part of my troops in the villages aforesaid in consequence of a great deficiency of tents and the inclemency of the season as well as for the purpose of protecting the military stores deposited there.

## *The Niagara Frontier Claims*

As stated by the Committee of Claims on January 23, 1817:

They have investigated the evidence adduced by the memorialists and find that most of the houses on the Niagara frontier were used by the Government as public stores, hospitals, or barracks. The public having no buildings of their own, were compelled from necessity to convert those of individuals to their own use, without, in many instances, consulting the feelings of the proprietors.

It further appears to the committee that the citizens in some instances, fearing what might be the consequences, remonstrated against the military occupation of their houses, and that assurances were given by American officers that if they were, in consequence, destroyed, Government would reimburse sufferers. Without deciding the question how far the usages of war would justify the destruction of private buildings occupied, your committee are unanimously of opinion that it is one of those cases in which a generous and enlightened Government would step forward in aid of the sufferers.

In what mode this aid is to be administered has also been a subject of deliberation with the committee. The military occupation was at different times nearly universal, and they are of opinion that no discrimination ought to be made between those to whose houses happened at the moment to be in the occupation of Government, and others who were equally sufferers, and recommend that the gross sum be distributed among the whole, in proportion to their respective losses. They therefore recommend that the sum of $340,000 be appropriated for this purpose.

The amount of losses returned to the commissioner, under the act of the last session, is $654,832.90, which may be assumed as the actual losses sustained. The Government has already paid for losses on that frontier $65,666.50, which, being subtracted, leaves $589,166.40. The committee are of opinion that, on many considerations which need not be stated, it would be improper to vote the whole amount of the actual losses sustained, and have therefore assumed the sum which they recommend to the House.

## Collins Boomer

As reported by the Committee of Claims on May 23, 1856:

> This claim is based upon the loss of a sloop loaded with provisions. The sloop was employed in 1813 in conveying American troops from the River St. Lawrence, and in consequence thereof was captured by the British, and towed across the river into Canada.
>
> The committee believing the facts to be as stated, and that the petitioner has never been remunerated for the loss of his property, report herewith a bill allowing him the sum of $1,000 without interest, in full payment of his claim.

In 1812, it appears Collins lived in Oswego, New York, and served as a drummer in Capt. George W. Clark's company in Col. Anthony Sprague's 55th Regiment of New York Militia at Henderson's Harbor, Jefferson County, New York. In 1813, he was a drummer in Capt. Daniel Ellis' company. In 1850, Collins lived in Ellisburgh, New York.

Collins Boomer was paid $3,000 in 1857, "in full payment for the sloop and provisions captured from him in 1813 by the British, in consequence of his employment of the sloop in the conveyance of American troops upon the River St. Lawrence, and towed across the river into Canada."

## Gad Pierce

As reported by the Committee of Claims on January 21, 1822:

> The petitioner, of Niagara, in the State of New York, alleges that during the late war against Great Britain, his dwelling-house was frequently occupied by troops and military stores, by order of officers in the service of the United States. It was taken possession of in the spring of 1813, and was constantly used as a military store house, and occasionally as a guard house, by order of John G. Camp, Deputy Quartermaster General. It was so used and occupied till the British burnt it in December, 1813. In consequence of the destruction of his house, with sundry articles of personal property, he has sustained a loss of $3,080.15, for which he asks Congress to grant him remuneration.
>
> In support of this claim, John G. Camp, the Deputy Quartermaster General, swears that at the time claimant's house was destroyed, there was deposited in it, by his orders, a quantity of arms and field ammunition; and also, that at the time it was destroyed by the enemy in 1813, it was used and occupied as a guard house by the troops of the United States.
>
> Ebenezer Hovey, another witness, swears that the house was occupied as a guard house under the authority of Major Benajah Mallory. The valuation of the property he believes to be just and true, as he was a near neighbor and had many opportunities of knowing the property. He was himself in the military service of the United States, was stationed in the house as one of the guard, and remained in it till the enemy entered it. He believes the house and other property were destroyed in consequence of the military occupation of the former by the troops in the service of the United States.
>
> Samuel Pierce, son of claimant, swears that he believes the property to be correctly valued; that he fled from the house with his father, carrying nothing with them but the clothes on their backs, and four feather beds, on the approach of the enemy.
>
> Other witnesses testify as to the correct

valuation of sundry articles of property, and sworn appraisers testify as to the value of the house.

The committee think the claim ought not to be granted. In support of this opinion, they refer to report in the case of Eli Hart, and to the several reports therein adverted to. The prayer of the petitioner ought not to be granted.

John Camp, of Virginia, was appointed a midshipman in the Navy on November 15, 1809. He resigned from the Navy on May 25, 1811, and was commissioned a 1st lieutenant in the 12th Infantry on March 12, 1812. He made captain on November 14, 1813, and acting deputy quartermaster general on May 20. On September 7, 1814, he was promoted to deputy quartermaster general as a major. He figured prominently in many claims during the war and was honorably discharged on June 15, 1815.

## Eleazer Bingham

As stated by the Committee of Claims on February 9, 1842:

The petitioner claims remuneration for a boat called *The Child of May*, and the cargo thereof, consisting of 350 bushels of apples, 36 bushels of potatoes, and 12 bushels of onions, which boat and cargo he alleges were impressed on the 4th day of October, 1813, while lying at Eighteen Mile Creek in the county of Niagara, and State of New York, by Capt. Joseph L. Barton, of the 15th Regiment of the United States Infantry, for the purpose of conveying the United States troops and munitions of war from Forts Niagara and George, whereby both boat and cargo were lost to the petitioner.

Also, the petitioner claims remuneration for damages done to a two-story dwelling-house, garden, and fences belonging to him in the village of Charlotte, at the mouth of the Genessee River while the house was in the occupancy of the United States troops in 1813 and 1814.

In support of his claim for the boat and cargo, the petitioner produces the deposition of Russell Whipple, who certifies that he was present at Eighteen Mile Creek in October, 1813, when Capt. Barton impressed the boat, and the cargo was thrown upon the beach of the lake and the boat was laden with soldiers and proceeded to Sackett's Harbor.

In support of the second item, he adduces the deposition of Simon Hunt, who deposes that he was a surgeon for the New York volunteer troops stationed at the mouth of the Genessee River in the village of Charlotte in 1814. While the troops were collecting and stationed at Charlotte, they occupied the house and buildings of Eleazer Bingham in April, May, and June of that year. During the occupancy of the buildings, considerable damage was done to them by the troops and to the fences, which damages were afterwards appraised by the deponent, Erastus Spalding, and Frederick Handford, at the sum of $350.

The committee find that the petitioner presented to the Secretary of the Treasury his claim done to the house, fence, and garden in 1819, which was rejected for the reason that too long a time had elapsed since the damages were incurred before they were presented to that Department under the act of 1816, and because the claim embraced items which were not admissible under the regulations of that Department.

It further appears that the petitioner presented to this House his claim for damages done to the house, fence, and garden in January, 1826, which was reported on unfavorably by the Committee of Claims, but for what reason does not appear. Nor does it appear that the petitioner ever presented any claim either to the Treasury Department or to Congress for the loss of his boat and cargo until the first presentation of his present petition in February, 1840.

It further appears that the deposition of Russell Whipple bears the date November, 15, 1839, 26 years after the loss is alleged to have happened, and the deposition of Simon Hunt is dated on the 19th day of October, 1841.

The committee has always required the occupancy to have been pursuance of an order of the commanding officer at the time, which fact must appear. And in relation to the damages done to the fences and garden, they were in the view of the committee, were trespass by the soldiers, for which they alone were liable, and not the government.

The committee, therefore, submit that the petitioner is not entitled to relief.

## Pierre Le Blanc

As reported by the Committee of Claims on May 29, 1834:

> Col. Richard M. Johnson, with a corps of Kentucky mounted volunteers under his command, encamped on the plantation of Pierre Le Blanc on the expedition to Canada in the fall of 1813 and used the forage of Le Blanc and burnt his fences for fuel, and took and killed a beef and two swine, the property of Le Blanc.
>
> The claim was presented to the commissioner of claims and testimony was taken. The Third Auditor afterwards rejected the claim for the want of proof in the first instant. The articles were taken by the order of an officer, and when that deficiency was supplied by the certificate of Col. Johnson, a further exception was taken, that the testimony of the officer who took the property was not produced, which was necessary under the regulations prescribed to govern the commissioner on claims.
>
> The committee, to supply the defects in the testimony, addressed a letter to Col. R.M. Johnson, making several inquiries of him relative to this claim. There is no doubt Col. Johnson, with about 1,200 men encamped on the plantation of Le Blanc over night. They subsisted their horses on the forage and grain of Le Blanc and they took his fences for fuel, and they killed a beef and two swine that belonged to him.
>
> Col. Johnson says whatever was taken for forage, fuel, or provisions was necessary for the public service; that the corps was not then furnished with these articles, nor with money to purchase them. He has no doubt they were taken, nor that they were worth $380.25, their estimated value at that time, and, as was proven by the testimony taken by direction of the commissioner of claims. He further states there was no wanton destruction of the property, and that it was taken by his order. Mr. Benjamin S. Chambers was his quartermaster, and he is now dead.
>
> Mr. Le Blanc was a Frenchman and wholly unacquainted with the English language and unacquainted with the mode of doing business. If the quartermaster had called appraisers and had made an estimate of the value of the property taken and given a certificate by which the owner could have been soon thereafter remunerated, but in the opinion of the committee, this was not the fault of Mr. Le Blanc, but the fault of the quartermaster.
>
> When it is considered that a corps of 1,200 men have been quartered for a night with their horses and have been sustained by the property of a citizen, the committee are disposed to think the amount asked is not unreasonable.
>
> The claim has lately been assigned by the administrator of Mr. Le Blanc, and without knowing whether a full consideration was paid for the claim, the committee were disposed to protect the interest of the widow and others, the representatives of Le Blanc, but on inquiry of Mr. Lucius Lyon, the delegate from Michigan, the committee became satisfied that McDonnell was entitled to the amount.

John McDonell, assignee of a claim of Pierre Le Blanc, was paid $380.25 in 1836.

Mons. Le Blanc lived somewhere along the 18-mile Rivière aux Écorces. The stream flows today through a heavily-populated area and enters the west side of the Detroit River at Ecorse, Michigan, about 8 miles southwest of Detroit.

# *Crysler's Farm*

John Crysler was born in Schoharie, New York, and settled in Dundas County. Canada. He represented the county in the Upper Canadian Legislature and was a captain in the county militia. His property near the bank of the St. Lawrence River near present-day Morrisburg, Ontario, offered expansive terrain for the drilling and training of troops, and his home served as headquarters for the British command, although the battle, in which he himself fought, was actually east of his farm and was generally known at the time as the battle of Williamsburg.

In the fall of 1813, Maj. Gen. James Wilkinson's troops left Sackets Harbor for Montréal and when they were met by Lt.-Col. Joseph W. Morrison's 800 British and Canadian regulars, militia, and Indians on November 13, Wilkinson was forced to retreat and was directed to set up winter quarters at French Mills, New York, right on the border with Canada.

A monument is located on the Crysler's Farm Battlefield Park at 13740 County Rd. No. 2, Morrisburg, Ontario.

## Denison Douglass

The petition of Denison Douglass, of Louisville, St. Lawrence County, State of New York:

> In the month of November, in the year of our Lord, 1813, a detachment of the army of the United States consisting of about 2,000 men, while on their retreat from the battle at Chrysler's Fields, arrived at memorialist's farm and encamped for the night. While your memorialist, with his family, were aiding and assisting the officers and soldiers, others took from the barn of your petitioner all his wheat, and oats, and other articles—the wheat and oats being then in the bundle—and carried them to the fields for the purpose of making beds.
>
> During the night, a large quantity of the fence was burnt by the soldiers. And your memorialist would further represent that for the space of twelve weeks afterwards, his dwelling-house was used and occupied as a hospital for the soldiers of the United States army, and that while they were in possession, they still continued burning the fence and to the amount of what is charged and their value.
>
> Your memorialist, therefore, begs that such remuneration may be made to him, as, in your sound judgment and discretion, may seem just and equitable: 14 bushels of wheat, at $2.00 per bushel, $23.00; 150 bushels of oats at $1.00 per bushel, $150; 20 lbs. of flax at 20 cents per pound, $4.00; 180 rods of fence at $1.00 per rod, $180; 7,000 feet of boards at 12 cents per hundred feet, $84. Total $446.

Douglass submitted a claim to Gen. Jacob Brown when he was at the Salmon River and was told any appraisal had to be made by army officers. Peter Sharp, of Louisville, who was a pilot on one of the boats carrying soldiers from Crysler's property, stated that he saw soldiers taking grain out of the barn and large fires from the rails.

Charles Whalen stated that Douglass's farm was entirely destroyed and vouched for the values requested, as did Griffin Place.

As reported by the Committee of Claims on December 19, 1827:

> It may be, and probably is, hard for the memorialist to sustain this loss, yet it was the duty of the commanding officer to have provided for his troops by contract, and not have suffered them to commit the depredations complained of, and the United States have not, in any instance, remunerated for similar trespasses committed. Where articles have not been furnished, such as the troops were by law entitled to, and the necessity of their having them existed, and the officer in command has proved this fact, and the private property has been taken for public use, the United States have made payment. No proof of this kind is made in this case. The committee think the petitioner has not proved his claim ant the prayer of the petition ought not to be granted.

## David Giffin and Samuel Hoag

As reported by the Committee of Claims on January 9, 1824:

> The petitioners represent that the army under command of General James Wilkinson, when descending the St. Lawrence River in the month of November, 1813, landed on the evening of the 5th day, and encamped on their farms during the night, and remained part of the following day, during which time the fencing on their farms was used by the troops for fuel, to the value of $75 on each farm, for which they ask payment.
>
> In support of their claim they produce two certificates signed by Thomas J. Davis, who it seems was appointed by Robert Swartout, then Quartermaster General, to estimate the value of the fencing thus burned by the troops, which represents the value thereof at $75 on each farm. Also a certificate signed by Joseph G. Swift, stating, among other things, that the fencing was necessarily used by the troops as fuel to cook and to warm the troops. Also a certificate signed by Robert Swartout

> stating that the appraisement made by Thomas J. Davis of damage done on the farms of Giffin and Hoag, was by his appointment. Also a certificate of General Jacob Brown, stating that fences to a considerable extent were consumed for fuel by the troops on the farms of Giffin and Hoag at the time stated by them, but says nothing as to the necessity of the fencing being thus consumed, nor of its value.
>
> From the testimony accompanying this case, the committee have no doubt the fencing of the claimants was destroyed by the troops to considerable extent, and from the certificates of Gen. Swift and Gen. Robert Swartout, it would seem, that the destruction must have been necessary, yet there are circumstances attending this claim, which cast a shade of suspicion on it, which the committee presume will be removed before a final decision is had on it. They therefore report a bill for its payment.

David Giffin and Samuel Hoag were paid $75 each in 1824.

## Jonathan Davis

As reported by the Committee of Claims on March 24, 1836:

> The petitioner was, at the commencement of the last war with Great Britain, a farmer living within a mile and a half of Fort Erie in Upper Canada. He took from Col. William Prescott, on the 30th of May, 1813, a parole while Col. Prescott was in command at Fort Erie.
>
> From the representations of the petitioner it would seem that his property had been subject to the alternate depredations of the American and British forces. While remaining on his farm under British protection, he states that by order of Gen. Peter Buel Porter, three horses worth $75 each, and one cow, worth $20, were taken from him, and that afterwards Lt. Patrick McDonough, under the command of Gen. Jacob Brown, received from the petitioner a quantity of wheat, oats, and hay, for the use of the army, estimated by the petitioner at $700, and for which Lt. McDonough promised to give him a receipt, which receipt the petitioner says he never obtained, from Lt. McDonough, he having been killed in the blowing up of the battery at Fort Erie.
>
> The petitioner states further that in consequence of his having left Canada, as he did in July, 1814, and entering the service of the American army under Gen. Brown, with two teams which he brought with him, his farm, worth $3,096, was confiscated and the British dragoons plundered him of various articles of property, estimated by the petitioner at $744. He states that the last service he performed for Gen. Brown's army was transporting baggage from Buffalo to Greenbush, and that he has not received compensation, nor for any of the property he lost.
>
> The petitioner now resides in Mercer County, Pennsylvania. He produces the certificates of reputable inhabitants of that county that he is a substantial good citizen, a man of truth, and entitled to entire credence. That the petitioner, as well as many others on that frontier, sustained heavy losses appears very evident, but the committee do not think the proof submitted to them shows a just claim against the government for any of the property lost by the petitioner, except the three horses and the cow.
>
> Frederick Tice and Elizabeth Tice swear that the facts set forth in the petitioner's statement are true. Thomas Davis, Nancy Davis, and Rachel Lindley, swear to their knowledge of the three horses and one cow having been taken from the petitioner in the manner by him set forth. These affidavits are regularly verified, and the character of Tice, in addition to the usual certificate of the officer administering the oath, is well supported.
>
> Dr. Cyrenius Chapin, of Buffalo, late lieutenant colonel, under Gen. Peter Porter, certifies that he was acquainted with the petitioner, Jonathan Davis, and he understood at the time referred to, and now believes, that he had three horses and one cow taken from him by a company of Indians under the command of Gen. Porter.
>
> Gen. Porter himself states that he does not know Davis, but that he did, for the reasons assigned, among which was an engagement on the part of the Indians, then about to enter upon an expedition into Canada, that they would not plunder private property, nor offer violence to private persons, agree to "allow them, on their return, to capture and bring over, for their own benefit, a drove of horses

and cattle, which were usually found feeding on the British commons below Fort Erie, most of which were supposed to, and many of which did actually, belong to the garrison, lately driven from that fort."

The General states that on his return from the excursion into Canada, about the 6th or 7th of August, 1813, he did, according to promise, permit the Indians to take and bring away most of the horses and cattle found upon the commons, amounting probably to 60 or 80 head; which were sold at auction, and the proceeds distributed among the Indians, who accompanied our troops. This transaction was submitted to and approved by General John Parker Boyd, then commanding at Fort George, for reasons which are given at large in Gen. Porter's statement among the petitioner's papers.

The committee are of opinion that under these circumstances the United States are bound in justice and good faith to remunerate the petitioner for property thus taken and they therefore report a bill for his relief.

As reported on January 2, 1839:

From the depositions of Loring Hodge and Frederick Tice it appears the petitioner resided near Fort Erie (Upper Canada) in the year 1814. He possessed a farm on which were wheat, hay, and oats. The crops were taken and used by the American army by order of Lieutenant McDonough. It further appears from the depositions of Mr. Hodge that Lt. McDonough said to the witness that he intended to give the petitioner a certificate for the property, and that Lt. McDonough was killed soon after. Mr. Hodge also estimates the value of the property at $1,698.

The committee find that this claim, together with claims for other property, was presented to this House at the first session of the 24th Congress, at which time it was accompanied by other testimony, and that the petitioner then valued the property at $700, which he now proves to be worth near $1,700.

The Committee of Claims reported against any compensation for the crops, and in favor of a part of the other claims. The committee are not insensible of the difficulties to be met in the establishment of a claim after the lapse of so song a time as has taken place in this instance, but they are clearly of opinion that the declaration of Lieutenant McDonough, as sworn to by Mr. Hodge, is not sufficient proof on which to grant money from the Treasury. They also think that the discrepancy between the petition exhibited two years since, and the proof at this time, is calculated to excite doubts as to the equity of the claim.

The committee therefore recommend the claim be rejected.

Jonathan Davis was paid $245 in 1838.

Patrick McDonough, of Pennsylvania, was commissioned 1st lieutenant in the 2nd Artillery on March 12, 1812, transferred to the Corps of Artillery on May 12, 1814, and died in the defense of Fort Erie on August 15, 1814.

In August 1813, Lt. George W. Hight was quartermaster at Fort George and responsible for purchasing wheat for troops, forage for horses, and whatever articles might be needed.

In September 1813, Gen. John P. Boyd wanted someone to scout out the British lines about 4 miles away and try to learn something of their intentions. Col. Winfield Scott's regiment of artillery was then at Fort George, and Scott approached James Rigden, who accepted an offer of money and a commission. That night Col. Scott escorted him past the "chain of American sentinels" and the next morning denounced him as a deserter. He then approached the British lines and was sent to their headquarters. He felt he had a chance of succeeding in his mission until a real deserter showed up, "one of Colonel Scott's most confidential sergeants" and said Rigden was an imposter. He was arrested as a spy and sent to a dungeon in Québec then put aboard the transport *Bostock*, sailing for England via Halifax to join a large convoy. The American cartel ship *Perseverance* was there with a number of British prisoners for exchange, and by eluding a sentry, he got aboard that ship just before sailing. Six weeks after leaving Québec he was back with his company in Upper Canada.

Between August 4 and September 21,

1814, British forces attempted unsuccessfully to take Fort Erie. They suffered heavy casualties in the assault, but unknown to the defenders, many British soldiers were sick and debilitated from exposure and the force was about to withdraw when the Americans left the fort and in the attempted rout, and also experienced heavy, unnecessary losses.

### *French Mills*

In the 1790s, a site on the Little Salmon River in upper New York, right on the present U.S.-Canadian border, was found ideal for building mills. Workers from Vermont and Canada came in and the village became known as the French Mills.

In November 1813, the town became the winter quarters for the Army and wounded from Crysler's farm arrived on November 13. After Brig. Gen. Leonard Covington, of the Light Dragoons, died the next day, the post was named Fort Covington.

Gen. Wilkinson set up his headquarters 16 miles away at Malone along with a hospital. Hundreds of wounded were inadequately cared for, many more fell sick with rheumatism, conditions at the hospital at Malone were hardly better.

Eventually, the post became a thriving community and detachments of the 9th and 31st Infantry were sent from Plattsburgh to guard the convoys of provisions, but the job, "was exposed and arduous duty."

An American expedition to St. Regis in October 1812, brought a response and in early 1814, British Colonel Hercules Scott's 103rd Regiment were approaching French Mills. Secretary of War John Armstrong directed Gen. Wilkinson to evacuate the post and send 2,000 troops from Gen. Jacob Brown's command, including the 23rd Regiment of Infantry, back to Sackets Harbor and take 4,000 to reinforce Plattsburgh.

The 400 or so sick and wounded at Malone were ordered to Burlington, Vermont, but during this evacuation, the British captured many, who were paroled, but all the supplies left behind, along with all those as far as the approaches to Plattsburgh were seized.

In February, Colonel Scott had possession of French Mills and that August, laid siege to Fort Erie.

In 1817, the town of French Mills was renamed Fort Covington and is on the National Register of Historic Places.

## Matthew McNair

Matthew McNair owned the schooner-rigged, flat bottomed boat *Columbia*, as reported by the Committee of Claims on February 15, 1822:

> The schooner *Columbia* appears to have been the sole property of the petitioner and was chartered to the United States by the boat's master William Gallagher, at Fort George, on the 18th September, 1813, to be manned and navigated at the expense of Gallagher, for the service of the United States on Lake Ontario.
>
> In November, 1813, the vessel was taken by the Quartermaster General, against the consent of the owner to convey General Wilkinson, &c. down the St. Lawrence to the French Mills, where the vessel was burnt by order of the commanding officer, because, from her size, she could not be brought up through the Rapids to the Lake, whence she was taken.
>
> The evidence shows the vessel to have been worth from $3,000 to $3,300. From the facts proved, the committee are of opinion that the petitioner is entitled to relief.

On May 7, 1822, he was allowed, "the value thereof, not exceeding $3,000, together with reasonable expenses for navigating said vessel while in the public service, crediting the United States with any sums of money paid to McNair on account of a contract of charter party for the same vessel."

McNair's boat was seized by Quartermaster Robert Swartout, of New York, who McNair sued in court and won. On January 3, 1821, Swartout petitioned Congress to be "indemnified against a judgment obtained against him for the loss of a boat impressed by him into the public service; whilst acting as quartermaster general of the northern army in the year 1813." McNair was paid $1,776.25 on November 6, 1822.

## Marinus W. Gilbert

Marinus Gilbert, of Watertown, Jefferson County, New York, had a brother, Thomas Gilbert, who was appointed sutler for the 13th Regiment at French Mills, and was furnished "with goods and articles necessary for the comfort of the troops, and such as are usual to furnish the troops by the sutlers."

After the order to evacuate, Gilbert employed Gardner White with 8 or 10 teams "to proceed from Watertown to French Mills about the 1st of February, 1814, to transport his stores back to Watertown," but immediately on arrival at the French Mills, he and team were impressed into the public service, "and he was informed and believes that all the others were also impressed."

Osmond Bannister bought a load of provisions and stores for the Gilberts to French Mills, from Watertown on or about the 1st of February 1814, and delivered them to Thomas Gilbert, "the clerk and agent of the petitioner, who retained him and team to return the load after it was unloaded."

Mr. Kaywood also brought another load and delivered it in like manner and was detained by Thomas Gilbert.

Benjamin Bull stated that he and Peter Parker each delivered a load of goods to Thomas Gilbert at French Mills on February 1. After delivering them to Thomas Gilbert, he wanted them to reload the wagons and take the goods back again because the post would soon be evacuated. They went to the store to reload and, "were there impressed and compelled to load with pork for the Army." Thomas strenuously objected, "declaring that he needed the teams to reload for Watertown, but was answered by the officer impressing the teams that he did not care, that he had authority to impress them and would have them, and took them." Bull and Parker were then compelled to accompany the Army to Plattsburg.

Thomas had charge of the 18 × 40 store, a 5-ton bateau, sails, and tools, and of removing all the goods for safekeeping during and after the evacuation of the post. After the order to evacuate, the Gilberts were able to remove a large amount of merchandise to the homes of Ebenezer Brownson, of Malone, Moses Chase, and possibly Reuben Hitchcock, but not everything was moved before Gen. Brown instructed Capt. John B. Hogan, assistant deputy quartermaster general, to "press all the teams that he could find in and about the camp for the purpose of moving the public stores." This would include Gilbert's teams, which he needed to remove the rest of his goods to a place of safety.

Moses Chase stated:

> Previous to the evacuation of the French Mills, a quantity of property said to belong to Marinus W. Gilbert was, by him and his agents, deposited at the house of his father in the town of Constable, viz: "one tierce of almonds, a quantity of raisins, a large sack of oats or crackers, a considerable quantity of cheese, one or more chests of tea, one or more barrels of spirits, a quantity of sugar, one barrel of crackers, a quantity of butter, all of which property so deposited this deponent cannot recollect, but that the same consisted of a number of sleigh loads, and was taken by the British troops and carried away. His father's house is about 5 miles from the French Mills."

Curtis Hildreth stated that he and ten or twelve others with teams went from Watertown to French Mills, "for the purpose of taking loads for Gilbert, as all were impressed on their arrival at the French Mills."

Henry Annable was a clerk of the Gilberts at French Mills in February 1814. A few days previous to the evacuation of the place, he said there were three teams at his store at the French Mills, "laden with goods which were unloaded and the teams were immediately impressed into the service of the Army by Captain John B. Hogan. Application was made to General Brown to have the teams restored, but in vain. Previous to the arrival of the teams, laden as aforesaid, the petitioner had a large quantity of goods on hand. He enumerates a large quantity of liquors, provisions, and dry goods taken by the enemy from Hitchcock's and Chase's, to which they had been removed for safe-keeping."

On February 5, 1814, Capt. Myndert M. Dox, Lieutenants Mason Ronalds, William Anderson, Jr., Reuben Humphreys, Robert Harrisson, Abraham Schuyler, and Ensigns Seth Johnson, Elisha Clark, and Abraham Howard, all of the 13th Infantry signed a note to Capt. Hogan:

> Mr. Gilbert, the sutler of our regiment, has a large quantity of valuable property on his hands. He wishes, in case the army moves from this place, to have it conveyed to a place of safety. The teams he procured for that service have been pressed for the public.
>
> The general good conduct of Mr. Gilbert since he joined our regiment induces us to request (if the public service will admit) that he may have the use of his teams now here for the purpose above mentioned. Your kind attention will oblige your obedient servants.

The request of the officer's was denied and Gen. Brown left on February 13 with British troops following the Americans. Gen. Brown had detailed 2nd Lt. James Young of the 6th Regiment as the rear guard, as he stated:

> I had command of the rear guard, left at Cantonment No. 1, with orders to set fire to all public property that might be left, together with the buildings occupied by the sutlers in the cantonment. Mr. Gilbert's was burnt among the rest. What property it contained, when set on fire, I cannot say. I observed a large quantity outside, and inquired of Mr. Gilbert why he had not taken it away sooner. He told me there had been teams ready for that purpose in the morning, and they were pressed by the army.

Ebenezer Brownson, of Malone, stated he had 15 barrels of rum, brandy, and whiskey; one large chest and one box of dry goods, a quantity of cod fish, a number of boxes of raisins and prunes, and another box of unknown goods, taken by the British on February 20, 1814.

It was reported that the British Capt. Grant took 2¾ barrels of pork, 210 pounds of tobacco, 54 pounds of almonds, 280 pounds of coffee, 160 pounds of dried beef, 500 pounds of cheese, 400 pounds of ham, raisins, brown sugar, 90 pounds of pepper and allspice, 50 pounds of chocolate, 100 pounds of rice, 3,000 Spanish cigars, and variety of clothes and hardware, and that Capt. Sherwood took a similar lot.

Marinus Gilbert obtained statements in 1816 from Ambrose Huntington, of Watertown, who was at French Mills and knew the Gilberts, stated Gilbert could have removed his property if he had the use of his teams and Lt. Robert M. Harrisson of the 13th Regiment of Infantry, and 2nd Lieutenants James Young and Seth Johnson, also of the 13th both concurred.

Some misunderstanding of the claims process ensued and Gilbert's petition wasn't presented until January 8, 1820, in part:

> Your petitioner, in the month of February, 1814, had a large amount of provisions, groceries, and clothing, of the first necessity for the use of the army of the United States at French Mills. At the time the troops were ordered to move from that place, your petitioner had his own teams there for the purpose of removing the property to a place of safety.
>
> By an order from the commanding general of the United States army, your petitioner's

teams were impressed into the United States service, and used in conveying away the property belonging to the United States army. In consequence of his teams being thus impressed, your petitioner's property to a large amount, was either destroyed by the officer commanding the rear guard of the United States army, by the order of General Brown, to prevent its falling into the hands of the enemy, or was captured by the enemy by reason of the impressment of his teams.

Your petitioner is aware of the many frauds that have been practiced on government, especially from this quarter of the country, but trusts that his papers will appear satisfactory.

On January 8, 1821, the Committee of Claims rejected the petition on the grounds that the teams Gilbert, "had engaged to remove his private stores were in the daily practice of coming to the camp to seek employment, or for the purpose of trade," and did not belong to Gilbert.

On October 11, 1821, Maj. Gen. Jacob Brown stated:

Mr. Gilbert's teams being pressed into the public service, there was no chance for him to save his property, as it was ordered that all stores, both public and private, that could not be moved, shall be destroyed, to prevent their falling into the hands of the enemy.

On January 4, 1822, Ambrose W. Huntington, of Watertown, said he was at French Mills and believed Gilbert could have removed his property, as did Dyer Huntington, Capt. Harrisson, and Seth Johnson.

As stated by Peter Hagner, the Third Auditor, on January 21, 1822, in part:

The petitioner had, in charge of his brother, Thomas Gilbert, at French Mills, a large quantity of sutler's stores. A few days previous to the departure of the army from that post, in February, 1814, some teams of the petitioner arrived with a fresh supply, which was immediately unloaded and the teams impressed into the public service. An order was issued by the commanding officer of the American army for the destruction of all stores, both public and private, which could not be removed to prevent their falling into the hands of the enemy, and, also for the destruction of the buildings occupied by the sutlers. The petitioner's brother and clerk, after the main body of the American army had left French Mills, and before the arrival of the enemy, effected the removal of considerable portions of the stores to Hitchcock's, Chase's, and Brownson's in whose houses, distant from 2 to 5 miles from French Mills, they were deposited for safe keeping. The residue of the property was destroyed under the order referred to by the officer commanding the rear guard of the American army.

Subsequently, the articles which had been so removed to Hitchcock's, Chase's, and Brownson's were, with some exceptions, taken and carried away by the British troops, and that the loss sustained by the petitioner was occasioned by the impressment of his teams, it having deprived him of the means of removing his property to a place of safety.

The deposition of Henry Annable, the petitioner's clerk, who has particularized many of the articles taken by the enemy, and estimated the gross value of the whole to have been, at actual cost, upwards of $3,500.

The property stated by Annable to have been destroyed by the rear guard consisted of a new log building, 40 by 18 feet, one story high, covered with boards and having two floors and two chimneys; a quantity of kitchen and shop furniture, sundry provisions, &c., and 5-ton bateau.

Claims for the remuneration for the destruction of property by order of the commanding officers of the American army, satisfactorily vouched, have been provided for by special acts, but it is not within my recollection that under any circumstances such a provision ever extended to the allowance for stores of sutlers so destroyed at the breaking up of an encampment, nor is it believed that in any instance has Congress authorized payment for articles taken by the enemy, as in the present case, from the dwellings of private citizens, without even an allegation that they were so taken, because the enemy considered them to be public property.

As stated by the Committee of Claims on January 8, 1827:

This claim is preferred upon the ground that, although it was private property, it was considered and treated as public, both by the enemy and our own officers, and destroyed or captured as such, and because the petitioner had provided himself with teams for the removal of his goods, and would have removed them beyond the reach of the enemy, but was prevented from doing so by their impressment into the service of the American Army, where they were employed in the removal of public stores.

The evidence of the petitioner seems to place his claim upon the broad basis of justice and equity, as well as to sustain it upon the plain and ordinary principles of the common law. It can be resisted only upon the assumption of interested and suspected testimony. Upon careful and jealous review of the testimony, your committee find no stronger reason for rejecting that of the petitioner, than may be urged against all testimony brought to support any other claim. The witnesses are, several of them, officers of the Army.

The enemy immediately occupied the post thus abandoned and scoured the country around. They sought and found the places where the petitioner's agents and clerks had deposited some part of his goods, and captured and destroyed the whole.

The loss thus sustained by the petitioner, from the nature of the case a matter of estimation, is stated to have amounted to about $4,000. The lowest estimate is $3,500. That this loss was occasioned by the impressment of the petitioner's teams, in pursuance of general orders, and in the necessary exercise of legitimate authority, for the removal of the Army, and the preservation of public property the committee are constrained to believe. The loss was the necessary and inevitable consequence of the act, by the laws and usages of war. Our own Army would have burned it, had it remained, and the enemy would have captured and destroyed it as public property had they not been prevented by the petitioner or our own Army.

They would therefore recommend that the claim be referred to the proper accounting officers of the Treasury to ascertain and settle the extent and amount of his loss.

Gilbert was paid $3,000 in 1828.

## Arthur McMillan

As reported by the Committee of Claims on January 9, 1833:

The depositions in this case were referred to the committee on motion and unaccompanied by petition. The claimant presents the following schedule of losses: One dwelling-house, burned by the British, $600; Furniture, beds, and clothing, $300; Provisions, pork, flour, beef, &c., $125. Total $1,025.

It is stated in the deposition of John McCrea that he resided in the town of Fort Covington, in the county of Franklin, in the State of New York in the year 1814. In the month of February of that year, Colonel Hercules Scott of the British army took possession of the town and burnt the dwelling-house of the claimant. He says the British officers told him the reason they burnt the house and destroyed the property of the claimant was that he piloted the American army and had been in the British camp as a spy. He thinks the account of the losses just and true.

George B.R. Gore testifies the house was burnt by the British troops and was worth $600.

The claimant states in his affidavit he acted as a guide to the American army. The British took possession of his house and burnt it with its contents. The amount contains a just estimate of losses he sustained and that he has never received any compensation.

To grant relief in this case would greatly compromit the liability of the United States to pay for the destruction of property by the enemy, far beyond any principle established by Congress. The ground of relief is that the claimant was in the military service. This did not authorize the enemy to destroy his property, which was not in any way in the occupation of the United States.

If it was a proper claim for relief the claimant should prove he was in the military service by other evidence than his own oath, or the testimony of a private individual. The committee do not think the claimant is entitled to be remunerated for his house by the United States.

An Arthur McMillan is shown as a private in Capt. David Erwin's company of New York militia.

## Elisha Button

As stated by the Committee of Claims on February 29, 1840:

The petitioner asks remuneration for property taken from him by the British army at or near French Mills in the county of Franklin, and State of New York, on the 15th day of February, 1814, viz: whiskey, cider, brandy, butter, cheese, oysters, shoes, one coverlet, and cash $3.00, valued in all at $672.36, all of which the petitioner alleges was lost by reason of the officers of the army of the United States pressing from him three teams which he had provided for the express purpose of removing his property to a place of safety, two of the teams being taken from him when in the act of loading the property. He shows, by the affidavit of others, the taking of the teams by the United States officers, and the taking of the property by the British army, and by the affidavit of Alfred Button, he shows the taking of a number of articles not included in the statement of petitioner, valued by witnesses at $143.51½, showing a loss of $815.87½.

The United States are bound by the Constitution to repel and protect each State from invasion. This being the duty of the United States, the right to occupy necessary stations, and to call to their aid all necessary means for the protection of the army and property of the Government, in cases of emergency, must be admitted. This right is believed to extend, when necessary, to the forcible taking of ships, boats, teams, provisions, &c., always paying a reasonable compensation for the use of property, and the value for what is not returned; but no collateral damage can, in any case, be allowed.

These are some of the necessary inconveniences under which individuals hold their property in the several States of this Union; and if their interests are sometimes prejudiced by reason of the necessary exercise of it by the Government, it is their misfortune, and one for which Government does not hold itself accountable.

*Resolved*, That it is inexpedient to grant the prayer of the petitioner.

## *Frauds at French Mills*

After the Act of April 9, 1816, was amended, claims filed by Nathan Goff, Samuel Gordon, Joseph Rossel, and Charles Dumpley for boats taken for the use of the army on the St. Lawrence River "excited suspicions as to the validity of the claims, and the decisions on them were suspended."

Maj. John B. Hogan was dispatched as an undercover agent to investigate claims. After further review and adjustments, he sanctioned the claims, but suspicions still remained and he looked further into claims filed at French Mills that were believed to be fraudulent. He met with one David Jones and was invited to join a scheme, and "believing Jones to be a consumate scoundrel, I deemed it justifiable to appear to fall into his views, with a view of obtaining a more correct knowledge of the validity of the claims I had in charge, than I could possibly ascertain in any other manner; although it was a course of conduct I by no means approved, yet I knew it was the only source whereby the government would be guarded from imposition."

He was then offered huge profits for a small investment and "should have $10,000 for a few weeks' work" and said he could make $100,000. He stated, "I was thunderstruck, and asked him how he could do it. He replied, he could muster up claims here to that amount, and could get witnesses to swear anything."

## *Newark*

The Old Fort Niagara State Historic Site features original buildings, living history exhibits, musket demonstrations, and a museum.

### John Dailey

John Dailey was a resident of Upper Canada who had extensive property in and around Newark when General Dearborn arrived and took possession of the area. In support of the American cause, residents turned over their houses for quarters for the troops, but after the Army evacuated the area, their property was confiscated by the British. They feared for their safety and sought protection from the American government and fled with them.

Dailey claimed losses of $30,000, "including the value of property owned by him after he had removed to the American side of the Niagara, consisting of goods, household furniture, and clothing estimated at $7,000."

He filed his claim when he was, "far advanced in life, and destitute of the means to enable them to live comfortably." Sen. Nathan Sanford, of New York, presented his petition on January 5, 1827.

As reported by the Committee of Claims on January 11, 1831:

> John Dailey resided in Newark, in the province of Upper Canada, for a number of years previous to the late war between the United States and Great Britain, and had, by his industry, acquired and extensive property consisting of five or six dwelling houses, two extensive tavern stands, and several stores, barns, sheds, and other buildings.
>
> When the American army took possession of the village of Newark in the spring of 1813, Dailey freely and cheerfully opened, for their use and accommodation, his houses, barns, and other buildings, and readily furnished them with whatever his stores of provisions afforded. His barns and stables were crowded with the horses belonging to the American troops, and his hay and grain delivered up for their supply.
>
> During the summer and fall, while the United States army occupied the village of Newark and adjacent towns, John Dailey exerted himself with great zeal and activity to promote the comfort of our troops and to contribute to the convenience and accommodation of the sick and wounded officers and soldiers of the army.
>
> In the fall of 1813, when the American army retired from Upper Canada, the village of Newark was burnt by order of the general commanding, and the extensive buildings of John Dailey, estimated to be worth more that $10,000, were destroyed in the general conflagration.
>
> Dailey, with his wife and seven children, accompanied the army across the Niagara River into the State of New York, taking with him such of his goods, furniture, and other personal property as remained to him after the wreck of his affairs.
>
> Soon after the petitioner moved into the State of New York, he deposited his furniture and goods in a barn in Lewiston, hired by him for that purpose. A few days thereafter, the goods and furniture, worth by estimation, several thousand dollars, were destroyed and burned, with the barn in which they were deposited, by a party of the enemy, which had crossed into the State of New York.
>
> From the numerous certificates and depositions of officers of the American army, and other persons, it fully appears that the loss of Dailey, in the whole, exceeded $30,000, and that he has been thereby reduced from circumstances of ease and affluence to poverty and want.
>
> In consequence of his well known love of liberty and his ardent admiration of our free institutions, he had, before the appearance of our army in Canada, been suspected by their authorities, and, after he retired to the State of New York, he was proceeded against as a traitor, and his property confiscated.
>
> John Dailey has, at sundry times heretofore, preferred his petition to Congress, setting forth his losses, and asking for relief. In 1818, a committee of the House of Representatives made a favorable report on his petition. The committee, on taking into consideration all the facts set forth and proved by the petitioner, are of opinion that he is entitled to some relief and remuneration, at least for the property furnished by him for the use and benefit of the United States army.
>
> The committee therefore report the accompanying bill.

John Dailey was paid $500 in 1831. Samuel Thompson also filed a claim for $10,000 in conjunction with Dailey's claim.

## *Lewiston*

### William Arbuthnot

On October 30, 1825, George McClure was deposed in Steuben County, New York:

> In the fall of 1813, the deponent commanded the American troops on the Niagara Frontier.

About the second week in December of that year, and after the detached militia had been discharged, their term of service being expired, he entered into a special agreement with the officers and soldiers of Col. Walter Grieve's 7th Regiment of Artillery to remain in the service of the United States one month longer, or until other troops would arrive for the defense of the frontier, which was then exposed to the enemy, and for this extra service, a certain bounty was paid to the officers and soldiers of the regiment, which special agreement was made and entered into by the advice and consent of the President of the United States.

The deponent ordered the regiment to quarter themselves in the village of Lewiston and occupy the private buildings, as such occupation was necessary, not only for the accommodation of the troops at that inclement season, but also for the defense of the village. The deponent does know that part of the houses in the village was so occupied until the morning of the 19th December, 1813, on which day the enemy crossed to the American side and destroyed the village and defeated and drove off the troops left there for its protection.

The village was then, and had been a deposit for arms, ammunition, and provisions for the troops of the army. A part of Col. Grieve's regiment was not discharged until near the last days of December, if they were then, as the deponent gave up the command to Major General Hull.

William Arbuthnot had a home on the bank of the Niagara River about 3 miles below Lewiston and about the same distance from Fort Niagara. In 1812, his daughter, Margaret, lived there when it was occupied by Lt. Robert Fleming, of the New York State Artillery, as William stated in a deposition on December 30, 1826:

During the late war he was situated on the bank of the Niagara River, 3 miles below Lewiston, and about the same distance from Fort Niagara. He had a large amount of property and was in good circumstances till the 19th of December, 1813, when the enemy crossed to take Fort Niagara, took your petitioner prisoner, destroyed his personal property, and, in a few days afterwards, destroyed his real property also. The house of your petitioner had been a guard-house from the commencement of the war, and situate only 200 rods from the Canada shore, there was frequent firing across the river each way. When the enemy came to the house, a guard was surprised and taken prisoners with your petitioner and his family, at which place was also two wagon loads of United States property also taken.

Your petitioner has presented his claim to the Third Auditor, by whom it has been rejected. The claim is yet in that office with testimony of the loss and value, which failed mainly because the building was not destroyed till several days after capture, the whole country being at the time, in possession of the enemy, and a portion of the time occupied by them.

Ezra St. John was deposed on October 31, 1825:

On the evening of the 18th December, 1813, in the performance of his official duties which devolved on the deponent as principal wagon-master acting under and in obedience to the order of John G. Camp, then a deputy quartermaster general of the United States, was at Fort Niagara.

After regulating the teams, property, &c., at the fort, he left it about 8 o'clock P.M. and proceeded on the road towards Lewiston until he came to the house of William Arbuthnot where he met two or three teams loaded with United States clothing. He, being fully authorized, ordered the teamsters to secure, in the best possible way, the property for the night, and proceed with it to the fort early the next morning. He was very particular in his direction, as he considered it a hazardous place, and as the property would not be deposited in the fort that night. He does not now recollect whether the teamsters began to unload before he left the house or not, but he thinks it probable they did unload, and put the property in the dwelling-house, pursuant to his order, where there was a guard of militia stationed, belonging as he believes, to Col. Grieve's regiment. The part of the regiment then on this part of the frontier, was in the United States' service, and commanded by Major Bennet. Bennet formerly resided near Cayuga Lake, State of New York. In that vicinity the deponent had relatives living, and from whom he has received information that Bennet was dead, and which he believed to be true.

He often passed the house during the war, and recollected well there was generally a guard kept at the house of Arbuthnot.

Daniel Field gave a statement on November 16, 1825:

During the late war he resided in Canada. A few days before the crossing of the British forces for the capture of Fort Niagara, which took place on the morning of the 19th December, 1813, he had been released from confinement as a prisoner of war at Fort Niagara. On crossing the river, being with the advance guard, he came to the house of William Arbuthnot, with whom he had been acquainted previous to the war, and knew it to be his premises.

At the house, a number of men were taken prisoners by surprise. He is unable to say whether they had or had not arms. The surprise was so great that if they had arms they had no chance, nor did they attempt to use them. There were as many as a dozen men. It was not yet daylight, and he did not accurately observe their dress. He well recollects viewing at this house, both within and without it, a large quantity of United States' clothing, such as shirts, great coats, &c., and which was taken by the British forces and recognized as public or United States' property. The British forces that remained proceeded with great caution in order to effect complete surprise, in which they succeeded.

The Committee of Claims sustained the rejection. Major Gen. Philip Rial commanded the British forces that crossed the Niagara. Artillery Capt. Alexander Cameron stated it was common knowledge that the British destroyed the houses and buildings in Lewiston, Black Rock, and Buffalo "to prevent their re-occupation by the armies of the United States, and that was understood by the armies of his Majesty in general employed in that expedition." The British also believed it would "prevent the American army from continuing its harbor for another year."

## Reuben Lewis

A claim filed by Roxanna Evans, as stated by the Committee of Claims on March 8, 1844:

This is a claim for the loss of a house in Lewiston, Niagara County, in the State of New York, and for money, household furniture, and goods to the amount of $1,500, burnt and destroyed by the British and Indians on the 19th of December, 1813, the day Lewiston was destroyed by them.

These facts are sworn to by the petitioner, but there is no evidence to show that the property thus destroyed was of the value mentioned by any specific valuation. The fact of its destruction, however, is proved by the evidence of William Coan who testifies that he was present and saw the property of Reuben Lewis, at that time the husband of the petitioner, destroyed, and from his knowledge of the property, he believes it to have been worth at least $1,500.

But if all the facts set forth were proved incontrovertibly, they would only establish a case of wanton destruction of private property by the British and their savage allies. Losses of this sort are the mere casualties of war, and have never been considered as imposing an obligation on government to indemnify the sufferers. The committee, therefore, recommend to the House that the petitioner is not entitled to relief.

## Lemuel Cooke

William Wadsworth was deposed on December 28, 1825:

During the campaign of 1812, he was a brigadier general of New York State Militia, then in the service of the United States. For several months of the summer and autumn of that year, he was stationed at and near the village of Lewiston under the command of Major General Solomon Van Rensselaer. This deponent, with their staff officers, quartered for several weeks at the house of Lemuel Cooke, situate on what is called the Ridge road, about 1 mile from the village of Lewiston. While there, the camp equipage or a portion of it, General Van Rensselaer and the deponent was brought to and used at and about the house of Cooke. Their servants were also there with all necessary cooking utensils, and considerable of our baggage, all which was brought and used there, pursuant to our orders or directions.

The deponent left that frontier after the battle at Queenston. Whether all the baggage or camp equipage which had been brought to Cooke's house by our order was or was not removed therefrom before the destruction of the building by the enemy in December, 1813, is unknown.

Signal services were rendered by Lemuel Cooke and his sons in taking charge of the boats which conveyed the troops that attacked Queenston battery—services which entitled Cooke and his sons to lasting gratitude, and which could only have been prompted by the holy zeal of '77, in which opinion it is believed Major Van Rensselear will concur.

Solomon Van Rensselaer was honorably discharged as a major in the Army on June 15, 1780, and became a lt. col. of New York Volunteers in 1812.

Laura Cooke was deposed on January 9, 1826, as stated:

She lived with her father, Lemuel Cooke, who resided about 1 mile east of the village of Lewiston, on the Ridge road. During the year 1812, Generals Van Rensselaer and William Wadsworth quartered at the house for several weeks with their staff officers and servants. During the time the officers quartered there, a considerable quantity of camp equipage was brought and used at the house. When the baggage and equipage was removed, several articles were left, viz. two camp kettles, several tables, and a cupboard, which remained at the house until the morning of the 19th December, 1813. This fact she knows because she was constantly at home and was in the habit of seeing them daily. There might have been, and probably were, other articles which composed the baggage of the officers.

She further recollects that at or about the time General John Chandler was taken prisoner in Canada in the year 1813 a man by the name of Blake deposited at the house a considerable quantity of baggage and camp equipage reputed to belong to General Chandler. The equipage and baggage was stored in a chamber of the house and remained there to her best knowledge until the 19th December, 1813. At the time the property was left, it appeared to be in charge of Blake and under his direction.

During the summer and autumn of 1813, there were many surgeons of the army quartered at different times at the house of her father, among the number the names of Doctors Mann, Beaumont, and Whitridge.

During that season, other officers, viz. Captains Leavenworth, Myers, and Lieutenant David Riddle, quartered at the house for a time. Lieutenant Riddle, at the time he was there, had in use, by his order and direction, a tent, the property of the United States. When Riddle left the Cooke house, the tent was left and remained there until the 19th December, 1813. The deponent hath been informed, and verily believes, that Lieutenant Riddle is now dead. She recollects that an officer by the name of Colwell or Caldwell, a captain or lieutenant in the army of the United States, during the fall of 1813, was brought to the house where he afterwards died. His sword and some baggage remained in the house until the 19th of December, 1813. Many military equipments and property belonging to different officers who quartered from time to time were left, but she cannot distinguish by whose order the same were brought.

Meshach Blake enlisted as a private in the 21st Infantry; Dr. James Mann was a hospital surgeon; Dr. William Beaumont was a surgeon's mate in the 6th Infantry; surgeon's mate Dr. Joshua B. Whitridge succeeded Dr. Mann.

Maj. Henry Leavenworth was in the 9th Infantry. Capt. Mordecai Myers was in the 13th Infantry; Lt. David Riddle was in the 15th Infantry.

Capt. Richard Caldwell of the 25th Infantry reportedly died on November 23, 1812, in New York.

Bates Cooke was deposed on January 9, 1826:

Bates Cooke saith that for several days previous to the 19th December, 1813, he had been at the house of his father, Lemuel Cooke, engaged in the care of a brother, whose leg had been amputated. About daylight on the morning of the 19th December, an alarm was given, and the family soon after left the house, about 15 minutes before the enemy came to the house. But a small portion of the household goods were removed, the alarm and sudden approach of the enemy preventing it.

The deponent, with a portion of the family, was overtaken by the enemy about 1 mile after leaving the house, but not captured. After passing about one and a half miles further from it, the deponent returned to near the place where the enemy had overtaken him for the purpose of getting a horse he had captured from the enemy. At that time he observed the house to be on fire, the flame was then just rising from the roof. The deponent left the house with the last of the family, at which time it was not on fire. He has much reason to believe, and does believe, that the fire was set by the enemy. There were but few of the American people passing the house after the deponent left it, the enemy then being within half a mile of it.

Dr. Beaumont was deposed on the 25th of January 1833:

I certify that at the time of the capture of Fort George, in Upper Canada, by the United States forces under the command of General Dearborn, in the latter part of May, 1813, I was attached to the United States army as surgeon's mate. In about two or three weeks after taking the fort, I was ordered to duty in the hospital established near Lewiston, State of New York, and to take charge of part of the wounded sent from Niagara to that place. The general hospital was established on what was called the Ridge road. Part of the sick were placed in barns, and some were sheltered in tents for want of buildings.

Near the hospital was the farm and residence of Mr. Lemuel Cooke, who owned and occupied a very good framed house, the only one of that description, I believe, in that vicinity. There were but very few other buildings near the hospital, and these made of logs and generally small and inconvenient. It was an object of solicitude and importance for the surgeons and officers, indisposed or sick, to get quarters at Cooke's. Although he kept not a public house, and it was very inconvenient to his family, yet he generally yielded to the solicitude of the medical and other officers, waived his own convenience, and accommodated the surgeons and other officers, who had the care of, and resorted to, the hospital during the summer of 1813.

Among the number who resided or adjourned there, besides myself, were senior surgeon Dr. James Mann, Drs. Joshua B. Whitridge and Henry Van Hoevenberg, I think, Maj. Henry Leavenworth, Captain Mordecai Myers, and 1st Lieutenant David Riddle, all of the United States army.

The building of Mr. Cooke was situated about one and a half miles from the enemy's position at Queenston Heights, on a plain below the hill and in full view from that post. I left Mr. Cooke's shortly before the army, under the command of General James Wilkinson, left Fort George to descend the lake, about the last week in September, 1813, leaving at that time at Mr. Cooke's Dr. Whitridge and Lieutenant Riddle and perhaps some others.

Mr. Cooke seemed warmly in favor of the war, and always willing to accommodate those who were engaged in its prosecution, and for which those accommodated, I am confident, felt very thankful, the more so as Mr. Cooke, only, had the necessary accommodations.

The reason why the hospital was not located in the village of Lewiston, as I understood, was because of its proximity to the Canada line, and for the benefit of greater safety and comforts of the sick and convalescents.

Meshach W. Blake testified on February 1, 1833:

I, Meshach W. Blake, of Monmouth, in the county of Kennebec, and State of Maine, do say that in 1813 I was with Gen. John Chandler in Canada. I enlisted in Monmouth and was with him until the time he was taken by the British. While with Gen. Chandler, I had care of his baggage, as I was employed by him for that purpose, and I attended to no other duty. I was not present with Gen. Chandler when he was captured, but was not far off. After he was taken, a flag of truce came from the British lines, I think in the forenoon of the next day, accompanied by one Capt. Brock, who brought to me a note from Gen. Chandler requesting me to forward to him certain baggage. I sent to him, agreeably to his request, I think, two trunks, which, as I supposed, contained clothing, and I am very positive that one trunk still remained with me; what it contained I cannot tell. All the baggage that thus remained behind with me was carried to Lewiston and deposited with one Cooke, who lived about a mile from the village. What his Christian name was I cannot tell.

The baggage was left there with the calculation that it would soon be transported to Sackett's Harbor. After depositing the baggage I went on to Fort George to Major Johnston's headquarters, who was one of Gen. Chandler's aid, but was not taken with the General. After staying at Fort George, I should think two or three weeks, I left there in company with the troops for Sackett's Harbor, where I learned the British had burned Lewiston, and that the house of Mr. Cooke, where Gen. Chandler's baggage was deposited, was burned with all its contents, and I have no doubt but that all the baggage then left was destroyed, as I had some property deposited in the same place, and I never afterwards saw or heard of either the General's property or my own. The baggage was carried to Lewiston by the order of Major Johnston and Capt. Tobey, both of whom belonged to Gen. Chandler's staff, and after his capture took the direction of his property.

Meshach Blake added information on February 1, 1833:

He was a waiter to General John Chandler, and had charge of his baggage at the time that officer was captured in 1813. The next day after General Chandler was captured, he sent to Chandler to forward to him certain baggage. He thinks he sent two trunks, which he supposed contained clothing, and he thinks one trunk remained. What baggage remained was carried to Lewiston and deposited with Mr. Cooke, near the village, and it was calculated it would be sent from thence to Sackett's Harbor. He then went to Fort George and saw Major Johnston, one of General Chandler's aids, but who was not taken prisoner with him. In two or three weeks he went to Sackett's Harbor with the troops, and there he heard of the burning of Mr. Cooke's house, and supposes General Chandler's baggage was burned. He had properly deposited in the same place, which he has never seen since, and has no doubt but all the property left at Mr. Cooke's was destroyed.

He says, "said baggage was carried to Lewiston by the order of Major Johnston and Captain Tobey, both of whom belonged to General Chandler's staff, and after his capture, took the direction of his property. I recollect seeing Captain Tobey at Lewiston while the baggage was there, and that Cooke agreed to send it down by water to Sackett's Harbor." He then states he is at a loss to recollect whether he went with the baggage to Lewiston, but says his impression is that Captain Tobey and himself accompanied it.

On the 18th of the same month, this witness gives another deposition, in explanation of the former, and says the quantity of baggage taken from Fort George to Lewiston and deposited at Cooke's was about half a wagon load. As to the agreement of Cooke to send it to Sackett's Harbor by water, he understood he was to send it by land when a safe chance should occur. Few, if any, vessels were then navigating Lake Ontario and he does not know that the baggage was ever sent for, or that a chance was ever presented for Cooke to send it to Sackett's Harbor.

Maj. John Johnson, assistant adjutant-general, and Capt. Charles E. Tobey were in the 21st Infantry. Maj. Johnson died on December 11, 1813.

As reported by the Committee of Claims on March 13, 1834, in part:

Blake speaks in very commendable terms of Mr. Cooke's hospitality and devotion to the prosecution of the war, and if the committee were to place this case on the good character of Mr. Cooke, and his attachment to the country, they would have no difficulties in recommending relief.

The questions, however, for them to decide are the military occupation of the house and the cause of its destruction. It is to be noticed that the testimony of Dr. Beaumont does not establish the military occupation of the house after September, 1813, when its destruction was on the 19th of the following December.

The principles established in the laws of 1816 and 1825 were that "the occupation should be ordered by an agent or officer in the service of the United States, as a place of deposit for military or naval stores or as barracks for military forces of the United States." The rules of evidence require all facts to be proven by the best evidence the nature of the case admits. If an officer or agent directs the occupation of a building, he is competent to prove the fact, and his testimony should not be dispensed with if it can be obtained. It has uniformly been required under all the acts and by the different committees to whom these cases have been referred, and secondary evidence has only been taken in cases where the best evidence could not be obtained.

The testimony of Blake is offered, as is supposed by the committee, for the purpose of proving the military occupation of this house. The committee think this witness's testimony is too confused, uncertain, and contradictory to be relied upon, but if it were true in every particular, the facts stated by him should be proven by an officer who directed the deposit. The committee do not perceive that the state of the case is changed by this additional testimony.

They will further remark that, in their opinion, the leaving of baggage in a house is not such a military occupation as justified the enemy in destroying this house, and brought the case within the provisions of the laws mentioned. Nor do they think the appearance of a few camp kettles about a house, when it is known they were sought for and obtained by private families as an article of convenience, should be taken as prima facie evidence that a house was in the military occupation of the United States; nor do they think if a sword was left in this house that such circumstances should be taken as prima facie evidence of a military occupation. And when Congress shall so decide, the committee fear, if our own citizens shall keep their arms and military accoutrements in their houses, the United States will be compelled to pay for such dwelling, should they be destroyed in time of war.

The committee would gladly recommend relief, if they could do so consistent with the wholesome principles heretofore established, but, in their opinion they could not without introducing an entire new class of cases. The prayer of the petitioner ought not to be granted.

## Solomon Hearsey

As reported by the Committee of Claims on May 11, 1838:

In December, 1813, his house near Lewiston in the County of Niagara, was occupied by the American troops stationed there who made deposits of provisions belonging to the United States at his house, in consequence of which, when the country was invaded, the British set the house on fire, and destroyed his property. While it was occupied by the American troops, they took a quantity of beef, pork, his household furniture, a barrel of brandy, and other articles.

He sets up a claim of $1,675 for property the enemy destroyed. He says he kept a tavern and that a company of militia, 120 in number, with 30 horses, were kept by him for the period of three months, for which he says he never received any compensation. He procured from the officers in command receipts specifying the length of time the militia were kept by him. He prays compensation for relief on account of his property being destroyed by the enemy and for the subsistence he gave the militia, and for the forage he furnished their horses.

Wishing to have his claim adjusted under the late act of Congress, he solicited Mr. Lee, commissioner on claims, to appoint commissioners to appraise his property, and to receive such proof as he should be able to offer, of his losses, and the causes of them.

He fixes in this petition on the year 1814 for the occupation of his house and says his house was taken by the enemy and partly destroyed in that year while he was in the public service. He lost much property when his house was taken, but does not know whether it was taken or destroyed by the American or English troops.

He then sets forth that he kept a tavern at Lewiston in the same year and that the United States troops took possession of his tavern-house and two other houses and stable, and occupied them 83 days, and would not let him have any use of them because the troops wanted the buildings for barracks. During a part of that time the troops had 30 horses in his stable and used his hay and grain. He also mentions they took two barrels of his pork and potatoes and burnt his fence.

He says he did not apply for payment under the act of 1816 because he understood his claim was not provided for in consequence of his not having public property in his house. He was surprised to see in Mr. Hagner's letter that such an application was made. Some years afterwards, he requested Bates Cooke, his representative in Congress, to make application for him, and that last year he employed a lawyer to make application for him.

In his first petition he says in the year 1816 or 1817 he procured an appraisal of his damages to be made out, amounting to $1,675, which, with proper vouchers and documents, were presented to Congress.

The first petition fixes the time when his property was destroyed to have been in the month of December, 1813. This is the time, he says in his letter of October 7, 1816, that the American troops occupied his house.

In his second petition he says the time the American troops occupied his house was in 1814.

In his first petition he says his property was destroyed by the enemy.

In his second petition he states his lawyer, in alleging his property was destroyed by the enemy made a mistake, and that he does not know by whom it was destroyed, the British or American troops. This discrepancy he notices.

In the letter mentioned he says the British set fire to his house and destroyed his property.

In the affidavit mentioned he swears he does not know what his damages were. He implicitly denies that he procured an appraisal of his damages by saying his property was appraised by Quinn and others. He speaks of an affidavit of Mr. Quinn as a stranger to him, in, in the following language: "a man who called himself Edward C. Quinn."

This Mr. Quinn was extensively engaged in getting up claims on that frontier at the time these papers were made out. He acted without authority from the United States. Extensive frauds were detected on that frontier about that time, which admonishes the committee to scrutinize old claims with care.

Quinn ostensibly appointed John Beach and Isaac B. Tyler to appraise Hearsey's property.

Major John Morrison testified that he was stationed at Lewiston in 1812, "and along the frontier along the Niagara River" and knew Solomon Hearsey, "who kept a tavern about 6 miles from the village of Lewiston in the years 1812 and 1813, during the war," and during the winter of 1812–'13, after Fort Niagara was taken, "the American troops took possession of the house and premises, and excluded him from the use and occupation during the whole of the winter."

Lt. Col. John Atchinston said he occupied Solomon Hearsey's stable for 20 horses for 14 days while at Cambria, but gave no certificate for forage either supplied or taken.

First Lieutenant Asa Lilly and 2nd Lt. Henry Jessup said 26 horses belonging to their company in Col. John Harris's regiment were kept at Hearsey's from March 5 until April 22, 1814. There was no captain there, and no quartermaster records for forage were found.

Lt. William Peters stated he commanded a detachment of cavalry and stabled five horses at Hearsey's from January 20 to March 19, 1814, and his detachment was discharged on March 22. No vouchers to Hearsey were found in their papers.

Capt. Peter Clarke, Capt. John Farwell, and Quartermaster Henry Polhemus were at Niagara that winter. Capt. Clarke certified 60 soldiers from his company quartered in two houses owned by Solomon Hearsey in the town of Cambria from January 25 to about March 15. Polhemus certified that a 20 × 30 foot log house had been occupied "by the United States troops of the detached militia, under the command of Lt. Col. Harris, for 65 days, and he issued a certificate on April 14, 1814." Harris's regiment was in service from January 8 to sometime between April 15 and 22, 1814.

Reuben Hurd and Reuben Huggins testified they knew Hearsey's buildings in Cambria and that he kept a tavern and his "dwelling-house was a comfortable tenement with six rooms, four of which had fire-places, and he owned another small house, his stables and barn were spacious and good, and that all the buildings were occupied by the troops of the United States in the months of January, February, and March, 1814."

The claim was rejected as all of these units were New York Militia.

## Peter Kindall

As stated by the Committee of Claims on February 12, 1817:

> In the month of July, 1814, the petitioner, with his wagons and team, was passing from Lewiston, in the county of Niagara, to Buffalo, with a quantity of goods. It was deemed necessary by General Brown to impress the wagon and team into public service for the purpose of transporting ordnance and stores from Lewiston to Scholassie, and the wagon was actually impressed by David Denman, assistant quartermaster general, by the order of General Brown.
>
> At the time the wagon was impressed, the goods with which it was loaded were taken out and a guard put over them; but the enemy advanced before they could be removed, and captured them, together with a variety of public stores.

Kindall was paid $509.97 in 1817.

## Ezra St. John

Ezra St. John was involved in a lawsuit by Bates Cooke and Capt. William Howard of the 25th U.S. Infantry. St. John paid him $31.00 on December 10, 1815, the cost of the suit.

As reported by Major John G. Camp, deputy quartermaster general, on July 28, 1815, from Buffalo:

> At the time the British crossed from Queenston to Lewiston, on the Niagara frontier, a man by the name of Bates Cooke said he shot a British Indian from one of the public horses and took possession of the horse, and claimed him as captured from the enemy. Information was given to the Commanding Officer that Bates did not take the horse from the enemy, but from one of our own Indians. He therefore directed Mr. St. John to take possession of the horse. Bates brought suit against both the Commanding Officer and St. John, in which he was cast. The within charge is for the costs.

The horse was described, "the little bay horse called Bully." St. John filed claims for the lawsuit and for property losses. As reported by the Senate Committee of Claims on February 8, 1830:

> The petitioner states that he lived at Lewiston, at the commencement of the late war; that he served as a volunteer until the arrival of troops to defend the frontier. In August he was drafted into the service, and was detailed as Superintendent of Artificers by New York Militia General Stephen Van Rensselaer, and was discharged in October.
>
> In the spring of 1813, he entered the service again and served as wagon-master until the 19th December when he and his family were made prisoners by the British Indians and on the same day delivered to British regulars and carried to Canada. His family were sent back, and in four days he was paroled and sent back to Lewiston.
>
> His house and its contents were burnt by the Indians. After his return he performed the duties of Quartermaster and Foragemaster under the orders of Major John G. Camp in the wagon department and after the army returned from Newark, he was ordered to Fort Erie as Issuing Commissary, and discharged the duty until the evacuation of that post. He was appointed Military Storekeeper at Williamsville, and to do the duty of Quartermaster and Foragemaster and Issuing Commissary to the hospital, and finally Auctioneer of the public property at Buffalo, Williamsville, and Canandaigua.
>
> All his accounts were promptly settled with the proper officers. He now asks compensation for the loss of personal property at the destruction of Lewiston, with interest on the amount; the loss of some carpenter's tools taken by, and for the use of the American troops, amounting to $24.75, and two bills of costs in defending a suit brought by Bates Cooke for the recovery of the value of a horse amounting to $128.
>
> On examination of this claim, the committee find that the amount of personal property was estimated by the Third Auditor at more than $7,000, which has been rejected by the Department as not embraced within the act for the relief of the Niagara Sufferers, and the committee do not recommend the extension of the provisions of that act to embrace personal property.

With respect to the carpenter's tools, they find a bill of the several articles and a receipt annexed, dated Buffalo, January 12th, 1816, from Maj. Benjamin Barton, Deputy Quartermaster General, for the sum of $24.75 in full, signed by the petitioner, stating that duplicates have been signed.

Attached to this receipt in the affidavit of Barton stating that the tools were received from the petitioner, and that he has never paid the petitioner; and also the oath of the petitioner that he has never received payment from any person whatever

This account appears to have been twice rejected by the War Department on the ground of the insufficiency of the testimony, the great length of time which had elapsed before its presentation, and the fact that there were disbursing officers in the Quartermaster's Department at that place, and in which the petitioner himself was employed for a portion of the time.

On finding that St. John had been paid $103 by the War Department, the claim for further money was rejected by the Committee of Claims on November 8, 1816.

He was paid $334.28 for the house by the Third Auditor and a claim for personal property referred to the state of New York, as "no allowance could be made by me, the law authorizing payment for buildings only." He continued to press his claims.

On July 13, 1812, New York Gov. Daniel D. Tompkins appointed Stephen Van Rensselaer military commander of the Northern Frontier. He accepted the position on condition that his cousin, Solomon Van Rensselaer, be appointed his aid-de-camp. Their headquarters were at Lewiston.

### Stephen Warren

As reported by the Committee of Claims on June 10, 1854:

The petitioner, of Niagara County, New York, asks compensation for property destroyed by the British and Indians during the late war with Great Britain, consisting of a house and household furniture, wearing apparel, wheat, hay, &c.; and it is alleged that the property was destroyed in consequence of arms and ammunition belonging to the United States having been deposited and being in the house at the time of its destruction.

The 9th section of the act of 1816 provides that any house or building "occupied as a military deposit, under the authority of an officer or agent of the United States, should be paid for, provided it shall appear that such occupation was the cause of its destruction." It appears that the petitioner and family were residing in the house destroyed at the time of its destruction, and, consequently, it could not have been used exclusively as a place of deposit for United States arms and ammunition; and the only proof upon that subject is contained in the affidavit of a single witness, who says, "that there were in the house, at the time it was burned, some United States arms and ammunition that were deposited by the United States soldiers, or by Sergeant Simons, one of the officers who had charge of them at the time they were left in the house."

The committee deem this proof insufficient to bring this case within the before-recited provisions of the 9th section of the act of 1816.

As to the personal property alleged to have been destroyed, the committee have only to say that there is no provision either in the act of 1816 or 1817 which authorizes compensation for personal property destroyed under the circumstances set forth by the claimant; and the committee are unwilling to extend the law to cases not within the range of its provisions.

## *Buffalo and Black Rock*

In 1764, a stream that ran into the eastern end of Lake Erie was named Buffalo Creek by British army cartographer Capt. John Montresor. The area was permanently settled after the Revolutionary War and became the county seat of Erie County.

In 1795, a community was established about 4 miles north of Buffalo on the Niagara River and became known as Black Rock due to the black limestone in the area. In the 1820s, the town became a contender for the end of the Erie Canal but lost out to Buffalo. A ferry service ran across the river from a landing about midway between the two towns to Fort Erie, Ontario, until 1951. In 1953 Black Rock was annexed by Buffalo.

## Samuel Perry

A claim presented by Comm. Oliver H. Perry, Samuel's son, as reported by the Third Auditor on February 6, 1837, in part:

> In one of the depositions, James Norton has testified that in September, 1812, Samuel Perry sailed a boat, of which he was one-half owner. The boat would carry about 70 barrels of salt. When the boat was at Buffalo, General Peter B. Porter, who was in the service of the United States, ordered the boat from Buffalo down to Black Rock to his store-house where it was loaded with 40 or 45 barrels of salt for Erie, Pennsylvania, and while pursuing her voyage near Sturgeon's Point on the American shore of Lake Erie, about 18 miles from Buffalo, a boat from the *Hunter*, a British armed vessel, captured her and took boat and cargo to the *Hunter*.
>
> The boat was a good substantial one with one mast and worth about $400, and when taken she had other property on board besides that put there by General Porter.
>
> Joshua Lovejoy testified that on the September 14, 1812, he shipped on board an open boat, then belonging to himself and Samuel Perry, 45 barrels of salt, on account and risk of General Peter B. Porter, who then acted as contractor's agent, consigned to Stephen Wolverton at the port of Erie. The boat sailed from the mouth of Buffalo Creek on the morning of the September 16 and when about 10 miles out, a British armed boat from under Point Abino put out after her and drove her on the American shore. The boatmen were obliged to abandon her to the enemy who cut away the mast and rigging, which, with the sails were left on shore. The boat and cargo were towed off by the captors to the British shore and has not since been recovered and that the boat was worth $120, and the necessary furniture $20.
>
> General Porter has testified that in September, 1812, he acted as the agent of Augustus Porter. The 45 barrels of salt was the property of Augustus Porter and was consigned to Stephen Wolverton, the agent of Augustus at Erie, to be by him applied to supply the troops of the United States in the State of Ohio.
>
> The other depositions relate to the schooner and appear to have been made by Daniel Barnes, John Wing, and Edmund Bunting. Barnes has testified that Samuel Perry, in September, 1813, owned the schooner *Eagle* on Lake Erie, of 40 tons burthen or thereabouts. He sailed her as master. In returning home from a voyage on Lake Erie, for and in the service of the United States in October, 1813, the vessel was in a storm, wrecked, or nearly so, on the shore of the lake near Erie and one man drowned. The schooner afterwards, at an expense of $200 or thereabouts, was partially repaired so as to enable her to be sailed to Erie, Pennsylvania, but a short distance from where she went ashore, where she was afterwards sold for $700. In his opinion she was worth $3,000 and that Samuel was about two months in the service of the United States, and never to his knowledge received any pay for the vessel or his own services.
>
> John Wing has testified that she was beached on the shore of Lake Erie in a violent storm or gale of wind near his house and he understood she was in the service of the United States and had sick troops on board when she went ashore. He supposed she was worth $3,000. After some repairs she was taken to Erie, about 3 miles, and sold for $700. She could not be kept from the shore by any management. The witness heard Samuel Perry say that he had never received any pay from the United States for his services, which he supposed was about $390.
>
> Edmund Bunting has testified that the schooner *Eagle*, in September, 1813, was at Put-in Bay on Lake Erie, with part of a regiment of troops in the service of the United States on board. She was in the service by order of an officer of the army of the United States. The witness heard an officer order Samuel Perry from Put-in Bay. That he obeyed, went to Malden. The schooner brought to Put-in Bay provisions for the army from Carrying River, Ohio. The witness is a militiaman in the service of the United States. In the latter part of September, or the fore part of October, 1813, he heard and officer of the army order Captain Perry to sail with some

sick troops on board to Erie. That he obeyed, but in a storm went ashore near Erie. The witness helped to get her off and he thinks Captain Perry was in the service of the United States for five or six weeks.

Daniel Barnes has testified that Samuel Perry married his daughter and came to see her at the witnesses house in the fall of 1813, when he informed her that while at Erie with his vessel loaded for a voyage, Commodore Oliver H. Perry ordered him to unload it and help to take his guns, ammunition, stores, &c. over the bar at Erie and put them on board the fleet. He did so and under the commodore's direction sailed with the fleet up the lake and continued in the service of the United States with his vessel till after the engagement between the American and British fleets sometime in October. While coming down the lake with some sick, wounded, and discharged soldiers of the army or fleet, he was by a violent gale driven on the shore of the lake about 4 miles from the harbor of Erie, and his vessel wrecked.

Samuel Perry was paid $108 by Quartermaster General John C. Bartlett for 12 days' service from Put-in Bay and Portage River to Detroit.

The boat was subsequently owned by Jacob Fowler & Co. and chartered by Capt. James McCloskey in 1814 to transport provisions for troops.

The claim was dismissed by Committee of Claims on February 14, 1837, after learning Samuel Perry had been paid, and stated, in part:

The fact that the Treasury Department was burnt more than 20 years after the transaction took place, and no claim having been presented within the lifetime of Samuel Perry, nor by his heirs, when the papers in the Treasury Department were in existence, the committee cannot allow this part of the claim.

## *Maj. John G. Camp's Statement*

Maj. Camp was deposed on August 20, 1816, as transcribed:

He was assistant deputy quartermaster general in the United States' service at Buffalo on the 29th of December, 1813, and in the command of that department, he accompanied the advance guard of the American army under the command of Col. Cyrenius Chapin when the enemy landed. This advance guard marched down below Black Rock to a battery near Congoquetta creek, where they encountered the enemy, who drove them back upon the main body of the American army, then at Black Rock under the command of Major General Hall.

On the morning of the 30th of December at daylight, the principle force of the enemy crossed the Niagara in open boats under the cover of artillery planted on the opposite shore and were met by the American army on their landing. A battle ensued in which the American troops were compelled to fall back upon Buffalo where some skirmishing took place. The principle part of the American army soon retreated and left the village of Buffalo defenseless. The firing, however, continued after the retreat of the main body of the American army from two pieces of artillery planted on an eminence in the village of Buffalo until the principle piece was dismounted and the enemy had approached too near to give time to remount it.

All hopes of being able to defend the town after this accident having vanished, Col. Chapin, at the request of the trustees of Buffalo, in which the deponent, being the only United States officer of the regular army then present, concurred, went to the British advance with a flag for the purpose of obtaining terms from the enemy. This deponent remained at Buffalo until Col. Chapin's return, who he met holding a paper in his hands which deponent understood from Col. Chapin to be the terms of capitulation, which guaranteed the safety of private property and private persons. Deponent was prevented from reading the articles of capitulation by the rapid approach of the enemy, who were then within half pistol shot, the enemy having possession of the eastern road. Deponent retreated with about 20 men up Lake Erie. The enemy took possession of the town of Buffalo at about 10 o'clock in the morning and burnt from four to five houses on their entrance and in the course of the day several more, all of which contained munitions of war and were barracks of United States' troops.

On the 1st of January they burnt the principle part of the buildings in the town and at night recrossed the Niagara.

About a week or ten days after the deponent met Lieutenant Connell of the 41st or 49th British Infantry bearing a flag to Black Rock, deponent entered into a conversation with Connell on the subject of the conduct of the British army at Buffalo, in which deponent charged the British with having violated the articles of capitulation, which Connell denied and declared that he knew very well what the articles of capitulation were; the British were bound by them to respect private property and private persons only. On entering the town of Buffalo the orders given to the British troops were in conformity to the articles of capitulation, namely, "to respect private property and private persons," that they found the town of Buffalo to be a military cantonment, in consequence of which it was destroyed and that they had destroyed nothing which they were not justified in destroying, both by the usages of war and the terms of capitulation.

The deponent was present at an interview between the Committee of Safety of the town of Buffalo and Gen. George McClure on or about the 20th of December, 1813, when the Committee remonstrated on behalf of the inhabitants against his occupying the town with his troops and stated that they had reason to apprehend the destruction of their property by the enemy should they ever obtain possession of the town, in consequence of its being in the military occupancy of the United States, to which Gen. McClure replied that he would pledge his honor that the government of the United States would indemnify the inhabitants of Buffalo for any losses which they might sustain and advised them to give up their houses peaceably and this deponent states further that the town of Buffalo was, in fact, a military cantonment at the time of its destruction and had been so for some time before. During the whole war, one part or other of the town was constantly in the military occupancy of the United States.

At the time of its destruction from 2,500 to 3,000 troops were quartered at Buffalo by order of Maj. Gen. Amos Hall, the commanding general. And public property, as this deponent verily believes, to the amount of $100,000 at the least was deposited in the town in different houses and that the following are the names of some of the persons whose buildings were occupied as barracks for soldiers or as deposits for military stores:

Mary Atkins, Jude Atwater, Zenos Barker, John Brunson, Robert Cain, Amos Callender, Messrs. Campbell, Benjamin Caryl, Cyrenius Chapin, James Chapin, Raphael Cook, Martin Daly, Ira Dickinson, Luke Draper, James Edsall, Elisha Ensign, Gilman Folson, Oliver Forward, William Gaird, Mr. Gilbert, blacksmith, Joshua Gillet, Seth Governor, Widow Governor, Vincent Grant, Eli Hart, Reuben B. Heacock, William Hodge, Sylvia Holmes, Ebenezer Johnson, Henry Kitchen, Joseph Landon, Lewis Le Coulteaux, Joshua Lovejoy, Timothy McKeowin, Norton & Davis, Ralph Pomeroy, Herman B. Potter, Elias Ranson, David Rees, John Root, Margaret St. John, Smith H. Salisbury, Oziel Smith, Stocking & Bull, Juba Storrs & Co., Storrs & Caryl, Mr. Stow, cabinet maker, Townsend & Coit, Ebenezer Walden.

The deponent further saith that all the houses in the village of Buffalo destroyed by the enemy were in the military occupancy of the United States and that the enemy passed a number of houses which were not in the military occupancy of the United States, and proceeded to the house of William Hodge, which is about two miles from the village of Buffalo, which was in the military occupancy of the United States, and destroyed the same.

The deponent further states that he is not, directly or indirectly, interested in the event of any claim from the town or village of Buffalo.

Militia Capt. William Hull's company was at Buffalo where he was a recruiting officer under direction of the Secretary of War. On December 30, 1813, he received orders from Gen. Hall at Batavia to take possession of whatever buildings he needed, "without the knowledge or consent of the owners."

Rowland Cotton was aid-de-camp to Brig. Gen. Timothy S. Hopkins under Gen. Hall and received the same orders.

Lt. Col. Thomas Dickson, of the Upper Canada Militia at Queenston, was at Lewiston in December 1813, stated Fort Niagara was taken by the British on December 19, 1813.

An Onondaga Indian chief named Peter Sky was a volunteer in Gen. Peter

B. Porter's command and was "struck by a British soldier with a gun" after chasing some enemy near Youngstown, seriously injuring his left shoulder.

The town of Batavia, New York, was founded in 1802 and was the county seat of Genesee County.

## John R. Williams

John Williams and his family left Detroit in August 1812 for Fort Erie. He eventually opened a store at Albany, New York.

John said the British allowed American citizens to remove their property and go aboard the schooner *Caledonia* on or about the first day of October 1812, "being then on his way to Buffalo, New York." The schooner was a merchant vessel and had two blunderbusses in the cabin, and pikes on deck, "intended to guard against attacks from Indians, as otherwise, while near shore or in narrow channels of water."

The schooner had left Malden and Detroit, "under a flag of truce at her masthead, which continued flying during her passage down the lake, and while anchored at Fort Erie."

In 1813 he purchased "a cargo of goods," including tobacco, from Levi Solomons at Albany, for shipment to Detroit, apparently in the care of Dennis Campau, who was the caretaker at his farm at Spring Wells outside of Detroit. After Perry's victory on Lake Erie, he was told the goods had been put in storage in John Brunson's warehouse at Buffalo on November 13, "for want of transportation," along with military stores in the same building. John wanted his goods removed to either Batavia or the Genesee River but Brunson had become quite ill and was unable to comply, and his goods were lost.

As he stated in a deposition:

> In August he was compelled to leave the country, and with his family and other American citizens, was sent away in the British vessel *Caledonia* bound for Fort Erie, a British post, nearly opposite Buffalo. On arrival off Fort Erie, in the month of October, himself and family, and other American citizens were taken away by means of small boats used as cartels, and, under appropriate flags, were taken to and landed at Buffalo.
>
> Owing to adverse winds and the lateness of the hour, he was prevented from landing his baggage and personal effects from the vessel and no communication was allowed between the vessel and the American shore after the setting of the sun.
>
> Shortly after his arrival at Buffalo he heard that an expedition was planned for the capture of the *Caledonia* and another vessel of the enemy then also lying at anchor off Fort Erie. He immediately waited upon Major General Amos Hall, of the New York militia, then commanding at Buffalo, and informed him of his property being left aboard the *Caledonia*, and received the assurances of General Hall that the property should be safely restored to him in case of her capture.
>
> During the succeeding night the vessels were captured by forces under Lt. (now Commodore) Jesse D. Elliott, of the United States Navy, and brought to the American shore. The *Caledonia*, unfortunately, was beached near Black Rock, whence the property on board was disembarked.
>
> The petitioner made every exertion to recover and secure his property but was almost wholly unsuccessful and that his personal property, to the value of $1,461, was lost or wholly destroyed. The *Caledonia*, so lying at or near Black Rock was completely within range of the British batteries, that as often as persons appeared upon the deck of the vessel, a hot fire was opened upon them, and the petitioner in this manner suffered much personal exposure and hazard in his attempts to land some articles of household furniture that had been left upon deck. The vessel was laden with furs, peltries, and other valuables, which were landed under the direction of the naval officer in command, during a constant fire from the opposite shore, and the property appears to have been placed for security in the public barracks at Black Rock, which, with most of their contents, were on the same day burnt and destroyed in consequence of hot shot having been thrown into them from the batteries.

John had a letter from Gen. Hall dated October 13, 1812, from Batavia certifying "a list of articles, the contents of two large, square trunks left on board the schooner *Caledonia* the day previous to her being captured." The trunks contained "two packs of deer, bear, raccoon, and various other skins worth $250, the total claim being $1,515.94, and other sundry articles received from John W. Macomb totaling $54.12."

The merchandise shipped from Albany to Detroit via Buffalo in October, 1813, and stored in John Brunson's warehouse at Buffalo and which was destroyed by the British on December, 30, 1813, was valued at £1,610 4s 4d.

Personal property could not be included and with the adjustment to the mortgage and bonds on his property near Detroit, John was awarded $93 in 1846.

## John Brunson

As stated by the Committee of Claims on May 17, 1830, in part:

> The claim is for the value of a house and store which were destroyed at Buffalo on the 30th of December, 1813, by the enemy because they were occupied by the order of an officer of the United States as a place of military deposit and for barracks and a hospital.
>
> It appears that there was some evidence that Lieutenant David Riddle was the officer who took possession of the house and store. This evidence, if it existed, is not now among the papers, nor is there any proof that the buildings were in the military occupation of the United States, except which is derived from the statement of John G. Camp, lately made, which he says in allusion to the house, "that if it had not previously been occupied by troops, with their baggage, arms, &c., I should assuredly have taken possession of it, as I did of part of almost every house in the village."
>
> And he further states his measures were necessary, owing to the inclemency of the weather, and that, when the inhabitants resisted, he set apart such rooms in their houses as would accommodate the family, and took possession of the residue of the houses.
>
> This statement seems to have been presented for the purpose of correcting some errors in his former depositions, and to prove that Lieutenant Riddle was at Buffalo at the time, or immediately preceding the time of its destruction, he further states that he knows there were some tents and a marquee in the store at the time of its being burnt. The statement of Major Frasier, made on the 8th of February last, is also presented for the purpose of proving that Lieutenant Riddle was at Buffalo on the evening of the 29th of December, 1813, and also on the morning of the 30th.

John Brunson, of Detroit, owned a home and outbuildings, and a warehouse in Buffalo. After Adm. Perry's victory on Lake Erie, goods shipped to Detroit were hampered by a lack of transportation.

November 24, 1813, John R. Williams (q.v.) stored goods in Brunson's warehouse. In late November or early December, an officer identified by Brunson as Lt. Ridley, "provost major of USA," put arms, tents, and munitions in his store alongside the goods belonging to John R. Williams and took possession of the buildings. He allowed his troops to use Brunson's house and store as a barrack and hospital. The British burned the place on December 30.

Brunson was reportedly "confined to his bed by sickness" at the time and remained sick for upwards of three months and was thus unable to remove any of his property. He claimed $775 for furniture, $3,500 for merchandise in his store, and was paid $5,340 in 1832.

## Ralph M. Pomeroy

As reported by the Committee of Claims on February 4, 1816:

> On the 24th of November, 1812, and for some time previous thereto, the petitioner, Ralph M. Pomeroy, owned and occupied a dwelling-house in the village of Buffalo, in the State of New York. That on the aforesaid day, a number of soldiers belonging to the United

States Army came to his house, broke it open, destroyed his furniture, and set the house on fire and burnt it. The petitioner prays to Congress to be paid the value of his house and furniture.

It does not appear to the committee, from the *ex parte* evidence of the petitioner, what was the cause of such wanton and unlawful conduct on the part of the soldiery. However much it is to be deprecated in those who perpetrated the offense, yet it certainly has created no obligation, moral or legal, on the government to pay for the injury. This principle has often been adopted, and is believed by the committee to be founded in a wise and just policy.

## Daniel Brayman

In 1814, Jabez Hull was a sutler at Black Rock whose goods were in a building owned by Daniel Brayman. As stated by the Committee of Claims on January 21, 1833, in part:

> On or about the 6th of November, 1814, Jabez Hull was in possession of a house at Black Rock having two rooms, one above the other, which he occupied for a shop or grocery store. Some time in that month a party of soldiers, in the night, burst open the door of the upper room and robbed it of every thing valuable. The party was supposed to be headed by Sergeant Penderghast, whose voice was recognized by one of the witnesses, who was at the time in the lower room.
>
> Several days after this event, another party of soldiers armed with muskets and bayonets, in the night, burst open the door of the lower room, threatened the life of Mr. Seely, who was in it, beat him severely, held him in duress for a considerable time, demanded the money of him and of another person in the room, gave repeated orders to fire and kill the damned rascals, and took such articles as they pleased out of the room, and retired.
>
> Several days afterward the house was taken down by the soldiers and demolished. A part of the materials were seen in the encampment of the artillerists, and bricks were carried in a direction to the encampment.
>
> Jabez Hull had, with the approbation of the commanding officer of the regiment for which he was the sutler, erected the walls of a log house within the encampment of the infantry, about 1 mile above Black Rock, and, during his occasional absence, these walls were torn down and carried away by the troops.

Hull complained to Gen. George Izard and filed a claim for $703.25, including $500 for the house, $60 for the log house, and $93.25 for "whiskey, cordial, casks, and kegs." Lt. Col. John McMahon, New York Militia, stated that sometime in October or November he gave orders to remove the buildings of Jabez Hull, and others there and in Buffalo, for use of the materials for barracks at Fort Erie. On November 2, he left Black Rock.

The house was actually owned by Daniel Brayman. Nathan Hull was Jabez's clerk. The soldiers were from Capt. Samuel B. Archer's company of light artillery. The claims were rejected as wanton destruction.

## Elisha Forster

His claim was detailed on January 19, 1827, but no action was taken:

> The petitioner states he was a mechanic at Buffalo during the late war with Great Britain, and had accumulated personal property to the amount of $3,200 or there about. He enlisted in a company of volunteers and served one year. In consequence of being in service, he was unable to remove his personal property to a place of safety when the enemy destroyed Buffalo in December, 1813, and the whole of his property was destroyed. He says that owing to ill health he has never been able to regain his former circumstances, but is now poor and, being advanced in life and much in need of compensation for his property, he asks relief.
>
> The petitioner asks to be compensated for the destruction of the following property: A quantity of hardware and saddlery valued at $1,255; finished saddlery work, $782; leather, $150; a set of tools, $150; furniture in his dwelling-house, $395.50; book accounts, $500. Total $3,232.50.

As reported by the Committee of Claims on March 24, 1836:

He states that he had frequently removed his property to a place of safety. At the time it was replaced he was in the service doing duty. His officers would not suffer him to leave it and secure his property. His saddlery and tools were in a room in the house of Mr. Landon, which he occupied for a shop; the house was occupied by the troops, and has been paid for, by reason of such occupation and destruction. He contracted a disease in the service incident to his fatigues and exposures from which he has not recovered. He lost all his property, is poor, has a large family, and prays from the peculiar hardship of his case for some relief.

However great the complainant's misfortune may be, it is such that the government does not repair, and the committee do not perceive that any new principle should be adopted in this case. They therefore move that the prayer of the petitioner ought not to be granted.

## Eli Hart

Eli Hart had a 32 × 34, 2-story house worth $4,250, a 25 × 36 store, a 28 × 28 store at $1,000, and long list of diverse goods a very well-stocked general store would have, including 83 gallons of "cognac brandy, 4th proof," block and tackle, 50 gallons of Jamaica spirits, tools, nails, seeds, leather goods, combs and mirrors, tobacco, kitchen and dining ware, 18 barrels of whiskey, Windsor soap, bedding, furniture, and 1,250 Spanish cigars, all worth $17,432.39.

He presented his extensive claim to the "executive department" under the act of April 9, 1816, but was rejected as not allowable under the act. It was then referred to the Committee of Claims, as reported on January 28, 1819:

The petitioner was the proprietor of a house and store in the village of Buffalo, State of New York, which, together with his merchandise and out-houses, were destroyed by the enemy in their predatory incursion into the United States on the 30th of December, 1813.

He alleges the destruction of his property was occasioned by his buildings being occupied for public military purposes, so as to make them liable to such disposition by the ordinary usages of war. A valuation of his buildings has been made by commissioners appointed under the authority of the United States. The amount is $6,670. The petitioner also claims $8,982.39 for personal property and merchandise destroyed in his buildings.

The petitioner adduces strong proof that his house was used as a laboratory for the purpose of making up fixed ammunition, and was at the time of destruction wholly in the public use. The store is proved to have contained muskets, knapsacks, and stores, by several witnesses. The invoice of the personal property is attested to be true, and charged at wholesale prices, by a person who has acted for several years previous to the 30th December as clerk to the petitioner.

The petitioner appears to have been resident as a proprietor and merchant at Buffalo some years before the war, and his stock does not seem to have been more valuable when destroyed than previously. He has received no part of the sum appropriated by the States of New York for the relief of the sufferers from British violence.

This is one of a large list of claims for property destroyed on the same occasion, and the committee are aware of the necessity of a strict investigation of its merits. The dwelling-house, in their opinion, stands clearly within the rule of allowance. The storehouse presents a case of more doubt, as the deposits seem to have been made with the owner's consent, and he continued to transact his own business as usual. Believing, however, that public property, wherever found, is fair prize of war, the destruction of it was an act the enemy might regularly do; and where the building was destroyed with it, as a necessary consequence, the committee are of opinion it would be just to reimburse the value to the owner.

The committee admit that the petitioner's claim for his merchandise is as imposing as any claim of the kind can well be, as he was a resident in business before the war, and his stock had not increased, and that it was destroyed in consequence of its contiguity to public stores; yet they cannot recommend the allowance. The merchandise was removable, and the petitioner must have been aware of the hazard to be incurred on a weak frontier, and to incur that hazard was a matter of choice which it would be unreasonable to suppose the Government should be held to insure. They therefore submit a bill allowing to the petitioner the appraised value of his buildings.

Corroborating testimony was given by John G. Camp and in 1826 Hart was paid $6,118.50. He subsequently filed another claim, as stated in 1859:

The petitioner states that previous to and during the war between the United States and Great Britain he was a merchant in the village of Buffalo, State of New York. At an early stage of the war, it became necessary for its preservation to place public property in buildings of individuals, as the United States had no public buildings in that section of the country. Petitioner, at the request of officers, received at sundry times, public property for storage and three of his buildings contained the property or were in the occupation of the United States on the 30th December, 1813, when the village of Buffalo was burned by the British. Petitioner claims $8,500 for his buildings destroyed and $8,902.39 for his stock of goods destroyed at the same time.

This claim was presented to the executive department of the government for payment under the Act of April 9, 1816, providing for property captured or destroyed while in the military occupation of the United States, but was rejected as not falling within the provisions of that act. But afterwards, by a special act of Congress in 1826, Mr. Hart was paid for his buildings the sum of $6,118.50, and he now claims the balance of $11,363.89.

The case was first presented to Congress in 1819 when an adverse report was made from this committee. Similar reports were made on the same case in 1820, 1821, 1822, and 1824. On the 3rd day of March, 1825, Congress passed an act to amend the act of 1816, and authorized the payment for houses destroyed by the enemy when shown to have been in the occupancy of the United States. Under this act the claim of Mr. Hart was re-examined by the Third Auditor and allowed for the sum stated, viz: $6,118.50. This, in the opinion of your committee, disposes of the claim for buildings.

The claim for merchandise destroyed is one of a large class of claims which have been uniformly rejected by Congress, and very properly so, for there is no principle of equity of justice which should render the government liable for store goods which the owners may move at pleasure and risk in the buildings at their own option. The whole Niagara frontier was destroyed, including property not in the occupancy of the government as well as that which was. The payment for the buildings was, in the opinion of your committee, improperly made, as their destruction was not the result of their temporary occupation by the government but the fate common to the whole frontier, resulting from an invasion by the enemy.

Major General Hall, in his testimony, says: "I am satisfied that one principal cause of said village being burnt was in consequence of its being a military deposit, and occupied as barracks by troops in the service of the United States."

By this testimony it appears that the whole village, and not any particular house or dwelling suffered from the military occupation by the troops of the United States. Indeed, Mr. Hart shows that there was an effort on the part of the enemy to prevent the destruction. John Lay, Jr., swears that, "he was taken prisoner by the enemy, and while in their hands heard several British officers say that an order had been issued for the saving of Cyrenius Chapin's house from burning, and consequently the store of Eli Hart, which was adjoining, would not be hurt, as the firing of said store would inevitably cause the destruction of the buildings of Chapin." To prevent the destruction of these buildings a guard was placed in front of Hart's store, and yet, as his buildings were destroyed after all these precautions, he claims, and has actually received pay for the same, because he happened to have in store goods belonging to the United States, while others whose property was destroyed at the same time do not pretend to have a claim upon the government.

Your committee perceive no grounds whatever upon which the claim for merchandise destroyed can be justified, and they, therefore, report back the case, with a recommendation that the prayer of the petitioner be not granted.

## Ebenezer Belden

As reported by the Committee on Military Affairs on February 5, 1857:

The petitioner prays to be reimbursed for losses sustained by his father, Ebenezer Belden, by the destruction of his stock of goods by the enemy at Buffalo, New York, on the 19th of December, 1813, when the storehouse occupied by him at that place was destroyed because it was partially occupied at the same time by military stores.

This claim was presented to the House of Representatives in the second session of the 15th Congress, but no final action was ever had upon it. On the 9th of April, 1816, Congress passed a law, "authorizing payment for property lost, captured, or destroyed by the enemy, while in the military service of the United States." The ninth section of this act required that evidence should be provided that the property destroyed, and for which payment was promised, was in military occupancy under the authority of an officer or agent of the United States, and a commissioner was appointed to take testimony and administer the law. Numerous cases were presented to this officer, and this one among them, and the testimony is taken before and certified by him. The law, however, was construed to extend only to houses, &c., and goods, wares, and merchandise, as charged in Mr. Belden's account, were in no instance paid for.

Michael Helms testifies that the store occupied by Ebenezer Belden was destroyed as alleged, whilst it was also occupied as a military depôt by the United States.

Ezra St. John testifies to the fact that the storehouse of Ebenezer Belden was also a depot for tents and other articles belonging to the United States, at the time it was destroyed.

Nathan Leonard, late a captain in the United States service, testifies that the storehouse, at the time of its destruction by the enemy, was also in the military occupancy of the United States as a deposit of forage by order of the United States quartermaster general.

Stephen Sparrow testifies to the same, and states that he believes the property was so destroyed in consequence of its military occupancy; and further, that he was, on December 19, 1813, the clerk or agent of Belden, and that the goods and effects as charged in the account accompanying Belden's memorial were in Belden's store and were therein destroyed, and that the goods are charged at New York prices with transportation added.

John Lay, Jr., testifies that he was a merchant and well acquainted with the prices of goods and that the prices charged in Ebenezer Belden's schedule of goods destroyed by the enemy in December, 1813, are reasonable and fair.

Reuben B. Heacock, also a merchant in Buffalo, testifies that he has known Ebenezer Belden as a regular merchant of respectable standing since 1808 until the destruction of the Niagara frontier in the winter of 1813.

From a review of this testimony it is manifest that Ebenezer Belden's property was destroyed in consequence of its being upon premises occupied in part as a military depôt, and such occupancy was by the order of an officer of the United States. There are numerous precedents on record of payments for losses sustained under similar circumstances, and there seems to be as much justice in providing for the payment of goods so destroyed as for houses, as authorized by the act of April, 1816, and the committee report a bill to pay the memorialist's claim.

William W. Belden, administrator of Ebenezer Belden, was paid $8,624.84 in 1857. Nathaniel Leonard was a captain in the 1st Artillery.

## Samuel May

Samuel Pratt owned a house and two warehouses. The house was apparently occupied by Elijah Leach.

Samuel died in August 1812, and was survived by his wife Esther and son Samuel. That December, Esther and Samuel became the administrators of the estate, and in 1816 filed a claim for $8,512 for three buildings and their contents. Leach testified the furniture and household goods in the house were worth $400 and the hardware, dry goods, and merchandise in one of the stores was worth $1,500. Augustus C. Fox and William B. Grant corroborated the estimates. Samuel valued it at $1,900.

Samuel died in 1822, leaving Esther as sole heir. Samuel May was the mortgage holder on the real property. As reported by the House Committee of Claims on July 5, 1832:

The bill is unaccompanied with any report, whereby the duty is devolved on this committee of concisely stating the facts of the case.

The bill proposes to allow Samuel May $3,150 for two stores or warehouses destroyed by the enemy at Buffalo on the 30th of December, 1813, while they were in the military occupation of the United States. The record title of these stores at the time of their destruction, together with a dwelling-house, was given in the name of Samuel Pratt. The claim for these buildings was presented under the acts of 1816 and 1825, by the representatives of Samuel Pratt, and Samuel May being the mortgagee, claimed the indemnity provided in the acts, and received the amount awarded for the destruction of the dwelling-house. The Third Auditor rejected the claim for the stores, the testimony not being satisfactory to him that they were in the military occupation of the United States, or used as places of deposit for military stores.

The positive testimony of John G. Camp as to the occupation of the white store, together with the testimony of Jonathan Baird, and the declaration of Mr. Granger, were outweighed in his opinion by historical accounts supposed to be correct by testimony taken in the case of Stephen Franklin, and by the reports made by the witness John G. Camp at the time, which conflicted with his testimony more recently taken.

For Mr. Hagner's views of the claim for the two stores, the committee refer to his letter to Mr. Wallach, dated November 9, 1825, and to his letter to J. Watson dated February 10, 1826, and to his letter to the honorable Benjamin Ruggles, Chairman of the Committee of Claims of the Senate dated January 12, 1832.

This committee was forcibly struck by the remarks of Mr. Hagner, and they created doubts whether the claim should be allowed. A letter was addressed to Mr. Camp, calling on him to remove the discrepancy that seemed to exist in the evidence; and his deposition, together with the deposition of William Baird, have been received together with a former deposition of Mr. Camp, and one given by Jonathan Baird.

Camp and Jonathan Baird testify positively to the military occupation of the white store and Mr. Baird testifies positively to the occupation of the yellow store, and their testimony is supported by other evidence. William Baird's testimony weakens, if it does not entirely remove, the objections raised by Mr. Hagner that were made by Mr. Camp at the time. The committee can well conceive that the reports of officers accounting for property lost during an invasion of the enemy, might be substantially, though not literally, correct, and that the arms and ammunition might be delivered out immediately before an engagement, without taking the ordinary receipts and vouchers. Such is proven to have been the case in this instance.

On the whole, without being more minute, this committee, with the aid of the additional testimony, concur with the Senate, and report the bill without amendment, and recommend its passage.

Samuel May was paid $3,150 in 1832, and filed a claimed for an additional $2,483.50, which was rejected in 1834.

## Conrad House

As reported by the Committee of Claims on May 11, 1838:

This claim is for the loss of buildings below Black Rock in December, 1813, by the burning of them by the British when they were in the occupation of the troops of the United States.

The deposition of Lorton Holden says he was a captain of a militia company in the 164th Regiment of New York Militia commanded by Col. Worthy L. Churchill in the service of the United States. On the 13th of December, 1813, he was in command of a detachment of militia occupying the buildings said to belong to Conrad House, situated on the bank of Niagara River about 6 miles below Black Rock, and the buildings were occupied until after the British had crossed over to the American side above the buildings.

David Wilkinson under date of the 23rd of December, 1836, testifies he was well acquainted with the house of Conrad House. When the British crossed on to the shore of the State of New York, about the 30th of November, 1813, the dwelling of Conrad House was occupied by a part of the American army as a guard-house, and was taken possession of by the British and burnt, together with the out-houses and barns thereunto belonging.

Conrad House was in the service and was detained after the destruction of his property nearly three months. He was too much reduced to bear the expenses of prosecuting his claim and that immediately after the war he moved on to the rapids of the Maumee in the State of Ohio where he has lived ever since. He estimates the losses of Mr. House at between $2,000 and $3,000.

David W. Hawley testifies he was acquainted with Conrad House at and before the burning of Buffalo by the British in the winter of 1813–'14, and that the house and other buildings were occupied by the American troops and that Conrad was in the service. He thinks the total loss must have been between $2,000 and $3,000.

William Scott testifies he resided below Black Rock. On the night previous to the burning of Buffalo and Black Rock, he was on the patrol-guard in company with Conrad House and that his dwelling-house was occupied by other American troops.

James Wilkinson states he was well acquainted with the petitioner and with his buildings. He particularly described the house and barn and said he resided about a mile from the buildings for some time previous and until the time the buildings were burnt, and often saw them in the occupation of the United States troops.

There is no evidence that the buildings were occupied by order of an officer. Proof of this fact is essentially requisite. Congress so decided when the act of 1816 and by the act of 1825 were passed.

Captain Holden does not say the buildings were occupied by his order, nor by the order of any other officer.

The enemy destroyed in their march 100 houses and they wantonly destroyed every thing they could—shooting down horses, cattle, sheep, and swine, and suffering them to lie where they fell.

William Scott mentions the house was occupied by Conrad House and other members of the patrol-guard. The inference is that Mr. House's family remained in the dwelling. A general estimation that his loss was between $2,000 and $3,000 is too vague and uncertain. This estimate may include personal property for which no compensation is given.

The prayer of the petitioner ought not to be granted.

Additional testimony was taken and an award of $575 was made on December 29, 1841. As reported by the Committee of Claims, in part:

> To show a military occupation of his house by proper authority, the petitioner presents the affidavits of General Timothy S. Hopkins and Captain Lorton Holden. The first was in command of the post at Black Rock at the period referred to by the petitioner, and says, "Captain Holden was ordered by me down the Niagara River, with a small detachment of horse troops as a patrol-guard and there being no public buildings for them to encamp, had to use private houses, when and where they occupied the private house of Conrad House. I was well acquainted with Conrad House and family and with his property, which had been destroyed by the British, which troops landed several miles above House's property, being occupied by my orders, and sanctioned."
>
> The house is said by one of the witnesses to have been 20 by 35 feet on the ground, and one and a half story high, built of hewn logs, and divided into two rooms with good chimneys, shingle roof and otherwise well finished, estimated to be worth $350. And the barn, said to have been a new frame building, 30 by 40 feet, at $225, total $575.
>
> For this amount the committee are of opining the petitioner is entitled to relief and herewith report a bill.

## Vincent Grant

As reported by the Committee of Claims on February 15, 1819:

> Grant prays indemnity for a storehouse, in back of which he resided, furniture, and merchandise, destroyed by the British in December, 1813.
>
> It appears in evidence that the cellar under the storehouse was occupied early in the war by order of the Navy agent on that frontier as a depot for the naval stores of the United States; that it continued to be so occupied up to the time of its destruction, and the claim is founded on the presumption that its destruction was owing to its being thus occupied.
>
> The committee might here remark that the burning of Buffalo was alleged to have been done in retaliation for the burning of Newark;

that buildings which were not used as depots shared the same fate with those which were; and that it is not probable the property of Mr. Grant would have escaped this indiscriminate conflagration, although it had not been occupied as a military depot. But as they wish to act on the most liberal principles which can safely be adopted, they rather incline to consider it as within the provisions of the act making compensation for property destroyed, and to recommend such allowance as this act and the evidence will justify.

With respect to the merchandise and furniture destroyed: as they would have admitted of a removal from the scene of danger, and as there is no satisfactory testimony of the quantity or value thereof, the committee do not consider them as proper subjects of allowance.

The building is described as framed, 36 feet long by 26 deep, two stories high, the front finished in the usual style of country stores, and the back part in a neat, plain manner, and occupied by Grant as a dwelling. It is differently appraised by different house carpenters, and is charged by the claimant at $4,250. The committee, however, have adopted the sum at which it was valued, under oath, by seven appraisers, viz. $3,350, which they believe to be a liberal allowance for a building of these dimensions and of this description; and for this amount the report a bill.

## George Winthrop Fox

As reported by the Committee of Claims on December 26, 1821:

The petitioner, of Buffalo, New York, states that he was the owner of a horse in the use of Daniel Fox, a private in the corps of mounted volunteers in the service of the United States, commanded by Colonel Cyrenius Chapin, and that Daniel Fox was captured, together with his horse and equipments, by the British troops at the Beaver Dams, in Upper Canada.

The horse and equipments are valued at $90, and for that sum the petitioner asks payment from the United States.

There is no evidence that the horse was in the service of the United States, on any conditions which were not applicable to other horses of mounted volunteers. What private agreement existed between the petitioner and Daniel Fox is not concerned to know; from it no claim could arise which would not be just, if the petitioner had himself been the volunteer; and the loss of the horse and equipments does not appear to have been occasioned by any of those incidents which have been admitted to create a liability on the part of the United States to pay for the horses of mounted volunteers.

The Committee, therefore, recommend that the prayer of the petitioner be not granted.

Lt. Col. Chapin's Detachment of New York Mounted Volunteers was at the Beaver Dams on June 24, 1813.

On November 12, 1845, Amanda King, "late widow and now administratrix of George W. Fox, late of the city of Buffalo, deceased, as well in behalf of herself as aforesaid, as for her only son George W. Fox, who is heir at law of George W. Fox, deceased" submitted a petition:

Immediately preceding and at the time of the destruction of the late village (now city) of Buffalo, on the 31st day of December, 1813, George W. Fox was in possession of and owned a large quantity of goods, wares, and merchandise, consisting of groceries, provisions, dry goods, boats, household furniture, and other effects, such as notes, books of accounts, wearing apparel, &c., which were destroyed, lost or captured by the British troops at the time and place above mentioned.

The property was never returned or restored to George W. Fox in his lifetime, nor to any person since his demise.

For many years previous to the war of 1812, George W. Fox, with others, came to Buffalo as the hardy pioneers in settling this new part of the country. After undergoing much of toil, suffering, and privation in the new settlement—in clearing up and tilling the land—by his industry and economy he had accumulated an amount of property, which, if not a competence, was at least a foundation for acquiring a more generous livelihood in the decline of life, with the prospect of an adequate support for his family.

But, in an evil hour, and at one fell swoop, the enemy of our common country invaded the then peaceful village of Buffalo, bringing death and destruction in their train.

The horrors of that night are easier imagined than expressed. While the good people within the interior of the State were safe from the attacks of an armed force, the frontier settlers were in constant dread. While the former were enriched by the enhanced value of their produce, the latter were ruined by actual invasion.

In a few short years after the memorable destruction of Buffalo, your petitioner was bereft of her husband (with one son surviving) and the necessary means of a comfortable living, which means your petitioner once, in common with her deceased husband, possessed but was deprived by an alien enemy, without any fault of the deceased or your petitioner.

Wherefore, in view of the premises, your petitioner respectfully submits to the consideration of your honorable body by the accompanying evidence of her losses, and respectfully asks of your honorable body relief by granting her an indemnity equal to the losses grievously sustained to be applied for her son and herself in such manner as your honorable body shall be deemed fit and proper under the circumstances of the case.

John Root and Seymour Whitaker testified and gave a value of not less than $2,000. Elisha Foster stated the same value, and testified, in part:

George W. Fox had possession of two grocery stores in which he had dry goods, ware, and merchandise, together with boats, which in number amounted to at least three or four, which were in the service of the United States and used as lighters, there being no harbor at Buffalo to carry freight from the mouth of the Buffalo creek for Perry's fleet, then previous to the destruction of Buffalo. On the 31st of December, 1813, the village was invested with militia and almost every house had more or less of soldiers quartered on the inhabitants of the village.

Sluman Harris said Fox sold dry goods, groceries, provisions, furniture, books and papers, tools, and operated a blacksmith's shop, "which was used by the fleet known as 'Perry's fleet' in loading and reloading the vessels."

As stated by the Committee of Claims on March 27, 1846:

It does not appear from the evidence submitted that the British were justifiable by those laws of war which are recognized by civilized nations in burning or in otherwise destroying the goods, wares, and merchandise of the petitioner. The act was clearly a depredation. Hence, under the laws of 1816 and 18125 redress cannot be had, nor can the committee recommend the claim, in violation of their spirit and true intent. The prayer of the petitioner ought not to be granted.

## Herman B. Potter

As stated by the Committee of Claims on January 23, 1822:

The petitioner claims payment for a dwelling-house valued at $700 and personal effects consisting of furniture, provisions, &c., valued at $423.50, said to have been destroyed by the enemy at Buffalo, on the Niagara frontier and in consequence of a military occupation by the troops of the United States.

John G. Camp, late a deputy quartermaster general, testifies, "That a dwelling-house owned by Herman B. Potter, situated in the village of Buffalo, was occupied by his order by troops in the service of the United States as barracks some time previous to and at the time of its destruction by the enemy on the 30th December, 1813."

Truman Kellogg also states that he commanded a company of militia in the service of the United States and in pursuance of an order from William A. Adams, acting quartermaster and aid to Major General Amos Hall, to quarter himself and company in any of the buildings at Buffalo, he went to the house of the claimant, which having forcibly entered, he occupied with his men till it was destroyed by the enemy. Several other witnesses testify to the value of the house and other property.

Until the last session of Congress, although the law of 1816 is silent on the subject of barracks, the term "military deposite" only being used, an entire occupation by troops—not merely transient—and continued up to the period of the destruction, had been regarded as the cause of it—a conclusion to which the committee had been led in consequence of the term "barracks" having been incidentally used in the explanatory law of 1817, although the latter law was evidently passed with the view of limiting the operation of the former on the subject of buildings. At the last session of Congress, however, the rule originally adopted by the committee on the subject of barracks was reversed in the House.

In the case of the present petitioner there is no pretense of any other military occupation than a very limited one as barracks, and hence the claim cannot properly be allowed.

## Ebenezer Averill

Averill's claim was presented on April 24, 1821. As reported:

> The petitioner claims pay for pasturing between 40 and 50 horses, for three weeks, in a field of his near Buffalo, which was taken possession of by officers in the service of the United States in the Fall of 1812, and occupied by a corps of artillery; and, also, for his fences used for fuel by the United States' troops. This claim has been heretofore presented to Congress, and the Committee of Claims has reported against its allowance in two instances, principally on the ground that the extent of the pasture was not proven, and that the commanding officer did not give any estimate of the probable benefit that the United States received from its occupation, and that it was not proven that the destruction of the fences was required by the necessities of the troops.
>
> At this session additional testimony is obtained, supplying the deficiency that existed heretofore. Col. N. Townsend states that the pasturage was worth, in his estimation, $50, and the fuel $20; that they were necessary, no other having been furnished, and that the acting quartermaster was without funds, or the amount would have been paid at the time.

Averill was paid $70 by the War Department in 1825. Possibly Col. Nathan Townsend. John Townsend was head of the New York militia and there is no record of an N. Townsend in the regular Army for that time period.

## Samuel Tupper

As stated by the Committee of Claims on March 22, 1830, in part:

> This claim is for a barn destroyed by the enemy on the farm of Samuel Tupper near the village of Buffalo on the 30th of December, 1813. It was part of a claim heretofore presented to the Third Auditor under the general law on this subject. An allowance was made to the amount of $3,120, but this item was rejected for want of the requisite proof to show that the occupation of this barn, for military purposes of the United States was by order of an officer thereof.
>
> There is no doubt that the barn was destroyed by the enemy, and that it was occupied as a place of deposit for military or naval stores, or both, at the time of the destruction, and for a considerable time before; and that the value of it which is proved to have been $450, ought to be paid, if it was thus occupied by an order of an officer of the United States. It is proper to remark that there is proof additional to that which was presented to the Third Auditor, and, in order better to understand the following evidence, it is proper to state that one barn has been paid for, and this claim is for another.
>
> John G. Camp, in his affidavit of January 21, 1817, says that he was a Deputy Quartermaster General, "and that he understood, and verily believes that the barn of Samuel on his farm was occupied as a store house for flour purchased and deposited therein by Col. Thomas of the Quartermaster's Department, and that a portion thereof was remaining in the barn at the time of its destruction."

William Baird testified on July 2, 1817, that "he knows that the barn of Samuel Tupper, Esquire, in the village of Buffalo, and on his farm, was occupied in the military service of the United States, and continued to be occupied in such service as a place of deposit for military stores and provisions, until the 30th day of December, 1813, when it was destroyed by the enemy, and the deponent verily believes the same was occupied by express order of Colonel Thomas, then in the service of the United States." David H. Sharp testified at the same time to the same facts.

Percia Tupper was paid $450 in 1832.

James Thomas, of Massachusetts, was commissioned captain in the Light

Dragoons on July 1, 1808, and resigned on November 1, 1811. On September 1, 1812, he came back as a deputy quartermaster general with the rank of major, and on April 13, 1813, was a quartermaster general with the rank of colonel. He was honorably discharged on June 15, 1813.

## Robert Kaine

Robert Kaine filed a claim for boards taken by the troops at Buffalo in 1812 and 1813 for the use of the United States army.

Kaine also filed a petition for certain services rendered during the late war on March 13, 1826, which was reported on unfavorably on December 29, 1829. A second claim for pay as a militia officer, loss of a horse and equipment, and property taken was presented on December 19, 1831, and on December 24, 1834, the Committee of Claims reported unfavorably on that petition.

Col. James Thomas, deputy quartermaster, stated that 7,000 to 8,000 feet of boards were taken for the "convenience and comfort of the soldiers" at Buffalo, but were not paid for at the time. His petition was presented several times, was finally approved on March 31, 1830, and Kaine was paid $187.50.

## Samuel Butler

As reported by the Committee of Claims on January 24, 1831, in part:

> The claim is for a horse, wagon, and harness, which the claimant says he lost while they were in the military service of the United States, at Buffalo, in the State of New York, in the fall of 1813. He states in a deposition that his team consisting of two horses, with his wagon and harness, were attached to the battalion of volunteers commanded by Major Parmenio Adams, and that, when the British crossed the river and landed at Black Rock, he volunteered and went into the ranks to defend Buffalo, and when he was thus engaged, his wagon and harness were burnt, and one horse was taken or killed by the enemy.

The committee needed more information and Third Auditor Peter Hagner responded on February 2, 1832, in part:

> Agreeably to my suggestion, the claimant has been required to designate who paid him for the services of his team, and he has named Captain John G. Camp. The accounts of this officer have now been searched and therewith has been found a voucher for a payment made by him to Samuel Butler for the services of a wagon and team.
>
> According to this voucher, which it will be seen is certified by Major General Amos Hall, the team was employed in transporting the baggage of Lt. Col. Worthy L. Churchill's 164th Regiment of New York Militia, a service different from that described in the deposition of the claimant. The voucher has no other date than that inserted in the receipt for its amount, 10th January, 1814. The whole period of service, however, of the regiment of Lt. Col. Churchill, as well as that of the battalion of Maj. Parmenio Adams, was only 17 days, extending from the 20th December, 1813, to the 5th January, 1815, as evidenced by the rolls for their pay, and this of course included the time occupied in marching from their homes or places of rendezvous and returning. As hire is charged in the voucher for 15 days, it follows that for 4 days at least, the payment was obtained beyond the time of the alleged loss. I do not see in his additional deposition, or in any other of the new testimony, any satisfactory information on this point.
>
> In consequence of his declaration that he volunteered into the ranks, sundry rolls of the militia in service have been turned over to see if they afforded any evidence of service by him, and on those of a small force, part of Major Adams's battalion and commanded by Lt. Joel Wright, the name of Samuel Butler has been found. He, however, appears to have been mustered and paid as a musician for the entire period of service, namely from the 20th December, 1813, to the 5th January, 1814. If he be the same person as the claimant, and from a comparison of signatures I should infer him to be so, it would seem that he must have been in the ranks from the commencement, and hence could not have been the driver of the team he had in service, but must have had one in his employ, and whose fault or negligence would, it is conceived, have exempted the United States from any liability to remunerate

for the loss, under the laws, before alluded to, as fully as any on the part of the claimant himself.

If the claimant is not the person named on those rolls, as the fact of his having volunteered into the ranks on the eve of the attack is the material one on which he predicates his claim, it ought to have been clearly established by an officer of the company in which he served. He has not even declared himself to whose company he was attached, nor has either Joseph Butler or Quartermaster Eliel Barber, and from the silence of the depositions of Major Adams, Captain William Sheldon, and Lt. Gilbert Dickinson, as to his having volunteered at all, it is presumable that they were unable to give any testimony to that effect.

The deposition of Lt. Dickinson mentions the value of the horse only, and which he estimates to have been $80. In the deposition of Joseph Butler, the sum mentioned has been altered from $60 to $90, and in the deposition of Johnson Bedel, of whom the horse is alleged to have been purchased at the latter sum, he has declared, not that the claimant gave him that price for the horse, but that at the time of the sale, in or about July, 1812, he was worth $90. More satisfactory evidence of the value of the property would have been considered necessary by me if the claim had been one on which I had power to act upon.

Samuel Butler was paid $180 for the loss of a wagon, harness, and horse, at Buffalo, in 1835.

Maj. Gen. Amos Hall gave Butler a voucher for $52.50 for 15 days' service at $5.50 per day and Butler signed a receipt, "Received, Williamsville, January 10, 1814, of Captain John G. Camp, assistant deputy quartermaster general, $52.50, in full of above account." On January 27, 1834, The Committee of Claims approved a bill.

Major Parmenio Adams, of Col. Philetus Swift's New York Volunteer Regiment, commanded a detachment of field, staff, and three companies commanded by Captains Daniel Kelsey, Abraham Matteson, and Jairus Crittenden from June 22 to September 30, 1813.

Samuel Butler enlisted as a private in Capt. Isaac W. Stone's company on May 6, 1814. In July he was a drummer in Capt. Kelsey's company.

## Joseph Webb

A claim filed by John B. Webb and others, as stated by the Committee of Claims on February 22, 1843, in part:

The petitioners set forth that their father resided in the village of Black Rock engaged in the business of baking bread and owned and occupied a new frame house filled in with brick, plastered and finished, 35 feet long by 22 feet wide, divided by partitions into suitable apartments, with two large stacks of brick chimneys, having fireplaces in each and worth in cash at least $1,000. He owned at the same time another frame building 30 feet long by 25 feet wide and 25 feet high, which was used as a bakery, well furnished off and was of the value of $700 or thereabouts.

On or about the 30th day of December, 1813, the United States troops, by order of General Hopkins, then in command at Black Rock, took possession of the buildings for the use of the government and continued in possession thereof until about the 30th day of December, when they were burnt and destroyed by the enemy.

Neither Joseph Webb during his lifetime, nor any of his heirs since have received any indemnity or compensation and they verily believe their destruction was owing to their being occupied by the United States troops.

Timothy S. Hopkins, of Amherst, Erie County, State of New York, in his deposition on the 13th of November, 1838, says he was a brigadier general in the militia of the State of New York. In the month of December, 1813, Major General Hull took command of the Niagara frontier and continued until the buildings in Buffalo and Black Rock were burnt and destroyed by the British.

By order of Major General Hull, deponent was stationed at Black Rock and took immediate command of the militia at that post. On or about the 20th day of December, 1813, he gave general orders to the New York militia to enter and occupy all or any of the buildings, public or private, dwellings or otherwise, in Black Rock that should become necessary for barracks or storehouses. From the 20th day of

December, 1813, to the time of said conflagration, a certain bakehouse belonging to Joseph Webb was occupied and used for the purpose of baking bread and supplying the militia with bread.

The aggregate amount of property lost by this devastating war on these frontiers rendered it impossible to be met by the resources of the national Treasury, if the principle upon which such claims rest was admissible. But no government can be expected to indemnify for losses arising to its citizens or subjects from the wanton destruction of private property by its enemy in time of war. Let that principle be once adopted, and it will operate as a premium to your enemies in time of war to avoid attacking your fortifications, armies, or other means of public defense, and steal upon your unprotected cities, towns, and villages, for the purpose of laying them waste, as the most effectual means of crippling the government, and rendering it incapable of performing its legitimate duty to the citizen, and defending the country against foreign invasion and final conquest.

The committee therefore think that the petitioners are not entitled to relief and that the prayer of the petitioners ought not to be granted.

Olivia Jennings, Benjamin Bidwell, and Peter B. Porter testified as to the facts.

## John Wilkinson

A claim presented by David and James Wilkinson for buildings owned by their father and destroyed by the British at Black Rock, as stated by the Committee of Claims on January 2, 1838:

The petitioners ask relief as heirs of John Wilkinson, deceased, for a house, barn, and out-houses destroyed by the British during the late war and situate near the Niagara River in the vicinity of Black Rock in the State of New York.

The petitioners account for this claim not having been earlier made that their father, after the destruction, was reduced to indigence and in the year 1814 removed to the State of Ohio, and not in a condition to prosecute the claim.

The petition is accompanied by the depositions of Conrad House, David W. Hawley, and William Scott, who all testify they were in the service of the United States at the time the property was destroyed, at which time, and for some time previous, the dwelling-house was occupied by American troops under and in obedience to the command of Captain Asa P. Haines, who was an officer in the United States service.

One of the witnesses states that he was one of the American troops quartered in the house when the British destroyed it. The witnesses further state that the house also contained a quantity or arms and military stores belonging to the United States army.

The destruction took place at the time the British crossed over and destroyed Black Rock about the middle of December, 1813.

Timothy S. Hopkins says he was a brigadier general in the service of the United States in 1813 and 1814 and commanded the post at Black Rock. For some time previous to the 1st of January, 1814, he gave general orders to captains and other officers to occupy all buildings from Black Rock down with troops and stores, and he verily believes that all or nearly all the buildings along the river were so occupied.

He further says that about the 13th December, 1813, Captain Haines proceeded down the river from Black Rock with a body of troops in pursuance of his orders. Several witnesses prove that Captain Haines died about 10 or 12 years ago. Some of the witnesses state the value of the dwelling-house to have been \$1,500 and other value it as high as \$2,000.

There is no proof that any part of the premises were occupied by the American troops when destroyed except the dwelling-house.

The committee are of opinion that the requisite proof that the dwelling-house was occupied as a military post under the authority of an officer of the United States, and that the destruction was in consequence of such occupation.

A bill is therefore herewith reported for relief in the sum of \$1,500.

As the result of further investigation by Peter Hagner, the Third Auditor, the claim was rejected on February 21, 1846, for lack of sufficient evidence to show John Wilkinson "was the true proprietor of the house," and that "the delay in presenting the claim is not satisfactorily accounted for."

## Joseph Sills

As reported by the Committee of Claims on January 23, 1822:

> The petitioner claims $1,000, the alleged value of two small dwelling houses, said to have been destroyed by the enemy at the village of Black Rock, on the Niagara frontier, and in consequence of a military occupation, as barracks, by the troops of the United States. John G. Camp, later a deputy quartermaster general, testifies that he has no interest in the claim, and that, by his authority, the buildings in question were occupied as barracks at the time they were destroyed, on the 30th of December, 1813.
>
> General Timothy S. Hopkins testifies that he was in the service at the time the buildings were destroyed, and that they were occupied by his order. Several other witnesses testify to the occupancy, and the value of the buildings, but all are silent as to the extent of the time they were occupied. It is believed, however, that from the history of the transaction, which will be found in the report referred to in the case of Herman B. Potter, that the occupation was a very limited one, and that the case does not differ in anything mentioned from the case above mentioned.
>
> The prayer of the petitioner ought not to be granted.

## James Beard

A claim filed by Harriet Beard, as reported by the Committee of Claims on April 4, 1840:

> The petitioner states that she is the widow of James Beard, who died in October, 1823. In the summer of 1812 they resided at Black Rock in the State of New York on the Niagara River where they owned and possessed a large farm. In the autumn of that year the crops—including the fences used as fuel and destroyed by the American troops under the command of General Smythe—were worth from $400 to $500.
>
> The army passed over the premises and part of them encamped thereon, and turned the horses, about 500 in number into the growing crops and entirely destroyed them.
>
> The claim of her husband for property destroyed by the enemy was presented to the commissioner of claims who was sent out by the government for that purpose, was ascertained by him to the amount of $888 and so reported to the government, but this amount did not include the property in question, but embraced other personal property taken and destroyed by the enemy at the time they invaded that country. But even that sum was never paid for the reason that it was personal property which had been taken or discharged, and the government has adopted the principle that personal property thus situated should not be paid for. After this decision, no further efforts were made for the indemnity until about 1837 when she was advised by a friend that remuneration might be obtained.
>
> The principle allegations are confirmed by the testimony of David Wilkinson, taken in 1837. The army consisted of about 3,000 or 4,000 troops, and about one-half encamped on Mr. Beard's farm and, Mr. Wilkinson says, were destitute of provisions. The army was commanded by Major General Alexander Smythe.
>
> The committee apprehend that this claim cannot be allowed until it shall appear, by the certificate of the officer in command that the occupation was by his command, that it was necessary for the public service, that the property was ordered to be taken by him, the necessity for it, and the value estimated at the time for which was alleged to have been destroyed by the troops. The Government does not hold itself responsible, never having adopted the act of the wrong doer, but leaves the aggrieved party to his remedy at law against the aggressor.
>
> With these views, the committee recommend that the prayer of the petitioner ought not to be allowed.

Alexander Smyth was an Irish-born Virginia lawyer and politician, for whom Smyth County was named. He was commissioned a colonel on July 8, 1808, in the Rifle Corps. On July 6, 1812, he was promoted to brigadier general as Inspector General.

In October 1812, at the loss at Queenston Heights, he found himself in the awkward position of being subordinate to Gen. Stephen Van Rensselaer, an inexperienced militia officer, whom he was ordered to replace.

On November 17 he proclaimed publicly his intention to invade Upper Canada, which naturally alerted the British, and, after failing at Frenchman's Creek, the invasion plan was put on hold.

He was then insulted by Gen. Peter B. Porter, who he challenged to a duel in December. Both fired once ineffectively and a parley was called. Porter attributed his comment to "irritation" and Smyth said he knew nothing of a derogatory nature about Porter. The matter was settled with a handshake, but on March 3, 1813, Smyth was "legislated out" of the service and went back to his law practice.

## Jasper Parish

Jasper Parish and his father were captured by Indians and Jasper grew up learning their language, later becoming an interpreter and Indian Agent residing in Canandaigua, New York.

As reported by the Committee of Claims on December 3, 1816:

> It is reported to the committee that the American army under command of Brigadier General Smyth, in the month of November, 1812, encamped on the farm of the petitioner, situate on the banks of the Niagara River. The weather being inclement, the soldiers made use of the fences, which were in good order and valuable, for fuel; and took out the bricks of a good dwelling-house for the purpose of making an oven with them. Besides the injury thus directly sustained, the petitioner states that he suffered materially from being unable to cultivate the ground, of which a large portion had been in a state of cultivation. For these injuries the petitioner asks Congress to reimburse him in the sum of $746.50.
>
> It appears to the committee that the injury complained of was the result of unauthorized acts on the part of the soldiery. Claims of the sort have often been before Congress, and have as often been rejected; no principle appears to be better settled. The reports of the Committee of Claims and the decisions of the House furnish abundant proof of that fact. A departure from the principle now would undo what has been done; would unsettle what was thought to be established. The consequences of such reversal will be readily perceived by the House. It is recommended that the prayer of the petitioner ought not to be granted.

Parish's claim was rejected again on February 11, 1824. As reported by the Committee of Claims on February 5, 1830:

> The claim of the petitioner is as follows: 342 rods of fence, at $1.25—$427; one log house, $130; loss of improving 21 acres at $4.50 per acre in 1813 and 1814—$189. Total $746.
>
> On the night of the 29th of November, 1812, the army under the command of Brigadier General Alexander Smyth, encamped on a farm of the petitioner's at the mouth of Conjockety creek, below Black Rock, with an intention of making a descent into Canada. The night was cold with a heavy fall of rain, freezing with snow, and that the rails were taken from the fences and consumed by the soldiers. General Smyth states that the weather was such as to render fires necessary. Although no orders were given to burn the fences, yet he credits the statement that they were burned.
>
> James Thomas, Deputy Quartermaster General, states that the troops suffered much from the inclemency of the weather and that to his knowledge they availed themselves of the rail fences in the vicinity of the encampment and burnt them in considerable quantities, which he then understood belonged to Jasper Parish.
>
> John G. Camp, then acting as Quartermaster to the 12th and 20th Regiments, testifies that the weather was very inclement, and extremely cold, that there was a scarcity of axes, and that it was absolutely necessary the soldiers should have taken such materials as would secure them against the inclemency of the weather. They did make use of the rails on the farm on which they were encamped, for fuel, and also burned a log house for that purpose. He says the farm belonged to Jasper Parish, and previous to that time was well fenced.
>
> Other witnesses speak of the destruction of the fences. Oliver Forward, Heman B. Potter, and Cyrenius Chapin, appraised the damages. The petitioner states the claim was presented

to the Commissioner of Claims under the act of April 9th, 1816, and allowed, but the Commissioner being arrested in the execution of the act, the money was not obtained.

It appears that the papers were delivered to him in the House of Representatives in 1820 and were mislaid. It appears that copies were retained and it is within the knowledge of one member of the committee that these were mislaid for two or three years by Mr. Dudley Marvin, formerly a member of this House.

A report was made adverse to an allowance in 1824. It was then considered requisite that the commanding officer should certify the articles were taken by his order. This rule has been relaxed since that period in a great variety of cases presented from Detroit and New Orleans. Officers were generally unwilling to expose themselves to the liability of being harassed by the institution of suits, and although they gave no positive orders to commit depredations like the present, still they knew they were committed, and did not express their dissent. The committee do not, in the least, recognize the doctrine that the United States are liable for all the trespass their troops may commit, the rule is understood to be, that when the United States fail to furnish the articles they are bound to provide, being absolutely necessary at the time for the sustenance or comfort of the troops and they take such articles from a citizen, the United States are bound to make payment to the injured person.

The petitioner states that the soldiers took the brick from the chimneys for the purpose of building ovens and then burnt the house. Mr. Thomas says nothing about the destruction of the house.

The committee do not perceive that it was necessary to destroy the house. In the inclement weather spoken of, the soldiers would have been more comfortable in the house than they could have been by its destruction. It was one of those wanton acts in which, in the opinion of the committee, the authority of the officer should have been interposed, if the meditated destruction was known to him, and if not the United States cannot be liable when the destruction of the house was unnecessary.

Damages have not been paid beyond the value of the articles taken. The committee do not think the petitioner should be compensated for a supposed loss of crops in 1813 and 1814 in consequence of his fences having been destroyed in 1812. The committee report a bill for the value of the fences destroyed, and reject the residue of the claim.

Jasper Parish was paid $427.50 in 1830.

## *The Niagara Sufferers*

As stated by the Committee on the Petition of the Niagara Sufferers on January 25, 1822, with respect to the petition of "Elias Ransom, and other inhabitants of the Niagara frontier, sufferers of the depredations of the enemy during the late war," in part:

> It is well known to the citizens of this state, that the losses sustained by the inhabitants of the Niagara frontier, in consequence of the depredations of the enemy, and the burning of the village of Buffalo, were very great, and that they are still suffering under the effects of these calamities, the circumstance of the times having been such as to impede and frustrate every effort to recover from their difficulties.
>
> In April, 1816, Congress passed a general law, making provision, "for the payment for property lost, captured, or destroyed by the enemy, while in the military service of the United States." Under this act, large compensations were made to many persons similarly situated with the present petitioners; and commissioners were appointed by a resolution of Congress to investigate the claims on the Niagara frontier. They made a very minute and patient examination of the subject, upon the spot where the principal losses took place, requiring legal testimony to support every charge, and reported thereon, fully and in detail, to the proper officers of the United States. The total amount certified by them to have been destroyed, at the valuation, appearing in evidence before them was $423,335.
>
> Unfortunately for the petitioners, attempts were made in various parts of the union, to obtain the allowance of numerous false or exaggerated claims, in consequence of which the whole swelled to so large an amount, that the president was induced to direct a suspension of the payments until further order.

The petitioners were therefore again obliged to repeat their applications to Congress, but from the financial difficulties which then embarrassed the national government, the pressure of other business, the competition of local interests, and other similar causes, the relief solicited has been hitherto postponed from year to year.

In the meantime, from the urgent necessity of their circumstances, the petitioners were compelled to resort to loans in order to raise the immediate means for the erection of dwelling houses, and the carrying on the several kinds of business, upon which they depend for their support and that of their families. For this purpose, the sum of $50,000 was obtained from the state on loan, as well as considerable sums by different individuals from the Bank of Niagara, which has since stopped payment, and is now indebted to the state to a large amount.

All this afforded but a temporary relief, and difficulties and embarrassments of all sorts have thickened upon them, and weighed them down. Though they are still confident in the equity of their claim upon the nation, as supported by the great principles and the reciprocal duties of allegiance and protection, by the authority of all civilized usage, by the obvious dictates of sound and enlightened public policy, all strengthened by the peculiar hardships of their particular case, yet hopeless of any immediate relief, they now, as their last resort, appeal to the magnamity of their own state, for that aid which the nation has hitherto refused.

The relief which they now solicit is not the full payment of all their losses, but merely a grant to the sufferers, of the debts due to the state by the Bank of Niagara, and a release or assignment for their general benefit, of the debt due by them to the state, under the loan of 1815, and secured by mortgage upon their lands.

These funds, there is great reason to believe, are now nearly lost to the state, or at best could not be realized but by the entire sacrifice of the property of the debtors, and the ruin of that part of the country. Thus the state, by making this grant, could hardly be a loser; while as the loans were originally advanced and would now be released for the benefit of all the sufferers, the state of New York would entitle itself to all their rights, and might urge its own claims in conjunction with those of the petitioners, with more decisive influence than could be done by the remonstrance or prayers of private citizens.

The committee, after much investigation of the subject, have agreed to report a bill in conformity with the prayer of the petitioners.

The following statement, founded upon information given by the Comptroller, will show their nominal amount of the funds proposed to be appropriated in compensation of the losses to the sufferers; by granting which, the state will entitle itself to a just claim upon the United States, to an equal value.

It was found the amount due for principal loans made out of the Treasury as of February 27, 1821, was $49,294.98 and adding interest and the bond of the Bank of Niagara and other charges the total came to $78,031.43.

The Act of January 29, 1822, outlined all the conditions and procedures and a report on February 14, 1822, listed the names of the borrowers, the amount of the loan, and the original loss, as shown:

Mary Atkins, $1,500; Moses Atwater, $1,000; William Baird, $1,330; Asaph S. Bemis, $400; Benjamin Caryl, $1,350; Benjamin Caryl & Lucius Storrs, merchants, $6,200; William Chapman, $350; Lemuel Cooke, $1,119.89; Amos Callender, $625; Henry M. & James Campbell, $2,256; James Chapin, $800–$1,000; Luke Draper (by Nathan Dudley), $700; Martin Daley, $2,000; Ira Dickinson, $1,352.06; John Desparr, $1,187.62; Jonathan S. Dodge, unknown; Samuel Edsell, $750; Elijah Ensign, $1,000; James Field, $650; Stephen Franklin, $1,250; Oliver Forward, $2,050; Gilman Folsom, $4,750; Vincent Grant, $500; Agnes Greensitt, $1,000; Joshua Gillet, $5,352.53; Jabez Goodell, $1,400; John Haddock, $3,375; Jonas Harrison, unknown; Reuben B. Heacock and Abel M. Grosvenor, merchants, $7,350; William Hodge, $3,000; Joseph D. Hoyt, $1,668; Ebenezer Johnson, $2,211.50; Robert Kaene, 1,625; Henry Ketcham, $1,275; Joseph Landon, grocer, $4,208; William Miller, $4,200; Herman B. Potter, $645.39;

Peter B. Porter, $450; Samuel Pratt, $1,690; Elias Ransom, $4,650; Davis Rees, $750; John Root, et al, $1,050 (assigned to Gaius Kibbe); Margaret St. John, $3,500; Nathaniel Sill, $2,250: Hez A. & Smith H. Salisbury, merchants, $1,937; John R. Smith, $875; Rufus Spalding, $1,000.25; Asa Stanard, $900 (assigned to Chauncy R. Sharp); Oziel Smith, $2,200; Juba Storrs, $500; Lucius Storrs, $300; Charles Townsend & George Coit, $2,500; Jacob Townsend, Sheldon Thompson, & Alvin Bronson, $1,570; Ira Tracy, $609.95 (but much greater); Samuel Tupper, unknown; Joseph Wells, $600; Ebenezer Walden, $4,176.41.

## *Fort Schlosser*

### Jacob B. Gilbert

As reported by the Committee of Claims on February 24, 1835, in part:

> The petitioner claims payment for a house and stable which were destroyed by the enemy on the Niagara frontier during the late war with Great Britain, and also for personal property which was in the buildings.
>
> Benajah Mallory, late major in the service of the United States, has given three depositions on this subject.
>
> In the first deposition dated the 25th of December, 1817, he states, "In December, 1813, I was appointed commanding officer at Fort Schlosser, on the Niagara frontier; and about the middle of the same month, I occupied the house of Jacob B. Gilbert, by placing a guard at Gilbert's house, and deposited public property therein. The house was a log house, and stood situated a short distance above the fort on the Niagara River."
>
> In his second deposition, which is dated the 6th of August, 1830, he states, "This deponent removed the public property about five miles further up the Niagara river, and deposited the same in the house and barn of Jacob B. Gilbert, residing in that place, which consisted of clothing, provisions, and a quantity of arms and military stores.' The house and stable of Jacob B. Gilbert were burnt by the British troops, then still having some part of the arms and munitions of war remaining in the buildings."
>
> He also states that a yoke of oxen belonging to Gilbert was impressed by the officers of the United States to convey the property, and remained in service from December, 1813, till the next fall.
>
> In his third deposition, which is dated the 25th of August, 1832, he states that, "I stored, as near as I now recollect, about 100 stand of arms and about 100 pounds weight of fixed ammunition at the house of Jacob B. Gilbert. The arms and ammunition remained in the house. The British found the property and burnt the same, together with his barn and some other buildings belonging to him."
>
> George Burgan, George Rogers, and Samuel Tiscom prove that the house and barn were destroyed by the enemy. The house was worth $600 and the stable $25. Burgan states that he was in the house about ten days before its destruction and saw muskets and other equipments.
>
> Asa Fuller proves the destruction of the house and says it was worth $800 and the stable $50.
>
> The evidence establishes the fact that arms and military stores were deposited in the house of the claimant by order of the commanding officer and that they remained there at the time of its destruction. On this proof the committee feel warranted in allowing the claimant $600, and for that sum report a bill.
>
> The personal property cannot be allowed, nor can any allowance be made for the yoke of oxen that was pressed into the service, as, for anything that appears, the claimant may have been paid for this at the time. The claim for the stable is also rejected.

Jacob B. Gilbert was paid $600 in 1836.

Fort Schlosser with four cannons was built by the British around 1760 at present-day Niagara Falls, New York, and named after Capt. Joseph Schlosser, a commander in the Royal American Regiment of Foot. It was occupied by American forces in 1812 and attacked on July 5, 1813. A historical marker located at the intersection of Niagara Parkway and Mackem St. near Chippewa, Ontario, states:

> At daybreak on July 5, 1813, a British and Canadian force consisting of some 35 militia

> and a small detachment of the 49th Regiment embarked in this vicinity to attack Fort Schlosser. This American depot (now within Niagara Falls, New York) was situated at the southern terminus of the Lewiston Portage and was an important military trans-shipment point. The attacking force, commanded by Lieut.-Col. Thomas Clark of the 2nd Regiment, Lincoln Militia, surprised the U.S. garrison and encountered little resistance. They captured a gunboat, two bateaux, a brass cannon and a substantial of small arms and supplies. While re-embarking, they were attacked by local American militia, but suffered no casualties.

The site is now a park, but nothing is left of the original fort.

Benajah Mallory was closely associated with Joseph Willcocks in Canadian politics and might have commanded a detachment of volunteers in Lt. Col. Willcocks' Canadian Cavalry Regiment of New York Militia.

Irishman Joseph Willcocks immigrated to Upper Canada, became a sheriff, and was elected to Parliament in 1807. He subsequently became embroiled in political disputes over land grants and was relieved of his duties. He then published a newspaper criticizing the government and sold out in 1812. In 1813 he enlisted Canadian volunteers in the service of the United States.

He was fatally wounded at Fort Erie on September 11, 1814, along with Lt. Thomas W. Roosevelt the same day.

## *Fort George*

Fort George, at present-day Niagara-on-the-Lake, Ontario, was built during 1796–1799 by the British. The fort was captured by American forces on May 27, 1813, and refortified, but abandoned after a British attack on December 19. In retiring across the river to Fort Niagara, the Americans burned the town, leaving the residents destitute in the middle of winter. This action was soundly condemned in Canada and at home by Americans. The British and Canadians eventually captured Fort Niagara and secured their territory.

The very impressive Fort George National Historic Site was restored by the Niagara Parks Commission as a reproduction of the actual fort with historic buildings, cannons, living history exhibits, and the original powder magazine, the only building to survive the American bombardment from Fort Niagara across the river in May 1813.

### John Bronson

As reported by the Committee of Claims on January 8, 1834:

> The petitioner claims of the United States the sum of $2,915.18, the value of a store of goods, which John Smith, his witness, says was destroyed in December, 1813, in consequence of his team being impressed by Colonel Samuel Hopkins in the service of the United States. A bill of goods, whose gross amount is the sum mentioned is made out and not signed.
>
> John Smith testifies he was at Fort George in December, 1813, when that place was in possession of the United States troops, and that, to his knowledge, whilst he was at Fort George, John Bronson sent a young man with a store of goods to the place some time previous, of the name of Hall, who attended the store as clerk, who received instructions from Bronson to remove the goods to Buffalo in the month of December. He assisted in packing and loading the goods, and whilst on their route, leaving Fort George, in Canada, after they crossed to the American shore, Colonel Hopkins, in the United States service, pressed the wagon, by which means the goods fell into the hands of the enemy, which were estimated by him and Hall at the time to be worth $2,900 or $3,000, and the boxes containing them were left on the road because they could not obtain conveyance.
>
> John Hammond testifies he was a wagoner in December, 1813, at which time a man of the name of John Smith was hired in the employ of John Bronson, who waited, and

often attended upon him when he was storing United States property in the premises of Bronson, which was afterwards burned by the enemy. He considered Smith to be a trusty and faithful man in whom Bronson appeared to place much confidence.

It will be seen by this testimony that no dates are mentioned, except the month of December, 1813, and were it a case for which relief could be recommended, the committee would require the testimony of the officer making the impressment, if alive, or, if not, of some other officer knowing to the fact of impressment, and who should be able to give dates and a narrative devoid of contradiction, and whose testimony should lay a foundation for the inference he might draw. As far as the circumstances in this case are disclosed, they do not come within any principle heretofore established by Congress. The committee recommend that the claim ought not to be allowed.

### George Ash

As reported by the Committee of Claims on January 2, 1839:

> The property destroyed by the British troops at the time they invaded the Niagara frontier in December, 1813, which belonged to the petitioner, was a dwelling-house occupied as a private residence, and its contents, consisting of various articles of household furniture and other personal property, which is enumerated in the petition.
>
> The house was not occupied as a military depot, nor as barracks for the military forces of the United States, nor in any other manner, by the order of an officer or agent of the United States. The personal property was either destroyed or carried away by the British soldiers and none of it was applied to the use of the American troops or the United States. It was the individual property of a private citizen and was not liable to the imputation of having been subjected to military use or occupation.
>
> Under such circumstances, its destruction was a wanton act of aggression on the part of the invading army, condemned by the usages of modern warfare, and in violation of the law of nations, as now expounded by the governments of all civilized countries. Under such circumstances, the loss must be borne by him on whom it happens to fall, unless he can compel indemnity from the aggressors. Hitherto, the government has never held itself bound to render indemnity for such losses, and with a view to uniformity in legislation, and to render equal justice to all, the committee have come to the conclusion that no remuneration should be granted in this case.

## *Newfane*

Newfane is a village on Eighteen Mile Creek (18 miles east of the Niagara River) on the south shore of Lake Ontario. The town of Olcott is at the mouth and Newfane is due south a little over 2 miles inland up the creek.

### James Van Horn

James Van Horn's claim was first entertained on February 18, 1818, after he had removed to Porter in Niagara County, New York. It was rejected and not pursued until much later for unknown reasons, but usually the financial embarrassment of the petitioner in old age. On January 4, 1854, he submitted another petition to Congress, as he stated:

> Your petitioner would represent that at the commencement of the war of 1812, and until the 25th day of December, 1813, he was the owner of a saw-mill and grist-mill, situated on the Eighteen Mile Creek, 2 miles south from Lake Ontario, and 18 miles east from Fort Niagara. The grist-mill was 30 feet square or more, besides a water or wheel-house, calculated for two runs of stones, with one run in operation, in every other respect finished for making flour, and worth at that time over $3,000. There was in the mill, on the 25th day of December, a quantity of wheat and flour, worth $1,000, and on the premises an unfinished hewed-timber house, 20 feet by 30 made of squared oak timber, two stories high, and a quantity of boards in the same to finish it with, worth $200.
>
> On the 24th day of December, 1813, a party of British soldiers from Fort Niagara, then

> in possession of the British, were dispatched down the lake to burn and destroy the tenements of the inhabitants and the mills of your petitioner. The party did proceed down the lake to the Eighteen-Mile Creek, burning and destroying the tenements of the inhabitants and the grist-mill, with the flour and wheat therein, and the block or timber-house of your petitioner, at the same time setting on fire the saw-mill, which was not burned, having, after the party left, been put out by Mr. Joseph Pease, who arrived on the spot soon after the party had left.
>
> You petitioner has not received any compensation from the government.

Reuben Wilson, of Wilson, New York, was called to testify and he stated that he lived in Porter at the time when the British came to his house and took him prisoner. The next day he and several others were marched to Fort Niagara where they were confined for one week, and he heard the Van Horn property had been destroyed.

Enoch Pease, son of Joseph Pease, stated he was "taken prisoner at the mouth of the Creek, and kept until a party went up and burned the mill" of Van Horn, after which he was released. He and his father went up and found the grist-mill burned and his father put out the fire at the sawmill.

Luther Wilson, also of Wilson, stated he was at the mill, "when on fire, just after the roof fell in, and saw a quantity of wheat burning in the mill—he supposes about 500 bushels." He said the British, who numbered 54, stayed at the home of one of the Kemps the night before they burned the mills.

On July 22, 1854, the Committee of Claims rejected the claim again.

## *Oswego*

The Oswego River flows into the south shore of Lake Ontario as the watershed for approximately one-fifth of the State of New York. The Indian traders in the area dealt in glass beads, axe heads, muskets, furs, wool blankets, and rum—generally used to get better deals. In 1722 a group of traders from Albany established a post on the west side of the river.

In 1727, in response to the construction of Fort Niagara by the French, William Burnet, governor of the Province of New York, ordered a fort built near the trader's post. In 1741, work began to reinforce the fort and, although poorly located and constructed, Fort Oswego remained England's primary fortification in the Great Lakes area for many years.

During the French and Indian War, Maj. Gen. William Shirley, governor of Massachusetts Bay, went to Fort Oswego to assist Maj. Gen. Edward Braddock in taking Fort Niagara. Braddock was expected to capture Fort Duquesne, but was defeated at Monongahela. Shirley then began improving the fort and renamed it Fort Pepperell, but it soon became known as Fort Ontario.

By 1810, although still in poor condition and lightly armed, Fort Ontario was intended to protect the supply route to Sackets Harbor, around 40 miles north.

In June 1813, Maj.-Gen. Sir George Prévost and Comm. Sir James Lucas Yeo attacked the post but were repulsed. The frigate *Montreal* was set on fire three times by hot shot and Capt. Stephen Popham received a severe wound to his right hand. Capt. Francis Spilsbury commanded the *Niagara*.

George Mitchell, of Maryland, was appointed major in the 3rd Artillery on May 1, 1812, and commanded the fort. He was brevetted colonel and cited for gallantry in repelling the attack.

On May 5–6, 1814, with a considerably stronger force, Lt.-Gen. Sir George Drummond and Comm. Yeo's forces seized and destroyed the fort. On May 12, Mitchell was transferred to the Artillery Corps.

The Fort Ontario State Historic Site at

1 East Fourth St., Oswego, New York, features the fourth reconstruction of the fort up to 1872 with living history exhibits, a picnic area, and guided tours.

## Nathaniel Jones

As reported by the Committee of Claims on February 13, 1824:

> The petitioner states that a boat belonging to him was taken into the service of the United States during the late war with Great Britain. While so employed in the summer of 1813 on Lake Ontario it was captured by the enemy together with its contents.
>
> The petitioner has produced the testimony of Colonel Jonas Cutting. He states that in the summer of 1813, he was in command of a detachment of troops of about 400 strong; that he was under orders to move them by way of Oswego to Niagara. On his arrival at Oswego, some of the bateaux provided by the Quartermaster proved leaky. He was under the necessity of unloading them, and Nathaniel Jones's keel boat was lying near the falls near Oswego. He informed Jones that he was under the necessity of having his boat go to Niagara. He said Jones concluded, after some hesitation, to go with his boat, and, accordingly, Capt. Collins's company of artillery were embarked on board and carried by Jones to Niagara, and there landed.
>
> Other testimony corroborates the above fact, and, furthermore, that the next day the boat was captured by the enemy on its return to Oswego.
>
> The Committee consider the case of the petitioner as coming within the 3rd section of the act of 1816, authorizing payment for property lost, captured, or destroyed by the enemy, while in the military service of the United States, and, therefore, report a bill for his relief.

Nathaniel Jones was paid $550 in 1824. Jonas Cutting, of Massachusetts, was appointed lieutenant colonel in the 25th Regiment of Infantry on March 12, 1812, and resigned on September 1, 1814. Stephen Collins was appointed captain in the 3rd Artillery on January 13, 1813, and honorably discharged on June 1, 1814.

## Elias Parks

As stated by the Committee of Claims on December 17, 1818:

> The petitioner alleges that he resided in the village of Oswego in the year 1814 and was engaged in mercantile business and was possessed of various goods, wares, and merchandise. On the 5th of May, in the year aforesaid, that being alarmed at the approach of the British to attack the adjacent fort and village, he procured a boat commanded by Captain Clark Warren to remove his goods to a place of safety up the Oswego River.
>
> The goods were put on board the boat and were about to proceed up the river when James T.B. Romayne, of the 3rd United States Artillery, interfered and forbid the boat from proceeding or leaving the harbor. Captain Warren having remonstrated against the detention, Capt. Romayne declared such were his orders from Lt. Col. George E. Mitchell, the commanding officer of the post, and if Capt. Warren did not comply, he would enforce the order by military guard.
>
> Capt. Warren, in pursuance of orders, proceeded to the eastern shore, discharged his cargo, and reported himself and boat to an officer stationed there. The goods were landed and two men left to watch over them. Shortly after this, the British attacked and carried the fort, took the goods, and wholly destroyed and carried them off. This loss the petitioner alleges happened to him in consequence of the orders and interference of Capt. Romayne.
>
> The petitioner further represents that he had sundry goods remaining in his store, besides those which had been put on board the boat, all of which the enemy took and destroyed or carried away. The petitioner asks such compensation as Congress think proper to grant.
>
> The committee think the petitioner cannot be entitled to any relief till satisfactory evidence be produced as to the two following points:
>
> 1st. The amount of goods on board the boat should be as distinctly ascertained as the nature of the case would admit;
>
> 2nd. It should be shown that these goods would have been transported to a place of safety had it not been for the interference and orders of Capt. Romayne.

Neither of these points is established to the satisfaction of the committee: they therefore recommend that the prayer of the petitioner should not be granted.

Congress chose to pay Parks $2,284 in 1822.

## Tuttle & Baker

As reported by the Committee of Claims on January 27, 1834:

The petitioner, William Baker, asks Congress to remunerate him for the loss of a quantity of butter, cheese, dried beef, and hams, which he says were captured by the enemy at Oswego during the last war which belonged to him and his partner and the value of which he claims as survivor, because he says the boat on which they were, was pressed into the service of the United States.

Dennis Tuttle states he was the clerk of the firm of Tuttle & Baker, and in the spring of 1814 he was sent to Oswego River on the lake, with a quantity of goods in a small sail boat, commanded, as he believes by Captain Ward; that the boat arrived at Oswego in the evening and at daybreak the next morning the British fleet was in sight of the harbor, and took possession of the place and fort the following day; and while endeavoring to get the boat containing the goods up the rapids, a short distance from the mouth of the river, the boat was stopped by a United States officer and unloaded at the foot of the rapids and given up. The deponent says he did all that he could to secure the goods, which were afterwards taken by the enemy. He cannot state the amount, but they were worth from $400 to $700, and he believes if the boat had not been taken, the goods would have been saved. He afterwards saw the goods in the possession of the British.

If it was a case where, according to the principles that have governed Congress, relief could be granted, the committee would require the statement to be proven with more certainty than it is by this deposition. The deponent does not mention the day nor the time when the boat was taken by the United States officer, nor what exertions he used to secure the goods after the boat was taken, nor on what his belief is founded that the goods would have been saved if the boat had not been taken, nor where he was when the goods were taken; and the inference is, from the deposition, that he was not in possession of the goods when they were captured.

Matthew McNair says he knows the United States officers pressed into the service several boats of the citizens in the spring of 1814, saying they should want them if they were obliged to retreat.

Peter D. Hugunin says he was knowing to several boats being taken into the service of the United States in the spring of 1814, when the British landed there, because they might be wanted in case of retreat. He recollects the enemy plundered the village considerably, but he does not recollect any individual losses.

The petitioner says he has not presented his claim before, because he did not know until lately that the United States paid for similar losses.

The committee are not aware that any such losses have been remunerated, but they know of many cases which have been rejected under the like circumstances. In the case of Mr. Gilbert, he provided himself with the means of removing his goods by procuring teams in three instances; and twice they were obtained at a distance from the camp, and beyond where the officers of the United States had attempted to obtain them. Congress granted relief in that case from its peculiar circumstances.

One of this committee, Mr. Rufus McIntire, was an officer in the United States army and at Oswego at the time mentioned in the petition. He is confident the deponents who have testified in the case are under a mistake as to the impressment of boats for the purpose of securing a retreat or any other purpose. They needed no boats to aid a retreat because that was up and not across the river. On the second day of the enemy's attack, and that on which he effected a landing, a part of the regular troops were stationed at the ferry on the east side of the river to be ready to cross over and meet the enemy, in case he should attempt to land on the village side of the river. The member of this committee referred to commanded the troops stationed at the ferry and is certain he nor any officer to his knowledge pressed any boat for the purpose of crossing. He recollects of but one boat, a large flat or scow, used at the ferry for crossing.

There might have been one smaller boat, but there was no other than what was ordinarily used, and appeared to belong to the ferry.

Captain Romaine was not the quartermaster, upon whom the duty would devolve to procure the means of crossing if any extra means were necessary. Captain Romaine was with the militia on the village side pitching tents, and making a show of force there, but his company was on the other side. There did not appear to be any lack of boats for crossing our small force, nor, so far as he recollects, was there any necessity to impress for that purpose a boat under the circumstances which the petitioner represents his to have been.

On the first day the enemy appeared before Oswego and cannonaded the fort, Colonel Mitchell, the commanding officer, dispatched this member privately to the village to advise the inhabitants to remove their property to a place of safety, and more especially a large quantity of salt that appeared much exposed; but the inhabitants did not seem inclined to take this advice. It was the wish of Colonel Mitchell for the inhabitants and others having property there, to remove it to a place of safety without creating any unnecessary alarm or manifesting any panic that might affect the minds of the troops under his command, by weakening their confidence in their ability to maintain the post. Hence, his message to them privately and in a form of advice.

The committee do not think the petitioner is entitled to relief.

Capt. James T.B. Romayne, of New York, was assigned to the 3rd Artillery on July 2, 1812, and transferred to the Corps of Artillery on May 12, 1814. Benjamin Romayne, of New York, was made a major in the Quartermaster Department on February 28, 1814.

## Elisha Ives

Elisha Ives, of New York, contracted with Capt. Melancthon T. Woolsey and lost his boat on Lake Ontario. He presented his petition on January 24, 1820, and on February 11, the Committee of Claims denied it. Further discussion ensued and in 1831 Ives was paid $1,200, as reported by the Committee of Claims on February 1, 1830:

It is satisfactorily proven to the committee by the testimony of Captain Melancthon Woolsey that during the late war, while he was in command at Oswego Falls, he employed a boat having a slip keel and schooner rigged to transport, in the month of May, 1814, ammunition and military stores from Oswego, in the State of New York, to Sackett's Harbor. The boat was entirely new, was owned by Elisha Ives, and that when Woolsey employed the boat, it appears the owner was unwilling to run the risk himself, and was told by Captain Woolsey he had no doubt, if she was captured that the United States would pay for her. He says he thinks this declaration had an influence on Mr. Ives' mind in embarking in the business. Ives went on board the boat as master and Midshipman Eaton as supercargo, and she proceeded to Sackett's Harbor with a load of military stores and, on return to Oswego for another load, was captured by the enemy off Stony Point without the fault of the owner and master. He says that there was no stipulation between him and Mr. Ives about the freight of the boat, and that he thinks she was probably worth $1,500.

Midshipman Eaton testifies to the capture of the boat. Nathan Johnson, John Byers, Midshipman Eaton, and William Vaughan, sailing-master, and one of the persons designated by the Commissioner to take depositions under the act of the 9th of April, 1816, say they were well acquainted with the boat, and that she was well worth $2,000. They describe her as being that kind of craft used in navigating Lake Ontario, and in descending the St. Lawrence to Montreal, called Durham boats.

This claim was presented to the Commissioner of Claims under the act of April 9, 1816, but it is not perceived that any decision was mad by him. It is known that he rejected several applications for similar losses because the craft was not what was intended by the term "boat" as used in the law. Congress, however, has put a different construction on the act and has granted relief in several cases he rejected on that account.

In this case no compensation was agreed on, and the idea is thereby excluded that the owner was to have a compensation commensurate with the risk incurred; for if his boat had not been captured, he would have been entitled to no greater compensation than his

> own and the services of his boat were reasonably worth, had no danger of capture been apprehended.

Elisha Ives was paid $1,500 in 1830. There is no record of a Midshipman Eaton in 1814, but Samuel A. Eakin was commissioned midshipman on June 18, 1812, made lieutenant in 1818, and died on October 30, 1822.

## Matthew McNair and Samuel Ward

Lt. Col. George E Mitchell ordered James Adams to seize a schooner and a smaller boat, "for the defense of Oswego, on Lake Ontario, in the State of New York" from attacks on May 5 and 6, 1814. The smaller craft belonged to Matthew McNair and the 18-ton schooner to Samuel Ward. Both vessels were captured by the British.

McNair sued James Adams for trespass based apparently on the fact that Col. Mitchell failed to issue a written order to Adams to seize the property, and Adams couldn't locate Col. Mitchell to obtain evidence in his defense. In August 1816, McNair was awarded $605.57 in damages. Adams didn't have the money so McNair ordered an execution of the judgment and the sheriff seized Adams' "goods and chattels, lands and tenements, the sole property of James Adams." The real property seized was Lot No. 72 in Hannibal, New York, which sold for $365 on an appraised value of $1,920.

Samuel Ward sued for his boat, which was appraised at $1,500, and recovered a judgment on January, 25, 1817, which Adams paid.

Four days later, on January 29, 1817, James Adams filed a claim for $2,185.56 to recover all the costs of defending the lawsuits, which he was awarded on March 25, 1817.

In January 1834, he filed another claim for $3,495.30 his legal costs, his lot in Hannibal, and included $1,764.95 in interest at 6 percent for 17 years. The Committee of Claims rejected it.

Matthew McNair resided in Oswego and died there on March 31, 1862, at age 88.

The identity of James Adams does not appear in committee reports. Maj. James Adams commanded a battalion of New York Militia in Col. George Fleming's regiment at Fort Oswego in 1812. Maj. Parmenio Adams' son James was involved in some court action, and a James Adams, Jr., was in Capt. Horace H. Watson's 3rd Artillery company, but would not likely be detailed to seize property.

## Alvin Bronson

In April 1814, Commodore Isaac Chauncey was at Oswego and became aware that a British attack was expected from Kingston. He wanted to remove "guns and other naval equipments" to Sackets Harbor, about 40 miles NNE, in case the town was captured. The cannon and equipment would be put aboard the new frigates *Superior* and *Mohawk*, building at Sackets Harbor. For security, the ordnance and stores had been taken to Oswego Falls, about 12 miles up the Oswego River.

Townsend, Bronson & Co. was the United States' Storekeepers at Oswego, Alvin Bronson being the sole member at the time. Comm. Chauncey put Capt. Melancthon T. Woolsey, the commander at Sackets Harbor, in charge of the venture and on April 4 he wrote to Townsend, Bronson & Co. at Oswego:

> I expect a large number of guns and a quantity of other stores at Oswego, the moment the boats can pass the Oneida lake. I wish you to prepare to forward them with as little publicity as possible, and to get those across the portage that don't run the falls.
>
> Do you wish to purchase the *Growler*? If you do, what will you give for her?

On April 6, Elisha Jenkins, the quartermaster general of the 9th District, wrote to the company:

> I wish you to employ such means as you possess for the immediate transportation to Sackett's Harbor of the principal part of U.S. provisions and stores on hand at Oswego; taking the whiskey and pork first in order, as being the most valuable.
>
> You will send invoices and procure triplicate receipts from such officers of the Quartermaster General's Department as may have charge of the United States' store at Sackett's Harbor. You will please to have this business attended to with as little delay as possible, the situation of Oswego being exposed to the attack of the enemy. I trust you will pay every necessary attention to the most rigid economy, consistent with dispatch.

On the 14th Chauncey requested Alvin Bronson, owner of the schooner *Penelope*, "the only suitable vessel that could be procured for this service," to load and deliver the stores. The schooner's master, Capt. Robert Hugunin, and crew would be aboard but the Navy would be in charge. Bronson then, "voluntarily and without any stipulation as to risk or compensation, placed his own vessel in this hazardous service, and under the direction and control of Captain Woolsey, conducted, however by the master and crew."

On April 17, Quartermaster Jenkins wrote to Bronson again:

> From information which I have just received, there is reason to believe that the British fleet has sailed from Kingston by this time, as they were in a state of readiness on the 14th instant.
>
> Oswego, under these circumstances, is exposed to a marauding visit, and if, on receipt of this letter, the United States' stores have not been forwarded to Sackett's Harbor, you will take the most prompt and effectual measures to have them removed to the falls, where there is a greater probability of their safety that at the village.

The schooner was loaded under the direction of Lt. George Pearce, one of two lieutenants, several midshipmen, and 15 or 20 sailors Capt. Woolsey had. Woolsey put a midshipman in charge of the schooner.

The *Penelope* made two successful voyages, bringing about 80 tons of stores, but on May 6, "while waiting at Oswego for her third cargo to arrive from the falls, and with a part of this on board, captured by the public enemy."

Bronson had told Capt. Huginin that if the enemy appeared off the harbor, "in the event of the capture of the fort," he was to scuttle the schooner, "in such manner as to baffle any attempt on the part of the enemy to raise and take her away," and this would have succeeded except for the midshipman Capt. Woolsey had put in charge, who was unfamiliar with the harbor and sunk the schooner in shoal water right next to the pier. The British later raised the schooner and salvaged it.

Capt. Hughinin stated, in part:

> From the manner in which I was deprived of the command, I did not feel authorized to proffer my "aid and advice" to the officer who superceded me. I think that an intimation from me, of that kind, would have been considered impertinent, if not abusive, by the officer to whom it might have been directed, as it certainly would have implied that I considered him incompetent to perform the duty to which he was ordered, unless he had requested it, which he did not.
>
> The day prior to the capture of the *Penelope*, after the enemy had been discovered to the westward, I proposed to Captain Woolsey to let me depart with the vessel, and go to the eastward and endeavor to escape, as I was confidant that Oswego would be taken by the enemy, which he refused to let me do. I considered myself and the vessel under the control of Capt. Woolsey, with the consent of Mr. Alvin Bronson, and do not believe that I was permitted to have the command of her merely because I was better acquainted with the coast and intermediate harbors, and would, consequently, be better able to escape capture than any officer Capt. Woolsey had with him, all of whom were, I believe, strangers to the lake.

On May 8, 1817, Capt. Woolsey submitted a report from Sackets Harbor:

> I do hereby certify that the schooner *Penelope*, owned by Alvin Bronson, was employed

by me in the service of the United States to transport guns and other equipments for the United States ships *Superior* and *Mohawk*, in the spring of 1814, from Oswego to Sackett's Harbor.

2d. There was no agreement made between Alvin Bronson and myself respecting the price of transportation or risk, though we were aware of the imminent danger there was of her being captured.

3d. The *Penelope* was of that class of vessels denominated (from the rigging) schooner. I have, however, seen on this lake vessels of greater burden, but of a different and more slender construction, usually denominated boats. She has a large open hatchway, and was peculiarly adapted for the reception of heavy guns and other bulky articles, and, upon this emergency and for this service, no other vessel so well calculated as the *Penelope* could be engaged.

4th. The schooner *Penelope* was loaded under my direction, by Lieutenant Pierce, of the United States navy, with heavy guns, shot, &c.; she was detained about two days after her arrival at Oswego for the United States ordnance, &c. to arrive from Oswego falls, where I had directed the deposit to be made, lest the enemy should capture Oswego and all the military stores at once, as the event proved they would have done.

5th. Previously to the capture of the *Penelope*, I had ordered a midshipman, with United States seamen, to take charge of her, and, in case the enemy should succeed in carrying the fort, to sink her with her cargo. This order was executed, but as he was not well acquainted with the harbor, he sunk her in water so shoal that the enemy succeeded in raising and taking her away. I am of opinion that, had she remained in charge of the owner or former master, she would probably, from their better knowledge of the harbor, have been sunk in such a manner as to have prevented the enemy from raising her during the short stay they made at Oswego, and that the owners would have afterwards recovered her as was the case with the *Henrietta*, a similar vessel to the *Penelope*.

6th. I also certify that I have given to Alvin Bronson a certificate, dated some months since, in relation to the *Penelope*, but not embracing certain facts which were not then, but now are, necessary.

Bronson sued Capt. Woolsey in the Oneida Circuit Court and prevailed, but on appeal the state of New York Supreme Court on November 18, 1819, "decided that Captain Woolsey was the agent of his government, and, while acting in good faith, could not be held personally responsible for the unfortunate and improper execution of his orders, but that the government ought to make good this loss."

Bronson then filed a claim for damages on December 14, 1821, and on December 12, 1822, it was rejected.

As stated by the Committee of Claims on March 22, 1820:

> The petitioner states that on the 6th day of May, 1814, a schooner called the *Penelope*, owned by him, was captured by the public enemy in the port of Oswego, and lost, occasioned by an officer of the United States having taken her from the charge and direction of the master. It appears by the evidence in this case that the schooner was employed by Captain Woolsey, of the United States navy, to transport guns, &c. from Oswego to Sackett's Harbor.
>
> It appears a suit has been instituted by Mr. Bronson against Captain Woolsey for the value of the vessel, and a recovery had in the supreme court of the State of New York for $3,830, the full value of the vessel. It also appears that Bronson's principal witness was the defendant himself, Captain Woolsey.
>
> The opinion of the court was that, "the interference of the defendant with the schooner was unlawful, and that he had strictly no right to take possession of the vessel, and deprive the captain of the charge and control vested in him by the owner; that, having done so, he was responsible as a trespasser; and whether the enemy afterwards did or did not capture the vessel was immaterial."
>
> The committee consider themselves bound to pay great deference and respect to the opinions of the judges of the highest court of law in the different States upon points of law, and would not in an ordinary case call them in question. The committee are also of the opinion that the Congress of the United States should be extremely cautious in doing acts which may in any way countenance or encourage trespass upon the persons or

> property of the citizens by the officers or soldiers of the United States.
>
> If Captain Woolsey has committed a trespass, no good reason is seen why he should not be answerable, as any other individual would be; or why his being in the service of the United States should make the United States responsible for his conduct when acting in his own wrong. They therefore recommend that the claim of Alvin Bronson not be allowed.

Alvin Bronson was paid $3,000 in 1824.

## *Ellisburg*

The meandering, 200-foot wide Sandy Creek flows into the eastern shore of Lake Ontario. The town of Ellisburg is 3½ miles east of the mouth, about 24 miles southwest of Oswego, and 20 miles due south of Sackets Harbor. Any sightings of the British on the Lake or activity at Oswego or Sackets Harbor usually caused alarm in the area and the frequent mustering of militia—time they could ill afford during the planting seasons.

British strategy in the area at that time was to intercept supplies going to the naval base and shipyard at Sackets Harbor and they established a blockade by anchoring the *Prince Regent*, *Princess Charlotte*, *Montreal*, and *Niagara* at strategic points.

Supplies for Sackets Harbor came all the way from the Brooklyn Navy Yard ending at the Oswego River. In April 1814, cannon, equipment, cables, and stores had arrived at Oswego for the frigate *Superior* and on the 21st, Comm. Chauncey directed Capt. Melancthon Woolsey to oversee the transfer of the goods. Owing to the blockade, he elected to load the supplies, including a huge anchor cable, into 19 boats which would be rowed along the shore and more difficult for lookouts to spot along the dangerous journey.

On May 18, as additional security ashore, Woolsey enlisted the help of around 125 Oneida Indians and that evening set out with 5 officers, 25 sailors, and 150 riflemen from Maj. Daniel Appling's Rifle Corps.

One of the large boats became disabled, and on the morning of the 19th the 18 remaining boats arrived at the Big Salmon River where they met up with the Indians, who then proceeded north along the road. They were observed by the residents of the area who also saw the 18 boats being rowed north and a number of soldiers and Oneida Indians around Little Sandy Pond.

The disabled boat had been found by the British and Comm. Yeo dispatched Capt. Stephen Popham's *Montreal* and Capt. Francis Spilsbury's *Niagara* to find and intercept any other craft.

Around noon on the 19th Woolsey reached the mouth of Sandy Creek, and when lookouts reported a gunboat and three barges approaching, Woolsey ordered his boats run up the creek and sent messengers to notify the residents of Ellisburg the British would be arriving and to muster the militia.

The next morning, the 20th, Capt. Popham spotted 18 masts in the marshes and the lack of fire from shore led him to believe their only cover was militia. They proceeded to capture a boat with two 24-pounders and had the large anchor cable for the *Superior*.

On the morning of the 21st, the British entered the creek and landed 200 seamen and marines on both banks. When the boats got to around a quarter mile of Woolsey's boats, their 68-pound carronade became disabled when they attempted to train their 24-pounders on the Americans, they were rushed and overwhelmed by about 150 riflemen, 120 Oneida Indians, militia, and cavalry. The British were obliged to surrender after the loss of 19 and around 50 wounded. Popham and Spilsbury were taken prisoner.

On June 1, Capt. Popham wrote a report to Comm. Yeo from Sackets Harbor and praised Maj. Appling's efforts in seeing to the treatment of the British wounded.

The major civilian feat was the carrying of the huge anchor cable for the *Superior* overland on their shoulders to Sackets Harbor. A marker on Smithville Rd. in Sackets Harbor states: "Route travelled by the men who carried the four-ton cable for the ship *Superior* twenty miles from Sandy Creek Battlefield to Sackets Harbor in June 1814."

After this defeat, and with the *Superior* launched, the British fleet retired to Kingston.

## John Otis

As reported by the Committee of Claims on May 23, 1856:

> The petitioner, previous to and since the year 1812, resided with his family near the mouth of Sandy Creek, where it empties into Lake Ontario, in the town of Ellisburg, in the county of Jefferson, New York.
>
> In the year 1814, a severe battle was fought at this point, known as "the battle of Sandy Creek," in which many persons were killed and wounded. There being no convenient quarters in which these unfortunate soldiers could be placed and cared for, Mr. Otis, upon the request of the surgeon, John McCauly, opened his doors and appropriated his dwelling, which for the space of 17 days, was used as a hospital, accommodating and furnishing 30 wounded prisoners, a surgeon by the name of Marsh, and two assistants, making in all 33 persons, with beds, rations, &c.
>
> In addition to this, Mr. Otis purchased and furnished a quantity of cotton cloth for the requisite covering and shrouds for the sick, three of whom died at this house or hospital. One bed was entirely destroyed; another was taken to Sackett's Harbor, on which was conveyed a sick soldier. The price of these beds was fixed at the time, with Surgeon McCauly, at $60.
>
> The committee deem it unnecessary to recount all the inconveniences and losses to the petitioner in consequence of such occupancy. While he and his family were thus deprived of the usual domestic comforts, they devoted their time and energies in administering to the numerous wants of the distressed inmates.
>
> The petitioner in due time presented for payment his account for services, &c., approved by General Edmund P. Gaines, to Samuel Brown, then acting paymaster at Sackett's Harbor, and was by him informed that there were no funds in his hands to pay with. The claim was afterwards, and repeatedly, presented for payment at the Quartermaster's Department at Sackett's Harbor, but was not paid, for the reason before stated.
>
> Mr. Otis prayed Congress to allow his claim and forwarded his petition and papers to Washington about four weeks previous to the burning of the Treasury building, since which time he has heard nothing of the application, and has never received any consideration for the services, &c., performed.
>
> The committee have had reference to the Treasury Department and find no evidence or record showing payment of this claim, or any part thereof.
>
> The facts alleged, and upon which this claim is based, are fully substantiated by Elijah Wright and Charles Hollister, residents in the county of Jefferson, who respectively state upon their oaths that they were captains of companies in the 55th Regiment New York Militia in the war of 1812. They were at the battle of Sandy Creek, and know that the wounded were taken to the house of the petitioner, and by him furnished with quarters and rations.
>
> Peter Doxater, a musician in the company of Captain Wright, swears that he was at the battle and assisted in taking these prisoners into the house. In addition, 15 aged and respectable persons, soldiers in the war and battle, have joined the petitioner in asking Congress to pay the amount claimed, which they assert to be justly his due.
>
> The committee are unanimous in the opinion that the services as set forth were performed by the petitioner, for which he ought to be fairly compensated, and therefore report a bill for his relief.

# *Clarence*

Clarence is 16 miles east of Buffalo. Batavia is 20 miles east of Clarence and 25 miles south of the south shore of Lake Ontario.

## Zebulon Ketchum

Zebulon Ketchum was a farmer and a private in Capt. John Sackrider's company in Lt. Col. Cyrenius Chapin's 3rd Regiment, New York Militia. He later served as an ensign in the 137th Infantry, 33rd Brigade, 1st Division, New York Militia.

He claimed $1,289 in damages for 26 acres of corn, 8 acres of wheat, and timber, fruit trees, and fences when troops camped on his property. He also wanted $12 for being compelled to transport sick soldiers from Clarence to Batavia. This service was certified by Acting Hospital Surgeon Joshua B. Whitridge.

On February 13, 1828, the Committee of Claims denied the claim:

> The evidence proves that the taking and destroying the corn and wheat by the soldiers of the United States was unauthorized and wanton, and that the remedy is against the trespassers, and not against the United States.

Dr. Whitridge, of Massachusetts, was possibly with the 9th Regiment of New York Militia in the service of the United States.

# *Champlain*

Champlain is about 3½ miles west of Lake Champlain and a mile and around a mile and a half from the Canadian border.

## Allen R. Moore

As reported by the Committee of Claims on January 11, 1822:

> The petitioner states that in the month of March, 1814, the troops of the United States, did, without his consent, enter into and occupy for some time, a large and convenient store, situate in the village of Champlain, in the state of New-York, the property of the petitioner. There were many articles of value in the store, which were either used by the troops, or by them entirely destroyed, viz: 12 pork barrels; 10 flour barrels; nearly one barrel of potash; 2 part hogsheads vinegar, say 100 gallons; 1 large sugar chest; 2 hogsheads, about 30 lbs. bees wax; 6 bushels of flaxseed; 5 weights, 6 lb. each, barrels of ashes; &c. which, together, are alleged to have been worth $133.70; and that damages were done to building, by cutting, and in various other ways to the amount of $38.
>
> To the above, a claim is subjoined for 1 cast iron stove, and some sheet iron pipe, worth $45, or more; and a small quantity of plug tobacco, worth $25 or more, exclusive of several articles of less value. This latter property is alleged to have been in a store in Plattsburgh, owned by the Messrs. Roswell and Edward Wait, and occupied by the petitioner, and burned by order of General Alexander Macomb, during the invasion in September, 1814.
>
> It having been intimated by the petitioner, that damages to the amount of about $25 done to his store, has been appraised in 1814, and included in the account of Aaron Smith, which, if found to have been paid, ought to be deducted from the present claim.
>
> Inquiry has been made by the Committee of the Third Auditor of the Treasury Department for information, who states:
>
> The regulations of the War Department provided for damages which be done to buildings occupied by the troops of the United States, and directed the manner in which they were to be ascertained. If the proofs necessary were produced, and the mode pointed out had been observed, it is not known why compensation was not made at the time. The Quartermaster's Department in that neighborhood having made many payments for like objects, about the same time. No payment appears to have been made to the petitioner for damages or rent, but it appears that payment was made in April, 1814, to Aaron Smith, the person named by the petitioner for rent of stabling, rooms occupied as barracks, and store occupied as barracks, in the village of Champlain, amounting in the whole to $38, but whether either of them were the building of the petitioner is not stated in the account.
>
> From the intimations of the petitioner and the facts stated by the Third Auditor, it may be fairly inferred that the payment to Aaron Smith was at least in part for the store of the petitioner. As to the personal effects alleged to have been destroyed, if it occurred, must

have been wanton, rather than authorized, for which no compensation can properly be made.

Upon the claim for property said to have been destroyed at Plattsburgh by the burning of the store of the Messrs. Waits, the committee have to remark that Congress passed an act on the 3rd of March, 1815, for the relief of the owners of buildings destroyed at Plattsburgh, on the settlement of which accounts, those of the Messrs. Waits were paid for, but no provision was made, nor was there any asked by the petitioner for any compensation for the property contained in the buildings, and no allowance has hitherto been made for any such losses growing out of the destruction of those buildings, and in the opinion of the committee, this, as well as the former part of the claim is inadmissible. They therefore submit that the prayer of the petitioner ought not to be granted.

As reported by the Committee of Claims on April 5, 1836:

The petitioner charges the United States with damages done in March, 1814, to his store in Champlain, in the State of New York, by the troops under the command of General James Wilkinson who occupied the store for barracks, and for sundry small articles destroyed by the troops at that time, the sum of $166.70. Of this sum, $28 is charged for damages done to the building, and the balance is made up by charges for casks, flaxseed, boxes, potash, vinegar, &c. which the petitioner states were left in the store previous to its being taken possession of by the troops, and were by them wasted and destroyed.

Nimrod E. Moore, the then Acting Assistant Deputy Quartermaster General, makes two affidavits. In the first, dated in November, 1815, he states that the troops took possession of the petitioner's store while much of his property remained in it, and the property was mostly destroyed while in their possession. In his subsequent affidavit, dated the 16th of June, 1817, he says he was ordered to provide quarters for the troops, and in compliance with that order, he cleared the store of the petitioner and gave them possession of it, and they damaged it in the manner certified by him heretofore.

There appears to be discrepancies in these affidavits, but the fact of occupancy seems by these and other affidavits to be sufficiently established. Several witnesses testify to the fact that the troops occupied the store for barracks. Joseph Pratt swears that after the troops had left the village of Champlain, at the same time alluded to, he and Captain Lanes were called on to appraise the damage done to the store in consequence of its occupancy, which they did, under oath, at a sum over $20, he thinks $28.

The remaining articles embraced in the petitioner's account are not of a character to be useful or necessary for the comfort or subsistence of the troops, and do not appear to have been appropriated by the order of any officer, to their use. If destroyed, it must have been such a wanton destruction as would implicate the soldiers or officers themselves, and not the government. There is, moreover, a vagueness and want of precision in the testimony touching these articles, which, if they were otherwise chargeable to the government, would render payment impossible without further specification as to quantity and value.

The petitioner has a further claim for a cast iron stove and a quantity of pipe connected therewith, and also some tobacco, which he alleges were in a building in Plattsburg, occupied by him as a store, and which, with the stove and tobacco, were burnt in September, 1814, by order of General Macomb. Payment has been made for the building, which belonged to the Messrs. Waits, but the petitioner says he has never been paid for the stove or the tobacco.

The only testimony aside from that of the petitioner, in relation to these articles, is that of William B. Underhill, then a clerk of the petitioner, who swears, in December, 1817, that during the defense of Plattsburg, in 1814, the store was consumed by fire and that a cast iron stove and pipe worth $40 or more, a small quantity of plug tobacco, and some other articles, the property of the petitioner, were consumed with the building.

The testimony as to the quantity and value of the tobacco and other articles is too indefinite to require further notice.

It may well be questioned whether a stove attached by a pipe to a building containing it, is not such a fixture, and so far forth a part and parcel of the building as to be justly estimated with it. In this case, the store has been paid for under the act of March 3, 1815, as appears by a communication from the Third Auditor to Mr. Charles Rich, a former member of Congress, dated in December, 1821, which is among the papers submitted to the committee. The petitioner states he has not been paid for the stove; but no reason is assigned why it was left in the store, nor it alleged that it might not have been removed.

If a stove thus circumstanced is not considered as a part of the building, it must come under the decisions often made by Congress, refusing to pay for personal property contained in buildings destroyed by the enemy in consequence of military occupancy, or by order of our own officers. In either case the committee are compelled to reject the claim, as well upon general principles, as upon the principles adopted at the Department, under the act of 3rd of March, 1815, as stated in the communication of the Third Auditor, above referred to.

The claim was submitted in 1816 to the commissioner of claims, Mr. Lee, who declined paying the charge for damages done to the Champlain store because the Secretary of War decided that damage done to real property was not cognizable in that case. He declined paying for the personal property in that store because damage proceeding from plunder and wanton destruction of soldiers was not provided for by the act of the 9th of April, 1816. It has been since submitted several times to different Committees of Claims. It was reported against, and the report committed to a Committee of the Whole House, in 1832.

Upon a careful review, however, of all the facts and proceedings in the case, the committee are of opinion that the petitioner should be paid for the use and damage of his store in Champlain while occupied as barracks and they accordingly introduce a bill.

Allen R. Moore was paid $28 in 1838.

## Aaron Smith

Aaron Smith claimed Gen. James Wilkinson's troops, on April 8, 1814, "burnt up and destroyed 15 rods of garden pine, made of posts and boards valued at $30.00; damage to gates, $4.50; one hog pen, $1.00; one horse house, $3.50; one barn and stable, $12.00; one large, red store belonging to Allen B. Moore, which was then in Smith's care, $25.00; and half a ton of hay used and destroyed in the barn, $4.00."

Samuel Ashman and Silas Hubbell signed affidavits in support of Smith's claim, and Joseph Pratt and Wilt Lane appeared as witnesses to the occupation and destruction of the buildings; Aaron Smith, Jr., for the garden and yard fences, and Anthony Graham for the hay. Smith had a certificate signed by Alexander McIlhenney of the 5th Regiment.

Major General Alexander Macomb commanded the Army at Plattsburgh and in 1830 was still in the Army at Washington. Papers were sent to him by Elisha Whittlesey for verification of Smith's claim and one for $108.25 from William Shute for "timber bark used in building huts for the army under General George Izard, and for corn, potatoes, and oats taken by the troops and destroyed in the field, and for fences burned and destroyed."

He replied on December 20 that he remembered the names but had no recollection of the damage. He said it was his policy, "to pay, forthwith, for all damages done by the troops under my command, or to give certificates which would enable the individuals claiming to procure payment from the proper disbursing officers," and that he was in command of the Champlain frontier until May 1815.

Shute had no evidence and his claim was disallowed. Capt. Smith died after falling off a horse on May 21, 1824, at Champlain, and his son, Elisha Lord, 18, died at Champlain on March 8, 1825. The legal representatives were paid $80, in 1835.

# *Chazy*

Chazy is about 3½ miles west of Lake Champlain and around 5½ miles due south of Champlain.

## Septa Fillmore

Capt. Fillmore's claim was first presented on February 2, 1816. As reported by the Committee of Claims on March 4, 1822:

The petitioner, of Chazy, in the state of New York, represents that he was a captain of a militia company in 1814. On the first day of September he was ordered, by Lt. Col. Thomas Miller, commandant of the regiment, to assemble his company and retreat before the enemy to Plattsburgh, which he accordingly did, and continued there in service till the enemy retreated.

The enemy, finding he was from home, and learning that he was in arms against them, took possession of his premises and remained there till the affair at Plattsburgh had terminated. They took and conveyed away, used, or destroyed his whole stock of family and tavern stores, with every article of furniture they could find in his house; also, the hay, grain, and other things in his barn and enclosures.

The petitioner states the losses to be equal to $919.08, and asks of Congress indemnification to that amount. Congress have uniformly decided that for losses occasioned by the wanton acts of an enemy, government could not be answerable. The claim of Septa Fillmore ought not to be granted.

From July 20 to November, 18, 1813, the 106 troops of Capt. Fillmore's company in Maj. John Roberts' 3rd Battalion of Lt. Col. Thomas Miller's 36th Regiment, New York Militia, were detached to the 40th Brigade at Plattsburgh, "in the service of the United States."

Septa died in 1829 and on December 29 of that year the claim was resubmitted by his widow, Eunice Fillmore, and then by children Nancy, Sabrina, Eunice, Fanny H. Luther, and Treviah North. It was again rejected on February 20, 1840.

## Nathan Carver

As reported by the Committee of Claims on March 2, 1832:

The petitioner presents an account against the United States for the sum of $334.79, of which $156.79 are for medicine and for medical attendance, administered to, and bestowed upon, different soldiers during the late war, at Chazy, in the State of New York, there being at the time no hospital surgeon at that place. The residue of the account is for the damage done to his dwelling-house by the troops under the command of Gen. Wilkinson, as also to his stable, for destruction of his board fence, for the destruction of two acres of a grove of sugar maples used for fuel, and for rent of his dwelling-house for barracks to a company of cavalry, as also for firewood furnished to the company, and stabling their horses.

The original bills for medicine and attendance made out against the United States, and proven by different persons, at whose houses the soldiers were, or who were knowing to the attendance of the petitioner are presented.

It is known that Chazy was near the lines and a place of much resort during a part of the late war, and that its position was suitable for leaving the sick as the militia were passing and repassing. Lieut. Graves testifies that he employed Dr. Carver to attend upon sick soldiers under his command. It would have been more satisfactory if like certificates had been obtained in all the cases, but the committee can easily conceive the impracticality of obtaining them where troops are passing and repairing, and only one or two soldiers from a company left for a few days to recruit in health.

Immediately after the petitioner sustained the damages he complained of, they were appraised by two men. They may be reasonable, but they are not satisfactorily proven. The occupation of the buildings and the destruction of the groves, should be proven by an officer in command, or, if dead, by some other officer who knows the facts, or who can put the committee in possession of the material circumstances attending the transactions of which the petitioner complains. He presents the following account:

September 12, 1814—One horse captured at Chazy by the British while in the military service of the United States, $60; new saddlebags for medicine, $3.00, medicines in them, $5.00; one bridle, $1.00, one new saddle, $10.00; 19 days' imprisonment of my person, being taken by the British at Chazy, in a lucrative professional business, the only practicing physician in town, $105. Total $184.

The petitioner supposes the property was in the military service of the United States because he says he was then attending on the sick soldiers, and that his horse and equipments were necessary for that purpose. It is to be noticed that the petitioner was not attached to the army, but was a citizen at large, and it appears from his own statement he was doing a lucrative professional business, and, with more propriety, he might have said his horse was in his private employ.

The United States have not, at any time, remunerated a citizen for his loss of business or of time because he has been taken prisoner by the enemy. The committee think this account is wholly inadmissible. The committee reserve the injury done to the property of the petitioner for further proof, and report a bill for his services as a physician, and for medicine furnished to the soldiers.

Lt. Graves is possibly Joseph Graves in Captain Martin Barney's company in Lt. Col. Clark Allen's 55th Regiment of New York Militia.

## Joel Byington

His claim was presented on December 5, 1817, as reported by the Committee of Claims on April 14, 1828:

The petitioner presents the following claim: To damages done by the troops of the United States to the dwelling-house, barn, outhouses, fruit trees, and fences, lying in Chazy village, while occupied by them.

To the house, $415.42; barn, $34.59; one outbuilding destroyed, $5.50; one hog sty destroyed, $19.00; apple trees destroyed, $12.00; 27 rods and 3 feet of board fence destroyed, $27.51; one bee house destroyed, $7.00; 13 rods and 4½ feet of picket fence destroyed, $40.00; plum trees destroyed, $24.00; currant bushes, vines, and shrubs destroyed, $13.00, for a total of $598.02.

He has received pay for the rent of his buildings from 8th of March, 1814, to the 2nd day of August, 1815, and for the barn, to August 25th, $263.50.

The proof is clear, that his buildings were occupied by the United States' troops for the period mentioned, and for the reason that the government had not furnished barracks for the troops at that place. The buildings were not very valuable when the troops took possession of them. The house was estimated to be worth $500, and the barn $100, by the oaths of two appraisers, appointed under a commission issued by Mr. Lee, then Commissioner of Claims; who also appraised the damages the petitioner had sustained by the deterioration of his buildings, and the destruction of his property, to be the amount set forth in the above account.

Two questions may be presented: 1st. Is the petitioner entitled to any compensation? And 2nd, if he is, to what amount? An individual leasing property and paying rent is liable if he does not leave the property in good repair; the ordinary use and decay excepted. It could not have entered into the conception of the parties at the time that possession was taken of a house worth $500, and a barn worth $100 that they were to be so reduced in value in less than two years, the one should be worth no more than $84.58, and the other $65.41, and the lessor only be paid $263.50.

The claim was rejected by the Commissioner of Claims because the President of the United States had decided, under the third section of the act of April 9, 1816, that no compensation could be given for damages sustained, for an injury done to the property mentioned in that section, short of a total loss.

Relief has, however, been granted in many instances by Congress, where buildings have been occupied by public authority, and a partial loss has happened, not within the contemplation of the parties at the time of the commencing the occupancy. On the principles of the common law, the lessee would be bound to make such repairs. The committee entertain the opinion that some compensation ought to be given.

2nd. To what amount? If from the value of the buildings is deducted the amount paid for their use, then the government will have had the use, without any compensation paid therefore. This is not consistent with the principles of justice. It is proven that the yearly value of the buildings, to rent for ordinary purposes, was $60 or $70; all over this sum was therefore paid in consideration of the occupancy to which the buildings were put: this excess ought therefore to be deducted. Taking $65 as the medium between the two sums, and for the time the buildings were occupied, and the rent will amount to $96.24, which deduct from $263.50, the amount paid, leaves $167.26, which deduct from $449.42, the deterioration of the house and barn, leaves $282.16; which the committee think ought to be paid.

Joel Byington was paid $282.16 in 1830 for the damage done to the house and barn, and in 1834 he was paid $148.01 "in full of his demand for damages done to his property by the occupation thereof by troops of the United States." He filed another claim for rent, which was rejected on February 29, 1840. Another claim was filed and rejected on September 16, 1850.

## *Plattsburgh*

Plattsburgh, New York, is 54 miles south of Montreal on the west side of the 77-mile long north-south Lake Champlain, fed by the Richelieu River from the St. Lawrence River. Plattsburgh is situated on the Saranac River which meanders in a southerly direction from Cumberland Bay. Beekmantown is 5 miles north of Plattsburgh and Mooers is 20 miles north.

The situation at Plattsburg was perilous from within as the soldiers of the 13th, 33rd, and 34th Infantries were not being paid. William Baily and Henry Delord were merchants as Baily & Delord who sold goods to the soldiers and when there was serious threat of mutiny, Gen. Macomb prevailed on them to give credit to the soldiers for their immediate needs, but the soldiers, "were marched, in many instances, to distant parts of the United States, without having been paid" and left the merchants in large debt.

William Baily and Elizabeth Sweetland, widow of Henry Delord, filed a claim for large amounts of money furnished to the 6th, part of the 10th, 29th, 33rd, 34th, 43rd, and 45th Regiments of Infantry, artillery, some dragoons, and artificers stationed at Plattsburg who were never paid. Bela Egerton was their principal clerk who swore money owed was between $25,000 and $30,000. The secretary of the treasury was directed to adjust and pay their account.

### Melancthon T. Woolsey

As stated by the Committee of Claims on January 7, 1819:

The petitioner claims $1,080 for injuries sustained from the occupation of his farm, at a place called Cumberland Head, near Plattsburg in the State of New York, in the years 1813 under General Wade Hampton, and 1814 by troops under General George Izard of the United States; and thus enumerates the several items of his claim:

Destruction of fruit, grain, &c., $200.

3,500 rails of cedar, burnt by the army for fuel at $50 a thousand, $175.

Wood cut on ten acres of woodland, all the woodland I had, and used for fuel and fortifications, $150.

A log-house, shingle roof, and plank floors, destroyed and burnt up—roof and chimney materials carried away to complete huts and tents, $30.

The destruction of a barn in 1813. Captain Henry Hall of the dragoons, put his horses into the barn and occupied it about a week; the stable and sides, including the great doors, the floor, and partition between the floor and stable, kicked entirely to pieces, stripped off and burnt up, $50.

Destruction of a nursery of 1,000 trees, 700 of which were of the best grafted fruit, fit to set out on ground occupied by the troops, $350.

Five acres of oats and potatoes, destroyed by public teams, $75.

In 1813 my fences were partly destroyed and the whole of about 20 cords of wood, drawn from the swap and piled for my family use; for which, together with a certain sum for the last item of this account, I was paid by Quartermaster General Thomas, the amount not recollected.

The committee think it is an honorable act in the petitioner to admit the payment of a part of his claim, although, "the amount not recollected," and that, by such admission, his claim ought by no means to be prejudiced; that, until the contrary be clearly shown, it must be regarded as satisfaction for whatever injuries might have been sustained in 1813, particularly when considered in connection with the rules of the War Department applicable to such cases of which the following is an abstract:

"When private lands and buildings are occupied by troops of the United States, a reasonable compensation shall be made to the proprietor by the quartermaster of the district or port; and, when the rate of compensation cannot be satisfactorily agreed on, discreet and disinterested persons shall be appointed by the quartermaster and the proprietor to appraise the rent, which will be settled by the quartermaster, and the damage paid."

They are therefore of opinion that, upon the testimony offered, no allowance can be made for injuries which might have been sustained in 1813, and, as there is no proof offered as to the portion of the claim which may have arisen from injuries sustained in 1814, a case is not made out which will entitle the claimant to any relief.

It appears the troops who camped on Captain Woolsey's property in 1813 were the Second Light Dragoons under Col. James Burn. Col. James Thomas was a quartermaster general in the Light Dragoons from 1813 to 1815.

## Joseph Emery

In February 1814, Joseph Emery, of Maine, was building a 20 × 40 foot house in Plattsburgh. That month he was away from home on duty in the 11th Regiment of Infantry when Capt. Alexander Parris and a "corps of artificers" arrived and proceeded to occupy part of the house, having no other quarters. On March 15 the house caught fire and burned down. After the war Joseph moved back to Maine and in January 1822, filed a claim for $500 for the house and personal property, which was rejected.

## Benjamin H. Mooers

General Mooers filed a claim for damage done by troops encamping on his property in 1813. Col. Melancton Smith, commander of the 29th Regiment of Infantry, stated on October 3, 1813, that the 4th and 29th Regiments were "encamped on the ground of Major General Mooers." Col. James R. Mullany, Quartermaster General, stated from Plattsburg on November 1, 1816, that he had not paid the account per Major James Rees's report. The claim was referred to the Committee of Claims a number of times and rejected for want of evidence. On April 27, 1836, the Committee reported:

The petitioner presents the following account, certified on September 20, 1833, by Melancton Smith and William Pitt Platt:

For damages done while the United States troops were encamped on his farm, and two picket guards: 1 ton of hay in cock, $7.00; destruction of corn and potatoes, $20; 2 acres of buckwheat destroyed, $20; about 700 rails, in fences, $14. Total $61.00.

The original paper at that time was not produced, it has since been found in the possession of a member who formerly represented the district in Congress where General Mooers resides.

Additional testimony was taken in 1834, and the case again presented. Without making any report, the deficiency in the testimony was pointed out by the letter. Lieutenant Aaron Walters gave his second deposition.

It is now proven that the grounds were occupied for military purposes; that hay was taken for the horses in the service, and for beds for the soldiers; that the corn and potatoes were used by the troops for food, principally; that the buckwheat was destroyed by encamping on the ground; and that the rails were necessarily used for fuel.

The committee think the petitioner entitled to relief. Interest has been requested, but is not allowed.

Moorers was paid $61 in 1838.

In 1776 and 1777, Benjamin Mooers was a lieutenant in the New York Militia. He was a nephew of Col. Moses Hazen and on March 20, 1778, was commissioned an ensign in his uncle's 2nd Canadian Regiment. In March 1780, he was appointed the regimental adjutant, and when the war ended in 1783 he moved to the vicinity of Plattsburgh, New York, and became a major land owner. On May 15, 1812, he was appointed a 1st lieutenant in the 23rd Infantry, and was in the battles at Sackets Harbor on July 19, 1812, and again on May 29, 1813. He resigned on June 13, 1813, and died on February 20, 1838.

## Nathaniel Z. Platt

Nathaniel Zephaniah Platt resided at Plattsburg, New York, "during the invasion in September." As reported by the Committee of Claims on June 5, 1834:

> The petitioner presents the following account, from September 6 to September 15, 1814:
>
> For house room and fuel for eight days for Maj. Gen. Mooers and suite, three rooms at $3 per day, $24
>
> Damages for breaking the stoop of the house, $25
>
> For the use of my carriage house for barracks 100 soldiers, eight days, $20.50
>
> For the use of my barn for 150 soldiers for quarters for eight days, $25
>
> For hay taken for horses and teams, at $3 per ton, $64
>
> For corn and oats taken for horses and teams, $60
>
> For fences destroyed and burnt by the troops, $30
>
> For 1,500 feet of boards taken by the troops under Gen, Mooers, for covering temporary barracks, and eventually destroyed by them, $15
>
> For damage done to my garden, including an acre of potatoes, $20
>
> Total $283.50
>
> The claimant swears the account is stated at reasonable and fair prices and that he has received no part of the money or given any voucher whereby any other person has, or could, obtain any money thereon.
>
> The committee sent the petition and papers to the Third Auditor for information. It appears that the petitioner has suffered this claim to remain dormant for more than 19 years, although an account was settled which commenced on the 1st of August, 1814, and ended on the 31st of December, 1814, which covers the very time embraced in this account. One item of that account is for the rent of houses and land; and another item is $60 for wood standing on 46 acres of land.
>
> It is singular the petitioner should not have presented all of his claims that existed at the same time. An agent was afterwards sent into that country to collect and register the claims, so that payment might be made where the claims were justly due, and this claim was not presented.
>
> All the testimony is of recent date, and would not have been received in support of claim on account of its insufficiency, if had been made out, and accompanied the claim at the time the transaction is said to have taken place.
>
> The committee submit that the prayer of the petitioner ought not to be granted.

Nathaniel Z. Platt was paid $283.50, in 1836.

Zephaniah Platt, Sr. (1704–1778), of Smithtown, Long Island, New York, married Anna Smith. In 1784, their sons Zephaniah (1735–1807), Nathaniel (1741–1816), and Charles (1743–1824) obtained a state land grant of 33,000 acres on the Saranac River that flows into Lake Champlain. The next year Charles and a number of others began building cabins and mills near the mouth of the river. Zephaniah is recognized as the founder of Plattsburgh, which was officially recognized in 1815.

Nathaniel married a girl named Phebe Smith and in 1771 they had a daughter named Hannah. Zephaniah married Mary Van Wyck and in 1775 their son Nathaniel Zephaniah Platt, the claimant, was born.

In 1791, Nathaniel's daughter Hannah married Benjamin H. Mooers, of New York, and she died in 1809. On May 15, 1812, he was commissioned a 1st lieutenant in the 23rd Infantry Regiment and resigned on June 13, 1813, to join the militia.

On April 21, 1812, the New York Militia was ordered reorganized into eight brigades of two divisions, and seven regiments. Major Mooers commanded the 3rd Regiment, 1st Brigade. William D. Ross was quartermaster of the brigade.

## Caleb Nicholls

As reported by the Committee of Claims on January 27, 1817:

> That in the month of September, in the year 1814, the village of Plattsburg was invaded and taken possession of by the British, then under command of Sir George Prévost, and that they remained in possession thereof for several days; that Plattsburg is within cannon shot of Fort Moreau; and the commanding officer of that fort, under the orders of the commanding general of the American army, then at that place, did order the artillery from the fort to play upon the houses near the court-house in Plattsburg for the purpose of dislodging the enemy; and that a firing was accordingly kept up from the fort for several days, between the 5th and 12th of September, 1814.
>
> The petitioner states that his store and office stood immediately under the guns of the fort and were fired upon from the 6th to the 11th of September, 1814, and that a cannon ball from the fort passed through a puncheon of St. Croix spirits, which then stood in the store, containing about 100 gallons, which, in his estimation, was worth $250, and which was all lost.
>
> There is no evidence whatever before the committee of the loss of the spirits as stated by the petitioner; but the committee are perfectly satisfied that the store and another house of the petitioner, both standing near the court-house, were materially injured by cold shot fired from the fort.

No record of a payment could be found.

Fort Moreau was an embankment built by the 6th and 29th Regiments of Infantry under Col. Melancton Smith. The site of the fort is indicated by a historical marker in Plattsburgh.

## Frederick Halsey

As stated by the Committee of Claims on March 4, 1822:

> The petitioner, of Plattsburg, New York, represents that while the British troops were at Plattsburg in September, 1814, Major-General Frederick P. Robinson and suite took quarters at his house. A regiment of dragoons of the British army used his hay and corn, &c., and altogether he believes they done him damage to the amount of $230.
>
> When the British army retreated, General Robinson delivered over to him 124 sacks of hard bread, then in a house of the petitioner, used by them as a commissary store, and a good wagon. This wagon and bread, the petitioner states, were delivered to him as indemnity for the damage done him by the troops. The bread and wagon, it seems, were taken by order of General Alexander Macomb, with other property left by the enemy, and deposited in the public stores for public use. The petitioner therefore asks payment of the government.
>
> The committee believe the reason the enemy left the wagon and bread, as also many other articles behind, when they retreated, was the inconvenience of carrying them away, and that the disposition made of such property by General Macomb, was proper and just, and recommend that the prayer of the petitioner be rejected.

The claim was pressed again and reported by the Committee of Claims on June 21, 1834:

> The petitioner presents the following account against the United States, to wit:
>
> Sold the British Government, by Major-General Robinson, while quartered at my dwelling-house in the month of September, 1814, during the invasion of Plattsburg, viz.
>
> 14 tons of hay at $10 per ton, $140; cord wood, potatoes, and other articles, allowed and audited by General Robinson, $63; total $205.
>
> In consideration of the above sum of $205, General Robinson, in behalf of his Government, sold, delivered, and put into my possession, as my property, and for my use and benefit, the following articles, to wit:
>
> 136 bags of hard biscuit, 100 lbs. per bag, is 13,600 lbs. worth at least 4 cents, $544; 1 two-horse wagon worth about $50; total $594.
>
> He then states that this property was left in his buildings, and after the enemy retreated, he stated the facts to General Macomb, who sent and took the bread away.

Cornelius Halsey, son of the petitioner, testifies under date of March 20, 1834, that he was personally knowing to the sale of the property to General Robinson, and the purchase made by his father, and that the wagon and biscuit were taken away by the order of General Macomb, as he understood and believes.

John Bleecker, under date of the 3rd of April, 1834, says he was a deputy quartermaster general and stationed at Plattsburg at and after the battle at that place in 1814. That he saw a quantity of hard biscuit, packed in bags, which he has no doubt came from the buildings of the petitioner, and it was so reported at the time. He says he heard it remarked that General Robinson was very kind to pay his debts in property which he was obliged to abandon, or words to that effect. The biscuit were afterwards sold at auction, on account of the government, under the direction of the commandant at that post, but deponent cannot positively state who acted as auctioneer. He further says that the British retreating army left behind them a number of wagons, which were afterwards brought into the American camp, but he has no recollection of the particular one mentioned in the annexed account.

He presented his petition to the House of Representatives on the 13th of February, 1818, in which he states his claim as follows: One of the British generals, viz. General Robinson, took his quarters at his house and while there, the general and his suite, Colonel O'Niel and his regiment of dragoons, and others, did take and convert to their own use, of his property, hay for more than 200 horses, corn, potatoes, and other provisions, firewood and rail fences, and many other valuable articles to the amount of $230, at a moderate estimation.

He then states that on the evening preceding the departure of the enemy, General Robinson paid over to him 124 sacks of hard bread, which were deposited in his house, together with a wagon, as a compensation for what the troops had received; that he related the circumstances to General Macomb, who ordered the articles to be taken away and sold.

It will be seen by this petition that the articles were said to have been taken by the British, and nothing is said about their having been sold by the petitioner to General Robinson. To corroborate this petition, Colonel Melancton Smith gave his deposition under date of January 27, 1818, and therein he said, "This deponent believes Halsey suffered much by the occupation of his premises, in burning, &c. by the British troops, from the 6th to the 11th September, 1814. On the 12th day of September, 1814, Frederick Halsey did apply to this deponent and informed him that the enemy, previous to their retreat after the action of the 11th September had given him a quantity of hard bread in compensation for the damages he had suffered; that he, however, considered it his duty to report the same immediately to the commanding officer."

Robert Cochran was the wagonmaster who took away the bread from Mr. Halsey's possession, and under date of January 29, 1818, he testified that the second or third day after the invasion of Plattsburg, he received orders to call on the reverend Mr. Halsey, and get a quantity of hard bread. When presenting the order to Mr. Halsey, he replied that he had received this hard bread in compensation for damages that the enemy had done him, then says, "If you will receipt this in behalf of the United States, you can take it." He then says he received 124 sacks and receipted for it.

M. F. Durand, under date of January 29, 1818, testifies he was a deputy barrackmaster and took from the reverend Frederick Halsey's premises 138 bags of hard bread and stored it in the public storehouse. He says the bread was afterwards disposed of by Major James Rees, deputy quartermaster general, at auction.

The statement of the witnesses that this bread was sold on public auction is not confirmed by an examination of the accounts of all the officers mentioned in the papers, or who were at that post at the time.

The articles said to have been transferred to the petitioners belonged to the British Government, and were the legitimate subjects of capture or destruction in time of war. Admitting the articles were purchased, it does not appear that there was any agreement as to the manner in which payment should have been made. It was, then, in legal contemplation, a purchase to be paid for in money. The debt remained undischarged until the fleet of the enemy had surrendered on the lake; and at the moment when he found himself obliged to retreat, and with so much precipitation as not to be able to remove all his baggage, the commanding general changed the character of these articles and made that private which before was public. If he could do this, he might sell or give away a park of artillery, or the ammunition, or the medicine chest, or any other public property.

In a letter which the petitioner addressed to General Macomb, under date of March 21, 1834, he says, "General Robinson, after delivering this property to me, directed his orderly to make out a certificate, stating that this identical property was on the 14th of September, destroyed in Plattsburg. This certificate, which his orderly wrote in my house, I saw and read."

If any evidence was necessary to confirm the committee in the opinion that the enemy was obliged to abandon this property in his retreat, it is here furnished. The delivering of property to more that double the amount of the debt, or the damages sustained, shows it was no ordinary transaction, and, as between two individuals under certain circumstances, it would be taken as a badge of fraud. Denying to the commanding officer of an invading force the right to dispose of public property when he is obliged to retreat, the committee cannot look upon the contract, if one was made, as being good and valid.

The committee think the petitioner is not entitled to relief and submit that the prayer of the petitioner ought not be granted.

Col. O'Niel is possibly Richard O'Neill of the British 19th Dragoons.

## Samuel Demarest

As stated by the Committee of Claims on February 1, 1830:

The petitioner claims $1,600, the alleged value of a house and sundry goods, wares, and merchandise said to have been destroyed by order of Maj. Gen. Macomb during the siege of Plattsburg, in 1814.

Gen. Macomb certifies, "That in the month of September, 1814, Samuel Demarest had a house in the cantonment at Plattsburg of about the value of $1,500, which he had erected to enable him to suttle for the army, for which he had permission of Gen. Wilkinson. In the defense of the post he was under the necessity of having it burned at the same time the cantonment was destroyed."

Two other witnesses testify as to the value of the building who estimate it at $550. The only witness who testifies as to the value of the goods destroyed, estimates them at $100, the principal part having been removed before the order of the General was executed.

The committee are of opinion that as the petitioner, for his own convenience, was permitted to erect his building within the cantonment, he cannot reasonably ask that any other protection should be afforded to his property than that which was afforded to the property of the United States. They therefore recommend that the claim be rejected.

As stated by Gen. Alexander Macomb on January 18, 1830, to Rep. John W. Taylor who requested information:

I am well acquainted with the facts set forth in the petition. The house for which he claims remuneration was a store constructed for the convenience of supplying the Army with necessities, and it was erected within the chain of sentinels by direction of the commanding officer in order to make his establishment more controllable, and, at the same time, more convenient for the troops.

He had been appointed by Gen. Wilkinson, sutler to the troops at Plattsburg, and it was an object with the General to have such a gentleman as Col. Demarest appointed, as he was looked upon as both respectable and capable of giving satisfaction. By placing his establishment within the chain of sentinels, it made it unnecessary for the soldiers to frequent the town to obtain those articles which they required for their comfort, or for their appearance. Col. Demarest's establishment was important to the comfort and well-being of the soldiers and he was very kind and obliging to them. His character was held in high estimation and he fulfilled the duties assigned to him with great propriety and satisfaction.

I was under the necessity of ordering his house to be burnt to prevent its being a cover to the enemy in approaching the fort on the South side, where, it was expected, the enemy would open trenches and make the most serious attack. The house was Col. Demarest's own property, and, on full consideration of all the circumstances with his appointment and services, I am of the opinion that he has a strong claim on the government.

## Clinton County Court-House

Clinton County, New York, 300 miles due north of New York City on Lake Champlain, was founded in 1788. Plattsburgh, with a population of 200, was the county seat and a small courthouse was built, Judge Charles Platt presiding.

A second courthouse was built in 1803, which the British occupied, along with the jail and several houses. Sgt. Robert Keith said Gen. Macomb ordered the buildings destroyed, as stated:

> Many red hot shot were fired into the buildings. The courthouse, jail, and several houses were set on fire and destroyed. These buildings standing on the hillside would have afforded the enemy a cover for the erection of forts and planting batteries. Their idea was to mask their operations, then destroying their barriers, open upon us with their heavy guns. But after the buildings were destroyed we could sweep the field with our 24 pound shot.

As stated by the Committee of Claims on April 1, 1816:

> In the month of September, 1814, when the British forces invaded the United States on the frontier of the State of New York, they took possession of a part of the village of Plattsburg and sought a cover from the American artillery at the fort near the village from a number of houses belonging to individuals and the court-house of the county of Clinton.
>
> In order to uncover and dislodge the enemy, General Alexander Macomb, who at that time commanded the American troops at that place, considered it prudent and proper to fire hot shot into houses for the purpose of destroying them. Among the number thus destroyed was the court-house of Clinton.

New York militia Major Reuben H. Walworth, Esq., also an officer of the court, was dispatched to Washington City to file an $8,000 claim for the destruction of the courthouse. On October 1, 1816, a third courthouse opened, but 20 years later it burned down. The present courthouse was built in 1889 at 135 Margaret Street.

## John Addoms

As reported by the Committee of Claims on March 30, 1836:

> The petitioner states that John Addoms had a claim against the United States for property used and damages done to his premises in Plattsburg by the United States troops during the last war amounting to about $700, which is still due and unpaid.
>
> It appears from the papers that John Addoms made out his account for property and damages as early as November, 1814, and that it was allowed by two commissioners appointed to examine it.
>
> For the damage done in breaking the ground and building forts on the farm, $100; 150 trees of a large size for military purposes, $100; fire wood and smaller timber, $50; 1,000 cedar rails destroyed, $30; 12 acres of meadow destroyed, the grass all trodden down, and damage done to pastures, $98; 4 acres of buckwheat destroyed, $30; 300 bushels of potatoes, $112.50; 400 bushels of apples carried away by the troops, $200; 5 cwt. of hay, $2.50; 1 plough taken and not returned, $10.
>
> And that the whole amount of the damage done by the United States troops amounts to $733.
>
> Plattsburg, November 21, 1814. Thomas Treadwell and Levi Platt.
>
> On the back of the account is the following order signed by Colonel Melancton Smith:
>
> "The Deputy Quartermaster General will pay the within account except the items for potatoes and apples."
>
> November 25, 1814.
>
> Smith, Colonel 29th
>
> Commanding.
>
> He wrote and signed the following certificate on the back of the account, explanatory of rejecting the items mentioned,
>
> "I hereby certify that I refused to order payment for the aforesaid articles of potatoes and apples because the United States troops were not encamped on the spot where they were taken or destroyed, and not because I doubted the correctness of the aforesaid appraisal.
>
> Melancton Smith."
>
> The account remaining unpaid, and application having been made to Mr. Lee, commissioner of claims under the act of March 9th, 1816, for payment, Mr. Lee appointed Joseph Watson and John Palmer, the latter being a

judge of the county of Clinton, commissioners to take testimony in this case. The commission bears date on the 18th of September, 1816.

Mr. Palmer only acted a commissioner.

He took the deposition of Thomas Tredwell, William Peters, and Abel Hoskins.

Thomas Treadwell was the person appointed on the part of the United States with Levi Platt, who was selected by John Addoms to appraise the damage the claimant had sustained.

He testifies to the building of a fort on the land of John Addoms, to its occupation, and to the damage to the farm by the erection of the fort. He identifies the paper containing the account which is among the papers procured from the Third Auditor's office, and the estimate of damages made by him and Levi Platt.

William Peters is very particular in his deposition. He says the land could not be leveled off or restored to what it was short of some hundreds of dollars. He is positive one hundred would not do it. He also testifies to the destruction of the meadow for that season, and of the buckwheat crop. Also to the use made of the apples and potatoes by the troops.

Abel Hoskins testifies substantially the same.

Thomas Moore's deposition was taken before Reuben H. Walworth, then a master in chancery. This witness also sustains the claim.

On the 8th of May, 1817, Mr. Lee, commissioner on claims, allowed $192.50 comprising the second, third, fourth, ninth, and tenth items. He would have allowed the first, fifth, and sixth items, amounting to $228, but for the opinion of the Secretary of War.

He rejected the seventh and eighth items amounting to $312.50, because they were not recognized by the commanding officer.

The first, fifth, and sixth items, amounting to $228 are for injury done to the land, and for the destruction of the grass on the meadow, and the buckwheat, by reason of occupying the ground as mentioned.

Whatever might have been the opinion of the Secretary of War as to the liability of the United States to pay for such damages under the act of April 9th, 1816, Congress has, at various sessions, passed special acts, remunerating those whose lands have been occupied for military purposes, the damages they sustained.

Where the face of the ground has been broken, it has been restored at the expense of the United States. Where crops have been necessarily destroyed in the prosecution of public works, or where the ground on which they were growing has been used for public purposes, the United States have paid for them.

The testimony in this case was taken in 1816, and fully proves the damages sustained by John Addoms.

Taking the apples and potatoes was without authority, and payment should not be made for them.

The committee think the sum of $228 should be paid and for this purpose report a bill.

Perceiving an endorsement on the back of the file in the handwriting of Mr. Hagner, and signed by him, of the following tenor, to wit: "No payment through this Department," and it being without date, the committee desired to know when he made it, in order to ascertain whether the sum allowed by Mr. Lee had been paid. His reply shows it was made before the 9th of May, 1817. It appears from a note he obtained at the Treasury Department that the sum of $192.50 was paid to Joseph Watson, as the agent of John Addoms, on the 17th of May, 1817.

John T. Addoms, the legal representative of John Addoms, was paid $100 in 1840.

## Plattsburg Residents

As stated in the Reports of the Committees of the House of Representatives, on January 11, 1822:

Your petitioners, the undersigned, beg leave to represent, that, at the late invasion of Plattsburg by the forces under the command of Lieutenant General Sir George Prévost, 1st Baronet, Governor General of the British North American Provinces, and commander of the forces, &c., it was thought expedient and necessary, and accordingly ordered, by Major General Alexander Macomb, command-ing the United States' army at Plattsburg, for the safety of that army, and the defense of the post, to set on fire, and destroy by hot shot, certain buildings in that village, which was accordingly done.

The buildings so destroyed belonged to the petitioners, whose names are hereunto subscribed, leaving them mostly destitute of dwellings: And whereas General Macomb, by his order, on the part of the United States, chose Peter Sailley, Esq., and the petitioners, on their behalf, Lewis Ransom, as appraisers, to settle and adjust the value of the buildings so destroyed. Whereupon the same were appraised, and the amount of the loss of each individual established at the sum annexed to his or her name, as to this petition is subscribed.

Your petitioners, therefore, pray legislative aid in their behalf, that they may be compensated for the injuries sustained:

Nathan Averill, Jr., $800; Charles D. Bachus, $1,750; Lois Baker, $180; Margaret Beaumont, $1,250; Noah Broadwell, $300; Enoch Chase, shop, $75; Daniel P. Clark, $200; John L. Foquet, $2,000; George Fraligh, $750; Benjamin Graves, sheriff, court-house of the county of Clinton, $5,000; Joseph I. Green, $300; Jonathan Griffin, $5,000; Henry Platt, store, &c. in possession of Jackson & Starks, $200; Levi Platt, $950; Henry Power's store, $750; James Savage, $1,150; Major A. Stone, $250; Joseph S. Thomas, $650; Edward and Roswell Wait, $1,800; John Wells, shop, $50; March 3, 1815.

Joseph S. Thomas filed a claim $1,105 for three buildings and was paid $650. He filed a claim for an additional $455, including $200 for a house taken down for lumber and bricks used for barracks, and $11 for wood cut on two acres, which were denied.

## *Youngstown*

### Samuel Wagstaff

As reported by the Committee of Claims on May 5, 1830:

The claim is for the loss of a house at Youngstown, which was destroyed by the British during the late war in consequence of its being in the military occupation of the troops of the United States. The claim was presented to the Commissioner of Claims under the act of April 9, 1816, and was afterwards transferred to the Third Auditor for his investigation and decision. He reported against the claim, and Samuel Wagstaff presented his petition to Congress on the 28th of December, 1826, and an unfavorable report was made by the Committee of Claims on the 22nd of January, 1827. The Third Auditor rejected the claim because the testimony did not satisfy his mind that the house at the time of its destruction was occupied by the troops of the United States by the order of an officer.

The claim is presented again with additional testimony. It is proven by Captain Nathaniel Leonard that the house was taken possession of by his order and occupied by the troops of the United States until its destruction on the 19th of December, 1813. Captain Frasier testifies that he occupied the house for a few days with his company in December, 1813, and that when he left it, it was taken possession of and occupied by the sick soldiers from Fort Niagara. Doubts have therefore existed as to the occupation by order of an officer from the apparent inconsistency in the depositions of Capt. Leonard and Capt. Frasier.

Capt. Leonard testifies that the house was occupied first by his order; Capt. Frasier testifies that subsequently he occupied it with his company and that when he left it, it was occupied by the sick from Fort Niagara under the care of Dr. Manley, and that he saw an order in the hands of Dr. Manley from Capt. Leonard directing him to take possession of the house, and that he saw the sick in it, on the 18th of December, 1813. Capt. Leonard testifies that he verily believes he gave an order to Dr. Manley, or Morely, to occupy any building he could obtain at Youngstown for the accommodation of the sick. The house was destroyed on the evening of the 18th, or the morning of the 19th, of December, 1813.

Jonathan Jones testifies that he occupied a house within 8 or 10 rods of the house of Mr. Wagstaff, which for some days previous to its destruction was occupied exclusively by the sick of the army. That he recollects distinctly hearing the cries of the inmates of that house at the time it was entered by the British soldiery and that the sick remained in the house under the charge of Dr. Manley until the enemy came and that Dr. Manley was killed, as he understood and believes.

Whatever might have been the doubts heretofore entertained about the occupancy by the order of an officer, the committee think, with the general evidence, that those doubts are dispelled, and herewith present a bill for the relief of the petitioner, referring the value of the house to the decision of the Third Auditor, on proof to be taken under his directions. Several witnesses appraised the value of the house at $1,000, but as, in several instances, the value of houses, as fixed at that time, have been considerably lessened, the committee prefer to give the case that reference, to making a decision on the present testimony.

Capt. Nathaniel Leonard commanded a company of United States 1st Artillery at Fort Niagara when the British attacked on December 18, 1813. He apparently was the senior officer, but was away at Lewiston at the time. The fort was poorly defended and it was reported that 65 Americans were lost, 15 wounded, and 344 were captured. The British held the fort until the end of the war.

Capt. Frazier is possibly 2nd Lt. Donald Fraser, of New York, an assistant deputy quartermaster general in the 15th Infantry in December 1813. He was brevetted captain on July 25, 1814, for gallantry at the battle of Niagara Falls, and major on September 17, 1814, for gallantry at Fort Erie.

## *Fort Erie*

The British built a fort in 1764 just south of present-day Fort Erie across the Niagara River from Buffalo, New York, as a post and port of embarkation for passengers and supplies going to the Upper Great Lakes via Lake Erie. A newer, stronger fort was started on higher ground in 1803, but in 1812 it was still under construction.

### Thomas D. Morrison

As reported by the Committee of Claims on July 6, 1838:

The petitioner, while a minor of 17 years of age, was a private in the company of Captain Charles E. Tobey of the 21st Regiment of United States Infantry. During the assault on Fort Erie by the British troops on the 14th of August, 1814, the petitioner shot a British officer dead on the field. There was found the sum of $800 about the person of the officer, which was regarded as the property of your petitioner, and given to him.

The petitioner deposes that, by the advice of those he confided in, he chose Benjamin T. Learned, who then commanded a company, his guardian. The guardian received all the money under an engagement to return it to him when he should be of legal age, and interest thereon. He has never been able since to obtain the money, or any part thereof, or to ascertain that any credit was given him for the money on the company's books, or any entry made in relation to the same, and claims indemnity for his loss.

Your committee, though they regret any loss should arise to the petitioner from a violation of his confidence, are not aware of any law or authority making the United States insurers of property thus situated, or any rule which could safely be established which could charge the government with his loss.

The petitioner is not entitled to relief.

Col. James Miller commanded the 21st Infantry at the siege of Fort Erie between August 4 and September 21, 1814. Capt. Tobey, of Massachusetts, reportedly resigned his commission on February 28, 1814.

### Schooner Tempest

In June 1814, Maj. Gen. Jacob Brown at Fort Erie issued orders to acquire water transportation, and directed Maj. John G. Camp, assistant deputy quartermaster general at Buffalo, to either contract for or impress, "all such small vessels or boats then lying in the harbor of Buffalo and Black Rock, as well as many others of like description, which could be found on the south shores of Lake Erie, as far up the lake as Cleveland, Ohio, to furnish transportation for his army into Canada."

On September 9, Gen. Brown ordered Major John B. Hogan, deputy quartermaster general, "to get the militia all across in the course of the night," and the next day Hogan paid Capt. Benjamin Napier $5 to transport troops from Buffalo to Fort Erie.

On board on September 10 were Capt. Napier, Isaac Cook, Peletiah Shepard, John Briggs, Mannah Briggs, Joseph Napier, the crew, and Anan Harmon, a passenger who had cargo aboard. Twelve days later, the schooner stranded on the "bar of Erie" and was lost. John Metcalf filed a claim for his goods that were lost on the *Tempest*, which was denied in 1842.

The owners believed the government owed them for their loss but they had no idea how to proceed. They eventually consulted Matthew Hubbard, an acquaintance, who described them as "illiterate and unlearned men." He advised them to obtain some evidence from Major Camp, which they apparently did, but in 1826, Hubbard and Nehemiah King consulted Elisha Whittlesey who told them further testimony from Major Camp, the officer who seized the vessel, would be needed. His whereabouts by then were unknown, but sometime in 1838 or 1839 he was located. On October 7, 1839, he wrote to Ohio Representative Joshua R. Giddings from Sandusky City, Ohio:

> The bearer hereof, Captain Cook, has again called upon me to give additional testimony in his case, for the payment of the lost schooner, the *Tempest*. My affidavit heretofore given, I think, is full as to taking in the service of the United States, and as the detention of the same until the army had been passed into Canada. The time since elapsed is so great that I cannot now recollect whether I paid for the use of this particular vessel at the time or not, but my accounts settled at the War Department will show as to that fact.

The claim was presented in 1841 and 1842 and denied. On May 16, 1850, the Committee of Claims, based on statements from Third Auditor Peter Hagner in January 1845, determined that $20 per day for detention would be reasonable and reported a bill for $200.

As stated by Hagner on December 30, 1841, in part:

> The petitioner represents that in September, 1814, he was on board of the schooner *Tempest* at Buffalo and was one-third owner of her, in company with Benjamin A. Napier and Isaac Cook. He and the other owners, together with the schooner and crew, were impressed into the service of the United States by Major John G. Camp (a subordinate under General Brown) for the purpose of carrying troops from Buffalo to Fort Erie.
>
> The schooner was well loaded and ready to start, and the owners then had on board about 250 barrels bulk of freight, which was, by the order of Major Camp, unloaded and placed upon the shore. The schooner was then controlled, directed, and used, together with her owners and crew, in the service of the United States, and otherwise delayed for about 12 days. During the time the owners and crew were kept entirely at the charge of the owners, both as it regarded the wages of the hands and the provisioning and boarding the crew. He is unable to state the precise number of times the schooner passed over from Buffalo to Fort Erie, but she went several times.
>
> The schooner would carry about 250 barrels bulk, and was built new at Ashtabula in the summer of 1814. Freight was high on Lake Erie at the time, and it was difficult to get it carried at any rate. The petitioner believes the use of the schooner and the services of the crew were well worth $20 per day while she was in the service of the United States. He has never received the least compensation for his own service or that of the crew or for the use of the schooner. No voucher for any payment to the petitioner or to either of the other owners for the services of the vessel could be found, and it is only with such a voucher that there was a probability of discovering the evidence in question. The petitioner has not declared that he acted as the master of the vessel, nor named the person who did so act. Any voucher for hire would likely to be made out in the name of the master, and that would be the name which would appear in the abstract of the disbursing officer who paid it.

Anan Harmon was deposed at Ashtabula, Ohio, on November 13, 1839:

> I, Anan Harmon, of lawful age, having been first duly sworn, on my oath depose and say: That, in the month of September, 1814, the schooner *Tempest*, of Ashtabula, owned by Benjamin A. Napier, Isaac Cook, and Peletiah Shepard, which was then lying in Buffalo creek, was pressed into the service of the United States, by Major John G. Camp, under an order from General Brown, as I was informed at the time, for the purpose of transporting troops from Buffalo to Fort Erie; and said schooner was employed in that business about twelve days.
>
> At the time said schooner was pressed into service, she was loaded and ready to sail for Ashtabula, for which port she was destined with her cargo. When pressed, the cargo was all taken out and relanded on the shore, exposed to the weather, as there were then no storehouses at Buffalo; and when the vessel was returned, the cargo, within twenty-four hours thereafter, was again put on board, and the vessel immediately sailed for Ashtabula.
>
> Soon after the schooner sailed, she was lost with her cargo in a very violent storm, near Erie, Pennsylvania. I was a passenger on board the schooner, and having some freight on board.
>
> During the time the schooner was in the service of the United States the weather was fair and the schooner could, I think, in that time, have made a voyage to Ashtabula and back to Buffalo. The vessel had a full freight, and the price of transportation was then high, and there was plenty of freight for the vessel, and the use of the schooner during the time she was detained from her owners in the service of the United States was worth $200 a day. Freight was then $5 a barrel from Buffalo to Erie, and $10 a barrel from Buffalo to Ashtabula. Said schooner had, when pressed, a cargo of about 250 barrels bulk of freight on board for Ashtabula.

Another shipper, Collin Wetmore, also testified as to freight rates on November 16, 1839, and Matthew Hubbard also swore to the facts on March 9, 1840.

Isaac Cook, Benjamin A. Napier, and Pelatiah Shepard were paid $200 in 1856.

The schooner *Experiment* was employed in June and July 1814, at $500 per month ($16.66 per day) and the schooner *Teazer* at $300 a month ($30 per day).

In July 1814, Gen. Jacob Brown was wounded and was succeeded by General Gaines until September 2 when Brown resumed his duties against medical advice.

Maj. John B. Hogan, a deputy quartermaster general at Buffalo, hired the schooner *Croghan*, the master and four sailors, from August 2 to September 8, 1814, for $25 a day.

In March 1814, the schooner *Lady of the Lake* was on the Navy List at Lake Ontario under Sailing Master Mervine P. Mix.

According to the Treasury Department, the schooner, *Lady of the Lake*, was impressed by a naval officer to transport troops and stores from August 2 to September 23, 1814, for $30.50 per day.

## Jacob G. Brown

Gen. Jacob Brown was severely wounded at Bridgewater, Niagara Frontier, on July 25, 1814, by a musket ball. He was attended to by militia surgeon Dr. Amasa Trowbridge who described the wound as "passing through the upper part of the right thigh, lacerating the external integuments, wounding the triceps femoris muscle, glands, and the great tendinous fascia of the thigh."

He recuperated for a few weeks at Buffalo, opposite Fort Erie, but on September 2, despite being "attended with much fever, pain, and feebleness, and yielding to high and patriotic impulses," he boarded a Navy schooner "to better direct the movements at the fort" and resumed command of the army, "then besieged on the Canadian side of the Niagara, from which perilous position he relieved it, after an arduous service, by the brilliant sortie from Fort Erie on the 17th of the same month."

This service, and the exertion and exposure in travelling from Buffalo to Sackets Harbor in November, aggravated his condition to the extent that by 1821 they, "brought on a derangement of the system." He was attended to by Dr. Trowbridge, who consulted with other physicians, but in October 1821, Brown became, "prostrated by an apoplectic stroke, which nearly destroyed life" and he was plagued by "a paralysis, prostrating him for the remainder of his life, and terminating in his death on the 24th of February, 1828." He left a wife, Pamela.

(26th Congress, 1st session, Report No. 204)

## The *Nighthawk*

Robert Swartout was awarded $2,800 on March 3, 1821, for expenses in defending a lawsuit by the owners of the *Nighthawk*. As stated by the Committee on Military Affairs on December 28, 1818:

> It appears that your petitioner was a quartermaster general of the army of the United States during the late war with Great Britain, that in that capacity he was attached to the northern army; that when that army was about to descend the river St. Lawrence, in the month of November, 1813, many of the boats and vessels that had been collected for that expedition were destroyed by a storm.
>
> General Wilkinson, then commanding, issued an order to your petitioner immediately to repair the deficiency occasioned by the storm, either by hire, purchase, or impressment of a sufficient number of boats; that, in fulfilling this order, your petitioner was under the necessity, in some instances, to resort to impressment; that, among the boats so impressed, was one called the *Nighthawk*, which boat, in the descent of the expedition, was fired upon by the British forts, and was destroyed.
>
> For the boats so impressed, an amicable arrangement was made with the proprietors, and they were compensated to their satisfaction, with the exception of this case. After your petitioner had finished his concerns as quartermaster general, and settled his accounts, in the year 1817, he was arrested in New York by a writ of the supreme court of that State, at the suit of the owners of the *Nighthawk*. He defended the suit, and pleaded on trial all the facts here stated; that, notwithstanding, judgment was given against him, and an award granted, which, together with costs, will amount to about $2,500; and he therefore prays remuneration.
>
> The committee are of opinion that this is a case deserving of relief. In the circumstances of war, such exigencies will frequently occur in which the commanding officer will stand justified in taking, by force, such necessaries, either for support or conveyance, as are indispensable, and which cannot be obtained by any other means. The descent of an army on an important expedition, at a season of the year which would admit of no delay, is considered one of those extreme cases of necessity in which an overstepping of the established legal rules of society stands fully justified. But even though it should be considered an unwarrantable step in a commanding officer, it is certain that the subordinate officer, bound to fulfill his commands, should not be permitted to suffer; and it is also certain that the individual whose property was forcibly taken and illegally taken away from him should be remunerated by the Government for whose use it was taken. They therefore ask leave to report a bill.

# Pennsylvania

## *Erie*

In 1753 the French built fort on a peninsula—Presqu'Ile—that creates a sheltered harbor on the south shore of Lake Erie. After the French were forced out in 1760 it was occupied by British troops and then in 1792 became part of Pennsylvania, known as Erie. The lake and town were named after the local Indian tribe.

The first naval vessels built there under the direction of Capt. Oliver H. Perry were the 20-gun brigs *Lawrence* and *Niagara*, completed in 1813. The builders were Adam and Noah Brown, supervised by Sailing Master Daniel Dobbins.

In 1988, construction started on an authentic, 123-foot replica of the *Niagara* and began sailing during the summer of 1992. The ship is owned and operated by the Pennsylvania Historical & Museum Commission and is homeported at the Erie Maritime Museum at 150 East Front St. A crew of 18 students and trainees sail on the Great Lakes and vicinity during May through October.

### Jonas Duncan

Jonas Duncan was a carpenter who arrived at Erie in 1799 with John Teel, his apprentice. They were two of the first builders in Erie and Duncan remained prominent in that trade for over 50 years. His petition was presented to the Committee on Naval Affairs on January 19, 1824, as reported on February 17, 1824:

> The petitioner states that in 1812 he was the owner of a house in the borough of Erie in the state of Pennsylvania which, without his consent, was taken possession of by the officers of the navy of the United States and kept in their use until 1816 when it was burnt. He has received no compensation for the loss or rent and prays a reasonable remuneration for the use of his property and for the loss of it.
>
> It appears to the committee from the deposition of Daniel Dobbins, a sailing master, that in November, 1812, he took possession of said house and used it in storing the United States' iron while building gun boats. It was subsequently used as a brickmaker's shop until the summer of 1814 when it accidentally burnt.
>
> John Hay and Peter Grawoss unite in deposing that the house was worth $100, and the rent was worth $35 a year. It will appear by a letter from Charles Hay, Chief Clerk in the Navy Department, that no payment has been made to Duncan. The committee are of opinion that a reasonable rent ought to be paid to Jonas Duncan.

Charles Hay reported that pursers, Samuel Hambleton and Ezekiel Solomon, the disbursing officers at Erie, reported that "a person named James Duncan was paid for house rent" and the name of Jonas Duncan did not appear in any record.

Jonas Duncan was paid $60 in 1824.

## *Gray's Ferry*

George Gray established an inn on the west bank of the Schuylkill River in the 1700s and took over operation of a ferry service that ran south of Philadelphia.

## Curtis Grubb

Curtis Grubb operated an ironworks in Lancaster, Pennsylvania, and enlisted as a sub-lieutenant on October 23, 1777, at Lancaster. As a colonel he commanded the Flying Camp at Lancaster during the war.

In 1805, he purchased Gray's Ferry Inn and married Eva Maria Kochersperger. The inn was known as Kochsersperger's Hotel.

As reported by the Committee of Claims on May 10, 1836:

> The petitioner presents the following account against the United States for himself and the owners of the Gray's Ferry estate,
>
> "For injuries sustained by him in having his property used or consumed by the United States troops, Pennsylvania volunteers, and the militia in the service of the United States, viz: 14 acres of young wheat and rye, and 480 panels of post-and-rail fence, and 200 bushels of turnips, in the months of April, May, August, and September, 1813, and summer months of 1814, whilst stationed on his then tenements near Gray's Ferry, on the river Schuylkill, in the county of Philadelphia, in the State of Pennsylvania, for which remuneration is claimed, $500."
>
> The petitioner is not the owner of the estate on which the depredations were committed, or the troops encamped; and to secure the United States against any liability to those who have the fee of the estate in them, the attorneys of the owners have signed a writing at the bottom of the above account, authorizing the remuneration to be made to the petitioner.
>
> Oliver Lindsay, under date of 8th of April, 1836, testifies that he resided on the estate. The Pennsylvania volunteers and militia, and also portions of the regular army, in the years 1813 and 1814, were encamped in the fields and enclosures of Curtis Grubb; that 480 panels of post-and-rail fence were used or consumed. A field of young wheat and rye of 14 acres, also a quantity of turnips, believed to be 200 bushels, and that a redoubt was likewise thrown up in the enclosure.
>
> This witness, nor any of the other witnesses, having estimated the damages specifically, and it not appearing why the property was used or consumed, nor how a letter was addressed to Mr. Grubb by the committee, on the 18th of April, 1836, pointing out the defects in the testimony.
>
> Mr. Lindsay's deposition was taken again on the 2nd of May instant, in which he says 480 panels of fence were used by the troops for fuel, worth 80 cents per panel; that the wheat and rye field was used for encampment and parade ground, and was worth $20 per acre; that the lot containing the turnips was used for the baggage wagons, gear, and like accoutrements belonging to the camp, and would have yielded 200 bushels, worth 25 cents per bushel; that to level the redoubt would cost $150, and that the rent of the ground, while in such military occupation, was worth $100.
>
> These sums amount to $964.
>
> Mr. Grubb says he was aware his account was much less than the actual loss sustained.
>
> Robert Milnor testifies to the throwing up the redoubt, and the destruction of the trees and fences on the fields, and that the position was important to prevent the enemy from entering the city.
>
> William Duncan says he was aid to Governor Simon Snyder; that he saw troops encamped on the premises, and has no doubt considerable injury was done by the frequent encampment on the estate.
>
> James N. Barker, late major United States army, testifies that the troops of the United States, volunteers, and militia, occupied the fields near Gray's ferry on the Schuylkill, in the immediate vicinity of which military works were thrown up for the defense of the city from 1812 to 1814, during which time he acted as assistant adjutant general.
>
> Robinson R. Moore officiated in the quartermaster's department and he testifies to the occupation of the premises, and to considerable injury being done.
>
> Col. John Thompson testifies to occupying the premises with a detachment from the 2nd Brigade of Pennsylvania militia, of 1,300 men, for 20 days in September, 1814, during which time the post-and-rail fence was much destroyed.
>
> U.N. Irvine testifies he estimated the damages done to the premises when they were occupied by Colonel John Thompson, and that they amounted to $250, and that when the premises were in his military possession, they amounted to $85. There were no

> funds in the hands of the quartermaster general to pay the amount. Since he left the army he forwarded them in a letter to Philadelphia, which letter, with the contents, has never yet come to hand, as he has been informed and believes.
>
> Other occupations having been proved than those mentioned by Mr. Irvine, and taking the testimony of Mr. Lindsay, the committee think the petitioner sustained damage to the amount claimed. The kind of injury is such as the United States have compensated in other cases. The committee report a bill herewith.

Curtis Grubb was paid $500 in 1838 "for the use and occupation of the farm at Gray's Ferry, on the Schuylkill during the late war for military purposes and for the crops and fences destroyed and for the expense of leveling a redoubt constructed thereon."

Robert Milnor was in Capt. William Rawle, Jr.'s, Troop of Cavalry, Pennsylvania Militia.

In March 1815, the home of Timothy Currin, located on "Market Street, between Schuylkill Sixth and Seventh Streets in Philadelphia" was taken for use as a hospital at $800 a year. The house was used between March 6 and June 6 for $200 by Dr. James Trimble, hospital surgeon.

## *Marcus Hook*

In the early 1640s a settlement in Pennsylvania about 43 miles up the Delaware River from the head of Delaware Bay, was known as Chichester and by the 1760s a section of the township was known as Marcus Hook owing to a geographical feature. The town was bombarded several times during the Revolutionary War and a blockade vessel was sunk in the river to prevent British incursion into the harbor.

As recorded on December 21, 1818:

> Mr. Anderson, of Pennsylvania, presented a petition of John Martin, and Hannah Peterson, and a petition of Joseph Dutton, respectively praying compensation for damage sustained in their landed property near Marcus Hook, whilst the same was occupied by the troops of the United States, in the late war with Great Britain.

Washington City was attacked on August 24, 1814, and on the 27th, Pennsylvania Gov. Simon Snyder wrote, in part:

> The recent destruction of the capitol of the United States; the threatened and probable conflagration of the metropolis of a sister State, and the general threatening aspect of affairs, warrant the opinion that an attack is meditated by the enemy on the shores of the Delaware.

With Philadelphia in danger, he ordered the militia of southwest Pennsylvania to "to hold themselves in readiness to march at a moment's warning." Where exactly to camp "by easy marches" to meet an attack on the Delaware River or Chesapeake Bay was discussed and Brig. Gen. Joseph Bloomfield, commandant of the Fourth Military District, suggested Marcus Hook. On September 15, 1814, he requested additional military forces from Gov. Snyder and the next day those militia forces were sent to Marcus Hook.

John Price built a grist mill in 1752, on the west side of Marcus Hook Creek and operated it until he died in 1806. It was then purchased by David Trainer, Sr., and the site, or near the site, became an encampment for Pennsylvania militia.

On October 7, 1814, Gen. Edmund P. Gaines assumed command of the Fourth Military District. Camp Gaines was located "just back of Marcus Hook cross roads," under the command of Maj. Gen. Isaac Worrall. Gaines was there on the 12th to review the troops.

Soldiers constructed earth berms and placed cannon to protect the town and garrison. Gen. Gaines made his headquarters at the home of Ann P. Marshall Price, the widow of Samuel Price, Esq., John Price's son, who died on May 20, 1801.

Anywhere from 5,000 to 10,000, mostly

Pennsylvania and Delaware militia, along with some regulars were stationed there. No attack on the state by way of the Delaware or Chesapeake materialized and the fortifications were abandoned in the fall of 1814. The companies were marched to Philadelphia and by Christmas all were discharged.

On March 3, 1823, the Secretary of the Treasury was authorized to pay Joseph L. Dutton, $450; John Martin, Samuel Peterson, and Hannah Peterson, $175, and Samuel Walker, $175, "it being for injuries done to their lands in erecting works of defense near the town of Marcus Hook, on the Delaware river in the fall of 1814."

The grist mill property is located at present-day 4358 Ridge Rd. in Marcus Hook.

# The Chesapeake Campaign

Two states, Virginia and Maryland, were within the same theater of operations.

The British formulated a plan to concentrate their forces in the Chesapeake Bay area, primarily to divert American forces from the campaigns in Canada and engage in retaliatory raids and seize or destroy public property. The location offered direct access to the capital at Washington City and Baltimore, a major builder of pesky privateers.

The north–south oriented Chesapeake Bay lies within the states of Virginia and Maryland, the lower part in Virginia to the west and Maryland to the east. The upper bay region is in Maryland. Fisherman Island, off Cape Charles, Maryland, marks the north entrance to the Bay and the Cape Henry Lighthouse in Virginia, about 11 miles to the south, marks the southern entrance. Norfolk and Hampton Roads is just west of Cape Henry at the mouth of the James River.

The Potomac River flows from the west about midway up the Bay and separates Virginia from Maryland. Washington is approximately 105 winding river miles in a northwesterly direction up the Potomac.

In Maryland, St. Mary's County separates the Potomac River from the mouth of the Patuxent River to the north by about 20 miles. Calvert County lies north of the Patuxent. There were no major cities on the Patuxent.

Going north up Chesapeake Bay from the mouth of the Patuxent about 45 miles is Annapolis and another 12 miles or so is North Point, and from there to the west about 6 miles is Baltimore. Havre de Grace lies at the head of the Bay another 30 miles or so from North Point in Hanford County.

In January 1813, a blockade was set up, trapping Capt. Charles Stewart's frigate *Constellation* at Hampton Roads. The first vessel reported stopped coming out of Chesapeake Bay was the *Emily* on February 5, which was allowed to turn back.

On June 22, 1813, the British mounted an attack on Norfolk but were repulsed by militia and *Constellation* crew at Craney Island.

Adm. Warren's second-in-command, Rear-Adm. Sir George Cockburn, noted for his dislike of Americans, was turned loose for the inland operations.

It was noted at this time that the aging Admiral Warren was suffering from some malaise, so during the winter layover of 1813–14 at Bermuda, he was relieved by Vice-Admiral Hon. Sir Alexander Cochrane. With the defeat of Napoleon, the year 1814 offered England greater opportunity in North America, freeing up ships and four experienced army divisions under Maj.-Gen. Robert Ross.

Admiral Cochrane maintained the blockade and raided shipping offshore while Adm. Cockburn and the troops set about destroying anything primarily of military value in the coastal and Upper and Lower Bay regions and along the tributaries.

On April 28, 1814, Adm. Cochrane wrote to Adm. Cockburn that the destruction of private property was in retaliation for the Americans, "savage conduct in Canada, where they have destroyed our towns in the most inclement of seasons of the year; it is therefore but just that retaliation shall be made near to the seat of their government from whence those orders emanated."

General Ross arrived in Bermuda in the summer of 1814 with 4,500 troops and reported to Adm. Cockburn. It would be the general's last glorious campaign for the Crown. It was later estimated the Chesapeake campaign prevented around 25,000 troops from going to Canada.

The claimants have been arranged chronologically by date regardless of location up to the battle at Bladensburg on August 24, 1814.

## *Commodore Barney*

In 1813, the mayor and city council of the Corporation of Baltimore became concerned for the defense of their city and took measures at their own expense to insure their safety, "having been advised and recommended by the officers commanding at Baltimore." The effort was sanctioned by the War Department, and for this effort the citizens contributed over $25,000 and the city borrowed $75,000 at 6 percent interest for the use of the Committee of Vigilance and Safety.

Under the direction of Lt. Solomon Rutter, a resident of Mobtown, the city obtained the row galley *Vigilant* and "employed a number of barges and look-out boats."

Since the port was blockaded, there was little work for seamen so most had left for Philadelphia and New York where wages were $16 a month. The city was then obliged to pay $12, $14, and $16 monthly wages.

In 1814, Washington detailed Joshua Barney as commodore of a flotilla, "for the defense of the Chesapeake and its tributary waters," but Baltimore had to man them. He had 12 barges built, and used the *Vigilant* and two gunboats.

Capt. Barney's son, William, a major in Lt. Col. James Biays' 5th Cavalry District, Maryland Militia, was stationed at an observation post at North Point. He left that position to join his father's little flotilla as commander of the *Scorpion*. Lieutenant Solomon Rutter joined the command on April 25, Lt. Solomon Frazier on the 26th, and Dr. Charles B. Hamilton joined as surgeon.

By May 1814, the little flotilla was anchored just below the mouth of the Patuxent River in Maryland to await the British spring offensive. William Barney was appointed a lieutenant in the Navy on August 18, 1814.

After the war, the city filed a claim with the War Department for reimbursement of wages, but, by law, could only reimburse the city for the sailors' wages at the rate of militia pay—$8 a month. In the end, all but $15,159.09 was paid and was still in limbo as of 1828, due mainly to financial records not being kept in accordance with federal practices.

The legal status of the *Scorpion* appears somewhat murky. As stated in ASP Naval Affairs, page 342:

> Cutter *Scorpion*. In March, 1812, the old gunboat *No. 59* was hauled up on the wharf. Cut down to her floor timbers, and thence rebuilt with much improvement; coppered, launched, and rigged completely new, with sails, water casks, and all her armament and stores; fitted out, and named *Scorpion*.

That was at the Washington Navy Yard as reported by Thomas Tingey, but no mention was made of the purpose for the overhaul. It was reportedly commanded by Lt. Edmund P. Kennedy at Norfolk in September 1812, and in March 1813, became flagship of the Potomac Flotilla to protect

Washington. With Kennedy becoming commodore, Lt. George C. Read assumed command.

*Scorpion* is reported to have arrived at Baltimore on February 18, 1814, as flagship for Barney's flotilla, but it seems unlikely his son, a major of militia, would command a vessel of the U.S. Navy.

In March 1814, the only *Scorpion* reported on the Navy List was a 2-gun schooner on Lake Erie. No commander was noted, but it was in fact at Sault Ste. Marie under Lt. Daniel Turner with officers of the 23rd Infantry aboard. On September 5, they were captured by the British on Lake Huron.

Two *Scorpions* would mean the Navy had two ships with the same name at the same time, normally a practice to be avoided.

There is no mention of the *Scorpion* in the city of Baltimore's accounting records with the War Department, only the *Vigilant*, and on February 26, 1859, the Navy Department provided the Senate, as requested, with a list of vessels that had been captured, lost, or destroyed since 1798. There is no mention of a *Scorpion* lost in Chesapeake Bay, only the one on Lake Huron.

## Joseph Jeans

The claim was filed by Joseph's wife, Elizabeth Jeans, after he died on May 20, 1813, and she had married James Randall. The petition was referred to the Committee on Military Affairs on December 31, 1821, and then sent to the Committee of Claims.

As stated by the Committee of Claims on March 8, 1826:

> The petitioners represent that in the fall of the year 1812, a wagon and five horses, with their gear, the property of Joseph Jeans, was seized and taken by impressment by order of Lt. Col. Dudley Evans of the Virginia militia, to transport the baggage, &c., of a detachment which marched under the command of Colonel Evans, to join the Northwestern Army. The wagon, horses, and gear was regularly valued at the time to the sum of $595. Two of the horses, valued at $175, died or were lost while in service.
>
> Joseph Jeans was also in the public service with the detachment of militia, and returned home sick, and shortly thereafter died. The derangement of his affairs in consequence of death prevented them from obtaining the voucher, to wit: the appraisement bill, at least they did not obtain it until the law had expired under which payment could have been made to them. They ask payment for the horses, the one valued at $95 and the other $80, amounting to $175.
>
> This claim has been before Congress heretofore, and reported against by the Committee of Claims, believing the testimony insufficient. Since which some explanatory testimony has been obtained, which is satisfactory as to the impressment and valuation of the property, and of the loss there can be no doubt.

Elizabeth was paid $175 in 1827 and an additional $61 was awarded on May 29, 1830, "that being the difference between the value of two horses impressed into the service of the United States in the year 1812, and never returned to Jeans, and the sum which Jeans has received for the use and risk of said horses."

## Stephen Harris

In 1811, the schooner *Trimmer* was owned by Moses Myers & Son, merchants. Thomas M. Corely contracted to purchase the vessel, but was unable to fulfill the contract and sold it to Stephen Harris, who hired John Jarvis, a ship carpenter at Portsmouth, "who fitted her up in complete order." Harris was subsequently offered $3,000 for the vessel but requested $5,000.

The memorial of Stephen Harris, of the borough of Norfolk, State of Virginia:

> During the late war with Great Britain, when the enemy's fleet was blockading the waters of Virginia generally, but particularly the port

> of Norfolk, and when serious apprehensions were entertained that it was the intention of the enemy to sail up to the town and bombard it, the commanding general ordered certain vessels then in port to be seized, carried down, and sunk in the channel of the river in order to obstruct the passage of the fleet. Among the vessels so seized and sunk was one, a schooner of about 120 tons belonging to your memorialist, then newly repaired and rigged for sea, for which he has never received compensation.
>
> Your memorialist prays that this subject may be considered, and that such compensation may be allowed him as the facts in the case may justify.

At the time the vessel was taken in March 1813, Brig. Gen. Robert Taylor ordered Capt. John Bramble to hire appraisers, with Harris' consent. Tristram Butler, James Williamson, Thomas Warren, John Frost, and George Chamberlain assessed the value, which they put at $450, and reported that to Capt. Hopley Yeaton, assistant quartermaster general at Norfolk. On August 17, 1813, Gen. Taylor authorized that amount, which Harris accepted. On October 21 he assigned his claim to Neil McCoull who in turn assigned it to Dr. George Murray, Esq.

Edward Chamberlain testified the vessel was worth $3,000 when Harris bought it. William A. Graves, who worked at the Jarvis yard, gave his estimate at $25 a ton when the schooner left the yard.

No further money was awarded, as stated by the Committee of Claims on February 13, 1835, in part:

> As the petitioner is convicted of falsehood in asserting that he has never received any thing, it will require very explicit explanation and incontrovertible proof, to entitle any claim he may set up for additional compensation, however much injustice may have been done to him in the appraisement of his vessel, to the favorable consideration of Congress. The committee recommend the rejection of the petitioner's claim.

No explanation was given for the very low assessed value.

## *The Cannon Foundry*

On Friday, April 30, 1813, John S. Skinner, the postmaster at Baltimore, was on board the British frigate *Statira* off Annapolis, presumably on some business, when Capt. Hassard Stackpole told him he would soon be hearing about a cannon foundry way up the Bay, which Admiral Cockburn had just gone to destroy. Skinner said he knew of no such foundry, but Capt. Stackpole had a map and pointed to the Cecil Foundry. Adm. Cockburn had the foundry and a few other targets in mind where he knew deposits of military stores were located.

With his flag on Capt. John Lawrence's brig *Fantome*, the *Marlborough*, *Maidstone*, *Mohawk*, and tenders *Highflyer* and *Dolphin* anchored off Turkey Point and early on the morning of April 29 around 180 sailors and 500 marines set out in 11 barges for the 14-mile trip up the Elk River to Elkton. They came first to the prosperous port of Frenchtown on the right bank. The alarm no doubt had been sounded, but all Maj. James Sewall of the 49th Maryland Regiment had was a four-cannon battery that was still under construction. That battery was quickly manned by militia under Captains Edward Oldham and William Garrett while Maj. Sewall organized other militia members in helping residents round up and evacuate livestock and load up merchandise and personal possessions into wagons for evacuation of the town.

At around 7 a.m. the British landing force arrived, routed the 40 or so militia manning the cannons, and by 1 p.m. the town was a smoldering pile of ash, along with a large store of Army supplies destined for Canada.

Elk Landing, just upriver, had been the jumping off point for the Redcoat's 40-mile march northeast to Philadelphia during the Revolutionary War. This time would be different. Accurate fire from

Forts Defiance and Hollingsworth stopped the illustrious admiral in his tracks.

Cockburn's next objective was across the upper bay in the Susquehanna River where he intended to pay Samuel Hughes a visit, but before setting off he anchored the *Marlborough*, *Fantome*, *Dolphin*, and *Highflyer* off Spesutie Island, apparently to take on water, provisions, and regroup. While there, he heard gunfire and saw the American flag being raised at the town of Havre de Grace at the mouth of the Susquehanna River. The town wasn't on Cockburn's list of targets, but this activity aroused his curiosity and he concluded that something important might be there and decided to investigate.

Soundings indicated the water was too shallow for ships to approach so Adm. Cockburn detailed Lt. George A. Westphal, first lieutenant of the *Marlborough*, to fit out a number of boats for a daylight assault the next morning. The boats with 150 marines and Lt. Westphal's company of Congreve rocket artillerists left at midnight on May 2 under Capt. John Lawrence. *Dolphin* and *Highflyer* followed behind. As the little flotilla made their way in, they found shoal water made a direct approach to the town closer than 6 miles impossible so they stopped and prepared for a daylight bombardment from the rocket boats.

At daylight, a "warm fire was opened," according to Adm. Cockburn, and was answered by two cannons from shore. As the boats were cautiously maneuvered in closer, it was noted the cannon fire decreased the further in they got and it soon became possible to go ashore.

When the marines landed, Lt. Westphal headed for the Concord Point cannon, from which about 40 militia had fled, and turned the cannon around and commenced firing at the militia, who were observed fleeing to shelter in the town.

Another cannon was still being operated by 2nd Lt. John O'Neill, of the 42nd Regiment of Maryland militia, who was forced to quit when he was injured, but he also had two muskets and returned fire with those until Lt. Westphal saw him and made him a prisoner. Cockburn wanted him shot, but he was held aboard ship with a few others for several days until his daughter Matilda, 15, came aboard and pleaded for his release.

Adm. Cockburn complained that the Americans, "no longer feeling themselves equal to a manly and open resistance, they commenced a teasing and irritating fire from behind the houses, walls, trees, &c.," until they were routed and driven from their "lurking places." With limited forces, Cockburn decided not to pursue the militia or residents who had fled into the woods. The only casualty noted was Lt. Westphal, who had been shot through the hand.

About 130 "stand of arms" was destroyed, and of the 60 or so homes and buildings in the town, anywhere from 20 to 40 were damaged to some extent, or destroyed, and all were looted of everything valuable.

Adm. Cockburn asked Howes Goldsborough, "if there was not a cannon foundry somewhere in the neighborhood" and he said there was. Cockburn said, "he knew as well as he did where it was, and he intended to pay it a visit."

William S. Coale approached Cockburn to enquire what would happen to his property and was told, "he should suffer no injury from them, that their object was to burn and destroy all public property he could come at." The admiral asked Coale how many soldiers were at the foundry and he was told "that a company of troops was stationed at the foundry and quartered in the houses there for some days."

The admiral told Capt. James Campbell, "that his principal object in coming to the foundry was to destroy public property, and asked him where the shot were, and if he knew anything about them."

## S. Hogg & Co.

Samuel Hogg, Thomas Burnside, Sr., and William T. Killpatrick were merchants at Havre de Grace, each having one-third interest in their store. Samuel and Thomas died soon after the war ended and William Killpatrick became insolvent, and "lost all direct interest in the subject." Thomas left a wife, Catherine, and a son, Thomas Jr.

Inheritance laws at the time prevented Catherine from claiming any interest in the property so she had to wait until her son, Thomas Jr. as lawful heir, became 21 years of age and they could file a claim. Catherine later married John Hogg.

As stated by Peter Hagner, the Third Auditor, on May 23, 1836, in part:

> In 1813, the citizens of that town resolved to place themselves in a posture of defense, and, accordingly, purchased ammunition, which was made up into cartridges and stored away until required, in the house of the firm because of its location near the point where it was supposed the enemy would land, and because of the willingness manifested by the members of the firm to afford every possible facility for the defense of the town. This accommodation, together with their stables for the use of the cavalry that had been collected to aid in the scheme of resistance, was gratuitously offered by the firm, and accepted by those who volunteered their services.
>
> On or about the 3rd May, 1813, soon after this preparation, the enemy made an attack on the town and burnt a part of it, including the storehouse and stables of the firm, and the whole loss sustained on that occasion by the firm in merchandise and clothing, amounted to at least $2,100, of which one-third part belonged to Thomas Burnside the elder. His private property consisting of furniture, &c., destroyed in his dwelling-house, was worth at least $150, making his entire loss about $850.
>
> One of the depositions appears to have been made by W.T. Killpatrick who has testified that some days previous to the attack, a number of quarter casks of powder for the use of the militia stationed there was lodged in the store and made up into cartridges.
>
> On the morning of the attack there was a quantity of it left in their store-room, which was found by the enemy and destroyed, and the loss of the firm of S. Hogg & Co. on that day in store goods and clothing amounted to at least $2,100. He has testified that some days previous to the attack, two casks of gunpowder, which had been purchased by the citizens of the place for the defense of the town, were placed in the second floor of their store, and there made up into cartridges by him and John O'Neill. A quantity of iron slugs was gratuitously given by William Cole and taken to the store, and then made into cartridges—part of which was taken for the defense of the place, and the balance which remained in the store was found by the enemy and destroyed. He believes this circumstance caused the wanton destruction of their property.
>
> He offered gratuitously the use of their stable some two or three days previous to the attack to accommodate a portion of cavalry who had come on to assist in the defense of the town. He believes this circumstance was known to the enemy from some observations made to him by one of the officers, Captain Lawrence, of the brig *Fantome*, to this effect: "We know you, sir. You wanted war, and you shall feel its effects."
>
> Thomas Courtney has testified that in May, 1813, the militia was called out to defend Havre de Grace. He commanded a company at Havre de Grace when some kegs of powder were received which was sent from Annapolis for the defense of the place and were deposited in the store of Messrs. Hogg, Burnside, & Co. Cartridges were made form the powder in the house and that when the British came to Havre de Grace they destroyed all of Hogg, Burnside, & Co.'s goods, the amount of which he never ascertained.
>
> John O'Neill remembers weighing gunpowder at the store to fill cannon cartridges and old iron for making langrage for cannons and this was some time before the British landed in Havre de Grace.
>
> John Donahoo recollects Hogg, Burnside & Co. had part of the gunpowder which was for the defense of Havre de Grace to be in their possession two days previous to the British landing.

The claim was denied by the Committee of Claims on May 23, 1838, as stated by Peter Hagner:

> The search for evidence of a presentation of

the claim, either to me or the later Commissioner has proved unsuccessful. It would not have been admissible by me even if the buildings had appeared to have been occupied by order of an officer or agent of the United States as places of deposit for military or naval stores at the time of destruction, as the loss of the firm would seem to have been confined to private property. The buildings are not alleged to have belonged to any of them, nor are they declared to have been used in the way mentioned in the depositions, at any time, by the order of an officer of the United States. It would seem to have been solely an affair of the citizens, and for any loss consequent on which the Commissioner had no authority to award an indemnity.

Capt. John Lawrence commanded the 18-gun brig *Fantome*, part of Adm. Sir John B. Warren's squadron.

## William B. Stokes

As reported by the Committee of Claims on February 27, 1817:

The petitioner was the owner of a house in the town of Havre de Grace, in the State of Maryland, when the British detachment arrived at that place in May, 1813, at which time it was destroyed by them. The petitioner represents his house as the value of $7,500. The evidence laid before the committee appears to have been taken under commissions issued by Richard Bland Lee.

It is set forth in the deposition of John C. Ridgely, a lieutenant of dragoons in the service of the United States, that on the Saturday before the British arrived at Havre de Grace, he reached there with a detachment of dragoons in pursuit of deserters and asked for quarters. Mary Sears, who kept the house of Mr. Stokes as a tavern, objected; but he insisted and did quarter there from Saturday until Monday when the British landed, and at the time had two deserters under guard in the house.

Subsequently he bore a flag to the enemy and remonstrated against the destruction of the house and was answered that it was a military depot. Abraham Jarrett, another witness examined, swears that he accompanied the flag and on remonstrating against the conduct of the British in burning the town, he was told by the admiral that many of the houses burnt were occupied for military purposes; that it was his determination to burn every house occupied for military purposes, &c.

The depositions of Ridgely and Jarrett are those only that go to touch the cause of the burning, and all they state amounts to no more than that this was a vague excuse of a vindictive freebooter for a disgraceful outrage on the usages of civilized warfare. The detachment of cavalry, it appears very evidently, adjourned in a public house over the Sabbath only; that they were there as persons passing casually, not in a military station, nor exercising any control over the house. The attempt to establish a military occupancy from the presence of militia is still more objectionable, as there were, it is believed, only the local militia present, and many of them residents.

That a British admiral, committing acts of the most flagitious desolation, should, when earnestly expostulated with against it, offer some pretense of justification at the expense of candor and truth, was to be expected—it was perfectly in character. But the committee think it would be erroneous to admit such authority to establish the fact of public occupancy. Mr. Jarrett says that many of the houses were alleged by the enemy to be occupied for military purposes. This would seem to convey the idea that Mrs. Sears's house was the strongest case, and that others are considered as eligible to allowance, even on slighter pretenses. Some, however, it is admitted, have been burnt wantonly.

The whole transaction the committee have no doubt was of the most lawless character, and they cannot admit for a moment that this flagitiously incendiary act should be at all palliated by the admission of such evidence to sanction it is an act of excusable warfare.

The committee believe this to be the first claim of a similar nature presented for the decision of Congress, and they apprehend that the extent in which like claims may be made gives to the decision that may now be had an importance that does not belong to the value claimed. While they regret an enemy, styling themselves as Christians, could commit acts of such aggravated turpitude, and that their fellow-citizens have been made the victims of such heinous depravity, they cannot feel the obligation on the government to make indemnity, nor discover any practical principle of justice that would allow it.

## Mary Sears

As reported by the Committee of Claims on January 10, 1820:

During the late war, Mary Sears rented, from William B. Stokes, a house, in Havre de Grace, and occupied it as a tavern. On the 3rd of May, 1813, the house, with all the furniture and other articles therein, was burned by the British, by which act the present claimant sustained a loss to the amount of $3,200. Application is, therefore, made to Congress for reimbursement.

The committee are unable to perceive that this claim has been provided for by any law or decision of Congress; and they therefore submit that the claim of Mary Sears ought not to be allowed.

## Charles Foreman

Charles Foreman, of Havre de Grace, "was engaged in making and trimming coaches when the British troops took possession of that place." As reported by the Committee of Claims on January 8, 1846:

The petitioner alleges that he was plundered of his property to the amount of nearly $2,000 by the British troops in May, 1813, during the war, while he was called to bear arms in defense of his country. The country was invaded by the enemy and the place taken, sacked, and plundered by them.

There is no legal evidence of his loss. Claims should never be allowed on the single oath of the claimant, and all ex parte testimony not of record should be given on oath. Besides, there is no principle of law or equity that binds the government to indemnify its citizens for losses sustained by the depredations of the public enemy in time of war. The committee are of opinion the claim ought not to be allowed.

## John Guest

John married Rebecca Hall in Hartford County, Maryland, on November 13, 1792. As reported by the Committee of Claims on March 12, 1828:

The petitioner's husband, John Guest, was the owner of a lot of tenements thereon erected, situate in the town of Havre de Grace, in the State of Maryland, in the year 1813.

The 42nd Regiment of Maryland militia, commanded by Colonel William Smith, was called into actual service, and that about 100 men, a portion of Col. Smith's command, were stationed in the tenements and premises and occupied from the 20th April until the 3rd of May, 1813, as the headquarters of the regiment. The premises was the place of deposit for arms and ammunition for the 42nd Regiment, and was used and occupied as such, until the 3rd of May, when the town was attacked and taken by the enemy, and the buildings burnt by the enemy in consequence of its being a military depot.

John Guest died 5th March, 1817, and the petitioner did not know until after the expiration of the limitation mentioned in the act of Congress that she would have been entitled to anything for the destruction of her husband's property.

Col. William Smith's testimony proves that on the 20th April, 1813, he stationed 100 men at Havre de Grace in a certain house which was occupied by the troops until the 3rd May, 1813. A considerable quantity of fixed ammunition and about six or seven kegs of powder were also placed in the house, it then being the arsenal and chief rendezvous for the militia. It was the first and main object of the enemy and consequently was burnt down with the smaller houses and appendages thereto belonging.

Thomas Courtney proves that a part of Col. William Smith's command was stationed in a frame house belonging to Mr. John Guest, of Philadelphia, and was considered by the British as a military depot. John O'Neill proves the same.

William Kirkpatrick proves the same and in addition states that a brick office attached to the premises was used by the militia as a place of deposite for arms, ammunition, &c., and that he assisted in taking out fixed ammunition on the 3rd of May, and that on the evening of the 3rd, on finding some difficulty in opening the place of deposit, the doors were broken open and ammunition handed out to the militia and that both houses were burned.

Paca Smith and William Williams prove that in 1813 the premises were worth $500. From the foregoing facts the committee are of opinion that the petitioner is entitled to relief and report a bill.

## Samuel Hughes

Samuel Hughes was born at Hagerstown, Maryland, in 1741 into a family of ironmasters from Lancaster, Pennsylvania.

After serving in Maryland's 3rd Regiment during the Revolutionary War, he decided to sell his interest in the family business and purchase the old Principio Ironworks on the Susquehanna River, about 4 miles northeast of Havre de Grace, in Cecil County, and which he called the Cecil Furnace. He eventually acquired a gristmill near the forge, extensive property, and business holdings and in 1785 was one of the incorporators of Havre de Grace in Hartford County. In 1803 he purchased the Jacob Giles, Jr., mansion on Mount Pleasant, and served as a town commissioner until 1809.

He had extensive experience in making naval ordnance and on August 4, 1807, wrote to Secretary of the Navy Robert Smith to say he would charge $133 per ton "for what cannon you may order, and if you will give me employment for all next year, I will furnish them at $130 per ton." Smith replied with an order for fifty 32-pounders and fifty 24-pounders, but said no money could be paid or advanced until appropriated by Congress, "which it is confidently expected they will do, in the course of the ensuing November."

John Conway was the clerk at the foundry for the previous eight years when war came in 1812 and later stated, "the guns and shot belonging to the United States were left there in deposit," and that Maj. Richard Simpson of the 30th Regiment of Maryland Militia sent a company to quarter at the works for the protection of the public property.

The Cecil Furnace was only 3 or 4 miles up the river so Adm. Cockburn went along with Capt. Lawrence and it was found, plundered, and destroyed, along with the gristmill.

Samuel Coale, a business partner of Hughes' and the manager at the foundry, said Adm. Cockburn told him, "that he had particular instructions from England to destroy this foundry, and that he was determined on this measure from the time of entering the Chesapeake Bay," as Coale stated later:

> From the tenor of the conversation he understood the admiral considered it public property, that at the time the British came, and for four years before, there were 13 long 24-pounders, and 22 long 32-pounders, with a considerable quantity of shot belonging to the United States left in deposit there, and at their risqué, as can be fully proved by reference to the Navy Department. For the protection of the property, a Major Simpson, who is now dead, sent a company of militia to the foundry about one or two weeks before the British came, which company, with their arms, was quartered in the house at the foundry, and the greatest part remained there till the British came in sight, when they retreated. When the troops first came there, they placed the shot belonging to the United States underground, which saved them, but the enemy spiked up and rammed the cannon with various materials.

Abraham Jarrett said he went aboard the frigate *Maidstone* to ask about Col. Hughes' foundry and gristmill and was told by Capt. George Burdett the mill was burned without his knowledge and should not have been burned, but the foundry "was a proper mark for destruction, and everything combined with it for the making of cannon."

Five vessels with a large supply of flour were also destroyed in the Susquehanna before the raiding party arrived back aboard ship about 10 p.m., "after 22 hours of constant exertion." They took six guns from Havre de Grace and disabled 45 others.

John Skinner stated later that he happened to be on board Adm. John Warren's ship *San Domingo* on the day Adm. Cockburn's expedition returned, and said he heard some of the officers mention the number of guns belonging to the United States they had destroyed at the foundry. From all the remarks and conversations of the British officers, he was convinced the destruction of the cannon was the object of the expedition, "and if it had not been for the public property, the expedition would not have taken place."

It was known the British remained in force for some time in the neighborhood of Caleb Dorsey's furnace, which they knew about as it was also on the map, and which they knew was undefended, but for some reason they didn't destroyed it. Skinner said he didn't know "their motives for this forbearance."

The total value of all of Samuel Hughes' property was estimated at $29,795. The value of undamaged property was $3,700, leaving a loss to Hughes of $26,095.

As reported by the Committee of Claims on February 3, 1818:

> The Committee of Claims, to whom was referred the report of the Commissioner of Claims in the case of Samuel Hughes, of the state of Maryland, praying the payment of $25,000 as compensation for the destruction of his cannon foundry and other buildings appurtenant thereto, by the enemy during the late war, have had the same under consideration, and offer to the House the following Report.
>
> From the evidence, the committee think it will be clearly seen that the claim of the petitioner does not come within the provisions of the act passed on the 9th of April, 1816. The foundry, and buildings appurtenant to it, cannot, in the judgment of the committee, be considered either as barracks or as a place of deposit for military stores. For such only did government provide payment by the act of 1816, and they therefore recommend to the House that the claim of Samuel Hughes, of the state of Maryland, ought not to be allowed.

Samuel Hughes made guns for the *Constitution*. The destruction of the ironworks was financially disastrous for Col. Hughes, and even after rebuilding, the debt was too much and he sold it in 1822 along with the mansion and his other properties.

Five vessels with a large supply of flour were also destroyed in the Susquehanna before the raiding party arrived back aboard ship about 10 p.m., "after 22 hours of constant exertion." They took six guns from Havre de Grace and disabled 45 others.

The Maryland Historical Society has a marker at the site of Fort Hollingsworth.

## The Elizabeth City Churchwardens

As reported by the Committee of Claims on December 23, 1829:

> During the late war, a bell belonging to the Episcopal Church of Elizabeth City Parish was used, by the order of the officer having the command at that point, to give warning to the surrounding country, of the approach of the enemy, and as a signal for relieving guard, and, while so used, was broken.
>
> The petitioners ask for an amount sufficient to pay the expense of recasting the bell, which is estimated at 25 cents per pound, which, with some necessary expense, the Committee think ought to be paid, and report a bill granting the sum of $130.50.

In 1610 a small group of survivors from Jamestown travelled about 30 miles southeast and settled on the north peninsula, now Cape Charles at the entrance to Chesapeake Bay. Since they had help from the Kecoughtan Indians they named their village Kecoughtan (Kiccoughtan), but after some trouble the settlement was renamed Elizabeth City in 1619 after the daughter of James I. In 1623, the settlers divided their land and church parishes into four "corporations" which were "coextensive with the parish," one of which was

Elizabeth City, which then relocated to the east side of the Hampton River.

In 1634 the whole of Virginia was divided into eight counties, one of which was Elizabeth City County. In 1705, the name of the main town became Hampton, but Elizabeth City was still used. The fourth structure was a fine brick building completed in 1728 by builder Henry Cary, Jr., of Williamsburg. The bell for the church was purchased in 1760 from the sale of lands donated by Alexander Kennedy.

In June 1813, about 400 Virginia militia were at Hampton under Maj. Stapleton Crutchfield. On the 24th, Adm. Sir John Warren landed a force composed partly from the 1st and 2nd Independent Companies of Foreigners, mostly French deserters and prisoners who were used as garrison troops and in some instances to relieve regular troops for more urgent duties. The militia was routed and from June 24–27, they ransacked the town and used the parish church for a barracks. After the shooting was over, many of the French troops deserted and engaged in looting, rape, robbery, atrocities, murder, and wanton destruction.

The shock of the raid caused membership to greatly decline and the church fell into decay. In 1824 efforts at restoration began and by 1827, when the work was nearly complete, the church was named St. John's, and consecrated by Bishop Richard Channing Moore on January 8, 1830.

Robert Lively and William Hope, churchwardens of St. John's Protestant Episcopal Church, Elizabeth City Parish, filed their petition to get a new bell on December 19, 1827, which was referred to the Committee of Claims.

Robert Lively was a merchant as Robert Lively & Co. in Hampton and was appointed by Gen. Zachary Taylor along with Robert Griffin to investigate the atrocities and make a report.

A historical marker states:

> As British Gen. Sidney Beckwith dispersed the local militia on 25 June 1813, Adm. Sir George Cockburn feigned an attack with barges at the mouth of the Hampton River. Hampton's water battery was abandoned and the British occupied the town. Their initial march in the town became known as the Sack of Hampton. There were reports that "at little Hampton, every horror was committed with impunity—rape, murder, pillage." These outrages became a rallying cry for the defense of the Chesapeake. By the end of June, the British left to raid elsewhere.

The churchwardens were paid $130.50 in 1830.

## *The* Asp

In July 1813, Midshipman James B. Sigourney's schooner *Asp* was patrolling with the *Scorpion* on Chesapeake Bay. On the 14th, they left the Yeocomico Creek and upon coming into the Bay were met by the British brig sloops *Contest* and *Mohawk*. The poor-sailing *Asp* was unable to escape and went back up the river. The British commenced firing and Sigourney, along with 10 of his crew, were lost and the *Asp* set on fire. After the British left, Midshipman Henry M. McClintock took the remaining nine crew back aboard and put the fire out and repaired the damage.

This incident caused great alarm in the area. Col. Thomas Downing ordered Major Pemberton Claughton, of the 37th Regiment, Virginia Militia, from Northumberland County, to occupy Mundy Point at the end of Mondays Neck, Virginia, on the Yeocomico Creek, "this position being considered the best in the upper parts of the county for the annoyance of an invading force."

### William T. Nimmo

William T. Nimmo's residence on the Lynnhaven River was known as the Pleasure House.

On the evening of February 5, 1813, the British burned a schooner and put the crew ashore at his home and made it known that Adm. John Warren was determined to obtain water and would send troops if necessary. It was reported that a party from the British fleet came ashore the next day with a flag of truce to land some prisoners at there.

As reported by the Committee of Claims on November 25, 1818:

> It appears from the testimony of Robert B. Taylor, the General commanding the troops of the United States stationed at Norfolk, for its defense in the year 1813, that the dwelling house (called the Pleasure House) and other buildings of the petitioner were occupied by his order and that this station was regarded as one of the most important outposts of the army.
>
> In the month of September, 1813, while the Pleasure House was occupied by a detachment of the army, the post was attacked in the night by a party of the enemy and the house was burned down by them.
>
> Littleton W. Tazewell states that from his knowledge of the dwelling house and other buildings destroyed by the enemy, together with information received from other sources, he believes that same were worth to the claimant $500. John Nevison gave evidence in corroboration of the statement made by Mr. Tazewell and General Taylor.
>
> From this testimony, given by characters of the first respectability, it would seem that the occupation of the houses, by the authority of an officer of the United States their destruction while so occupied, and the value of them, are facts, most conclusively and unquestionably established.

William Nimmo's claim was presented on December 10, 1817, and he was paid $500 in 1824.

## George J. Knight

The Yeocomico Creek is a tidal tributary of the Potomac River in Virginia just over a mile long. The town of Kinsale sits between two branches of the headwaters.

George Knight was a merchant in Baltimore who owned the schooner *Experiment* and employed Capt. George McDuell to trade in the Chesapeake Bay and its tributary waters.

In April 1814, the *Experiment* was heading down the Potomac from Alexandria, in the District of Columbia, to St. Mary's City, about 80 river miles downstream and then north up the St. Mary's River just around Piney Point.

On April 13, Midshipman Richard Mackall's Navy 3-gun schooner *Asp* left the Washington Navy Yard with cannon and towing a raft made from pieces of masts intended for the construction of the frigate *Java* at Baltimore.

After he had left, the Navy Department was informed that a British squadron was off the mouth of the Potomac and orders were sent to stop the *Asp*. Mackall was informed that the enemy's squadron was at anchor a small distance below Blackstone's Island, in the Potomac and on April 28 he put in at Ludlow's landing and wrote to Comm. Thomas Tingey that for the safety of the raft and goods he should move further up the river.

At this time lookouts spotted the *Experiment* and Mackall hailed and stopped them. Capt. McDuell was informed of the reports of the British and that, as his vessel was not a swift sailor with a tow and he needed to insure the protection of his naval stores, he needed a faster vessel, "as a lookout vessel to proceed down the river and reconnoiter the enemy."

Capt. McDuell had received strict orders not to engage in any activity that would endanger the schooner or the property of others on board as cargo so he declined Mackall's "request." Mackall explained that as a naval officer he was authorized to employ lookout vessels and ordered Capt. McDuell to continue down the river, which he then felt he had no option of refusing, so he proceeded, "keeping as near the shore as possible."

On rounding Piney Point just at dusk, they suddenly saw the British squadron. No escape upriver was possible owing to the wind blowing downriver so he decided the best escape was to head due south across the Potomac for Yeocomico Creek, but on going up a little way, they went aground.

Capt. Allen S. Dozier's company of militia was stationed just above the mouth of the creek and saw the stranded schooner. Upon request, they assisted all night in trying to get the schooner refloated, but were unsuccessful.

Capt. William L. Rogers commanded a company of Army troops about two miles from the *Experiment* and also went to their assistance, arriving just as a large British barge, "under cover of a heavy armed schooner," was approaching. Rogers opened fire but was outgunned and forced to cover. The British also tried to free the vessel but couldn't so they set fire to it and left. Rogers went back aboard and tried to put the fire out but wasn't able to. He testified later he thought the schooner was 80 to 100 tons and worth around $2,000 to $3,000.

Capt. McDuell filed a formal protest with the collector at the Port of Yeocomico.

George Knight suffered such severe losses in Baltimore that he moved to the western part of New York to take up farming. Then, on February 10, 1830, his house burned down and destroyed all of his records.

Knight's claim was referred to the Committee on Naval Affairs, which reported favorably on December 23, 1831. On February 2, 1838, Congress approved a further $1,500 for his schooner to equal the lowest amount of the estimated value of the vessel.

The Committee of Claims reported on July 7, 1838, and rejected the entire claim for want of evidence that the vessel was ever impressed.

George J. Knight was paid $2,000 in 1832.

## *St. Leonard's Creektown*

As stated by the Committee of Claims:

> The unexpected advance of the British troops upon the villages bordering the Patuxent River in 1814 found this section of the Union wholly unprepared.
>
> In June, 1814, when the enemy ascended the Patuxent River, within 28 miles of Washington City, there was not a breastwork nor a fortification of any description—not a solitary cannon planted to sound an alarm, or check their progress to the Capitol of this Union. What was to be done?
>
> Under these trying circumstances the commanding officer did not hesitate. He lost no time in strengthening his position and fortifying himself in the best manner time and circumstances would allow. If the necessity exist, then that case has arrived, in which the government may take private property, or endanger its safety, for the public defense.

Adm. Cockburn became aware of Commodore Barney's flotilla and vowed to destroy it. Barney's boats patrolled around various areas and when an advance force was spotted on June 1, 1814, Barney chased them until the 74-gun *Dragon* appeared off Cedar Point in the West Yeocomico River in Virginia. Barney then sailed up the Patuxent about 4 miles to the shallow waters of St. Leonard Creek.

The creek runs in a northerly direction about 9 miles from the mouth of the Patuxent River to form the eastern part of a small peninsula in Chesapeake Bay. The town of St. Leonard is about 2 miles north of the main waterway.

On June 8, a British frigate, a brig, and two schooners ascended the Patuxent and anchored at the mouth of St. Leonard Creek and readied several barges to go up the creek.

Barney's boats opened fire and the British retreated. In response to this situation, the Maryland militia under Major Michael Taney was called out. This was repeated two or three times until June 10 when the British arrived with 21 barges, a rocket boat, and two schooners. A major battle commenced up the creek with both sides eventually breaking off, and the British retreated to their anchorage at the mouth of the creek.

To break the blockade, Barney sent for reinforcements from Washington. A detachment of District of Columbia mounted volunteers under Maj. John Peters in the service of the United States was dispatched and Marine Capt. Samuel Miller with 120 Marines and five 18-pounder artillery pieces was sent. The artillery failed to perform as expected when Barney commenced his attack owing to their poor location and he was forced back up the creek and was blockaded by the enemy.

## John Broome

As reported by the Committee of Claims on April 12, 1836:

> The testimony shows that the dwelling-house of John Broome was situated near the Patuxent River in Calvert County, Maryland. In June, 1814, the British armed vessels sailed up the river within the vicinity of his property.
>
> Colonel Michael Taney, then in command of a regiment of militia, upon observing British forces proceeding towards the dwelling ordered a detachment of the militia to march and take possession of the same in order to defend it in case the enemy should land and approach it. The detachment remained in possession of the house a short time, probably less than a day, and vacated it. Four days afterwards, the British forces landed and destroyed the house with fire.
>
> The evidence in the case does not show that the property at the time of its destruction was occupied by order of an officer of the United States as barracks for the troops or as a place of deposit for military or naval stores. On the contrary, the United States troops, which had been placed there for a short time to protect the property had been withdrawn from it four days previous to the time of its destruction. And there is nothing in the evidence to contradict the inference that the petitioner was in the full and uncontrolled possession of the property at the time it was destroyed.
>
> The petitioner has exhibited no certificate of an officer or agent of the United States to sustain this claim. To obviate the necessity of furnishing such evidence, he has shown that Colonel Taney has left the State of Maryland, and that the other officers in general are dead, or have moved away.
>
> The committee recommend the petition of John Broome be rejected.

As reported by the Committee of Claims on January 8, 1839, in part:

> The witnesses now speak of the house of the petitioner as having been an important point of attack or defense in reference to the rear of the flotilla and troops, and account for its destruction by the enemy in that way. In the opinion of the committee, there is nothing in this suggestion. The house was occupied by our troops but for a day or less, while the enemy appeared approaching towards it, and by a detachment under the immediate command of the house. The occupation was evidently intended for the protection of the property. As soon as the enemy retired, the troops evacuated the house, and four days afterwards it was burnt by the enemy. It is true that a detachment of our troops attempted to reach the house on the day it was destroyed and were driven back. But it is evident they were sent to repel the enemy and protect the house, and not to occupy it. Had it been a point of so much importance both to our troops and the enemy, as represented by the witnesses, the occupation would have been a continued one.
>
> The committee concur fully in the views taken by the Committee of Claims in their former reports, and recommend that the petitioner is not entitled to relief.

The claim was again rejected on August 20, 1842.

## Richard Mackall

Mackall filed a claim for the destruction of his tobacco warehouse by British troops in June 1814. He said his building was used by American troops for military stores. Reports were made against this claim by the Committee of Claims on April 15, 1836, February 22, 1837, and

January 27, 1839. Thomas Billingsley and Benjamin Slye testified.

As reported by the Committee of Claims on February 4, 1851:

> On the 8th of June, 1814, the 36th Regiment of United States Infantry, then stationed in St. Mary's County, Maryland, was ordered to Calvert County, Maryland, for the protection of the flotilla under the command of Commodore Barney, then blockaded in St. Leonard's creek by two British frigates, and other smaller armed vessels. A part of this regiment, in order to elude the British naval force then having the command of the Patuxent River, was ordered to march to Benedict, and there to cross the river and effect a junction with the American forces at St. Leonard's creek. After this portion of the 36th Regiment had crossed the river, they landed upon the farm of the petitioner, and, by the order of the officer in command, the tobacco-house of the claimant was taken possession of, and all the baggage of the regiment deposited therein. On the same day a sergeant's guard was left in possession of the tobacco-house and military stores until the regiment should reach St. Leonard's, a distance of 20 miles, and procure the means of transportation.
>
> When the enemy came up the river, some eight or ten days thereafter, they fired on the guard of the house, and, leaving an armed schooner at anchor, proceeded up the river, captured several American schooners, which they loaded with tobacco, and returned to their vessel, left at anchor, opposite the house of the petitioner. The enemy then landed, took one of the United States soldiers a prisoner, and burnt the tobacco-house with its contents.
>
> It further appears from the testimony that the occupancy of the petitioner's tobacco-house by the United States soldiers continued for eight or ten days prior to its destruction, and that whilst so occupied, on the day before the house was burnt, an American officer arrived from the encampment at St. Leonard's with wagons to transport the military stores from the house of the petitioner, but being discovered by the enemy, they were fired upon and compelled to retire without effecting that object, and on the next day the enemy landed and destroyed the house and its contents.
>
> It also appears from the testimony that the tobacco-house when burnt contained three crops of tobacco, estimated at 30,000 pounds, and one crop of wheat estimated at 500 bushels, which, with the house, was totally destroyed.
>
> Your committee are of opinion from the facts above enumerated that the petitioner is equitably entitled to claim of the United States the fair value of his tobacco-house, wheat and tobacco, so destroyed by the enemy.

## Joshua Cullumber

As reported by the Committee of Claims on December 21, 1835:

> The petitioner states that in 1814 he owned a schooner of upwards of 50 tons burthen in St. Leonard Creek, loaded with lumber for Baltimore. Prior to his departure, Commodore Barney's flotilla ran up into the creek, and was there blockaded by the enemy. He removed the rigging and sails of his schooner to a barn some distance and was prepared with augers to sink his vessel should it become necessary.
>
> When Barney escaped with his flotilla and ran up the Patuxent, he left John Geohegan in possession of a quantity of stores, munitions of war, &c. Geohegan came with a body of men and forcibly took his vessel to carry away the stores, munitions of war, &c., threw his timber overboard, and went and got the sails and rigging, and put to her. The British captured and burnt her.
>
> The reason of his delay in prosecuting his claim was that he was ignorant that the government would pay for property taken and destroyed under such circumstances.
>
> The petitioner is sustained in every statement he makes by the testimony of Thomas Travers who swears he was an eye witness of the whole transaction and gives a more intelligent account of the matter than the petitioner, except the reason of his delay in which he is sustained by the honorable Mr. Stoddard, who states that he heard the case and gave it as his opinion he was entitled to relief from the government.
>
> A bill was reported in this case on the 8th of January, 1835. Having examined the case again, and concurring with the former committee, a bill is herewith presented.

Joshua Cullumber was paid $1,000 in 1836. He enlisted as a private in Capt.

William Clare's company, 31st Regiment of Maryland Militia, on July 18, 1813, and was discharged near St. Leonard Creek on July 22, 1814. John Geohegan was a sailing master who served from September 16, 1813, to April 15, 1815. Thomas Travers was a private in Capt. John Travers' company of 48th Regiment Maryland Militia.

## *The First Battle at St. Leonard Creek*

On June 8, the British commenced firing on Barney's boats. One sailor was lost and a boat set on fire. Sailing Master William Barney, the commodore's son, led efforts to extinguish the flames. On June 10, the British began salvage operations on a damaged schooner aground and retired.

### James J. Pattison

A timely claim was filed and on October 17, 1816, commissioners were appointed by Richard Bland Lee but on January 23, 1818, the claim was rejected. In 1825 it was examined again and remanded to Peter Hagner, the Third Auditor, "who considered the testimony insufficient to justify payment for the property."

As reported by the Committee of Claims on March 3, 1836:

> The petitioner claims pay for a house and furniture burnt in June, 1814, by a detachment of British troops in consequence, it is alleged, of the occupancy of the house and premises by the Maryland Militia under the command of Colonel Michael Taney. The house stood on the Patuxent, near the mouth of St. Leonard Creek, in Calvert County, Maryland.
>
> The flotilla of Commodore Joshua Barney were anchored in the creek, and threatened by the British commander. It was to protect and defend Commodore Barney that the militia under Major Taney were called out.
>
> William Hooper, on the 14th of October, 1813, swears that he was a dragoon in Captain John G. Mackall's troop of horse and was ordered, in June, 1814, near the mouth of St. Leonard's Creek. When the troop arrived in camp, they found no provisions, and they were ordered by Colonel Taney to make Pattison's house their quarters and to go, without delay, to quarters. When they arrived there, they found a detachment engaged in providing provisions for the regiment from the farm of Pattison. The troop fed their horses in the stables and yard and used and occupied the house every day until the house was burnt by the enemy. They used corn, straw, and provisions of every kind during each day they remained there—being no other house near, where they could be supplied. The troop was often paraded in the yard, in full equipage, the house being every day visited by the officers of the encampment.
>
> Captain Horace Fuller swears, on the 2nd of January, 1833, he was present on a visit at the house in the summer of 1814, "that whilst there he saw the American troops, which were stationed near the dwelling house of Pattison to defend the flotilla commanded by Commodore Barney, daily visit his house and farm, and procure sheep, breadstuffs, salt, and other necessaries for the subsistence of the troops, the sheep being killed in the yard and hung up in trees, and cooked in the kitchen." He further saw corn, fodder, hay, and straw, taken for the cavalry, which were also stationed near his house, some of the troops occupying the dwelling during every hour in the day. The enemy were in sight and in full view during all the time, and could see what was going on.
>
> The American sentinels were stationed near the dwelling house and he stated at the time to the troops that he believed the enemy would destroy the house in consequence of their occupation, which he firmly believes was the cause. He states that the family of Mr. Pattison left the house some days before its destruction, but that he remained there and was in sight at the burning, and that the occupancy of the troops was continued up to that time.
>
> The petitioner was at the time, on duty as commandant of a company of the troops.
>
> A witness, John Broome, deposes that the major of the regiment, Stephen S. St. John, is dead, and that Colonel Taney, has been many years out of the State. He is understood to be in Texas.

The facts here set forth, taken in connection with the testimony of Richard S. Parran and Joseph Reynolds, who were then taken prisoners on board different vessels of the British squadron, and both testify to the declarations of the English officers, that Pattison's house was burnt on account of its being a military stand, and occupied by the militia.

The value of the property destroyed appears to have been differently estimated at different periods and by different persons. In a paper attached to the report of the commissioners in December, 1816, purporting to be a statement of James J. Pattison's claim, and signed by him, the house is estimated at $5,000, and the furniture burnt and destroyed, at $300.

A witness, George Stone, examined by those commissioners, and who represents himself as well acquainted with the property, both before and after the burning, says the house was worth $5,000 and the materials remaining were worth $800.

Leaving the value of the property destroyed, $4,200, besides the furniture, which the committee do not consider under the decisions heretofore made by Congress, a fair charge to the United States. The committee adopt this estimate and report a bill for that amount.

James J. Pattison was paid $4,200 in 1838. Capt. Mackall's company belonged to the Lower Battalion of Militia of St. Mary's County.

## John G. Mackall

In 1817 Capt. Mackall filed a claim for a house, $6,000; kitchen and out-house, $1,000; furniture, $600; and grain, $200, total $7,800. The claim was approved once, but rejected several times. The legal representatives pursued the claim, which was finally rejected. As stated by the Committee of Claims on March 8, 1860:

It appears by the deposition of Maj. James Walker and Capt. George McWilliams that on the 11th day of June, 1814, they, with others, accompanied Lt. Neale of the United States army with dispatches to Commodore Barney, then blockaded by the enemy in St. Leonard's creek. They crossed the Patuxent River and went to the claimant's house where they procured horses and then proceeded to the commodore. On their way back they saw the claimant, who stated that he was away from home on duty, and obtained his consent to their stopping at his house and refreshing themselves. Finding on their reaching it, on account of the absence of some of their company, they could not recross the river that night, they lodged in the house.

On the following morning, when crossing the river, the British barges were in sight and were making for the shore which they had just left, and fired at it several guns, and that Lt. Neale was dressed in uniform and wore his sword.

It appears by the deposition of Sgt. James D. Denton and Capt. Benjamin Gray, of the company he commanded, that on the 15th of June, 1814, the enemy ascended the Patuxent River in a schooner and 14 or 15 barges. A part of the company, about 60 in number, was stationed within 150 yards of the claimant's house for its protection, and Capt. Gray and Sgt. Denton went to the house and found there a person by the name of Crane, who resided with the claimant in the capacity of a schoolmaster, and having informed him of the right of their visit, he objected to any opposition being made to the enemy, as they were too many in number for the captain's command, and required him and Sgt. Denton to leave the house, which after some persuasion they did, and retreated with the company. When they were at the claimant's house they were in full view of the enemy.

It appears by the deposition of George Posey, a member of Capt. Gray's company, the company having halted within 150 yards of the claimant's house, that on their retreat they were fired at by the enemy's troops.

It appears by the deposition of Edward Truman that a few days after the burning of the claimant's houses he saw Mr. Crane, who stated he had been requested by the claimant to stay at his house and endeavor to protect it. The British officer who first entered the house told him it should not be burnt, but he was ordered to the river as a prisoner of war, and when he arrived there an officer said to him he had seen some militia about the house, and it should be burnt.

It appears further by Sgt. Denton's deposition that Crane told him that he heard some

British officers say the claimant's house was burnt in consequence of their seeing the militia in it.

James Jones, in August, 1814, had a conversation with a British officer respecting the burning of the claimant's houses, in which the officer said they were burnt in consequence of one of the British marines having been wounded near them, and that no other houses were burnt at the same time and on the same shore except Capt. John Browne's.

Dr. John Dare was well acquainted with the claimant's buildings and that they were worth the following sums: Dwelling-house, $4,500; out-house, $500, and materials remaining after the destruction, $5.

Capt. Gray and Sgt. Denton were with Col. Taney's 31st Regiment, Maryland Militia. Maj. Walker and Capt. McWilliams were with Lt. Col. Henry Ashton's 45th Regiment, Maryland Militia. Lt. Neale is possibly Maryland native 2nd Lt. Francis J. Neale of the 36th Infantry.

## George W. Biscoe

George Washington Biscoe, was a merchant and an officer of militia, who had a large amount of tobacco stored in the Benedict warehouse, at Magruder's Ferry, and at Nottingham when the British arrived in June, 1814.

The affidavit of George Biscoe:

> A company of militia acting under my orders as major of the 17th Regiment were posted at Magruder's warehouse for its defense, and when the British barges ascended the river on or about the 17th of June, 1814, so soon as they were discovered by Captain Joshua Naylor (the captain in command) to be in reach of his fire, he commenced firing upon them from behind the warehouse and continued to do so until his ammunition was expended. The enemy immediately landed and the militia retreated. The enemy burned the warehouses with all the tobacco contained therein.

Jesse Selby and James Baden, of Capt. Naylor's company, testified they were stationed at Magruder's and believed their presence there was the reason the warehouse was burned. Captain Naylor died in 1825.

As reported by the Committee of Claims on March 26, 1832, in part:

> Maj. George W. Biscoe, then commanding a detachment of Maryland militia, in order to aid in arresting the progress of the enemy then advancing on Washington, used a large quantity of the petitioner's tobacco deposited in the public warehouse in the village of Nottingham, in erecting a breastwork to shelter and defend his men against the attack of the enemy.
>
> The militia were compelled to retreat and the enemy possessed themselves of the tobacco, and destroyed or converted it to their use. The petitioner therefore prays Congress to pass a law to indemnify him for his property thus seized on by an officer in the service of the United States for a public purpose, and whereby it became lost to him.
>
> George W. Biscoe testifies that a part of the claimant's tobacco was used by his order, as commanding officer at Nottingham, for the purpose of erecting a breastwork for the defense of that place; and to the exception of three or four hogsheads, he is confidant, out of the sale he made to petitioner of 105 hogsheads, that the remainder was carried away by the enemy.
>
> He states that a captain in command reported to him his encounter with the enemy at Magruder's warehouse. He stated that on the approach of the enemy's barges, he posted his men behind the warehouse, situated within 30 yards of the shore, and there commenced and continued for an hour or two a fire of musketry, being, at the same time, under cover of the warehouses. He was finally compelled to retire when the enemy landed, and set fire to the warehouses, which were accordingly destroyed.

His claim was rejected on the ground that the buildings and tobacco were private property.

### *The First Landing Attempt at Benedict*

On June 20, 1814, British forces from the *St. Lawrence* and *Narcissus* attempted to land at Benedict but were repelled by militia and artillery.

## *The Second Battle at St. Leonard*

On June 26, 1814, Barney's flotilla was supported by artillery and infantry and was able to break out of the creek and head up the Patuxent. The British burned St. Leonard and continued up the Patuxent in pursuit.

### John Ireland

John Ireland claimed, "a tobacco warehouse 48 feet long, 24 feet wide, 12 feet high, with sheds on two sides and a shed at one end worth $2,500; and of a dwelling and store occupied by Hezekiah Cobreth, the dwelling 14 feet long, 16 feet wide, and 10 feet high, and a store joined thereto 18 feet long, 16 feet wide, and 10 feet high, with a shed 18 feet long and 12 feet wide, worth $2,000."

The claim was rejected after testimony of Benjamin H. Mackall, Aquilla G. Brown, and William Spencer, who said the only structures burned in St. Leonard's Creektown were Mary Frazier's house, John Ireland's storehouse, Hezekiah Cobreth's kitchen, and a tobacco-house on John Ireland's farm outside of town.

John A. Webster, commander of one of the barges testified. As stated by Comm. Barney on January 27, 1818, from Baltimore:

> I never was more surprised than, in reading the proceedings of Congress, to find that Mr. John Ireland had petitioned to be paid for a house (tobacco-house I suppose), said to have been burnt by the British on account of having been occupied, &c., by men belonging to the flotilla under my command. If the house in question was the tobacco house at St. Leonard's creek, the petitioner can have no claim whatever on that account. The place where it was situated was a common landing, and where I had established tents, &c., near the house for the purpose of receiving stores and provisions from Baltimore and the city of Washington. Some few small sails were laid upon the rafters and tobacco to keep them from the weather; but the sails and every other article were removed from that place to Huntington court-house, some time before the British landed and burnt the house. It never was occupied by my men except in the instance cited.
>
> After the battle of the 26th June, 1814, in which we drove the blockading squadron from before the creek, the flotilla moved up the creek opposite Huntington, and received on board from that place all the sails, stores, and materials of the flotilla, nothing being left but some round shot and iron ballast, near the said house on the landing; so that the destruction of that property had no connection with the flotilla, any more than the destruction of Mr. James Pattison's house had with the militia; for Pattison would not suffer a man to go on his place for its defense, but declared he would shoot the first man that attempted to do so, rather than trusting to the enemy than the protection of the militia. This statement was made to me immediately after his declaration and soon after his house was burnt, which could have been defended with ease, had not Mr. Pattison prevented it.
>
> I do hope, sir, if any more claims are made, in which myself, or the officers and men of the flotilla, are mentioned, that I may be referred to, when a true statement shall be made for the satisfaction of Congress.

### Henry Gardiner

The Committee of Claims rejected the original petition on January 31, 1838. After Henry's death, Eleanor pursued it, as stated by the Committee of Claims on January 30, 1857:

> The claim is for the value of the dwelling house and barn alleged to have been destroyed by the British in the war of 1812 upon the farm of her husband, St. Charles county, in the State of Maryland.
>
> It is alleged that the battle of St. Leonard's creek was fought upon the farm of Mr. Gardiner in 1814, and that regular soldiers of the United States and militia were stationed on a

portion of the farm, and that this fact occasioned the battle. In the deposition of Samuel Turner taken in 1836, he states that he was quartermaster or deputy quartermaster of the militia in 1814. The militia were encamped a short distance from the farm. The farm was visited by the militia for the purpose of reconnoitering and viewing the enemy, and that some few days after the arrival of the British vessels at the mouth of the St. Leonard's creek, the buildings on the farm were destroyed. He further states that the battle of St. Leonard's creek, fought by the United States troops, was fought on this farm.

There is nothing whatever to show that the buildings in question were ever occupied for military purposes, or that their destruction was a consequence of their having had a military character imparted to them at any time, and your committee, therefore, respectfully recommend, for the reasons given in their report on the case of Rinaldo Johnson and Ann E. Johnson, that the claim of the memorialist be rejected.

No date is shown for the loss, but it's noted as being in St. Charles County. St. Leonard Creek is in Calvert County. The landings at Benedict took place in St. Charles County where the Gardiners lived, and Nottingham, where the Rinaldos lived, is in Baltimore County.

Henry was born on May 10, 1766, in St. Mary's County and married Eleanor Sothoran on September 18, 1800. Daughter Elizabeth was born March 15, 1814. Henry died on June 23, 1820.

## Rinaldo Johnson

Rinaldo and Anne E. Johnson lived in Nottingham, 8 miles from the tobacco they had at Magruder's, and saw the smoke from the burning warehouse in June 1814. They filed the original claim, and were succeeded by Thomas Rinaldo Johnson and Sarah A. Nuttrill, as stated in December 1849:

Those they represent were proprietors of upwards of 100 hogsheads of tobacco, which were stored in the Maryland inspection warehouse at Magruder's in the year 1814. At the time the tobacco was stored there in June, 1814, or thereabouts, the British troops or sailors, on a predatory excursion, were fired upon by the American troops stationed in and about Magruder's warehouse. After the ammunition of the American forces was exhausted they retreated and the British forces immediately after landed and burned the warehouse and its contents, including the tobacco belonging to the estates your memorialists represent.

Your memorialists refer for proof of their claim to the affidavits and reports of committees of Congress, by which it will be shown the quantity of tobacco belonging to them, which was stored in the warehouse at the time of its destruction, and also that the burning of the same was in consequence of its occupation by the American troops.

Gen. Biscoe and James Baden both stated the Rinaldos had 80 hogsheads in Magruder's.

The claims for tobacco used as breastworks were denied, as stated by the Committee of Claims on January 9, 1857, in part:

The fact that they were employed did not in any way provoke the destruction or carrying off of the property actually lost.

An officer is no more authorized to take hogsheads of tobacco than he would be bales of hay or any other kinds of merchandise to construct the fortifications he may think advantageous to him; and if he should venture to do so, he would be responsible to the owners of the property for any damage done to it in consequence of its being put to such use, or for its entire value if it should be lost or destroyed.

The government is by no means bound for all the acts of its agents. Acts of so extravagant and mischievous a character as those spoken of are never within the scope of their powers, and they who do such acts must be alone answerable for them.

But this is not all. If an officer in the military service of the United States were to be stationed at a point where field-works of any kind were requisite for the defense of the position, and he were to fail to throw them up in the ordinary way immediately on his taking his command, and afterwards should be driven to the necessity of employing any of the property he was sent to protect for improvising a defense, he should be brought before a court-martial for misconduct and incapacity, and be expelled from the service in disgrace.

The claims that were approved occurred when the premises were actually occupied by the militia on authority of an officer and were remanded to the Secretary of the Treasury to determine the price per hogshead. It was reported the British took and destroyed 3,000 to 4,000 hogsheads of tobacco, which had great value in Europe.

## Mary Frazier

In 1810, Mary Frazier was the head of a family in Calvert County of seven persons and ten slaves. The original petition was presented by Charles M. Frazier, but his name was deleted with no explanation. As stated by the Committee of Claims on February 19, 1818:

> Mary Frazier claims $800 compensation for the loss of a frame house in Calvert County on the Patuxent River, alleged to have been destroyed by the enemy in consequence of it being occupied by Commodore Joshua Barney as a hospital for the United States flotilla.

Comm. Barney responded to the Committee of Claims from Baltimore on February 15, 1818:

> I have the honor to receive your letter of the 13th instant, and would have answered it by return of post, but was desirous of obtaining Dr. Hamilton's report on the subject of Mary Frazier's claim for a house burnt in Calvert County by the British. I was always informed that the house was not burnt. However, if was burnt, the case is as follows:
>
> 1st. A small house was occupied by a few sick men belonging to the flotilla, in the town of St. Leonard's, in Calvert county.
>
> 2nd. It was not occupied by my orders.
>
> 3rd. It was some short time (a few days) after we left St. Leonard's creek that the British burnt the tobacco-house and several other houses in the town of St. Leonard's; but I am very confident, if Mrs. Frazier's house was burnt, it was not in consequence of the sick men having occupied it for a few days, for the house where Dr. Hamilton lived was not burnt, although several officers, sick and wounded, had occupied it. If the house which Mrs. Frazier claims was burnt, and was the one which my men occupied, it was a wretched hovel, being deserted and vacant at the time, without windows, and entirely open, being a small one-story frame and entirely rotten, and, if valued at the very highest, could not be worth more than $50; and in this opinion I am supported by Dr. Hamilton, who also informs me he was solicited to occupy the house, and I now believe with a view to make a claim for it in case of accident; but as several other houses were burnt at the same time, I do think our occupation of it was not the cause, for, at Nottingham, I occupied a large house, where all my sick and wounded lay six or eight weeks; and when the British took that place, they did not molest it. But, sir, the fact is, that in Calvert County, and particularly at St. Leonard's, the inhabitants were more the enemies of our officers and men belonging to the United States service than they were to our enemies the British.

As further stated by the Committee:

> The committee feel it a duty to observe that this second letter from Commodore Barney affords additional proof of the danger of attending the admission of *ex parte* evidence. The evidence before the Commissioner of Claims, and reported by him to the House, appeared very suspicious before any other information had been received. If it had been unsuspected, still the committee would have thought that the case did not come within the provisions of the act of April, 1816. But since the information has been disclosed, it most evidently appears that the claim of Mary Frazier ought not to be allowed.

Mary pursued the claim, as reported by the Committee of Claims on February 25, 1835:

> This claim was presented in the name of Mary Frazier, petitioner's name being erased, to Mr. Richard Bland Lee, late commissioner, and subsequently to Peter Hagner, the Third Auditor. On what grounds the latter rejected

it, does not appear, but Mr. Lee rejected it for want of proof that it was occupied at the time of its destruction.

In 1818, the Committee of Claims made an unfavorable report in consequence of a letter dated from Commodore Barney dated February 15, 1818. The committee would have been compelled to have reported unfavorably, for the want of proof of its occupancy, but that proof having been since supplied, it becomes the painful duty of the committee to scrutinize the letter of Barney, for, if that is to be relied upon, the claim is barred forever.

Barney, in the first place, says he was informed the house was not burnt. 2d. That it was not occupied by his orders. 3d. If it was burnt, it was several days after his troops left it. 4th. Dr. Hamilton informed him that he was solicited to occupy the house.

William Spencer swears he was in St. Leonard's when the British landed, and saw them set fire to Mary Frazier's house.

Col. William Clare states that he was in sight when the house was burnt. Aquilla G. Brown, Thomas Edmonds, and others swear same.

With this proof, the committee can come to no other conclusion than that it was burnt.

As to the second objection that it was not occupied by his orders, Dr. Charles B. Hamilton states that he occupied it as a hospital for the sick and wounded for a considerable time, but does not say that it was by the order of the commodore, but it is to be presumed that it was by his order as Hamilton was the surgeon of the flotilla which lay almost during the whole time of its occupancy in its immediate vicinity, and the commodore must have known that it was occupied as above stated.

As to the third objection, Col. William Clare, sustained by four other witnesses, swears that it was burnt on the same day that our troops left it, and Clare and one other witness say that, as the British approached, our troops retreated, and they burnt it. Clare further states that he commanded a squad of militia in sight of the place and saw the whole transaction, but had not force sufficient to prevent it.

As to the fourth objection, Dr. Hamilton swears he did not know who owned the house.

As to the value of the house, Comm. Barney says in his letter that it was a rotten, wretched hovel, framed, and only one story high, worth not more than $50.

One witness swears it was worth $750; two, that it was worth $500, one of whom is a mechanic.

With these facts proven by so many witnesses, the committee are bound to believe that the house was occupied by our troops, that it was burnt in consequence of such occupation immediately after they retreated from it, and the occupancy was not by contract, and that it was occupied by order, or at least consent of the commanding officer.

It does not appear why this claim was presented in the name of Mary Frazier, with Charles M. Frazier's name erased, until the last session of Congress when it was presented in petitioner's own name.

In 1817, one witness proved it worth $750. Deduct $8 for materials not destroyed, leaves $742. In 1834, three state its value at $800. Deduct $8 for materials not destroyed leaves $792.

Charles Hamilton was commissioned a surgeon's mate on April 2, 1811, and became a surgeon on April 15, 1814. He left the service on April 12, 1826.

## Charles J. Catlett

Charles J. Catlett was a merchant who lost 4 hogsheads of tobacco at Cedar Point, 115 at Magruder's Ferry, and 149 at Nottingham. He incurred one of the largest losses, and became a prominent and persistent claimant.

Catlett wrote to George Biscoe for information to support his claim, and Briscoe responded on February 27, 1832, from Washington. He was then a government surveyor and inspector and brigade commander of Maryland militia:

> You request information on the subject of the defense of Magruder's warehouse in June, 1814, by a detachment of militia acting under my orders. In reply I have to state that the captain in command reported to me his encounter with the enemy at that place. He stated that on the near approach of the British barges under the command of Commodore Robert Barrie and Colonel James Malcomb of marines, he posted his men behind the warehouses, situated within 30 yards of the shore,

and that so soon as his fire of musketry could be deemed effectual, and continued to do so for an hour or two being under cover of the warehouses. Finally, his ammunition being expended and he was compelled to retire, the enemy then landed and set fire to the warehouses, which were burned.

I am aware that you sustained considerable loss of tobacco there and elsewhere on the Patuxent River, from the circumstance of your having purchased of me more than 100 hogsheads, which, with the exception of a few, say to the best of my recollection, four or five of the warehouses here, were either burnt in Magruder's warehouses at the period above stated, or were carried away by the enemy on their retreat from the city of Washington to the shipping at this place.

At one period I used the tobacco in the warehouse here for military purposes, a part of which I recollect, was your property, having sold it to you.

Wishing you success in your appeal to Congress, I remain truly your obedient servant.

On July 2, 1836, Congress authorized Peter Hagner, the Third Auditor, to settle the claim of Charles J. Catlett, "under the Acts of April 9, 1816, and March 3, 1817, for tobacco which belonged to him at Magruder's warehouse, Cedar Point warehouse, and Nottingham warehouse, all in the state of Maryland; and was lost, captured, or destroyed, by the British or American troops." (6 Stat. L. 673)

On December 30, 1836, Hagner advised the Second Comptroller of the Treasury that he believed the losses did not come within the acts cited. In January 1837, the Comptroller concurred and the Committee of Claims was "discharged from the further consideration of Charles J. Catlett."

Charles persisted with his claim and in 1841 President Tyler, "ordered a statement of the value of the tobacco to be made out and reported to him." This was done by Auditor Hagner and submitted on September 20, 1841. The next day, Tyler authorized a partial allowance and on the 23rd ordered the claim re-examined, "and if they could not allow it, to report specially to him their reasons for disallowance." On the 28th Hagner again ruled against the claim as did the Attorney General, but on the 29th the claim was allowed, "by direction of the President," and Catlett was paid $8,861.99.

## Benedict I. Heard

As reported by the Committee on Claims on January 15, 1835:

The petitioner states that he was the owner of a plantation on which there was a valuable brick house and other buildings near the river Patuxent, in the State of Maryland; and that about the 1st of July, 1814, a detachment of the Maryland militia under General Philip Stuart was encamped in the neighborhood of this plantation as a corps of observation, and to check the marauding parties of the enemy; and that about the 10th day of that month a party of British troops landed on his plantation and commenced slaughtering his cattle.

General Stuart sent a detachment of 150 men for the purpose of cutting off the retreat of the British troops. Upon the approach of the militia, the British troops fired upon them and immediately fled to their boats. The militia pursued, and continued to fire upon the enemy until checked and compelled to retreat by the fire of a British ship of war.

The detachment of militia then returned to the encampment of General Stuart about two miles from the dwelling house on said plantation. Early the next morning a party from the British landed and burnt the petitioner's house and other buildings, which, as the petitioner says, were of the value of $8,000.

The petitioner alleges that the destruction of his buildings was occasioned by the attack made by the militia upon the British troops on his plantation on the preceding day, and asks Congress a remuneration for his loss.

All the legislation of Congress on this subject has proceeded upon the principle that the buildings which had been used by the troops of the United States as barracks, or had been used as places of deposit for public property by the order of an officer or agent of the United States, and destroyed by the enemy when thus occupied, in consequence of such occupation, constitute a just claim upon the government for remuneration, to the extent of the loss of the owner; but if that destruction of buildings by the enemy, when unauthorized by the rules of civilized warfare, imposes no obligation upon the government to indemnify the sufferer for his loss. The facts in this case, as stated by the petitioner, afford no evidence that his buildings were used by troops of the United States as barracks or for the deposit of public property. It is evident from the testimony in the case that the destruction of the petitioner's buildings by the enemy was wholly unauthorized by the acknowledged rules of civilized warfare.

The committee submit that the petitioner is not entitled to relief.

On September 6, 1814, Gen. Philip Stuart wrote to an unidentified person:

> The bearer Lieut. Benedict I. Heard who has acted as adjutant to my Brigade from the first of June 'till the present time is desirous of obtaining a commission in the Army of the United States. Mr. Heard's property (in St. Mary's City) has been all burnt and destroyed by the enemy on account of his use—full & energetic services in defense of his Country. I am particularly acquainted with Mr. Heard & have to request your interference in his behalf.

Eight days later, on September 12, Lt. Heard was at North Point as a volunteer with Ensign John Wilmot and 78 members of Capt. David Warfield's Baltimore United Volunteers. Other volunteers were Pvt. Philip Gover, of Capt. Aaron R. Levering's company of Independent Blues; Pvt. Thomas T. Bond, of Capt. Charles Pennington's Baltimore Independent Artillerists; Richard B. Dorsey, of the 1st Baltimore Hussars; Hammond Dugan and Leonard Matthews apparently joined Warfield's company later.

On September 16, 1814, Lt. Heard was commissioned an ensign in the 14th U.S. Infantry and made lieutenant on October 1.

Ensign Wilmot was cited for "conspicuous bravery" and promoted to lieutenant on October 8. The Baltimore United Volunteers was organized on July 29, 1811.

## James T. Sothoron

As reported by the Committee of Claims in February 1836:

> Alexander Lyon, Joseph B. Burroughs, John B. Burroughs, and Hanson Burroughs, testify that they were private soldiers in a company of Maryland militia commanded by the petitioner and were encamped, with other troops, under the command of the late General Philip Stuart near the farms of the petitioner during a part of the summer of 1814.
>
> In the early part of July they were ordered by Captain Sothoron, together with others, to march down upon his farm on the Patuxent River and occupy his houses, as a corps of observation. The guard of troops did, according to his orders, occupy the houses, both dwelling and out-houses, for the space of 30 days, when they were driven therefrom by the enemy landing and attacking them with a superior force. They effected their retreat with difficulty, leaving behind their baggage, ammunition, and provisions, and that the enemy fired cannon into the house, damaged and nearly destroyed the dwelling, and burnt a large barn with upwards of 40 hogsheads of tobacco, and pulled down other houses, such as the granary, quarters, &c.
>
> When the troops were driven from their first position, they retreated to an adjoining farm, also belonging to the petitioner, and occupied the dwelling-house and buildings upon it. The next day the enemy pursued them, drove them from their new position, injured and nearly destroyed the dwelling-house, and burnt a large barn containing 123 pounds of tobacco.
>
> They further testify that the troops under the command of General Stuart had not, at the time they were ordered to occupy Sothoron's houses, any tents at all, and the detachment had no other shelter from the weather than the houses of the petitioner.
>
> John B. Burroughs testifies that about three or four days after the burning of the petitioner's barns and the damage done to his dwelling-houses, he heard a conversation between his father and the British officers at his father's house, during which conversation the British officers declared, "that it was their orders to burn and destroy all property occupied by the militia in any way, and if

that property had not been so occupied, they would not have burnt and destroyed it."

The character of the persons who testify to the above facts is vouched for by the certificates of Charles C. Egerton, William Ford, and William Floyd, three justices of the peace.

The petitioner alleges in his memorial that, while under the command of General Stuart and encamped with his company about 5 or 6 miles from the river, he was ordered by General Stuart to detach a portion of his company, under the command of a subaltern officer, to march down upon Sothoron's farm, there to occupy his houses, and remain as a corps of observation. Against this order the petitioner alleges he remonstrated, stating the consequences that might result from such occupancy, but he was nevertheless obliged to comply with the order, and did detach a part of his company for that service accordingly, which was the cause of the destruction of the petitioner's property by the enemy.

It will be perceived that the facts stated applied as well to the loss of the personal property as of the real estate of the claimant, and that he asked, in his former application, to be remunerated for the latter only.

The committee are not disposed to give sanction to the practice of dividing claims, by listening, without good reasons, to a second application, when the subject of it was involved and should have been considered with the first. In this case, however, it is shown by the evidence that the petitioner was induced, by advice of members of Congress who had charge of his former petition, to postpone his claim for loss of personal property, and to ask, at that time, indemnity for the destruction of his buildings only, as coming within the principles of the act of 1816.

It is difficult to draw a distinction, in equity, between a claim for loss of buildings and of the personal property they contain, and as the petitioner was entitled, according to the evidence, to remuneration for the loss of the former, he is, as we believe, for that of the latter.

The committee, therefore, recommend the passage of the accompanying bill.

Philip Stuart was born on February 18, 1752, to John and Frances Stuart in Virginia. He was a lieutenant in the 3rd Continental Dragoons during the Revolution, was wounded at Eutaw, and transferred to the 2nd Artillerists and Engineers. He married Mary Fell Bayne on December 15, 1792, in Prince Georges County, Maryland, resigned his commission on November 15, 1800, and was elected to Congress in 1811 and served to 1819. He was appointed brig. gen. of the 5th Brigade, Maryland Militia, on March 23, 1814, and died on August 14, 1830.

James was in Lt. Col. Henry Ashton's 45th Regiment of Maryland Militia. George Burroughs was a sergeant in Capt. Wilson Cawood's company in the 45th Regiment; Alexander Lyon was a corporal, and Basil, Hanson, Philip, and William Burroughs were privates in Cawood's company.

James was paid $7,500 in 1836, and the Senate approved the claim on February 4, 1848. The Secretary of the Treasury issued a decision on May 8, 1849, and Sothoron was paid an additional $12,070. James was married to Elizabeth C. Sothoron. On February 23, 1843, Elizabeth A. Sothoron married Hezekiah Burroughs.

## William Kilgour

William Kilgour's very valuable and extensive plantation, extending two miles from the river, was destroyed during the same raid that wrecked the Sothoran place, right next door, and for the same reason, as a deposit for military stores. It was occupied in July 1814 by Capt. William Woodburn under orders from Maj. John Chappelier, 1st Battalion, 45th Regiment of Foot.

In 1836, Kilgour put his claim in the hands of Daniel Fraser and in July it went to U.S. Attorney for the District of Columbia, Francis Scott Key. As reported by the Committee of Claims on January 27, 1837:

In this case, George N. Alvey testifies that during the late war with Great Britain he was frequently on the premises of Capt. William

Kilgour, bordering on the Patuxent River, that as frequently he saw some of the Maryland militia there. He has seen them exercising, while there, and shooting at the barns, a few rods only from the dwelling-house, and has seen some of the holes made in the side and ends of the barns by their balls. He has also frequently seen arms, ammunition, and cartouch boxes belonging to the militia, placed away in the dwelling-house. On one occasion he saw an officer of Col. Henry Carberry's regiment there, who remained all night, and who stated the baggage of the army was ordered to be brought there.

He further says, that he was near, and in sight on the day and at the very time the British forces landed, marched up to the dwelling of Captain Kilgour and set fire to and burnt down the barns containing Kilgour's tobacco and other property.

Several other witnesses testify, substantially to the same facts.

The petitioner charges the United States for several negroes, a quantity of tobacco consumed in his barns, some cattle, and other personal property, and with the value of two barns, in all amounting to $4,360, and interest $5,689.80—making $10,049.80.

He credits the United States with cash received under the first article of the treaty of Ghent, $1,120; by interest, 8 years, $537.60, and by subtracting the credit from the debit, he strikes a balance in his favor due on the 20th of April, 1836, to the amount of $8,392.20. He estimates the barns at $150.

The testimony does not prove a military occupation of the barns for any purpose whatever. If they were occupied, and if they were destroyed in consequence thereof, the tobacco and other property destroyed in the barns do not furnish a claim against the United States, according to former decisions. The claimant is not entitled to relief.

William Kilgour subsequently died and his claim was taken up by his son and executor, James E. Kilgour. In 1840, Francis Key told James that he was awaiting action. Key died on January 13, 1843, and James wrote to his son and executor, Philip B. Key, asking about the papers and was told in 1848 they were with Addison & Tucker. The claim was rejected in 1857 as the details of losses being too vague at that time.

In 1848, testimony was taken from Alexander Lyon, Joseph B. Burroughs, and John Chappelier, as reported on April 11, 1850:

The evidence is clear and conclusive that William Kilgour, deceased, was living upon the Patuxent River, in the State of Maryland, and county of St. Mary's during the war with Great Britain, in 1814, and at the time the British ascended the river. The premises, as well as the dwelling and barns and outbuildings were used frequently and commonly for purposes of depot and quarters by the forces in the service of the United States, by order of commanding officers.

In ascending the river, the British landed at his plantation, and that the premises of Kilgour were so occupied on the day and at the time they so landed. The British in consequence of such occupation marched upon the premises, routing the American forces, and then burned two barns, rifling the dwelling-house, and destroyed and carried away with them tobacco, wheat, carriage, and much other personal property, for which no compensation has ever been made.

The committee beg leave to refer to the case of James F. Sothoran, as being almost identical in facts, as being adjoining plantations, for the more minute particulars. And they present herewith a bill for the relief of the petitioner.

Col. Carberry commanded the 36th Infantry Regiment in Maryland. William Kilgour served in Maj. Adam Whann's 8th Regiment of Maryland Militia Cavalry.

## Michael Fenwick

In 1790, Michael Fenwick was a planter in St. Mary's, Maryland, with a wife, two daughters, and six slaves.

In 1814, the farm was occupied by troops and much damage was done, but apparently Michael never filed a claim. In time, Caroline, a minor child at the time, became the sole heir and married Robert Brooke.

In 1834 they filed a claim for $5,000, and Caroline was recognized as heir "and perhaps the only one of Michael Fenwick, deceased." She swore under oath that her father, "owned a plantation on which the destroyed property was situated, near the bank of the Patuxent River, St. Mary's County, Maryland." Ignatius Fenwick appeared and said he was a private in Lt. Col. Francis Newman's 4th Cavalry District during the war, and gave some conflicting testimony. His relationship to Caroline was apparently unknown, and on December 24, 1834, the Committee of Claims tabled the petition.

Ignatius Fenwick is shown as a private in the 4th Cavalry District and in Lt. Col. Athanasius Fenwick's 12th Regiment, Maryland Militia.

Additional witnesses were subsequently found, including Capt. Gerard N. Causin, 1st Lt. Samuel Greenwell, Sgt. Bennet Stone, Quartermaster-sergeant Thomas Spalding, and Pvt. George Plater of the 4th Cavalry Maryland Militia, and Capt. William Floyd and Pvt. Joseph Rockhill in Lt. Col. Fenwick's regiment.

Caroline retained William L. Brent, Esq., and the claim was presented again. On February 6, 1838, the Committee of Claims stated:

> The petitioners ask compensation for certain buildings destroyed by the enemy in the late war with Great Britain; which buildings were on and near the bank of the Patuxent River, and were, as the petitioners represent, in the military occupation of a corps of American cavalry, under the orders of an officer at the time they were burnt by the enemy.
>
> This claim was presented to the commissioners appointed under the act of the 9th of April, 1816, and depositions were taken for that purpose, but a very slight examination of the evidence now submitted in support of the claim is sufficient to show that the interest of the claimant, Caroline Fenwick, (then a female infant) was not understood, or was grossly neglected by those whose duty it was to guard it.
>
> The report of the commissioner represents the claim as not coming "strictly within the letter, though it seemed to fall within the equity of the 9th section of the act of the 9th of April, 1816, inasmuch as the houses were not in the actual possession of the military force at the time of their destruction." Compensation was therefore refused.
>
> A correspondence of great length has been carried on between the Third Auditor and William L. Brent, Esq., the agent of the petitioners, and as the administrator of Michael Fenwick, deceased.
>
> The evidence consists in part of two depositions of Captain Gerard N. Causin, commander of the company of 4th Cavalry which was, or had recently been stationed on the farm of the petitioner, Caroline, (then Miss Fenwick) when the buildings on it were burnt by the enemy. The second deposition of Captain Causin states that he occupied the house of the petitioner, then Caroline Fenwick, by the orders of General Philip Stuart; and that immediately after his arrival at the house with his troops, he rode down to the river with a party of his company and was, as he believes, seen by the enemy from their ships, then in the Patuxent River, in full view.
>
> He further says that during his stay at the house, he ordered Lt. Samuel Greenwell to select a private room for the officers, and a label written and put over the door of the room, "officers' quarters," or words to that import, and that to the best of his recollection, the label was left sticking over the door, "when by an order from his general, he left the house with his troop. On the day after he had occupied the house, the enemy came and burnt all the houses on the plantation, and he verily believes it was in consequence of having been occupied by the troop of horse under his command."
>
> From this evidence it must be understood that Captain Causin meant to represent himself as having been in command of his company when he occupied the house of the petitioner, Mrs. Brooke, and that his actual occupancy of it had ceased the day preceding its destruction, and that, "he received orders from his commanding officer to occupy the houses, and that he left the house in a hurry, in consequence of an order from the general, and omitted to take down the label, and he believes, and it was generally understood, that the houses were burnt in consequence

of having been so occupied by the troop of cavalry."

It would be found that Sergeant Bennet Stone, Quartermaster-sergeant Thomas Spalding, Pvt. Ignatius Fenwick, and Pvt. George Plater, all of whom belonged to the company, corroborate the evidence of Mr. Greenwell relative to the command, and the absence of Captain Causin at the time.

George Plater, who says, "that when the troop temporarily left the houses, it was still under the command of 1st Lieutenant Greenwell, and that they left their forage for their horses in the out-houses under the care of a certain Joseph Rockhill, intending to return, and that they did return on the following day and found the houses in flames."

Bennet Stone proves that the dwelling-house on the farm was occupied by the officers and some two or three gentlemanly troopers, considering themselves the officers' equals, and that one of the barns was occupied by part of the men, and the other barn and stables by their horses and those of the baggage wagons, whilst the other men and horses were kept as a picket-guard at the tobacco warehouse on the creek upwards of a mile from the dwelling and barns, and that the men and horses and forage there occupied the warehouse, dwelling, and storehouse, and cooked in the kitchen. The stable at that place was small, and was not made use of, and he cannot recollect as to the occupation of the carriage-house and negro houses. Thomas Spalding concurs with Stone in this statement.

In conclusion, Plater says several troops occupied every house upon the premises during their station upon Cole's creek.

The value of the buildings at the time of their destruction is proved by a number of witnesses. William Floyd and Thomas Spalding give the following description and valuation of the buildings, other than the dwelling-house, burnt by the enemy on the farm of Michael Fenwick:

Brick entry, 16 by 10, $179; brick kitchen, 20 by 16, $320; brick smoke-house and meat-house, 14 by 12, $150.

Large barn, 50 by 30, built of the best and most substantial wooden materials in the best and workmanlike manner, and covered with shingles, $350.

Stabling-house, 50 by 12, of good and substantial materials, covered with shingles, $278.

Two large corn-houses, each 30 by 16, built of good and substantial materials, covered with shingles, $179.

A public tobacco inspection warehouse, 150 by 100, and one inspection room with scales and weights, built of strong, heavy, and solid timbers, and covered with shingles, sufficiently large to contain 1,000 hogsheads of tobacco, $3,725.

A store-house at the warehouse, 20 by 16, built of good and substantial wooden materials, covered with shingles, $398.

A dwelling-house at the warehouse, 32 by 14, built of good and substantial wooden materials, covered with shingles, $771.

A kitchen at the warehouse, 20 by 16, built of good and substantial wooden materials, covered with shingles, $312.

William L. Wheatley and Vincent Camalier testify to the correctness of the estimate.

Francis Spalding testifies that he lived in the immediate neighborhood of the burnt buildings, and gives a minute description of them. Other witnesses testify as to the description and value of the buildings, estimating them at about $7,000, excluding the dwelling-house. Some of them make a higher estimate, but the decided preponderance of the evidence is in favor of $7,000, and for that amount the committee report a bill.

On March 3, 1839, the Secretary of the Treasury was directed to pay to the legal representatives of Michael Fenwick $7,000, "in full satisfaction for buildings other than the dwelling-house destroyed by the enemy on the state of the deceased, during the late was with Great Britain."

Gerard Blackstone Causin was an attorney and a member of the Maryland House of Delegates. He was a captain in the 4th Cavalry District. Maryland was divided into eleven Cavalry Districts, the 4th being Charles and St. Mary's Counties under Maj. James Thomas.

Samuel Greenwell enlisted as a private in Col. John R. Fenwick's 12th Regiment of Maryland Militia and was attached to Maj. Thomas' 4th Cavalry Regiment. Brig. Gen. Philip Stuart, commanded the 5th Brigade, Maryland, militia.

## William and Richard H. Reeder

As reported by the Committee of Claims on May 20, 1842:

> This claim is for damages sustained by injury to a house and furniture belonging to one of the petitioners and the father of the other, by the British during the last war.
>
> The petitioners represent that the house, situate on the Patuxent, in Maryland, in 1814, "was by the commanding officer of the militia then on duty, taken possession of and used as barracks by a detachment therefrom for the purpose of reconnoitering and reporting the movements of the enemy, whose ships were then in the river."
>
> It is also represented that in consequence of such occupation, the enemy, "destroyed the dwelling house inside and out, as to leave but little more than the frame, thereby rendering it useless and uninhabitable until repaired." Their furniture was taken off and destroyed by the enemy, and also that another house on the farm was destroyed.
>
> This claim was first presented to Congress in March, 1840. It does not appear that any application was ever before made to any Department of the government for relief. The reason given for delay is that one of the petitioners, for ten years last, before February 2, 1840, had been out of the country, and a part of the time out of the State (meaning, as the committee suppose, the county of St. Mary's), and the other petitioner had, at the day last mentioned, "but recently arrived of age." No reason is given why the elder petitioner did not make application for compensation during the 16 years from 1814 to 1830, nor does it appear when the father of the other died.
>
> The great lapse of time is not regarded as an absolute bar to the claim, though there does not appear to be any satisfactory excuse given for the delay, yet it requires greater caution in looking into the evidence.
>
> It appears that the militia, from which the detachment was sent to the house of the Reeders were under the command of Col. Henry Ashton. Ignatius Pike says he was of this detachment, and was, by order of Col. Ashton, "sent to the house of Thomas A. and William Reeder, on the Patuxent, for the purpose of watching and reporting the movements of the British." The committee do not consider it proper to take other evidence than that of the officer who gave the order, until a sufficient cause is shown for not providing that better evidence.
>
> The evidence as to the extent of the damage is altogether too vague and indefinite to enable the committee to adjust the amount to which the claimants should be allowed if the proof of military occupancy and destruction in consequence thereof were satisfactory. It has not been the practice of Congress to allow for personal property destroyed with houses that were used for military purposes, though found by the enemy in such houses. No witness estimates the damage done to the house alone. No witness states the value of the house or the cost of repairing it. Whether the militia under Col. Ashton were in the service of the United States or not does not appear.
>
> The committee recommend that the petitioners are not entitled to relief. Pvt. Pike was in Fenwick's regiment.

## Benjamin Hewitt

Benjamin Hewitt, of St. Mary's County, Maryland, filed a claim for $280 for a slave "who was conveyed from the United States on board the British fleet in the year 1814 and not recovered by Hewitt." A fund was allotted by the British Government under the 1st article of the treaty of Ghent for slaves, and by convention the estimated average value was established for the payment of slaves by a Board of Commissioners pursuant to the convention heard the claims.

A report was made on April 18, 1834, granting relief, and again by the Committee on Foreign Affairs on March 25, 1836:

> The petitioner asks compensation for a slave carried from the United States by the enemy during the last war from the money remaining undistributed of the fund allotted by the British Government as indemnity for claims of this description.
>
> He alleges, as the reason of the postponement of the application to so late a period that the paper which constituted his proof had, after his claim had been presented to the board of commissioners, been mislaid in the hands of the agent to which he had

confided it, and has only been recently discovered among the papers of this person on his decease.

The facts are sufficiently established and the committee are informed that there remains of the fund referred to, a sum sufficient to cover the claim of the petitioner. They have not thought themselves called upon to inquire whether the present be a case properly relievable by the terms of the treaty and convention under which the board of commissioners to distribute the fund allotted by the British Government was formed. To the board belonged the decision as to the class of cases to which payment was due, and the committee do not feel at liberty to assume the revisal of the exercise of that authority. It appeared that the board established no system of regulation for its government, but awarded on each case on the circumstances. a case of award exactly analogous to that of the petitioner, duly authenticated, having been produced to the committee, as they have regarded it as a sufficient foundation for a favorable consideration of that of the petitioner, and accordingly report a bill for his relief.

Hewitt's proof was mislaid at the State Department, but on March 3, 1839, Congress awarded $280.

## *The Northern Neck*

The Northern Neck is the land between the Potomac River and Rappahannock River to the south. The Yeocomico River at south end of the mouth of the Potomac River.

Mundy Point is at the end of Monday's Neck in Northumberland County, Virginia, in the Yeocomico River.

In July 1814, Lt. Col. Alexander Parker's 111th Regiment of Virginia Militia, Westmoreland County, prepared for the defense of Northern Neck, "in consequence of the landing of the enemy in different parts of the county."

Around July 25, 1814, Capt. Arthur Middleton marched his company of artillery to Kinsale and caused a breast work to be thrown up on the beach.

On August 3, 1814, Colonel Thomas Downing ordered troops to march immediately to the Yeocomico River to repulse the enemy who were advancing up the river.

### The Calvert County Levy Court

The courthouse in Prince Frederick, the county seat, was burned on Tuesday, July 19, 1814. As reported on December 10, 1817, by Commissioner Richard Bland Lee, of the Office of Claims:

> This claim is brought forward by the Levy Court of Calvert County, in the state of Maryland, to obtain compensation for the court house and jail, alleged to have been destroyed by the enemy in consequence of having been in the military occupation of the United States as a military deposit.
>
> The court house is valued by the claimants at $5,000 and the jail at $1,800.
>
> George W. Crane deposes that sometime previously to the burning of the court house by the enemy, they key of the court house was demanded of him by Captain Solomon Rutter, a commander of one of the boats belonging to the United States' flotilla under the command of Commodore Barney. Upon deponent stating his belief that there was no key belonging to the court house, Captain Rutter remarked that he must obtain possession of it, if he should be obliged to break open the door. Afterwards, Captain Rutter, with a number of men whom the deponent supposed to belong to the flotilla, took possession of the court house and deposited therein a number of arms and other military stores. The sick and wounded men were also brought to and accommodated. The court house remained in Captain Rutter's occupation till a few days before its destruction by the enemy.
>
> Elizabeth Crane deposes that when the enemy came she was there and, in conversation with some of the British officers, solicited them not to burn it. They replied that if Commodore Barney had not been harbored in it, they would not have come to it, nor burnt it.
>
> Thomas Billingsly deposes that on the day on which the enemy burnt the court house, a British officer told him that he, with a parcel of troops, had been to the court house in

consequence of hearing that Commodore Barney was there, and under the expectation of meeting him there. On the British officer's arrival at the court house, Commodore Barney had gone away, but that the appearance of huts having been erected, the exercise of cannon on the ground before the court house, manifested its having been made a military stand, and that, therefore, the British officer had caused the court house to be burnt.

Dr. Thomas Hamilton, surgeon to Commodore Barney's flotilla, deposes that in the summer of 1814, he, together with Captain Solomon Rutter, second in command of the flotilla, took possession of the court house, and occupied it for some considerable time as a hospital for the sick and wounded, and also a military store house to keep medicinal and other stores, and for other purposes. Around the court house cannon were placed, and it was guarded as a military post, and, as such, would have been defended against any equal force of the enemy.

John Ireland, John T. Patterson, and Alexander Skinner depose that in their belief, the court house was worth at the time of its destruction, $3,100. This latter sum, deducted from the former, leaves a balance of $3,000 as the actual loss of the claimants.

No proof has been offered of the occupation and destruction of the jail.

The claimants depose that they have not received anything from any officer, agent, or department of the government of the United States for the destruction of their court house. They did not agree with any officer or agent of the United States to run any risk on account of the use or employment in the public service. They have not received any other voucher or certificate relating to their claim from any officer or other person, at any time, except what is now exhibited before the commissioners. In consequence of Captain Rutter's being at sea, as they have been informed, their diligent and proper endeavors to procure his testimony have failed, and that the evidence which they have offered is the best which they could procure in the case.

On February 18, 1818, Commodore Barney wrote to the Committee of Claims, in part:

I have received another letter from General Philip Stuart requesting me to state what I know respecting the destruction of the Calvert Court House, occasioned, as he says, by the occupation of it by my men. This is another misstatement, as my men never occupied the Court House, having tents, &c., for their use near it.

Commodore Barney died on December 1, 1818, leaving his wife, Harriet. The Committee of Claims rejected the petition again on December 22, 1822. As reported again by the Committee of Claims on March 2, 1837:

This claim has been many times before the Committee of Claims, but the evidence in support of it has, in no instance, brought it within the provisions of the acts of Congress to allow indemnity in such cases. Reports of the committee, 18th of December, 1817; 10th of January, 1820; 6th of December, 1822; and on the 18th and 19th of December, 1823.

These reports were all adverse to the claim, on several grounds: 1st. That the military occupancy of the court-house by the troops of the United States, by order of the officer in the service of the United States did not appear so clearly made out as not to admit of doubt; and if so occupied, the evidence adduced went to show that the court-house had been evacuated by the military of the United States two or three days before its destruction by the enemy, and no satisfactory evidence to show a continued use of the house up to the time of its destruction. Upon such grounds, all those reports, in the opinion of the committee, are to be sustained.

Additional testimony in support of the claim has been referred to this committee, by which it clearly appears that the court-house was, by order of Commodore Barney, occupied some two or three weeks preceding its destruction, as a hospital for the sick and wounded sent from the flotilla under his command; also, as a receptacle for some prisoners and their guards, and as a deposit for some naval stores landed from the flotilla. It also appears that about the same time several corps of the United States troops made this a place of rendezvous and encamped near and around the court-house. And though it appears that, by order of Commodore Barney, on the near approach of the enemy, his men stationed in the court-house evacuated it on

Saturday, and that it was not destroyed until the Tuesday following.

Evidence is now before the committee to show that several military munitions were, in the hurry of evacuation, left in the building, which manifestly demonstrated to the enemy the public use to which the building had been, and thus was held. One or two of the witnesses state that the British officer directed this building to be destroyed under the conviction that it was in the military use of the United States. All testify that no private property was injured. On the contrary, in one instance it was carefully protected, and many respectable witnesses express the belief that the court-house was destroyed in consequence of its military occupancy, as aforesaid, of which occupancy evidences remained in the house at the time of its destruction, as is stated by one respectable witness.

This claim is to indemnify for a court-house and jail destroyed by the enemy. The Levy Court of Calvert County estimate the value of the court-house at $5,000, and the jail at $1,800. Commissioners duly appointed under the authority of Richard Bland Lee, Esq., to ascertain the loss of the court-house find it to be $3,000. It has nowhere been alleged that the jail was at any time in the military use of the United States; and, as no notice has, for that obvious reason, been taken of it heretofore, nothing need now be said in regard to it. In regard to the court-house, the evidence now adduced, and all the circumstances of the case, conduct the committee to the opinion that it ought to be paid for, according to the valuation reported by the commissioners. A bill is therefore reported in conformity with that opinion.

Dr. Thomas Hamilton actually served in Lt. Col. Kennedy Long's 27th Regiment of Maryland Militia and Lt. Col. Jacob Small's 39th Regiment of Maryland Militia.

## Elizabeth Thompson

On July 20, 1814, about 1,000 British marines from Adm. Cockburn's fleet went ashore at Nomini Creek in Virginia, a tributary of the Potomac, then continued on the next morning.

As reported by the Committee of Claims on March 7, 1834:

The American officers and troops had entered the house of Mrs. Thompson and were obtaining some hasty refreshments when the enemy coming suddenly upon them in considerable number drove them off, actually firing upon them whilst in the portico and yard. The enemy were not probably accurately informed in what home the soldiers and officers of the guard had been stationed, but they actually found some of them in the dwelling-house, and, on reaching the house, found some spirits and water which had been hastily left exposed in the open portal of the house, and which, from some cause, they suspected were poisoned, and thus left for the purpose of falling into their hands, and military accoutrements and provisions were found in the storehouse which had been occupied by the soldiers.

The certificate of William G. Furman, supposed to have been given about the time of the transaction, states with minuteness the approach of the enemy and the abandonment of the house. He did not see the house burning, but he went near to where it stood the next day after it was burnt, and saw the ruins of the home. From his statement, the house could not have been in the military occupation of the United States. Finding the enemy was ascending the river, he went to the house of Mrs. Thompson, and found her and several ladies in distress and he walked with them until they got into their carriage and were conveyed away.

This witness had been ordered to take 10 or 12 troopers and proceed to the ferry at Nomoni to watch the movements of the enemy's boats; and after they had left the home of Mrs. Thompson, he met Gen. Hungerford and Col. Parker, with Col. Glascock's troops, and he saw them afterwards at Mrs. Thompson's house observing the movements of the enemy, who were upon the point of landing. They soon landed, entered Mrs. Thompson's yard, and fired upon the party to which the witness belonged, and in a short time the American troops retreated from the superior numbers of the enemy. He thinks the enemy, as they came in sight of the house of Mrs. Thompson, discovered that he and his party were soldiers, and that, on their nearer approach, they discovered Gen. Hungerford, Col. Parker, and others retiring from the house, and when the enemy fired he says the troop was in sight of the house, and not far from it, and Col. Parker's regiment, which they saw drawn up in battle array against them, commenced its retreat not far from Mrs. Thompson's.

Samuel Templeman gave his deposition on the 6th day of December, 1816, and he thinks the landing at Nomoni was about the 21st of July, 1814. He says the landing at Nomoni ferry, where the warehouses stood, was occupied by a military force as a boat guard. He saw Mrs. Thompson when she was leaving her estate, and understood Col. Parker, with his troop, had taken a station at Mrs. Thompson's dwelling-house near the ferry on the hill. He, with others, went down and met Gen. Hungerford and Col. Parker retreating, and he gave it as his opinion that the only reason which induced the enemy to burn and destroy the property of the estate of Mrs. George Thompson and Mrs. Elizabeth Thompson were, 1st, that the place was occupied by a boat guard; 2d, that the tobacco warehouses were considered public property; and 3d, because Col. Parker, with a military force, took a stand at the dwelling-house in sight of the enemy, and while they were advancing up the hill.

Samuel Templeman, James Montgomery, and William Franklin estimated the property destroyed, consisting of the buildings and their contents, to have been $10,319.40. James Douglass, whose deposition was taken on the 6th of February, 1820, testifies that he occupied the storehouse at Nomony ferry until he was broken up by the British, which house was the property of Mrs. Thompson. From the spring of 1812 until the landing of the enemy on the 21st of July, 1814, the boats were collected at that place, and a guard of the militia was posted there to prevent the elopement of the negroes to the enemy. When the British landed, there was a detachment of the militia at that place, and on their retreat there were left in the storehouse some arms, ammunition, and other military apparatus, there being a house attached to the store, which the guard had always used as a barrack. Mrs. Thompson's house, storehouse, and all the buildings attached, were destroyed, except one negro cabin. The witness was on board the British fleet shortly afterwards, when Captain Robert Ramsay asked why it was that the military apparatus was lodged in the storehouse. He explained the cause, and says he knows nothing of the motives of the enemy.

William G. Furman does not know whether a boat guard was posted at Nomoni ferry, near to Mrs. Thompson's, just before the time when the houses were burnt by the British soldiers and concludes by saying he has always confidently believed that the burning of Mrs. Thompson's property was occasioned by the military show on the spot, and by the presence of a large part of the Westmoreland regiment of militia, quite near, probably in sight at the time.

Col. Parker gave a certificate of what he recollects, which is dated on the 19th March, 1832. He does not recollect whether a guard of militia, denominated a boat guard, was stationed at the ferry at the time of the destruction of the buildings, or if there was, he says, it must have been placed there by his order. He was there when the enemy landed, with a small detachment of cavalry, and he intended to have resisted the enemy, but the artillery did not arrive in season. He says he has no doubt the intention of the enemy was, in entering the river, to destroy the warehouses. When he arrived at Mrs. Thompson's house, the boats of the enemy were in sight and a considerable force soon landed. The Americans retreated and retarded the movements of the enemy by occasionally halting and making a show of resistance by which he supposes the court-house was saved in Westmoreland county.

The next morning found all of Mrs. Thompson's houses were burnt, he says, "their cause, as I understand, was that the militia had left poisoned spirits at the house for them to drink. A bottle or two of spirits had been left in the porch by the troopers, in consequence of their being driven away unexpectedly, and this circumstance gave rise to the suspicion. A flag of truce was sent to their fleet a few days afterwards, borne by Maj. Lomax, and I have among my papers a letter from Admiral Cockburn admitting that the suspicion had been entertained. I have said that the militia were then in the service of the State of Virginia. Of this I am confident, they were soon afterwards taken into the service of the United States."

If poisoned spirits had been left in this house, that would not have justified the enemy in setting fire to these private buildings, but there is no pretense that the spirits left in the porch were poisoned, and the committee think the destruction of these buildings was a wanton act of the enemy, such as so frequently marked his footprints whenever he effected a landing. The loss is a severe one, and one the committee would recommend to the favorable consideration of Congress if they could do so without violating the rules established by Congress. The petitioner is not entitled to relief.

Gen. John P. Hungerford commanded the 14th Virginia. Col. Richard E. Parker commanded the 111th Virginia. Capt. George Glasscock was in Col. Parker's regiment. Maj. Lomax is probably Mann Page Lomax.

### Benjamin H. Mackall

As reported by the Committee of Claims on March 3, 1836:

> Some time about the 1st of August, 1814, the troops under the command of Col. Michael Taney, being a part of the 31st Regiment of Maryland Militia, by order of the commanding officer, took possession of an out-house belonging to Benjamin H. Mackall, of Calvert County, in the State of Maryland, for the purpose of more effectually defending themselves against a detachment of the British forces, then in the immediate vicinity. A skirmish shortly after ensued, and after exchanging a few shots it was found necessary that our troops should vacate the house, which they accordingly did by order of their commanding officer, whereupon the enemy immediately advanced upon and burned the out-house.
>
> This claim has been rejected from an apparent discrepancy in the testimony of Major Stephen St. John taken in 1816, and that of Colonel or Major Taney taken in 1828, upon the ground that both swear to being in actual command at the same time. The committee think that upon a close examination of the language used by these deponents, that no such discrepancy will be found to exist.
>
> Major John says, that he "gave orders to James D. Denton, orderly sergeant under his command, to take possession of an out-house." Col. Taney says that "a small guard was stationed in a house on the farm of Benjamin H. Mackall in 1814, which guard were a part of the militia then on duty by order of this deponent."
>
> Thus it will be found that the troops were in immediate possession of the house by order of John, and that the troops thus stationed there were a part of the militia then on duty by order of Taney. The facts of the case appear to be clearly made out in the estimation of the committee, which, with the proof of two witnesses that the property was worth at the time of its destruction $210, have induced the committee to conclude the petitioner is entitled to relief and report a bill.

The legal representatives of Benjamin H. Mackall were paid $210 in 1838.

James D. Denton was a sergeant in Hodgkin's and Taney's 31st Regiment of Maryland Militia. Theodore Hodgkin and Michael Taney were both lt. cols. in the 31st Regiment. Benjamin Mackall reportedly died at Baltimore on June 25, 1840.

## *The Yeocomico Creek Landing*

Mundy Point is at the end of Monday's Neck in Northumberland County, Virginia, in the Yeocomico River.

On August 3, 1814, about 500 British sailors and marines from Adm. Cockburn's fleet landed at Mundy Point. Capt. William Henderson lived there and along with 30 Northumberland County militia assisted in fortifying the position, but they were forced to retreat to the courthouse. Three days later the British advanced along the Coan River, a tributary of the Potomac.

### William Henderson

Capt. Henderson submitted a claim for $6,140, as reported by the Committee of Claims on March 6, 1818:

> In this case, the witnesses state that a company of artillery, commanded by claimant, was stationed at Monday's Point and that anterior to and on the 3rd of August, 1814, a

dwelling house and new storehouse, situated at said point and owned by the claimant were ordered occupied as barracks.

Very early in the morning of the 3rd of August, the enemy in numbers greatly superior, attacked the claimant's command, who, after a sharp conflict, retreated in good order, when the enemy set fire to, and consumed, all the buildings on the point and then pursued claimant's command into the country, and at a distance of about 6 miles from the point—claimant's command having eluded the enemy's pursuit—set fire to and destroyed a house, store, and out houses, the property of the heirs of Rodham Davis, and in the occupancy of the claimant. His household and kitchen furniture, goods in the store, and other property—very little of which is enumerated—to "about the value" of $3,280, was also destroyed.

Witnesses also state that there were deposited in the house in which claimant lived, four boxes of artillery cartridges, and one box of carbine cartridges in the store, which the enemy "discovered and either destroyed or carried away."

The witnesses also state that the dwelling house which was used as barracks was a frame of a single story, "about 20 feet in length, by 20 feet in width," in which, they state, was about three tons of clover hay, and 25 bushels of oats. The new storehouse, which they also state was used for barracks, they say was about 36 feet by 16, and in that, it is alleged, was 7 tons of hay.

The committee are at a loss how to reconcile the facts that are here attempted to be proven, to wit: that a house and store of the above dimensions, should be occupied as barracks, while their contents consisted of no less than 10 tons of clover hay, and 25 bushels of oats, and from the examination of this case, and many others which they have had under consideration, they are perfectly satisfied that until it can be ascertained what witnesses mean, by certain expressions which they evidently borrowed from the law of the 9th of April, 1816, such as, "occupied as a military deposit," "barracks," &c. &c. it is extremely difficult, if not altogether impracticable, to determine who are, and who are not, entitled to remuneration for their losses.

The committee deem it proper here to remark that from the known wantonness of the late enemy, in his almost indiscriminate destruction of property wherever he effected a landing, it is fair to presume that buildings have not been destroyed in consequence of a military occupation, except in cases where it is in proof, that no other buildings in the vicinity of those thus occupied have been destroyed. Nor can they perceive any safe rule for determining that a building has been burned in consequence of a military occupancy, except it shall appear that the burning was necessary to effect the destruction of military supplies, or some other legitimate object of civilized warfare.

In the case of William Henderson the evidence is very uncertain as to the fact of the burning being in consequence of a military occupation. The witnesses say all the buildings at Monday's Point were burned, but are silent as to the fact whether there were, or were not, other buildings there than those which were necessarily consumed with such as are alleged to have been used as barracks.

From the deposition of Gen. John Hungerford it is fair to presume that other buildings were destroyed. He states that Capt. William Henderson, "was pursued several miles by the enemy, who wantonly burned and destroyed several houses and other property." But admitting the buildings to have been destroyed in consequence of a military occupation, the evidence is too vague and uncertain as to the amount of damages to authorize an allowance. The committee therefore recommend that the claim be rejected.

Capt. Henderson pursued his claim and obtained a transcribed statement from Col. Hiram Blackwell:

The claimant some weeks prior to the 3rd of August, 1814, was directed by Col. Downing to occupy with his company of artillery a situation on Monday's Point. After the enemy had landed, the brigade of Gen. Hungerford was called out and a detachment from the regiment was ordered by him to cooperate with the claimant. Col. Blackwell, then a major, marched with the detachment under his command to Oyster Shell, just above Monday's Point, where, after remaining some days, he received orders from Gen. Hungerford to return with the detachment to Northumberland courthouse where the principal part of the regiment was embodied and to direct the

> claimant to remain with his company at Monday's Point. With this order Col. Blackwell complied on the 31st July.
>
> Early on the morning of the 3rd August, the claimant was attacked by a strong force of the enemy's barges, and after a most gallant resistance, was compelled to retreat. The enemy then landed, set fire to and consumed all the houses at Monday's Point and pursued the claimant's command several miles up into the country and burnt the dwelling house and storehouse occupied by him, the property of the heirs of Rodham Davis, deceased.
>
> The dwelling house and storehouse at Monday's Point were used by the claimant's company at the time of the attack as barracks, that they had been so used and by the company of Capt. Thomas Beacham at intervals of alarm, frequently in 1813, and generally by the claimant's company when the enemy were in the Potomac in 1814 prior to their destruction. This was done by the orders of Col. Downing and was from necessity, the regiment not being sufficiently provided with tents, and that Col. Blackwell understands and believes that a considerable quantity of ammunition belonging to the claimant's company was deposited in the storehouse and dwelling house and is convinced that the occupation of the houses at Monday's Point as barracks and of the dwelling house and storehouse as military depots, was the cause of their destruction by the enemy.

Lt. John Fulks, Sgt. Thomas Brann, and Pvt. William Dameson, Jr., former members of Henderson's company corroborated the facts, as did John Lunsford, Henderson's store clerk, and George Miskell, an acquaintance. On December 6, 1820, Major Pemberton Laughton, of the 37th Regiment Virginia Militia, was deposed by Samuel Crall, justice of the peace for Northumberland County:

> After the burning of the United States' gunboat *Asp*, near Kinsale by the British in 1813, Captain William Henderson, whose company of artillery was attached to this affidavit's battalion, was ordered to occupy, with a part of his command, the place called Monday's Point, on the Yeocomico River, whenever the enemy made his appearance in the Potomac, this position being considered the best in the upper parts of the country for the annoyance of an invading force.
>
> This affiant, also, directed Henderson to throw up breastworks, or fortifications, and Henderson accordingly erected three defenses, which afterwards proved of essential service in the attack made by the British at that place. The orders were given under the direction of Colonel Thomas Downing, the commandant of the 37th Regiment of Militia, and who is now dead.
>
> The fortifications consisted of a breastwork, composed in front of large logs covered very thickly with earth and sods, and a ditch in the rear. The other two were thrown up on the beach and composed of a large mound of sand in front and a ditch in the rear. So much importance did the enemy attach to the first mentioned battery, that after obtaining possession of the place, they entirely destroyed it.
>
> This affiant states further that he witnessed the attack on Monday's Point on the 3rd of August, 1814, from a position on the opposite side of a large creek. Captain Henderson continued to fire upon the British barges from the two batteries which were manned until some of the enemy were in the act of leaping on shore, when he affected a retreat with the loss of an artillery piece. The enemy then landed and burned the whole of the houses at the Point, all of which belonged to Henderson.
>
> The company of Henderson, when stationed at the place, occupied the dwelling house and new storehouse as barracks, sleeping, and being sheltered from the weather therein, and cooking in the dwelling house and kitchen. That such occupation was necessary for the well-being of the company, which was destitute of tents.
>
> The ammunition and provisions for the use of the company were kept in some of the houses; that the whole of such occupation was by the authority of Colonel Downing. This affiant is well convinced that the houses were burned by the enemy in consequence of the military occupation of the same, and the gallant resistance he met with from the little band of Henderson.

On December 31, 1821, the Committee of Claims rejected Henderson's claim pursuant to the Act of April 9, 1816, but reported an award of $2,765.

## Hannah Davis

As reported by the Committee of Claims on December 20, 1820:

> The petitioner claims payment for a dwelling house, store house, and other out buildings, situate in Northumberland County, Virginia, occupied by Capt. Henderson, and destroyed by the British on the 3rd of August, 1814, in consequence, as alleged, of being used as places of deposit for military stores. The amount of claim is $3,223.
>
> The case was reported on at the last session of Congress by the Committee of Claims, which was adverse to the petitioner. At that time the claim of Capt. Henderson for destruction of his buildings at Munday's Point and for his personal effects burned and destroyed in the buildings of Hannah Davis, had been reported on by the committee and was referred to a Committee of the Whole House; it was, therefore, deemed sufficient by the committee to refer the House to their report in the case of Capt. Henderson, as the two cases were intimately blended and connected together.
>
> The report of the committee on the claim of Capt. Henderson having been subsequently confirmed by the House, and this case again referred to them, they have thought it their duty to re-examine the evidence, the result of which has been a conviction in their minds that this case is much less entitled to the favorable consideration of Congress than was that of Capt. Henderson as a dwelling and store house distant from Munday's Point about 6 miles in the country, occupied by his family, and filled with the ordinary household goods, and store goods.
>
> Although it is in evidence that there were a few boxes of artillery cartridges lodged there, and perhaps three or four broken muskets, the committee have yet to learn that this circumstance imported to property thus situated, such military character as authorized its destruction by an enemy. Therefore the claim of the petitioner ought not to be granted.

## William W. Scott

As reported by the Committee of Claims on January 9, 1839:

> The petitioner was a non-commissioned officer in a company of artillery in Northampton County, Virginia. Hearing that the British were landing at a place called Sandy Point, he immediately repaired to that place on horseback for the purpose of joining his company. On his arrival, he found the enemy's barges very near the shore, and firing having commenced, his horse took fright and fled into the bay in the direction of the enemy's barges, and was taken on board together with a bridle and saddle. The petitioner states that he pursued his horse as far as he could do so with safety to himself, but was unable to prevent his capture. He asks compensation, which he estimates at $100, and the saddle and bridle, which he values at $11.25.
>
> There is no principle established under which this claim can possibly be allowed. It is not pretended that the horse was directly or indirectly in the service of the United States. The petitioner, being a member of a foot company, for his own accommodation and convenience, rides his horse to the place of rendezvous, dismounts from him for the purpose, it is presumed, of performing his military duties, and the horse taking fright, deserts to the enemy.
>
> The committee can only regard the case in the same light as if the petitioner's horse had been captured by the enemy from his stable or pasture.
>
> The petitioner is not entitled to relief.

Sandy Point at that time was part of a plantation near Mundy Point owned by Horatio and John Gibson. In 1818 they sold the property to Henry Mayer. It is known as the youthful home of George Washington's mother, Mary Ball. The Sandy Point State Park offers camping, picnic facilities, and sandy beaches.

## Charles G. Layton

The petition of Charles Layton of December 15, 1845:

> The petition of Charles G. Layton, of the county of Essex, and State of Virginia, respectfully represents that in 1814 your petitioner was possessed of a certain sailing vessel called the *Albert Gallatin*, of the value of $1,800, which was usually employed in the transportation of grain and other commodities between the different ports and landings

on the Chesapeake Bay and its tributaries. While thus employed, the vessel was pressed into the service of the United States and used for the transportation of troops, arms, ammunition, &c., and while engaged in their service, and whilst your petitioner was himself in the service, and at a distant point, the vessel was captured by the enemy and carried off and destroyed, so that your petitioner suffered the loss arising from the necessary delays to which he was established in procuring another vessel.

Your petitioner further represents that he placed his claim in the hands of a friend for the purpose of having it presented to the proper accounting officers of the Treasury for settlement, but, upon presenting it there, was informed that under a late act of Congress, no claim against the United States of more than six years standing can be legally acted upon, or even examined, without a special act of Congress to that effect.

Your petitioner is therefore placed under the necessity of bringing his application before your honorable body, and relying with strong evidence upon the high sense of justice which distinguishes so eminently the Representatives of a free and enlightened people, would most respectfully pray the enactment of a law directing the proper officer of the Treasury to examine and report upon his claim, and at the same time make provision for the payment, together with interest, and such damages as your petitioner may be justly entitled to.

As stated by the Committee of Claims on May 5, 1846:

This claim originated about 32 years ago, and is now first presented for payment. The petition does not state by what agent the vessel was taken into the service of the government, or whether the taking was by competent legal authority, and for a justifiable purpose. The appraisement of the value of the vessel by persons who had merely seen it 31 or 32 years before cannot be relied on with certainty, for it is clearly impossible to recollect the value of the several vessels one may see during a long series of years. If this claim was just, and no legal impediment existed, why were 32 years permitted to elapse prior to its presentation? Why is not the name of the officer who impressed the vessel furnished to Congress, together with his authority to impress? Why was not the value of the vessel proved at a time when the citizens at the port whence it sailed knew its value, and could correct any error of statement?

The petitioner says he would have presented it to the accounting officers of the Treasury, but for the law prohibiting the payment of claims of more than six years standing. This law, it will be recollected by the House, is of very recent date, and the long delay, therefore, fails to be accounted for.

The committee, from these and other considerations, are constrained to recommend that the prayer of the petitioner ought not to be granted.

No date is shown for the impressment. Charles Layton was a lieutenant in Lt. Col. Elliots Muse's 109th Virginia Regiment.

## Thomas Beacham

The claim was filed by heirs Thomas C., George L., James W., Samuel L., and Nathaniel G. Beacham.

As stated by the Committee of Claims on February 13, 1835:

The petitioners state that about the 1st of August in the year 1814, a party of the British landed at Munday's Point, and, after destroying much property at that place, marched to the residence of their father and found in his barn a quantity of arms which had been there deposited by order of Colonel Downing, the commandant of a regiment. They set fire to the barn and it was actually consumed with all its contents, and departed without destroying any other property.

Their father was taken prisoner and remained a prisoner to the end of the war, and they state as a reason for their long delay in applying to the government for remuneration for their loss, that they were minors at the death of their father, which occurred several years since, and that there was no person capable of acting who took an interest for them. They now ask to reimbursed for their loss.

This claim was presented to Congress in March, 1832, in December 1832, and in December, 1833, but does not appear to have been acted on.

It was noted that Capt. William Henderson's home at Munday's Point was destroyed before they set off for the Beacham place. Lt. Col. Thomas D. Downing commanded the 37th Regiment of Virginia Militia.

The petitioners have taken additional testimony; the case, now made out by proof, is that the British landed at Munday's Point, near the residence of Capt. Henderson, whose property they destroyed, and marched to the residence of the father of the petitioners and burnt an out-house or barn, and then returned without destroying any other property. The barn had been a place of deposit for some time of public arms, by order of Col. Downing, to be distributed amongst the militia as occasion might require. A considerable number of arms were in the barn at the time it was burnt.

The father of the petitioner was a captain of militia and was taken prisoner by the enemy, and kept a prisoner until the end of the war. It is proved that Col. Downing is dead. The time of his death is not shown, but the deposition proving his death was taken in February 1832. The Hon. Mr. Chinn states he died shortly after the war.

The value of the barn is proved to be between $600 and $700. The facts are proved by the depositions of Samuel Cralle, Snyder T. Hudson, James S. Hale, William B. Lewis, John Damerson, John Claughton, and Thomas Bell, the latter of whom was a lieutenant in Capt. Thomas Beacham's company.

It is a well settled principle that where property is in the military occupation of the government, whether in time of war or peace, and is destroyed during that occupation, an obligation is imposed upon government to remunerate the owner for the loss. The property in question must be regarded as being in the military occupation of the United States. It is fairly inferable that the destruction of the property by the enemy was in consequence of that occupation for they left undisturbed the dwelling-house and all other houses on the premises, some of which proved to have been within 100 yards of the barn.

The committee think the petitioners are entitled to relief and report a bill in their favor.

The legal representatives of Thomas Beacham were paid $600 in 1836.

## William Forbes

In July 1814, Lt. Col. Alexander Parker's 111th Regiment of Virginia Militia, Westmoreland County, prepared for the defense of Northern Neck, "in consequence of the landing of the enemy in different parts of the county."

Parker was deposed on January 23, 1823:

> On or about the 24th of July, 1814, apprehending a descent upon that part of the county contiguous to Kinsale, on the river Yeocomico, he, as the officer then commanding, gave an order to Capt. William Middleton, of the artillery, to proceed to that place and throw up such temporary defenses as time would permit in order to aid in repelling the enemy if they attempted to land. And also an order to Quartermaster Richard T. Brown to furnish the entrenching tools, &c. as might be necessary for that purpose. This order was obeyed, and the place including the houses belonging to the estate of William Forbes, deceased, which were immediately at the spot, was occupied by the troops.
>
> On the 23rd of July, General John P. Hungerford was appointed to command the force, then assembling from different quarters. But the order did not reach the Northern Neck until about the 25th or 26th when he took command, and immediately marched, with all his disposable troops to Kinsale, arriving about daylight of the very day whereon the enemy landed first at Monday's Point and drove Capt. William Henderson from that place, and, afterwards, at Kinsale.
>
> On their return from the pursuit of Henderson, they were seen re-embarking and proceeding up the river to the latter place, which was now occupied by the General with his whole force, but on their nearer approach, it was withdrawn, for what reason this affiant does not know, unless it was deemed untenable, with the exception of two companies under Major Robert L. Yates, of King George, who volunteered to stay and attempt its defense. They were quickly driven away with the loss of one man killed in Capt. Pitt's company of infantry, and the enemy landed in full view of Hungerford's brigade, and burnt the warehouses on each side of the river, and the dwelling and store house at Kinsale, which

had been occupied as barracks for the troops and in which provisions, &c. were stored.

This affiant has never considered Kinsale as a military post, when it was taken and burnt by the enemy, and the heirs of Forbes to be justly entitled to retribution for their loss.

General Hungerford stated on February 4, 1823:

> In July, 1814, I was appointed to the command of the troops that were called into service for the defense of the Northern Neck, and part of them were stationed at Yeocomico church near Kinsale. Captain William Middleton was detached to that place for its defense with a company of artillery. Previous to the destruction of Kinsale by the enemy, the troops were marched there from Yeocomico church, as it was apprehended they intended to visit that place. The British fleet then lay off the mouth of Yeocomico.
>
> Early in the morning of the 3rd of August, we discovered the enemy ascending Yeocomico River, with considerable force, in tenders and barges. They landed on the east side of the river, about two miles below, at Monday's Point, and, after great depredations at that place, and in the neighborhood, re-embarked for Kinsale.
>
> Sensible of their great superiority in numbers and knowing that we should be much exposed on a bleak shore to their cannon, it was thought proper to retire. Major Robert L. Yates, however, with two volunteer companies under their command, were immediately sent back, and, after being much exposed to the racking fire of their cannon, was forced to retreat with the loss of one of his men. The British landed, plundered, and burnt the houses and carried away a great deal of property. The houses at Kinsale were generally occupied by the troops. In fact, we had then only partially been furnished with tents.

Capt. James Cox stated on December 10, 1817:

> I was in service during the late war and held the commission of captain in the 111th Regiment of Virginia Militia. I was stationed at Kinsale at different times with the company under my command. The dwelling house was occupied by the officers as a barrack and that on the day of the enemy's attack, a number of militia were in the dwelling house procuring rations of meal, which had been procured for them. The kitchen was used by the militia for cooking; the storehouse was occupied as a barrack, and also as a depository of ammunition and provision, and that one of the granaries was occupied as a barrack. The occupation of the houses was made under the authority and by the direction of John Turberville, deceased, at that time major of the 111th Regiment of Virginia Militia. Major Turberville died in October, 1815.

Capt. William Middleton stated on December 18, 1817:

> The dwelling house, store house, and granary at Kinsale, in the county of Westmoreland, belonging to the orphans of William Forbes, were occupied as barracks and used as depositories of provisions and military stores, and were destroyed the 3rd of August, 1814. Under the orders of Major John Turberville, commandant of the 2nd Battalion and 111th Regiment, I marched with my company of artillery about the 25th of July, 1814, to Kinsale and caused a breast work to be thrown up on the beach between the dwelling house and store house, from which I was ordered to retire, but a little while before the enemy effected their landing.

The heirs of William Forbes claimed a frame dwelling house, 42 × 30 in good repair, with 4 rooms on one floor and 5 above, with cellars under, \$3,000; new framed dwelling house, 18 × 16 used as a nursery, annexed to the dwelling house, \$500; new framed house, a kitchen, 18 × 16, \$300; framed granary, 20 × 16, \$300; framed storehouse and counting room with dutch roof and cellars under, 30 × 20, \$2,000; new close jointed log granary, 20 × 16, \$300; one old log granary by the dwelling house, 20 × 20, \$50; framed smokehouse, 10 × 10, \$150; framed pigeon house, 14 × 14, \$100; tobacco warehouse for inspection of tobacco, with a shed at one end and two prize beams, in good repair, 60 × 24, \$1,000. Total \$7,700.

Gordon Forbes was one of four children of William Forbes, "who, some years before the war had been bereaved of both father and mother, left dependent on a small property for support, and the chief revenue arising from that property, derived from the houses now under consideration. Severely, however, this blow was felt, he is sensible that any appeal founded on this ground would be alien to the principles which must regulate the decision of his case."

As stated by the Committee of Claims on January 23, 1824:

> The committee are of opinion that the petitioners are not entitled to any relief. The hostility of the enemy during the late war was marked with a character peculiarly licentious and extravagant. At every point where he landed, devastation and pillage appear to have been his only objects. In the instance before us, a claim is made for property destroyed at Kinsale, to the amount of $7,700. But, on the other side of the river Yeocomico, opposite Kinsale, the property of our citizens was also destroyed. It could not therefore be urged that the occupation at Kinsale was the cause of the destruction, when the same destruction equally awaited property on the opposite side of the river, where, it is believed, no occupation is pretended. The law, it will be remembered, requires that occupation must be the cause of destruction, before any claimant can be entitled to indemnity.
>
> This conclusion will be fortified by a knowledge of the various acts of predatory and licentious warfare committed by the enemy. In Louisiana, Virginia, Maryland, in this city, and on the Niagara frontier, the same ruthless spirit appears to have marked his course. No one could say, for example, that the Capitol of the United States was destroyed in consequence of its having been in the military occupation of government. Yet this and other monuments, "dedicated to the arts," were doomed to the assaults of barbarous invasion. For losses of this description, no government can or ought to be held responsible; because the resources of no nation would be adequate to meet so varied and extensive a demand.
>
> The claim of the heirs of William Forbes, deceased, ought not to be granted.

In 1836, John Burke claimed to be a tenant "in possession of the houses belonging to the heirs of William Forbes," in which he had "the usual quantity of furniture, new, and of good quality" and also "the usual quantity of kitchen furniture; that he had a good assortment of goods in the store-house, that in the granary he had 900 to 1,000 bushels of grain, and that in the other houses he had a considerable quantity of flour, salt, sugar, coffee and other groceries" for which he filed a claim, which was denied every year between 1836 and 1842.

As stated by the Committee of Claims on February 22, 1843, in part:

> It appears that a detachment of American troops had been stationed a short distance from Kinsale for some time previous to the 3rd of August, 1814. A few days previous, this detachment was quartered at Kinsale, and the buildings at Kinsale, then occupied by the petitioner, and owned by one Forbes, consisting of a dwelling house, store, and out buildings, were occupied by the officers and soldiers. On the morning of the 3rd of August, the troops left Kinsale and retired some distance into the country. At this time the petitioner was absent from home, and had furniture, goods, provisions, &c., in his buildings, where it was considered as safe as it would have been considered in any other place in the vicinity.
>
> Mr. Burke returned on the 3rd, and, finding that the troops had evacuated Kinsale and that the enemy were advancing towards it, he applied for and obtained permission to call for volunteers to repair to that place to defend his property. He collected a force, repaired to Kinsale, and was there met and attacked and driven back by the enemy, who set fire to and burned his rented buildings and the property contained in them, of very considerable value.
>
> This is one among the many cases of great loses and hardship by the calamities of war. The petitioner suffered severely, but the committee do not discover any thing in the case to distinguish it from ordinary cases of the destruction of private personal property by hostile armies. This building had been occupied as barracks by our troops previous to the attack, but the movable property which they contained was subject to the control of the petitioner. The military occupation of the buildings, probably subjected them to the

character of military property, and rendered them legally liable to destruction by the enemy.

Such, however, was not the condition of the personal property. That was not in any way, by impressment or contract, taken into military or other public service. It is said that the officers slept in the beds of Mr. Burke, and that his cooking utensils were used by the soldiers, but it does not appear that this was by order of an officer against the assent of Mr. Burke, nor that any act of the officers or soldiers was interposed to prevent the removal of any part of the property from those buildings.

It has been suggested that some of the property which was destroyed was needed for the troops, and that the means of transporting it away were taken into the service of the American army, wherefore it became the duty of Mr. Burke, as a good citizen, to let that part of his property needed by the troops remain, and impossible for him to remove the other parts of it.

The evidence not only does not show that Mr. Burke desired to move his property away, but that it was considered safe at Kinsale. But it will hardly be contended that the government, by the impressment of teams and wagons into the public service, become liable for the loss of property for the want of those means to move it away from danger. The flour and other articles needed by the troops, if it had been permitted to remain at Kinsale for that purpose alone until it was purchased for the use of the army, was kept there at the risk of the owner. The risk would not be transferred until the property passed.

The committee recommend that the petitioner is not entitled to relief.

Gordon Forbes, John A. Parker, and Robert M. Forbes, "heirs at law of William Forbes, deceased," were paid $2,100 in 1836.

## Baldwin M. Leland

As stated by the Committee of Claims on February 15, 1830:

The petitioner represents that during the late war sundry detachments of militia were stationed on his farm in Northumberland County in the State of Virginia, by which he sustained great injury. On one occasion soon after the troops had kindled their fires to prepare their breakfast, the enemy was attempting to land, and the forces were hurried away for defense, and neglected to put out their fires and the consequence was a valuable woods was almost entirely ruined, the fencing for miles, enclosing valuable crops of corn, wheat, and cotton, was entirely destroyed, and estimates his loss at about $2,000.

The committee feel sorry to say that the case of the claimant is one of those casualties which frequently occur in times of peace, as well as war, which the government cannot be responsible for.

Henry H. Travers testifies that he was a Captain of a company of militia stationed by order of Col. Thomas D. Downing, who was in the United States' service, on the lands of the petitioner, at different times from some time in 1813 till the latter part of 1814.

On the 3rd day of August, 1814, he was thus stationed, when he was ordered by Colonel Downing to march immediately to Yeocomico River, to repulse the enemy who were advancing up the river. At the time of the reception of this order, the men had just kindled fires for the purpose of cooking breakfast. Being thus hastily marched off, the fires were left unextinguished, in consequence of which they communicated to the fencing, woods, crops, &c. The quantity of corn destroyed was not less than 300, nor more than 350 barrels; that of wheat, not less than 200, nor more than 250 barrels. The damage in other articles of the crop was not less than $150 nor more than $200. The damage done to the fencings and woods was not less than $300 no more than $500.

His farm adjoins that of the petitioner and that he is well acquainted with its productions, that the price of corn in the Spring of 1815 was from $3.50 to $4.00; that of wheat from $1.00 to $1.75.

He further states that at the time of the destruction of property, the petitioner, in consequence of his station in the regiment as contractor, was totally prevented from paying any attention to his farm. The Colonel and all the field officers died shortly after the war.

Thomas Oldham, a sergeant in Captain Travers' company substantiated the facts. George Downing, a lieutenant commandant of a company of the 37th Regiment, was stationed just below the rendezvous of the petitioner, and testified the militia failed to put out the fires and the damage was $1,000 to $2,000.

Capt. William Henderson stated the petitioner was absent and unable to defend his property, as did William Sett.

## John King

As reported by the Committee of Claims on March 8, 1842:

> The petitioner represents that on the 3rd day of August, 1814, his dwelling-house, then situated in the county of Richmond, was set fire to and destroyed, with its contents, by a detachment of British troops during the continuance of the late war between that country and the United States.
>
> At the time it was consumed it contained a large quantity of arms and other munitions of war that had been deposited there by order of Captain Edward J. Northum, a regular commissioned officer of the State militia, but who was then in the service of the United States, and prays to be remunerated for the loss he sustained on that occasion.
>
> It appears from the testimony that a company of Virginia militia, under command of Captain Edward J. Northum, was mustered as in the service of the United States from the 21st of July to the 30th of August, 1814, inclusive, and that prior to that time, a quantity of arms had been deposited in the petitioner's house by order of said captain, and that the same was very generally used as a place of rendezvous by the military in that region of the country. The militia, of which the company formed a part, received their pay from the State of Virginia, but which was subsequently reimbursed by the United States, and the rolls are on file with the accounts of the State against the United States.
>
> The petitioner was a member of the company, and appears to have been taken prisoner by the enemy on the very day that his house was consumed and transported to Canada where he remained some time in con-finement.
>
> It is proved that a portion of those arms were in the house at the time it was consumed, and from the fact that only two other buildings in that neighborhood were destroyed, both of which were similarly occupied, your committee have no doubt but that the burning of the petitioner's house was induced by the arms and other munitions it contained. The principle being well established that the government is bound to pay for property destroyed by the enemy, when in the actual possession of its own troops, or employed and set apart by some competent authority as a place of rendezvous or deposit for public stores; the committee herewith report a bill for the relief of the petitioner.

John King was paid $900 in 1842. Some units of Virginia Militia were called up in the summer of 1814 to protect the Richmond area.

## Mottrom Ball

On October 4, 1813, about 3,000 British infantry landed at the Coan River, drove off the militia, and captured three schooners with cargoes of tobacco, arms, ammunition, and general merchandise. Among the raiders were around 50 former slaves who had been liberated by the British and inducted into their service, as part of thousands of slaves who joined the British forces during the war.

As stated by the Committee of Claims on March 10, 1818:

> The petitioner claims payment for a dwelling-house and kitchen, with sundry property therein contained, near the mouth of the Coan River, Northumberland County, Virginia, destroyed by the enemy on the 7th of August, 1814, in consequence (as he alleges) of the houses being occupied as barracks at that time by troops in the service of the United States, the value of which he estimates at $1,400.
>
> It appears by the evidence in this case that troops were stationed on claimant's farm in the year 1813, and some huts erected and works of defense thrown up near to claimant's dwelling-house; that this encampment was continued, and troops stationed there in August, 1814, at the time of its destruction by fire. One company of troops, which had arrived there about ten days previous to the latter date, without tents, did, by order of

the commander of the regiment (who is since dead) take possession of claimant's house and kitchen (the claimant having recently removed therefrom) and used the same as barracks until the morning of the 7th of August, when the enemy appeared in considerable force off Coan. Several of their own tenders entered the river and commenced a fire with artillery on the American troops, who, finding that resistance was unavailing (the enemy being able to cover the landing of their troops under a fire from heavy artillery aboard their vessels) retreated.

When the enemy landed, they burnt the dwelling-house and kitchen and huts erected by the troops, and leveled the works of defense, &c.

Your committee are of opinion, that, from the permanent encampment of troops on the farm and near the dwelling-house, the erection of huts and works of defense thrown up, the dwelling-house and kitchen occupied by soldiers only did impart to said houses such a military character as gave the enemy a plausible pretext for their destruction as public property, and gave the petitioner a just claim on the Government.

Dr. Ball was paid $1,400 for his buildings on Old Court House Point in 1819. Dr. Ball attended medical school in Glasgow, Scotland, and on January 25, 1800, married Martha Turberville. Son Spencer was born on February 24, 1801, at Woodberry, the family's 1,200-acre plantation.

Dr. Ball was a surgeon in Lt. Col. Downing's 37th Regiment and died in 1849.

Spencer married Mary L. Dulany. They had a son, Mottrom Dulany Ball, who was a colonel in the 11th Virginia Cavalry during the Civil War and a pioneer settler in Alaska.

## Richard Hall

Queenstown, Maryland, was attacked by 300 British troops on August 13, 1814. Lt. Col. Philip Reed commanded the Maryland militia against Captain Sir Peter Parker, who died in the battle, which became known as the Battle of Slippery Hill.

William Grason, governor of Maryland, was deposed at Annapolis on November 15, 1841:

In the month of August, 1814, I belonged to a company of artillery, which, with other militia, amounting to about 300 men, was stationed at Queenstown, on the eastern shore of Maryland, for the purpose of protecting the adjacent country.

The British then occupied Kent Island with a large force, and surrounded it with their ships so as to cut off all communication between the island and the main land.

An attack was made upon Queenstown some time in August, but on what day I do not recollect, by the whole British force consisting of about 2,000 regulars under the command of Sir Thomas Sydney Beckwith, and a large body of sailors and marines commanded by Admiral Cockburn. The attack was made about daybreak, and the militia, being unable to defend the place, left it in the possession of the enemy.

I returned to Queenstown immediately after the enemy left it, and found that no house in the town had been pillaged or destroyed, and that no injury had been done to the inhabitants. The house of Mr. Richard Hall stood some short distance from the town at the public landing place where the attack was made by the sailors and marines.

With several other officers and members of the artillery company, I had occupied a room in Mr. Hall's house, where we slept on the night preceding the attack. I saw the condition of his house in an hour after the British left it, and found that considerable damage had been done to his beds and other furniture. I was also informed by him and his family that provisions, liquors, and other articles of value had been taken away or destroyed.

The artillery company and the rest of the militia were stationed in the town where they remained till they were compelled to retreat, but the cannon had been occasionally placed in Mr. Hall's yard for the purpose of firing at a mark. Whether this circumstance and the occupation of part of his house as before mentioned caused the pillage and destruction of his property, I am not able to determine.

Mr. Hall is now dead, and his widow, Mrs. Henrietta M. Hall, is about to claim compensation from the government for the injury sustained, and it is at her request that I have made this statement.

As reported by the Committee of Claims on May 20, 1842:

This claim is for damages sustained by injuries to the house, personal property, and farm of the husband of the petitioner in Maryland by the British army during the last war.

The only evidence is the affidavit of Gov. William Grason, of Maryland. This affidavit was made in November, 1841. The petition was presented and referred February 14, 1842, and the damages alleged to have been sustained in 1814. No cause for delay in presenting the claim appears.

It does not appear that the house in question was occupied as a military deposit. Gov. Grason was of the Maryland militia and on duty at Queenstown near which the house of Mr. Hall was situate. He had occupied a room in Mr. Hall's house, and with others had slept in the house on the night before the attack by the British upon Queenstown, in which the house and property of Mr. Hall were injured.

This claim, in the opinion of the committee, is for various reasons wholly inadmissible. It is sufficient to note that there was not such military occupation of the building as would, in any event, make the United States liable for the injury to the house. The committee recommend that the petitioner is not entitled to relief.

Thomas Beckwith was an army officer who was appointed lieutenant colonel in the Rifle Brigade in 1803 and served in Denmark, Hanover, Spain, and Portugal. In 1810 he was appointed a deputy quartermaster general and in 1813 was an assistant quartermaster general in North America. He also commanded landing parties.

## The Schooner *Islet*

As reported by the Committee of Claims on January 5, 1816:

The petitioners, William O'Neal and Robert Taylor, were owners of the schooner *Islet*, which in the month of June, 1814, then lying in the river Patuxent, they chartered to the United States as a store-ship to the flotilla commanded by Commodore Joshua Barney, upon the following terms: The petitioners were to find a sufficient number of seamen to navigate the vessels, the captain of the vessel to be under the orders of the commander of the flotilla, to carry such quantity of naval stores as was agreed on, and her safety in every respect, to be at the risk of the owners; for which services and risk the United States agreed to give the petitioners the sum of $10.00 per day.

On the approach of the enemy, in August, 1814, it was deemed prudent by the commanding officer of the flotilla to blow it up to prevent its falling into the hands of the enemy, but the schooner *Islet*, which was left in the care and management of Captain Taylor, was run up the river and sunk by him to prevent the vessel and stores from falling into the hands of the enemy: the vessel has not since been raised. The petitioners pray of Congress a compensation equal to the value of the vessel, and such further relief as my be just.

The committee are of opinion that the petitioners, having undertaken in their contract to be at all risks of the vessel, and the vessel having been sunk by its commander, are entitled to no relief.

Brig. Gen. Philip Stuart commanded the 5th Brigade of Maryland Militia, Col. Cook the 2nd Regiment.

## *The Landing at Benedict*

In August 1814, Sailing Master Joseph Middleton was stationed near William T. Nimmo's Pleasure House at Lynnhaven Inlet near Cape Henry, Virginia—an excellent vantage point for lookouts. On the early morning of the 16th he spotted ships of all sizes entering Chesapeake Bay, which he numbered at 22. British reinforcements had arrived for the march to Washington City. Middleton assumed at the time their objective was Norfolk, about 15 miles to the west, and dispatched an express rider to warn them of an impending attack. But then he noticed the ships were heading north up the Bay with the tide and wind.

When Adm. Cockburn got to the

mouth of the Potomac River, he split his force, one part going up the Potomac and the other continued north for the Patuxent River. The objective was a pincer movement toward Washington City.

On August 19, the Patuxent contingent anchored off Benedict, Maryland. Most American regular forces were in Canada leaving the Maryland militia to face the invaders. The troops aboard were under the command of Major-General Robert Ross, who would never return home. The troops set up camp to prepare for the march north along the Patuxent to Upper Marlboro and then westerly for the roughly 35 mile overland march to Washington. The navy was to seek out and wreck Joshua Barney's little fleet.

When word of the enemy's presence became known to Barney, he sent word to Washington, and then departed with the sailors and Marines, leaving his gunboats and barges in charge of 2nd Lieutenant Solomon Frazier with orders to burn everything if the British arrived, and then head for Washington.

The alarm of the landing was given, and the superintendent of the armory at Harpers Ferry, James Stubblefield, issued arms to around 100 employees and volunteer citizens. The next day they embarked in four boats and all during the trip could hear cannons and observe fires. The volunteers elected George W. Humphreys as captain.

To meet this threat, a call for 15,000 troops to serve under Brig. Gen. William Henry Winder went out, but in the end only a few hundred volunteers showed up.

## Dr. John Gray

Betty H. Beard, Stephen Beard, and James W. Gray, heirs of Dr, John Gray, deceased filed the claim. Dr. Gray's widow, Betty, married Stephen Beard and in 1836, Capt. Philip Pindell, of Anne Arundel County, Maryland, informed Betty that she might have a valid claim so she pursued it.

As reported by the Committee of Claims on January 11, 1839:

> The memorialists, during the late war between the United States and Great Britain, resided on the Patuxent River in the county of Calvert and State of Maryland, and owned and possessed valuable real and personal estate there. In the attack made by the British army on the city of Washington in the year 1814, great depredations were made on the estate by the army. Their fleet anchored opposite to, and their men landed on the farm of the memorialists. They commenced their work of destruction by carrying off cattle, sheep, hogs, and crops of grain, and completed it by burning the dwelling-house and all the buildings on the farm to ashes.
>
> The amount of property thus destroyed appears, by the testimony and appraisals filed in the case to be $5,050. It appears also from the testimony the property had, through fear of attack, been abandoned by its owners several days before its destruction, and that the American troops occupied it for their accommodation till the near approach of the British forces induced them to leave the place. On their departure, the British troops landed and destroyed the property for which the memorialists claim indemnity.
>
> The act of Congress of April 9th, 1816, and the acts in amendment on which this claim depends, provide for the payment of all damage sustained by the destruction of buildings by the enemy during the late war which were occupied by the authority of an officer or agent of the United States as barracks or places of military or naval stores, at the time of their destruction, provided the destruction was occasioned by such occupancy.
>
> In this case there is testimony calculated to induce the belief that the property was destroyed in consequence of its having once been in the possession of the American troops. Yet, in the opinion of the committee, there is no proof of occupation by order of an officer or agent of the United States at the time the property was destroyed, which can authorize them to report a bill for relief. They therefore report that the prayer of the petitioners ought not to be granted.

As reported by the Committee of Claims on April 4, 1840:

The memorialists set forth in their petition that John Gray, deceased, in the summer of 1814, owned a farm on the Patuxent River in the State of Maryland, on were erected a dwelling and out-houses, which were taken possession of by the troops of the United States about the time the British fleet were ascending the Potomac River.

The buildings were taken possession of by order of the officer then commanding the troops. The buildings were occupied as barracks or quarters for the accommodation of the officers and men until a force was landed from the British fleet, which drove our troops from the farm and burnt the buildings.

Dr. Gray seems to have died soon after the close of the war, and the petitioners state that they resided on the farm in the interior of Anne Arundel County, and were not aware that their claim upon the government would be recognized until the year 1836, when they, for the first time, learned that other claims of the same description had been paid by Congress.

Colonel Michael Taney, who commanded the militia troops, had left the county and gone west, where it was difficult to find him until further time had elapsed.

The original petition was presented to the House of Representatives in December, 1837, and referred to the Committee of Claims and at the 3rd session of the 25th Congress an unfavorable report was made thereon.

Since that time, additional proof has been furnished, particularly the depositions of Colonel Taney, John Smith, and several other less important witnesses. It is also shown that the dwelling-house was worth $3,000; four negro-houses $1,000; two barns $1,000, total $5,000, for which sum the committee herewith report a bill.

A sworn statement by William G. Jones on July 3, 1837:

I was the manager to Doctor John Gray on his farm, lying on the Patuxent River, at the time the British army made an attack on the city of Washington. Previous to their advance on the city, their fleet anchored off Shirden's Point, opposite the farm—the channel of the river running within a few steps of the shore—and on seeing our light infantry posted there, they seemed to be much enraged and commenced a heavy fire from their fleet at our light horse, who retreated behind a hill. On landing they took me prisoner and treated me very roughly and asked me if there was not a large body of troops behind the hill and in the pines. My answer did not satisfy them. They then fired several hundred balls at the hill, in the mean time landing their men and giving them orders to scour the pines.

Being disappointed in coming up with our troops, they searched the houses and finding a canteen, one of their soldiers placed it on a bayonet and raised it in the air, saying to one of their officers, "We have found them out. Their militia has been stationed here." They also said they had been informed by a colored man named Bill, who had escaped to them, that the farm belonged to Captain Gray, and he was then in the army. They appeared much exasperated and gave orders to their men to fire the buildings, which was done.

Finding in one of the barns some prime cedar timber, they ordered their men to take it on board their ships. They likewise carried off a large crop of oats, wheat, and corn, saying it would do for their cows on board. Also all the vegetables and the stock of cattle, sheep, and hogs. One of the officers abruptly called me to him, as I feared to take me on board, and told me to clear myself, that if I had anything in the house he would give me but one hour to take it away, and that if I did not, he would have the house burnt over my head. Soon after I left it, it was in flames.

I have no doubt, from all the circumstances attending the destruction of the property, that it was caused from the facts hereinbefore related—their finding the canteen in the house; the American soldiers being quartered in the place; and their supposition that the farm was the property of Captain Gray.

I concur in the estimation of the damages made by Mr. William Wood, of Calvert County, in every particular, amounting to $5,050.

On August 5, 1837, William Wood stated:

I was a near neighbor and lived at that time adjoining the farm of Doctor John Gray. On the advance of the British army towards Washington City, they discovered the American troops were stationed on the farm, and our light horse on the hill. Their fleet was anchored near the shore, opposite the farm, and under cover of a heavy fire, they landed a large number of their men. I suppose they fired five or six hundred shots. I saw them destroy or take away a large crop of oats, wheat, and corn, also the stock on the farm consisting of cattle, sheep, and hogs. They then set fire to, and consumed the dwelling-house and all the buildings on the place, and I have every reason to believe that the destruction of the whole of this property was in consequence of their discovery of our troops having been quartered on the farm, and also of their having been informed by a colored man who went to them that the farm belonged to a Captain Gray, who was at that time in actual service in our army, and who was also a brother to Doctor John Gray.

There is a very high eminence on this farm, perhaps more so than any on the Patuxent, which afforded a full view of the movements of the enemy, and from which our army kept a lookout, and could observe the British spying our men. They appeared to be much enraged on landing, to find in the house some soldiers' accoutrements, which induced them to believe our militia had been quartered in the house. From my knowledge of this property, having resided a number of years thereto adjoining, I believe the following statement to be a fair estimate of the loss or damages sustained: the dwelling-house, $1,000; two tobacco houses, $1,000; four quarters, $400; overseer's house, $200; one corn house, $150; two out-houses, $200; 600 bushels of oats taken away, $300; 300 bushels of wheat taken away, $600; crop of corn destroyed and taken away, $600; 26 head of cattle, $264; 50 head of sheep, $100; 40 hogs, $86; the furniture in the house, &c., $150, amounting in the whole to $5,050.

James Mackall was deposed on September 8, 1837:

I was living adjoining the farm of Doctor John Gray at the time that a part of the British fleet came up the Patuxent River and anchored off opposite the land, and landed several hundred men who marched up and set fire to the houses and to the grain stacks. I saw them burning. The reason given by Captain Joseph Nourse, the British officer, for this destruction of property, was, because the American troop of horse was stationed there, which troop was commanded by my brother, John G. Mackall, since deceased, this troop of horse being stationed there for some time during the time of the fleet's being in the river.

Colonel Taney stated on September 23, 1837:

In the year 1814, I commanded a regiment of militia in Calvert County, State of Maryland. During the time the British fleet was in the Patuxent River, I ordered a part of the militia to occupy the houses on the farm of Doctor John Gray, near the river, and within a short distance of some of his farm-houses; part of the English fleet then lying opposite the farm near Shirden's Point. These houses were burnt by the British. I myself, with many of the officers and men, were frequently passing through the fields in full view of the British. This house was burnt in consequence of being so occupied.

William N. Laughlin's sworn statement of February 14, 1838:

While the British fleet was in the Patuxent River, I was a non-commissioned officer in Captain Jacob Franklin's company of military in the month of July, in the year 1814, when the British fleet was in the Patuxent River.

On our arrival there, we were placed under the command of Colonel Michael Taney and were ordered by him to take possession of Doctor John Gray's house and use it for our barracks. From that farm and house we got rations. The salt beef and pork we got from that house, and the sheep we obtained from the farm. We butchered them in the yard, and hung them up in the trees in full view of the British fleet. We also cooked the meat in Gray's kitchen every day, and occupied his house every hour of the day, till the morning the British showed signs of landing their force. We retreated and, on the evening of the same day they burnt his dwelling-house. I was informed afterwards they burnt all of the buildings on the place. I further state that while there on duty, I was one who assisted to carry Colonel Thomas Simmons on board of the British fleet with a flag of truce, who has since deceased. While on board of the fleet, I heard the British officers say they would burn and destroy the property of Doctor Gray in consequence of the American troops being stationed there, and this destruction occurred on or about the 21st day of August, 1814.

Capt. Rezin Hammond was deposed on February 22, 1838:

> During the time the British fleet was in the Patuxent River, Colonel Michael Taney commanded the military of Calvert County. When our troop of horse, commanded by Captain John Hall, got to Calvert County, we were attached to Colonel Taney's regiment and subject to his orders. We were requested by him to quarter at the house and farm of Doctor John Gray, late of Calvert County, deceased, our headquarters. Our quartermaster, Richard B. Watts, who is since deceased, provided rations for the troops, and grain, hay, and fodder for our horses. Our meat was cooked in Doctor Gray's kitchen. We had free access to the buildings for our accommodation and out-houses for our horses. We occupied them day and night. We were there on that expedition on or about ten days. This event of our services to the State took place in the latter part of July, or the first of August, in the year 1814. After this, we were discharged.

John Smith was deposed on April 3, 1839:

> I was a volunteer in Captain Jacob Franklin's company. He was ordered by the governor of the State to march to Calvert County to the farm of Doctor John Gray. When we got there, Captain Franklin ordered his company to occupy the buildings of Doctor Gray. I do further testify that I heard Colonel Taney order Captain Franklin to occupy the house of Doctor Gray for their accommodation—the officers in the dwelling, and the men in the kitchen and other houses of the place.
>
> The family of Doctor Gray had left their home on account of the British fleet then lying in the Patuxent River, at or near Shirden's Point, in full view of the buildings, and within cannon shot of them. They were near enough to see our troops occupying the building, parading in and near the houses—both foot and troopers.
>
> Colonel Taney gave orders to get provisions from that farm, no other place being near where we could get supplied. We cooked our rations in the houses; we occupied them eight or ten days—perhaps more—until the British landed their force under a heavy fire of cannon. They drove us out of the houses, and on the same day we left the building they set fire to and destroyed the whole of them and everything on the farm. I saw them burnt and destroyed.
>
> I am acquainted with Mr. William G. Jones, who, as I been informed, has given testimony in this case. He was manager for Doctor Gray at the time. As far as comes to my knowledge, there is but one person now alive who belonged to Captain Franklin's company. He was a non-commissioned officer whose testimony has been taken.
>
> I very frequently heard it mentioned by our officers and men that the British would burn this property on account of its being a military post or station. Colonel Taney, in company with other officers, was frequently passing and repassing through the fields on this farm in full view of the fleet. I have no knowledge of Colonel Taney at this time. If alive he must be a very old, infirm man. Many years past he went to the west and, I understood to Texas.
>
> My early occupation was that of a carpenter, being acquainted with the value of buildings. Their property was in good repair, and I do consider Mr. William Hooper's valuation a very reasonable one for those buildings. I do state as follows: the dwelling to be worth \$3,000; two barns worth \$1,000; the other buildings worth \$1,000, making in the whole, \$5,000, exclusive of all other property.

Taney married Monica Brooke on June 25, 1771, in St. Mary's County, Maryland, and they had children Michael T., Roger, Augustus, Octavius, Dorothy, Sophia, and Ann. Monica died in 1814.

As to Taney's absence, it was reported that on July 1, 1819, Taney killed John Magruder, a neighbor, in a duel. On the 15th, apparently fearing legal action, he put all his property in the hands of Roger and Octavius and fled to Virginia. In March 1820, it was reported he fell off a horse in Loudon County, Virginia, and died. He was reported buried in Calvert County and his property sold off. Others said he had "gone west" or to Texas and had not been heard from since. He was found, quite obviously, at the elderly age of 87, and submitted a statement.

The first Michael Taney came to Maryland in 1660 and was high sheriff in Calvert County from 1685 to 1689. Several Michael Taneys followed and intermixed with the Brooke and Neale families.

Son Michael became a planter; Octavius C. was a private in the 31st during the war, became a physician, and married Jane Gray in Baltimore in 1819, was elected a state senator, and died in 1832; Roger Brooke became a justice on the U.S. Supreme Court; Augustus served in John Hood's 32nd Regiment of Maryland Militia during the war. Dorothy married William Diggs in May 1798; Sophia Brooke married Robert Neale in 1826; and Ann married Thomas Rochester on September 12, 1801.

## James Plunkett

As reported by the Committee of Claims on June 20, 1834:

> Since the presentation of the petition, Henry R. Taylor has deceased. Jane Taylor was formerly the wife of James Plunkett, of the city of Washington, and the claim is for a horse impressed into the military service of the United States during the late war, that belonged to James Plunkett.
>
> Benjamin King testifies that he was the captain of a militia company and that he took for the service of the United States, for the purpose of conveying ordnance to Captain Miller, a grey horse belonging to the late James Plunkett, then residing at the Navy Yard of this city. This was three days before the battle at Bladensburg. He says he was then a captain of militia and was also attached to the service of the United States in the Navy Yard, and that he was transferred from Miller's command to that of Commodore Barney's and was taken prisoner with his corps on the day of the battle. He says this horse was never restored to his knowledge or belief, and that if it had been, he, having impressed the animal for the service of the United States, and having, on his release from captivity, returned to Washington, where he has resided to the present time, must have known if the horse was ever restored.
>
> Jane Taylor states in her deposition that the horse was impressed, and never restored to Captain Plunkett, her late, husband, nor to any of the family. She says its value, with the value of the saddle, bridle, martingale, cushion, &c., amounted to $150, and that their cost to Captain Plunkett was that sum.
>
> There is no further testimony of the value of the horse and equipments, and this the committee do not think is sufficient to establish the value. Under the conviction that the horse was impressed, and not returned, the committee report a bill, referring the question of value to the Third Auditor, to decide upon evidence to be submitted to him by the claimant.

Jane Taylor was paid $150 in 1836. James Plunkett married Jane Carlin at Alexandria, Virginia, on March 16, 1812.

Benjamin King was a master blacksmith at the Navy Yard and in a militia company organized at the Yard by naval architect William Doughty called the Navy Yard Rifles. The unit was under the command of Maj. Robert Brent of the 2nd Regiment of District of Columbia Militia. In late August they were ordered to Bladensburg for the defense of the Capitol. Capt. James Miller was stationed at the Marine Barracks in Washington City and also left for Bladensburg.

# *Commodore Barney Trapped*

Barney's boats got into shallow water above Pig Point in Anne Arundel County, Maryland, with the British in hot pursuit. When lookouts saw the British coming around the point on August 22, he had no option but to destroy the boats to keep them out of British hands, which was done by Lt. Solomon Frazier, except for one boat that was captured. The sailors and Marines then headed overland for Washington.

## Schooner Henry

The claim of John Pritchett, as reported by the Committee of Claims on January 28, 1842, in part:

The petitioner presents a claim for the expenses of raising and repairing the schooner *Henry*, of Georgetown, in the year 1814, burnt and sunk under the following circumstances:

In the spring of the year 1814, the petitioner, as master and owner of the schooner, shipped at Baltimore, for Washington, 60 barrels of tar, worth, as the petitioner states, $12 per barrel. The vessel sailed from Baltimore with this cargo, which the petitioner says was shipped for his own private account in the month of May, 1814, and upon the voyage to this city fell in with the United States flotilla, then upon the waters of the Chesapeake, and under the command of Commodore Barney.

A British fleet was then in the bay lower down, and as the petitioner says in great force; and he says, "Commodore Barney was extremely anxious to prevent the tar from falling into the hands of the enemy's ships, of which they stood in great need," and therefore prevented the petitioner from proceeding with his schooner and cargo, and ordered him to remain under the guns of the flotilla. While the petitioner thus remained, with his vessel, in the company of the fleet, the enemy approached in great force and compelled Commodore Barney to retreat to the Patuxent and the commodore ordered the schooner to take a position in front of the flotilla, so as to keep his armed vessels between her and the enemy. In this form the retreat was continued to the highest navigable point of the Patuxent, while the enemy, in very superior force, made constant close pursuit. The destruction of the retreating fleet by the enemy being thus rendered unavoidable, the commodore ordered the destruction of the whole, the schooner of the petitioner, as well as his flotilla, and the order was immediately executed by firing the vessels. In this way the schooner was burnt to the water's edge and sunk.

During the following year, the petitioner caused the schooner to be raised and repaired at an expense of little short of $3,000, which, together with the loss of the tar, he states caused his embarrassment and ruin, and that he has never recovered from those losses. For them he now prays indemnity from the government upon the ground that an officer of the government had taken possession of his property and ordered its destruction, and that it was so destroyed for public purposes.

The petitioner makes oath to the truth of the statement contained in his petition, "according to the best of his knowledge and belief," but there is nothing found with the papers, from the commodore or any other officer having command, to show that the schooner was arrested upon her voyage, detained, or destroyed, by his order.

John A. Webster, a witness, makes affidavit that he was a sailing-master in the flotilla at the time, and confirms, generally, the statements made in the petition. In reference to the arrest of the schooner and her detention, he uses the following language: "In the month of May, of 1814, the schooner *Henry*, of Georgetown, District of Columbia, John Pritchett, master, was brought to by the flotilla in Chesapeake Bay, and found to have on board a quantity of tar then on a voyage from Baltimore to the city of Washington, in the District of Columbia. Commodore Barney was apprehensive that the schooner, if permitted to proceed on her voyage, would be captured by the enemy's vessels, then not far off, and the cargo on board, consisting of tar, having been reported by Captain Pritchett to be purchased by him for Commodore Tingey, of the Navy-yard at Washington. Commodore Barney was of the opinion that if the vessel was permitted to pass, would be captured by the enemy's vessels, then not far off, and that the cargo of naval stores, or tar, on board, would be applied by the enemy as stores on board his public ships, being an article of which they stood in great need of at the time," and hence ordered the vessel to be arrested and detained, and then the witness gives the same account substantially of her destruction as is given by the petitioner.

The deposition of John Peck proves that he was pilot of the *Scorpion*, one of the vessels of the flotilla, and that he helped to blow up the barges of the flotilla, in the Patuxent, under the express order of Commodore Barney, and that the order embraced the destruction of the schooner *Henry*, "to prevent the enemy from taking possession of her," but he says nothing of the manner or causes for the arrest and detention of the schooner.

John Keynau is a third witness, who testifies that he was present at the destruction of the flotilla, and two schooners, being a hand attached to one of the barges of the flotilla, that Captain Frazier was, at the time, "in command or in charge of the flotilla," and that Captain Frazier was the officer by whose order the flotilla and schooners were destroyed, one of which schooners he says was the *Henry*, of Georgetown, John Pritchett, master. This witness says nothing of the manner or causes for the arrest and detention of the schooner.

It is worthy to remark that neither the petitioner nor any of the witnesses speak of the destruction of the tar, and the only mention, in any of the papers, from which it can be inferred that compensation for that composes a part of the claim, is that in the petition, stating that 60 barrels of tar, worth $12 each, composed the cargo, and the following sentence in that paper, viz: "That in the following year, 1815, deponent caused said schooner to be raised and rebuilt, the expense of which was nearly $3,000, which added to the freight and cost of her cargo, produced a loss that effectually ruined him."

Accompanying the papers is testimony intended to show, very particularly, the cost of raising and rebuilding the schooner, and a long bill of particulars, and with prices of a very extravagant rate where they are specified, in case the character of the charges are properly understood; the whole being footed at $2,913.01½.

No testimony is offered to show the fact of the shipment of the tar, its value at the time of the shipment, its destination or object, beyond the statements of the petitioner himself, and no evidence of its destruction by the burning of the schooner is presented.

The committee are not familiar with cause and effect in these operations, but it would seem to them that if 60 barrels of tar, properly stowed in this small schooner, had been burnt by the burning of the vessel, the wreck which would have remained would scarcely have been worth raising for repair, while it would seem quite possible, if the vessel was properly scuttled before she was fired, that her upper works might have been consumed by the fire, as they are represented to have been, without injury to this cargo.

The committee are not prepared to say they would make the single circumstance of the elapse of time a ground of the entire rejection of the claim, but, connected with the other circumstances which are presented in the case, they are not prepared to say a claim is made out at all. The presence of an overpowering enemy's fleet in the waters of the Chesapeake was well known in Baltimore, and over a large extent of the adjacent country, when the schooner left that port for Washington. It was not reasonably to be expected that she could pass round to the mouth of the Potomac without coming under the observation of that vigilant enemy, and she and her cargo would be lawful prize, according to the laws of nations and the laws of war, regardless of what that cargo might consist, or who might be the owner of vessel, or cargo, he being an alien enemy. The cargo actually consisted of naval stores of an important character, and especially to a fleet which had been long at sea, as had that enemy's fleet from the other side of the Atlantic. Indeed, it seems to have come to be well understood on board of our fleet, that the ships of the enemy were in pressing want of this very article, and the committee leave it for the Senate to determine whether that fact would have been likely to be made known to our hostile fleet, before it was in the commercial city from which the schooner took her departure, and where a supply of the article might reasonably be expected to be found.

If the same thing had happened at the place of destination, would he have been better that his schooner and cargo were delivered into the hands of a victorious enemy uninjured, than that the vessel was sunk, and her upper works burnt to the water's edge, in the upper Patuxent, thus leaving the hull, to say nothing of the cargo, to be raised and repaired in the following spring, so as to be a vessel navigating the same waters for which she was originally destined, up to the year 1829, at least, full 15 years after her partial destruction?

The committee can form no such conclusions from the facts and premises here presented, and they therefore respectfully recommend that the prayer of the petitioner ought not to be granted.

## Richard Woodland

No specific date is noted for this incident. Dorchester County is directly across Chesapeake Bay from St. Mary's and Calvert County. As reported by the Committee of Claims on March 16, 1822:

The petitioner was an inhabitant of Dorchester County, Maryland, and in 1814 was the owner of a schooner called the *Betsey*, of the value of about $1,200. In the summer of the same year she lay in the Patuxent River at the time the United States flotilla commanded by Commodore Barney was blockaded there. To avoid the enemy, she was carried up the river to Pig Point where she lay when the United States' flotilla was destroyed by order of the United States' officers. The petitioner's vessel was destroyed at the same time, but whether it was destroyed by our own officers, by the enemy, or in consequence of its contiguity to the flotilla when it was burnt, he is unable to state. He prays Congress to pass a law allowing the value of the vessel.

The committee are of opinion that the claim of the petitioner does not come within the usual rule of allowance. The destruction of his vessel is one of the casualties of war, in which individual sacrifice must yield to the public good. The particular manner of its destruction is not proved, nor is it distinctly stated by whom it was done. The committee recommend that the prayer of the petitioner ought not to be granted.

Pig Point is about 40 river miles up the Patuxent on the east side of the river.

## James Goddard

As reported by the Committee of Claims on December 20, 1816:

In the year 1814, the petitioner was the assistant collector in the Fifth Collection District of the State of Maryland, and at that time resided in Upper Marlborough Town. He states that, for the necessary and convenient management of the duties of his appointment, he usually kept in his house a number of papers belonging to the office of the collector; and that, upon the approach of the enemy to the town in the month of August, 1814, he took the precaution to convey to a place of safety, about 8 miles distant, all the papers relating to the revenue, except some stamp paper, which was closely and secretly locked up in his desk at home. When the enemy came to Upper Marlborough, they destroyed his house and property, and the petitioner states that he believes it was in consequence of his being a collector of the revenue.

This case involves the same principle which has often been decided by Congress. The property of the petitioner was private property, and, according to the usages of civilized warfare, entitled to protection. Upon this ground, the committee are of the opinion that, according to decisions heretofore made by Congress, the petitioner is not entitled to relief.

The port city of Nottingham was the base of the Navy's Chesapeake Flotilla. In August, 1814, the townspeople fled in terror on hearing of the British approach, as did the residents of Upper Marlborough Town, with exception of Dr. William Beanes. They arrived on August 21, and the next day camped just outside Upper Marlborough Town where Maj. Gen. Robert Ross, the British commander, prevailed upon Dr. Beanes for the use of his house for headquarters.

Dr. Beanes was later arrested as a spy and taken aboard the British ship *Tonnant*. Lawyer Francis Scott Key was retained to secure his release and went out in the cartel ship *President* and while on that vessel, witnessed the bombardment of Fort McHenry on September 13.

## George W. Biscoe

George W. Biscoe sought relief under the first article of the treaty of Ghent, "for the loss of the schooner *Speedwell*, captured in the Patuxent River by the British on August 22, 1814, and which was in the waters and within the territorial jurisdiction of the United States on February 17, 1815, the day of the exchange of the ratifications of said treaty, and was carried away out of the territorial jurisdiction of the United States, in violation of the first article." On June 5, 1858, Congress decreed his award "shall not exceed $2,000."

Biscoe's claim was submitted to a board of American commissioners to examine claims filed under the Treaty of Ghent and was disallowed, "not from any want of credit in the testimony offered, but because it does not come within the treaty, as expounded by the award of the Emperor, and what is stated at large in the opinion given in the Alexandria cases."

The Committee on Foreign Affairs took it up and on February 6, 1838, and chose to uphold that decision.

Biscoe filed another claim, as stated by the Committee of Claims on January 24, 1857:

> The memorialist represents that he was the owner of the schooner *Speedwell* in 1814, which was at that time a new vessel and engaged in trading between the port of Nottingham, on the Patuxent, and the city of Baltimore; that this vessel was captured in the Patuxent River on August 22 by the British fleet, which had ascended the river in pursuit of the flotilla of Comm. Barney; that after its capture the schooner was converted into a tender to the *Royal Oak*, a British man-of-war; and that she was lying off the city of Mobile in the waters of the United States, at the date of the exchange of the ratifications of the treaty of peace between the United States and Great Britain in February, 1815.
>
> The claim is made under the First Article, in the following words: "All territory, places, and possessions whatsoever taken by either party from the other shall be restored without delay and without causing any destruction or carrying away any of the artillery originally captured in the said forts or places, and which shall remain therein upon the exchange of the ratifications of this treaty, or any slaves or other private property."

The *Speedwell* was first used to transport troops, stores, and provisions "up the various rivers and creeks," and afterwards "employed by Sir Pulteney Malcolm as a tender to his Majesty's ship *Royal Oak*, bearing the admiral's flag." The schooner went back to England with the fleet and in 1828 was employed in the West Indies.

Major Archibald W. Hamilton testified that he was held prisoner on the *Speedwell* on February 17, 1815, when it was lying off Mobile between Dauphin Island and the mainland.

At trial, His Imperial Majesty found for Biscoe on April 22, 1822. When Biscoe filed his claim for the *Speedwell*, the British fund had a balance of $4,112.89.

The territorial waters were then defines as "Three maritime leagues of the line of the coasts as any portion of its soil which is in actual cultivation by its inhabitants." Briscoe's claim was rejected on August 27, 1828, for lack of proof that "the vessel was in the waters of the United States when the treaty took effect."

## *Bladensburg*

When the British were unexpectedly observed heading toward Bladensburg, about 5 miles NNW of Washington, Gen. William Winder's forces were concentrated there. Comm. Barney's sailors and Marine artillery arrived and were stationed with other artillery units on the road to Washington, about 700 yards past Tournecliffe's bridge about 1.7 miles southeast of Bladensburg with orders to destroy the bridge on approach of the British.

On August 24, Gen. Winder's forces were defeated and the British continued on to Washington while Royal Navy ships anchored just below Alexandria.

When Comm. Barney was seriously wounded by a musket ball, Admiral Cockburn and Gen. Ross were very kind, immediately paroling him and detailing a surgeon to attend to his wound. Barney's wound amounted, "to a total disability, and resulting in his death, after extreme suffering. The ball which lodged in his right thigh could not be extracted, though repeated efforts were made by the most skillful surgeons, and caused his death." He died on December 1, 1818, at Pittsburgh. The ball was extracted and sent to the Navy Department. He left a wife, Harriet, who was granted financial relief in May 1840.

### Charles Todd

On April 27, 1816, the accounting officers of the Navy Department were authorized to settle the claim of Charles Todd, of Virginia, for a wagon and horses that were impressed in the service of the United States and for tobacco, which he lost, "in consequence of the wagon and horses being impressed." Todd's property was seized and lost during the battle at Bladensburg.

## Henry and Robert Sewall

The original claim was filed by Robert Sewall. As reported by the Committee of Claims on January 25, 1819:

> On the retreat of the American forces from Bladensburg on the 24th August, 1814, a party of Comm. Barney's men, then a portion of that force, threw themselves into the home of the petitioner and made an attack from said home upon an advance of the British army under the command of General Robert Ross, by which attack General Ross's horse was killed, one or two of his men also were killed, and several were wounded.
>
> This adventure and heroic party were immediately overpowered by the British force; three of them were taken prisoner in the house, whilst the remainder made their escape by flight.
>
> The house of the petitioner, thus made a block-house of by this gallant little band, was instantly set on fire by order of General Ross, and destroyed with all its costly furniture. The house had been deserted by its inhabitants, the proprietor having several months before removed to his farm in Prince George's County for the summer, and his son, William Sewall, in whose care the house had been left by his father, was then employed in the militia who had been called in to service some time before, when the enemy threatened thee adjacent country.
>
> A claim for remuneration for this house and furniture was before made to Congress, and by that body ordered to be sent to the Commissioner of Claims, under supposition that the case was embraced by the ninth section of the claims law. The commissioner takes the same into consideration, and finds that, inasmuch as it is not proved that the house was occupied by order of the commanding officer, the claim does not come under any power of awarding indemnity that he possesses, and therefore surrenders the papers, that the petitioner may again appeal to Congress.

As reported by the Committee of Claims on April 7, 1820:

> The petitioner claims payment for a dwelling-house and furniture burnt and destroyed by the enemy on the 24th of August, 1814. The evidence which the claimant relies on to establish his claim is a conversation with officers of the British army; that the invading army was fired on from this house when they entered the city, by which fire General Ross's horse was killed, and some of the men killed or wounded. For this reason, it is alleged, the house was burned.
>
> The prayer of the petitioner ought not to be granted.

As stated on February 28, 1844:

> There is no evidence submitted since the foregoing report was made that goes to change the facts or the nature of the occupation established by them, which is substantially that several of Commodore Barney's sailors, on their retreat, threw themselves into or behind the house and fired on the advanced guard of the enemy as they approached the city, killed General Ross's horse, and, as alleged, killed and wounded some of his men. General Ross, in his verbal statement of the case to Mr. Sewall in the presence of Richard W. West, says that he was fired upon by a part of the American army from that house, his horse killed, and some of his men killed and wounded. In consequence he felt it to be his duty to set fire to and burn the house for the purpose of making an impression, which he did with reluctance, as it was his intention to respect private property while in Washington. And he adds, as his opinion, that as he was fired upon from this house by a part of the United States army, after the flag officer had returned and reported that he had seen nobody in arms, and without opposition, and had caused his trumpet to be sounded, indicating his intention to enter the city, the United States government should pay for the property thus destroyed.
>
> The opinions of General Winfield Scott, General Nathaniel Towson, and others have been obtained with a view of showing what, in their judgment, constitutes the rule of action in military warfare, in relation to taking possession of private property under such circumstances.

Gen. Scott says, "that a detachment or number of men belonging to a retreating army closely pressed, may throw themselves into any house or building and make a blockhouse of it for the purpose of checking and harassing the enemy in their advances, and that such occupation must be considered by the rules of warfare as under the command of their officers."

Gen. Towson says, "It is not only competent for subordinates to assume the responsibility and order troops to occupy the buildings, but it is imperiously their duty to do so if, in their judgment, the advance of the enemy may be checked, or any important advantage obtained by it."

These sailors evidently availed themselves of the shelter afforded by this house to fire upon their enemy as they passed through the city. They could not have taken this position with a view of "checking the advance of the enemy" for the purpose of covering the retreat of their own army, or any part of it, or of obtaining any important advantage, or assisting it in any military movement. The United States forces had separated, and that part only which did not enter had passed on to or through Georgetown, leaving the city entirely at the mercy of the enemy. No good could, therefore, have been expected to result from the attack upon the enemy by those men.

From a careful examination of the facts and evidence, the committee are of opinion that they do not bring the case within the provisions of the act of 1816. The petitioner is not entitled to relief.

The Sewalls were paid $10,000 in 1834.

## James Meads

The deposed petition of James Meads, dated October 6, 1845:

> On the 24th day of August, 1814, whilst he was with the United States army in Washington City, the British army, passing his residence between the long old fields and Bladensburg, stole from him two valuable horses worth at that time at least $80 each. They cut two pairs of blacksmith's bellows to pieces in his blacksmith shop worth $30 each; broke to pieces all the tools in the shop and two fowling pieces, one was new and cost $16—the other was worth about $8. The value of the tools destroyed he cannot accurately estimate, but should think they were worth $12.00.
>
> After they left Washington and your petitioner got released from the army, he made every effort he possibly could to get his horses again, but could not succeed, nor could he get any remuneration from them for the property destroyed.
>
> Your petitioner is now 63 years old, has been unfortunate in business, and is now poor and infirm and scarcely able to earn a livelihood by his daily labor. He prays your honors consider his care and pass a bill for his relief, and, as in duty bound, he will ever pray, &c.

Hector Mitchell, 65, a resident of Bladensburg, gave a sworn statement in support on October 6, 1845, and Frances Meads was deposed on October 7, 1845:

> I do certify that in 1814 I lived in the immediate neighborhood of James Meads. On the 24th of August, 1814, I was at James Mead's house when the English army passed on their way to Washington. Some of them came in the house and searched all of the rooms down stairs. An officer took two guns belonging to Mr. Meads out of the house and broke them in pieces in the front yard on some stones. Some of the men went in the blacksmith shop and destroyed the bellows and other tools in the shop. This I was an eye witness to. I did not see the horses stolen, but know of Mr. Meads having lost two valuable horses, and of his being in search of them for some weeks afterwards. I do not think he ever got them again, of this I am not certain, as I left the neighborhood shortly after the battle.
>
> I am the widow of William Meads, brother of James Meads, and am now 66 years old.

James W. Lowe was deposed on January 27, 1846:

> I do hereby certify that in August, 1814, my father lived within about 2 miles of Mr. James Meads. I was a volunteer at the battle of Bladensburg. After the battle, we returned to Montgomery court-house. I was there one day and a night, and then got liberty to go home. I went by Mr. Meads' house on my way home. I saw the two blacksmiths bellows that had been cut to pieces by the English army. The blacksmith's tools were very much injured

and some taken away. Two guns had been destroyed by them. Mr. Mead afterwards gave me the barrel of one of the guns. Two of his horses were stolen; they were very valuable horses. Mr. Meads and Mr. Mullican went down to Benedict where the British lay at the time, after the horses, and were searching for them several days, but could not get them. I do not know the real value of the horses and things destroyed at the time, but know that one pair of the bellows was nearly new and the guns were very valuable. I was in the habit of going to Mr. Meads every day at that time, after I came back, and was about 18 years old.

As stated by the Committee of Claims on March 5, 1846:

The petitioner alleges that the British, in 1814, near Bladensburg, stole his horses and destroyed his property while he was with the army of the United States in the city of Washington.

The government of the United States does not pay for losses, damages, or destruction of property committed by the enemy, unless the property, at the time of its loss, damage, or destruction, was in the use and service of the government. The property in this case was not in the use or service of the government, and the loss must be borne by the owner. The petitioner is not entitled to relief.

## Henry Knowles, Sr.

As reported by the Committee of Claims on June 3, 1834:

The petitioner states that his horse and cart were impressed into the military service of the United States, together with his slave, soon after the battle of Bladensburg and that his horse was never returned.

George W. Humphreys, late a captain of the volunteer riflemen in the United States service certifies under the date of June 7, 1833, that being ordered by Gen. Winder to proceed with his command to Baltimore, and not having the means of transporting his baggage, he pressed the petitioner's horse and cart to transport his baggage, and then gave a certificate in due form, which he says Mr. Knowles states, as he has before, that this certificate is lost. He knows nothing of the value of the horse. Henry Knowles, Jr., testifies the horse was worth $100. The petitioner states under oath that his horse was impressed into the United States service and not returned, and that he never received any other horse or other property or money in lieu thereof, or any other consideration whatever.

Mr. Hagner has furnished the committee with a copy of the account for the use of the horse and cart and copies of the certificates to prove that the horse was impressed.

Joseph P. Malin, a private, certified that he was present when Ensign Russel pressed the horse for the purpose of conveying baggage on the way towards Baltimore. Captain Humphreys certified that Malin was a private in his company and was detailed to impress a wagon or cart for the transportation of baggage belonging to his company from Montgomery courthouse towards Baltimore by the direction of the assistant quartermaster general, Major Ferdinand Marsteller. A horse and cart were impressed, which he believed to be the property of Henry Knowles.

The committee are satisfied from this evidence that the petitioner's horse was impressed and that he was not returned. They are not able, from the testimony, to fix upon what was the value of the horse, and they will report a bill leaving this to be decided by the Third Auditor.

George Washington Humphreys, of Jefferson County, Virginia, who served in the 8th U.S. Infantry in 1799, and was honorably discharged on June 15, 1800. He became a successful merchant and on August 23, 1814, joined around 50 others with James Stubblefield, the superintendent of the Harpers Ferry Arsenal, to head for Washington City with rifles from the arsenal.

The members had no uniforms, only their usual clothing. On the way down in boats Humphreys was elected captain of their company of riflemen. He was then ordered to Baltimore. Capt. David Porter commended the company for firing on British vessels in the Potomac at Alexandria as stated in the Norfolk Gazette on September 17, 1814:

In the woods on the left, a company of riflemen from Jefferson County, Virginia, under

> Capt. George W. Humphreys, greatly distinguished themselves by a well directed fire on the enemy's decks, as did a company of militia under the command of Capt. Gena, who was posted by me on the right.

Porter noted that one rifleman from Humphreys' company was lost and one sergeant and four privates wounded.

Joseph Malin enlisted in the Volunteer Corps of Riflemen from Jefferson County, Virginia, on August 20, 1814, at Charlestown, Virginia, and was discharged on September 30, 1814, at Charlestown. He later became a judge in Ohio.

Ferdinand Marsteller was appointed assistant deputy quartermaster general in the 5th Military District—Maryland and Virginia—on July 17, 1813.

## *Washington City*

On the evening of August 23, 1814, Adm. Cockburn and Gen. Ross found sleeping quarters at Melwood, Maryland. At around 2 a.m. on the morning of the 24th, Lt. James Scott arrived from the fleet with a message from Adm. Cochrane. It was an order not to attack Washington and directed them to return to the fleet. Ross felt the order should be obeyed, but Cockburn said they had come too far and to turn back now and not face a weak militia that could not possibly defeat Ross's troops would be a grave dishonor to the service and do far more harm to their personal reputations than any discipline for disobedience. Moreover, Cockburn believed they would have the support of Parliament. Ross reluctantly assented, a decision that would cost him his life.

### Edward Barry and George Hodge

As reported by the Committee of Claims on January 5, 1818:

> It appears that Edward Barry is a sailing master and George Hodge a boatswain in the Navy Yard of the United States. Previously to the 24th of August, 1814, they were in the employment of the government in the Navy Yard at Washington and for their convenience, and the promotion of public service, they had quarters assigned them in the yard.
>
> Upon the approach of the British, the Navy Yard and other public property at that place were destroyed by order of the Secretary of the Navy. The property of the petitioners was also destroyed in the conflagration, and they petition Congress to pay them its value.
>
> It further appears from the statement of Commodore Thomas Tingey that the petitioners were so busily employed in preparing measures for executing the orders of the Secretary of the Navy as to have had no opportunity to rescue their own property from the impending danger.
>
> After an attentive consideration of the facts submitted to them, the committee are inclined to think that had the petitioners been active, or exerted a diligence proportionate to the pressing necessities of the case, they might have saved their own property. That they did not save it is proof to the committee of neglect or inattention on their part.
>
> Another reason for not granting the prayer of the petitioners is that the property of officers and soldiers lodged in barracks, and which is of such character as to be attached to their persons or profession, cannot according to any rule with which the committee are acquainted, be paid for by the government if it should be destroyed by the casualties or accidents of war.
>
> The committee therefore think that the prayer of the petitioners ought not to be granted.

It wasn't stated exactly what the two were employed to do at the Navy Yard or why the tools and equipment they used belonged to them. Barry was later "Master of the Yard" at a yearly salary of $660.10, and George Hodge was "Boatswain of the Yard" at a salary of $420.10. Barry was sailing-master at the yard for a long time and died on May 13, 1830.

On July 14, 1832, Congress awarded Barry $568.45, "in full compensation for property destroyed in the conflagration of the Navy Yard at Washington in the year

1814," and the heirs of George Hodge were awarded $824.18 on March 2, 1833.

## Alexander McCormick

As reported by the Committee of Claims on January 20, 1819:

> In the year 1814, when the city of Washington was taken possession of by the British, the petitioner was engaged in the performance of military duty and absent from his home. The petitioner's store on Capitol Hill, in this city, was broken open by the enemy on the 24th of August, 1814, and goods rifled and taken away by them to the amount of between $8,000 and $10,000. The house of the petitioner, if not strictly a military deposit, became in some measure so, and that, too, without knowledge or consent of the petitioner, as a part of a company of militia had taken possession of his house on the 23rd of August by order of Captain Clark.
>
> On the 24th following, Carter's company and parts of several other companies stopped at the petitioner's house, five or six of whom were left there sick, and numbers of them left their arms and accoutrements there, which were found by the enemy upon their arrival. The enemy were about setting fire to the petitioner's house, but were prevailed on to desist by some females of the neighborhood.
>
> The committee do not hold the opinion that the occupation of the petitioner's house made it a military depot or barracks in the proper sense and meaning of the terms; nor are they convinced that the goods stated to be stolen and taken away were stolen and taken away by the enemy, or that such depredations were committed because the house was regarded as a public storehouse or barracks. They therefore think that Congress cannot interfere.

## Andrew Villard

As reported by the Committee of Claims on January 2, 1818:

> The petitioner was for many years employed in the Ordnance Department by the United States. Upon the approach of the enemy in August, 1814, he was ordered by that department to take immediate charge of a certain wagon loaded with public property, and conduct it to a place of safety in the interior. With this order he complied, being allowed no time to provide for the safety of his own property, nor room in the wagon for a few articles belonging to him. He remained with the public property committed to his care at Leesburg, Virginia, till he was recalled, and on his return found the house he had occupied, his furniture, and tools, entirely consumed by fire. The loss thus sustained is estimated at $580, and indemnification to that amount is asked of Congress.
>
> The petitioner further states that the house containing his property was destroyed by authority under the control of government; that by his prompt attention to the safety of public property, he was prevented from having his own transported across the river beyond the reach of the conflagration, and that, on leaving Greenleaf's Point, he had the promise of the commanding officer that his effects should be removed, if necessary, but of this last statement he has adduced no proof.
>
> Admitting all the statements of the petitioner to be fully proved, the committee are of opinion that the principle upon which he asks indemnification is wholly inadmissible. The petitioner was superintendent of artificers in the service of the government, and never can it be supposed that he should have been permitted, in the hour of danger, to prostitute the dignity of his office, or to neglect the service required of him, to attend to his own private affairs.
>
> The fact that the buildings and other public property were destroyed by the order of Col. Decius Wadsworth is also immaterial in the present case. The residence of the petitioner in the houses of the government was also no doubt both a privilege and a benefit conferred on him. If he derived such advantages from that situation, he ought unquestionably to take it upon himself all the risk and danger to which it was liable. In the progress of a war, government may often find it prudent, as in this case, to destroy their own property; and if necessary the property of officers and soldiers should meet a similar fate. It is a misfortune to be lamented, but for which no compensation can be demanded.

Col. Wadsworth commanded the Ordnance Department. Andrew Joseph Villard also invented an improved gun carriage for which he requested $100.

## William Essenbeck

As stated by the Committee of Claims on January 7, 1818:

> The petitioner was a messenger in the office of the Secretary of the Treasury and was resident in a house, the property of the United States, near the office on the 24th of August, when it was destroyed in the conflagration then having occurred, together with his furniture, of the value as he alleges, of more than $300.
>
> The petitioner states he has been employed as messenger for more than 24 years, and is still retained in public service as assistant messenger on half pay. In the case of Mr. Villard, of the Ordnance Department, and of sailing master Barry, and boatswain Hodge, of the navy yard of this place, the committee believe no allowance has been made, though several times petitioned for. In these cases the destruction was by orders from the government and the parties were proved to have been in the discharge of their duties at the time of, and previously to the destruction of their furniture. In the case of the petitioner, the destruction was by the enemy, which is a principle, it is believed Congress have no case thought allowable. The committee therefore report that the petitioner have leave to withdraw his petition.

## William H. Washington

On December 3, 1814, Corporal Philip Boilia was deposed at Washington by Justice of the Peace Daniel Rapine:

> Be it remembered that personally appeared Philip Boilia, corporal in the United States army, and said that on the 24th August he was stationed with five privates over a quantity of public stores which had been deposited in a frame house, said to belong to Mr. William H. Washington, at the foot of the Potomac bridge in Alexandria county; that he was ordered to take care of the stores by Lieutenant Nehemiah Baden and to blow up the stores if the deponent was attacked by the enemy; that on the 25th August, about three o'clock, P.M., as soon as the storm that day had ceased, the deponent saw a British officer who came to the draw in the bridge, on the Virginia side and soon after returned; that a number of British soldiers were, at the same time, at the millhouse on this side of the river; that the draws on the bridge had been raised the night before and kept up, but were blown down during the storm, and the chains that raised them were broken; that soon after the officer on the bridge returned, a cannon shot was fired at him, the deponent, from the Point; and this deponent thinking that the enemy intended an attack, and not having the means to prevent the enemy passing, as the draw was broken, blew up the stores with powder and retired with the men to a hill near the place; that the explosion destroyed the house entirely, there being a quantity of ammunition and powder in the house.

Boilia certified his statement by making his mark, which Rapine witnessed. The Committee of Claims reported on December 19, 1814:

> The petitioner owned a small house, situated in Alexandria county, near the western end of the Potomac bridge; that on the 24th of August last, a quantity of public stores was removed from Greenleaf's Point by order of Colonel Decius Wadsworth and deposited in the house for safe keeping: a corporal and five men were stationed at the house to protect the public stores and to prevent them from falling into the hands of the enemy. The command of the stores was given to Lieutenant Baden, who directed the corporal, in case of attack by the enemy, to blow up the stores and retire from that place.
>
> It appears from the affidavit of the corporal that he apprehended an attack by the enemy and under that impression, blew up the stores and destroyed the house.
>
> Whether the destruction of the house was necessary to prevent the public stores from falling into the hands of the enemy is a matter of opinion to be formed by the facts submitted to the House. The committee are of opinion that, inasmuch as the officer to whom care the public stores were committed thought it prudent and proper to destroy the house and stores to prevent the latter coming to the possession of the enemy, the petitioner should be paid the value of the house.

Clement Sewall operated a ferry service across the Potomac and between August 28 and October 27, 1814, ferried expresses and baggage wagons of troops raised in Virginia for the defense of the District.

## John Rose, Sr.

As reported by the Committee of Claims on May 14, 1834:

> The following is a clause in the contract by which models and tools were brought to the Navy Yard, to wit: "That for and in consideration of the terms hereinafter specified, John Rose shall construct, erect, and put into efficient operation all the materials and machinery necessary for block-making and pump-making upon the most improved methods within his knowledge, and with all practicable speed, bringing with him to the aid of the work all such tools, models, and machinery, as he now possesses, applicable to the completion of the whole."
>
> It appears that Mr. Rose was an ingenious mechanic who had served with distinguished credit to himself and usefulness to the government of France, in consideration of which he had the privilege given to him by a special decree issued by the Emperor Napoleon in August, 1805, to quit France and to go to Russia, Sweden, Denmark, or the United States of America. He chose to come to the United States. To the privilege of emigration was extended that of bringing with him a number of models of his own invention, his mechanical apparatus, drawing, mathematical instruments, and tools of every denomination—the study and labor of 40 years.
>
> The improvement he had made in making blocks and pumps was that which the Navy Department contracted with him to apply to the public service in the Navy Yard at Washington.
>
> By the clause cited above, he was bound to bring with him his models, tools, and machinery applicable to the business about which he was employed. They were, then, by the very terms of his contract, taken into the public service, and he could not have withdrawn them without violating his contract. The foundation of all the paying for property lost, captured, or destroyed, during the late war, is, that the property was in the public service. The committee lament that justice has not more promptly been done in this case. They think most of the claim allowed is within the letter of the act of March 3, 1815, "for the relief of sundry persons in the service of the United States, in consequence of the destruction of their tools by fire at the Navy yard," and that it is within the spirit of the act of April 9, 1816.

The heirs were paid $2,500 in 1834.

## John Hansborough

A. H. Hansborough, the heir of John Hansborough, filed a claim. As stated by the Committee of Claims on April 12, 1842, in part:

> On or about the 24th of August, 1814, the British fleet said to be commanded by Captain James Gordon, when ascending the Potomac River, lay off the mouth of Potomac Creek, within a few miles of Fredericksburg. General William Madison, commanding the Virginia militia, then in the service of the United States, stationed a strong picket guard on the banks of the creek at a place called Belle Plains, where it was supposed the enemy would attempt to land if his object were Fredericksburg.
>
> A schooner belonging to the petitioner lay at anchor at the wharf at Belle Plains in the mouth of Potomac Creek and the schooner was destroyed by the enemy, as alleged, for its military occupation by the United States troops, for which indemnity is claimed of the Government.
>
> Captain Carter C. Allan says in his deposition of the 8th of February, 1840, "that a part of the forces was stationed for duty immediately behind the schooner, and that as the enemy approached in his barges, armed with cannon (9-pounders as it was believed) and filled with officers and men. The first fire of the American troops was from the direct and immediate rear of the schooner, and the first fire of the enemy's cannon was aimed at the vessel, behind which the militia had been stationed by order of their officer. The militia had no cannon, nor any other than small arms (muskets and rifles) for some time, and were of course driven back by the artillery of the enemy. As soon as the British could safely seize the vessel, which lay between the hostile parties, they seized its possession and destroyed it by fire.

I believe the schooner was destroyed because it was in our use as a protection, for they had power to destroy other property and vessels and I never heard of their doing so at that time."

In addition to his former statement, and in answer to questions propounded to him by the Hon. Linn Banks, he says: "As to using the schooner for a position to view the enemy, that was very needless, for the enemy was in very full view of his own motion, and as long as the British had cannon and we small arms to contend with, we wanted as little view of him as could be taken. As soon as our artillery came up we beat off the enemy, but not until he had set the schooner on fire."

He further says, "the forces under his command were in possession of the schooner for the purpose of defending themselves against the fire of the British, and also as a rampart behind which the men could fire back with their small arms." Other witnesses testify to the same effect.

From the full view of the evidence, the committee are of opinion that the claim does not come under the provisions of any act authorizing payment for property lost, captured, or destroyed in the late war.

Capt. Charles Shackelford, of the Virginia militia, testified to the facts presented:

On the night of the 24th of August, 1814, I was posted at the landing on Potomac Creek called Belle Plains, by order of General William Madison, who then commanded a brigade of Virginia militia in the service of the United States. The British fleet lay just off the mouth of the creek. General Madison's brigade, and a part of another brigade, lay in the immediate vicinity of this landing.

At the landing, Mr. John Hansborough's schooner lay at anchor. I had command of the picket guard consisting of infantry and riflemen. In the night my sentinels were doubled, and a part of my command was stationed directly behind the schooner. In the morning the enemy approached us in his barges filled with armed men and also carrying 9-pounders in his barges, for one of the balls fired was afterwards weighed. He also fired grape and canister shot, and one of the men was wounded by a cannon ball.

As the enemy approached he fired his cannons upon the post and my men fired first from the rear of the schooner. The enemy kept up his fire for some time with his artillery, and the schooner was cut loose, seized, and burnt by the British.

My men took their position in rear of schooner by my orders and its seizure and destruction was the consequence. I did not hear of the enemy's destroying any other private vessel than Mr. Hansborough's as they ascended the river. There was a public warehouse near the landing and a dwelling house also in point blank shot of the enemy, both of which they could have destroyed, but they did not destroy or burn either.

After some short time, a company of artillery came up and after they began to fire cannon at the British, they fled, but they burnt the schooner before they retreated.

I concur with the statement of Major Allan, then in the service with me from the same brigade, and then marching from the county of Culpepper. I also add that Captain John S. Barbour was aid-de-camp of General Madison. We received our orders through him, and he visited the picket guard in the night as officer of the grand rounds.

Ensign William Foster, then 58 and a resident of Ohio, also testified in this very lengthy hearing, which would have been settled by the Committee of Claims very quickly in 1820.

## *The Navy Yard Ropewalks*

### Daniel Renner and Nathaniel H. Heath

In August 1814 there were three ropewalks at the Washington Navy Yard owned by Renner & Heath, Tench Ringgold, and John Chalmers, Jr. On August 24, 1814, on the anticipated arrival of British forces, a hasty attempt by yard officers to burn the facilities to keep them out of British hands failed. The next day, Rear Admiral Sir George Cockburn arrived on Capt. John Wainwright's 80-gun *Tonnant* and completed the destruction of the Yard.

The ropewalk owners filed claims and on August 13, 1816, Tench Ringgold & Co. was paid $18,749.89, "in consequence of its military occupation by the United States."

Renner & Heath submitted a claim for $31,510.75, and on February 16, 1819, Congress directed the Treasury Department to settle the claim of Daniel Renner and Nathaniel Heath, "on account of cordage, spunyarns, and hemp, burned in their ropewalk on the 24th day of August, 1814, upon their exhibiting such proof of the quantity and value of said articles, considering the circumstances they were under at the time, as shall be satisfactory to the officers aforesaid," up but not to exceed $19,803.60.

As reported by the Committee of Claims on November 19, 1814:

> The petitioners were owners of ropewalks in the city of Washington, in which was contained a large quantity of spun yarns and navy cordage, all of which was destroyed by the enemy in his late incursion into this city.
>
> On or about the 20th of July, last, one of the petitioners, Mr. Heath, applied to Mr. Southerlin, the owner of some long boats then lying in the Potomac, and engaged of him five of them to transport his cordage and yarns up the river, if the enemy should invade the city. On the 18th or 19th of August it was deemed expedient, by Gen. Winder, to impress the boats of Mr. Southerlin, for the purpose of transporting the troops across the Potomac, which were kept in the employment of the Government until after the invasion of this city.
>
> On the 20th of August the petitioners applied for the boats, according to contract, for the purpose of removing their property, when they were informed that they were impressed. It also appears to the committee that on the 22nd of August the petitioners employed a wagon and nine or ten carts for the purpose of removing the property, but the wagon and two or three of the carts were impressed by the officers of the departments to remove the public papers and property; and that seven of the carts employed, after taking loads from the ropewalks out of the city, refused to return to haul any more for the petitioners, apprehending, if they did, they would be impressed into the employment of the Government.
>
> It is also stated, and believed, that after that day and before the enemy entered the city, carriages were not to be had in the city to remove the property. The loss to the petitioners, exclusive of the price of the ropewalks, is estimated at about $24,800; they ask of Congress to be reimbursed to the amount of their loss.
>
> The committee are of opinion the Government is under no obligation to pay for the property. The destruction of private property by the enemy in the progress of the war is much to be regretted and highly deprecated; but when it does happen it is to be considered, between the Government and its citizens, as one of the calamities of war. It may be presumed that the circumstances of the boats, wagons, and carts being impressed by the Government to perform services valuable to it, may create some equitable considerations in favor of the petitioners. It is, however, believed by the committee, not to be sufficient to authorize them to allow the claim.

On January 17, 1817, the committee added:

> Admitting, however, that the property was of that public character which would have authorized its destruction by the enemy, it does not appear in this case that the petitioners were prevented from saving such of their property as they could have removed by the impressments made by the officers of the Government. It appears that on the 22nd of August, of the ten carts employed by the claimants seven were not impressed, but took, each of them, one load from the walks and afterwards, of their own accord, left the service of the petitioners. Had that number of carts continued to haul the cordage and yarn till the enemy came into the city on the evening of the 24th, there can be no doubt it would have been removed.
>
> The committee are of opinion the petitioners are not entitled to relief.

Daniel Renner's wife, Mary S. Renner, pressed the claim, as reported by the Committee of Claims on July 24, 1846:

> When the city of Washington was threatened with invasion, he had on hand in his walk near the Navy-yard a large quantity of cordage, rope, and twine, suitable for the public

use. Justly fearing, in case of invasion, the destruction of his property by the enemy, he employed in season a sufficient number of "long-boats" to remove all the stock from his manufactory to a place of safety beyond the enemy's reach, but the long-boats were taken away from his service and impressed into the service of the United States to remove Young's brigade across the Potomac by order of General Winder.

He then obtained carts, but these were impressed by the government to remove books and papers from the public offices. He then hired wagons, but these were also impressed by the United States to remove the property of the public, and though he at first remonstrated, he acquiesced in the patriotic decision that "private considerations give way for the public good."

Thus deprived of every means that industry and vigilance could make available, frustrated by the government in three energetic efforts to save his property by removal, he was compelled to leave it to its fate.

The enemy soon after entered the city, discovered the naval stores in his walk, set fire to and totally destroyed all his stock, implements, and buildings. Compensation was made in part by the government for the cordage destroyed, but no compensation has been made for the ropewalk destroyed. The ropewalk contained cordage, &., evidently marked as public property. The contents being fired by the enemy, the building inevitably shared its fate, and was consumed. But for the government preventing the removal of the naval stores by impressing for its own use the owner's means of transportation, the walk itself would have been empty and unoccupied and would not have been destroyed. Private property, according to the usages of civilized warfare, is always respected.

The committee deem the petitioner entitled to the value of the ropewalk destroyed by the enemy on account of its having stores within it which, but for the interference of the government, would have been removed and saved, as its destruction was an inevitable consequence upon the destruction of the moveable property.

The committee therefore report a bill.

On June 20, 1848, the Senate Committee of Claims rejected the claim, and on March 31, 1856, the House Committee of Claims approved it.

## John Chalmers, Jr.

On July 16, 1803, John Chalmers received permission from the president "to occupy and use as a ropewalk, a portion of the public reservation in the city of Washington called The Fort" and there were public buildings nearby.

As reported by the Committee of Claims on November 7, 1814:

> On the 29th of March, 1814, the petitioner and the Secretary of the Navy entered into a contract for the manufacture of cordage for the United States' frigate *Java* upon the following terms: The Navy Department was to furnish him at Baltimore with Russia hemp and Kentucky yarn in such quantities as might be found convenient, and he should require which was to be manufactured in good navy cordage, sufficient for the complete equipment of the frigate. For every pound of hemp and yarn delivered to the petitioner he was to return a pound of cordage to the Navy agent, free from expense to the United States; so that his profit and compensation for his labor and art in manufacturing consisted in the difference in the weight of the hemp and yarns, increased by the quantity of tar used in the manufacture. It was also understood by the Secretary of the Navy and Mr. Chalmers that the raw material thus delivered was to be at the risk of the United States, in the event of loss by fire.
>
> The petitioner commenced manufacturing the cordage and had prepared and delivered to the Navy agent at Baltimore upwards of nine tons, and had a considerable quantity ready to deliver when, on the approach of the enemy towards Baltimore, in the month of September last, the ropewalks in which the cordage was manufacturing and then deposited was set on fire by order of General Thomas M. Forman, who then commanded the Maryland militia at that place; in consequence of which the rope-walks were destroyed, and with them about 30 tons of Russia hemp belonging to the Government, and all the labor and profit of the petitioner, except that part of the hemp which had been

delivered. He asks of Congress to reimburse him to the amount of his actual expenditures, in the purchase of tar, and the money which he has paid to persons employed in the manufacture of the cordage.

The committee are not in possession of facts which would authorize them to determine whether the destruction of his property was necessary: if it was not, however much they might regret and deprecate that work; yet they are of opinion that under the circumstances of this case, the individual who sustained the loss should at least be reimbursed by the Government to the amount of his claim.

Further reports on February 28, 1818, January 4, 1820, as January 8, 1821, rejected the claim on the grounds the property was "wantonly and lawlessly" destroyed by the enemy. As reported on March 5, 1824, in part:

The petitioner claims payment from the United States for a ropewalk and other property therein contained, also a barn, with rye and oats therein, altogether estimated at $5,967.38, stated to have been destroyed by fire during the invasion of the British army of this city in the month of August, 1814. He states that he erected this rope-walk about the year 1803 on the public ground and near to the public buildings at Greenleaf's Point in order to be convenient to supply cordage for the Navy.

Levi P. Cole says he was the Steward of the United States' Hospital at Greenleaf's Point on the night of the 14th of August, 1814. When the troops under Col. Wadsworth retreated to the Point, they set fire to the public buildings, and that the flames communicated to a large pile of wood stored up between the buildings and the claimant's rope-walk, and from the wood to the south end of the rope-walk and that a part of the rope-walk was burned. The next day, 25th, some of the British troops came down to the Point and set fire to the north end of the rope-walk in which was the hemp and other property of the claimant, and thereby the balance of the walk, with its contents, was consumed, except about a half a dozen rod of rope-walk in the middle, as also a barn containing rye and oats.

Dr. James Ewell states that on the morning after the capture of Washington, in his endeavors to save private property, he made an attempt to save the rope-walk of John Chalmers from destruction when it was observed by the enemy that they would spare nothing that made in favor of our Navy, and that from what they said it appeared they viewed it as public property.

After the British retreat from Washington City, Dr. Elwell, a hospital surgeon's mate, found shelter for 47 wounded British soldiers who had been left behind. On August 26, Elwell prevailed on Dr. William Baker, a surgeon, to help out, which he did. All had broken limbs and wounds that needed constant attention and dressings changed. On August 30, Gen. John Mason, "commissary for prisoners," put Hospital Surgeon Dr. Charles Worthington in charge of Dr. Baker, a Navy veteran of Tripoli, under whom Baker refused to serve, as beneath his dignity, and he left.

Dr. Baker said his services would have easily amounted to $1,000 in private practice. He was later paid $60. Dr. Worthington earned $145 a month, and Dr. Elwell $78 a month.

## *The Washington City Bridges*

### Eastern Branch Bridge Company

Between around 1795 and 1800 the company built a toll bridge in Washington City over the Eastern Branch of the Potomac River from the Southern Termination of 11th St. E., known as the 11th Street Bridge.

After war was declared, the consensus of military commanders was that Washington City wasn't in any great danger, seeing no military advantage to the British. President Madison did not entirely agree and Brig. Gen. William H. Winder, commander of the 10th Military District, which included the capital city, did what little he could over about six weeks to shore up defenses, but the city remained poorly defended.

The British arrived via the Patuxent River on August 19, 1814, and as they advanced on Washington City, American forces crossed the Eastern Branch bridges to the Washington Navy Yard, and on August 24, the bridges were ordered burned.

The Eastern Branch River was subsequently renamed the Anacostia River.

### Anacostia Bridge Company

Benjamin Stoddert was born in Maryland in 1751, went into business, was wounded at Brandywine during the war, and after the war went into exporting tobacco. He owned the land that would become Washington City and in November 1797 incorporated the Anacostia Bridge Co. in Maryland, owning most of the stock, and built a bridge from his land, the first to cross the Potomac River. He was appointed the first Secretary of the Navy on May 18, 1798, and served as interim secretary of war from June 1–12, 1800. He resigned as Navy secretary in the spring of 1801 and returned to business but lost considerable investments in real estate. He died on December 13, 1813.

The petition of Thomas Ewell, agent for the bridge company, was presented on November 4, 1814. Ewell was a physician and chemist who married Benjamin Stoddert's daughter Elizabeth and was co-owner and manager of the bridge company.

### Washington Bridge Company

On February 5, 1808, Congress authorized Robert Brent, Daniel Carroll, Thomas Monroe, James D. Barry, Frederick May, Samuel Harrison Smith, Jonah Thompson, Jonathan Swift, Thomas Powell, Cuthbert Powell, Elisha Janney, and Charles Alexander to act as a board of commissioners and sell up to $200,000 worth of stock in the Washington Bridge Company for the purpose of building a draw bridge across the Potomac River from the foot of Maryland Ave. in the City of Washington to Alexander's Island. It had to be at least 36-feet wide, "for the passage of travelers, horses, cattle, and carriages, with a secure railing on each side at least four feet high, of which six feet shall be appropriated to the purpose of a way for foot passengers, and shall be separated from the carriage way by a good and sufficient railing at least four feet high." A center section at least 35-feet wide over the main channel for the passage of vessels and two wharves were required, both toll free. Another smaller draw section 15 feet wide was required over the Maryland Channel. Various tolls were charged for foot, horse, and carriage traffic.

This was the second bridge across the river. In August 1814, the British set fire to the northeast end to stop American defenders and the Americans set fire to the other end to keep the British bottled up. Both fires were extinguished before major damage was done.

On August 10, 1816, Samuel Eliot, treasurer of the company, was paid $23,099.78. Daniel Carroll was the proprietor of the Washington Hotel, also destroyed by the enemy, and he was paid $27,093.50 on September 14, 1816.

## *Fairlee Creek*

### Henry Waller

In late August 1814, Captain Sir Peter Parker, RN, was ordered to take his 38-gun frigate *Menelaus* to the Upper Chesapeake Bay and land marines to draw American militia away from the impending attack on Baltimore in September, burn every structure from which enemy fire might ensue, and, as was their custom, seize and carry off every slave they could find.

On Sunday, August 28, 1814, the *Melelaus* stopped offshore opposite Henry

Waller's 308-acre farm, upon which was a fine two-story home, numerous outbuildings, and a large apple orchard and cornfield befitting a very prosperous enterprise. Waller had purchased the property from Col. James Lloyd in 1807.

Royal Marines under Lt. Henry Crease landed at Fairlee Creek in Kent County and at 10 a.m. encountered mounted militia on Waller's property. Lt. Crease ordered everyone back aboard and requested Capt. Parker to fire Congreve rockets and commence shore fire from the ship's 18-pounders, which he did, and that afternoon the Marines returned and engaged the militia, while, "the Waller house was burning most furiously and all the out houses and corn stalks," according to Lt. Benjamin G. Benyon on the ship.

As reported by the Committee of Claims on June 27, 1834:

> When the bill passed the Senate, the direction to the Third Auditor was general to ascertain the value of all the property that belonged to Henry Waller that was destroyed. This committee, from believing that the principle established by a long course of legislation would be enlarged if the bill became law, moved to amend it so as to confine its provisions to the buildings that were destroyed.
>
> At the last session of Congress, a bill similar to the one now before the committee passed the Senate, and, being referred to this committee, they recommended rejection.
>
> The committee regret to differ from the committee of the Senate in deciding claims, but having examined the legislation of Congress relative to the liability of the United States to pay for property destroyed during the late war, and finding that personal property has been excluded, except under peculiar circumstances, they cannot, until decisions of both branches of the National Legislature shall be reversed, after a full discussion, consent to enlarge the liability of the United States, and thereby invite the presentation of claims long since rejected.
>
> The property whose value is now claimed is described in the deposition of William B. Wilmer as being 900 bushels of wheat, farming utensils, hay, straw, and some furniture, valued by him and James Bowers and Philip Taylor at $1,554.
>
> The payment for property is urged on the ground that the buildings have been paid for, which contained the property, and they were destroyed so suddenly that their contents could not be removed and, therefore, that the destruction of the personal property was necessarily consequent upon the destruction of the buildings. The same facts existed in the destruction of the buildings on the Niagara frontier, in Michigan, on the Chesapeake and Delaware Bays, at Havre de Grace, and at all the other places where the enemy destroyed the buildings of our citizens, and the same reasons have been urged why personal property the buildings contained should be paid for; but Congress has decided, when legislating generally upon these applications, that the United States were not liable to make restitution.
>
> The bill from the Senate for the relief of Henry Waller ought not to pass.

After the attack and destruction, Waller sold the property to Richard Frisby, another nearby landowner and planter who likewise filed a claim, and in 1829 retained attorney Francis Scott Key to press his claim. One of the rockets that hit the house was saved and is on display at the Fort McHenry National Monument and Historic Shrine in Baltimore.

## Richard Frisby

As reported by the Committee of Claims on December 16, 1818:

> The petitioner represents that he is the owner of a farm on Fairlee Point, situate on the waters of the Chesapeake, in Kent County, on the eastern shore of Maryland, which forms the peninsula between the Chesapeake Bay and Fairlee Creek. This high point of land being an eligible situation for observing the movements of the enemy, a detachment of militia was generally stationed there to watch the British, and to communicate intelligence to the commanding officer. The militia at all times enjoyed the privilege of occupying any part of the buildings, and of taking anything from the farm which their necessities might require.

About the close of the summer of 1814, when the memorialist was constantly and actively engaged as a member of the Committee of Vigilance and Safety of the city of Baltimore, in preparing for defense against the threatened attack of the enemy, a squadron commanded by Sir Peter Parker, ascended the Chesapeake Bay and anchored opposite his farm.

After a variety of hostile and harassing movements, which were constantly watched by the unceasing vigilance of the gallant veteran General Philip Reed, availing themselves of the decided advantage which they possessed in having the exclusive command of the water in a country everywhere intersected with creeks and rivers, they crowded their barges with men and landed on the opposite side of Fairlee Creek.

This stratagem succeeded in drawing off the militia from the farm where they had been that morning in considerable force; and while General Reed was under rapid march to the head of Fairlee Creek, and was hastening to the defense of the property on the opposite shore, a signal was given from the fleet that the militia were now absent from the farm. They suddenly recrossed the creek, set fire to the buildings, wheat, corn, hay, &c.; seized and forcibly carried off four servants, his most valuable negroes; and destroyed, with a wanton and barbarian hand, every thing within their reach.

The bursting out of the flames gave the first notice to General Reed that the enemy had returned. Instantly he wheeled about his gallant troops and flew to the spot where the British were carrying on their disgraceful work of destruction. But the moment the enemy discovered the militia rapidly advancing, they precipitately fled to their boats.

Richard Frisby was paid $2,000, in 1838. He initially claimed $8,490 when the original report was made on March 20, 1818, and which the Committee of Claims rejected in its entirety.

He claimed compensation for his dwelling-house; granary, $1,000; corn-crib with sheds, $350; stable, $500; large barn, with carriage-house, $600; 1,500 bushels of wheat at $1.75 per bushel, $2,625; 10 barrels of corn at $4 per barrel, $40; and slaves William, 25, $440; Ephraim, 22, $460; Solomon, 20, $500, and Peregrine, 17, $200.

The Committee found it improbable that all that property was destroyed "in consequence of its military occupation." A house, yes, but they found it "ludicrous" a stable and the slaves were lost to military occupation and stated: "If government pays for the houses, it is just as necessary to pay for the negroes, because the same motive which produced the destruction of the one led to the stealing of the other" and denied the entire claim.

As reported by the Committee of Claims on May 28, 1836:

The petitioner asks compensation for several buildings and a quantity of grain and other personal property destroyed by the British in August, 1814.

The property was situated on the eastern shore of Chesapeake Bay, in the county of Kent, in the State of Maryland, at the mouth of Fairlee Creek. It does not appear from the papers referred to the committee, that any other buildings than the dwelling-house were occupied for any purpose by the troops which were called to that point for the defense of the country. The attention of the committee has been directed to the evidence which details the purpose for which the dwelling-house was occupied, and which goes to show that its destruction was during, and in consequence, of such occupancy.

The personal property not being, as the committee understand by the former decisions of Congress, recognized as a proper subject of charge to the United States, is also disregarded.

As to the dwelling-house, the testimony of Brigadier General Philip Reed, who commanded the militia called into service at the time and place referred to, is that the house and grounds were the most eligible position for a lookout station in that vicinity. The house and farm were constantly used as such station, while the enemy were up the bay. The horse-picket was ordered to be stationed at Mr. Frisby's house at nights, from whence to send out patrols to the shore, the house being for this purpose, a barrack. The house lay directly in the way from the main body of troops to the shore. He had been, in the course of the service, with officers and troopers at Mr. Frisby's house. Detachments, patrols, or videttes, being perpetual while the enemy were in the waters of that neighborhood.

James E. Barroll testifies that, "with three others of the cavalry attached to Colonel Reed's militia regiment, I was sent to Farlie on the evening of the burning. Part occupied the house as sleeping quarters, while the other part patrolled the shore. I was in the house that evening when the guard from the shore came in, stating that one of them was sick, and requesting those of the second watch to turn out, which we did, and proceeded to the shore. The sick trooper and his companion proceeded to camp instead of remaining in their quarters at the house.

About daybreak in the morning I discovered the barges of the *Menelaus* frigate in motion towards the Fairlie shore. My fellow trooper was dispatched with notice to General Reed, and I afterwards reported the intelligence that the enemy was landing. Before the militia came up, the property was fired by the British. The dwelling-house on the Fairlie estate was occupied as a guard-house for several nights by detachments from Captain Wilson's troop of horse, attached to the regiment of Maryland militia commanded by Colonel Philip Reed."

Captain Wilson states that "the dwelling-house in question was occupied by a guard of American troops for a number of nights preceding the burning, and that in a conversation with Lieutenant James Seagrove, of the *Menelaus* soon after the battle of Caulksfield, and when an exchange of prisoners was about taking place, he stated that they were directed to burn and destroy all houses occupied by armed American troops."

The same facts as to the occupancy, the burning and declarations of English officers at other times, are confirmed by the testimony of other witnesses.

Another fact, testified to by some of the witnesses, and which is not without some force in the view of the committee, is this: that other buildings and property, equally within the power of the British forces, and which were frequently visited by them without injury, were situated in the immediate neighborhood. The names of the owners are given, and a diagram submitted to the committee, exhibiting the relative position of these farms and buildings, and it appears that the only buildings burnt were those of the petitioner, and one belonging to Mr. Henry Waller, which were the only buildings occupied for military purposes. Mr. Waller's house was paid for by the United States, some three or four years since.

The committee are of opinion that the claim of Mr. Frisby is just, and well established.

The value of the house, as it was estimated in October, 1818, by William Matthews and William Skirver, commissioners appointed by Richard Bland Lee in April, 1818, was $2,000. The testimony taken under the commission does not appear to have been satisfactory, nor was it so considered by a committee of the first session of the 18th Congress, who reported against the claim. Since that time, other testimony has been procured, particularly as to the nature and extent of the occupancy of the dwelling-house, by which this committee are convinced that the claim of payment for it is well founded and that the valuation given is a reasonable and fair one. They ask leave, therefore, to report a bill.

The British landing force under Captain Sir Peter Parker was defeated by Gen. Philip Reed's militia. Frisby had left the property a short time before it was plundered and set on fire.

## *North Point*

On the evening of Saturday, September 10, 1814, a British squadron of 55 ships under Vice-Admiral Sir Alexander Cochrane arrived at the mouth of the Patapsco River. On board the transports were 4,700 sailors, soldiers, and marines. The army commander was Major-General Robert Ross.

The transports carrying the troops anchored in Old Road Bay off North Point while the others continued toward Baltimore Harbor and Fort McHenry, about 8 miles away. At 3 a.m. on the 12th, the troops began going ashore with their supplies, including artillery. Their march would be around 9 miles along Long Log Road to the Philadelphia Road and then 3 more miles or so to Baltimore. By 6:30 they were ready to move out and began forming columns. At 7 the sound of drums and bugles pierced the quiet countryside and the march began. General Ross famously said, "I will take Baltimore if it rains militia."

Waiting about 6 miles away near the intersection of Trappe Road was about 3,000 Maryland militia. Brig. Gen. John Stricker's 3rd Brigade—"City Brigade" or "Baltimore Brigade"—of Maryland Militia. Maj. William Pinkney's 1st Rifle Battalion, 3rd Brigade, Maryland Militia, and among them were Pvts. Henry McComas and Daniel Wells of Capt. Edward Aisquith's company of Sharp Shooters.

Another mile or so behind Gen. Stricker was Lt. Col. William McDonald's 6th Regiment of Baltimore Militia.

Both McComas and Wells were lost at the battle of North Point and Capt. Aisquith died in April 1815.

As recorded:

> The tradition in the Wells family was that Wells and McComas concealed themselves in a clump of bushes near a spring and that Ross stopping there to get a drink of water was shot by the two boys and thereupon their bodies were riddled with bullets.
>
> The company of Captain Aisquith was present at the battle of Bladensburg, and McComas had a plume shot out of his hat. There he saw General Ross and on his return to Baltimore remarked that should he see him again he would know him.
>
> The tradition of the McComas family was that when Henry bade his family good bye on leaving home he said, "Here goes for a golden epaulette or a wooden leg."
>
> When the sharpshooters were ordered to retreat he and Wells lagged behind and McComas said, "I see a mark," to which Wells replied, "So do I." Each took shelter behind separate trees and fired simultaneously. As the officer fell, the British fired several volleys in the direction of the tell-tale smoke and both youths fell dead. McComas was apparently reloading his gun as when found the ramrod was half way down the barrel. It is probable that he had stepped from behind the tree in order to ram home the charge when a bullet struck him and passed through his heart. Wells, who was only a few paces off, was shot through the back of the head.
>
> Both were buried in the same grave in a churchyard on Broadway, where Johns Hopkins Hospital now stands, and the bodies were subsequently removed in 1858 to their present resting place.

This obviously would have to have been told to the families by a third party know. A "military expert" later examined the scene and determined that Ross was actually shot by someone in Capt. Benjamin Chew Howard's company of Mechanical Volunteers, but that somehow remained unknown.

Major-General Ross was buried at St. Paul's Church in Halifax on the 29th. To Ross's credit, he had a sharp disagreement with Adm. Cockburn about wantonly destroying private property not used by the enemy, which he refused to do, and threatened punishment for anyone in his command who did. Cockburn was known for his virulent dislike of Americans.

The battle only slowed the British advance, and Gen. Stricker was forced back to the defense of the city. The militia held the British in check while the frigates and bomb ships moved into position to attack Fort McHenry, the last main defense of the city. When that failed, the British withdrew and marched back to North Point.

Military authorities ordered the burning of any manufacturer the British would find useful, such as rope making and naval stores.

Caught up among the British ships was an American lawyer named Francis Scott Key, on board an American truce ship tied up alongside a British tender several miles from Fort McHenry. He was able to see the 30 × 42-foot flag flying over the fort.

Adm. Cockburn gained fame in 1815 for transporting Napoleon into exile at St. Helena.

## Bernard Todd

Navy Captain Joshua Barney had a son, William B. Barney, who was a major in Lt. Col. James Biays' 5th Regimental Cavalry District, Maryland Militia. On March 23, 1813, Maj. Barney wrote to Brig. Gen. John Stricker, of the 3rd Brigade, Maryland Militia, that the home of Bernard Todd at North Point was ideally situated and suited to accommodate a detachment of cavalry troops for reconnaissance and guard duty.

On May 14, 1814, Maj. Barney took command of the gunboat *Scorpion* in his father's Chesapeake Bay Flotilla, and on August 19, 1814, he enlisted in the Navy as a lieutenant.

In September 1814, Bernard Todd was a private in Capt. Tobias E. Stansbury's company of 6th Regiment of Maryland Volunteer Cavalry when an imminent British attack was expected. Maj. Gen. Samuel Smith, commander of the 3rd Division Maryland Militia, ordered Lt. Col. William McDonald of the 6th Regiment to occupy the house.

Bernard died on September 13, 1816, apparently without ever filing a claim. He was survived by his wife, Mary Shaw Todd, and children Thomas Jefferson, Nathan Green, Richard Montgomery, George Washington, Elizabeth Frances, and Sarah Ann.

In 1832, his heirs hired an attorney. On December 29, 1845, the surviving heirs, wife Mary, son Richard, daughter Elizabeth Porter, William Shaw, John A. and Sarah A. Diffenderfer, and Vincent and Rachel R. Green, filed a petition and stated, "the papers, with others, were placed in the hands of an attorney, but were misplaced, and but recently found, and as your memorialists have suffered greatly in consequence of the destruction of their property and are illy able to sustain the loss thereof."

The property as claimed lost:

One large frame dwelling, 35 by 40 feet, two stories high, $1,600.
One frame kitchen, 25 by 30 feet, one story and a half, $300.
House and kitchen furniture, $250.
One large frame barn, 40 by 43, two stories, $950.
One large frame stable, 30 by 60, one story and a half, $500.
Sheds attached to stable, sufficient to contain 60 head of cattle, $500.
Four log houses for workshop, carriage, and poultry house, each 20 feet square, one story, $200.
About 600 bushels of wheat, and 400 or 500 bushels of rye, corn, and oats, $1,200.
15 tons timothy hay, $240.
80 or 90 head of hogs, $300.

Several witnesses were called, including 1st Lt. Lyde Goodwin in Capt. Henry Wilson's 6th Cavalry District company, who swore that the "above described premises was occupied in the year 1814 by militia in the United States service and at the time of conflagration, by a vidette guard in said service."

Other witnesses were Capt. Jonas Green, commander of a company in the 6th Cavalry District, and Thomas S. Jones, also in Capt. Stanbury's company.

Cpl. Eli Simpkins, Pvt. Robert Benson, and Pvt. Caspar Prince, members of Capt. James Sterett's company of 1st Baltimore Hussars in the 5th Cavalry District, testified in early 1834, that they were a "piquet guards" on September 12 under orders of Maj. William Jackson of the 5th Regimental Cavalry District.

Lt. Nicholas Brewer, 1st Sgt. Richard Bell, and Pvt. Isaac Turner, in Capt. Peter Galt's 6th Regiment Maryland Militia, testified that they were also stationed at the Todd residence headquarters on orders of Maj. Gen. Smith. Capt. Stansbury also testified.

Local residents John M. Gorsuch, an ensign in the Fells Point Riflemen, and Joshua Shaw valued the property at $6,732.

As reported by the Committee of Claims on May 4, 1846:

> The memorial sets forth "that during the late war with the British, Bernard Todd resided at North Point and was in possession and owner of a dwelling-house and other property, which, on the night of the 11th of September, and morning of the 12th of September, 1814, were occupied by our troops, as also several times previously, especially in 1813 when it was occupied by a detachment of infantry from Baltimore under the command of Col. William McDonald and on that account was soon set on fire by the British and totally destroyed together with a great quantity of grain, stock, &c." and prays compensation for the property thus destroyed.
>
> This case has never been presented to the proper department for adjudication and settlement, and no testimony obtained to establish the claim prior to 1834—nearly 20 years after the alleged destruction of the property.
>
> The testimony establishes the fact that the property was occupied temporarily by a detachment of American troops from Baltimore in April, 1813, but there is no proof of occupancy from April, 1813, to September, 1814—so that the military occupancy of the property in 1813 cannot avail the memorialist in this application, the occupancy not having been continued, but evidently abandoned.
>
> It is, however, alleged that the property was occupied by our troops in September, 1814, and at the time of the landing of the British forces at North Point, and in consequence of such occupancy, was destroyed by the enemy. From the testimony it appears that a vidette guard of three men, by order of the officer in command, was stationed at North Point on the evening of September 11, 1814, but they were not ordered by the officer to take possession of the dwelling-house of Mr. Todd. They, however, did, during the night of the 11th of September, enter the house in question, if not contrary to orders, at least without any order from the commanding officer, and on the morning of the 12th September, at the approach of the enemy, retreated, soon after which the property was set on fire and destroyed.
>
> The testimony in the case is unsatisfactory and somewhat contradictory. The military occupation by the vidette guard, without authority, is not of such character as to bring the case within the provisions of the acts of Congress heretofore passed providing for the payment of property lost, captured, or destroyed, &c., by the enemy, and upon no principle of general policy ought this claim, at this late day, to be allowed. The prayer of the memorialists ought not to be granted.

As reported by the Committee of Claims on February 29, 1848:

> During the years 1813 and 1814 the residence and out buildings of Todd at North Point were occasionally occupied by the American troops under the command of the officers for military purposes. That they were so occupied on the night of the 11th of September, 1814, until driven from it by the British forces, who then burnt all the buildings containing a large amount of personal property, and that, by the burning of the buildings, some other property not in them was fired and consumed also.
>
> The committee are convinced from the proof that the destruction of the property was owing to the fact that it was occupied for military purposes by our troops, and that compensation ought to be made for it. They are not prepared to say that the amount at which the property is valued, proposed to be paid for, should be allowed for, and have thought it most prudent to refer that matter to the proper department to ascertain, and settle according to what may be shown to be just and right.

The legal representatives of Bernard Todd were paid $4,315 in 1853.

## James Maglenen

As reported by the Committee of Claims on January 15, 1839:

> The petitioners allege that James Maglenen was a private in Captain James Horton's troop of light horse volunteers at Baltimore in the late war. In September, 1814, a horse, with a saddle, bridle, and pair of pistols belonging to James was impressed by order of Colonel James Biays and Captain Horton, then in the service of the United States, for the purpose of sending an express to North Point to ascertain if the British forces were about to land, and the horse died in the service and the articles were lost and no payment or satisfaction has ever been made therefore.

> Their father died many years ago, leaving them with very scanty means of support and they pray for relief.
>
> The material facts stated in the petition are supported by Daniel Fosbenner and William Brannan and they state the horse was worth $100. The petitioners estimate the value of the equipments at $30.
>
> It is also proved that Colonel Biays died many years ago and that Captain Horton died about two years ago.
>
> The committee are of opinion that the claim is just and equitable and the petitioners should be allowed and paid the sum of $130.

Susanna T. Lea, widow and administratrix of James Maglenen, late of the city of Baltimore, was paid $130 in 1858.

This claim was filed in 1837. During the 25th and 27th Congresses it passed the House of Representatives, but failed in the Senate, chiefly for "want of time." It was again reported favorably by the Committee of Claims on January 4, 1841, and Committee on Military Affairs and the Militia on August 7, 1856. The heirs were finally paid in 1858.

James was from Ireland and was naturalized on December 13, 1808, at Baltimore.

## Juliet Eliza Sollers, Tobias E. Stansbury, Jr., and William Stansbury

Elisha Sollers married Sarah Partridge on May 3, 1798, at Baltimore and they farmed land on the Patapsco River known as Sollers Point. Their only child, Juliet Eliza, was born on March 17, 1804. Elisha died in 1809 and it appears Sarah married John Wright on May 23, 1809.

In his will, Elisha had appointed Hickman Johnson, a county assessor and husband of Ann Sollers, as legal guardian for Juliet, then a minor child, who inherited Sollers Point. Johnson rented the land, dwelling, and out-buildings to Capt. Tobias Stansbury, Jr., and his son, William. Tobias commanded a company in the 6th Cavalry District of Maryland Volunteers.

The property was burned by the British on the night of September 13, 1814. Tobias Stansbury filed a claim and Hickman Johnson submitted a petition on Juliet's behalf in November 1817.

Witnesses and potential witnesses were contacted, and Beale Randal, who was a major in the 15th Regiment of Maryland Volunteers, was deposed on January 19, 1818, as recorded:

> Beale Randal deposes that on the 11th of September, 1814, he commanded a battalion of Riflemen belonging to the Maryland militia, but then in the service of the United States, and stationed near Baltimore, under the command of Gen. Samuel Smith, also of the Maryland militia, but then in the service of the United States.
>
> On the 11th September, 1814, in obedience to the orders of Gen. Smith, he marched with his command to Soller's Point, about seven miles from Baltimore, and arrived there at night. Having no baggage wagons and no tents, he took possession of and occupied with his troops the houses on a farm, which he understood and believed at the time belonged to Juliet Eliza Sollers.
>
> On that night and part of the next day, 12th September, and the day of the battle between the Baltimore troops and the British forces, about 1 o'clock P.M., which was about the time the battle commenced, a part of the British fleet got under way and stood up the river towards Baltimore. At the same time several barges came up Bear Creek, in the rear, and fired six or eight rockets and round shot in a direction towards the houses occupied by the troops under his command, one of which set on fire an old field. Some of the vessels of the fleet had by his time passed up the river above the houses and other vessels were abreast of them in full view.
>
> Capt. Wilson's troop of horse was stationed with his company and they were all in uniform and fed their horses near the houses. Some of the militia under his command were also in uniform and the enemy had a distinct view of them.
>
> The deponent then ordered his battalion to retire, apprehending that the enemy would pass in their barges up Colgate's Creek and cut off his retreat. The enemy afterwards burnt the houses on the farm and he has every

reason to believe that they did so in consequence of their having been occupied by the militia as a military post.

Commissioner of Claims John P. Harris rejected the claim on January 19, 1818, for lack of evidence that the property was occupied by the United States or that it was destroyed by the enemy.

The Stansbury's sued for the crops destroyed, as reported by the Committee of Claims on March 2, 1818:

> From the evidence adduced in this case, it appears that sometime in the night of the 11th of September, 1814, a company of cavalry commanded by Captain Benjamin Wilson, and a battalion of riflemen commanded by Major Beale Randal, arrived at the farm of the claimants and took possession of the dwelling-house and as such of the out-houses as were not filled with grain and hay and occupied the same till about 1 o'clock the next afternoon when a squadron of the enemy ascended the river, and, on coming up against the house, commenced a discharge of rockets and shot. Some of the rockets, it is alleged, fell very near the house, upon which the troops retreated, and several of them, who are witnesses in this case, state that when they were about half a mile from the farm, they discovered that two stacks of hay upon the farm were on fire.
>
> Frederick O'Brien states that he resided on a farm situate immediately on the Patapsco River, near the city of Baltimore, and adjoining the farm of the claimants. That on the night of the 13th of September, 1814, a party of the enemy came to his house with lanterns and proceeded to the farm of the claimants and burnt their dwelling-house, granary, barn, and a large brick building called the still-house, but which for many years had been used as a granary or barn, and that "there were many houses and farms in view, and convenient to the property, but that none of the houses except those of the claimants were burnt by the enemy."
>
> The claimants allege that their property of the description and value set forth in the following list was destroyed, viz:
>
> Wheat in the straw, the production of 53½ bushels sowing, 10 bushels to one sowing, amounting to 535 bushels at $1.50—$802.50; Oats in the straw, the product of 68½ bushels sowing, averaging 15 bushels to one sowing, amounting to 1,027½ bushels, at 75 cents—$770.62½; Wheat and oat straw—$175; 6 tons of timothy hay, at $20—$120; 30 barrels of corn, at $4—$120; Crop of flax—$20; 30 bushels large potatoes—$30; Farming utensils, $75; one seine and rope, $150; household and kitchen furniture consisting of mahogany bedsteads, tables, &c., $160, amounting to $2,423.12½.
>
> If the burning of the property was in consequence of a military occupation by the United States, the claimants are entitled to remuneration, and that such was at least a pretext for the burning, is pretty evident, if the witness O'Brien is to be believed, who states that no other buildings were burnt, although there were many in the vicinity.
>
> The committee are, however, of opinion that the evidence is insufficient to establish any part of the claim, there being none except the affidavit of one of the claimants, who states, "that the foregoing estimate is just and true, according to the best of his knowledge and belief," and the affidavit of Colonel Josias Green and Thomas L. Jones, who, without saying anything as to their means of knowledge, "depose and say that they have no personal knowledge of the burning and the property of Tobias E. Stansbury, Jun., and William Stansbury, by the British on the 13th of September, 1814, but that they have heard and believe that the same was burnt and destroyed by them, and that the estimate, sworn to by Tobias E. Stansbury, Jun., is a correct estimate of the damage sustained on that occasion."
>
> Admitting the evidence was perfectly satisfactory as to the loss, and the amount of it, the committee are of opinion that a case is not made out in which, by a law of the 9th of April, 1816, or upon any other proper grounds, the claimants would be entitled to relief, unless the government should proceed upon the principles of remunerating for all losses resulting from the acts of the enemy, whether lawful or otherwise.
>
> The buildings of the claimants were partially occupied by troops of the United States, from some time in the night of the 11th of September until about 1 o'clock in the afternoon of the succeeding day, and were destroyed on the night of the 13th. It is therefore believed

that, unless the committee are altogether erroneous in the view they have taken on the subject, it cannot be said that the burning was justifiable on the grounds of a military occupation. They therefore recommend it ought not to be allowed.

On November 3, 1824, Juliet married Augustine Taney, at Baltimore. The British had also burned the Taney home. Augustine and Juliet pursued the claim, and the property was independently appraised at $9,475 by David Willson, Caleb Arnest, and Thomas Murray, of Baltimore.

On December 21, 1825, Gen. Smith was deposed:

> To prevent the enemy from getting in the rear of General John Stricker's 3rd Brigade, he detached the Light Infantry under the command of Maj. Randal the day before the battle at North Point, the 12th September, 1814, with orders to proceed to the mouth of Bear Creek to watch the motions of the enemy. Maj. Randal did proceed, and on his return reported that he had been at the mouth of Bear Creek and had remained there till the enemy had discharged several rockets at the spot where his corps had been stationed. The houses were afterwards burnt by the enemy, and as they destroyed no other houses in the vicinity, he believes the houses and other property were destroyed inconsequence of their having been occupied by the detachment under Maj. Randal.
>
> The deponent gave no order to occupy the houses, but they being on the spot, and the corps having no other covering, would of course occupy the houses, and they were occupied, he understood, by order of Maj. Randal, a militia officer, then in the service of the United States.

As reported by the Committee on Claims on January 26, 1827:

> It appears that Juliet Eliza Sollers, on the 11th September, 1814, was owner of a farm on Patapsco River below and near Baltimore called Soller's Point when the British army and squadron were approaching that city during the late war on which farm were houses, and other improvements valued at $6,600.
>
> On the 11th day of September, 1814, by order of General Samuel Smith, who commanded the American force, Major Beale Randal, with a detachment of Riflemen or Light Infantry, and also a detachment of Cavalry, was ordered to Soller's Point to watch the motions of the enemy, at which place Major Randal arrived after dark on that day and took up their quarters there, the officers sleeping in the house, and the soldiers in the out-houses and barn of the petitioner, and cooked their rations near the houses, next day.
>
> The detachments retired from the houses about 1 or 2 o'clock on the 12th in consequence of the approach of the enemy, by whom a few rockets and round shot were fired in a direction towards the houses. On the night of the 13th of September, the enemy landed on the Point and burnt the houses.
>
> The claim was transferred to the Third Auditor of the Treasury for settlement under the act of March 3, 1825, by whom it was disallowed for reasons contained in his letter to Hickman Johnson dated 14th October, 1825.

Third Auditor Peter Hagner explained to Hickman Johnson that he was authorized to settle claims, "for no other buildings than those which were occupied by order of an agent or officer of the United States, either as barracks for the military forces of the United States, or as places of deposit for military or naval stores," and the evidence did not sustain that.

On July 14, 1832, the Third Auditor was "directed to ascertain the value of the buildings, the property of the wife of Augustine Taney before her intermarriage, which were destroyed by fire by the enemy during the late war, on Soller's Point, near the city of Baltimore." The term "intermarriage" implies there was some connection between the two families.

Peter Hagner again disallowed the claim. Augustine Taney filed his own claim and was paid $6,600 in 1832. As stated by the Committee of Claims on June 12, 1832:

> It is proven that Juliet Eliza Sollers, on the 11th of September, 1814, then a minor, but, since intermarried with Augustine Taney, owned a farm on the Patapsco River, below, and near to Baltimore, called Sollers Point, on which were houses and other buildings. On

the 11th day of September, Major Beale Randal, by order of Gen, Samuel Smith, took a position with his command at Sollers Point, together with a company of cavalry to watch the movement of the enemy and remained there through the night of the 11th, the officers occupying the house, and the soldiers the out-houses; and, until about the middle of the 12th, when the enemy having proceeded up the river towards Baltimore, and a number of barges having ascended Bear Creek in the rear, and discharged a number of rockets and round shot, the position was abandoned by the American troops, and not re-occupied.

Maj. Randal says in his deposition given on the 8th of December, 1827, that on the 11th of September, 1814, he was ordered by Gen. Smith to march with his command to Sollers Point. He arrived there after night and took up his quarters in the dwelling-house and the men took up their quarters in the out-houses. He does not recollect the precise orders given at the time, but is certain that the soldiers would not have occupied the houses without his orders and directions.

From this and much other evidence, the committee think the fact of military occupation from the 11th until about the middle of the day on the 12th is satisfactorily proven, and that our troops were driven from the buildings by the enemy, and that the enemy having advanced up the river and up Bear Creek, prevented a re-occupation of the point by our troops, if they had been disposed to have taken possession of it.

From the time our troops abandoned the point until the enemy descended the river, which was on the evening of the 13th, when the houses were destroyed, the point was in the possession of the enemy. During the night of the 13th, a part of the enemy's force went to the houses thus previously occupied with lanterns in bags and set fire to the buildings and destroyed them, but set fire to no other buildings in the neighborhood.

The committee cannot doubt that the buildings were destroyed in consequence of their having been in the military occupation of the troops of the United States. The buildings, for all military purposes, had assumed the character of public property, and as such was the legitimate object of destruction by the enemy. Such is a main principle in all the laws passed for the relief of those whose buildings have been destroyed. The character was in no wise changed by the circumstance that our troops were driven from the buildings because the enemy had the complete and entire control of them, and it was not in the power of the United States to put the proprietor in possession, before the time the buildings were destroyed.

This case does not come strictly and literally within the letter of the law, but it does, in the opinion of the committee, within its true spirit and meaning. If the enemy had retired without destroying the buildings, and the temporary possession they held of that section of the country had been restored to the United States, the case would be different. If the buildings had not been re-occupied by our troops, the enemy would not have been justified by the principles of civilized warfare in destroying them, if he had afterwards returned, because their character of public property would have been changed.

The committee recommend the passage of the bill.

Capt. Benjamin Wilson, Jr., was in the 6th Cavalry District, which his father commanded. Beale Randal was commissioned a captain in the 36th Maryland Militia in October 1807 and in 1809 was elected to the state legislature. On July 8, 1813, he was appointed major in the 2nd Regiment, brigade major of the 11th Brigade, and in July 1814 major in the 15th Regiment. He was promoted to lt. col. on November 12, 1814.

## *Baltimore*

### Anxiety at Hepbrontown, Maryland

On September 15, 1814, Lt. Col. William Spencer's 33rd Regiment of Maryland Militia was at Hepbrontown, in Kent County, "and that great anxiety was felt by the commanding officer and other officers and men of the regiment to know the result of the attack on Baltimore by the British and the movement of the enemy."

Private Samuel Kerr, who had his own

horse in Capt. Matthew Tilghman's company of infantry, was detailed by Col. Spencer to go to Elkton in Cecil County, "to ascertain the result of the attack and the subsequent movement of the enemy." He completed the mission in one day, but the trip was so arduous, the horse died from exhaustion soon after.

Col. Thomas Hepbron, serving under Col. Spencer, and Ensign James Millward in Capt. George Spey's company witnessed the unfortunate event.

## *Baltimore Ropewalks*

John Calef, Jacob Shinnick, Schoultz & Voegeler, and Christian Chapman operated ropewalks and filed claims, "on account of the destruction, by the United States, of their rope-walks, and other property therein deposited, in the vicinity of Baltimore."

Acsah Calef was the legal representative of John Calef. On September 19, 1814, Brig. Gen. Thomas Marsh Forman, of the Maryland Militia, responded to the Committee of Claims from his camp at Hampstead Hill:

> I hereby certify that in consequence of discretionary power invested in me by Maj. Gen. Samuel Smith, commanding officer at Baltimore, I ordered the rope-walks near my lines, in the possession of Jacob Shinnick, to be set on fire and consumed on the evening of the 12th instant. The ropewalks at the time contained the tools of the trade, some hemp, and some yarns. I also, at the same time, and under the same circumstances, directed a common frame stable in pasture of Mr. Shinnick to be set on fire and consumed.

On November 16 he added:

> Although it was decidedly evident that the three ropewalks in front of my lines must be destroyed the moment the enemy appeared before them, yet I did not obtain Maj. Gen. Smith's permission to burn them until Monday evening, the 12th September. It was then impossible to remove any thing, and notice to the owners would have been useless. Indeed, from my knowledge of the demand for wagons and carts to remove the inhabitants after the enemy had landed at North Point, I do not think that teams could have been procured to remove bulky articles.

On November 22, Maj. Gen. Smith replied:

> I do certify that the ropewalk owned or occupied by Jacob Shinnick was situated directly in front of the lines, and under battery within the command assigned to Brigadier General Forman; that ropewalk and two others were so close to the works that had they remained, and an attack been made by the enemy, they would have afforded such a cover as would have enabled him to have approached close to the works undiscovered. It became necessary to destroy them; nor did I give the discretionary power to Gen. Forman until the attack of the enemy appeared certain. Their destruction was postponed as long a prudence permitted, nor were they destroyed until it became absolutely and indispensably necessary.

### Thomas Sprigg

Thomas Sprigg was a merchant at 90 Dugan's Wharf and lived at the corner of Pearl and Fayette Streets. His ropewalk was ordered burned by Brigadier General Thomas Marsh Forman, commander of the 1st Brigade (Cecil and Hartford Counties), 2nd Division of the Maryland Militia.

### Hugh McDonald

As stated by the Committee of Claims on March 3, 1837:

> The petitioner resided at Baltimore during the late war, and was a member of Captain John Hanna's company of Fells Point Light Dragoons. In the month of August, 1814, Lieutenant Stephen W. Pennell, of the navy, took the horse of McDonald to go as an express to St. Leonard's creek on public business relative to the United States flotilla under the command of Commodore Barney. The horse was returned in about ten days, and from its usage and starvation died soon afterwards.

His value was $100. The claim was rejected in 1831. The petitioner has since taken other testimony which has satisfied the committee that relief should be granted. A bill is herewith reported.

## Edward Evat

His home in Baltimore was occupied by Army troops for barracks and burned in 1815. His petition was presented on February 8, 1816. He was eventually paid $1,338.81 for his house and property. He was paid $1,338.81 in 1823, "being the value of a house burnt while occupied by the American troops, provided that there shall be deducted whatever amount may have been paid for the hire or use of the house."

# *Vessels Sunk for the Defense of Baltimore*

## Port and Harbor Defense Act

> The President is hereby authorized, whenever the same shall be deemed necessary for the defense and security of any of the ports and harbors of the United States, to cause to be hired or purchased, hulks, or other means of impediment to the entrance of ships or vessels of the enemy, to be sunk with the consent of the proper authority of the state in which such port or harbor may be, and the same to be removed whenever in his opinion it may be done with safety to such ports or harbors.
>
> Sec. 2. To defray any expense which may be incurred under this act, the sum of $250,000 is hereby appropriated.
>
> July 16, 1813. (3 Stat. L. 18)

On August 24, 1814, the people in Baltimore could see a glow in the sky and smoke billowing up in the air to the southwest. It was Washington City, 35 miles away, on fire. The British had arrived at the capital from their victory at Bladensburg, and the residents rightly believed the Redcoats would soon be on their way to Mobtown, then the third largest city in America and a beehive of shipbuilding.

Fort McHenry and the Lazaretto Battery on either side of the approach to the Inner Harbor were manned and ready and gunboats were stationed between them. Maj. Gen. Samuel Smith got citizens busy building various defensive works as residents from Maryland, Virginia, and Pennsylvania arrived to offer help. Comm. John Rogers sent sailors and Marines from the Philadelphia Navy Yard to help, and by then it was estimated the city had anywhere from 15,000 to 20,000 defenders with 60 to 100 cannons.

Vessels were sunk that successfully protected the Inner Harbor and town and on March 7, 1815, Secretary of War John C. Calhoun wrote to Col. Paul Bentalou, quartermaster general at Baltimore:

> As the owners of the vessels which were sunk at Baltimore will now become very importunate, and as you probably cannot raise them fast enough to meet their wishes and expectations, you may, therefore, permit individuals to raise their own vessels for a stipulated sum, or in such manner as may, in your opinion, be compatible with the public interest, as it is my wish that you should give every facility to the raising of those vessels which may be consistent with economy and the public interest. As there no doubt will be many applications to Congress, by individuals owning those vessels, for compensation and damages, by injuries either to their vessels or rigging, while sunk, it would be advisable that such damages should be duly ascertained, in such manner as you may think best, at the time the vessels are respectively raised, and a report thereof made to this office.

In 1816, Col. Bentalou hired Thorndike Chase, a ship carpenter; John Snyder, a ship joiner; and James Cordery, a ship chandler to survey the raised and Refitted vessels, which they valued at $115,600. In 1816, those owners were paid $15,188.50 for damages, but considerable dissension and appeals to Congress ensued over the amounts paid to all owners, especially for demurrage, the amount of money a common carrier could or would have made if not for the lawful or unlawful detention by a public authority.

On December 17, 1821, Baltimore Mayor Edward Johnson wrote a letter to Secretary Calhoun:

> I have just been informed that the owners of the vessels that were sunk at the entrance of this harbor in the month of September, 1814, are without a settlement with the United States for the injuries they sustained from the application of their property to the public use.
>
> As the presiding officer in this city at the period alluded to, the transactions incident to its defense came under my notice, and I deem it my duty, as an act of justice, to comply with the wishes of the owners of the sunken ships, to make this communication to you, as the proper organ of the General Government. The United States officer then commanding at this post having made a requisition on this city (at the instance of Commodore Rodgers) for a sufficient number of vessels to obstruct the channel-way near Fort McHenry, in order to prevent the enemy's ships' passage into the harbor, the local authorities, with great confidence in its prospect of efficient defense, readily met the requisition, and authorized the commodore to take possession of and sink any vessels he could most readily obtain.
>
> The moment had arrived when this important post was at its utmost peril, and our most skillful officers had their attention and anxiety fixed on this entrance, not only as the least prepared for defense, but as the very course through which the enemy calculated on passing with his naval forces. The emergency was limited to a moment; but, by the unequalled exertions of that intelligent officer, Commodore Rodgers, that moment sufficed to provide a barrier of about 25 vessels of all descriptions.
>
> The bombs from the enemy's ships were thrown over McHenry before all the vessels were sunk; it was therefore not possible either to select vessels destined to be sunk, or to remove from those indiscriminately taken even the most valuable articles. It was then seen that these vessels would be materially deteriorated, and their materials and articles on board lost and destroyed; but the exigency and procedure admitted of no delay. The local authorities, however, satisfied that the justice and equity of a fair and full compensation being made to their owners would be recommended to the nation, as well as by the high sanction of the procedure by the public functionaries, as by the united opinion of the citizens and the official acknowledgement of the enemy's commander. The vessels remained sunk a considerable time after the war terminated, which subjected their owners to great loss in being deprived of their services at a period particularly advantageous for commercial pursuits.
>
> It can hardly be necessary for me now to state that the sinking of the vessels chiefly, if not entirely, saved the city from destruction. The application was highly judicious, and made at a period when some or all of their owners were in contact with the enemy's troops at North Point. Many of the owners are to me personally known as men of respectability in wealth, influence, and public zeal; and I do most earnestly recommend their case to the consideration of the Government.

On April 26, 1822, Congress allowed $40,563.32 for demurrage and an additional $38,154.21 for raising the vessels.

John S. Stiles, the heir of George Stiles, deceased, whose ship *Fabius*, brig *Aid*, and schooner *Ann* were salvaged and returned, believed full compensation for demurrage had not been made, "during the time the vessels were in the public service." The original claim was for $16,281.10. The Navy Department paid $5,486.92, leaving a balance of $10,794.18.

On February 27, 1823, the Committee on the Judiciary recommended he be paid that amount, and on March 3, 1825, the Secretary of the Navy was authorized to re-examine the claim and allow John compensation for the detention of the vessels from February 17, 1815, to the time when they were delivered to the owner, "and from thence to the termination of the period necessary to repair the injury done to them by sinking: according to the intent and meaning of the act of Congress passed on April 26, 1822."

On May 7, 1824, the Secretary of the Navy reported that 12 of the vessels "were so injured as to be worthless, and were left as wrecks, or sold for a few dollars." The value of these vessels were proved to be worth $73,079.30. A total of $9,991.60 was realized by the owners from salvage sales from the wrecks.

As reported by the Committee of Claims on January 17, 1826:

> The petitioners have heretofore applied to Congress for a remuneration for the injury they have sustained and by several acts passed for their relief, the following sums have been allowed and paid. Under the act making appropriations for the military service of the United States, passed the 29th of April, 1816, there was paid to the petitioners (no application being made by them) the sum of $15,188.50 for damages sustained, "for articles lost from and injured on board of the vessels."
>
> By the act of April 26, 1822, there was also granted and paid to the petitioners the sum of $40,363.82 for detention from the 17th of February, 1815, the period peace took place with Great Britain, until the vessels were raised and restored to their owners, and a reasonable time allowed for repairing the injuries they had sustained. By the act of March 3, 1825, there was allowed and paid the additional sum of $10,680.33 to John S. Stiles, the legal representative of George Stiles, deceased, for the detention of the ship *Fabius*, brig *Aid*, and schooner *Ann*, agreeably to the provisions of the aforesaid act of the 26th of April, 1822. The whole amount which has been paid to the petitioners by the United States, under the above recited acts of Congress, for detention and damages, amounts to $66,232.65.
>
> Those vessels were raised by the Quartermaster General, under an order from the Secretary of War, for which the United States have paid $38,154.21. None of this last sum, however, accrued to the benefit of the heirs of George Stiles.
>
> The petitioners, believing that they have not received a just indemnity and full satisfaction for their vessels, ask further remuneration from Congress. The petitioners claim the full value of the vessels at the time they were taken, where a total loss accrued, in consequence of their being sunk—twelve and a half percent on the value of those that were refitted, for deterioration and hidden injury—an additional allowance for specific damages—and demurrage from the 10th of September, 1814, the time they were taken by the United States, until the 17th of February, 1815, the date of the peace between this country and Great Britain.
>
> The committee have carefully examined the documents and evidence in support of the claim of the petitioners, and after much labor and difficulty, have come to the conclusion that it would be proper and just to allow them the value of such of their vessels, at the time they were taken, as were totally lost in consequence of their being sunk, deducting therefrom the amount of moneys they have received for detention and damages, and the price for which the wrecks may have sold.
>
> The committee are also of opinion that the owners of the remaining 12 vessels, which were refitted, are entitled to a reasonable allowance for deterioration, or hidden injury. The following extract from the Secretary of the Navy's report, before referred to, will show the nature of the injury, and the amount of damages sustained: "The vessels were strained and weakened in such a way, that, although they might be repaired, they could not be rendered so strong, safe, and lasting as before they were sunk, and could not be insured on as favorable terms. Much evidence is presented on this point, and the opinion of skillful men, showing a deterioration of twelve and a half percent."
>
> The committee are of opinion that the payment of that sum to the petitioners would be right and reasonable.
>
> The committee are also of opinion that no allowance in the nature of demurrage ought to be made for the detention of the vessels from the 10th of September, 1814, until the 17th of February, 1815. The history of the times, as well as other more direct evidence, goes to show that it was almost impossible to employ them to any advantage or profit, the British during that time having command of the Chesapeake and closely investing the city of Baltimore itself.
>
> The Secretary of the Navy in his report presents the statement of three intelligent merchants, which shows that during this time there were "partial shipments, at a very high freight, say from $8 to $10 per barrel of flour to the West Indies; but it is impossible to designate among the sunken vessels any that would have been employed at that time."
>
> Upon a review of the case, the committee

are of opinion that notwithstanding there may be something like an equitable claim under the two last items, which has been rejected, yet, taking all the circumstances of the case into consideration, they believe that full and ample justice will be done to the petitioners by the payment of the value of the vessels which were totally lost, deducting what has been heretofore paid for detention and damage, and the prices for which the wrecks may have been sold; and by the payment of twelve and a half percent for deterioration on the value of those vessels that were refitted.

The committee therefore report a bill for their relief.

George Stiles was paid $10,680.33 on March 3, 1825. In 1826, $9,501.50 was paid for damages, and $22,059.92 for demurrage under the act of April 26, 1822. A balance of $31,526.38 was then left. The evidence was submitted by all the owners to the House and Senate Committees of Claims. None of the claims for additional money were approved.

## Vessels Requisitioned and Final Status

*Adriana*, ship, Samuel Smith and James A. Buchanan, owners. Raised and refitted. John Connyngham testified in 1823 he knew the ship and believed it was worth $20,000. The owners were paid $300 for damages, and $1,458.76 for demurrage. The ship was repaired for around $3,000.

*Aid*, brig, George Stiles, owner. Refitted, claim litigated as stated.

*Ann*, schooner, George Stiles, owner. Refitted, claim litigated as stated.

*Ann*, brig, Thomas and Samuel Hollingsworth owners. Raised and refitted. Repairs were reimbursed at $155 and demurrage $879.77. After the vessel was raised, it was sold at public auction to Samuel Grace, master ship carpenter, for $45. Another master ship carpenter, Joseph Benson, said the sale price was $150. Grace said he spent about $1,600 to convert the brig to a schooner, but he offered no value.

*Betsey*, brig, Samuel Sterrett, agent for the owners. Total Constructive Loss. Appraised at $1,350; $150 paid for damages, and $972.70 for demurrage, and sales of goods, $281. Filed a claim for $93.30.

*Blanche*, brig, Levi Claggett owner. Raised and refitted. Eli Claggett stated on November 26, 1823, that Levi purchased the brig for $2,500 in June, 1814, and spent $1,000 to $2,000 on repairs. Levi Claggett was mortally wounded by a bomb during the attack on Fort McHenry, and Eli was the administrator of his estate. The vessel was raised, and some repairs were done and then "sold her on account of the estate for $3,150." The estate was paid $547 for damages and $885 for demurrage. No further money was awarded.

*Chesapeake*, ship, John Donnell owner. Raised and refitted. Damages were $640 and demurrage $4,841.22. A further claim for a value of $30,000 when taken, based on values given by Jacob Adams, a merchant at Baltimore, and shipmasters John Grosh and John Conayngham, who "knew the ship long before she was sunk." When raised and repaired in 1815, they offered a value of $20,000. Discrepancies were found in documents produced on January 29, 1821.

*Columbia*, schooner, Timothy Baker, of Barnstable, Cape Cod, owner. Raised and refitted. Baker was paid $140 for repairs, and $442.85 for demurrage. On September 6, 1823, Nathan Tyson stated, "the repairs, or the greater part of them, were made indispensably necessary from the great injury the schooner had sustained from being sunk." On January 5, 1824, Benjamin Clap, a Baltimore merchant, stated the vessel was consigned to his house in 1814 and was worth about $1,800, and the cost of repairs was $2,299.13, much more than the vessel was worth to begin with.

*Eliza*, brig, Thomas Chase, of Annapolis, owner. Total Constructive Loss. Capt. William Massicot, of Baltimore, valued the ship at $4,000. Chase was paid $529 for damages, $1,376.05 for demurrage, and realized $1,750 from salvage "sales of wreck." On January 29, 1821, the *Eliza* was valued at $3,000.

*Enterprise*, schooner. Owners J. Valentine, Luther Bixley, and Simpson Clark, of Boston, consigned the vessel to Vose & Worthington for sale, but it was taken prior to sale. Total Constructive Loss. Raised in 1815 and valued at $415 as is, which was paid, along with $495.11 for demurrage. The rigging, anchors, etc., were sold by James Brundige, Vose & Co., of Baltimore, in 1815 for $209 cash.

*Fabius*, ship, George Stiles, owner. Refitted, claim litigated as stated.

*Father and Son*, brig, John Craig and Edward Wynn owners. Wynn sold his one-half interest to Craig for $1,250 prior to 1813. Total Constructive Loss. Craig was paid $250 for damages, $250 for demurrage, and received $200 for sails, etc. He claimed another $669.21 for detention, "of a vessel not to be regarded as his own property and condemned in 1815 as not worthy of repair" and was paid that amount. He filed another claim for $1,380.79.

*George*, brig, William Patterson & Sons owners. Total Constructive Loss. Henry Worthington, a Sailing Master, stated on September 11, 1823, that he knew the *George* prior to 1810, and in January, 1811, signed on for several voyages. In May, 1812, they arrived in Baltimore from Cadiz, which concluded the last trip. He believed the value was $6,000 at that time. The owners subsequently abandoned the vessel as "unworthy of repair, and became a wreck." Patterson received $247 for damages, $1,602.94 for demurrage, and $2,000 for salvage. On January 29, 1821, Patterson gave a value of $10,000. Archibald Kerr said $8,000 to $10,000.

*India Packet*, ship, Levi Hollingsworth owner. Total Constructive Loss. Purchased in April, 1812, for $5,000; repaired from June 15, 1813, to May 31, 1816, at a cost of $7,873.30 and restored to Hollingsworth on May 16, 1815. Sales of salvaged items from the wreck totaled $1,142. Hollingsworth was paid $1,553 in 1816 and $2,890.73 in 1822.

*Mars*, ship, Henry Payson & Co. owner. Henry P. Sumner, a partner in the ship broker firm, stated that Obed Mitchell & Sons, of Nantucket, consigned the ship to them for sale in 1812, "provided the sum of $4,000 could be obtained," but prior a sale it was sunk. Total Constructive Loss. Payson was paid $649.50 for damages, $1,904 for demurrage, and $915.25 for sales.

*Nancy*, ship, Robert Barry owner of one-half purchased from Washington Hall in October, 1811, for $6,015.47, but only $4,500 was given. The ship was insured for $10,700 on April 20, 1812. Total Constructive Loss. Restored to owner on August 10, 1815, which Barry denied was ever done, and 85 days were allowed for repairs. He was paid $1,000 for damages, $3,846.15 for demurrage, $596.55 for "materials sold" for a total of $5,242.70. For some reason the ship was not allowed by wharfingers at their piers. Barry was allowed to moor the ship at the Sugar House wharf near Harris's Creek but it came loose and drifted inside the Lazaretto and stuck in the mud. He filed a claim for $10,000, which was denied on the grounds he could have prevented the unmooring.

*Packet*, schooner, Thomas and Samuel Hollingsworth owners. Surveyed and found "rotten and sunk." Total Constructive Loss. The owners were paid $200 for damages, although property of the United States, $537.40 for demurrage, and they realized $231.20 in salvage sales. The owners claimed the vessel was worth $1,500 when taken, leaving a balance of $531.40.

*Rosanna*, sloop, Dr. Thornton and others of Washington City owners. Total Constructive Loss. Paid $200 for damages, $700.53 for demurrage, and $262 in salvage sales. The sloop was moored at Joseph Benson's wharf when taken and he believed it was worth $1,500 when taken. Nathan Warren said $2,400, and John Miniton said $2,500. Commodore Tingey gave his opinion to Thornton as $2,600 after repairs.

*Sally*, brig, James H. Causten owner. Raised and refitted. Richard Walters sold the Sally to Causten on June 4, 1814, to Causten, who commenced repairs and Walters then thought the brig was worth $5,000. Neither one stated the sale price. Causten stated the *Sally* was in good condition when sunk; irreparable damage totaling $1,000 was done, and repairs after raising were $3,589.03 with $5.00 a day demurrage totaled $6,059.03, and the government owed him $5,384.03. In May, 1816, the brig was sold by Josep Cromwell, Causten's agent at San Salvador, for $7,133, which included $1,000 worth of salt loaded at the Cape de Verd Islands. On January 29, 1821, Causten valued the brig at $4,600. He later claimed a value of $8,000, "but some of the items constituting this amount had no imaginable connection with the cost of the repairs or the worth of the vessel." He claimed wharfage, the cost of depositions, travel, and custom house fees, etc. The cost of repairs in 1814 were $1,327.59; 1815, $4,215; and 1816, $949.50.

*Scioto*, ship, Smith & Buchanan owners. Raised and refitted. The owners were paid $755 for damages and $1, 804.76 for demurrage. On September 19, 1823, master ship carpenter Stephen Benilliant testified he knew the ship for several years and did the repairs after being raised, for which he charged $451.05. No further money was awarded.

*Scudder*, schooner, Eli Claggett owner. Declared a Total Constructive Loss in 1815 with damages assessed at $2,750, which the owner was paid. The government became the legal owner of the vessel, but Claggett was paid $1,204 for demurrage in 1822, and he collected $500 for sales from the wreck. Filed a claim for $2,752.05.

*Swallow*, brig, Peter Rescaneire or John Hanna and others owners. Raised and refitted. They received $715 for damages and $1,003.95 for demurrage. In February, 1815, Matthew Pascal bought the vessel at public auction for $6,200, "with all her claims on the United States for damages; that the vessel was much injured by sinking and raising, being broken in the hull, copper, bottom, and otherwise, and her cables, camboose, and other articles on board were destroyed." The repairs cost $1,400. On October 14, 1817, the brig was insured for $6,500 by the Chesapeake Insurance Co. On January 29, 1821, the owners estimated the value at $3,700 when taken. No further allowance was made.

*Telegraph*, schooner, James Orr, owner. The schooner was apparently omitted in the original report of the sunken vessels or was simply damaged and not actually sunk. Orr's petition was presented on January 8, 1817, and he was paid $250 in 1819 by the Secretary of War for, "the value of a certain schooner called the *Telegraph*, taken and sunk for the defense of the harbor of Baltimore, in the year 1814."

*Temperance*, ship, Charles F. Kalkman owner. Raised and refitted. Received $800 in damages and $2,217 for demurrage. Elie and John Despeaux testified the ship was in good condition when taken and they did $3,205.09 worth of repair work, "but these witnesses make no discrimination between the repairs which were, and those which were not rendered necessary by the sinking of the vessel." No money was awarded.

*Thomas Wilson*, ship, John Donnell owner. Declared a Total Constructive Loss but raised on July, 10, 1815, and sold two years later for $2,000 to Jacob Adams, who spent $10,000 on restoration then sent the ship to sea. For his claim Donnell valued his ship at $42,000. He was allowed $11,669.65 after surveys of $17,000, $20,000, and $25,000. The ship was lost at Java on its fourth voyage.

## *Black Point*

### William Jett

On October 4, 1814, 3,000 British troops landed at Black Point and Ragged Point on the Coan River in Northumberland County. From there they proceeded to Heathsville. As reported by the Committee of Claims on April 11, 1834:

> The petitioner asks Congress to pay him the amount contained in the following account, to wit:
>
> 8 barrels of whiskey, say 264 gallons at 6*s*. per gallon, $264; 2 barrels of brandy, say 66 gallons at 9*s*. per gallon, $99; groceries and dry goods, $300; 4 feather beds at $30 each, $120; books, $100; and clothing, $100. Total $983.
>
> He says he was a citizen of Northumberland County, in the State of Virginia during the late war, and commanded a company of riflemen in the service of the 37th Virginia Regiment of Militia, and was commanded by the colonel of the regiment to repel, if possible, the landing of the enemy in the county. He was compelled, after giving them a fire, to retreat. The enemy having effected a landing, proceeded on their march to the court-house, and entered a store then in the occupation of the petitioner, a part of which was used as a barracks, and wantonly destroyed the property contained in the account. He proves the value of the property by his brother, Joseph H. Jett, who was his clerk.
>
> Samuel Downing testifies he was the oldest captain in the regiment and in the absence of Col. Thomas Downing, his brother, he commanded the regiment. All the regiment had been dismissed except about 90 men. He states he gave orders to Capt. Jett to march to Black Point, a distance of about a mile from the court-house to prevent, if possible, the landing of the enemy. This, however, they were unable to effect, and after giving them a fire, the detachment had to retreat. The enemy marched to the court-house and did considerable damage to public and to private property.

He says Capt. Jett owned and kept a store at the court-house, and that the counting room of the storehouse was occupied as barracks for the men composing the company.

Randall R. Kirks testifies he was a member of Capt. Jett's company and went to prevent the enemy from advancing; that having fired on the enemy at Black Point they were obliged to retreat and fired on the enemy again at the court-house. The enemy marched to the court-house, broke open the store of the petitioner, and took or destroyed a large quantity of goods and clothes of the petitioner. Several beds were ripped open and destroyed, and he says the store and counting room were used as barracks and as a place of deposit and that the company had no other place designated as barracks.

If the claim had been for the destruction of the store, to prove it was occupied as barracks, the committee would have required the evidence of the officer thus converting the store to the use of the United States to be produced.

As this company was only temporarily called out or remained in service, the other part of the regiment having been dismissed, the committee would have been required evidence in explanation of what the witnesses understood by the occupation of the store as barracks; whether they slept there, or cooked and dressed provisions there, &c.; but admitting the store to have been occupied as barracks, and the goods to have been destroyed as stated, still the United States are not bound to pay for such loss by any principle heretofore established.

The petitioner is not entitled to relief.

## *Tracey's Landing*

The 1 mile by 3½ mile Tilghman Island lies 120 miles up Chesapeake Bay. About 11 miles to the west across the Bay is Herring Bay, into which Herring Creek flows. Across the creek to the south is Town Point, about 17 miles north of St. Leonard. About half a mile up Herring Creek is Tracey's Landing in Anne Arundel County, Maryland, where a tobacco warehouse was located and the leaf was graded, classified, and weighed for shipment. James Tongue owned the land.

In October 1814, around 1,000 British troops went ashore on Tilghman Island and set up camp. They apparently were in search of provisions, water, and stores, and made forays across the Bay to Town Point.

Comm. Barney stored ammunition at Tracey's Landing. The claim of James Tongue for a tobacco storage and inspection warehouse at Tracey's Landing; John Scrivener for a house at Town Point; and William Hodson for a house, windmill, and out buildings at Town Point were noted. Tongue was paid $1,837.78; Scrivener, $3,840; and the legal representatives of Hodson, $9,646.17 in 1842.

It was noted that all military occupancy was by militia not in the service of the United States. Sgt. Walter Wyvill of Capt. Thomas T. Simmons' company of the 2nd Regiment of Maryland Militia, and several others, said they were ordered out by the governor of Maryland "to repel and keep off the enemy." As stated:

> The dwelling-houses of Scrivener and Hodson, at Town Point, were abandoned by the families which occupied them, and being thus vacant, were, together with their outbuildings, occupied at pleasure by the militia when there, as was also the tobacco-warehouse; and the witnesses state that the men had no tents, and that these buildings contributed to their protection and comfort when upon duty there, and afforded places of deposit for their arms, and the like, when they left upon their temporary absences to attend to their private concerns at home.

### John Scrivener

John Scrivener was a lieutenant in the 2nd Maryland Regiment. His petition stated:

> John Scrivener respectfully states that he held a farm at the mouth of the creek leading from the Chesapeake Bay to Tracey's landing tobacco inspection warehouse, which is about half a mile from the mouth of the creek to Tracey's landing warehouse. And as the mouth of this creek was very narrow, about 50 yards wide, a piece of cannon was placed

at the mouth of Tracey's landing creek for the protection of the tobacco warehouse, and the tobacco therein, and for the protection of the neighborhood generally.

There were two dwelling-houses, out-houses, and a wind-mill, also at the mouth of the creek. One of the dwelling-houses and some of the out-houses belonged to your petitioner, and the other houses and wind-mill belonged to William Hodson, now deceased.

Your petitioner states that the militia rendezvoused at the mouth of the creek, and these houses afforded considerable convenience to the militia while acting here on duty. On the day the British took possession of Tracey's landing tobacco inspection warehouse, your petitioner, being a commissioned officer in the company of militia commanded by Captain Thomas Simmons, now dead, he with some other of the militia made an attack on the British barges as they were passing at the mouth or narrows of the creek, where it empties into the Chesapeake Bay, with the piece of cannon. The fire was returned by a good many pieces of cannon from the British barges, which being too numerous and powerful for the militia, we were compelled to retreat.

The British landed, spiked the cannon, gave many hearty cheers, took possession of all the houses at the mouth of the creek, burnt them down, together with a quantity of corn in the corn-house on his farm, and also burnt some hogsheads of tobacco belonging to him in Tracey's landing warehouse.

Your petitioner verily believes that the property was destroyed on account of the militia making an attack on the British barges, and the houses here located being used by the militia while rendezvousing at the mouth of the Tracey's landing creek.

Your petitioner prays your honorable body will make such remuneration for the property belonging to him, which was burnt by the British during the late war as is just and right; and your petitioner in duty bound will ever pray.

John's claim was rejected on June 21, 1836, since, "the petitioner's houses were not occupied for military purposes and destroyed in consequence of such occupation."

Similar claims were filed by James Tongue, John S. Skinner, and William Hodson. As reported by the Committee of Claims on July 6, 1838:

The three cases being similar in their character and sustained by the same evidence, the committee have thought it best to consider them together in one report.

These cases were before the committee at the second session of the last Congress, but not being then sustained by sufficient evidence, they were suffered to lie in order to enable the claimants to adduce additional evidence.

As now presented by the evidence they stand as follows: James Tongue claims the value of a tobacco ware-house destroyed by the British at Tracey's landing. Each of the other claimants claims the value of a dwelling-house destroyed in like manner at Town Point.

It may be necessary to add that the commander of the British forces justified the destruction of the buildings to Mr. John S. Skinner on the ground of their being occupied by the American troops.

The reason of the claimants not having sooner applied for relief, as assigned by themselves, was that one Patterson, whose property was destroyed under similar circumstances, applied to Congress for relief soon after the war and his petition was rejected. He applied again, a few years since, and obtained relief.

As to the value of the property destroyed, it is established by the appraisement under oath of John Collinson, William J.W. Compton, and Thomas C. Denny, that the ware-house was worth $1,837.78. It is further established by James Tongue, Samuel Gover, and John Collinson that the buildings belonging to William Hodson, deceased, were worth $3,968.39.

Scrivener states that the valuation of his property is among the original papers, but such valuation is not to be found, and there is no evidence to show the value of his buildings destroyed. While the committee believe him entitled to relief to the amount of that valuation, they cannot report a bill in his favor for want of evidence. Therefore, they leave his claim, without prejudice, to be hereafter reported upon.

They now report a bill for the relief of James Tongue and the representatives of William Hodson.

According to the Committee of Claims a claim submitted by Matilda Drury was submitted with James Tongue's petition. The Third Auditor rejected it for lack of evidence, but the claim never got to the House for deliberation, and on February 22, 1837, stated "she should produce the testimony required by Mr. Hagner to entitle her to relief."

She said her brother, Capt. William S. Tillard, who died shortly after the war, had for 22,386 lbs. of crop tobacco at $16 per 100 lbs. ($3,569.82), and 7,948 lbs. of second tobacco at $14 per 100 lbs. ($1,112.27) in the tobacco inspection warehouse.

James Tongue stated he was a near neighbor to William Tillard, and "he was a good tobacco maker, and possessed of a soil adapted to the growth of tobacco of a superior quality, such as sold soon after the late war from $13 to $17 per 100 pounds."

It wasn't stated what relation Matilda had to Capt. Tillard, other than being his sister, but apparently she was recognized as his legal heir.

The 23×45-foot Tobacco House No. 2 is on the National Register of Historic Places.

## William T. Swann

Frances Swann, of Washington, D.C., and the widow of William T. Swann, filed a claim for five hogsheads of tobacco that was "partly destroyed, and partly taken away by the enemy, at various public warehouses on the Patuxent River in consequence of the military occupation of the warehouses by the troops of the United States, a part of the tobacco being at Magruder's warehouse and the other part at Nottingham warehouse."

The claim was rejected on February 25, 1845, as it "appears to be unsupported by any testimony of a nature to constitute a legal demand upon the Treasury."

## *The Tobacco Warehouses*

As the British pressed inland in 1814, they encountered resistance from militia posted at warehouses full of tobacco. Two of the major locations were Magruder's, 9½ miles northeast of Benedict in Prince George's County, and Nottingham 14 miles north of Benedict in Charles County, Maryland.

Forays were made inland in June 1814, when the British were looking unsuccessfully for Comm. Barney and they were met by militia.

In 1661, Alexander Magruder built a warehouse and landing to export tobacco. The original location of the warehouse and landing is unknown, but Magruder's Ferry Rd. still exists, and subsequent warehouse sites have apparently been identified.

Nothing is left of the original village of Nottingham, other than Nottingham Rd., in Upper Marlboro. Other warehouses were located at Hunting Creek, Lower Marlborough, Piscataway, Bladensburg, Georgetown, Cedar Point, Blue Plains, Broad Creek, Pile's warehouse, and Chaptico.

Comm. Barney requested militia to be stationed at Nottingham.

Word of the munitions at Tracey's Landing got to the British and in October 1814, around 275 British troops from Tilghman Island crossed over to Town Point on the 27th. Five militia manning a cannon were quickly routed, and the troops proceeded up Herring Creek to Tracey's Landing.

The Committee of claims stated:

> During the spring of 1814, Commodore Barney, commanding the American flotilla in the Chesapeake, in order to lighten his vessel, deposited a considerable quantity of munitions of war in the tobacco ware-house at Tracey's landing belonging to James Tongue, and left a detachment of men to guard the same. The stores and munitions of war were gradually removed over land to the Patuxent for the use of the flotilla—probably a small

remnant remained at the time of the destruction of the ware-house.

In October, 1814, the British fleet, in considerable force under Admiral Sir John Warren, appeared in the Chesapeake, in the neighborhood of Town Point and Tracey's landing. A detachment of militia were ordered to take post at those two points for the defense of the ware-house, where a large quantity of tobacco was in store, and of the neighboring country. This detachment occupied the ware-house and the dwelling and out-houses of John Scrivener and William Hodson at Town Point for barracks.

The position of Town Point was a stronger one, and well calculated to effect the object for which it was occupied, the creek at its mouth being but about 50 yards wide. The governor of Maryland sent a cannon to the detachment there for the purpose of aiding its defense.

The British boats, at length, entered the mouth of the creek and were immediately fired upon by the detachment, the cannon being fired from between the houses of Schrivener and Hodson, which were about 60 yards apart. Being much superior in ordnance and numbers, they succeeded in dislodging the American militia from their position. They then proceeded up the creek to the ware-house of Tongue at Tracey's landing, where the portion of the detachment attempted to defend themselves by making a bulwark of the hogsheads of tobacco, but they were unsuccessful and were compelled to evacuate their position. The British troops being in possession of the two posts considered themselves justifiable under the usages of war in destroying the ware-house and the two dwelling-houses, &c. occupied by the American troops as barracks, which they accordingly did, scrupulously abstaining from, and studiously avoiding, injury to any other property.

Tobacco at that time was generally divided into two qualities called crop or first quality, and seconds or second quality, and it was the general custom, when a whole crop was sold together, to rate the crop at $2.00 per 100 lbs. "higher than seconds."

A hogshead was a barrel containing 100 to 140 gallons. Loaded with tobacco, the weight varied between 600 and 1,800 pounds depending on the leaf. Standard measures used in shipping tobacco into the 1940s were based on leaf from Kentucky, Virginia, and South America.

It was estimated the British carried off or destroyed 3,000 to 4,000 hogsheads. The product had great value in Europe.

## *Tappahannock*

### Austin Brockenborough

Dr. Austin Brockenborough's petition, dated November 24, 1815:

Austin Brokenborough, of Tappahannock, in the county of Essex, Virginia, respectfully represents that on the morning of the 1st of December, 1814, whilst the enemy were ascending the river and approaching the town of Tappahannock, the place of his residence, and whilst he was busily engaged in removing his family, furniture, and effects to a place of safety, he was deprived by a press-master of the only means he then possessed, or could at this time command. This officer, without the knowledge of your petitioner, seized from a servant two horses, the only two he then had, whilst they were employed with a wagon in removing his goods and effects, alleging, as your petitioner is informed, that the public service required them.

So soon as your petitioner was appraised of the fact, he made a representation of his situation to the highly respectable commandant of the regiment, who, at first, promised to surrender the horses, but afterwards declined so doing, saying that the safety of the artillery and the protection of the neighborhood depended upon the service of the horses. The consequence was that the horses were retained in the public service and your petitioner's furniture and effects left to the mercy of the enemy, who landed shortly after and committed the most wanton waste and destruction, to the amount of not less than $1,000, exclusive of the loss sustained in consequence of being thus unable to remove valuable servants who would otherwise have been out of the touch of the allurements of the enemy.

Your petitioner has been uniformly

influenced by a proper sense of patriotism, and could give ample testimony of his readiness on that occasion, as well as on others, to make sacrifices, and endure loss and privation, in common with his fellow citizens, when the public welfare required it, but feeling that a portion of the calamities which then befell him arose from the fact that the preservation of public property, and the protection of the country, were preferred to his private rights and interest, he relies upon the justice of your body to lighten this individual pressure, which bears with peculiar weight upon him and prays that he may be reimbursed and remunerated in the sum of $1,000.

Your petitioner would further remark that the fact of the invasion of this place by the British in 1814 has now become a part of the history of the country, and the fact of the mischief and destruction committed on the property of your petitioner is acknowledged, and particularly spoken of in a work called, "The Life of a Sailor," written by a British midshipman, who was then engaged in that identical service.

In regard to the other material facts herein charged, your petitioner would beg leave to refer to the affidavits of William L. Waring, the press-master, and Colonel Archibald Ritchie, the commandant of the regiment, and Thomas Gresham and Thomas M. Henley, two highly respectable citizens.

Affidavit of Lt. Col. Archibald Ritchie, commander of the 6th Regiment, Virginia Militia, dated November 27, 1815:

I do hereby certify that when the enemy was ascending the river Rappahannock, I arrived in the town of Tappahannock about dusk on the evening of the 30th of November last. When I got to town, I found not more than 15 persons in all, and not one-half of that number subject to military duty, and heard from good authority that the enemy was under sail not more than 5 miles below, and had every reason to expect that the town would be attacked and carried in the course of the night. As the people of the town had employed what few horses belonged to the place in removing their effects, it was impossible to procure horses there to remove the pieces of artillery and a quantity of ammunition then in the place. I directed an officer to go into the country and to impress as many horses as would remove the cannon, &c. from the town for that night, intending, if the militia would collect in a justifiable force in the course of the night, or before the enemy did come up, to bring some of that cannon back in the morning and attempt the defense of the place.

Early in the morning I ordered an officer to go out and impress as many horses as would bring in one or two pieces of artillery and a sufficiency of ammunition, &c. The first horses the officers met were two belonging to Dr. Austin Brockenborough, of Tappahannock, returning to town to remove the Doctor's effects. Those horses the officer impressed and with them brought one piece of artillery to town. The Doctor represented his situation to me and solicited a discharge of his horses. This I considered to do if others could be procured, for I began to despair of being able to defend the place as but few of the militia had come in during the night and morning and the enemy was not more than 3 miles below town, exhibiting a large force, from the numerous vessels composing the squadron. Other horses could not be procured and I was obliged to retain the Doctor's to preserve the piece and ammunition, &c., which had been brought into town.

I have no hesitation in saying that the Doctor sustained considerable loss in being prevented from removing many articles of value by the impressment of his horses, the value of which he can better appreciate and determine than any other person. Doctor Brockenborough is a gentleman of much standing and character here, and great faith is due to whatever he may say or set forth.

In the successful prosecution and termination of the war, and in the prosperity and honor of the country, Doctor Brockenborough felt, and continues to feel, as lively an interest as any citizen.

The doctor's claim was rejected by the Committee of Claims on April 4, 1840, as being personal property wantonly destroyed by an enemy.

## Lawrence Muse and William Gordon

Muse claimed one warehouse 24 by 60 feet, three stories high, $6,000; sundry articles including beef and pork, $320. As reported by the Committee of Claims on February 23, 1818:

> The former claims $6,320, the alleged value of a tobacco warehouse and sundry articles contained therein, situate in Tappahannock, in Virginia, and burned by the enemy on the 2nd of December, 1814, on account of its being used by the United States as a place of military deposit, and the latter claims compensation for 83,567 lbs. of tobacco destroyed in the warehouse.
>
> The only evidence of a pretended military occupation of the warehouse is to be found in the affidavit of Buller Cocke, a Navy agent of the United States, and Robert Weir. The former states that about the 8th of August, 1814, he was engaged, by order of the Secretary of the Navy, in the transportation of a quantity of provisions from Washington, for the use of the Army, then stationed at Norfolk, and that he found it necessary to engage Lawrence Muse to receive the same at Tappahannock and superintend their transportation to Washington, which, he alleges, was done with all the attention and dispatch that the occasion required.
>
> The latter, Robert Weir, states that in the month of August or September, 1814, Buller Cocke did engage the claimant to receive the provisions and other naval stores, "which were at different times sent by Cocke and were received by Lawrence Muse in his warehouse."
>
> About the 1st of December following, the enemy ascended the Rappahannock River, took possession of the town of Tappahannock and set fire to his warehouse, which was entirely consumed, together with sundry valuable articles therein.
>
> It is in proof that the warehouse was destroyed on the 2nd day of December, 1814, but there is no evidence of there having been any public property in or near the warehouse subsequent to the months of August or September of the same year. The committee therefore submit that the claims of Lawrence Muse and William Gordon ought not to be allowed.

The claim was again rejected on February 15, 1822.

## Joseph Janney

Janney filed a claim for $7,655.75. As reported on December 8, 1818, by Richard Bland Lee, Commissioner of Claims:

> Archibald Ritchie, Lt. Col., commandant of the 6th Regiment of Virginia Militia, received information on the 30th November, 1814, that the enemy were ascending the river Rappahannock, doubtless with a view to seize upon and plunder the town of Tappahannock. That he, the same evening, repaired to Tappahannock and soon after his arrival directed Major Samuel Muse to issue an order to Joseph Janney, then commandant of a company of militia, to assemble his company and to station it at a place called Bowlers, on the Rappahannock, about 10 miles lower down the river than the town—that the claimant in obedience to the order, did promptly assemble his company to watch the movements of the enemy; to protect the farms in the neighborhood from pillage by the marauding parties of the enemy, and to prevent the negroes from seizing the boats on the river and going off to the enemy.
>
> The claimant remained with his command at Bowlers until the 4th December, the day on which the enemy descended the river and until he was driven from his position by superior numbers of the enemy.
>
> The enemy took possession of the place called Bowlers, in the afternoon of the 4th—that all the houses at that place were the property of and occupied by the claimant—that the claimant's company was barracked in some of the houses—and that all, or the greater and most valuable of the houses were burned by the enemy on the evening of 4th December, 1814.
>
> John Saddler states that he was ensign in the claimant's company and stationed at Bowlers at the time the British came—that the company occupied the houses belonging to the claimant. That he saw an order from Major Samuel Muse, who acted under the authority of Col. Ritchie, directing the claimant to assemble his company and remain at Bowlers until further orders, with a view to partly watch the movements of the enemy—that the claimant with his company did assemble and remain at Bowlers till Sunday the 4th December, 1814, when they were driven from the ground by superior force of

the enemy, except for a small space of time; when the claimant had started for Tappahannock, but in meeting Captain Layton, who delivered orders from Col. Ritchie to remain at Bowlers, he immediately returned with his company.

Charles G. Layton states that he knows the houses of the claimant were occupied by a company of militia under the order of the colonel commandant of Essex County; that when he waited on the colonel to get a flag to go down with his vessel in which the British had taken, the colonel told him to tell the claimant to remain at Bowlers until further orders; that on his return to Bowlers he met the claimant and his company going to Tappahannock where the colonel was, and that as soon as he delivered the orders from Colonel Ritchie, the claimant returned to Bowlers with his company, and there remained till driven from his ground by superior force of the British when they immediately put fire to the buildings.

Francis Smith states that he was attached to the claimant's company and joined it about 1st December, 1814, at the place called Bowlers; that during the stay of the company there they had the use of the claimant's houses for their accommodation, viz. the dwelling house, storehouse, and cabins, and some of the men slept in one of the granaries, in all which they slept kept their arms, ammunition, and baggage.

He understood they were stationed at Bowlers in consequence of orders from the colonel commandant and thinks he saw an order to that effect. On Sunday evening, the 4th December, they were compelled by superior force to retreat and abandon their post, that the enemy immediately took possession, and burnt and destroyed whatever they found and that he believed the houses would not have been burnt if they had not been occupied by the company.

Richard Barnes stated that in the month of December, 1814, a few days after the British expedition of light vessels had descended the river Rappahannock, he rode to Westmoreland court-house on private business; that while he was at the court-house, he was in company with Lieutenant Anson of the British navy, who, in the course of conversation on the conduct then pursued by the enemy, openly advocated all the acts and outrages committed by his countrymen, and appeared particularly to justify the burning of some of our villages and dwellings, as measures of retaliation for alleged outrages said to have been committed by our forces on the Canada frontier, and that on an inquiry from him as to their motive for burning the claimant's houses, Lieutenant Anson replied that the claimant had made barracks of his house or houses.

William Oliver and James Cauthorne, master workmen and skilled in the art of building houses, state that the dwelling house, one storehouse, and two granaries were worth $4,300 and that the walls and other parts remaining of those houses are worth $300.

Thomas Collins, Jr., states that he was the principal clerk of the claimant, that he was well acquainted with all the property in the store, dwelling, and ware houses, that at the time of their destruction he knew there were in them 80 barrels of corn, 140 bushels of beans, 30 bushels of peas, 170 bushels of wheat, a pair of scales, 4 half bushel measures, 100 bushels of salt, a parcel of stone ware, 1 barrel of rectified whiskey, 1 barrel of linseed oil, some common whiskey, some apple brandy, several articles in the store, and many article of furniture in the dwelling house, all of which were destroyed or taken off by the British and that from a calculation he believes the articles were worth $1,310.25.

It is satisfactorily proved that the dwelling house, storehouse, cabins, and one of the granaries were occupied as barracks. It does not appear that another granary was actually occupied as barracks, but being it is presumed, regarded by the enemy, who does not appear to have made nice distinctions, as appurtenant to the same military post, it was also burnt with other buildings.

In the estimate of damages, this granary is comprehended with the other buildings, which after deducting the value of the ruins, are stated to have been all worth $4,000. The estimate by the witnesses of furniture and other goods in the houses amounts to $1,340.25. [$5,340.25]

The claimant, however, estimates his loss in personal property only at $1,155.75, which would reduce the aggregate loss to $5,155.75.

The claimant, though of foreign birth, is represented to have been a strenuous, brave, and faithful officer during the late war, and to have merited the particular notice of Commodore Porter, at the White House.

The Committee of Claims stated on December 8, 1818:

> The evidence reported to Congress at the last session, by the late Commissioner of Claims embraces a pretty full, and it is believed, correct review of the facts and circumstances attending this case. The committee beg this to be considered as comprehended in their report, and to refer to it the attention of the House.
>
> It does not appear to the committee that the petitioner has any just or legal demand against the United States.

Janney's claim for $7,655.75 was taken up again and on January 2, 1822, it was rejected again in the Senate.

As stated by the Committee of Claims on March 3, 1851, with respect to Joseph Janney and others:

> The losses of the petitioners appear to have been very considerable, on account of military operations of the enemy during the late war with Great Britain. The petitioners, as it appears from the testimony, had large quantities of tobacco in store in the Maryland warehouses, located on the waters of the Patuxent River and the Chesapeake Bay—all of which was captured, burnt, and destroyed by the enemy.
>
> The extent to which the government has extended its legislation in remunerating losses to individuals who have sustained injury by the condition of the war, has been to indemnify where the injury resulted from its occupation and use of property. The fact is supported by unquestionable testimony that the warehouses were occupied by our troops as a shelter and protection, and the tobacco used and converted into a fortification. This was a conversion of private property into the public use, and would grow out of that state of necessity which is superior to all laws, and flows from what the civilians called the eminent domain, which belongs to all governments, and is founded on the irresistible dictate and impulse of self-preservation. Every writer, in treating of the rights of the sovereignty, says, that when a nation is at war, it has a right to avail itself of all its means.
>
> The rule laid down in the laws of Congress is that if the United States, in the prosecution of a war, occupy and use the property of a citizen for military purposes, so as to make it the legitimate object for capture and destruction, according to the rules of civilized warfare, and, if in consequence of such occupancy, the enemy be drawn upon and do capture and destroy it, the owner shall be compensated out of the public treasury.
>
> This is manifestly right, and it is no more than simple justice, under the provision of the constitution which prohibits the taking of private property for public use without just compensation. See the case of John S. Stiles, adjudicated in the 27th Congress, 2d session. He claimed indemnity for vessels sunk for the defense of the city of Baltimore in 1814. The Judiciary Committee of the Senate say that, "it is the duty of the government to make compensation for them, and the damages which their owners had sustained." Also, the act for the relief of sundry citizens of Baltimore for the sinking of vessels at the mouth of the harbor of Baltimore. Also, an act for the relief of James Orr for schooner *Telegraph*, sunk in defense.
>
> The facts established in support of these claims are similar in detail to those which were deemed sufficient in the case of James T. Sothoron, for whose relief a bill was passed at December session, 1848. In that case, Mr. Bradbury, on the part of the Committee of Claims of the Senate, recognizes the principle of indemnity, and lays down the rule that personal property should be paid for in all cases where property has been used for belligerent purposes and offensive military operations. Such being the established legislation of the country, as indicated by the foregoing cases, the committee see no reason why they should depart from the principles heretofore recognized.
>
> Upon careful examination the committee have found the following cases to be included within the precedents and principles above stated, to wit: The legal representatives of Joseph Janney; the legal representatives of General Robert Young; the legal representatives of William Morsell; and the legal representatives of Colonel Samuel Tilliard; and the cases of Christopher Neale, assignee of Jerome and Gerard Plummer, and the case of George W. Briscoe. They therefore report a bill in common for their relief.

## John McCarty

As reported by the Committee of Claims on February 19, 1836:

The petitioner asks pay for a house burnt on the 5th of December, 1814, by the British troops at Farnham, in the county of Richmond, in Virginia, which he alleges was burnt in consequence of its having been made a place of deposit for arms, provisions, and ammunition belonging to the United States, and perhaps because it was a house in which a collector's office and post office were also kept.

It appears by the depositions submitted that the 41st Regiment of Virginia Militia had been called out, in whole or in part, at different times during the late war. Their usual place of rendezvous had been Farnham, and that the cellar of the petitioner's house had been generally used as the place of deposit for whatever ammunition and other military stores were from time to time remaining on hand.

William Settle, the quartermaster of the regiment, swears that the regiment was ordered in October, 1814, to Lancaster County, and on its return the deponent deposited arms, ammunition, provisions, &c. in the house of the petitioner. He further says he saw the British set fire to the house on the 5th of December.

Capt. Foushee G. Tebbs, commanding a rifle company attached to the 41st Regiment, says that he frequently, during the war, made Farnham his place of rendezvous. Upon one or two occasions he drew, by order of his commanding officer, arms, ammunition, &c., from the house of the petitioner, and that by his orders, arms, ammunition, &c. were frequently deposited in the same place.

Farnham was made, by order of the colonel, the rendezvous of the regiment on the 5th of December, 1814, at which time and place an action occurred with the British, and the deponent swears he verily believes there were public arms, ammunition, and stores in the house at the time it was consumed, and that its destruction was in consequence thereof.

Col. Joseph Palmer was acquainted with the property and the facts, and swears he has no doubt the burning of the house was in consequence of its containing, at the time, munitions of war. He states several circumstances which support this opinion.

Lieutenant Edmund Northern, of the rifle company, corroborates the statement of deposits having been from time to time made of military stores in the house of the petitioner.

Olivia Downman states that one of the British officers informed her that McCarty's house was burnt because it contained camp kettles, ovens, whiskey, &c. munitions of war.

Mary S. Saunders states, in a conversation with a British officer, she thinks it was Captain or Lieutenant Hamilton, she was, by him, told McCarty's house was burnt because munitions of war were found in it.

This claim was rejected in 1828, principally, it is believed, on the facts disclosed in the affidavit of Dr. Horace Wellford.

Dr. Wellford went with a flag to attend professionally an American officer who had been wounded in the skirmish and taken to the enemy's camp as a prisoner. While there, the Doctor observed petitioner's house in flames, and remonstrated against the cruelty, inasmuch as the petitioner was a man deaf and dumb from his birth, industrious and respectable as a mechanic, and would lose all the little property he had been long laying up.

The British commander inquired of a Major Williams why the house was fired, who replied that there was a quantity of brandy in it, upon which the soldiers were getting intoxicated. The commander expressed much regret; said he had been given orders that no houses should be burnt, and offered to pay for the building, which the deponent did not think proper to accept. This deponent has been some years dead, but in his lifetime expressed to Col. Palmer, whose deposition has been before referred to, and to an honorable member of this House, whose statement is before the committee, his full belief that the spirits referred to by Major Williams, formed a part of the stores placed in McCarty's cellar by Settle, the quartermaster, and also his belief that McCarty's house was burnt on account of its military occupancy as a depot for stores belonging to the United States.

On the whole, the conviction made on the minds of the committee, by all the facts and circumstances before noticed, that this house was destroyed in consequence of the use which had been made of it for the benefit of the United States. this conviction is strengthened by the additional fact, that the

> British troops burnt no other building, and destroyed no other private property on a march of 7 miles into the country and on their return, through a populous part of Virginia, and passing, in all directions, buildings and property as likely as this to have attracted their attention, but for the character given it, by its being used as a place of deposit. The committee therefore recognize the claim as within the law.
>
> Of the value of the house, the estimate made by Col. Palmer, corroborated by the opinion of Lt. Northern, fortified as the testimony of these gentlemen, and indeed all the witnesses who have deposed in this case, are, by the assurance of the honorable member of this House before referred to, is satisfactory to the committee, and they report a bill for $1,000, the valuation put upon the building by the gentlemen above named.

The legal representatives of John McCarty were paid $1,000 in 1838.

## John Haile

As reported by the Committee of Claims on February 24, 1818:

> The petitioner states that in the month of December, 1814, the enemy entered the town of Tappahannock and in consequence of his house being used and occupied as a custom house, in which the public records were kept, set fire to and destroyed the same with its contents. The petitioner begs leave to further state that although the house was his own property, it was evident the enemy destroyed it in consequence of its being used as a public office, and he therefore prays Congress to grant him remuneration.
>
> The committee think that the petitioner cannot, under the law of April, 1816, or any other law with which they are acquainted, be entitled to relief. They therefore recommend that his prayer be rejected.

## Charles M. Collier

On January 7, 1824, Congress authorized $1,000 be paid to Charles M. Collier, "in full for the loss of his packet boat, the *Huntress*, captured by the enemy during the late war, while in the service of the United States."

Capt. Charles Miles Collier was from Virginia and a member of the House of Burgesses from 1819 to 1828, when he died. His petition was presented on December 7, 1821.

## The *Friendship*

Nicholas H. Bell filed a claim, as reported by the Committee of Claims on February 7, 1838:

> The petitioner states that he, with other citizens of the United States, were the owners of the schooner *Friendship*, of Vienna, in the State of Maryland. In January, 1815, she sailed from Vienna for the port of Baltimore freighted with corn and wood. On the 8th January she was captured by a British armed vessel commanded by Captain Fibb, and with her cargo was burnt and destroyed. She was of about 68 tons burden, and was worth about $1,008.
>
> The facts set forth in the petition are confirmed by the affidavit of Thomas L. Moore, taken on the 25th day of November, 1837, in which he states that he was on board the schooner *Friendship* at the time of her capture by the British.
>
> The committee entertain no doubt of the truth of the allegations made by the petitioner, and they are equally clear that the case does not entitle the petitioner to the relief prayed for. The injury is one incident to a state of war, and is one of the evils which the citizens of a belligerent nation are destined to suffer, and presents one of the considerations which should be deliberately weighed by those into whose hands the destiny of nations is confided, before resort is had to this last appeal of nations by which the lives and property of the citizens are periled, and by which the accumulated avails of individual frugality, industry, and enterprise are so often sacrificed and destroyed.
>
> The vessel, when she was captured and destroyed, was engaged in a commerce which was no doubt commendable, and promised a reasonable reward for the hazards which the owners were encountering, owing to the perilous conditions of our coasting trade and the

activity and vigilance with it was watched and regarded by the enemy. His vessels of war were hovering around our coasts for the purpose of visiting upon our citizens and our country the evils incident to the existing state of things. For aught that appears, the government were deriving no benefit from the services in which this vessel was engaged. She was in no sense in the service of the United States, and to consider the government standing in the light of an insurer to the citizens for all the property they may have had afloat at this inauspicious period, would be changing the risk from such as were interested, and who ought to encounter it, to those who had none.

The capture and destruction of this vessel having taken place after the treaty of peace was signed at Ghent by the plenipotentiaries of the two governments, but before the ratification thereof, may hereafter present a question worthy of consideration, and upon this point the committee intend to express no opinion, but it cannot now be regarded as a sufficient reason for disregarding all rules previously established in settling claims arising from the loss of the property of our citizens captured or destroyed by the enemy during the late war with Great Britain.

No claim of the kind now presented has ever been yielded to by the government, and a just regard to public policy and the interests of the United States it is believed require that the prayer of the petitioner should be rejected.

# Missouri

## *Missouri Claims*

### Joseph Hertich

As reported by the Committee of Claims on January 20, 1835:

The petitioner states that himself and Joseph Perkins were joint owners of a keel-boat. Sometime in the year 1812 they sent the boat under the care of an agent from Ste. Geneviéve, in Missouri, to Louisville, in Kentucky, for the purpose of returning with a load for them, but that while there the boat was pressed into the service of the United States for the purpose of transporting public stores to Vincennes, in Indiana.

The boat was loaded with public stores and some articles belonging to the petitioner, the whole being placed under the care of their agent having charge of the boat. The agent, without their authority, having made an agreement with the agent of the government for conducting or piloting the boat, not in the capacity of agent of the petitioner, but on his own account. A part of the understanding being that the private property should be taken out, and other public property put in the boat, should it be necessary.

The petitioner also states that in prosecuting the voyage to Vincennes, the boat was wrecked and lost. Some of his private property was entirely lost, some damaged, and some saved, and believes that the most of the public property was saved.

The partnership existing between Joseph Perkins and himself was dissolved after the boat left St. Geneviéve, by which he became sole owner, and consequently subject to the whole loss. He prays that an adequate compensation be made to him for the loss of the boat, and so much of the cargo as belonged to him, estimating the boat at $300, and the boat and other property on board at $500.

It appears from the statement of William Sampson, who acted as the agent of the government in the case, that the boat was pressed into the service of the United States, but that John W. Buckner, whom he believed to be the owner, finding that the boat must go, agreed to take on board the public property, and to navigate the boat on his own account, agreeing to depend on the Deputy Quartermaster General for compensation. The agent says that he offered to employ a pilot to convey the boat through a difficult pass, which was declined by Buckner, and in about half an hour the boat was staved and sunk. The agent, William Sampson, with another witness, states that the boat, "when taken into the service of the United States, was worth $140."

The committee have thus recapitulated the principal facts deemed essential in the case, and are of opinion that the circumstance of the boat's being pressed into the public service in such a manner as to put it out of the power of the owner or his agent to resist the authority by which it was so pressed, gives the owner an unquestionable right to demand remuneration for the loss. But the property belonging to the petitioner, also in the boat, being placed there by the petitioner's agent without any agency or direction on the part of the government, should not be paid for.

The committee have assumed the valuation of the boat made by William Sampson, agent of the United States, and John A. Lapsley, under oath, and report a bill, allowing to the petitioner the sum of $140.

Joseph Hertich was paid $140 in 1836. Hertich and Joseph Perkins lived in Ste. Geneviéve and did business as Hertich & Perkins, and Perkins as Perkins & Co.

Hertich served as justice of the peace in 1816–17. His name is sometimes seen as Hertick.

## James Alexander and Ira Nash

A claim involving James Alexander, Ira Nash, Reuben Gentry, William Monroe, and others, as reported by the Committee on Indian Affairs on January 13, 1836:

> It is shown by the petitioner that during the late war with Great Britain in the year 1813, the United States removed from their own country, some 300 miles distant, and located within the limits of the Territory, now the State of Missouri, near the center thereof, and in the immediate vicinity of a flourishing white settlement called Boonslick, a number of Indians, a part of the Sac and Fox tribes, who then expressed an unwillingness to take any part in the war against the United States. It was, however, soon observed that small parties of these people were frequently breaking off from their new residence to join the hostile tribes; taking with them horses and such other property belonging to the whites as came within their reach.
>
> At length, some fifteen months after their location as aforesaid, although at all times kindly received and treated by the white inhabitants of Boonslick, the greater portion of those Indians removed their families to a distant point on the route to their former residence from whence the warriors returned to the settlement, collected a large drove of stock consisting of cattle, horses, &c., belonging to the white inhabitants, and destroyed much other property, which they could not take away, and then, with their plunder, returned to Rock River and joined the hostile party of those nations. The petitioner was one of the sufferers on that occasion. His house was robbed of its furniture; his corn crib, with 250 bushels of corn, burnt, and three horses were killed. The damage he sustained is estimated at $403.
>
> It is further shown that the petitioner had in his charge five barrels of saltpeter, which belonged to Doctor Ira Nash, and which was also destroyed at the same time and place, and by the same Indians. It also appears to the satisfaction of the committee that Nash lost a valuable mare and two colts estimated at $350, which were taken away by the Indians in the course of their depredations, as aforesaid, in the summer of 1814.
>
> Your committee are of opinion that the facts set forth in the prayer of the petitioner are clearly established, and that the claim of the petitioner, as well as that of Ira Nash, for the barrels of saltpeter, valued at $225, and the value of the mare and two colts, before mentioned, ought to be allowed: therefore report a bill for their relief.

James Alexander was paid $403, and Ira Nash $575 in 1836.

In 1799, Daniel and Rebecca Boone, of Kentucky, had two sons, Nathan and Daniel, when they moved to what became St. Charles County, Missouri. One day the two boys noticed animals licking wet ground and discovered it was actually a salt spring. They determined it could produce salt, a valuable commodity, but it would be a labor-intensive project so in 1805 they went into business with James and Jesse Morrison. Large amounts of firewood were required to boil the brine in iron kettles, leaving salt at the bottom, which was then packaged and shipped to St. Louis by keelboat and sold for $2.50 a bushel.

The trail from the new village to the works was known as Boone's Lick Road and an ill-defined area became known as Boonslick. In 1821, William Becknell, the works' manager, sent wagons to Santa Fe and Boone's Lick Road became the Santa Fe Trace, which became U.S. Highway 40, and today's Interstate 70.

The old salt works is a Missouri State Historic Site located off Highway 187 in Boonsboro, Missouri. Hiking is required to get to the site of the salt well, furnace, and ash heap. Parking and amenities are located at visitor's center.

## Louis Roy

The claim was filed by Robert Johnson, heir of Louis Roy. As stated by the

Committee on Indian Affairs on January 16, 1839:

> The administrator states in his petition that in the year 1815, Louis Roy was a resident of the county of St. Charles, in the then Territory of Missouri, and that in April of that year, certain Indians of the Sac, Fox, Pottawatomi tribes entered the Territory and destroyed or took away property of Louis Roy of the value of $700.
>
> The petitioner makes the statements set forth not from any personal knowledge of their truth, but according to his belief founded upon information derived from others. The only evidence is the affidavit of Joseph Roy, taken before a justice of the peace containing general statements of the injuries alleged and from which the witness had not a particular knowledge of the transaction.
>
> The depredations complained of were the acts of hostile bands of Indians, and the principle has never yet been recognized by Congress that the government should be held responsible for injuries inflicted on the property of our citizens under such circumstances. It is only when property is taken or destroyed by Indians at peace with the United States that government has made compensation as provided by the Intercourse Act of 1834.
>
> The committee are therefore of opinion that the claim should not be allowed.

# Kentucky

## *Kentucky Claims*

### Thomas C. Withers

As reported by the Committee of Claims on January 20, 1826:

> The petitioner's wagon and team were taken into the service of the United States, first by contract, and retained afterwards by impressment; which wagon and team, (with the exception of one horse) never were returned to the petitioner.
>
> On the 8th day of May, 1820, a law was passed authorizing payment to be made to the petitioner for the full amount of the appraised value of his wagon and team and gear with the exception of the one horse, with a provision to deduct therefrom the amount which had been paid to him for the use of the property; which payment has accordingly been made, but the petitioner thinks himself entitled, not only to the value of the property thus lost, but to all pay he has received for its use. To this part of the claim the committee will only remark that the same rule was applied to this case which has been applied to other similar cases, and that the committee know of no rule more just.
>
> A claim is now made for the wages of the wagoner who drove the team, while employed by contract. This part of the present claim is, no doubt, just, and would have been provided for in the former law if it had not then been expected that, as no claim was made, the wagoner had received his monthly pay; it, however, on examination, was found, that said wagoner was in the service 57 days, to which add reasonable time to return home from the place of discharge, say ten days, in all 67 days; for which service the petitioner ought to be paid, and for which a bill, at the rate of $10 per month, is herewith reported.

Withers was from Kentucky and was paid $187 in 1825 and an additional $177 by the War Department in 1827.

### Presley N. O'Bannon

As reported by the Committee of Claims on April 20, 1836:

> The claimant presented a petition at the 1st session 19th Congress, praying to be compensated the value of a horse, which, he said, he had furnished to a man by the name of Landy Sumner, a volunteer from the State of Kentucky, in 1813, under the command of Governor Isaac Shelby.
>
> In that petition he stated that he supposed the horse had been stolen or died.
>
> William Whitsett testified that the horse was rode to the Canada border and was either lost or died in the United States service, and was the value of $86.
>
> An adverse report was made by the Committee of Claims on the 6th of January, 1826, on the ground that the petition did not state the cause of the loss, nor was it proved by the testimony. A suspicion was entertained by the committee that, as the horse was said to have been rode to the Canada border, and as no account was given the rider, nor the cause of the loss, the rider had probably gone into Canada.
>
> The petition was sought for at the Clerk's office, but the committee was informed that Colonel Johnson withdrew it on the 8th of February, 1830. He informs the committee that he sent the papers to Mr. O'Bannon by mail, at his request, to obtain further testimony.
>
> General Whitsett now testifies he has a perfect knowledge of the fact that O'Bannon did furnish the horse to Sumner, which was

> appraised at $86, and was rode by Sumner in a company commanded by Whitsett to the lake, or border of Canada. Summer was there dismounted from his horse by order of the commander-in-chief, and the horse was turned into the big pasture with many others, and that on the return of the troops from Canada, diligent search was made for the horse, but could not be found. He further testifies that he brought Sumner part of the way back towards Kentucky without the horse.
>
> The Hon. Mr. Joseph Underwood says he should give credit to the witness in the subject about which he has testified. He also informs the committee that the petitioner was with General William Eaton at the capture of Derne, and is incapable of preferring a claim against the government for a horse, unless he had in truth lost one.
>
> The testimony of General Whitsett removes the objections heretofore made and the committee herewith report a bill.

Presley Neville O'Bannon was paid $86 in 1838. He was a lieutenant in the Marine Corps when Derna on the coast of Tripoli was attacked on April 27, 1805. He was given a sword by a Mameluke chief whose design became a standard issue to Marine officers in 1825 that remains to this day.

O'Bannon was noted to be the first American to fly the nation's flag over a captured foreign city. He is the namesake for the Navy destroyers *O'Bannon* 177 and 450.

Capt. William Whitsett was paymaster in Col. Samuel Caldwell's 1st Regiment of Kentucky Mounted Volunteers and also served as quartermaster. His company mustered at Newport, Kentucky, on August 31, 1813. Pvt. Sumner is also shown in Col. Philip E. Barbour's 10th Regiment of Mounted Kentucky Volunteers.

## James Smith

Robert Brackenridge, of Kentucky, was appointed captain in the 2nd U.S. Regiment of Rifles on March 17, 1814, right after its organization on February 10. As stated by the Committee of Claims on January 8, 1830:

> It appears to the Committee to be proven that the petitioner's horse, of the value of $80, was impressed into the service of the United States in the year 1814 by Capt. Robert Brackenridge and for which he has received no compensation.
>
> The case was presented some years since to the Third Auditor for settlement and rejected for want of Capt. Brackenridge's certificate of impressment, or some evidence that Capt. Brackenridge was dead. Evidence of the death of Capt. Brackenridge is furnished in a letter written by the Hon. Mr. Wickliffe. It appears from the deposition of Mr. Alney McLean, formerly a member of the House from the State of Kentucky, that the papers of James Smith were put into his hands to obtain pay for the loss of his horse. He brought them to Washington and he thinks, presented them to Congress, and that he entertains the opinion that the certificate of Capt. Brackenridge was among them. The papers alluded to by Mr. McLean cannot be found, either in the Clerk's office or in the Auditor's office. The persons who were called on by Capt. Brackenridge to appraise the horse have moved without the State of Kentucky, and to parts unknown to the petitioner, but the value of the horse is proven by Joseph Fuquay, Jr., to have been worth from $75 to $80. The petitioner swears that the appraisers valued the horse at $80. Mr. McLean says he thinks the papers he had proved the value of the horse at $80.
>
> The Committee believing that the weight of the evidence fixes the value of the horse at $80, a bill for that amount is reported.

James Smith was paid $80 1830.

## Anthony G. Willis

As stated by the Committee on Military Affairs on February 18, 1851:

> The petitioners state that in the year 1814, Anthony G. Willis was the owner of a wagon and team in Kentucky, where he lived, and that he had Benjamin T. Rowe employed in driving said team.
>
> At Lexington, Kentucky, whither wagon and team had been driven with a load of hemp, Captain George Stockton, an officer of the United States Army, being in great need of the means of transportation for his troops, pressed wagon and team and driver

into service, and were carried beyond Dayton, in Ohio, towards the Canada line, and subsequently back to Nashville, Tennessee, laden with wounded soldiers of the regular Army.

They further state that wagon and team and driver were kept in the active employ of the government till the services amounted, according to the rates of pay then established and allowed, to the sum of $251, and that Capt. Stockton gave a certificate for that sum. The certificate was sent on to Washington for payment by the representative in Congress from the district in which Willis lived, and that the accounting officer rejected it because it contained an interlineation. They further state that every effort was made to have the voucher corrected, but that, owing to the distance at which Willis lived from Capt. Stockton, and the fact that Stockton was absent from home when the agent of Willis went to see him, it was not done till Willis died, leaving his children, all minors and wholly incapable of transacting business. The administrators subsequently endeavored to get a proper voucher, but with like want of success. The family and their friends have been endeavoring from that day to this, through the various representatives from that district in Congress, to get the claim allowed and paid, but all in vain.

They state, further, that Willis was poor, and having a large family, the denial of this just demand was a peculiar hardship. It is also fully proven that the voucher was lost by being left at the house of Stockton for correction.

Your committee would state that all the material facts in the petition are proven to their entire satisfaction. The proof is clear and satisfactory that the wagon and team were the property of Anthony G. Willis, and that Rowe was employed by him to drive it; that it was pressed into the service of the United States in time of war by an officer of the army, and rendered the service for which compensation is claimed, and that the service was certified by the officer to be worth the amount claimed.

It is not pretended that one cent of the claim has ever been paid. The difficulty is simply this: one officer of the government, after appropriating the property of a citizen to the public use without his consent, and by a hard military rule, carelessly made an interlineation in the voucher; and another officer of the government seized upon the interlineation as an objection to it and refused payment.

Thus the uninformed but innocent citizen is driven back and forth from one of the government agents to another, as wholly unable to reconcile their action, or get his money, as he was to prevent the forcible appropriation of his property in the first instance.

Your committee are of opinion that the prayer of the petition ought to be granted, and recommend that under the peculiar hardships of the case the sum of $500 be paid the petitioners, in full satisfaction of the principal and all claim for interest thereon.

The executors of Anthony G. Willis were paid $251 in 1854.

An interlineation is the alteration of an original document, specifically by writing between the lines.

It appears Anthony Willis lived in Adair County, Kentucky, and married Harriott Bowmar, 14, on September, 14, 1811. They had children Ann (September 12, 1812); Benjamin (October 4, 1814); Mary Jane (April 11, 1817); Almira (November 27, 1819); and Julia (January 31, 1822). Harriet died on May 20, 1837.

In 1776, George Stockton, 31, raised by Indians and late of Virginia, and his half-brother, John Fleming, went by canoe down the Ohio River to settle in the wilds of Kentucky, apparently for personal reasons. In 1787, George established Stockton Station.

John Fleming died at Fleming Station in 1794, and Stockton founded a town he named Flemingsburg, plotted in 1796. Fleming County was established in 1798 from land donated by Mason County with Flemingsburg as the county seat.

George was captain in Col. Richard M. Johnson's Regiment of Mounted Kentucky Volunteers. On May 20, 1813, he joined the Army and was appointed captain in Col. Thomas Dye Owing's 28th U.S. Infantry, organized on January 29, 1813. As of May 31, 1814, Stockton was on recruiting duty at Flemingsburg and on July 1, he marched his recruits from Olympian Springs.

In the early 1800s, a mineral spring was discovered near Fox Creek which became popular with locals and then tourists. A hotel was built and another spring, Bell Grove, was also located near Fox Creek.

Mud Lick Creek, a medicinal spring, in Bath County, Kentucky, about 8 miles southeast of Owingsville, was originally owned and improved in 1791 by William Ramsey, whose interest was mining salt. In the early 1800s it was purchased by Thomas Hart who renamed it Olympian Springs, after the local 1,200-foot Mount Olympus. In August, 1803, John Kennedy commenced building a 47-mile road to Lexington. When Hart died, the resort was purchased by Col. Thomas Owing. A historical marker commemorates the site.

Capt. Stockton was transferred to the 3rd Infantry on May 17, 1815, and he resigned on May 1, 1816.

## Jonathan Lowe and John Daniel

Jonathan Lowe owned a boat that was impressed into the military service of the United States on the 6th of December, 1814, to convey a corps of Kentucky militia to New Orleans.

John Daniel owned a ferry flat employed by order of Major-General John Thomas, for the Kentucky detached militia in December 1814.

Both assigned their assigned claims to John Pollock who filed the petition. Pollock presented two vouchers as evidence:

Smithland, December 6, 1814.

Colonel Richard Taylor, Frankfort, Ky.:

Sir: Five days after date please to pay to Major Jonathan Lowe, on order, $104, for one flat bottom boat, taken of him for the use of the Kentucky detached militia, under the command of Major General John Thomas.

Thomas P. Dudley,
Dep. Qr. Mast. Gen. of Ky. detached militia.

Smithland, December 8, 1814.

Colonel Richard Taylor, Frankfort, Ky.:

Sir: Five days after date to pay to Mr. John Daniel, on order, $40, for the use of one ferry flat, and services rendered by order Major General John Thomas.

Thomas P. Dudley,
Dep. Qr. Mast. Gen. of Ky. detached militia.

As reported by the Committee of Claims on June 3, 1834:

The petitioner states that he put these claims into the hands of Mr. Baldwin, representative from Allegheny County, Pennsylvania, in 1819, (the same not having been paid by Colonel Taylor when presented, immediately after their date, because he had no funds) with the request that he would obtain the money, which was not paid, because the vouchers did not contain evidence they were "due and not paid." Whereupon he sent the drafts to Thomas P. Dudley, and obtained his certificates written upon the back of them, as follows, to wit:

I do hereby certify that Major Jonathan Lowe is entitled to $104, for one flat bottom boat, taken from him by order of Major General John Thomas, for the purpose of transporting the Kentucky detached militia, ordered to reinforce Major General Jackson, as specified in the within draft. Given under my hand, at Winchester, Kentucky, the 15th November, 1819. Thomas P. Dudley, late deputy quartermaster general of Kentucky detached militia.

This draft, with this certificate upon it, was afterwards presented at the Third Auditor's office for payment, when Mr. Hagner endorsed the following note upon it: "Act of 9th April, 1816, has expired. No provision for this claim exists. 5th February, 1820."

On the other draft, Mr. Dudley endorsed the following certificate, to wit:

I do hereby certify that John Daniel was entitled, and that, in consequence of the above transfer, Major Jonathan Lowe is entitled to the within $40, as specified. Given under my hand, at Winchester, Kentucky, the 15th November, 1819. Thomas P. Dudley, late deputy quartermaster general of Kentucky detached militia.

The assignment referred to in this certificate is as follows: "Mr. Taylor: Sir: Pay the within to Jonathan Lowe, and oblige yours, John Daniel. December 10, 1814."

The facts are fully set forth in the petition, and the petitioner says he, nor Jonathan

Lowe, nor John Daniel, have received any portion of the money contained in said drafts; and the truth of the petition is verified by the oaths of John Pollock and Jonathan Lowe.

The committee are satisfied from the evidence stated and set forth in this report, that the petitioner is entitled to relief.

John Pollock was paid $144 in 1836.

Smithland is the county seat of Livingston County, Kentucky, located at the confluence of the Ohio and Cumberland Rivers. The little town, population about 240, was incorporated on March 8, 1843.

# Tennessee

## *Tennessee Claims*

### John Topp

Topp's petition was presented from Nashville on December 20, 1819, as reported by the Committee on Military Affairs on April 20, 1824:

> The petition of John Topp, a citizen of the state of Tennessee, humbly represents to your honorable body, that some time in the year 1812, a cantonment was established on the lands of one Andrew McNairy, near Nashville, for the use of the troops of the United States. It so continued in the occupation of different troops for two or three years during which time the troops crossed the line of McNairy's land and entered the land of your petitioner, and thereupon cut and carried away the timber of about 15 acres for the use of the troops.
>
> He should have applied for payment of the injury thus done to his property at an early day after the injury had been done, but Col. William P. Anderson had been ordered away on public service and so remained away so long that when he finally obtained his certificate and attempted to obtain pay under the law of April 9, 1816—that law had expired and his claim was therefore judged inadmissible. He now humbly asks your honorable body to reward to him, by law, the same measure of justice that other citizens in like circumstances have received and as in duty bound, he will ever pray, &c.

On September 4, 1818, Col. Anderson was deposed, as recorded:

> Col. William P. Anderson says that some time in the year 1812, then in command of the 24th Regiment of Infantry, by the advice and command of Brig. Gen. James Winchester, who then commanded in this quarter, selected a spot of land in the neighborhood of Nashville supposed to belong to Andrew McNairy, but under the control of the Hon. John McNairy, where the necessary buildings and huts were built for the use of the United States' troops. It was intended to procure the necessary wood for the use of the troops on the land of McNairy, but the troops without the knowledge of the affiant, had cut across and over the line of McNairy's land and did actually cut and carry away to the cantonment a quantity of the timber, which was most excellent timber, belonging to Mr. John Topp. The timber was very valuable, but to what amount I am unable to say.
>
> This affiant was afterwards ordered away upon distant service and before Mr. John Topp had ever obtained any certificate of the amount of timber or the value thereof. This cantonment was also used for the 39th Regiment afterwards, and perhaps for other United States' troops, and was so continued for a considerable time afterwards until the year 1814, and it is probable those troops also may have fallen into the same mistake.

Topp requested Peter Randolph and Jeremiah Perry to assess the damage and they reported $300. John Topp was paid $300 in 1824.

Col. Anderson's regiment marched from Knoxville, East Tennessee, to Canada, and to Fort Niagara. Corporal Peter Rambo enlisted for 18 months in the summer of 1812 at Sevierville in Capt. Francis Armstrong's company, with Lt. Michael Toomy, and was captured and sent to Québec until exchanged on September 8, 1814.

## David Henley

As reported by the Committee of Claims on January 28, 1819:

> The petitioner had received about the 23rd December, 1797, a considerable sum of arms which were intended as collateral security for a debt due from certain persons to Edward Fox, and the petitioner made himself accountable to Edward Fox for the same. The debt not being paid, the arms became the property of right of Edward Fox and the petitioner was instructed to sell them. They remained in the petitioner's hands until the 18th day of October, 1813, when a part of them, to wit: 19 muskets, were impressed into the service of the United States by order of General John A. Cocke, of the Tennessee militia.
>
> The facts have been satisfactorily established before a commission, ordered by Commissioner Lee, as to the taking and estimating the value at $230. The committee report a bill for its allowance.

Col. Henley, of Knoxville, Tennessee, and agent of Edward Fox, presented his petition on February 7, 1812, and was paid $228 in 1820.

## Henry Williams

Williams was from Tennessee. As reported by the Committee of Claims on January 26, 1818:

> The petitioner states that on the 25th of November, 1814, his wagon and team were pressed into the service of the troops of the United States under the command of General William Carroll, then about to descend the river to New Orleans.
>
> In the mouth of Red River on the Cumberland, his wagon and two horses were precipitated from the ferry boat into the stream, in consequence of which the two horses were drowned.
>
> The petitioner further states that as the ferry boat was also impressed into the public service, he is unable to recover the value of the horses from the owner of the boat and prays Congress to pass an act directing the quartermaster in West Tennessee to pay him $100, the value of the two horses lost.
>
> It appears satisfactorily to the committee that the horses were precipitated into the river through the misconduct of the persons having charge of the ferry boat. If then it had been satisfactorily proved that the wagon and team were impressed in the public service, still the committee would be unable to discriminate between this case and one of wanton depredation, or unauthorized violence on the part of the soldiery, for which government has never deemed itself responsible.
>
> They therefore submit that the prayer of the petitioner ought not to be granted.

Gen. Carroll commanded three West Tennessee Militia regiments at New Orleans. The 2nd regiment was mustered in November 1814, and went down to New Orleans on the Cumberland, Ohio, and Mississippi Rivers.

# The Mississippi Territory

The Territory of Mississippi was established on April 7, 1798, and included the future state of Alabama. Mississippi was admitted to the Union on December 10, 1817, and Alabama on December 14, 1819.

The major disturbance in the Territory during the War of 1812 was the split among the Creek Indians. Once the shooting began in 1812, the numerous Indian tribes again got caught between the British invaders and American expansion into the Northwest Territory, primarily in Ohio, the Mississippi Territory, and Florida.

In 1812 American troops entered Spanish East Florida to curb British influence and their Seminole allies. Volunteers from East Tennessee undertook a hazardous 700-mile expedition against the Seminole Indians with regular army troops under Lt. Col. Thomas A. Smith. William Cocke, of the Tennessee mounted gunmen, served as a colonel of infantry in the army of the United States for two months.

Claims were filed for property damage by residents, which were heard by the Superior Court at St. Augustine, Territory of Florida, and judgments entered. On June 26, 1834, Congress limited awards to those who "were actual subjects of the Spanish Government," and that no award would be paid for depredations committed in East Florida, "previous to the entrance into that province of the agent or troops of the United States."

By this time, a considerable amount of intermarriage between Indians and non–Indians had occurred, which resulted in the emergence of prominent "half-breeds," some of whom became chiefs with western names. The Cherokees and Creeks never got along and the Creeks were split to the point of civil war over ceding land to the United States and the forced removal from Indians from their lands. It was a complicated mix of political loyalties, family ties, and intrigue.

The Creeks who opposed the United States became known as Red Sticks because of the color of a club they carried. They were universally viewed by Americans as allies of Great Britain, although no British troops took part.

The attack on the fortified residence of Samuel Mims, known as Fort Mims, by around 800 Red Sticks William Weatherford—Chief Red Eagle—on August 30, 1813, in which 553 people had taken shelter under Maj. Daniel Beasley galvanized the military response. As stated by Gilbert C. Russell, former commander of the 3rd Regiment of Infantry, and a Creek War veteran:

> In 1813, a little more than a year after the declaration of war against England, the great body of the Creek nation made war upon the frontier settlements of the Mississippi Territory, including the half-breeds and Indians then living along the Alabama River who remained friendly to the United States, and laid the whole country east of the Tombigee nearly a waste.

The Tombigee River starts in northeast Mississippi and flows south and southeast to the Alabama River, which becomes the Mobile River that empties into Mobile Bay.

Samuel Moniac was one of the early claimants and proved British involvement in attacks on American settlements. He was "a friendly Creek Indian of the half blood." Like many others of the day, he could not write so his sworn statement was recorded on August 2, 1813, by Mississippi Territory Judge Harry Toulmin:

> About last of October thirty northern Indians came down with Tecumseh who said he had been sent by his brother the Prophet. They attended our Council at the Tuckabatchee, and had a talk for us. I was there for the space of three days, but every day whilst I was there, Tecumseh refused to deliver his talk, and on being requested to give it said that the sun had gone too far that day. The day after I came away he delivered his talk. It was not till about Christmas that any of our people began to dance the war dance. The Muscogees have not been used to dance before war but after. At that time about forty of our people began this northern custom, and my brother in law [Josiah] Francis who also pretends to be a prophet, was at the head of them.
>
> Their number has very much increased since and there are probably now more than a half of the Creek nation who have joined them.
>
> Being afraid of the consequences of a murder having been committed on the mail route, I had left my house on the road and had gone down to my plantation on the river. I stayed there some time. I went to Pensacola with some steers, during which time my sister and brother who have joined the war party came and got off a number of my horses and other stock and thirty-six of my negroes. About one or two and twenty days ago, I went up to my house on the road and found some Indians camped near it, who I tried to avoid but could not.
>
> An Indian came to me who goes by the name of High Headed Jim, and who had been appointed to head a party sent from the Tuckautatchee Town on the Tallapoosa, on a trip to Pensacola. He shook hands with me and immediately began to tremble and jerk in every part of his frame, and the very calves of his legs would be convulsed, and he would get entirely out of breath with the agitation. This practice was introduced in May and June last by the prophet Francis who says that he was so instructed by the Spirit.
>
> High Headed Jim asked me what I meant to do. I said that I should sell my property and buy ammunition and join them. He then told me that they were going down to Pensacola to get ammunition, and that they had got a letter from a British General, which would enable them to receive ammunition from the Governor. That it had been given to the Little Warrior and saved by his nephew when he was killed and sent down to Francis. High Head told me that when they went back with their supply another body of men would go down for another supply of ammunition and that ten men were to go out of each town and that they calculated on five horse loads for every town. He said that they were to make a general attack on the American settlements and that the Indians on the waters of the Coosa and Tallapoosa and on the Black Warrior were to attack the settlements on the Tombigbee and Alabama, particularly the Tensaw and fork settlements. That the Creek Indians bordering on the Cherokees were to attack the people of Tennessee and that the Seminoles and lower Creeks were to attack the Georgians, that the Choctaws also had joined them and were to attack the Mississippi settlements. That the attack was to be made at the same time in all places, when they got furnished with ammunition.
>
> I found from my sister that they were treated very rigorously by the chiefs and that many particularly the women among them two daughters of the late General McGillivray, who had been induced to join them to save their property were very desirous to leave them but could not.
>
> I found from the talk of High Head that the war was to be against the whites and not between the Indians themselves, that all they wanted was to kill those who had taken the talk of the whites, viz. the Big Warrior, Alexander Cornell, Capt. Isaac, William McIntosh, the Mad Dragon's son, the Little Prince, Spoko Hauge of Tallassee Thicksico. They have destroyed a large quantity of my cattle and burnt my house and my river plantation as well as those of James Cornell and Leonard McGee.

The celebrated Alexander McGillivray was a Scotch-French-Indian of Creek extraction who served in the British, French, Spanish, and American armies.

Samuel joined the American forces and might have served under Gen. Jackson. His son, David Moniac, was the first West Point appointee from Alabama and the first Native American to graduate from West Point. He served as a major in the Alabama Mounted Creek Volunteers in the Second Seminole War and a lieutenant in the 6th U.S. Infantry Regiment.

## *Mississippi Territory Claims*

### Samuel H. Garrow

As reported by the Committee of Claims on March 18, 1818:

> It appears that near the close of the late war, a sloop called the *General Jackson* belonging to Garrow & Wilson was in the service of the United States for the purpose of transporting troops to Mobile Point for the defense of Fort Bowyer and that after landing the men, she was captured by the enemy.
>
> Garrow, in the month of January, 1817, presented his claim for the value of the vessel to the Commissioner of Claims, who made a report in favor of allowing $3,500 deducting therefrom any sums which might have been paid to Garrow. The Secretary of War, in revising his report, obtained from the Third Auditor a certificate stating that John A. Watson (since deceased), who acted as assistant deputy quartermaster general, and who is said to have impressed the sloop, had made a return to that office of outstanding claims against government in that quarter, in which it was stated that $800 were due Garrow & Wilson for the hire of the *General Jackson*. Opposite the return, it was remarked by Watson that he had understood the owners had to pay $600 for the ransom of the vessel. The Secretary of War authorized an award for $600. From this decision the claimant appeals to Congress, averting that it is erroneous and contrary to the 3rd and 5th sections of the act of 1816.
>
> The committee are of opinion that the petitioner is not entitled to receive from the government more than $800, the hire of the vessel. They cannot understand the return of John A. Watson, assistant deputy quartermaster general, in any other light than as evincing a contract between him and the petitioner, and the $800 stated to be due for the hire of the vessel to transport troops to Mobile Point, a considerable distance, is certainly sufficient to cover the risk incident to such service. Besides, it does not appear the vessel was captured in consequence of having been in the public service as she had landed the men and had retired to Bon Secour Creek as a place of safety.
>
> The committee submit a resolution that the prayer of the petitioner be rejected.

### Morgan Brown

Morgan Brown, of Georgia, filed a claim for a horse lost while transporting provisions from Fort Jackson during the Creek war, "for the use of the quota of Georgia militia." As he stated to Justice of the Peace John Gilmore on October 10, 1820:

> During the campaign in the Indian nation under Major General John H. McIntosh he had employed, by and in the service of the United States, a wagon and team under the care of William and John Roughton, and that one of the horses was a chestnut sorrel mare, about ten years old with a blazed face and all her feet white; value $130. The mare was lost and said to be stolen by the Indians and when she was found, somewhere near the Tallapoosa River in the neighborhood of Fort Jackson, her throat was cut.

As stated by the Senate Committee of Claims on December 8, 1820:

> The claim of the petitioner is for a horse stolen from a team and killed at Fort Jackson on the Tallapoosa while the team was in the service of the United States during the late war with the Creek Indians. Although there is not, and cannot, be any positive proof that the horse was taken and killed by the hostile Indians, yet the circumstances are such as to leave little doubt that this was the fact. Although this

case is not strictly within the letter of the law making provision for horses killed in battle, it would seem to the committee to come fairly within the spirit of that law. The committee therefore recommend the allowance of the claim and report a bill accordingly.

On January 30, 1822, the House denied the claim for lack of sufficient evidence.

In 1717, the French, at the behest of the Alabama Indians—members of the Creek Indian Confederacy—built Fort Toulouse as the furthest eastern post in the Louisiana Territory. The post served as a trading center for deerskins sold to French and British traders.

The competition between the French and British interests blew up in 1754 into the French and Indian War, part of what became the Seven Years' War. The French were defeated in 1763 and Louisiana was ceded to England and Spain. The French settlers then moved to the area around present-day Opelousas, Louisiana.

The site of the old French fort became an Indian village until the United States fought the Red Sticks. In 1814, Gen. Jackson established Fort Jackson at the site and it was used until 1817. The original brig at the fort was used as Montgomery County's jail after Alabama became a state.

The Fort Toulouse–Fort Jackson Park offers restored buildings, year-round living history demonstrations, and reenactments at 2521 W. Fort Toulouse Rd., Wetumpka, Alabama.

## David Tate

On May 18, 1826, Congress authorized the Secretary of the Treasury to pay David Tate $218 for forage, "impressed by the officers of the United States, in the year 1814 for the use of the army."

David Tate was David Moniac's uncle and a resided on Little River, Alabama, whose corn and fodder were taken. His petition was presented on January 8, 1821. He was paid another $107.50 on April 6, 1826, and a further $218 later the same year.

## Benjamin S. Smoot

Benjamin Stoddert Smoot, the nephew of Benjamin Stoddert, the first Secretary of the Navy, was born in Maryland in 1781. Sometime in the early 1800s he moved to Baldwin County, Alabama, and on March 22, 1804, President Jefferson nominated him to the Senate for confirmation as an ensign in the 2nd Regiment of Infantry. On February 25, 1807, he was promoted to 2nd lieutenant, fought Indians, and on April 1, 1809, left active duty service and transferred to the militia.

He was then appointed sheriff of the District of Washington in the Mississippi Territory and around this time married Harriet Mims, 16, a daughter of Samuel Mims. Harriet's father, Samuel, had a large plantation in Baldwin County on the east bank of Tensaw Lake with a stockade which was called Fort Mims.

On January 9, 1812, he resigned as sheriff and recommended Dr. Samuel Perry as his replacement to acting governor Henry Daingerfield.

Smoot then went into business with Dennison Darling as Smoot & Darling, sutlers for the 2nd Regiment, and hired Curtis Lewis as their agent and clerk.

Dennison Darling was born in Vermont in 1753, moved to Alabama, delivered mail, was a collector of customs in 1810–11 at Fort Stoddert and married Sarah Mims, daughter of David Mims, a director at St. Stevens Bank.

On December 17, 1814, he joined Maj. Diego McBoy's 14th Regiment of Mississippi Volunteers as a private and was discharged on March 20, 1815. On December 21, 1819, Darling was appointed justice of the Washington County Court, Alabama Territory, and on April 17, 1820, registered in Washington County as an auctioneer. He died at age 53 on March 26, 1827, at St. Stephens and thus ceased to be a party to the claim. No heir or legal representative came forward to take up the claim.

According to testimony from Capt. Abraham L. Sands, the regiment was disbanded in 1815 for lack of funds to pay the soldiers, who were still owed about twelve months' pay. Soldiers were normally allowed to trade with the sutlers to the amount of half their pay and in some cases to a larger extent, but the paymaster didn't receive funds until the spring of 1816. Smoot filed claims, as many sutlers did, to recover the debts due and from deserters or deceased soldiers.

On December 29, 1818, a petition from Smoot, of Mobile, Alabama, was presented for the loss of a house at Fort Bowyer, "destroyed by order of an officer in the army of the United States, in the late war with Great Britain." Major William Lawrence was in command of Fort Bowyer.

A statement was written by Smoot at Washington City on December 17, 1830:

> Your petitioner, Benjamin S. Smoot, of Mobile, Alabama, represents that he was sutler to the Second Regiment of the United States Infantry from 1809 to 1815; that he, with his partner in business, Dennison Darling, erected about the year 1814, at Fort Bowyer, a storehouse, which was of the following dimensions, viz: 35 feet long by 18 feet in width, and a story and a half in height, of good materials, weather-boarded, floored, and ceiled, and fitted with all necessary appurtenances, and that just previous to the attack on this fort by the land and naval forces of Great Britain in 1814, the commanding officer had said storehouse demolished, in order that it might not afford to the invaders a shelter.
>
> In testimony of the above, your petitioner begs leave to refer to the deposition of Maj. Reuben Chamberlain, then of the Second Infantry, who was present at the attack above mentioned, and that of Mr. Curtis Lewis, the agent and clerk of the sutler. These gentlemen estimate the cost of the storehouse at about $1,000; but this amount is not within $500 of the actual expense incurred in its erection. By the loss of this house your petitioner has sustained a loss of at least $1,500, independently of a very considerable loss in goods by their hasty removal and deposit in an insecure and exposed situation. Your petitioner therefore asks that the amount of his house may, with legal interest, be paid to him.

Reuben Chamerlain was a captain at the time of the attack. The Committee of Claims and the Committee on Military Affairs rejected the claim on February 4, 1831, as stated:

> The petitioner was sutler to the Second Regiment of the United States Infantry from the year 1809 to 1815, and that he, with his partner in business, Dennison Darling, erected, in the year 1812, at Fort Bowyer, a storehouse, 35 feet long and 18 feet wide, one story and a half high, of good materials; that the commanding officer, by and with the advice of his subordinate officers, on the approach of the British land and naval forces at that place in 1814, ordered said storehouse to be demolished and destroyed to prevent its being occupied by the enemy as a shelter, and as a point from which to attack the fort, it being in musket shot of the same. The building is proved by the witnesses to be worth $1,000.
>
> The committee are of opinion that, as the property of the petitioner was destroyed by the order of the United States to prevent its being useful and advantageous to the enemies of the country, he is entitled to relief.

While this was in the works, Smoot filed other claims. On January 29, 1813, Smoot's petition as, "late sheriff of the District of Washington, in the Mississippi Territory, praying compensation for services rendered as Marshal of the said District" was presented.

On March 9, 1818, a petition from Smoot and others from Mississippi was presented "praying to be confirmed in their title to a tract of land including the town of St. Stephens, in the Alabama Territory."

On February 14, 1825, Smoot filed a claim, "praying for compensation for injuries sustained by his wagon and team, in the service of the United States, in the year 1818."

Their claim for the house was reported on "unfavorably" again by the Committee of Claims on January 30, 1826.

On January 13, 1831, he again presented a petition for compensation for services "rendered by him in the capacity of Marshal of the State of Alabama," which was referred to the Committee on the Judiciary.

Benjamin S. Smoot was paid $1,000 in 1831. Harriet died in 1826 and Smoot married Anne McGuire in 1831. He died in 1844 at Mobile.

## Joshua Kennedy

Kennedy, of Mobile County, Alabama Territory, was deposed on November 1, 1817, by Judge Harry Toulmin, and presented his claim in January 1818, to Richard Bland Lee, Commissioner of Claims:

> During the late war between the United States and Great Britain, your petitioner was possessed of a mill and other buildings in Mobile County, which were fortified or picketed in, and occupied as a fort or barracks by a detachment of the troops of the United States, then under the command of Brigadier General Ferdinand L. Claiborne, who were stationed at the saw mill for the purpose of protecting the settlement adjacent, and enabling the mill to continue in operation whilst sawing plank for the use of Fort Bowyer.
>
> The mill was destroyed by the enemy, viz. the Creek Indians, then in alliance with Great Britain in the month of September, 1813, soon after the fall of Fort Mims. The property destroyed actually within the pickets was worth $9,000, though more property adjacent to the mill of the value of $2,000 or $3,000 was, at the same time, destroyed—for none of which he received any compensation.
>
> Your memorialist, therefore, humbly prays that a commission may issue to one or more persons, authorizing them, or either of them, to take the testimony of such witnesses as may be produced, relative to the claim of your memorialist against the United States, under the authority of the laws in such cases made and provided.

As reported by the Committee on Indian Affairs on June 4, 1844, in part:

> The facts, as stated by the petitioner, and substantially verified by his proofs are that in 1810 he was the owner of land on the Tensaw River, south of latitude 31° north, which country, by proclamation of President Madison, was declared to be under the protection of the United States, and was taken possession of by them.
>
> Under this assurance of the government, petitioner improved his land by building his dwelling-house, a saw mill, cotton gin, cotton press, &c., and as a trading post, he had on hand during the war with Great Britain, and in the year 1813, large quantities of cotton, rope, cordage, baling rope, and lumber. The mill and a portion of the premises were stockaded and occupied by the troops of the United States under the military orders of an officer of the government.
>
> In 1813, after the massacre of Fort Mims, which was distant about 14 miles, in the panic which followed that event, the troops were hastily withdrawn from his premises, which were shortly thereafter entered by the hostile Creeks and all the buildings and personal property were destroyed by fire.

A summary of the testimony was presented:

> William C. Vaughn (overseer for Mrs. Hollinger) proved Kennedy a rich merchant, to whom all cotton planters on the Tombigee and Alabama Rivers used to sell their crops. Sold Mrs. Hollinger's crop to him for that year for $2,200. Proves that this lot of cotton, and much more, together with the cotton-house, mills, &c., were burnt by the Creeks. Proves the occupation by the United States, as a fortified and armed place of defense, the cause of the destruction.
>
> George Stiggins proves that he was going down the Tensaw in a boat from a quarter to half a mile from the mills. Heard the Indians, and saw the light of the fire; was afterwards told by a half-breed named John Cook that he was with the band of hostile Creeks who burnt "Kennedy's mills."
>
> Andrew Milton proves that he was a United States soldier stationed at Kennedy's mills, which were stockaded—"occupied as a fort." On the fall of Fort Mims, the soldiers retreated from Kennedy's mills, leaving them as an unoccupied fort. Shortly after, the mills were burnt.
>
> James Conway proves Kennedy's mills, houses, and cotton buildings very valuable.

Proves they were burnt by the Indians, by matters found on the ground after they had retired—such as carcasses of sheep, &c. Cause of the burning was their having been occupied and fortified by the United States. Other mills in the vicinity, and houses above and below, not molested.

J. Pierce was at Kennedy's mills 1st September. Saw them with a stockade about them occupied by United States troops who retreated on the fall of Fort Mims.

Nicholas Cook proves the mills to have been an out station of Fort Mims under the command of the commander of that fort, Major Daniel Beasley. Was then enclosed with strong timbers; port holes cut. Heard Major Beasley order trench to be dug in front, and pickets to be driven.

Mills new, best machinery he ever saw. Loss by destruction of mills and contents, $15,000 to $20,000. The troops and all the inhabitants retreated to Mobile.

Some days was informed by a man named George Stiggins that "Kennedy's mills" were burnt. Afterwards, went with Kennedy to the place where his mills had been burnt, and it was evident from appearances—remains of sheep, broken arrows pointed with iron, war clubs, &c.—that the hostile Indians had been there.

William Pierce says "Kennedy's mills" were stockaded on or about the 1st September, 1813, and United States troops stationed there, who retreated on fall of Fort Mims, leaving the mills an "unoccupied station."

William Kitchen proves the occupancy and fortification of the mills by United States troops. Saw Captain Beasley there. Troops retreated from the mills the day after fall of Fort Mims. The mills shortly after burnt—supposed by Indians, as all the inhabitants had fled, as deponent knows; family of his father being the last which fled. The mills were very valuable and a large quantity of cotton in the gin, which was burnt.

Samuel Kitchen says "Kennedy's mills," 14 miles south of Fort Mims, occupied by order of Gen. Claiborne as an armed garrison or stockade a month previous to the massacre at Fort Mims, the detachment under the command of Major David Beasley. Shortly after the massacre at Fort Mims, the soldiers retreated from the mills in terror. Shortly after the retreat of the soldiers, the mills and all connected with them were burnt by the Indians. The mills and contents destroyed worth, at a low estimate, $15,000.

Aaron Barlow proves the occupancy of the mills, their enclosure and fortification by United States troops latter part of 1813, shortly before the massacre at Fort Mims. After the fall of Fort Mims, it was said that a large body of Indians was approaching to attack them. The soldiers retreated to Mobile, "leaving the mills as an unoccupied fort." Loss from $20,000 to $25,000. The mills very large and complete; best deponent has seen in the State.

Joshua Kennedy, deceased, was awarded $6,500 in 1854. Kennedy's petition was rejected several times and finally approved on January 28, 1845. The allowance for restitution was grounded in the treaty with the Creek Indians of August 9, 1814, and ratified on February 16, 1815, "in which the country where the petitioner's premises were situated was purchased." The hostile Creeks were "under the lead of the celebrated Francis."

After the massacre, Samuel A. Edmondson was chosen by Gen. Edmund Gaines as an express rider to go to Nashville, about 500 away, and convey and order to mobilize the Tennessee militia, "to obtain a military force to protect the infant settlements, and to succor his command, and secure the public property from falling into the hands of the Indians." The trip took 12 days of hazardous travel and when he returned in depleted health, Gaines gave him $100.

## John Randon

Peter Randon was deposed under oath on February 1, 1848, by George Y. Bright, "second justice of the peace for the parish of Orleans." As stated on March 24, 1848, by Gilbert C. Russell, the administrator of John Randon's estate:

> John Randon—a half breed—a man of large property consisting of plantations, slaves, stock, &c., &c. When Fort Mims fell, he with his wife and one daughter were killed, one

daughter taken prisoner, and his son Peter was one of 17 men that escaped with life from the havoc.

The amount of losses of Randon's estate was proved before Judge Harry Toulmin, either $6,000 or $8,000. The property taken off and destroyed consisted of negroes, cattle, horses, &c., &c. At one time Weatherford had, as he told me himself, 300 slaves that he had taken from the half-breeds and white people, most of which were recovered towards the close and after the war, but many were killed and starved to death. Weatherford made the men fight, and the Indian negroes were just equal to the red men themselves.

On January 7, 1851, the Office of Indian Affairs in the Department of the Interior reported that John Randon's name could not be found in the original list of claimants and the Second Auditor reported the claim was presented after the $85,000 had been expended.

As reported by the Committee on Indian Affairs on January 29, 1851:

The memorial of Peter Randon, of the city of New Orleans, and State of Louisiana, respectfully showeth: That during the war in 1813 and 1814 with the hostile Creek Indians, the father of your memorialist, John Randon, a friendly half-breed Creek Indian, sustained losses by the ravages of the enemy in the destruction of his houses, horses, cattle, sheep, household furniture, a negress slave, and other property, to the amount of $5,925—a full and authentic account whereof is now on file in the office of the War Department, in the city of Washington.

At the siege of Fort Mims, John Randon, and also his mother, and nearly every member of his family, were slain by the enemy.

In the year 1817 an appropriation of $85,000 was made by Congress to indemnify those who had sustained losses in the Creek War, which was disbursed by Governor Mitchell, but unfortunately proved insufficient, and the claim of your memorialist was never reached. Your memorialist is now the sole living representative of John Randon, and being in destitute circumstances, is compelled to appeal to Congress for relief.

Randon's claim was for 7 horses at $75 each, $505; 7 houses at $100 each, $700; 100 sheep at $4: $400; 20,000 weight seed cotton at 37½ cents, $700; 1 negro girl, aged 10 or 12 years: $300; 300 cattle at $6: $1,800; house and household furniture and farming utensils, $600; 100 hogs at $3: $300; 1,200 bushels of corn at 50 cents: $600.

Gilbert Russell, the representative of John Randon's estate, whose claim wasn't settled at the time, stated many years later:

Of the justness and truth of the claim of Peter Randon, as administrator of his father John Randon's estate, I have no more doubt than I have of anything that I ever witnessed; and but for the avarice and trickery of the agent in 1817, he, with all the others for whom the $85,000 was intended, would have had the amount of their accounts as proved before Judge Toulmin. Mitchell was dismissed for his conduct, or, to avoid dismissal, resigned.

Gilbert Russell also remarked about John Randon's investments:

He embarked the money in an African speculation; the negroes were seized by the marshal before they got from St. Mary's through the Creek nation. David Mitchell could not refund the money, but got credit for goods—invited fictitious claims to the amount of near a million dollars, and paid with these goods at high prices, and took receipts to the amount of $85,000.

Those for whom the sum was intended got one-fifth, one-sixth, one-seventh, or one-eighth of their claims in money. Some got nothing, because they would not go after it.

## Richard Tarvin

As reported by the Committee on Indian Affairs on January 22, 1858:

Richard Tarvin, alias Richard Farrin, was a friendly Creek Indian in the war between the United States and his tribe in 1813–'14, and sustained loss by the depredations of the hostilities to the extent of $600, as reported by General David B. Mitchell, the agent of the federal government.

The heirs of Richard Tarvin, alias Richard Farrin, deceased, were paid $600 in 1858.

Depredations, by definition, can include destruction of property or loss of life and limb. The $600 was paid to Neal Smith, the administrator of Richard Tarvin, of Baldwin County, Alabama.

## *Indemnity for Friendly Indians*

The right of friendly Indians to file claims "for losses sustained in consequence of the claimants taking part with, and remaining friendly to the United States" was based on a letter from Gen. Thomas Pinckney to Col. Benjamin Hawkins, agent for the Creek tribe, dated April, 23, 1814, in which he stated the terms on which peace would be granted to the hostile portion of the tribe, in part:

> The United States will retain so much of the conquered territory as may appear to the government thereof to be a just indemnity for the expenses of the war, and as a restitution for the injuries sustained by its citizens, and the friendly Creek Indians.
>
> You will please, sir, communicate these terms to the friendly Indians, and enjoin them, in the prosecution of the war against such as may continue hostile, to abstain carefully from injuring those who may be returning with the intention of making their submission. You may likewise inform them that the United States will not forget their fidelity; but, in the arrangements which may be made of the lands to be retained as indemnity, their claims will be respected; and such of their chiefs as have distinguished themselves by their exertion and valor in the common cause, will also receive a remuneration in the ceded lands, and in such manner as the government may direct.

On August 9, 1814, Gen. Andrew Jackson concluded the Treaty of Fort Jackson with the Indians which transferred millions of acres of Indian land to the United States, but, with respect to the property claims, Jackson said his power, "did not extend to embrace by treaty or capitulation the promises contained therein." The Indians then refused to sign unless the promise of restitution was sent to Washington along with the treaty, which Jackson agreed to do.

On August 29, 1815, the War Department informed Col. Hawkins, "that it is the wish of the President that you should proceed to the liquidation of the claims of the friendly Indians to indemnify them upon the principles of General Pinckney's and your letter to them."

The report made by Hawkins would be sent to the War Department, "to be laid before the President for his ultimate decision and approbation." On April 1, 1816, Hawkins submitted his report, but stated it was "imperfect, from the peculiar situation of affairs there, and cannot be otherwise till all the hunters are in, which is not expected till the last of next month."

After Samuel Moniac was paid $12,595 in 1816, "all the Indians, half-bloods, and white Indian countrymen appeared before Judge Toulmin in the summer of 1816, stated their losses, valuing their property at the then lowest prices of the country, and proved their accounts by such testimony as would have been admitted in any court of justice."

The claims Col. Hawkins submitted amounted to $108,415.12½ and he stated the "just claims" would not exceed $100,000.

Benjamin Hawkins died on June 6, 1816, and a Creek delegation went to Washington to meet with Secretary of War William Crawford. They spent the winter of 1816–17, "attending to the business of their people," and the claims reported on favorably totaled $78,360.75. Congress then appropriated $85,000.

Secretary of War Crawford addressed them: "You have been a long time detained here; but our great council does business slowly, and you wanted to know, before you returned, how much money they would give your people as a compensation for their property that was destroyed by the hostilities during the late war. The law which was passed on that subject authorizes the President to apply $85,000 to that object. The money will be sent to your agent to be divided among the sufferers in proportion to their losses."

David B. Mitchell was appointed agent for the Creeks and on March 18, 1818, he submitted an account in which he stated that a little over $100,000 was still due as his total for claims presented was just under $300,000, but were "reduced by the chiefs" to $195,417.90. After applying the $85,000 appropriated, a balance of $110,417.90 was left.

On March 29, 1819, Secretary Crawford told a Creek delegation that any additional money could only be appropriated by Congress and on January 6, 1820, said the claims would be submitted to the Committee on Indian Affairs and if approved by Congress would be promptly sent to David Mitchell.

David Brydie Mitchell was a native of Scotland and settled in Georgia where he became a lawyer, judge, mayor of Savannah, governor, and general in the militia. He resigned as governor to accept an appointment as an Indian agent.

Around 1820, Mitchell was accused by John Clark of smuggling slaves into Georgia for sale in Alabama and on March 4, 1821, he was dismissed from his position. Some alleged the accusation was false.

In April 1824, the Committee of Ways and Means, after being directed to, "enquire into the expediency of making an appropriation to compensate the friendly Creek Indians for property lost and destroyed during the late Creek war," reported that it was inexpedient to make any further appropriation on the grounds that the $85,000 was intended as full compensation and that Col. Hawkins stated at the time that the chiefs would have been satisfied with $60,000.

As the petitions from the Mississippi Territory were presented at various times and may have encountered irregularities, the claimants are listed here according to the first date of the Committee report. Not all involve the Creek War.

## *Petition to the State of Alabama*

On February 15, 1832, "sundry individuals belonging to the Creek Indians" petitioned the legislature of Alabama for assistance from the Government, to wit: Thomas Armstrong for Josiah Fletcher, Dixon Bailey, James Bailey, Lauchlin Durant, James Earles, Charles Elhert, David Hale, William Hollinger, Arthur Sizemore, Lynn MacGhee, Zachariah MacGirt, David Moniac, William Oliver for his wife Polly Jones, Simmoice for David Tate (deceased), Arthur Sizemore, George Stiggins, and John Weatherford.

As reported by the Committee of Claims on May 15, 1838:

> The Legislature of the State of Alabama, on the 23d of December, 1837, passed a joint memorial addressed to the Congress of the United States, asking remuneration for those individuals who have sustained losses in consequence of the late war with the Creek Indians, and in that memorial it is represented that many of the citizens of Alabama, residing in that portion of the State lately occupied by the Creek nation of Indians, have been subjected to great pecuniary losses in consequence of depredations committed upon their property by hostile Indians of the Creek tribe in the prosecution of their savage warfares against the white settlers.
>
> In many instances the hostile Indians have devastated plantations by destroying the then growing crops; they have burnt dwellings and other necessary houses; they have carried away and appropriated to their own use, personal property of great value to the owners, and many of their citizens were compelled to abandon their homes to secure their personal safety by reason whereof their property was destroyed, the amount of which injuries and losses the memorialists could not undertake to estimate.
>
> Relief is asked on the ground that the

United States are bound to protect the citizens and to preserve their property.

The memorialists further represent that during the war many crops were destroyed and considerable property appropriated from necessity by Indians who were friendly, by troops engaged in the military service of the United States, and also by troops who flocked to the standard of their country at the requisition of the governor of Alabama and who were not mustered into the service of the United States, which they say should be paid for, and they pray that an appropriation may be made for that purpose.

There is no evidence to sustain the memorial. The committee have given to the subject all the examination and deliberation that are due to the sufferings of a portion of our citizens, and to the character of the memorialists, and it would be much more gratifying to their feelings to allow the claims than to reject them, if they could do so in the conscientious discharge of their duty, and be sustained in their decision by precedent, and the settled policy of the government.

The committee admit the government of the United States is bound to protect the citizens of Alabama in their persons, and to preserve their property to the fullest extent that any government is bound to its citizens, but it does not follow from thence that the government becomes the insurer of the property of such citizens.

The government is equally bound to protect the property of our citizens employed in commerce as it is to give protection to those whose capital is employed in agriculture. If the Malays, or pirates, should seize a vessel, murder the crew, and take the cargo to their use, no one would say the United States were bound to remunerate the loss. A misunderstanding may exist between the government and a foreign power, by which the millions employed by our citizens in commerce and navigation may be swept from the ocean and rendered valueless, and yet no one would remunerate the sufferers from the Treasury of the United States.

Thousands of such sufferers now exist, and they have combated poverty for years without relief. Such is the case with those who have suffered by Indian depredations on the frontiers, as the settlements have progressed southwest and west, and by those who suffered during the war with Great Britain which commenced in 1812. Every section of our country has, at some period, been a sufferer for the common benefit of the whole Union, and if an accurate and just account were taken, it would be found that the losses have been distributed with a tolerably even hand.

The principle laid down may have been departed from in a very few cases, but from the haste in which business is sometimes transacted, or from inadvertness; but if any such cases exist, they are too few for precedents, and should not be taken as varying the principle.

If the amount of this class of claims in 1800 was an impediment to making a favorable report, how fearfully has it increased in the years that have intervened, within which we have had an embargo, a non-intercourse act, a war with England, a violation of our neutrality by the belligerent powers of England and France, and almost a constant collision with some of the Indian tribes, by which the property of our citizens has perished at our wharves, or been destroyed on the ocean and on the land. The obligation of the government is not to remunerate such losses, but to prevent their occurrence as far as is practicable. This the memorialists do not allege has not been done.

It is not expedient to grant the relief prayed for in the joint memorial of the Senate and House of Representatives of the State of Alabama, in General Assembly convened, approved on the 23d day of December, 1837.

## Six Claimants

On August 3, 1854, the Committee on Military Affairs reported six "friendly Creek Indians" presented claims after the $85,000 had been distributed as reported by Gen. Mitchell, to wit: Lachian Durant was paid $582; Arthur Sigemond, $1,420; John Simmance, $1,163; Peter Randon, $5,925; and Tallmassee Emanthlan, $80, for a total of $9,770.

As reported by the Committee on Indian Affairs on January 22, 1858:

By the treaty negotiated with the Creek tribe at the close of the war, the United States guaranteed indemnity to those Indians who had remained friendly to our cause, for whatever property they had lost during the war by the common enemy.

Claims were presented against the government for such losses, on the part of the friendly Creeks, amounting, in the aggregate to $195,417.90, all of which has been provided for and paid by Congress. In addition to the claims embraced in the amount, a supplemental abstract of claims was presented by General Mitchell in favor of six other friendly Creek Indians, amounting, all together, to $9,770. Among these latter claimants is found the name of Richard Tarvin, alias Richard Farrin, and his damages were assessed at $600.

Of the half a dozen claimants included in the supplemental abstract of General Mitchell, the sum of $5,925 were paid to Peter Randall in an act passed by the 33rd Congress. The claims of Arthur Sigemond for $1,420, and of John Simmance for $1,163 were provided for in the Indian appropriation bill of last Congress.

# Georgia

## *Georgia Claims*

### Joseph G. Posner

Joseph G. Posner and Sylvia S. Posner lived in Jefferson County, Georgia, in a house called Richmond Bath. Joseph died in 1812. Maj. William Schley was a Georgia politician and one of the executors of his estate. A claim was filed by Sylvia, as stated by the Committee of Claims on June 12, 1832:

> This case was examined on the petition of William Schley, executor of Joseph G. Posner at the 2nd session of the 19th Congress, and at the 1st session of the 21st Congress, and unfavorable reports were made against the claims. The committee was not satisfied that the house was occupied by the order of an officer. There was evidence of occupation anterior to the time of the destruction, but not at the time the house was destroyed by fire.
>
> It appeared from the evidence that Captain Richard Proctor was the last officer who was in command at the Richmond Baths, and his testimony was not obtained, nor was the omission accounted for. It appears from a statement recently made by Mr. Hunter that the residence of Captain Proctor is not known, if he is alive. Mr. Schley put the claim on the ground that the buildings were occupied by contract made with General Thomas Flournoy, and that the occupation was to be without compensation, and evidence was introduced to prove such contract, which was not satisfactory to the committee. If there was a contract, as was set up by the executor, the committee required it to be proven by General Flournoy himself. He stated, in a certificate, that his headquarters were at a place called Richmond Bath, belonging to Joseph G. Posner. This was during the summer of 1812.
>
> Extracts from different official reports have been obtained from the Adjutant General's office by which it appears that Bath was established as a rendezvous for the troops on account of its healthy position, and the unhealthiness of Louisville; and it further appears that it was so occupied through the years 1812 and part of 1813.
>
> On the 22nd of August, 1814, the Assistant Adjutant General reported that his papers had been consumed by fire at Bath, which occasioned delay in making his report. The committee has inquired, and been informed, that Bath was not the name of a village or town, but was a watering place owned by Mr. Posner, and that the buildings consisted of a large house, occupied as a tavern, with several out buildings.
>
> John Colvin, a soldier, was stationed at the house at the time it was burnt, and states that it was supposed to have happened by placing some light wood near to the fire, which caught fire, which was communicated to the ceiling, and then to the roof. Taking the whole testimony together, the committee come to this conclusion: that this place called the Richmond Bath, was established as a place of rendezvous for an indefinite period of time, to be used as long a troops might be recruited in that quarter; that the soldiers used the out buildings, and the officers occupied the mansion house, which was occupied a part of the time as a tavern, but that, at the time it was burnt, it was not so occupied, but that it was used as quarters for the officers. The committee could have wished more conclusive evidence, but the bill from the Senate is reported to the House with the proof, and its passage recommended, after adopting an amendment, that the amount be paid to Joseph G. Posner's representatives.

Louisville is the county seat of Jefferson County. Thomas Flournoy served in the Georgia militia, was commissioned a brigadier general in the Army, and commanded the Seventh Military District. John Colvin was a private in Capt. John Thom's company in the 2nd Regiment of Virginia Militia, and Capt. Richard Proctor was in the 5th Regiment of Virginia Militia.

## John Ross

Charles Ross and Samuel Breck, "surviving executors of John Ross, deceased," filed a claim for "damages which they have sustained in consequence of the occupation, by the troops of the United States, of Point Peter, in the state of Georgia, in the loss of the rent of the farm, and of the wood, and other fuel thereon."

April 27, 1816. (6 Stat. L. 173)

As stated on the historical marker in St. Marys, Georgia:

> In 1795 a cannon battery constructed on the Point Peter peninsula became the southernmost fortification in the First System of U.S. coastal defenses. Vacated in 1802, it was reoccupied and strengthened in 1808 to provide support for the enforcement of the Embargo Act and the prohibition of the international slave trade. In 1812, former Georgia governor George Matthews, led the unsanctioned invasion of Spanish Florida from Point Peter. On January 13, 1815, during the War of 1812, a British force overwhelmed 116 U.S. regulars here, destroying the fort and barracks. After the U.S. acquired Florida in 1819, the post was abandoned.

On June 10, 1815, John Ross wrote to Peter Early, the governor of Georgia, to report rampant robbery and vandalism in the area, particularly by Indians.

# Louisiana

The first Gulf Coast settlements the French founded in 1699 were known as La Louisiane. The mercantile system established was based on the same principles as the British-American colonies and were expected to produce a return on the investment, but were not as successful as hoped, but still attracted settlers.

In 1743, Pierre de Rigaud de Vaudreuil became governor when the colony was still struggling, but he managed to establish relations with the Chickasaw and Choctaw Indians and commenced a program of public works, forts, and churches. Despite these efforts, the colony did not thrive and on November 3, 1762, France ceded La Louisiane to Spain, which the residents resented, but they managed their affairs until 1766 when Gov. Don Antonio de Ulloa arrived. Sensing the mood of the population, Ulloa made no changes in administration, but when certain economic changes were proposed, a rebellion broke out and Ulloa was kicked out two years later. Spanish rule everywhere was generally on the harsh side, and the next year when Lt. Gen. Alejandro O'Reilly arrived with ships and 2,000 soldiers, the rebellious ringleaders were arrested and caused no further trouble.

In 1800, when Spain gave Louisiana back to France, the colony was still relatively poor with around 7,500 residents and. In 1802, Napoleon appointed Pierre Clément de Laussat governor and the population and prosperity exploded. When Laussat arrived in 1803, the population had reached about 50,000. In August he was told France was giving Louisiana to the United States. He took formal possession from Spain on November 20, and on December 20 Louisiana was transferred to the United States to the great annoyance of Great Britain.

The Louisiana Territory was established on March 3, 1805, and the state admitted to the Union on April 30, 1812. It is the only state whose legal heritage does not come from English common law, and their legislature did not subscribe to the 1892 Uniform Commercial Code until 1990.

Britain's defeat of Napoleon in the spring of 1814 released resources for the American war. Washington City was burned without accomplishing much militarily, and the effort to put Baltimore's shipbuilders out of business failed.

## *Baton Rouge*

### John Harding

Harding and others were the owners of 15 boats that apparently were impressed by Gen. Philemon Thomas at Baton Rouge. As stated by the Committee of Claims on January 26, 1820:

> With respect to the boats, the testimony is defective in the extreme; it being no where proved even that the claimants sustained the loss for which they claim compensation. Some of the evidence appears to have been

taken under a commission issued by the late commissioners, which is not with the papers. And the original order of Gen. Philemon Thomas and other papers connected with the claim, referred to in the deposition of John Harding, one of the claimants, as having been thereafter forwarded to Washington, are not produced.

The owners were paid $720 in 1820 and $180 in 1825 under a supplementary act. Maj. Gen. Philemon Thomas commanded Louisiana militia at Baton Rouge in 1814 and 1815.

## *New Orleans*

Sieur de Bienville wanted a town named after the Duc d'Orleans and after considerable opposition as to its location, it became, in 1718, what is now New Orleans.

Vice-Admiral Sir Alexander Cochrane believed capturing New Orleans and controlling the Mississippi River would greatly weaken and divide America. After Parliament approved an expedition, Adm. Cochrane planned use Jamaica for the staging area and to anchor his troopships as close as possible to the city. Troops would then be transported in barges to Lake Borgne and then head west overland to New Orleans.

Around this time, Commodore Daniel T. Patterson at New Orleans had his hands full dealing with Jean Laffite's piracy enterprise on Barataria Bay and on September 16 raided his base and captured six schooners and a number of other craft.

Spies were everywhere, lips were loosened by liquor, bravado, sexual overtures, or torture, and information from various locales was bought and sold. With a friendly ear or two open, Patterson learned the British were going to attempt to take New Orleans. He immediately informed Gen. Andrew Jackson, commander of the 7th Military District at Mobile, Alabama. Jackson had just become available after defeating the Red Stick Creeks and he arrived at New Orleans on December 1. His first job was to organize a makeshift army of regulars, militia, and reformed pirates, but his primary concern was the British cutting off his supplies from Mobile.

The naval station at New Orleans had been sadly neglected by Navy Secretary William Jones, despite warnings, and to make matters worse, President Jefferson, the "pinchpenny pacifist" in Washington, chose to build 257 small gunboats instead of one or two frigates. After Napoleon was defeated, the Royal Navy had 219 ships of the line and 296 frigates.

Patterson then had very limited resources, no deep draft ships, and could in no way repel a British invasion at sea. But he knew the sandbars, shoal water, and strong currents would prevent the British from approaching the town from the Gulf so any expedition would have to come overland from the east. The entire area was a huge quagmire of lakes, inlets, islands, swamps, marshes, canals, and plantations.

The closest the 50 British vessels with 7,000 aboard could get to New Orleans was the Chandeleur Islands, about 50 miles due east where they arrived on December 8.

## *Lake Borgne*

When British barges were reported at Pensacola, Patterson sent Lt. Thomas Ap. Catesby Jones to Lake Borgne with five gunboats, a tender, and a dispatch boat on December 9 with orders to deploy his vessels at his discretion for surveillance and interdiction, if possible. Jones was in *Gunboat No. 156* and on the 13th the British were sighted. Jones planned to move to Fort Petite Coquilles at the entrance to Lake Pontchartrain if the British force was too large to engage, which it was, but the wind and shoal waters prevented their escape and he was obliged to anchor off Malheureux Island.

At dawn on December 14, British Capt. Nicholas Lockyer's barges with 1,200 soldiers and 42 cannons spotted the gunboats and rowed in to attack. As stated later, Jones was wounded, by a ball, "which passing through the joint of the left shoulder, and taking a downward course, lodged in the body between the blade and the ribs, where it still remains—at times causing painful inconvenience, with the irreparable loss of the injured joint." Jones was knocked into the water, but could not swim, and was saved by Thomas B. Parsons, who entered the Navy in 1808 from the merchant marine and was assigned to *Gunboat No. 22* under Sailing Master Brown, possibly Eli Brown, whose life Parsons also saved.

Ten American sailors were lost, 35 wounded, and 86 taken prisoner, including Jones. All their stores, personal effects, and money were looted, including $100 in personal funds belonging to Jones.

That same day, December 14, Admiral Cochrane sent Capt. Robert Cavendish Spencer, 23, of the 20-gun post ship *Carron* to reconnoiter a route to New Orleans along with Army Lt. John Peddie, and a coxswain. Spencer spoke several languages and the three disguised themselves as locals. When they encountered a fisherman/smuggler from Bayou Bienvenue, Spencer hired him as guide. He took them up a creek from the bayou and from there the trio made their way across to the Jacques Philippe Villeré plantation on the Mississippi River. The scouting party returned on the 18th without having been seen.

On December 20, British soldiers from the 4th, 85th and 95th Rifle Brigades, rocketeers, and 100 engineers assembled on the western shore of Lake Borgne and early on December 23, an advanced party arrived at the Jacques Philippe Villeré plantation and occupied Jacques' house for their headquarters.

About 30 British troops from the 85th and 95th Brigades scouting for American sentries supposedly captured Gabriel Villeré who lived near the Villeré Canal. He supposedly had been ordered by Gen. Jackson to block up the canal but had not done so. He managed to escape and proceeded to cross the river to alert Jackson of the British presence.

Another plantation owner named Pierre Denis La Ronde spotted the force, which he estimated at about 1,800. He escaped detection, and reported to Gen. Jackson. That day, the Navy's schooner *Carolina*, fired on the "British bivouac" and that night Jackson made an attack on the British, but was forced to fall back to the canal. The British regrouped and on the 28th mounted another indecisive attack.

Whether any British barges made it to the Mississippi River, or what part the Villeré canal, other canals, or Bayou Bienvenue played in Gen. Jackson's eventual victory seems to vary with each historical account.

Jones and the other prisoners were released in January 1815, and a Court of Inquiry was convened to examine Johnes' conduct. He was absolved of any dereliction of duty at Lake Borgne, and, despite the loss, Jones was credited with significantly delaying the British arrival at New Orleans. He was, however, passed over for promotion, and on December 22, 1815, wrote to President Madison to plead his case to no avail.

In 1816, he filed a claim for the money, clothing, and personal effects he and his crew lost. Claims for lost personal property, with the exception of pursers and sutlers, were generally denied, but in this case the Committee of Claims was subsequently overruled, as was the claim of Thomas Shields.

Jones was promoted to commander on March 28, 1820, and subsequently became involved in a number of events, including the acquisition of California from Mexico. His name appears in several versions in print, but he signed it *Thos: apC. Jones* in a clear, firm hand on documents at the Naval Academy's Nimitz Library. His name appears in the Naval Registers as "Thomas Ap. Catesby Jones."

The location of Fort Petite Coquilles is known, but nothing is left of the structure.

## Thomas Shields

Thomas Shields was purser in the Navy at New Orleans in 1812. He had three claims, arranged by the date of the incident:

The loss of Purser's stores, as stated by the Committee of Claims January 4, 1819:

> The memorialist states that Commodore John Shaw, whilst he commanded the naval forces of the United States on the New Orleans station, caused to be built a public storehouse for the use of the United States. This storehouse was built at the Bay of St. Louis on a lot belonging to the memorialist and by him voluntarily tendered for that purpose. The house at the time of the attack of the enemy at that point, on the 13th of December, 1814, contained stores, for the supply of the crews of vessels attached to that station, belonging to the memorialist of the value of $4,887.96.
>
> Previous to the attack of the enemy, the memorialist had erected, principally at his own expense, a small gun battery for the protection of the store and the property contained in it, from which a fire so steady and well directed was kept up that the enemy was baffled in his several attempts to effect a landing, till the night of the 13th of December, 1814, when a positive order was received by the person having charge of the store, from Lieutenant Jones, commanding the detachment of naval force on the station, directing the same to be blown up and destroyed, which was accordingly done.
>
> Adjacent to the public store was a building belonging to the memorialist and materials for other buildings of the value of $1,693.10, to which fire produced by the burning of the public store, extended, whereby the building and materials were totally destroyed.
>
> The memorialist states his whole loss occasioned by the burning of the public store, to the amount of $6,581.06, for which he prays remuneration from Congress, if they shall think his claim just.
>
> The committee are of opinion that it is supported by the testimony exhibited. The stores which were properly destroyed by the burning of the public storehouse, by order of the United States officer commanding on the station to prevent their falling into the hands of the enemy, were lodged at that place by the memorialist for the use of the naval force in the neighborhood. They were of the kind and quality always furnished for such purpose, by pursers in the Navy, which was the office held by the memorialist, and the public store from which they could be easily and quickly put on board the vessels requiring them, appears to have been the most natural place for their deposit. That independent of the merits of the memorialist, in voluntarily tendering a situation for the erection and use of this building for public purposes, and erecting a battery principally at his own expense, the committee think, under all the circumstances of the case, compensation ought to be made to the memorialist for the loss of the stores and his house and building materials adjacent to the storehouse and consumed by the fire which caught from the burning of the same, and for this purpose they herewith report a bill.

For the loss of stores on Lake Borgne, as stated on January 13, 1819, by the Committee on Naval Affairs:

> The memorialist states that during the invasion of Louisiana by a British force, in the winter of 1814, he, in his capacity of purser in the Navy on the New Orleans station, furnished five gun-vessels of the United States, then stationed in Lake Borgne, with stores and necessaries for the supply of their crews, to the amount of $2,492.08.
>
> On the 14th December, the gun-vessels, then under command of Lieutenant Thomas C. Ap. Jones, were attacked by a superior force, and captured after a gallant resistance; that by reason of the capture, the memorialist lost the whole of the stores so furnished for the use and comfort of the crews, and prays remuneration from Congress.
>
> The committee find, upon examination, that the stores above stated by the memorialist were his private property, consisting of sugar, coffee, knives, combs, &c.; that by the

regulations of the naval service, the purser is authorized to sell to the crews of the vessels articles of the above description at a limited but liberal advance; that this privilege is, generally speaking, very profitable to the purser, and is no doubt one of the great inducements to the attainment of that appointment in the naval service, generally sought after, the committee believe, with solicitude.

The committee have not been able to find that the public have heretofore made good any losses of this description, though doubtless many have occurred. Were this a solitary case, the committee would feel a strong disposition to make good the loss, on account of the general good conduct, patriotism, and public spirit of the memorialist, which is abundantly proved. But the committee must act upon principles applicable to all cases of a similar nature.

The hazard incurred in cases of this kind in time of war is an ordinary one, and perfectly understood, it is presumed, by all persons encountering it. It is met for the chance of the profit on the sales of the articles; which premium, the committee think, ought to cover the risk, and that the United States ought not to be considered as insurers in cases of this description.

The committee recommend that the prayer of the petition ought not to be granted.

For losses while held as a prisoner, as reported by the Committee on Naval Affairs on December 29, 1818:

The memorialist states that he was a purser in the Navy on the New Orleans Station during the time of the invasion of that part of the United States by the enemy during the late war with Great Britain. On the morning of the 15th of December, 1814, he was ordered by Commodore Patterson, commanding naval officer on that station, to proceed under the protection of a flag of truce on a special mission to the commander of the British fleet, then in the neighborhood of Lake Borgne. On reaching the enemy there at the mouth of Pearle River, Admiral Cochrane, the commander, through motives of caution, as he alleges, thought it proper to detain him as a prisoner, and he was accordingly kept in confinement till the 13th of January, 1815.

On his return to New Orleans he suggested to Commodore Patterson, the idea of an attempt to harass and cut off part of the enemy on their retreat, which from observation of their position and movements, he thought, although hazardous, likely to succeed. On the memorialist volunteering in the enterprise, it received the sanction of Comm. Patterson, who put at his disposal such open boats as could be obtained, one of which, a launch, mounted a 12-pound carronade, the only piece of ordnance the memorialist had under his command. With the exception of munitions of war, 5 boats were fitted out at the private expense of the memorialist, which were manned with about 50 hands, chiefly volunteers. This force under the command of the memorialist, notwithstanding all their exertions, were unable to commence operations against the enemy till the night of the 19th of January when he captured one of their barges and made prisoners of 54 men, whom he delivered at the headquarters of General Jackson, without any loss on the part of the memorialist.

The memorialist further states that on the 21st of January, he succeeded in capturing seven of the enemy's barges with 78 men and in burning a large and valuable coppered transport. By this time the enemy had succeeded in regaining their shipping when the memorialist returned to New Orleans.

The memorialist states that nothing but the heavy losses sustained by him during the invasion of Louisiana would have induced him to make application to Congress for remuneration for any exertions made by him, believing, as he does, that the person of every good citizen, and his means also, ought to be at the disposition of the government in times of emergency, but from the circumstances above mentioned, he is induced respectfully to present himself to the notice of Congress and ask for his services such remuneration as Congress may think they deserve.

The committee have considered the case of the memorialist and are of opinion that it is substantially correct according to the evidence produced. They further state that from the letter of Commodore Patterson, the conduct of the memorialist is placed in the most favorable point of view on account of his voluntary and patriotic exertions to serve the cause of his country.

The committee are of opinion that the case does not come under the provisions of any law making compensation for prisoners taken, inasmuch as the memorialist was in the service of the United States, and the vessels which he used belonged to the public as well as their munitions of war. in searching for a rule by which they think he ought to be made in this case, they think the principle of that law, which allows $20 for each person on board an enemy's vessel sunk or destroyed in action by an equal or inferior force most applicable and report a bill grounded on that standard compensation.

## Nathan Winteringer

His claim was presented to the House of Representatives on the February 2, 1824, and referred to the Committee on Military Affairs. On the 24th of January 1826, it was presented to the Senate, referred to the Committee on Military Affairs, and was discharged from consideration on March 23. On April, 14, 1834, it was again presented in the House and referred to the Committee on Military Affairs and tabled. It was presented again on December 12, 1834, and rejected. It was presented again on January 7, 1836, and referred to the Committee on Military Affairs, where it was discharged from further consideration on February 4, and was then referred to the Committee of Claims.

As reported by the Committee of Claims on March 3, 1836:

The petitioner, a citizen of Jefferson County, Ohio, states that on the 6th of October, 1812, he fitted out a keelboat from Steubenville for a trading expedition upon the lower Mississippi under the charge of Ralph Foster. The boat had 349 barrels of apples, 20 barrels of flour, 4 barrels of whiskey, 2 barrels of cider wine, and 1 barrel of cider, besides the necessary stores for the use of the boatmen.

The boat arrived at New Orleans on the 14th of December, 1814, with the whole cargo except 8 barrels of apples and 10 barrels of flour sold at Baton Rouge and Natchez. While at Natchez, the captain engaged with Mr. Prior, of the house of Jelly & Prior, merchants at New Orleans, for a full freight of sugar and cotton from New Orleans for Pittsburgh.

On the 17th of December martial law was declared in the city by the commanding general and the captain was told by Mr. Prior he could not attend to delivering the freight under martial law. The captain could do no business, the city being closely guarded by sentinels. He states that on the 17th of December, orders were given for the boatmen to enroll themselves or they would be pressed into the service of the United States. Captain Foster, with his hands and most of the other boatmen, volunteered their services for the defense of New Orleans, and the property in their charge, and elected Robert Sprigg for the captain of their company.

That these boatmen volunteered and a company being formed, they were kept constantly engaged in drawing arms and ammunition, and in training until the 22nd December, when they marched below the city to join in its defense.

He says the cargo was watched, as well as the situation of the captain and the hands would permit until the 23rd of December when they were ordered below New Orleans. The cargo of the boat, which had been fastened to the bank, was lost, estimated at $1,600, plundered of the entire cargo, and the question is, whether, under the circumstances, the United States should pay the petitioner the loss sustained. He further states that his boat was worth at the time $900, and could have been sold for that sum if the captain had not been taken into the service as mentioned, but after the return of peace the captain was obliged to sell the boat to procure the means to return home, for $150. He says the loss he sustained ruined his property, and left him with a family, to work daily for his sustenance.

The facts as related by the petitioner are substantially established by the testimony. It is proven that the boat was used by the United States to transport troops across the river after the cargo was pillaged. There is no testimony to show how long the boat was in the military service nor what would be a reasonable compensation for its use, nor that its use was not paid for by a disbursing officer. The petitioner states it was sold by his agent, and he does not raise any claim against the United States for the use of the boat.

The United States have not been considered the insurers of the property of her citizens against the depredations of thieves, nor against wanton acts of violence, even when they are compelled to enter the military service to protect the country from invasion. In this instance, the enrollment of Captain Foster and his men was voluntary.

There is no excuse given for leaving the cargo on board of the boat. Prudence required that the cargo should have been stored, and it would have been extraordinary, being left on board of a boat, if it had not been pillaged, whether in a state of war or peace.

The case is one, however, aside from any negligence on the part of the person who had charge of the boat that cannot be relieved without establishing new rules and principles.

The committee, conforming to former decisions, submit the petitioner is not entitled to relief.

The claim was again reported on unfavorably by the Committee of Claims on September 16, 1850.

## Robert Fulton

Robert Fulton died on February, 24, 1815, at age 49, and was survived by his wife, Harriet, 28, son Robert, and daughters, Julia, Cornelia, and Mary. He left no estate so the family filed a claim for the seizure and impressment of his steamboat *Vesuvius*; his invention of steam-powered floating batteries, "for the defense of the coasts and harbors of the United States, and his services in superintending the construction of the steam frigate *Fulton*." In February 1826, the United States sued the heirs over the amounts claimed.

Mary died on March 24, 1826, and the surviving heirs pursued the claim. On June 23, 1836, Congress passed Resolution No. 9:

*Resolved*, That the petition and papers of the heirs of Robert Fulton, be referred to the Secretary of the Navy, to state an account between the United States and said heirs, by debiting them with all the moneys paid to Robert Fulton, and not settled on the books of the Treasury Department.

*Second*. To credit the heirs with all moneys advanced or expended by Fulton, in and about the business of the United States, committed to his care, or about which he had an agency.

*Third*. To credit the heirs a compensation commensurate with the value and importance of the services rendered by Robert Fulton, to the United States, in inventing a system of coast and harbor defense, and in testing its utility so far as he was employed or engaged to render such services by the authorities of the United States, or when such services were recognized as having been rendered for the United States, previous to, or during, the late war with Great Britain.

*Fourth*. To credit the heirs with a just and equitable compensation, for the detention of the steam-boat *Vesuvius*, at New Orleans, from the 13th of December, 1814, to the 12th of March, 1815, both days inclusive, being the time the boat remained aground by reason of her being impressed into the service of the United States, and grounded when in service.

Sec. 2. That the Secretary of the Navy be authorized to take such further testimony as he shall think necessary and that he ascertain what defense was made to the suit in favor of the United States, against the representatives of Robert Fulton in the Southern District of New York, and what composed the items of set-off to the claim of the United States.

January 3, 1837, Secretary of the Navy Mahlon Dickerson credited the heirs $50,000 for detention of the *Vesuvius*; $60,000 for the invention of the steam-powered floating batteries; and $25,000 for superintending the construction of the steam-frigate.

Fulton was credited for receiving $5,000 for developing experiments with torpedoes, and another $5,000 for carrying them out, and was also paid $40,000 to transport troops, "making the balance due to Mr. Fulton's heirs $100,000." On appeal, the Committee of Claims reduced balance due to the heirs to $76,300, as stated:

As stated by the Committee of Claims on February 15, 1844:

The steamboat *Vesuvius* was impressed into the public service by order of General Jackson, as early as the 30th of December, 1814,

> and that afterwards, and while under the control of persons in the United States service, she grounded, and could not be got off until the 12th of March, 1815.
>
> The Hon. Edward Livingston, late Secretary of State, who acted a conspicuous part in the trying scenes at New Orleans, states that the steamboat *Vesuvius* was taken into the public service by impressment; that she was not hired for the service—it being one that would have exposed her to destruction or injury from the enemies batteries, the captain was very averse to her being taken; that cannon were put on board of her; that it was intended that she should be brought down the river to enfilade the enemy's ranks on their march, if they should attack ours; that the water having fallen, she grounded, and was left dry on the sand-bars about 100 feet from the water's edge; that he was sent up by the general with orders to employ a company of boatmen which had been embodied at the city to try to set her afloat; that they attempted to do so in various ways, but without success; and that she remained there until the next rise of water.

The Committee of Claims reduced the award to $76,300, as stated:

> For the detention of the steamer *Vesuvius*, impressed into the public service at New Orleans by order of General Jackson, from the 30th December, 1814, to the 12th March, 1815,—being 73 days at $600 per day, $43,000.
>
> For the invention of the steam battery, $60,000.
>
> For services as naval constructor in building the steam frigate *Fulton*, five percent on the cost ($250,000), $12,500, for a total of $116,300.
>
> Advances made by the government for the transportation of troops, which became unnecessary in consequence of the conclusion of the war, $40,000.
>
> Balance due to the heirs of Mr. Fulton, $76,300.

Capt. Robeson De Hart, master of the *Vesuvius* said his ship was the only steamboat between Louisville, Kentucky, and New Orleans in the winter of 1814–15, "and as she arrived at New Orleans during the great alarm occasioned by the appearance of the British army before the city, her services might have been worth to her owner during the campaign, (which lasted between three and four months) from $800 to $900 per day."

It was intended on December 27, 1814, to contract with the *Vesuvius*, *Ætna*, *New Orleans*, and *Natchez* to transport troops and munitions on the Mississippi and the steamboat Buffalo on the Ohio River, but the war ended. Word of the end of hostilities was not known at New Orleans until three days later, "but not according to the terms of the contract, nor in fulfillment of the same."

On August 7, 1846, the heirs of Fulton were paid $76,300, "in full of the claims of Fulton against the United States for inventing floating steam batteries and superintending the steam frigate *Fulton*, for the detention of, and damage to, his steamboat *Vesuvius*, and for the great benefits conferred on the country by his improvements in the application of steam to navigation."

## Francis Larche

As reported by the Committee of Claims on May 11, 1830:

> While the British army lay before New Orleans in the Winter of 1814 and 1815, the commanding General on that station issued an order to the Mayor of New Orleans and the Syndic of the suburbs to procure carts, horses, and drivers for the use of the army. In consequence of this order, the cart, horse, and negro man, Antoine, belonging to the petitioner, were impressed and sent to the lines of the American army on the 1st day of January, 1815, where the negro man was killed by a cannon ball from the British batteries, while in the service of the United States.
>
> The subject is one of much delicacy, and the committee are not disposed to increase or add to the excitement which a discussion of it has, within a few years past, created. The Committee of Claims have endeavored in their decisions to be governed by the principles established by laws relating to the allowance of claims against the United States by the decisions of Congress in the same or in analogous cases.

At a former Congress, when a similar case was before the committee, they directed an inquiry to be made of the Register of the Treasury, whether slaves were paid for during the American Revolution, when they were killed in the military service, and they were informed that no instance of the kind could be found.

The first claim presented since the late war was that of Andrew Montgomery, 1st session, 14th Congress. The petitioner was a lieutenant in the rifle corps and at the battle of Fort Mims, his waiter, a slave, was killed, or run off, or was captured and carried off by the Indians. The committee said that, "where an officer took a slave into the service, the United States ought not to be liable for the value of the slave if he should be killed, or by other accident, be lost to the owner."

The next claim for the loss of a slave was presented by William P. Lawrence at the same session. Mr. Lawrence was a surgeon in the army and on the return of the Tennessee militia he was ordered to remain at Bogue Chilito in the State of Louisiana and attend upon the soldiers who were afflicted with a contagious disease. Nurses could not be obtained, either from the line of the army or the inhabitants. Dr. Lawrence was obliged to put his slave into the hospital to nurse the sick, where he contracted the same disease and died. The claim was rejected on the ground that the United States were not liable to pay for the slave.

The next claim was presented by Basil Shaw at the 1st session 15th Congress. Mr. Shaw was Assistant Adjutant General and took his slave into the service with him, who was killed by a cannon shot on the morning of the 8th of January, 1815, while in the service, and attending to his duty. The committee say, "They are decidedly of the opinion that Congress is under no obligation whatever to remunerate the petitioner." No principle of legislation is perhaps better settled than this, that for such losses government cannot be liable.

The claim of Robert Evans for a slave who died in the service from fatigue was reported against at the same session. A claim of Jacob Parkhill was rejected at the 1st session 16th Congress, and that of P.S. Lendy at the 1st session 17th Congress.

Similar claims have since been rejected. It may be said that the cases referred to are for slaves that were voluntarily taken into the service: there is that difference between those cases and this; but the question of impressed slaves seems to have been discussed and decided on. And, when the bill authorizing further payment to sufferers during the late war was under consideration on the 24th of January, 1825, Mr. Forsyth moved to amend it so as to provide payment for slaves lost in the public service. The motion was negatived by a large majority, only 48 members rising at that time in its favor.

With these different reports, and the decisions of Congress, this committee do not conceive that they would be justified, whatever might be their own opinion, in recommending relief. They concur, however, in the principles contained in the reports and decisions and move that the bill from the Senate for the relief of Francis Larche be rejected.

## William Flood

As stated by the Committee of Claims on February 16, 1816:

> The petitioner owned and occupied a valuable dwelling-house, together with a valuable mill and other out-houses on the west side of the Mississippi, previous to the month of December, 1814. On the 27th of that month, the plantation was taken possession of by Brigadier General David B. Morgan, under an order from General Andrew Jackson, then commanding the United States troops in New Orleans and its vicinity, and the houses occupied by the officers and troops under his command.
>
> On the morning of the 8th of January, 1815, General Morgan was attacked by the enemy, forced from his position, and the houses of the petitioner, together with his mill and timber, at the same time destroyed by the enemy. It appears to the committee that the property was destroyed on account of its being occupied by the troops of the United States, and for the purpose of preventing barracks being again erected for the defense of New Orleans. No other buildings at that place, or in the neighborhood, were destroyed; and it was known to the enemy that the mill of the petitioner had furnished the timber with which the batteries had been constructed.

Dr. Flood joined Gen. Jackson's forces during the battle. He died suddenly in

April, 1823, at age 48, and is the namesake for Flood St. in New Orleans.

## Jacob Purkill

As reported by the Committee of Claims on January 20, 1819:

> In November, 1814, the petitioner hired a fine negro man named Arche to a certain James Edwards, commander of John Will's barge *Kitty* for a voyage to New Orleans and back to Eddyville, on the Cumberland River.
>
> On the December 17 following, when the barge arrived at New Orleans, the black men among whom was the slave of your petitioner were all impressed by order of the commanding general for fatigue duty, and were sent to cut away the timber in and about the Bayou St. John where they were constantly in wet, and in deep mire. So dreadful was the condition of these laborers that the greatest rigor was necessary to keep them to their duty, and Arche worked incessantly 27 days in the mud and water. By this means he fell sick and very shortly died of a disease of his lungs.
>
> The loss sustained by your petitioner in the death of this man is estimated at $700, and as he is informed by the commissioner for property lost, captured, or destroyed, that his authority under the law only extended to actual losses at the time of service, and not to consequential losses, he prays that Congress will feel the justice of his claim, and grant him compensation for a loss of property, which is as grievous to him, and as certainly the consequence of taking property into the public service, as if the death had taken place during the time of his labor at the Bayou St. John.
>
> The committee are of opinion that the uncertain character of this, and all claims resting upon consequential losses, forbids them to be allowed. The facts appear to be established, that the servant was impressed into the public service; that he was brought from that service in bad health, and that he subsequently died. There is no proof, nor is the case susceptible of proof, that the servant would not have died before his return, if he had not been impressed, as such property is at all times held subject to those casualties which destroy health and life. The voyage to New Orleans must at all times be considered as hazardous, and the more so in time of war; and the petitioner must be supposed to have hired his servant with a full knowledge of this increased risk. The committee are also of opinion that to grant the prayer of the petitioner would establish a bad precedent, and open a wide field for claims where consequential damages may be alleged. The petitioner have leave to withdraw his petition.

## Pierre Lacoste

Pierre Lacoste claimed 20 acres of plant cane and 50 acres of fence destroyed. As reported by the Committee of Claims on February 2, 1819:

> The losses for which the petitioner prays indemnity were losses occasioned by the destruction of the British at the time of their invasion of Louisiana. It does not appear from the evidence that the British caused the destruction in consequence of any use which the United States' troops made of the buildings or of the plantation but that the injuries sustained had been committed subsequently to the time when the houses had been used and the plantation occupied by the United States' troops and stores.
>
> The committee, therefore, recommend that the petitioner have leave to withdraw his petition.

# *The Battle of New Orleans Sufferers*

On January 8, 1815, Maj. Gen. Andrew Jackson's army fought British forces under Maj. Gen. Sir Edward Pakenham at New Orleans. American preparations for the defense of New Orleans caused significant damage to the numerous plantations in the area.

Major General Jackson directed the quartermaster general of the Seventh Military District to appoint a commission to "assess the damages occasioned by the troops of the United States, in the neighborhood of the city of New Orleans," as reported by the Committee of Claims on January 6, 1819:

That in pursuance thereto, they repaired to the several places hereinafter designated, in order to ascertain the nature and extent of the damages sustained by the individuals hereinafter mention, which they found to consist of two distinct classes: one being for damages done to the real estate and improvements, the other for moveable property consumed or destroyed by the army.

The first they considered it their duty to estimate, and for that purpose carefully examined the respective premises, requiring of the several claimants a particular description of the buildings that have been totally destroyed, which were compared with such traces of their having existed as could be found, and the whole estimated in equity to the best of their knowledge.

The other class of losses, consisting of provisions, furniture, wood, &c., consumed by the army, but of which no regular proof could be furnished, the commissioners considered would be more properly presented in the form of attested accounts made out by the parties, accompanied with such evidence as they were in possession of, and which they have subjoined to this report.

On the left bank of the Mississippi between Camp Jackson and the city of New Orleans.

The claims in the first class were numbered and described in various detail. Some may be elsewhere in individual acts and reports:

No. 1—John Rodriguez country seat, "on which the line of defense was established," $1,857 for outside property and $5,829 for furniture, books, and cattle.

No. 2—Marie Macarty (Widow McCarty): Home occupied as headquarters for Gen. Jackson, $800 in damage. Totally destroyed: Two pigeon houses on brick pillars, $250; a 30 × 18 shed, $300; a 14 × 20 coach shed, $150; two Negro houses, $120; a 16 × 25 store house, $300; 38 acres of post and rail fence, $460; and 16 acres pale fence, $560. Total $2,940. Furniture destroyed, $1,219.

No. 3—François B. Languille: Country house occupied as the head quarters of Gen. Carroll. Damage to dwelling, $300; damage to storehouse, $25. Entirely destroyed, corn house, out buildings, stable and fence, $2,250. Cattle and provisions taken, $2,848.

No. 4—John Pettit, brickmaker who claimed $3,864 in damages for a 20 × 60 dwelling house, $1,800; a 50 × 100 brick kiln and shed, $1,080; two tempering beds and utensils, $450; 3 Negro houses, $300; a kitchen and hen house, $100, 10 acres pale fence, $214; furniture, firewood, bricks, &c., $1,786.

No. 5—Joseph McNeil: Dwelling house damage, $195; kitchen destroyed, $350; stable and corn house, $180; privy, $65; a Negro house, $40; large double gate, $60; small double gate, $25; bake oven torn down, $20; 21 acres pale fence, $450. Total $1,385.

No. 5—Col. Samuel B. Davis: Damage to country house, $195; buildings destroyed: 50 × 12 shed, $100; 12 × 15 kitchen, $200; 12 × 16 Negro house, $60; hen house, $60; 3½ acres pale fence, $75; 11 acres post and rail fence, $140. Total $835.

No. 5—Mons. De la Chenaye, a resident tenant on the property, claimed $286 for cattle and poultry consumed by the Army.

No. 6—Rosalie Picou Deslonde: "House occupied as a general hospital." Damage to the dwelling, $500; damage to a store, $150; 24 × 14 kitchen destroyed, $400; 20 × 10 coach house destroyed, $120; five Negro houses destroyed, $400; a large double gate cut down, $60; 28 acres post and rail fence, $343; 12 acres pale fence, $254. Total $2,227. Provisions, &c., $532.

No. 7—Larunte Segur: "The former proprietor of the last mentioned property, claims for a quantity of spars said to have been on the place at the time of the invasion, and to have been used for the fortification." Total $3,748.

No. 8—Barthelemy Louis Chauvin-Delery: 53 acres of rail fence destroyed, $650; 20 acres of rail fence destroyed, $204; 4 acres of pale fence destroyed, $87; brick kiln fence, $22; roof of a brick kiln shed destroyed, $300; two Negro cabins, $50; damage to sugar house, $72; seven garden gates, $150; three tempering beds for brick making, $330. Total $1,865.

No. 9—Marie Adelaide Lecomte Purnas: 50 × 42 brick kiln shed destroyed, $600; 5 Negro cabins, $250; 3 tempering beds for brick making, $291; damage to store, $36; 72 acres post and rail fence, $915; 30 acres post and rail fence, $642. Total, $2,734. Provisions, $1,387.

No. 10—Salomon Prevost: A gardener's house destroyed, $300; 80 acres post and rail fence, $980; 26 acres post and rail fence, $506; 5 gates and fastenings, $120. Total, $1,966. Hay and corn, $5,411.

No. 11—Madame Dupré: "A sawmill torn down to erect the second line of defense," $4,000; brick kiln shed No. 1, $1,000; brick kiln shed No. 2, $550; brick kiln shed No. 3, $400; 2 tempering beds for brick making, $200; 14 Negro houses, $1,150; 7 gates and doors, $56; damage to dwelling and outhouses, $200; 97 acres post and rail fence, $1,183; 12 acres pale fence, $256. Total $8,995.

No. 11—Lewis H. Guerlain: 26 acres post and rail fence, $317; 2 ½ acres pale fence, $53; damage to a house, $50. Total $420. Firewood, garden stuff, &c., $1,103.50.

No. 12—François Duplesis: 10 acres post and rail fence, $122; 20 loads of hay, $160.

No. 13—Corporation of the city of New Orleans. Damages to their property occupied by a troop of horse, $654.

No. 14—Mons. Cervillier: Damage done to his house on the left bank of the Mississippi above the city of New Orleans, and in the neighborhood of Generals Varrol and Coffe's camps. $200.

No. 14—Mons. Ducro: 13 acres post and rail fence destroyed, $160. Damage done to the dwelling and sugar house, $100. Total $260.

No. 14—Robert Avart: Damage done to his dwelling house, $100. Provisions, &c., $2,002.

No. 15—Madame L. Avart: 2 acres post and rail fence, $25; hay, oats, &c.

No. 16—Pierre Laurent: 25 acres of fence, $305. Hay, oats, &c., $1,288.

No. 17—Robert Avart's widow: 95 acres post and rail fence, provisions, wood, &c., $1,160.

No. 18—Widow Rousseau: 10 acres post and rail fence, $122, provisions, wood, &c., $941.

No. 19—Joseph Lefebvre: Gardiner, on the right bank of the river, at and near Gen. Morgan's camp. Garden stuff, poultry, &c., $1,657.

No. 20—John Caslanedo: 9 acres post and rail fence, $11, damage to his house used as a hospital, $25, 1½ acres pale fence, $36. Total $171. Garden stuff, hay, wood, &c., $2,924.

No. 21—Maurice Bertrand: Garden stuff, hay, wood, &c., $301.

No. 22—Barthélemy and Pierre Jourdan: "Destroyed by fire by order of General Jackson." 70 × 20 dwelling house, $4,000; kitchen, $500; sugar house mill, &c., $12,000; saw mill, $4,000; sugar refinery, $150; rice mill, $400; large grange, $400; large store house, $1,800; coach house, $100; 2 fowlhouses, $140: 2 pigeon houses, $200; 10 double Negro houses, $1,500; a small store house, $150; 96 acres post and rail fence, $1,171; 13 acres pale fence, $278. Total $26,789. A crop of sugar and molasses in store when burnt, farming utensils, &c., $8,978.

No. 23—Pierre Cazeland: Saw mill burnt, $6,000. Carpenter's tools, &c., $2,438.

No. 24—Jacques H. Boisgervais: Saw mill burnt, $4,000; 26 acres of fence, $208. Total $4,208. Sundry articles taken or destroyed by the army, $1,046.

No. 25—Bartholome Duvergé: Opposite the city, brick kiln on the margin of the river destroyed for the purpose of erecting a battery; a brick kiln shed, $700; roof, &c., of the kiln, $1,000; 2 tempering beds, $200; damage to the levee and the furnace, $200. Total, $2,100.

No. 25—Mons. Bertionniere's Camp Bertonniere: On the Chef Menteur Road, 24 acres post and rail fence, $292; labor to fill up the ditch on his plantation, $100.

No. 25—Francis Dreux: 10 acres post and rail fence, $122.

No. 25—Madame Leafroy Dreux: Cattle killed on her farm, $1,500.

No. 26—Jean Baptiste Colson: 5 acres post and rail fence, $61; 2 cart loads of hay, $16.

No. 27—Daniel Clark executors: 20 acres of post and rail fence, $244.

No. 27—Pierre Guéno: 4 acres post and rail fence, $50.

No. 27—Mons. Cousin: Bayou St. John, 18 acres post and rail fence, $220.

No. 27—Josephine Allard: 4 acres post and rail fence, $50. Cattle, &c., $372.

No. 28—Alexander Milne: Bake house on the bayou opposite Fort St. John, $200; a house on the bank of Lake Ponchartrain near the fort, destroyed by order of the military commandant, $2,000; damage to a house occupied by a picket guard in advance of the fort, $550.

No. 28—The New Orleans Navigation Company: Materials taken for the use of the fort at Bayou St. John, $438.

No. 29—Jean Baptiste Joublan: Superintendent of the Navigation Company, a billiard table destroyed, $180.

No. 29—A. R. De Menard: Damage done to his house in the suburb of De La Course, used as a guard house for a troop of cavalry, $139.

No. 29—Pierre Louis Le Ray: Compensation for a Negro, a cart, and 3 mules taken into requisition. The former died in the service, and the cart and mules were lost, $795.

No. 30—Michel, Deirell, & Co.: Damage done to 2 boats whilst in the service, $213.

No. 31—Francis Leirche: A freeman of color claims compensation for a Negro taken into requisition and killed at the lines, $600.

No. 32—John Mouchon: Two mules killed in the service of the United States, $143.

No. 33—La Barre La Contoure: Two mules killed at the lines, $146.

No. 34—Louis Barthelemy Macarty: "intersected by the third line of defense"; fences destroyed, $96.

No. 35—Marie Montreuil: "Plantation intersected likewise by the third line of defense." Fences destroyed, $141. Damage sustained, $8,700.

The commission further stated:

In addition to the foregoing, a third and distinct class of claims has been presented to the board, consisting of losses and damages sustained by individuals, whose property was alternately in possession of the American and British armies, and as it would be impossible for the commissioners to discriminate between the damage occasioned by either, they have subjoined hereto the respective claims for the consideration of the authority to whom the present report may be referred, and which are as follows:

Ignace Delino alias Chalmet, the proprietor of a sugar estate adjacent to Gen. Jackson's camp between the American and British lines, the buildings of which were fired and blown up by order of the American commander. (A).

Mons. Antonio Cruzat, son-in-law of Mons. Chalmet, residing in his house, for his furniture, &c., destroyed. (B).

Mons. P. Duverge, son-in-law of Mons. Chalmet, residing in his house, for his furniture, &c., destroyed. (C).

Mons. Antoine Bienvenue, a sugar planter, next adjoining the above, his house occupied by the enemy and materially injured by the shot from our line. (D).

Col. Pierre Denis de la Ronde, a sugar planter adjoining Mons. Bienvenue. (E).

Major General Jacques Villeré claims for damages stated to have been done by the American Army, per his account and vouchers, (F).

Mons. Jumonville de Villiers claims for damages stated to have been done by the American Army, per his account and vouchers, (G).

Messrs. Baily and Rinker, planters at the English Turn, per account and vouchers. (H).

Thaddeus Mayhew, proprietor of a plantation and saw mill on the right bank of the river, his account and vouchers. (I). Loss by depredations of the American troops: 3 beds and bedding, $60; crockery ware, $20; 6 chairs, $15; 3 tables, $18; 1 writing desk, $20; clothing and 2 trunks, $150; kitchen furniture, $20; 12 spades, $30; 12 hoes, $24; 4 axes, $8; 1 chest of carpenter's tools, $100; 2 lanterns, $3.50; 6 lamps, $5.75; one-half barrel of molasses (16 gals.), $12; 12 pounds of coffee, $4.50; 50 pounds of bacon, $6.25; 1 pair steel yards, $8; 1 jug of lamp oil, $3.50; 15 cords of wood, $45; 1,000 pickets taken from fences, and labor to replace, $150; 6,000 feet of plank burnt by guards stationed near the mill, $240; 2,000 slabs, $80; damage to house and out-buildings, $200; 2 plantation boats, $50. Total, $1,273.50. Loss by whom uncertain, in consequence of setting fire to the bridge, saw mill, and lumber on the morning of the 8th of January, 1815. Saw mill with all the utensils, $6,000; 200,000 feet of boards at $4, $8,000; 12,000 feet of scantling at $5, $600; a bridge across the canal of saw mill, $200. Total, $14,800.

Joseph Lefebre's petition was rejected on February 9, 1819, for lack of evidence.

## Robert Avart

As reported on February 29, 1832, by the Committee of Claims:

The claim is for the destruction of 97 acres of post and rail fence, and for injury done to a dwelling-house by the army under the command of General Jackson in the vicinity of New Orleans. It appears that General Jackson appointed commissioners to estimate the damage done to the plantations in that quarter by reason of their military occupation and that the commissioners estimated the damage sustained by widow Avart, by the destruction of 95 acres at $1,160.

In order to ascertain whether the award had been taken at the Treasury Department to be final and as to the liability of the United States to remunerate them, the committee addressed a letter to Mr. Hagner, seeking the desired information. It appears that other evidence has been required. The claims presented against the United States for injury done to buildings, fences, and lands in the vicinity of New Orleans during the military operations there have generally been referred to the accounting officer of the Treasury for settlement. The committee will report a bill for that purpose in this case.

The commissioners referred to appear to be Richard Relf, Pierre Foucher, and Benjamin Morgan. Avart is referred to in other documents as François Robert Avart, owner of 8½ arpents for over 40 years in the Committee on Private Land Claims of February 10, 1834, report, and there is reference to a Madame L. Avart.

## Jumonville de Villiers

As reported by the Committee of Claims on February 3, 1817:

> That in the months of December, 1814, and January, 1815, the American troops, called to the defense of New Orleans, and commanded by General Andrew Jackson, were stationed on the plantation of the petitioner; that while so stationed there, it became necessary to use for fuel, for the use of the troops, a quantity of fencing, and the petitioner request Congress to pay him the value thereof, and also the value of a quantity of sugar cane and sugar which he states were used by the troops of the United States.
>
> The committee are of the opinion that the fencing having been made use of for fuel, which could not have been procured of the ordinary kind, from the nature of the service, and the circumstances under which the troops were collected for the defense of New Orleans, the claimant is entitled to relief do far as respects the vale of the fence, but that the Government cannot be liable for the destruction of the cane or use of the sugar, it being neither necessary for the service nor for the sustenance of the army. Pursuant to this opinion, they report a bill authorizing payment for the fence only.

De Villiers was paid $650 in 1817.

## Antoine Bienvenue

As reported by the Committee of Claims on February 3, 1817:

> The claimant was owner of an elegant and well-furnished house situated below the city of New Orleans, and between the positions occupied by the American and British armies in December, 1814, and January, 1815. In consequence of this situation of the house and the two armies, it afforded a shelter to the British army, and was, by General Jackson, ordered to be fired on with hot shot for its destruction. It was several times fired on by Commodore Patterson and set fire to, which was extinguished by the British forces. In consequence of the destruction of the house and furniture, and other houses adjacent to the dwelling-house, the petitioner has sustained considerable injury. The committee are of the opinion he is entitled to relief.

Reported again by the Committee of Claims on February 20, 1822:

> The claim of the petitioner is for damages done to his dwelling-house, out-houses, and other property, and for property destroyed and taken away during the invasion of Louisiana in the late war with Great Britain.
>
> It appears from the evidence that during that invasion, between the 23rd December, 1814, and the 19th January, 1815, the Americans had erected several batteries on the right bank of the Mississippi River—one opposite the plantation of the petitioner, about six miles below the city of New Orleans.
>
> The enemy, having advanced up the river and occupied the plantation of one Chalmet [Ignace Martin de Lino de Chalmette], was dislodged by the American batteries firing the houses, &c., and compelled to fall down the river to the plantation of the petitioner, of which he took possession and made a stand, using the houses and other edifices as protection from the American fire.
>
> In this situation, the enemy exerted himself to keep possession of the position, and the Americans to dislodge him from it, and red hot shot was used by order of the commanding officer from the batteries to destroy the edifice and everything on the plantation calculated to afford protection, aid, or comfort to the enemy, whereby the petitioner's dwelling-house was several times fired by the

> Americans and extinguished by the enemy, and some stacks of rice being fired, communicated to a number of negro cabins standing near, and consumed them.
>
> Much damage was done to the petitioner's property of various kinds, as well by the American as the British, and personal property to a large amount was destroyed or taken away and lost to the petitioner.
>
> It does not appear from the evidence that any part of that property was taken into possession or used by the American army, except 30 or 40 spades, taken by order of the commanding officer to cut the levee, stated to have been worth $50 or $60, and to have been lost to the owner, but the loss is not satisfactorily proved, with the exception of which, the committee cannot perceive anything in the petitioner's case to distinguish it from the common misfortunes of war, to which individuals are liable, nor anything in the conduct of the American army to distinguish it from the ordinary necessities of war, in which private mischief must be suffered for the public good.
>
> Therefore the prayer of the petitioner ought not to be granted.

Antoine Bienvenue, Pierre (Peter) Lacoste, and Jacques Villeré filed claims for slaves taken from their plantations by the British and on December 23, 1817, the Committee let the issue lie on the table pending negotiations with the British.

## Don Juan de Castañedo

As reported by the Committee of Claims on February 3, 1817:

> The petitioner owned a plantation and house situated on the right bank of the Mississippi below New Orleans, and that a battery was erected by order of the commanding officer in front of the house and close by it; in consequence of which the house received much injury from the British artillery.
>
> The petitioner had also a quantity of wood and hay taken from him and used by the army. The committee are of the opinion the petitioner is entitled to relief.

He was paid $630 in July 1817. Don Juan de Castañedo was the alderman and treasurer of the City of New Orleans.

## Ignace Martin de Lino de Chalmette

On March 1, 1817, the accounting officers of the War Department, "were authorized to audit and settle the claims of the legal representatives of Ignace Chalmet Delino, deceased, on account of the destruction of the property of Delino, and of Anthony Cruzat and L.P. Deverges, in the vicinity of New Orleans, by order of Major-General Andrew Jackson."

The officers were authorized to appoint "three good and discreet citizens, who shall repair to the plantation of Delino, where the property is alleged to have been destroyed, and there diligently inquire what property may have been destroyed and to make a just appraisement to the accountant of the War Department."

Ignace Martin de Lino de Chalmette owned a sugar plantation. On seeing the British marching towards them, Chalmette, his family, and their slaves fled their mansion and property in the direction of Gen. Jackson's troops. The Chalmettes reportedly stayed in a home on Bourbon St. in New Orleans and on returning home on February 2 found nothing but charred remains. His financial ruination and the loss reportedly led to Chalmette's death eight days later at age 59 from anxiety and stress. His heirs sold the property in 1817 to two wealthy free black brothers, Hilaire and Louis St. Armand.

Antonio Cruzat was the son of the lieutenant governor of Upper Louisiana. He married Victoire de Chalmette and was treasurer of the City of New Orleans. Ignace Martin de Lino de Chalmette is the namesake for Chalmette, Louisiana, in St. Bernard Parish.

The heirs were paid $55,476 in 1817.

## Marie Montreuil

The claimant was identified only as "Madam Montreuil." It appears Roberto

François Gauthier de Montreuil owned a plantation right next to the Macarti Plantation outside New Orleans. On June 21, 1783, Roberto married Marie Marthé "Mannette" de Macarti, 18, in New Orleans. After he died 1797, Marie Montreuil continued the work of managing the plantation until she died in 1837.

Madame Mannete owned two slaves: Lolotte, who she freed in 1827, at age 34, and her sister Adele, whom Lolette purchased from Mannette soon after. The sisters took Montreuil as their surname.

During the War of 1812, defensive works were started on the Montreuil Plantation after the January 8, 1815, battle, but were never finished. What would have been the last line of defense against the British were described by Capt. H.D. Jones of the Royal Artillery in March 1815:

> It is entirely different from the other two, having a ditch of 12 feet broad and 6 feet cut expressly. It is well flanked. On the right is an inclined redoubt with its gorge palisaded. At 500 yards from the river is a flat bastion of brickwork for musketry only. The line continues from this to the wood. The redoubt on the right has a good command from being constructed upon the levee. The parapet on this line is in an unfinished state.

On February 3, 1817, the Committee of Claims recommended relief and in 1817 Madam Montreuil was paid $7,715.

## Pierre Cazeland

Cazeland filed a claim for the destruction of his sawmill and property, by order of General David Morgan.

Gen. David Bannister Morgan commanded Louisiana and Kentucky militia in the defense of a battery of guns commanded by Commodore Daniel Todd Patterson on the west bank of the Mississippi, which, if taken could fire on Andrew Jackson's then unprotected troops. As it happened, Gen. Morgan was overrun and the battery was lost, but his forces held out long enough for Jackson to entrench his troops. Cazeland's mill was probably burned to keep the British from using it as a shelter or fortification. He was paid $6,584.40 in 1817.

## Jacques Philippe Villeré

On June 15, 1815, Villeré presented his original claim to Gen. Jackson for $12,000 for "30 arpents of sugar lands, destroyed by an inundation occasioned by the filling up of a canal, by order of General Jackson during the invasion of Louisiana."

In response to this, three commissioners were appointed by joint agreement who submitted their report to the Treasury Department.

On June 26, 1815, Villeré submitted another claim for $5,370 to the commissioners appointed by Gen. Jackson for supplies furnished the Army, which apparently complicated the process, but which was paid.

On November 12, 1816, he filed another claim, which increased the total to $7,890:

> 100 cords of wood burnt by the American troops, $400; 20 acres of sugar cane stock to plant 100 acres, $1,200; 147 arpents of fence, used for fuel, $2,053; 20 arpents of levee, supported by pickets used for fuel, $432; almost all the doors, windows, and floors of two houses destroyed and burnt; a negro cabin burnt, all the other mush injured, and all the planks, weather boarding, a barn taken and used for fuel, $1,500; posts enclosing 140 acres used for fuel, $1,470; 20 acres of mole, taken and burnt, $300; the canal stopped and filled in the widest and deepest place for more than six acres, and the expense of opening, $1,000.

Third Auditor Peter Hagner awarded $5,000 for opening the canal, including $1,500 for rent of the land for one year. On November 12, 1816, Villeré filed another claim for $2,500, "after the inundation had subsided, a year before he had affixed the value at $1,200."

Because there were two separate

accounts, a new commission was appointed, and Villeré's claim went to $17,000.

In support of Villeré, Hugues Lavergue offered a sworn statement and was deposed by Gallien Preval on January 28, 1820, at New Orleans:

> On the 20th of January, 1815, his Excellency, James Villeré, now governor of the state of Louisiana, and then Maj. Gen. of the 1st Division of the militia received from Maj. Gen. Jackson, then commanding the 7th Military District, and order to fill up the canal on his plantation. At the time the river Mississippi was low its waters did not enter the canal, which was shut up pursuant to the order.
>
> In the month of February he was the bearer of a written statement made by James Villeré of the losses he had sustained on his plantation. This was delivered to Maj. Gen. Jackson, who said he would make his best efforts to have the losses remunerated by the general government.
>
> At the time Gen. Villeré furnished this written statement to Gen. Jackson, he did not, and could not, include the damages which he afterwards experienced by filling up the canal because those losses could not have existed at a time when the waters of the Mississippi were still low and could not get into the canal.
>
> It was not before the beginning of May that the Mississippi became so high as to empty into the canal and that the damages occasioned by the overflowing of its waters on Gen. Villeré's plantation, in consequence of the shutting up of the canal, did take place during the months of May and June.
>
> This deponent has read the act of Congress passed for the relief of Gen. Villeré and that understanding that Mr. Hagner has granted him the sum of $5,000 only. The decision of that officer was influenced by the written statement made by Gen. Villeré without including those occasioned by the overflowing of his plantation. This deponent has deemed it his duty to make this deposition in order to elucidate a point which has been so injurious to the interests of the general, and to prove that when Gen. Villeré made a written statement of the depredations committed on his plantation, he could not have mentioned a loss which had not yet taken place.

As reported by the Committee of Claims on January 29, 1821:

> The petitioner claims compensation for 130 arpents of sugar lands destroyed by an inundation occasioned by the filling up of a canal by order of General Jackson during the invasion of Louisiana in the year 1814–15, which he estimates at $12,000.
>
> By act of Congress of the 3rd of March, 1817, settlement was directed and a reasonable allowance has been made for opening the canal and one year's rent allowed for the sugar lands.
>
> On the 26th of June, 1815, the petitioner presented a statement, on oath, of the nature and amount of his claims to the commissioners appointed by General Jackson to appraise supplies furnished to the army, of the sum of $5,370. Accompanying his petition to Congress, on which the act for his relief was passed, was another account to which the petitioner made oath on the November 12, 1816, in which claim was increased to $7,890.
>
> The act of his relief authorizing a discretionary settlement of his claim for property consumed as fuel, for opening his canal, and a year's rent for sugar lands, the proper officer was led, from the difference between the two accounts, stated on oath by the petitioner, to appoint a new commission, which resulted in swelling the claim to the extraordinary amount of $17,000, and which evinces the extreme uncertainty of the amount of such injuries. It is very obvious the act of Congress, in allowing a rent for the sugar lands inundated in consequence of the stoppage of the canal, meant to relieve, in a liberal manner; but, under no view of the case can it be supposed a greater sum than then demanded, much less such an extraordinary increase of the petitioner's demand, was contemplated.
>
> The Committee are of opinion that the documents furnished by the petitioner conclusively invalidate his claim. His first statement on oath is dated the 26th of June, 1815.
>
> The deposition of Hugues Lavergne, taken 28th of January, 1820, sets forth: he believes it was in the beginning of May, 1815, that the inundation of the petzitioner's lands commenced, and that he is positive it was during the months of May and June. It follows, then, that the petitioner's first demand had not been authenticated till the inundation had subsided, and he must have been as well qualified to judge of his loss then as at any time subsequent time; but, on the 12th of November,

> 1816, his charge for sugar cane plants is put down $2,500, to which, after the inundation had subsided, a year before, he had affixed the value at $1,200. He has been allowed and paid $1,300 for rent, and this on the valuation of the best appraisers, made in the year 1817. These appraisers had no authority to ascertain or affix the value of any damages but as rent for the grounds inundated.
>
> The Committee are, therefore, clearly of opinion that the petitioner has been fairly and fully compensated for all he has a right to demand of the public. They are, at the same time, aware that the petitioner has great merit as a citizen and a soldier in the late war, and that he suffered most severe and ruinous losses from the vision of the enemy and the chance of war. While they feel the truest sympathy for his sufferings, they can discover no principle by which he can have further legislative relief without violating those rules of justice which they think should never be departed from. The documents submitted to the Committee are annexed. They therefore submit the following resolution.
>
> *Resolved*, That the prayer of the petition ought not to be granted.

Maj. Gen. Jacques Villeré, owner of the plantation "Conseil" about 10 miles below New Orleans on the Mississippi River, commanded the 1st Division of Louisiana militia.

Villeré was paid $5,000 in 1817, and went on to serve as Louisiana's first native-born governor from 1816 to 1820.

## Jumonville de Villiers

Jumonville de Villiers filed a claim for a fence used as fuel by the troops of the United States. On February 14, 1816, the Committee on Military Affairs reported on the claims of Nicholas Boilevin, John de Lassize, and de Villiers, and stated:

> That no doubt exists on the minds of the committee as to the truth of the facts disclosed in the petitions; the losses complained of, resulting from a barbarous warfare carried on by the ferocious inhabitants of the wilds, as well as by the regular forces of His Britannic Majesty, have been most severe on the unfortunate petitioners. Whether it becomes the magnanimity of a Government whose only object should be the protection and prosperity of all its citizens to dispense relief in cases like these, and thereby to cause the war to fall equally on all, is a question which the committee believe is placed beyond their cognizance, in consequence of the course heretofore pursued by Congress in regard to losses sustained during the war—a course which seems to indicate that indemnity is due to all those whose losses have arisen from the acts of our own Government, or those acting under its authority; while losses produced by the conduct of the enemy are to be classed among the unavoidable calamities of war, and do not entitle the sufferers to indemnification by the Government. The losses of the petitioners belong to the latter class, and therefore the committee, yielding to what is believed to be the settled purpose of Congress.

## Barthélemy and Pierre Jourdan

The claimants are identified only as brothers "B. and P. Jordon" who are most likely Barthélemy and Pierre Jourdan, who filed a claim for $40,917.80, "for sundry property destroyed and damage done to their sugar plantation on the right bank of the Mississippi, below New Orleans, during the invasion of the British army in the years 1814 and 1815," and "wantonly burnt and destroyed by the enemy, contrary to the rules of warfare among civilized nations."

Items included 1 sugar house, $12,000; a refining house, $150; a barn and stable, $400; a magazine and apparatus, $1,800; a coach house, $100; 2 poultry houses, $140; a kitchen, $500; 2 pigeon houses, $200; 10 negro cabins, $1,500; a granary, $150; a rice mill, $400; fences, $1,449; 56,880 pounds of sugar, "burnt in sugar-house," $4,834.80; 120 barrels of molasses, $1,800; corn and hay "in part used by United States troops," and the balance burnt, $1,220; sugar cane plants, "used and destroyed by United States troops," $1,400.

On February 16, 1818, the Committee of Claims reported:

Whatever propriety there might be in paying for some part of the property, a want of sufficient evidence of its loss or destruction forbids it, no other evidence being offered in support of this part of the claim but the oath of one of the claimants; nor is it stated whether said property was destroyed by the enemy or the United States troops.

Further investigation and appraisals were conducted and on January 20, 1819, the Committee of Claims stated:

The petitioner's plantation, situated on the right bank of the Mississippi, was occupied during the campaign of 1814–15 by Gen. Morgan's detachment of troops. On the 10th January, 1815, an order was given by Gen. Jackson to destroy all buildings and other property that might interfere in the defense of his position. In pursuance of this order, your petitioner's large house and other outhouses were all burnt by Gen. Morgan, together with all the greatest part of their contents and that the fences were all consumed, and much damage done to the plantation by throwing up military works. Several of your petitioner's buildings were also destroyed by the enemy preparatory to his attack on the American lines.

The statements here made are, in the opinion of the committee, satisfactorily proved by evidence taken under commissioners on the part of the United States. Separating the houses burnt by the enemy, and much of that portion of the claim made for various articles not so satisfactorily proved to have been used or destroyed, the committee have decided to report in favor of the claim, so far as to indemnify the petitioners for the houses burnt by General Morgan, by the order of General Jackson, and for the molasses and sugar destroyed with them.

Additional items included a mansion-house and saw-mill, $8,000, two negro slaves, sugar molds, empty sugar hogsheads, sundry farming utensils, and household and kitchen furniture carried away and valued at $4,274. Damage done to the plantation, "by digging and throwing up the earth for works of defense," stated at $600. A total of $28,043.80 was awarded.

As stated by Zachary Smith in 1904:

Commodore Patterson removed from the *Louisiana* a number of guns, which he placed in battery in front of Jordon's plantation, on the right bank, with which he did important service to the end of the campaign. This formidable battery was formed to give a deadly flanking fire on the enemy's ranks from the opposite bank of the river. It was manned and served by sailors, mostly landed from the *Carolina* when she was burned. They had been enlisted about the city after the gunboats were destroyed; men of all nations, not a third of them speaking the English language. The constant daily fire of this battery caused the British to fall back from Chalmette's and Bienvenue's houses and to seek safer quarters in the rear, after the artillery duels of the 28th.

## Francisco Baltazar Langeville

As reported by the Committee of Claims on March 22, 1820:

The bill is intended to provide payment for property said to have been destroyed in the neighborhood of New Orleans during the invasion by the enemy in 1814–'15, while in the occupancy of the troops of the United States.

The support of the claim is the affidavit of Richard Relf, Benjamin Morgan, and Peter Fouchers who state that, "after the retreat of the enemy they were appointed by the quartermaster general, under orders from General Jackson, to ascertain the nature and amount of the damages caused to several persons," and that, "they repaired to the country seat of Francis B. Longville, where, after a careful and minute examination of the premises, they have found and estimated the damages done to his real estate as follows:"

Damages done to the dwelling-house, occupied as quarters by General Carroll, $300.

To the store-house, $25.

The following buildings entirely destroyed: a corn house, $300; an out-house 27 by 25 feet, $300; a kitchen and small house adjoining, $150; a bake house, $350; and stable, $50.

18 acres of standing fence, $385; 32 acres post and rail fence, $390.

Total $2,250.

General William Carroll wrote to General Jackson on March 4, 1815:

The owner of the plantation and house

occupied by me as quarters during our stay at the camp below New Orleans has called upon me to certify the damages he sustained. I have barely to remark, that a fine garden, his out-houses, or a part of them, and all his fences, were completely destroyed; his dwelling-house was much injured, by seven or eight 18-pound balls passing through it.

This being one of a large class of cases, and of great apparent hardship, and which in the opinion of the committee, do not come within any rule settled by Congress which would authorize an allowance; and the other branch of the Legislature having come to a decision in which the committee have not felt it their duty to concur, they have deemed it proper to present to the House somewhat in detail the views which they have taken of the question, and to which they have been led by the nature of their inquiries, connected with the events of the last war.

During the prosecution of that war, losses have been sustained by the citizens, of all the variety of character, and from as various causes and incidents as the most fruitful imagination could suggest; and, as they could be traced directly or indirectly to the events of a war declared and prosecuted by the government, an opinion seems to have been entertained that payment may rightfully be demanded from the Treasury to their full amount, whatever be their description, or from whatever cause produced.

It is believed by the committee that a rule which would authorize an allowance in this case would produce to the country much more of evil than benefit; and, as the testimony does not satisfactorily show that the property for which the petitioner prays to be compensated was taken and used for the public service, they recommend that the bill be indefinitely be postponed.

Francis B. Languille, or his legal representative, was paid $2,250 in 1821.

## Rosalie Picou Deslonde

As stated by the Committee of Claims on December 11, 1820:

The petitioner alleges she was possessed of a plantation with sundry buildings and other improvements thereon situated below New Orleans, and that during the invasion by the enemy in December, 1814, and subsequently her dwelling-house was occupied as quarters for some of the officers and a hospital for the sick and wounded, and while so occupied, her house, out-houses, fences, &c. were damaged or destroyed, as set forth in the following schedule, viz:

28 arpents of 4 and 5-rail fences burned for fuel, $343; 210 feet close garden fence burned for fuel, $254; 5 negro houses burned for fuel, $400.

1 kitchen, framed on sills, weather boarded, shingle roof, two rooms and double chimney, $400; 1 coach-house, two rooms, $120.

Damage done to mansion-house while occupied as a hospital from December 23 for the sick and wounded, $500.

1 large gate, $60; an out-house greatly damaged, $150, for a total of $2,227.

To the foregoing a claim is subjoined for hay, corn, beans, tables, sheep, cows and calves, pickets piled in the yard, "destruction of a garden in full crop," and three months' rent of the house. These latter items are estimated at the sum of $802.

The damages to the real estate appear to have been assessed in the first instance by commissioners under an order from General Jackson, and at the sum stated in the schedule and established subsequently by testimony taken under a commission from the late Commissioner of Claims. Should compensation be made for any part of the alleged injuries, it is believed it should be confined to the real estate, respecting which the proof is probably as satisfactory as it is practicable to obtain; but in regard to the personal affects, there is none but the statement of the petitioner.

At the present, as well as at the former sessions of Congress, the committee have bestowed upon the claims from the vicinity of New Orleans the most deliberate and careful attention, but have found it altogether impracticable to come to any satisfactory conclusion respecting them. There is probably no provision of the constitution which ought to be regarded more sacred that that which forbids the taking of "private property for public use without just compensation," and it is believed there are none which will be found more difficult in their just application, particularly when applied to the occurrences of war, such as happened near New Orleans where there was a sudden invasion by the enemy at an unexpected point, and the retreat of the inhabitants, equally sudden, the concentration of a large military force, mostly militia, and all without any previous preparation either of barracks or fuel, and at an inclement season. Under these circumstances the property of the citizens seems to have fallen almost an indiscriminate sacrifice, not from the will of the government or its officers, but from circumstances over which neither had any control; and consequently could not have been avoided but by yielding it up to a still greater sacrifice by the enemy.

Notwithstanding there are no known rules or established usage of the government which would seem to authorize an allowance in a case thus involved in obscurity, the committee are nevertheless of opinion that in a case of such extreme hardship as the one under consideration, and several others in the vicinity of New Orleans, it would best comport with the dictates of sound policy that, in the exercise of the discretion of Congress, some relief should be granted and for that purpose a bill is herewith reported to authorize a payment to the petitioner to the amount of the injury alleged to have been done to the real estate.

Rosalie P. Deslonde was paid $2,227, in 1821. Rosalie was born in 1775 and married Barthélemy Jourdan. After he died, she was involved in a dispute with Ann M. Jeter over the ownership of two young male slaves, "Archer" and "Bob" owned by her late husband. She then apparently married his brother, Pierre Barthélemy Jourdan. Rosalie died on January 4, 1835, at age 60, in Orleans, Louisiana.

Barthelemy and Pierre both served as privates in Pierre Denis De la Ronde's 3rd Regiment, Louisiana Militia during the War. Other Jourdans were 2nd Lt. Noel and private Celestin in Michel Fortier's 1st Battalion, Louisiana Militia, and Daniel in Jean Baptiste Plauché's Battalion, Louisiana Militia, and Francis Jourdan.

## John Rodriguez

John Rodriguez was an attorney who represented himself, "to be the owner of the land on which was erected the works of defense by the army under the command of Major General Jackson, about four miles below New Orleans on the left bank of the Mississippi, and on which was fought the battle on the 8th of January, 1815."

His 4 foot deep by 20 foot wide canal was the "line of defense" for the city of New Orleans. The Battle of Rodriguez Canal occurred between December 28, 1814, and January 1, 1815, between Gen. Jackson, Maj. Gen. Pierre LaCoste's battalion of free blacks, the 2nd Louisiana Militia, and British Lt. Gen. Sir Edward Parkenham and Maj. Gen. John Keane. Gen. Jackson directed his engineers to construct a 30-yard wide earthwork on the Macarty Plantation, which was behind the Rodriguez property, and they apparently used his soil. The work was done by slaves, militia, and regular Army. Parkenham was successfully repulsed.

As stated by the Committee of Claims on June 12, 1834:

> The petitioner has made applications to Congress for compensation for the losses he sustained in the damage done to his plantation and houses occupied by the troops of the United States under command of General Jackson when defending New Orleans, and for the losses he sustained in the removal and destruction of his personal property by troops.
>
> Shortly after the retreat of the enemy, General Jackson instituted a commission to examine and report the injury done to the property of the citizens by the troops of the United States while in their military occupation, and the petitioner presented his claims, amounting in all to $7,686, of which $1,857 were for damages done to real estate, and consisted of household furniture, farming utensils, cattle, horses, books, &c. said to have been taken away or destroyed. The commissioners estimated the damage done to his houses as follows, to wit:
>
> A stable and coach-house, $200; four negro quarters, $120; a pigeon house, $100; a kitchen, $50; damages to a dwelling house, $300; damages to an adjoining house, $150; ten and a half acres of pale fence, $220; 26 acres of post

and rail fence, $317; a double gate and seven garden post and rail fences, $100.

The petitioner applied to Congress for relief at the second session of the 16th Congress and the Committee of Claims reported a bill for his relief, on the 20th of December, 1820. This bill proposed to allow him the damages estimated by the commissioners, and an act was passed for his relief on the 2nd of March, 1821.

Application having been made for further relief, the committee made unfavorable reports on the 21st of December, 1824, and on the 6th of February, 1826. Additional testimony having been presented, the committee reported a bill in favor of appropriating $883, the balance of the damages due to him for digging and using earth for works of defense, and for materials to enclose the plantation and gates, which passed during the 21st Congress.

The account first presented to Congress exceeded the one presented to the commissioners, the former being $9,894, and the latter, as mentioned above, being $7,686. The committee, not having the account presented to the commissioners before them, are unable to state how this difference arose.

The estimation of the damages done to the buildings, as fixed by the commissioners, is taken from the report of the committee at the 2nd session of the 16th Congress, recorded in book 5, page 26, to which this committee refer, and make the same a part of this report. That report refers to one made at the same session in the case of Rosaline P. Deslonde, and is recorded in book 5, page 4.

This seems to have been the first case for damages done to buildings under the like circumstances, in which the committee reported in favor of making an allowance. The question whether the United States are liable for damages done to personal property by those in the military service, when the property has not been taken into the service by contract or impressment, but where the buildings containing it have been occupied in the face of an enemy, for the purpose of preventing that enemy from laying waste and subjugating the country, is discussed with great ability.

The committee came to the conclusion that the United States were not liable, and such has been the uniform decision of the committee and of Congress since. The committee do not find themselves at liberty to disregard these decisions.

John Rodriguez presents his petition at this session, in which he adverts to the previous action of the committee and of Congress on his claims, and he discusses at large the duties of the government towards her citizens, as he understands them. He complains of the great delay that has taken place in the investigation of his claims and the very partial relief that has been given him.

The committee sent to the Third Auditor's office for the papers that had been lodged there after the passage of the acts referred to, to ascertain whether there was any claim overlooked by the former committees, or improperly decided. They find but two items not passed upon, under the general classes of damages to houses, or to the injury or destruction of personal property, and these two items are—

For eight cart loads of hay, at $8 each: $64; 40 barrels of corn at $1 per barrel, $40.

If these articles were taken and not paid for, the petitioner is undoubtedly entitled to be paid their value.

There is testimony, "that the army, while stationed on said plantation, made use of some provisions, fowls, pigeons, hay, corn, firewood, vegetables, &c. that were found on said plantation; that the implements of husbandry were taken to work at the fortifications, and lost while at that service." This testimony is the most specific of any that is discovered, to sustain the items mentioned above, and it introduces a claim not heretofore noticed in any of the receipts, to wit, for his implements of husbandry which were taken for the works and not returned.

If the implements spoken of were necessarily taken for the purposes of defense, and not returned, their value should be paid when their loss, in the manner mentioned, is ascertained.

General Jackson gave his deposition in relation to the petitioner's claims on the 25th of November, 1826, and, after describing the position of his camp, which was on the plantation of the petitioner, and after mentioning the raising of the breastwork and parapets, and the occupation of the petitioner's buildings as head quarters, and the injury they sustained by the shot of the enemy, he says, "the fences and part of the growing timber in the swamp were necessarily consumed for fuel by the troops." He closes his deposition by stating that he appointed commissioners to estimate the damages all the property had sustained that was occupied by the troops; but whether the damages were assessed or paid to Mr. Rodriguez, he does not know.

The print describing the ground and the line of battle is among the papers, by which it appears that the battle was fought on the plantation of the petitioner; the American troops having been protected by an embankment formed in part by a canal, and enlarged by earth dug up after the position for resisting the enemy was selected. The evidence shows that the buildings of Mr. Rodriguez were occupied from the 23rd of December until after the retreat of the enemy, but the precise day the occupation ceased is not mentioned.

The committee do not find any testimony that the petitioner has been paid for this use of his buildings. If such payment has not been made, in the opinion of the committee, it is a proper subject of charge against the United States. The committee do not propose now or hereafter to disturb any decision made by former committees, nor to introduce any new principle, but to indicate to the petitioner, whose case, in many particulars, is an extreme hard one, that, on proof being made that his hay and corn and timber or wood were taken and necessarily used, and that his buildings were occupied by contract or impressment, for a definite period of time, are such ordinary charges as have uniformly been paid, when substantiated by evidence. As the case is now presented, the committee submit the following resolution:

*Resolved*, That the Committee of Claims be discharged from the further consideration of the papers of John Rodriguez, and that they lie on the table.

On March 2, 1821, he was paid $1,857 "in full for the injuries sustained by him, in consequence of his plantation and buildings having been occupied by the troops of the United States, during the invasion of New Orleans, in the year 1814 and 1815." On April 7, 1830, he was paid an additional $823, "for damages done to his plantation by digging and using earth for works of defense during the late war, and for materials and labor to repair said plantation."

His famous canal is little more than a depression in the ground in Mereaux in St. Bernard's Parish.

## Alexander Milne

It is assumed this was the young Scottish immigrant, Alexander Milne, Jr., born in 1842, who arrived at New Orleans in 1776 and entered business selling hardware and eventually manufactured bricks used to rebuild New Orleans after two very destructive fires. He invested heavily in real estate and owned a large amount of land along Lake Ponchartrain. He built the Port Ponchartrain Lighthouse and a rail line to Milneburg from the French Quarter. In his will he left a substantial sum of money to build two orphanages, one for boys and one for girls. Milneburg is now a neighborhood in New Orleans.

Milne claimed $500 for, "A bake house on the Bayou opposite fort St. John," and "A house on the bank of Lake Ponchartrain near the fort, destroyed by order of the military commandant," as reported on December 28, 1818, by the Committee of Claims embedded in a long list of claims related to those of Thadeus Mayhew. Milne's claim was presented to Congress on Friday, November 27, 1818, along with eleven others and ordered referred to the Committee of Claims.

Alexander Milne was paid $2,500 in 1821, "for the losses sustained by him in the destruction or injury of his building, and other property, by the troops of the United States, during the invasion of New Orleans by the British, in the years 1814–15."

## Joseph McNeil

Joseph McNeil's plantation was about 4 miles below New Orleans. He claimed damage to his dwelling house, $195; kitchen destroyed for fuel, $350; a stable and corn house, $180; a privy, $65; a negro house, $40; a large double gate, $60; a small gate, $25; a bake oven torn down, $20; and 21 acres of pale fence used as fuel, $450. Total $1,385.

As stated by Dr. David C. Ker, hospital surgeon, on February 3, 1817:

> I hereby certify that as hospital surgeon of the United States army during the invasion of Louisiana by the British in 1814 and 1815, several houses in the vicinity of Camp Jackson on the left bank of the Mississippi were employed as hospitals under my direction and occupied as such by proper authority.
>
> Among others, a dwelling house belonging to Joseph McNeil was thus taken by public authority for the use of the army, and in consequence of such use and occupation, much injury and damage was done to the house, and that there was a total destruction and consumption of a kitchen attached to the premises, and of the fences, gates, &c.
>
> I further certify that the estimate of damage above made by Joseph McNeil is, in my opinion, reasonable.

Jacob Knabb, who lived on the property, stated that Dr. Ker, "belonging to the Tennessee troops" came to house and said he was ordered to occupy the house, "and that I saw many of the soldiers tearing down and carrying away the picket fences, and at the time I told them not to destroy the property. They answered that they were ordered to do so."

James Lambert, late a private in Capt. Peter V. Ogden's company of Louisiana Light Horse Militia, and a carpenter working for McNeil, said he witnessed the destruction.

Shortly after the British left "from the island of Orleans" a commission composed of Benjamin Morgan, Richard Relf, and Pierre Foucher was appointed by the quartermaster general, "for the purpose of examining and assessing the damages which individual property had sustained at the different encampments near the city of New Orleans from the occupancy by the troops of the United States."

McNeil was one of a group of prominent Americans doing business in New Orleans. Others were Daniel Clark, William Hulings, Evan Jones, James Mather, and George Morgan.

McNeil's claim was rejected on February 17, 1820, then re-examined. Joseph Lefebvre filed a similar claim for hospital use by Gen. Morgan, "commanding the Louisiana drafted militia" and, "for carrying away of materials from his plantation for fortifications; the employment of his negroes, horses, oxen, and carts, in the public service, and the consumption and destruction of his provisions by the troops."

His claim was rejected by the Committee of Claims for lack of evidence and sent to the Treasury Department for adjudication.

Joseph McNeil was paid $700 in 1821.

## Bartholome Duvergé

March 2, 1821, Congress authorized $2,100 be paid to Bartholome Duvergé, or his legal representatives, "in full for injuries and losses sustained by him, in consequence of the use and destruction of his property, by the troops of the United States, during the invasion of New Orleans by the British, in the winter of 1814–15."

## Pierre de la Ronde

De la Ronde left his plantation and joined Gen. Jackson's army on December 3, 1814. On the evening of December 23, a detachment of Louisiana cavalry with their wounded occupied the plantation and helped themselves to anything they needed for themselves or their horses. Gen. John Coffee's troops encamped in the cane field, which was completely consumed or burned to prevent the British from seeking shelter in it. Other troops came and went until the evening of the 28th when the British arrived and drove everyone off and they remained there until the night of January 18, 1815.

Several witnesses reported seeing U.S.

troops carrying off every conceivable item that could be carried, leaving the house and outbuildings stripped bare.

A total loss of $40,008.38 was claimed, to wit: a field of sugar cane, $7,920; 40,000 pounds of sugar, $11,200; 15,320 fence pickets, $1,932; provisions, liquors, wine, preserves, coffee, spermaceti candles, $2,743.10; earthen and glassware, $245.50; bedding, clothes, furniture, kitchen supplies, $2,502; poultry, sheep, cattle, horses, $3,110.50; firearms, powder, shot, $126; farming and carpenter tools, $664; carriages, bridles, saddles, $860; library books, $300; negroes, $7,200; 200 cords of wood, $400; destruction and damage to buildings, $794.28.

De la Ronde was compensated only for the articles actually used by the U.S. troops for their sustenance—food, fuel, and forage, there being no provision in the law for any other compensation. He was paid $5,770.50 in 1821, "in full for injuries sustained by him, in consequence of his plantation and buildings, having been occupied by the troops of the United States, from the 23rd to the 28th of December, 1814."

## Jumonville de Villiers

As reported by the Committee of Claims on February 20, 1822:

> During the late invasion of Louisiana by the British, after the enemy had landed near the city of New Orleans, in order to prevent him from bringing up his cannon and other ordnance to the city, General Morgan, commanding the Louisiana militia, caused the levee to be cut through at or near the plantation of the petitioner on or about the 24th of December, 1814, whereby the greater part of the plantation was inundated, and remained so until after the departure of the invading army from the State.
>
> In consequence, the petitioner suffered great losses in the destruction of his sugar cane standing on the plantation and of the cane plants in the ground, and in the expenses of repairing the levee, appraised at $19,250 by certain citizens of Louisiana.
>
> The committee are of opinion that this injury was done in the necessary operations of war, and the United States are not liable for the individual losses sustained by that inundating, and therefore the prayer of the petitioner ought not to be granted.

## Joseph Abell

Maj. Gen. John Thomas, commander of the Kentucky troops "at the battle below New Orleans," wrote: "By my order, and for the transportation of my troops in the public service, a batteau, the property of Joseph Abell, was taken and not returned, of the value, as I believe, of $40, for which Abell has never received compensation."

On December 30, 1829, the Committee of Claims rejected his petition on the ground that there was no evidence the boat was lost, only that it wasn't returned. The Third Auditor also discovered that Col. Richard Taylor, deputy quartermaster general, advanced a "considerable amount" of money by the United States for the purchase of boats to bring Kentucky troops down to New Orleans by water, but the accounts and vouchers were "alleged to have been destroyed by fire."

## Edward McCarty

The petition was filed by Jean Noël Destrehan, father of Marie Elèonore Destrehan, who married Edmond de Macarty. They had two children, daughter Mirtille and son Edmond Jr. Edmond Sr. appointed Barthélémy Macarty as tutor to the children.

Edmond Sr. was born on June 30, 1782, and died on the Macarty Plantation on Bayou Chapitoulas on November 13, 1814, at age 32.

On April 6, 1816, possibly because Marie had become ill, Jean Noël filed a petition with James Pitot, judge of the Court of Probates, "in and for the Parish and city of New Orleans" on behalf of the children and stated an inventory of the estate had been made and there was no "necessity to the taking of a new inventory" and requested that he be named guardian of the children.

Edmond Jr. died on October 19, 1816, and Marie died on November 16, 1816, leaving Mirtille as sole heir, along with a grandson, Edmond Macarty. Jean Noël Destrehan petitioned the Probate Court to allow the grandson one-half of the estate and Barthélémy Macarty agreed to a family meeting to convene on February 27, 1819, to discuss details.

The heirs of Edward McCarty, deceased, were paid $2,940, in 1822.

## John Pellet

Edward White Robertson, of Louisiana, presented the petitions of Joseph McNeil, Bartholome Duvergé, Pierre Denis De La Ronde, and John Pellet on December 22, 1817, "praying for compensation for damages committed on their landed estates and other property, by the American and British armies during the military operations in the neighborhood of New Orleans, in the months of December, 1814, and January, 1815." The claims were ordered referred to the Committee of Claims.

John Pellet was paid $3,864 in1822, "in full for losses sustained by him in the destruction of his buildings and other property during the invasion of New Orleans in the winter of 1814–15."

## Thaddeus Mayhew

Thaddeus Mayhew owned a plantation called Belvidere and a saw mill on the right bank of the river about 6 miles below New Orleans and was one whose property was in possession of both American and British troops. It was certified in a report by a commission appointed by Gen. Jackson that Mayhew's loss caused by American troops was $1,253.50 out of his total claim of $14,800 for a bridge, saw-mill, and lumber burned on the morning of January 8, 1815. Mayhew's overseer, Luther Howe testified on May 13, 1815, about the destruction, but he couldn't say who did it. Gen. David Morgan stated, "The saw-mill belonging to the claimant, together with the wooden bridge which crossed the canal on which the saw-mill stood, as also a large quantity of lumber, consisting of cypress boards, planks, and slabs, were, on the 8th day of January, and during the retreat of the enemy, set on fire and totally destroyed by the enemy."

Commodore Patterson stated: "As the enemy tore up and destroyed by fire the platforms of his batteries, the enemy also burnt the saw-mill and lumber." Another witness, Samuel Packwood, said he also believed the property was destroyed by the British.

Mayhew claimed the bridge and saw-mill loss and rebuilding cost would be $6,000; 200,000 feet of cypress at $40: $3,000; and 12,000 feet of scantling at $50: $600.

After exhaustive legal research, the committee stated:

> The total absence of a standard price in the valuation of the lumber furnishes an irresistible inference to the prejudice of the petitioner. To supply defects which in every view of the case, must seem to be intentional, would require the exercise of a patience of which the committee are not possessed, and which, it is presumed, they cannot be expected to practice. The committee, therefore, recommend the following amendment to the bill, to wit: Strike out the words, "fifteen thousand eight hundred and ninety-eight dollars and fifty cents," and insert "one thousand two hundred and ninety-eight dollars and fifty cents."

Thaddeus Mayhew was paid $715 in 1824.

## Gonzales & Colmanero

Gen. Thomas Flournoy commanded the 7th Military District at New Orleans and between March 1813 and April 1814 was extremely concerned with security, "in the event of alarm occasioned by insurrection or a sudden eruption of the enemy."

Don Ramon de Lenares Gonzales and Don Ramon de Calmenero were permitted to load three Spanish vessels for La Vera Cruz but when the collector at New Orleans apparently received word of the impending embargo law they were refused clearance. Gen. Flournoy then ordered the vessels unloaded and detained, "to the great injury and loss of the petitioners," as stated on March 1, 1814.

The owners sued in the District Court for the Eastern District of Louisiana in May 1825, and prevailed. Gen. Flournoy submitted a petition for relief, which was forwarded to the Committee on Foreign Relations, who found the embargo did not pertain to friendly foreign vessels loaded with provisions, and the general was paid $3,684.83 in 1828.

## Marigny D'Auterive

On December 17, 1814, William W. Montgomery, quartermaster of the 4th Regiment, Louisiana Militia, hired a cart belonging to Mons. Marigné Dauterive at $2.50 a day for service until January 24, 1815, for a total of $95. The cart was used by Capt. Anthony Doriocourt's 2nd Company and certified by Maj. Aldre St. Amand and Col. George W Morgan, commander of the regiment.

On December 31, 1814, Lt. Louis Viales gave D'Auterive a certificate at "Suburb La Course" for the services of three slaves named Bling, Warwick, and Fidel, "for the service of the military government" by order of Gen. Jackson. Warwick was to drive the team delivering the wood.

On June 24, 1815, Lt. Viales stated:

> I, the subscriber, syndic of the Upper Suburb of the city of New Orleans, declare that on the 31st of December, 1814, I put in requisition of an order of Gen. Jackson, transmitted to me by Mr. Nicholas Girod, Mayor of this city, a negro named Warwick, belonging to Mr. Marigny D'Auterive, and that the negro being employed at the works of the lines at Camp Jackson, received two gunshot wounds from the enemy, one in the left arm, and the other on the left eye, the last of which is incurable, and the first, although healed, has left a weakness in the arm which makes it difficult for him to use it. Wherefore, to put a just value for the damage to the negro, I have summoned Messrs. Baptiste Bouttet and Joseph Lavigne, both inhabitants of this parish who declared that the negro had lost his original value to the amount of $200. The negro being perfectly well known by the subscriber before receiving the wounds. Hereto is also annexed the certificate of the Surgeon, and the costs of attendance, and an account of the time lost by the negro. In witness whereof we have hereunto signed, this 24th June, 1815.

In 1826, D'Auterive filed a claim for $1,095 for the horse and cart, and $24 for medical services, $15 for a month of his time lost, and $200 "for the value of the injury done to him" for a total of $239, who was wounded at Camp Jackson on January 1, 1815, and attended to by Dr. P. Beaudaquin.

As reported by the Committee of Claims on December 28, 1829:

> The committee has several times reported in favor of allowing a compensation to the petitioner for 95 cords of wood, necessarily taken by a body of horse commanded by General Carroll at the attack by the British on New Orleans proven to be worth $8 per cord, amounting to $750, and for the use of a cart, horse, and driver from the 17th of December, 1814, to 24th January, 1815, at $2.50 per day.
>
> The committee, as to these items, entertain the opinion heretofore expressed, and report a bill, similar in all respects to a bill passed by the House, but which was not definitely acted on in the Senate.

The claim for Warwick was rejected by the Committee on the grounds that a slave was property in one sense, but a person in another, as when impressed for government service as any other person might be.

This set off a furious debate over the legal status of slaves. Could they be pressed into federal service and their owner compensated? Could they be seized under the 5th Amendment and set free with just compensation to the owner? This was at the time the American Colonization Society was seeking federal funds to establish a homeland for freed slaves in Liberia.

John Leeds Kerr, of Maryland, summed it up:

> The question has gone forth to the People, and you cannot now stop the current of the public mind upon it. No matter how needlessly it may have been brought up; no matter what disavowals or admissions gentlemen may now think it wise, or prudent, or liberal, to make; the question has been raised—whether slaves are property?—but not in those general terms, I admit, but whether they are property in the view of this General Government, insofar as it may have power to affect them in certain exigencies of State, and in which the owner is to be indemnified for any loss or injury sustained by him thereby. And it is our solemn duty to meet and to decide in on the claim of the individual now petitioning for redress. It is because I regard this question as vital to the interests of a large portion of the citizens of this country, and of those too, whom I have the honor to represent, that I was opposed to the recommitment of this bill, and now advocate a decided vote in favor of this amendment.
>
> Gentlemen now say, some of them at least, that they do not deny the general proposition that slaves are property; yet they do not contend that, *pro hac vice*, they are not property, and they are not to be considered as such, when taken or lost or injured in the public service. Here then is the issue: we aver that slaves are property; so declared by law, and so held in the view of the Constitution. It is the report of this committee with the bill, which will make up the record of our judgment here, and if you had permitted this amendment to be dropped, because of the insignificant amount of the claim of Marigny D'Auterive, or now reject it, you establish a precedent to be quoted on all future occasions, against the most important claims, and against the redress for the most serious individual losses, and I have no doubt it would be set up by some as a solemn decision on record, that slaves are not property.

(Register of Debates in Congress, Volume IV, January 18, 1828)

Marigny d'Auterive was paid $855 in 1830 for 95 cords of wood and for the use of a cart, horse, and driver, from the 17th of December 1814, to the 24th of January 1815.

## Widow Dupré

Bayou Dupré was located in the marshes off Lake Borgne within 2 miles of the Mississippi River and 10 miles below the city. Dupré's canal, along with Bayou Bienvenue, was considered to be a strategic site. The Dupré plantation was occupied in January 1815 by a number of unarmed Kentucky troops from Brig. Gen. John Adair's command as a reserve force. Upon encamping, they began breaking up their flatboats and getting materials for shelter and fires against the dampness.

The original petition was for 1 saw-mill torn down to erect the second line of defense, $5,000; 2 brick kiln sheds, $2,000; 1 brick kiln shed, $8,000; 2 tempering sheds for brick making, $300; 14 Negro houses, $1,400; 7 gates and doors, $56; damage to dwelling and out-houses, $300; 97 acres of post and rail fence destroyed, $1,142.75; damage to the cultivation of the farm (hay and oats), $3,000. Total $14,254.75.

Commissioner Richard Bland Lee rejected the claim, as did Third Auditor Peter Hagner, and the Secretary of War. Commissioners appointed by Gen. Jackson assessed the damage at $8,995 for a saw mill pulled down to make room for a fortification at the same location, $4000; 3 brick sheds destroyed, $1,950; 2 tempering beds for brickmaking destroyed, $200; 7 gates and doors, $56; 14 Negro cabins, $1,150;

damage to dwelling and out-houses, $200; 97 acres of post and rail fence destroyed, $1,182; and 12 additional acres of post and rail fence destroyed, 256. Total $8,995.

Lee allowed $2,795, the difference between the two sums, but this was rejected by the Secretary of War, based on a report by Hagner, and Widow Dupré was paid $6,202.94, in October 1817, and which was approved by Gen. Jackson's commissioners.

In 1828, it was called to Peter Hagner's attention that the amount paid, "was made for personal property alone, and did not include any of the items in the account which had been thus rejected, and for the payment of which the application is now renewed."

As reported by the Committee of Claims on January 13, 1830:

> The petitioners claim $3,000 for the damage to the cultivation of the farm.
>
> The nature of the damage is too indefinite to grant relief. Where the United States have occupied the grounds of an individual as a military station, reasonable rent has been paid, and where the grounds during such occupation have been dug up to construct works of defense, the rent has been paid, and, in addition thereto, such an amount as would restore the soil to its original position. But in no instance has a compensation been given to remunerate for the loss of an anticipated crop. It is necessary for the petitioners to set forth the injury done to the land, and prove the amount expended in remedying that injury.
>
> The Committee think the petitioners are entitled to relief, to the amount of the estimate of the Commissioners, and for that amount a bill is herewith presented.

The heirs or representatives of Widow Dupré, deceased, were paid $8,995 in 1830.

# APPENDICES

## The Lost, Captured, or Destroyed Property Act of April 9, 1816

The relevant sections:

Sec. 3. That any person who, in the late war aforesaid, has sustained damage by the loss, capture, or destruction, by the enemy, of any horse, mule, ox, wagon, cart, boat, sleigh, or harness, while such property was in the military service of the United States, either by impressment or contract, except in cases where the risk to which the property would be exposed was agreed to be incurred by the owner, if it shall appear that such loss, capture, or destruction, was without any fault or negligence on the part of the owner; and any person, who, during the time aforesaid, has sustained damage by the death of any such horse, mule, or ox, in consequence of failure on the part of the United States to furnish the same with sufficient forage, while in the service aforesaid, shall be allowed and paid the value thereof.

Sec. 9. That any person who, in the time aforesaid, has sustained damage by the destruction of his or her house or building by the enemy, while the same was occupied as a military deposit, under the authority of an officer or agent of the United States, shall be allowed and paid the amount of such damage: *Provided*, It shall appear that such occupation was the cause of its destruction. (This section was amended by the Act of March 3, 1825.)

Ten more sections detail the administrative procedures for paying for goods taken and for processing claims.

(3 Stat. L. 261)

Richard Bland Lee was appointed Commissioner, and between July 1 to December 17, 1816, Bland and his assistants adjusted 850 claims and awarded $229,693.15.

Between July 19 and December 27, 1816, the Treasury Department paid out $226,194.90 in claims for Property lost, &c. while in the Military Service of the United States, under the act of April, 9, 1816.

On April 20, 1818, all unadjusted claims were transferred to Peter Hagner, the Third Auditor.

## Amending the Act of April 9, 1816

That any person having a claim for a building destroyed by the enemy during the late war, under the ninth section of the act to which this is an amendment, and of the act to amend the same, passed the third of March 1817, which shall have been presented to the commissioner of claims, appointed under the act aforesaid, at any time before the 10th of April 1818, and which was not paid under said acts, nor finally rejected by said commissioner, may, within nine months, hereafter, present the same with the evidence to support it, to the third auditor of the treasury, for examination and adjustment, and if he shall be satisfied the building or buildings for which damages are claimed, was, at the time of its destruction, occupied by order of any agent or officer of the United States, as a place of deposit for military or naval stores, or as barracks for the military forces of the United States, he shall proceed to assess the damages, and certify the amount of payment, in the way pointed out in the act first above referred to, which shall be immediately paid out of any money in the treasury not otherwise appropriated. *Provided*, That if the auditor shall be satisfied the evidence before him is insufficient to enable him to correctly to decide between the United States and the claimant, he may, on giving notice to the claimant, cause other evidence to be taken: *And provided*, *also*, That no payment shall be made under the provisions of this act, where the property destroyed was occupied under a contract with the owner, and at the risk of such owner.

Sec. 2. That the amount which shall appear to have been paid to the owners, as rent for the use or occupation of their property, shall be deducted from the amount directed to be paid to them under this act.

Sec. 3. That, in the case the whole amount of claims presented and allowed, under this act, shall exceed the sum of $250,000, then, and in that case, the claimants, shall, respectively, receive only their ratable proportion of the sum of $250,000, to be liquidated by the said auditor, in the adjustment of the amount to be received by such claimants respectively.

March 3, 1825. (4 Stat. L. 123)

Sec. 9. of the December 6, 1816, Payment for Revolutionary War Claims Act authorized the payment for property "lost, captured, or destroyed by the enemy while in the military service of the United States."

## War of 1812 Restitution for Slaves

On December 30, 1814, the Treaty of Ghent ended the war while the British commander, Maj. Gen. John Lambert, was planning his attack on New Orleans. Having failed to defeat Gen. Jackson's "motley collection of militiamen, creoles, and pirates," he proceeded to Mobile Bay.

In mid–February 1815, copies of the peace treaty arrived. Gen. Jackson then demanded that the owners of slaves who had been carried away in Louisiana by British troops when they retreated from the Island of Orleans be compensated pursuant to Article 1, which Lambert refused to do, claiming the British interpreted the article differently than the United States.

The relevant portion of the article stated:

> All territory, places, and possessions whatsoever taken by either party from the other during the war, or which may be taken after the signing of this Treaty, excepting only the islands hereinafter mentioned, shall be restored without delay and without causing any destruction or carrying away any of the Artillery or other public property originally captured in the said forts or places, and which shall remain therein upon the Exchange of the Ratifications of this Treaty, or any Slaves or other property.

On December 27, 1815, the House was debating the section of an act which provided payment for "pressed horses, carts, &c." William Mayrant, of South Carolina, moved to include "slaves used as drivers of wagons, as sailors, laborers, &c. employed or pressed into the service of the United States, and lost, captured, or destroyed by the enemy." The motion was seconded, but a "considerable majority" rejected it.

On September 17, 1816, the United States proposed, "that the question should be referred to the arbitration of some friendly Power" and the Russian czar became involved in settling disputes.

On January 24, 1825, when the House was debating relief for the Niagara sufferers, John Forsyth again suggested including slaves, and which again was opposed, but 48 members approved.

On November 13, 1826, Great Britain agreed to pay $1,204,960 "as an indemnity for slaves and other property carried away," and on March 2, 1827, Congress passed legislation, "for the adjustment of Claims for Slaves, and other property, taken away in violation of the First Article of said Treaty." A commission was set up to hear claims, and between December 29, 1827, and January 27, 1829, a total of $406,438.21 was paid out. Awards were reported by the Treasury Department in their annual "An Account of the Expenditures of the United States for the Year 1828." The claimants were paid 75 percent of the amount awarded by the commissioners.

The report shows the date the payment warrant was issued, name and state of residence, number of slaves claimed, and the amount paid. Some claimants were reported deceased at the time and are marked with a † symbol. The names of the heirs or legal representatives of the deceased are not shown.

Claimants are arranged here by State of residence. Some owners had slaves that were taken in states other than their residence.

### *District of Columbia*

†Landon Carter, of Alexandria, 1, $210; †Thomas Davis, 1, $210.

### *Alabama*

John B. Borzage, 1, $292.50; †Honore Collins, 1, $292.50; Nicholas Cook, 1, $292.50.

### *Georgia*

Isaac Abrahams, 1, $292.50; George D. Ashton, 1, $292.50; †Richard Atwell, 1, $292.50; †Chapman Austin, 1, $292.50; †John Borum, 2, $585; †Mary Borum, 2, $585; James J. Bourne, 1, $292.50; John J. Brooke, 3, $877.50; Bushrod M.F. Beacham, 1, $292.50; †Charles I. Carroll, 2, $585; Sarah Cox, 1, $292.50; †Thomas Dade, 1, $292.50; †John Darby, 1, $292.50; †Poulain Dubignon, 21, $6,142.50; †Charles Floyd, 2, $585; †Joshua Foley, 1, $210; †John Frazier, 14, $4,095; Thomas Harwood, 1, $292.50; James Hopewell, 1, $292.50; †Ezekiel Hudnal, 1, $292.50; Charles Johnson, 2, $585; Ann R. and Elizabeth M. McCarty,

6, $1,1631; Daniel McNeil, 1, $292.50; James Miller, 1, $292.50; †Sally Nutt, 2 in Georgia, $585; †Alexander Parker, 1 and other property, $787.50; †Littleton Savage, 2, $585; Louisa C. Shaw, 1 and other property, $10,318.50; †Robert Shield, 1, $292.50; †William Somerville, 4, $1,005; †John Stratton, 1, $292.50; †David Stuart, 1, $292.50; John Teasdale, 1, $292.50; Samuel Wapples, 1, $292.50; William Ward, 1, $292.50; George Wilkinson, 1, $292.50; Benjamin Williams, 2, $585; †Benjamin Williams, 1, $292.50; †Rebecca Wright, 1, $292.50; †William Wroe, 1, $292.50; Anna F. Wylly, 1, $292.50; John A. W, 1, $292.50; Susan C. Wylly, 1, $292.50.

### *Louisiana*

Widow Barjac, 1, $292.50; Jourdan Brothers, 2, $870; Jean B. Dufossat, 1, $435.

### *Maryland*

Francis Abel, 1, $210; Anthony Addison, 1, $210; †Benjamin W. Allen, 4, $840; †David Avis, 2, $420; William Bailey, 1 in Ga., $292.50; Elizabeth W. Ballard, 13, $2,730; Levin W. Ballard, 1, $210; Charles D. Barrow, 2, $420; Aquilla Beall, 1, $210; Rebecca Beard, 1, $210; Isaac Beauchamp, 1 in Ga., $292.50; †Thomas Beauchamp, 3, $630; Zachariah Berry, Sr., 3, $630; Thomas Billingsly, 1, $210; †George Biscoe, 1, $210; Josiah Biscoe, 2, $420; Margaret Biscoe, 5, $1,050; †Thomas Blake, 2, $420; John T. Bond, 2 in Va., $420; †Samuel Bond, 3, $630; Henderson S. Boteler, 1, $210; James E. Bourne, 5, $1,050; Isaac Bowen, 3, $630; Peregrine Bowen, 3 in Va., $630; Charles Bowie, 3, $630; †John B. Bowie, 1, $210; †Thomas Bowie, 2, $430; Harriet Brooke, 1 in Va., $210; Alexander Broome, 2, $420; †James M. Broome, 7, $1,770; John Broome, 2, $420; †John H. Brown, 1, $210; †Henry Bullen, 1, $210; Elizabeth Carvell-Bryan, 1, $210; †Richard Bryan, 3, $6300; Edward H. Calvert, 1, $210; Charles J. Carroll, 3, $630; Juliana Carroll, 1, $210; †Margaret M.A. Carroll, 3, $630; Thomas K. Carroll, 2, $420; Nicholas Causin, 1, $210; †Seneca Cheseldine, 1, $210; †Ann Chew, 1, $210; John H. Chew, 1, $210; Charles Claggett, 2, $420; †Benjamin Clocker, 1, $210; †John Coad, 1, $210; Edward Colbourne, 1 in Ga., $292.50; Hezekiah Colberth, 5, $1,050; Mary M. Coombs, 16, $3,360; †Ann Dare, 2, $420; †John Dare, 1, $210; William C. Dawkins, 13, $2,730; James Dawson, 2, $420; James D. Denton, 1, $210; †William Dixon, 3, $630; †James Duke, 1 in Ga., $292.50; James Duke, 8, $1,680; Mary Ann Broome-Duke, 1, $210; Robert Dunkinson, 1, $210; Howard Duvall, 1, $210; Sarah Dyson, 1, $210; William Eareckson, 1, $210; †Jeremiah Edelin, 1, $210; †Walter Edelin, 1, $210; Jesse Edwards, 1, $210; Benjamin T. Fendall, 5, $1,050, and 1 in Va., $210; †John Fitzhugh, 1, $210; Henry Fontaine, 1, $210; Josias B. Ford, 2 in Va., $420; Jacob Freeland, 1, $210; Richard Frisby, 4, $840; John P. Gale, 1, $210, and 1 in Ga., $292.50; Elizabeth Gantt, 2, $420; Edward Gantt, 2, $420; Thomas C. Gantt, 1, $210; †Robert Gardiner, 2, $420; †Mary Gest, 2, $420; †John Goodhand, 2, $420; †Marmaduke Goodhand, 4, $840; John M. Gray, 1, $210; Josias Green, 1, $210; Alexander Greene, 3, $630; †Pitt Hall, 1, $210; Richard T. Hall, 1, $210; †Richard Hammett, 1, $210; †Robert Hammet, 1, $210; Benjamin Hance, 2, $420; Joseph Handy, 1, $210; †William Harris, 1, $210; Jonathan Harrison, 6, $1,260, and 1 in Ga., $292.50; Thomas Harwood, 1, $210; †Martha Hatton, 1, $210; Nathaniel Hatton, 1, $210; Basil Hatton, 1, $210; †Henry Hatton, 2, $420; Edmund Heard, 1, $210; †Winifred Heard, 1, $210; †Josiah W. Heath, 2, $420; Elizabeth Barnhouse-Hebb, 1, $210; †Rebecca Hellen, 1, $210; Walter Hellen, 2, $420; Tilghman Hilleary, 2, $420; †John Hodges, 1, $210; Elizabeth I. Hungerford, 1, $210; Mary Hungerford, 3, $630; Thomas B. Hungerford, 1, $210; †Violetta Hungerford, 1, $210; John C. Ireland, 5, $1,050; John K. Jackson, 1, $210; †John M. Jenkins, 2, $420; †Ann E.

Johnson, 3, $630; Arthur T. Jones, 3, $630, and 5 in Ga., $1,462.50; †Caleb Jones, 8, $1,680; Mordecai Jones, 1, $210; William Kilgour, 4, $810; Joshua King, 4 in Va., $840; Philip King, 1 in Va., $210; Thomas E. King, 1, $210; Harris Legg, 1, $210; †Thomas Lewis, 1, $210; Margaret Lowry, 1, $210; Thomas Lynch, Jr., 2, $420; †Ann Mackall, 1, $210; Benjamin H. Mackall, 20, $4,200; †John G. Mackall, 1, $210; John Mackall, Jr., 12, $2,520; Pricilla Maddox, 1, $210; John R. Magruder, 4, $840; Sarah Marshall, 1, $210; Richard B. Mason, 3, $680; Thomas L. McCubbin, 1 in Va., $210; Elizabeth K. McKay, 5, $1,050; John Miles, 1, $210; †Andrew Montgomery, 1, $210; †Jonathan Morgan, 2, $420; †Thomas B. Moreland, 1, $210; †Charles Muse, 1, $210; †Aquilla Nelson, 4, $840; Lewis Neth, 1, $210; Daniel Norris, 1 in Va., $210; †Henry M. Ogle, 18, $3,780; George Parker, 1, $210; Jane Parran, 6, $1,260; Alexander Perry, 1, $210; Benjamin Phillips, 5, $1,050; John R. Plater, 49, $10,290; James Pumphrey, 1, $210; Isaac Rawlings, Jr., 1, $210; Juliet Rawlings, 3, $630; Sarah Rawlings-Sedwick, 1, $210; Susannah Rawlings, 3, $630; William Reeder, 1, $210; Edward Ringgold, 2, $420; †Jacob Ringgold, 1, $210; Richard Ross, 1, $210; †William Sasseer, 1, $210; William A. Schoolfield, 1, $210; John Scrivener, 2, $420; †Nicholas Sewall, 24, $5,040; †Robert Sewall, 17, $3,570; Neale H. Shaw, 1 in Va., $210; William T. Simmons, 1, $210; Andrew Skinner, 1, $210; †Levin Skinner, 1, $210; Artimisia Skinner, 1 in Ga., $292.50; Thomas Smith, 1, $210; Ann Sollers, 4, $840; †James M. Sollers, 1, $210; Henry Somerville, 1, $210; †William Somerville, 4, $1,005; †William A. Somerville, 8, $1,680, and 1 in Ga., $292.50; †William C. Somerville, 4, $1,050; †Ann Sprigg, 6, $1,260; John T. Stoddert, 2 in Va., $420; John G. Stuart, 1 in Ga., $292.50; William Sudler, 2, $420; †Michael Taney, 21, $4,410; †Philemon Tanner, 5, $1,050; James M. Taylor, 1, $210; †Peter U. Thompson, 5, $1,050; †Bernard Todd, 2, $420; †Jacob Tolson, 1, $210; John Tucker, 3 in Va., $630; †John Turner, 1, $292.50; Samuel Turner, 1, $210; Trueman Tyler, 2, $420; Nathaniel Washington, 1 in Va., $210; Gustavus Weems, 1, $210; Walter Wells, 3, $630; †William Whittington, 4, $810; George Wilkinson, 5, $1,050; Benjamin Williams, 19, $3,990; †Thomas Williams, 1, $210; William Williams, 1, $210; Martha Wilson, 14, $2,940; †Miel Wise, 6, and 1 in Ga., $922.50; †John Wood, 5, $1,050; †Frances Wrightson, 2, $420; †Robert L. Young, 4, $810.

### *Mississippi*

John J. Jourdon, 7, $1,470.

### *South Carolina*

William B. Smith, 1 in Ga., $292.50.

### *Virginia*

William Alderson, 1, $210; †Benjamin Alexander, 1, $210; †Thomas Allen, 1, $210; †Anthony Armistead, 4, $840; †Robert Armistead, 1, $210; †Mary Ashton, 3, $630; Thomas B.B. Baber, 1, $210; Thomas Badger, 1, $210; Elijah Baker, 6, $1,260; Robert Bailey, 12, $2,520; †Susannah Bailey, 3, $630; Robert Baily, 3, $877.50; †David Ball, 5, $1,050; James Ball, 2, $420; Joseph Ball, Jr., 1, $210; Mottrom Ball, 5, $1,050; †William Ball, 1, $210; †Stephen Barnes, 11, $2,310; James Barren, 1, $210; Daniel W. Beacham, 6, $1,260; †Thomas Beacham, 2, $420; Alice O. Beale, 3, $630; †Matthew Beard, 1, $210; Sydnor Belfield, 2, $420; Charles Bell, 1, $210; Thomas Bell, 1, $210; †Levin Belote, 1, $210; William Bernard, 1, $210; Ann W. Berry, 3, $630; Alexander Berryman, 1, $210; Francis Berryman, 2, $420; †Willoughby N. Berryman, 3, $630; †Thomas Biggs, 2, $420; Sally Billups, 1, $210; Ann Biscoe, 1, $210; †George Blackwell, 1, $210; †James Blake, 1, $210; George Booker, 1, $210; John Booth, 1, $210; William Boush, 17, $3,570; †Carter Braxton, 2, $420; Polly Bray, 1, $210; Winter Bray, 1 in

Ga., $292.50; †George Brickhouse, 3, $630; Austin Brockenborough, 2, $420; John Brooks, 1, $210; Richard T. Brown, 1, $210; †Eliza Buckner, 16, $3,360; †Jonathan Bunting, 1, $210; †James Burwell, 1, $210; Joseph C. Cabell, 35, and 7 in Ga., $9,397; John Campbell, 4, $840; Nelly Candiff, 1, $210; †Daniel Carmichael, 2, $420; John Carpenter, 3, $630; †William Carpenter, 3, $630; †Charles Carter, 22, and 5 in Ga. $6,082.50; †Charles B. Carter, 4, $840; †James Carter, Jr., 2, $420; †Joseph Carter, Jr., 1, $210; Miles Cary, 11, $2,310; Thomas Cary, 3, $630; John Chandler, 3, $630; Thomas Chandler, 4, $840; William C. Chandler, 7, $1,470; †Daniel M. Chichester, 2, $420; Cyrus Chilton, 1, $210; †Martha Chisman, 2, $420; James Chowning, 1, $210; William Chowning, 1 in Ga., $292.50; †John Christopher, 3, $630; Samuel Clarke, 5, $1,050; Pemberton Claughton, 12, $2,520, and 2 in Ga., $585; Elizabeth and Kitty Claughton, 6, $1,260; †Pemberton Claughton, Jr., 4, $840; Lucy Clements, 1, $210; †John Cockarell, 14, $2,940; Ann Coleman, 2, $420; †Edward Coles, 1, $210; †Elizabeth Coles, 4, $840; Joseph Coles, 2, $420; †Richard Coles, 4, $840; Samuel Collard, 1, $210; †Joseph Conway, 10, $2,100; †James N. Cooper, 6, $1,260; †John Cooper, 13, $2,730; †Gawin Corbin, 2, $420; †Elizabeth Cornick, 1, $210; James Cornick, 1, $210; John Cornick, 1, $210; Lemuel Cornick, 2, $420; †Mary Cornick, 1, $210; †Thomas Cornick, Jr., 3, $630; †William B. Cornick, 1, $210; Abraham Costin, 1, $210; William Costin, 7, $1,470; John Cottrell, 1, $210; Ann Cox, 1, $210; Carlos Cox, 8, $1,680; †Peter Cox, 3, $630; Peter C. Cox, 27, $5,670; †Polly Cox, 1, $210; Thomas M. Cox, 6, $1,260; †John Cralle, 3, $630; †Carter Crafford, 1, $210; Kenner W. Cralle, 21, $4,410; †John Crandol, 1, $210; †John Critcher, 1, $210; Fielding S. Crow, 1, $210; Nancy Crowder, 1, $210; John C. Crump, 5, $1,050; †Henry Curtis, 1, $210; †Thomas Custis, 1, $210; William P. Custis, 2, $420; Francis T. Dade, 1, $210; Langhorne Dade, 2, $420; Henry P. Daingerfield, 2, $420; †David F. Davenport, 2, $420; Lindsey O. Davenport, 1, $210; Arthur L. Davies, 10, $2,100; †John Davis, 1, $210; †Davis Day, 4, $840; †Josiah L. Dean, 2, $420; †Molly Demerit, 1, $210; John T. Deggs, 3, $630; †William Deggs, 1, $240; †William Dixon, 9, $1,890; Thomas Dobyns, 5, $1,050; Allen S. Dozier, 2, $420; †Joseph Doulin, 3, $630; Samuel Downing, 2, $420; †Thomas D. Downing, 2, $420; Fanny Downman, 1, $210; Harriot I. Downman, 2, $420; James W.P. Downman, 1, $210; Olivia Downman, 2, $420; Rawleigh W. Downman, 10, $2,100; Nancy Dugan, 5, $1,050; Robert Dunn, 2, $420; †John Dunton, 2, $420; William Dunton, 1, $210; †John Elliott, 1, $210; Frances Elliston, 1, $210; †William Eskridge, 6, $1,680; †William Eustace, 1, $210; Kemp Evans, 1, $210, and 1 in Ga., $292.50; James Ewell, 2, $420; John Eyre, 8, $1,680; †William Eyre, 6, $1,260; Henry Fairfax, 1, $210; †James N. Fitchett, 1, $210; Joshua Fitchett, 4, $810; Richard Fitchett, 1, $210; †Solathiel Fitchett, 1, $210; †Thomas Fletcher, 11, $2,310; John K. Floyd, 14, $2,940; William H. Forrester, 1, $210; †Joseph Fox, 2, $420; Elizabeth C.B. Gibbons, 1, $210; †Griffin Garland, 2, $420; †William S. Garner, 1, $210; †William Garner, 1, $210; William S. Garner, 24, $5,040; Henry L. Gaskins, 7, $1,470; †John Gibson, 1, $210; William Gibson, 1, $210; †Richard M. Glasscock, 1, $210; †Frances Goffegan, 1, $210; James Goffegan, 1, $210; John Goffegan, 2, $420; John M. Gray, 2, $420; Thomas Griffin, 5, $1,050; John Grinstead, 1, $210; Kendal Groten, 1, $210; †Benjamin R. Haile, 2, $420; †William Hallet, 1, $210; †William Harcum, 1, $210; †John H. Harmanson, 3, $630; †James Harvey, 1, $210; †Thomas Harvey, 6, $1,260; †Thomas Hathaway, 3, $630; †John Hayes, 7, $1,050; †James H. Haynes, 1, $210; †John Haynes, 4, $840; Bridgar Haynie, 1, $210; William Hazard, 2, $430; James Headley, 5, $1,050; William Henderson, 1, $210; Sena Anderson-Hicks, 1, $210; †William A.

Hipkins, 1, $210; Abraham B. Hooe, 6, $1,260; Thomas Holland, 1, $210; George Holt, 2, $420; †Calthorpe Howard, 1, $210; Henry Howard, 1 in Ga., $292.50; †William H. Hudgins, 1, $210; Richard Hudnall, 5, $1,050; Sally Hudnall, 2, $420; Sally Hudnall & Polly Taylor, 3, $630; †Thomas Hudnall, 1 in Ga., $292.50; †Warner Hudnall, 1 in Ga, $292.50; †William Hudnall, 1, $210; Esther Hughlett, 2, $420; John Hughlett, 2, $420; Thomas W. Hughlett, 1, $210; †John Hull, 3, $630; John G. Hunt, 1, $210; †James Hunter, 1, $210; Isaac Hurst, 1, $210; Maria Hutt, 9, $1,890; John Ingram, 2, $560; Josias Ingram, 2, $560; Sally Ingram, 1, $280; Thomas Jacobs, 2, $420; Nancy Hunter-Jenkins, 1, $210; Francis Jervis, 1, $210; Thomas Johnson, 1, $210; James Johnston, 1, $210; John Jones, 1, $210; Thomas Jones, 1, $210; Walter Jones, 11, $2,310; †William Joynes, 1 in Ga., $292.50; Adam Keeling, 4, $840; John T. Keeling, 7, $1,470; †Walter Kellum, 2, $420; †William Kent, 1, $210; Richard Knott, 2, $420; †Mary Lackey, 2, $420; Samuel Lamkin, 1, $210; †Hillery Land, 1, $210; Philip Langley, 1, $210; †William G. Langley, 1, $210; †William Lane, 6, $1,260; †Benjamin Lansdell, 2, $420; John Lansdell, 1, $210; †Eleanor Ann Lee, 20, $4,200; Baldwin M. Leland, 1, $210; †Charles Leland, 1, $210; †John Lewis, 8, $1,680; Lawrence Lewis, 1, $210; Richard Lewis, 3, $630; Samuel Lewis, 16, $3,360, and 2 in Ga., $485; †John Lovett, Sr., 3, $630; †John S. Lovett, 3, $630; Catherine Lowry, 5, $1,050; †Ethel Lyon, 1, $210; †George Mallicote, 3, $630; Thomas Mallicote, 1, $210; Elizabeth G. Manson, 1, $210; Joseph Marmaduke, 3, $630; †Thomas Mason, 1, $210; †Lee Massey, 3, $630; †William Mathias, 1, $210; †Susanna Mayo, 1 in Ga., $292.50; James McAlpine, 1, $210; Ann R. and Elizabeth M. McCarty, 27, $5,670; †Elizabeth McCarty, 2, $420; †Tarplay McCarty, 3, $630; †William J. McClanahan, 1 in Ga., $292.50; †Jesse McKinney, 1, $210; †Timothy McNamara, 1, $210; †Catherine Meredith, 2, $420; †Thomas Meyers, 4, $840; John Middleton, 1, $210; Lucy R. Miller, 1, $210; Thomas Miller, 1, $210; Newman Miskell, 2, $420; †William Mitchell, 1, $210; John Morris, 3, $630; †Nancy Mosely, 1, $210; †Frances Mountford, 1, $210; †Thomas Nelson, 1, $210; †William Norris, 1, $210; †Presley Neale, 3, $630; †Eppa L. Neasome, 2, $420; †Edwin Nelms, 5, $1,050; Peter Nelms, 1, $210; John Nelson, Sr., 1, $210; George D. Nicholson, 1, $210; Elizabeth J. Nimmo, 1, $210; Edmund Northern, 1, $210; George Northern, 2, $420; †Jacob Nottingham, 4, $840; John Nottingham, 1, $210; †Levin Nottingham, 1, $210; Lewis Nottingham, 1, $210; †William Nottingham, 8, $1,680; William Nottingham, Sr., 1, $210; William Nottingham, Jr., 8, $1,680; Walter Nutt, 4, $840; Polly F. Beacham-Oldham, 1, $210; Hiram L. Opie, 1, $210; †John Paine, 2, $420; †Charles Palmer, 1, $210; Rawleigh Palmer, 1, $210; Thomas Paramour, 2, $420; †Nathaniel Parish, 1, $210; †Alexander Parker, 2, $420; †George Parker, 3, $630; Jacob G. Parker, 1, $210; †Thomas Parramore, Sr., 1, $210; †Elizabeth Parsons, 1, $210; Margaret Parsons, 1, $210; †William Parsons, 1, $210; †John Patterson, 2, $420; Emanuel Peck, 1, $210; Harriot Peck, 2, $420; †John C. Peck, 4, $840; Ransdell Peirce, 1, $210; †Cyrus Pinkard, 1, $210, and 1 in Ga., $292.50; John Plummer, 1, $210; †Thaddeus Pope, 1, $210; George S. Powell, 1, $210; James Powell, 6, $1,260; †Mary Powell, 1, $210; Sarah Purcell, 1, $210; †John Redman, 2, $420; †Peter C. Rice, 3, $630; †Ann Richards, 1, $210; †Robert G. Robb, 1, $210; †Zerobabel Roberts, 1, $210; John Robins, 5, $1,050; Temple Robbins, 1, $210; †William Robinson, 1, $210; †George Rogers, 1, $210; Margaret Rose, 14, $2,940; William Routt, 1, $210; Thomas Royston, 1, $210; †Charles Sandford, 2, $420; Nancy Sandy, 2, $420; †Mary Ann Savage, 3, $630; †Littleton Savage, 1, $210; †Severn Savage, 1, $210; †William Savage, 2, $420; †George Scott, 1, $210; †Benjamin Sedwick, 1, $210; †Richard Selden, 1, $210; John Self, 1, $210; Edward

Seymour, 1, $210; Richard L. Shackelford, 1, $210; †Joseph Shearman, 3, $630; James Shelton, 3, $6300; †Robert Shield, 2, $420; †Samuel Shields, 1, $210; Smith Sheppard, 2, $420; John Silverthorn, 1, $210, and 1 in Ga., $292.50; †John Skinner, 5, $1,050; Catherine Smith, 1, $210; †George Smith, 1, $210; James Smith, 2, $420; John B. Smith, 1, $210; †John M. Smith, 1, $210; William B. Smith, 1, $210; Thomas S. Spady, 1, $210; Edward Spence, 1, $210; John B. Steele, 1, $210; Thomas Stowers, 3, $630; †Benjamin Stratton, 2, $420; Sally Cox-Straughan, 8, $1,680; †David Stuart, 1, $210; John G. Stuart, 2, $420; Beverly Stubblefield, 1, $210; John Stubblefield, 5, $1,050; †Simon Stubblefield, 1, $210; Eliza Conway-Sutton, 1 in Ga., $292.50; Judith Sutton, 1, $210; John Sydnor, 1, $210; †Philip Tabb, 1, $210; William Taliaferro, 7, $1,170; †Edmund Taylor, 1, $210; †Polly Taylor, 3, $630; John B. Thomas, 3, $630; †William Thomas, 2, $420; †George F. Thornton, 2, $420; †Pope Tiffy, 1, $210; †Philip Tignor, 1, $210; †Mallory Todd, 1, $210; †Moore F. Tomlin, 7, $1,170; William B. Tomlin, 1, $210; †Thomas Towles, 1, $210; Benjamin Thomas, 2, $420; †Ann Thompson, 1, $210; Elizabeth G. Thompson, 1, $210; †Frances Thompson, 1, $210; Henry H. Travers, 1, $210; William Truss, 1, $210; †John Turberville, 34, $7,140; †Benjamin Turner, 2, $420; John D. Turpin, 1, $210; †John Tyson, 3, $630; Nancy Underhill, 2, $420; Elizabeth Waddey, 1, $210; †Shapleigh N. Waddey, 1, $210; †Thomas Watts, 11, $2,310; Hezekiah P. Westcoat, 1, $210; †William Waring, 2, $420; Westerhouse Widgeon, 1, $210; †William Waring, Jr., 10, $2,100; John H. Washington, 3, $630; Sarah Washington, 1, $210; Edmund Watson, 1, $210; †Mary White, 16, $1,260; Obedience White, 2, $420; †Henry Whiting, 2, $420; Thomas Whittington, 10, $2,100; Nathaniel Widgen, 3, $630; John Wilkins, Sr., 1, $210; †Peter Wilkins, 2, $420; †Robert Wilkins, 3, $630; John S. Williams, 2, $420; Margaret Williams, 1, $210; Samuel S. Williams, 4, $840; William S. Williams, 2, $420; Mary Wills, 1, $210; James R. Wilson, 1, $210; John Winder, 10, $2,100; John H. Winder, 1, $210; †Tully R. Wise, 6, $1,260; Sidney Wishart, 1, $210; Bennet Wood, 1, $210; †William D. Woodhouse, 7, $4,470; †Samuel Wornum, 1, $210; †William Wroe, 2, $420; †John Yeatman, 3, $630; †George Yerby, 2, $420; †Nancy Yerby, 2, $420; †Thomas Yerby, 2, $420; Henry Young, 1, $210; William Young, 1, $210.

## Claims Filed for Vessels at the Treasury Department Under the Act of March 2, 1827

Benjamin T. Fendall—$2,000 estimated value of schooner *Little Eliza*. $1,050 paid on April 3, 1828, for "slave property" and $210 on June 4, 1828, for one slave. Nothing was paid for the schooner.

McFadden & Harris, sloop *Chance*—nothing paid.

Michael Tiernan—$3,217.37 estimated value of schooner *Caroline*. $1,582.96 paid on July, 31, 1827.

Robert Barrick—$4,000 estimated value of schooner *Independence*. $3,000 paid on April 22, 1828.

Blackwell Chilton—$600 estimated value for sloop *Harriet*. Nothing paid.

John Dudley—$300 estimated value of a boat, anchor, and cable. $2,730 paid for 13 slaves on December 24, 1827, and $932.88 on September 13, 1828. Nothing for the boat, anchor, and cable.

Caleb Redman—$700 estimated value of schooner *Harriet*. Nothing paid.

Joel Thomas—$400 estimated value for one 20 to 30-ton vessel. Nothing paid.

James Caze & John Richaud—$8,000 estimated value of the ship *Victory*. $12,210.75 paid on December 17, 1827.

Jeremiah, Gideon, and William O'Brien and John Holway—$1,500 estimated value of schooner *Washington*. Nothing paid.

## The Court of Claims

The various committees were always burdened with numerous claims, but by the 1850s, petitions from private citizens to Congress were becoming so numerous, particularly the Revolutionary War pension claims, that Congress created a special court of three judges to handle all future claims against the federal government, and on February 24, 1855, President Pierce signed it into law (10 Stat. L. 612).

The first judges nominated on March 3, 1855, were John James Gilchrist, of New Hampshire; Isaac Newton Blackford, of Indiana; and Joseph J. Lumpkin, of Georgia. Lumpkin declined the appointment and was replaced by George Parker Scarburgh, of Virginia. The court was set up as a standard court, the United States being the defendant and represented by the Attorney General's office. Plaintiffs obtained their own counsel, which soon became a thriving business in the nation's capital.

The Court heard its first case in the Willard Hotel in May 1855, and in July moved to the Supreme Court's chamber in the Capitol building basement. Shortly after they were allocated their own rooms in the basement. The cases primarily involved the same class of claims—the taking and loss of private property, military and civilian pay allowances, breach of contract, and the very numerous claims put into special classes like the French Spoliation and Indian Depredation claims.

The one exception to this court that made it different from a standard civil trial, was that the court was strictly fact-finding in nature and did not render a binding judgment. Like the various Committees, the Court took all the evidence and wrote a report with their recommendation Their findings and conclusions were sent to the appropriate Congressional committee, which could then either accept or reject the court's decision. The committee, in turn, presented the opinion to Congress, who then appropriated the money or rejected the claim.

The Court's published reports were bound in their own volumes of court reports. The court functioned until 1982.

# Bibliography


Bailey, Thomas A. *A Diplomatic History of the American People*. New York: Appleton-Century-Crofts, 1958.

Bennett, Marion T. *The United States Court of Claims*. Washington, D.C.: Committee of the Bicentennial of Independence, 1976.

Bertram, Mike. "Water and Fire—The Power Behind Valley Forge." *Tredyffrin Easttown Historical Society History Quarterly*, Vol. 41, No. 3, Summer 2004.

Billon, Frederic L. *Annals of St. Louis in its Territorial Days*. St. Louis: Nixon-Jones Printing Co., 1888.

Chappelle, Howard L. *The History of the American Sailing Ships*. New York: Bonanza Books, 1935.

Clinton County Military Association. *The Battle of Plattsburgh*. Plattsburg: Plattsburgh Republican, 1843.

Clute, Penelope D. *Clinton County Courts*. The Historical Society of the New York Courts, 2014.

Coggins, Jack. *Ships and Seamen of the American Revolution*. Harrisburg: Stackpole Books, 1969.

Deeben, John P. "Stealth Warfare Along the Monongahela: Rangers, Scouts, and Spies in Western Pennsylvania Militia Units, 1791–1795." *Western Pennsylvania Genealogical Society*, Vol. 36, No. 3–4, 2010.

Dobbins, Capt. William W. *History of the Battle of Lake Erie and Reminiscences of the Flagship Lawrence*. Erie: Ashby & Vincent, 1876.

Drake, Samuel Adams. *Old Landmarks and Historic Personages of Boston*. Boston: James R. Osgood & Co., 1873.

Draughon, Ralph, Jr. *Down by the River: A History of the Baton Rouge Riverfront*. New Orleans: U.S. Army Corps of Engineers, 1998.

Emerson, Edgar C., ed. *A Descriptive Work on Jefferson County, New York*. Boston: The Boston History Co., 1898.

Everest, Allan S. *The War of 1812 in the Champlain Valley*. Syracuse: Syracuse University Press, 1981.

Graves, Donald E. "Atrocities at Hampton in 1813." *War of 1812 Magazine*, June 2009.

Greene, Jerome. "The New Orleans Campaign of 1813–1815 in Relation to the Chalmette Battlefield." http://www.nps.gov/history/history/online_books/jela/lost_riverfront/Part_1.pdf.

Herringshaw, Thomas W., ed. *Herringshaw's Encyclopedia of American Biography of the Nineteenth Century*. Chicago: American Publishers' Association, 1905.

Jacobs, Moira Ann. *Profiles of Patriots: A Biographical Reference of American Revolutionary War Patriots and Their Descendants*. La Vergne: Author House, 2016.

Keeler, Lucy Elliott. *93rd anniversary of the battle of Fort Stephenson: reinterment of remains of Major Geo. Croghan, beneath the monument erected in his honor on Fort Stephenson, Fremont, Ohio. Thursday, August 2, 1906*. Ohio State Archeological and Historical Society, 1907.

Long, Capt. Oscar F., USA. "Quartermaster's Department." *The Army of the United States: Historical Sketches of Staff*. Edited by Theophilus Francis Rodenbough and William Lawrence Haskin. New York: Maynard, Merrill, & Co., 1986.

Lord, Walter. *The Dawn's Early Light*. New York: W.W. Norton, 1972.

Lossing, Benson J. *Pictorial Field-Book of the War of 1812*. New York: Harper & Bros., 1869.

Marine, William M. *The British Invasion of Maryland*. Baltimore: The Society of the War of 1812 in Maryland, 1913.

McNair, Frederick V. *Handbook for Naval Officers*. New York: D. Van Nostrand, 1920.

Miers, Earl Schenk, ed. *The American Story*. New York: Channel Press, 1956.

Mooney, James L., ed. *Dictionary of American Fighting Ships*. Washington, D.C.: Navy Department, Office of the Chief of Naval Operations, Naval History Division, 1959.

Moore, Cyrus. "The Ohio National Guard Before the Militia Act of 1903." Master's thesis, Kent State University, 2015.

Muller, H. Nicholas, III. "Jay's Treaty: The Transformation of Lake Champlain Commerce." *Vermont History*, Vol. 80, No. 1, 2012.

Omohundro, John, and Susan. "The War of 1812 in St. Lawrence County." *The St. Lawrence County Historical Association Quarterly*, Vol. 56, No. 3, 2011.

Paulos, Anastasia, and John E. Kille. "The War of 1812 in South Anne Arundel County." *Anne Arundel County History Notes*, Vol. 45, 1–10.

Quaife, Milo M. *Chicago and the Old Northwest, 1673–1835*. Chicago: University of Chicago Press, 1913.

Reseck, Shirley Ann Duvall. *William Duvall*. Bloomington: AuthorHouse, 2013.

Robertson, William Spence. *Essays in American History: The Beginnings of Spanish-American Diplomacy*. New York: Henry Holt, 1910.

Rowland, Eron O. *Mississippi Territory in the War of 1812*. Jackson: Mississippi Historical Society, 1921.

Sheads, Scott S. "Henry Waller's Farmhouse." *Maryland in the War of 1812*, 2011. https://maryland1812.com/.

Smith, Zachary E. *The Battle of New Orleans*. Louisville: John P. Morton, 1904.

Stevens, William G. *The Story of Our Navy*. New York: Harper & Brothers, 1918.

Syrett, Harold C., ed. *The Papers of Alexander Hamilton*, Vol. X, December 1791–January 1792. New York: Columbia University Press, 1966.

Taylor, Robert L. *The History of the Potomac Bridges in the Washington Area*. District of Columbia, Department of Highways, 1957.

Torres-Reyes, Ricardo. *1779–80 Encampment: A Study of Medical Services; Morristown National Historical Park*. Washington, D.C.: National Park Service, 1971.

Treasury Department. *An Account of the Receipts and Expenditures*. Various editions.

Walker, Anne Kendrick. *Backtracking in Barbour County: A Narrative of the Last Alabama Frontier*. Richmond: The Dietz Press, 1941.

Wheeler, George A. *History of Castine, Penobscot, and Brooksville, Maine*. Bangor: Burr & Robinson, 1875.

Wheeler, Richard A. *History of the Town of Stonington, County of New London, Connecticut*. New London: Day, 1900.

Winter, Nevin O. *A History of Northwest Ohio*. Chicago: Lewis, 1917.

Workmaster, Wallace F. "The Forts of Oswego." *Northeast Historical Archaeology*, Vol. 2, Article 3, 1972.

# Index


Abbott, James 78, 85
Abbott, Joel, Jr. 122
Abell, Joseph 355
*Acasta* 39
Adair, Gen. John 358
Adam, Capt. Nathaniel 74
*Adams* 57, 59
Adams, Jacob 293–4
Adams, Capt. James, Jr. 186
Adams, John 7
Adams, Sec. John Q. 70
Adams, Capt. Nathaniel 74
Adams, Maj. Parmenio 172, 186
Adams, QM William 170
Addison & Tucker, Esqs. 238
Addoms, John 202
Adele (slave) 346
*Adriana* 293
*Ætna* 338
Agnew, George 98
Agnew, Nancy 98
*Aid* 291
Aisquith, Capt. Edward 282
Alabama 320
Alabama, Indian petition to 327
Alabama River 317
Albany, New York 161
*Albert Gallatin* 249
Alburgh, Vt. 44
Alden, David 60
Alexander, Charles 278
Alexander, Pvt. Henry 121
Alexander, James 308
*Alice Taylor* 1
Allan, Capt. Carter 273
Allen, Col. Clark 195
Allen, Ebenezer 49
Allen, Col. John 88
Allen, Capt. Joseph 111
Ally, Moses 16
Alvey, George 237
Amanda 125
American Colonization Society 358
Amherstburg 68, 71, 89
Amringe, John 21
Anacostia Bridge Co. 278
Anderson, Albert 19
Anderson, Elbert, Jr. 21
Anderson, Col. John 83, 90–1
Anderson, Col. William 315
Anderson, Lt. William, Jr. 144
Angus, Lt. Samuel 12
*Ann* 292
Annable, Henry 144–45
Annapolis, Md. 216
Anson, Lt. (Br.) 302
Antoine (slave) 338
Antwerp, New York 29
Appling, Maj. Daniel 189
Arbuthnot, Margaret 149
Arbuthnot, William 148
Arche (slave) 340
Archer (slave) 351
Archer, Capt. Samuel 163
*Ariel* 13
arms and ammunition 51, 60, 73, 102, 118, 161, 165, 179, 185, 202, 217, 218, 220–21, 250, 255, 268, 271, 296, 298, 304, 316, 318
Arms, Lemuel 23
Armstrong, Allen 56
Armstrong, Capt. Francis 315
Armstrong, Sec. John 142
Armstrong, Thomas 326
Arnest, Caleb 287
Arnold, Gen. Benedict 63
Arnold, James 9
Ash, George 181
Ashman, Samuel 193
Ashtabula, Ohio 206–7
Ashton, Col. Henry 230, 237, 240–1
*Asp* 223–24, 248
Aston, Capt. Samuel 128
*Atalante* 39
Atchinston, Col. John 155
Audrain, James 81
Audrain, Peter 83
Auglaise River 128
Avart, François Robert 344
Avart, Madame L. 344
Avart, Robert 343
Averill, Ebenezer 171
Avery, Griswold 52
Avery, John 51

Babcock, Thomas 46
Baden, Lt. James 230, 232, 272
Baie Missisquoi 14
Bailey, Dixon 326
Bailey, James 326
Baily, William 196
Baily & Delord 196
Baird, Jonathan 167
Baird, William 168, 171
Baker, Timothy 293
Baker, William 17, 184
Baker, Dr. William 11, 17, 277
Ball, Mary 249
Ball, Mottrom 255
Baltimore: defense 214, 290; ropewalks 289; supplies from 231; vessels sunk 293
Baltimore "City" Brigade 282
Baltimore Independent Artillerists 236
Baltimore Independent Blues 236
Baltimore United Volunteers 236
Bangor, Me. 58, 159
*Bangor Packet* 58
Banister, Osmond 143
Bank of Niagara 178
Banks, Hon. Linn 274
Bannister, Col. Asahel 31–4
Barataria Bay, La. 332
Barbee 129
Barbee, Col. Joshua 129
Barber, QM Eliel 173
Barbour, Capt. John 274
Barbour, Col. Philip 311
Barclay, Comm. Robert 135
Bare, Pvt. George 116
Barker, Maj. James 210
Barlow, Aaron 323
Barnes, Daniel 159
Barnes, Richard 302
Barney, Comm. Joshua 214, 225, 227, 233, 242 –3; died 243; 257, 262–7, 283, 289, 296
Barney, Capt. Martin 195
Barney, William 214, 228, 283
Barrie, Comm. Robert (Br.) 234
Barroll, James 281
Barry, Sailing Master Edward 270
Barry, James 278
Barry, Robert 294

Barrymore, Maj.
Bartlett, QM John 159
Bartlett, Jonathan 57
Barton, QM Maj. Benjamin 157
Barton, Capt. Joseph 137
Batavia, New York 161, 191
Baton Rouge, La. 331
Baxter, John 57
Bay, Col. Robert 116
Bayard, William 19
Bayley, William 43
Bayou Bienvenue 358
Bayou Chapitoulas 355
Bayou Dupré 358
Bayou St. John, La. 340
Beach, John 155
Beach, QM Luman 122
Beacham, Capt. Thomas 248, 250; heirs, George, James, Nathaniel, and Thomas 250
Beal, Joseph 23
Beall, Gen. Reasin 117
Beanes, Dr. William 265
Bear, George 116
Bear Creek, Md. 285
Beard, Betty 258
Beard, David 73
Beard, Harriet 175
Beard, James 175
Beard, Pvt. Joseph 121
Beard, Parthenia 73
Beard, Stephen 258
Beasley, Maj. Daniel 317, 323
Beaudaquin, Dr. P. 357
Beaugrand, Jean 91–2
Beaumont, Dr. William 151
Beauport, Can. 89
Beaverdams, Can. 132–4, 169
Beckwith, Sir Thomas 256
Bedel, Johnson 174
Beekmantown, New York 196
Belden, Ebenezer 165
Belden, William 166
Bell, Nicholas 305
Bell, 1st Sgt. Richard 283
Bell, Lt. Thomas 251
Bell Plains, Va. 273
Bellamy, Aaron 45–6
Bellamy, Maj. Justus 45
Belle Plains, Md. 273
Bellfontaine, Ohio 125
Bellinger, Col. Christopher 11
Benedict, Jane 26
Benedict, Gen. Thomas 24, 26, 29
Benedict, Md. 227; first landing 230; second landing 257, 269
Benilliant, Stephen 295
Bennet, Maj. 149
Benson, Joseph 293–4
Benson, Pvt. Robert 283
Bentalou, QM Col. Paul 290
Benyon, Lt. Benjamin 279
Bermuda 10
*Betsey* (brig) 293
*Betsey* (sch) 265
Beyea, Capt. John 55
Biays, Col. James 214, 283–84
Bidwell, Benjamin 174
Bienvenue, Antoine 344
Big Darby Creek, Ohio 130
Big Spring, Ohio 125
Big Warrior (Indian) 318
Biggs, Jane 110
Bill (slave) 259
Billingsley, Thomas 227
Bingham, Eleazer 137
Biscoe, Maj. George 230, 232, 265, 303
Bissel, Col. Daniel 38
Bixley, Luther 293
Black Point, Va. 295
Black Rock, New York 13, 133, 151, 157–8, 161, 168; 174, 176; claimants 178–9
Black Swamp, Ohio 121, 125
Black Warrior River 318
Blackwell, Col. Hiram 248
Bladensburg, Md. 262; battle 266, 268
Blake, Pvt. Meshach 151
Blanchard River 124–25
*Blanche* 293
Bleecker, QM John 200
Bling (slave) 357
Bliss, QM John 18
blockade 10, 40
Bloomfield, Gen. Joseph 211
Blue Plains, Md. 298
Board of War 8
Bob (slave) 351
Boerstler, Col. Charles 133
Bogardus, Col. Robert 42–3
Bogue Chilito, La. 339
Boilevin, Nicholas 348
Boilia, Cpl. William 272
Bon Secour Creek, Ala. 319
Bond, Pvt. Thomas 236
Boomer, Collins 136
Boone, Daniel & Rebecca 308
Boonslick, Mo. 308
Bordeau, Joseph 89
*Bostock* 141
Boteler, Edward 76
Bourgea, Jacques 77
Bourgoud, Antoine 89
Bouten, Samuel 40, 42–3
Boutte, Baptiste 357
Bowen, William 28
Bowers, James 279
Bowlers, Va. 301
Bowyer 319, 321
Boyce, Adj. Richard 116
Boyd, Gen. John 133, 141
Brackenridge, Capt. Robert 311
Bradbury, Capt. Francis 46
Brady, Robert 39
Bramble, Capt. John 216
Branard, Reuben 56
Brann, Sgt. Thomas 248
Brannan, William 285
Brayman, Daniel 163
Breck, Samuel 330
Brent, Maj. Robert 278
Brent, William, Esq. 239
Brevoort, Henry 19
Brewer, Lt. Nicholas 283
Brier, Andrew 124–5
Briggs, John 206
Briggs, Mannah 206
Bright, George 323
Brittain, Capt. Philip 48
Broad Creek, Md. 298
Brock, Gen. Isaac 12, 63, 68
Brockenborough, Dr. Austin 299
Brockville, Can. 24
Bronson, Alvin 186
Bronson, John 180
Brooke, Robert 238
Brooklyn Navy Yard 189
Brooksville, Me. 58
Broome, John 226, 228
Brown, Adam 209
Brown, Aquilla 231, 234
Brown, Sailing Master Eli 333
Brown, Gen. Jacob 11, 22, 25–28, 140–1, 143, 145, 156, 205, 207
Brown, Jesse 34–5
Brown, Morgan 319
Brown, Noah 13, 209
Brown, Overton 96
Brown, QM Richard 251
Brown, QM Maj. Samuel 23, 190
Brown, William 75
Brown, Dr. William 75
Browne, Capt. John 230
Browning, Meshach 115
Brownson, Ebenezer 143–4
Brownstown, Mich. 68
Brundige, James 293
Brunson, John 162
Brush, Adelaide 85
Brush, Capt. Elijah 69, 79, 84
Brush, Capt. Henry 90
Bryant, Philip 38
Buchanan, James 293
Buckner, John 307
Bucksport, Me. 58
Buffalo, New York 13, 134, 151, 157–8; claimants for homes as barracks or storehouses 160, 162, 171–4, 205
Buffalo Creek 157–8, 170, 207
Bulkeley, John 28
Bull, Benjamin 143
Bullock, Capt. Richard 64
Bully (horse) 156
Bunting, Edmund 158
Burdett, Capt. George 221
Burget, Lt. John 129
Burgon, George 179
Burke, John 253
Burlington, Vt. 13, 46–7, 142
Burlington Heights 80

Burn, Col. James 197
Burnett, Gen. William 30–1, 33
Burnside, Catherine 218
Burnside, Thomas, Sr. 218
Burr, Timothy 20
Burroughs, Pvt. Basil 237
Burroughs, Sgt. George 237
Burroughs, Pvt. Hanson 236–7
Burroughs, Pvt. John 236
Burroughs, Pvt. Joseph 174
Burroughs, Pvt. Philip 237
Burroughs, Pvt. William 237
Busseron Creek, Ind. 110
Butler, Col. John 81
Butler, Joseph 173
Butler, Paul 117
Butler, Samuel 172
Butler, Tristram 216
Buts, Jna. 23
Button, Alfred 148
Button, Elisha 146
Byers, Capt. David 75
Byers, John 185
Byington, Joel 195
Byxbe, Moses 117

Caldwell, Capt. Richard 151
Caldwell, Col. Samuel 311
*Caledonia* 161
Calef, Acsah 289
Calef, John 289
Calhoun, Sec. John 47, 290
Calvert County Levy Court 242
Camalier, Vincent 240
Cambria, New York 155
*Camden* 58
Cameron, Capt. Alexander 134, 150
Camp, Elisha 17, 23
Camp, QM John 136–37, 149, 156, 159, 163, 165, 171, 173, 176–7, 205
Camp Jackson 354, 357
Campau, Dennis 161
Campbell, Duncan 19
Campbell, Capt. James 217
Campbell, Col. John 123
Campeau, Jean 75
Canada, Nathaniel 52
Canadian Cavalry Regiment, New York Militia 180
Canandaigua, New York 157, 177
Canfield, John 24
Cape Henry, Va. 213, 257
Cape St. Vincent, New York 20
Carberry, Col. Henry 238
*Carolina* 333, 349
*Caroline* 368
Carpenter, Ira 116
Carroll, Daniel 278
Carroll, Gen. William 316, 349, 357
*Carron* 333
Carrying River, Ohio 158
Carver, Dr. Nathan 194
Case, Loudon 47
Cass, Col. Lewis 68, 79, 83–4, 101, 117
Castine, Me. 54, 57–8
*Catherine* 11
*Catherine Eliza* 40
*Cato* 58
Cattlett, Charles 234–5
Caulksfield, battle 281
Causin, Capt. Gerard 239
Causten, James 294
Cauthorne, James 302
Cavendish, Capt. Robert 333
Cawisa farm 81
Cawood, Capt. Wilson 237
Caze, James 57
Cazeland, Pierre 346
Cecil Iron Foundry 216
Cedar Point, Md. 225
Chalmers, John, Jr. 274, 276
Chalmet, Ignace (alias) 343
Chamberlain, Edward 216
Chamberlain, George 216
Chamberlain, Maj. Reuben 321
Chambers, QM Benjamin 138
Champlain, New York 191
*Chance* 368
Chandler, Gen. John 151, 153
Chapin, Col. Cyrenius 133, 140, 159, 165, 170, 176, 191
Chapin, George 34
Chapin, Luther 71
Chapman, Christian 289
Chappelier, Maj. John (Br.) 237
Chaptico, Md. 298
Charlotte, New York 137
Chase, Moses 143
Chase, Thomas 293
Chase, Thorndike 290
Chateaugay, New York 36
Chauncey, Comm. Isaac 11, 12, 19, 24, 33, 44, 186, 189
Chazy, New York 44, 193
Cherokee 317
*Chesapeake* (ship) 293
*Chesapeake* (navy ship) 9
Chesapeake Bay 211, 213
Chicago 102–3
Chickasaw 331
Chief Red Eagle 317
*The Child of May* 137
Chillicothe, Il. 82
Chilton, Blackwell 368
Chippewa 75
Chittenden, James 66
Choctaw 318
Church, Col. 29
Church, Daniel 25
Church, Harvey 29
Churchill, Col. Worthy 167, 172
Cicot, François 77
Cicot, Jean 77
Claggett, Eli 293–4
Claggett, Levi 293
Claiborne, Gen. Ferdinand 322
Clap, John 293
Clare, Col. William 228, 234
Clarence, New York 190
Clark 104–5
Clark, Andrew 72
Clark, Daniel 354
Clark, Ens. Elisha 144
Clark, Capt. George W. 136
Clark, John 326
Clark, Pvt. Jonathan, Jr. 61
Clark, Joseph 24
Clark, Simpson 293
Clark, Lt.-Col. Thomas 181
Clark, Thomas 44–5
Clarke, Col. Isaac 14, 46
Clarke, Capt. Peter 155
Claughton, John 251
Claughton, Maj. Pemberton 223
Cleveland, Ohio 12, 205
Clinton County New York Court House 202
Clough, Dr. Nathan 120
Coale, Samuel 221
Coale, William 217
Coan, William 150
Coan River 255
Cobreth, Hezekiah 231
Cochran, Robert 200
Cochrane, Adm. Sir Alexander 213, 281, 333
Cockburn, Adm. Sir George 40, 213, 216, 225, 244, 246, 256–7, 266, 270
Cocke, Buller 301
Cocke, Gen. John 316
Cocke, Col. William 317
Coffee, Gen. John 354
Coffman, Isaac 110
Cogswell, William 15
Cole, Levi 277
Cole, William 218
Coles, Edward 104
Coles, John 41
Colgate's Creek, Md. 285
Collier, Capt. Charles 305
Collings, William 110
Collings, Zebulon 110
Collins, Capt. Joel 64
Collins, Gen. Oliver 23
Collins, Capt. Stephen 183
Collins, Thomas, Jr. 302
Collinson, John 297
Colt, Col. Samuel 31
*Columbia* 142
*Columbia* (sch) 293
Colvin, Pvt. John 329
Committee of Claims 3
Committee of Finance 15
Committee on Military Affairs 3
Comparet, Jean 83, 103–4
Compton, William 297
Comstock, Col. Asa 52
Concord Point 217
Confederacy, Creek Indian 320

Congoquetta Creek, New York 159
*Congress* 62
Conjockety Creek, New York 176
Connecticut 50
Connecticut River 50
Connell, Lt. (Br.) 160
Conner, James 80
Connyngham, John 293
Constable, New York 143
*Constellation* 213
*Constitution* 222
*Contest* 223
Conway, James 322
Conway, John 221
Cook, Isaac 206
Cook, John 322
Cook, Nicholas 323
Cooke, Bates 152, 156
Cooke, Laura 151
Cooke, Lemuel 150
Cooper, David 75, 79
Coote, Capt. Richard 51
Cordery, James 290
Core, Adj. John 115–16
Corely, Thomas 215
Cornell, Alexander 318
Cornell, James 318
Corning, Lt. Malachi 48
Cornwell, William 40
Corps of Artificers 197
Corps of Artillery 141
Cortelyon, Peter 43
Cotgreave, Col. William 129
Cotton, Adj. Rowland 160
Court of Claims 41–2, 44, 57, 76, 369
Courtney, Capt. Thomas 218, 220
Couture, Catherine 91–3
Couture, Jean 91–3
Couture, Medare 93
Covert, Morris 40
Covington 143
Covington, Gen. Leonard 142
Cowles, Leonard 116
Cox, Capt. James 252
Craig, John 294
Craig, Capt. Thomas 104
Cralle, Samuel 248
Cramer, Pvt. John 80
Crane, Elizabeth 242
Crane, George 242
Craney Island, Va. 213
Crawford, Sec. William 104, 325
Crease, Lt. Henry (Br.) 279
Creasley, Dr. Eliakim 15
Creek 317, 325
Crittenden, Capt. Jarius 174
*Croghan* 207
Croghan, Col. George 64, 77, 81, 85, 100
Cromwell, Josep 294
Crook, Lt. Robert 80
Crooks, James 14
Crooks, William 14
Crosby, Ebenezer 13
Crosby, John 57–9
Crown Point, New York 46
Crutchfield, Maj. Stapleton 223
Cruzat, Antonio 345
Crylser, John 138–39, 142
Cullumber, Pvt. Joshua 227
Cumberland Head, New York 196
Cumberland River 316
Cunningham, Joseph 127
Currin, Timothy 211
Curtis, Lt. Daniel 113
Cushing, Gen. Thomas 51–2
Cutting, Col. Jonas 183
*Cuyahoga Packet* 68, 71

Dadd, Billy 53
Dailey, John 147
Daingerfield, Henry 320
Damerson, John 251
Dameson, Pvt. William, Jr. 248
Dana, Josiah 57
Danbury, Ohio 71
Daniel, John 313
Darby Creek, Ohio 130
Dare, Dr. John 230
Darke County, Ohio 126
Darling, Dennison 320
Darling, Capt. Thomas 60
Darragh, Alexander 30
D'Auterive, Marigny 357
Davidson, John 115
Davis, Hannah 249
Davis, Jonathan 140
Davis, Nancy 141
Davis, Rodham 247
Davis, Thomas 140–1
Dawson, James 111
Dayton, Ohio 65, 68, 115, 125, 312
Dean, Aaron 126
Dearborn 102, 112
Dearborn, Gen. Henry 11, 16, 28, 45, 63, 132, 147
Debois, Hannah 42–3
de Calmenero, Don Ramon 357
de Castañedo, Don Juan 345
Decatur, Comm. Stephen 40
de Chalmette, Ignace de Lino 344
de Chalmette, Victoire 345
defiance 87, 130, 217
Defiance, Ohio 129
De Hart, Capt. Robeson 338
de la Présentation 24
De la Ronde, Col. Pierre 351, 354
de Lassize, John 348
de Laussat, Gov. Pierre Clément 331
Delaware 75
Delaware, Ohio 116
Delaware River 211
de Lenares Gonzales, Don Ramon 357
Delino, Ignace 345
Delord, Henry 196
Deltz, Peter 115
de Macarty, Edmond 355
Demarest, Col. Samuel 201
Demari, Jacques 75
Denman, QM David 156
Denny, Thomas 297
Denton, Orderly Sgt. James 229, 246
Dequindre, Antoine 77, 81
des Compes Labadie, Elizabeth 75
des Compes Labadie, Theresa 75
desertions 58, 123, 223
Deslonde, Rosalie 350
Desnoyes, Peter 80
Despeaux, John 295
Destrehan, Jean 355
Destrehan, Marie 355
Detroit 10, 63, 67, 69, 112
Detroit, Mich. 16, 63; settlement of claims 85; surrender terms 69
Detroit River 63, 66
de Vereges, L.P. 345
de Villiers, Jumonville 344, 348, 355
Dickerson, Sec. Mahlon 15, 337
Dickinson, Lt. Gilbert 173
Dickson, Col. Thomas 134, 160
Dill, Andrew 123
Disbrow, Henry 65–6
Dixon, Joseph 62
Dixon's Point, Me. 62
Dobbin, Col. Hugh 30–1
Dobbins, Daniel 11, 209
Dodge, Gen. Richard 19, 20
*Dolphin* 46, 216
Dolway, William 20
Donahoo, John 218
Donnell, John 293
Dorchester County, Md. 264–5
Doriocourt, Capt. Anthony 357
Dorsey, Caleb 222
Dorsey, Richard 236
Doughty, William 262
Douglass, Charles 13
Douglass, Dennison 139
Douglass, James 245
Dow, Capt. Thomas 53
Downing, Lt. George 254
Downing, Capt. Samuel 295
Downing, Col. Thomas 223, 242, 248, 251, 254
Downman, Olivia 304
Dox, Capt. Myndert 144
Doxater, Peter 190
Doxey, Joseph 47
Doxsey, Samuel 41
Dozet, Joseph 89
Dozier, Capt. Allen 225
*Dragon* 225

Drinkwater, Pvt. West 54, 60
Drummond, Lt.-Gen. Sir George 134, 182
Drury, Matilda 298
Duane, New York 45
Ducharme, Capt. Dominique 134
Ducktrap, Me. 61–2
Dudley, John 368
Dudley, Lt. Peter 96
Dudley, QM Thomas 313
Duffield, Margaretta 42–3
Dugan, Hammond 236
Dumpley, Charles 148
Duncan, Pvt. Ingraham 61
Duncan, James 209
Duncan, Pvt. John, Jr. 60–1
Duncan, Jonas 209
Duncan, Pvt. Kingsbury 60–1
Duncan, Pvt. Samuel 60–1
Duncan, William 210
Dupré, Widow 358
Durand, M.F. 200
Durant, Lauchlan 326
Durham boats 185
Durkee, Marshall 75
Durocher, Laurent 91
Dutton, Joseph 211
Duvergé, Bartholme 354

Eadus, William 30
*Eagle* 39, 46, 158
Eakin, Midshipman Samuel 186
Earl, Comm. Hugh 14
*Earl of Moira* 14
Earles, James 326
Early, Gov. Peter 330
Eastern Branch Bridge Co. 277
Eastport, Me. 54, 57
Eaton, John 25
Eaton, Midshipman 185
Eaton, Gen. William 311
Eckford, Henry 13
Ecorse, Mich. 138
Eddyville, Ky. 340
Edgar, John 127
Edgecomb, Capt. Noah 55
Edmonds, Thomas 234
Edmondson, Samuel 323
Edwards, James 340
Edwards, Mary 29
Edwards, Rowland 74
Egerton, Bela 196
Egerton, Charles 237
Eighteen Mile Creek, New York 137, 181
8th Regiment Maryland Militia Cavalry 238
85th Rifle Brigade 333
Eldred, Julius 84
11th Regiment of Infantry 37, 46, 123, 198
11th St. Bridge, Washington, D.C.
Elhert, Charles 326
Eliot 62
Eliot, Robert 62
Eliot, Me. 62
*Eliza* 293
*Eliza* (brig) 293
Elizabeth City, Va. 222; church wardens 222
Elk River, Md. 216
Elkton, Md. 216, 289
Elliot, Capt. William 88
Elliott, Comm. Jesse 12, 161
Ellis, Capt. Daniel 137
Ellisburg, New York 189
Ellsworth, Israel 15
Elwell, Dr. James 277
Emanthlan, Tallmassee 327
Emery, Joseph 197
*Enterprise* 293
Ephraim (slave) 280
Episcopal Church 222
Erie 77, 142, 205
Erie, Penn. 12, 159, 209
Erwin, Capt. David 38, 147
Essenbeck, William 272
*Essex* 46
Eustis, Sec. William 68, 113
Evans, Col. Dudley 215
Evans, Robert 339
Evans, Roxanna 150
Evat, Edward 290
Ewell, Dr. Thomas 278
"Exempts" 31
*Experiment* 207, 224

*Fabius* 291, 294
Fairlee Creek, Md. 278
*Fantome* 216
Farnham, Va. 304
Farr, Bennet 34
Farrin, Richard (alias) 324
Farwell, Capt. John 156
*Father and Son* 294
Fellows, Benjamin 37
Fellows, John 34
Fells Point, Md. 263, 289
Fells Point Light Dragoons 289
Fells Point Riflemen 283
Fenwick, Col. Althanasius 239
Fenwick, Caroline 238
Fenwick, Pvt. Ignatius 239
Fenwick, Michael 238
Ferris, Capt. Archibald 46–7
Fibb, Capt. 305
Fidel (slave) 357
Field, Daniel 150
Fielding, Daniel 124
15th Regiment Maryland Militia 285
15th Regiment of Infantry 44, 137, 151
5th Brigade Maryland Militia 237
5th Brigade New York Militia 27
5th Maryland Cavalry District 214, 283
5th Regiment Indiana Militia 110
5th Regiment of Infantry 69, 194
5th Regiment Virginia Militia 330
50th Regiment Maryland Militia 115
55th Regiment New York Militia 136, 190, 195
Fillmore, Eunice and children 194
Fillmore, Capt. Septa 194
*Finch* 46
Findlay 124–5
Findlay, Gen. James 64, 68–9, 124
Findlay, Ohio 125
Finney, Joseph 47
Fire Island, New York 40
1st Baltimore Hussars 236, 283
1st Battalion Louisiana Militia 351
1st Division Louisiana Militia 347
1st Independent Company of Foreigners 223
1st Maryland Rifle Battalion 282
1st Regiment Essex Militia 71, 88
1st Regiment Kentucky Militia 88
1st Regiment Kentucky Mounted Volunteers 311
1st Regiment Light Dragoons 13
1st Regiment Michigan Militia 66, 69, 75
1st Regiment of Infantry 63, 112–13, 116
1st Regiment of Royal Scots 134
1st Regiment Ohio Militia 120
1st U.S. Artillery 128, 167, 205
Fitzgibbon, Lt. James 132–4
Fitzhugh, Elizabeth 34
Five Medals (Indian) 112
Fleming, Col. George 186
Fleming, John 312
Fleming, Lt. Robert 149
Fleming Station, Ky. 312
Flemingsburg, Ky. 312
Fletcher, Josiah 326
Flood, William 339
Flournoy, Gen. Thomas 329, 357
Floyd, Capt. William 237, 239
*Fly* 54
Foley, James 76
Forbes, Gordon 252, 254
Forbes, Libeus 45
Forbes, Robert 254
Forbes, William 251
Ford, Nathan 24, 25
Ford, Peter 122
Ford, William 237
Foreman, Charles 220
Forman, Gen. Thomas 276, 289
Forster, Elisha 163
Forster, Capt. Thomas 13

Forsyth, Maj. Benjamin 24, 26, 29
Forsyth, Thomas 102–03
Forsythe, Dr. William 64
Fort Covington, New York 142
Fort Erie, Can. 161
Fort Jennings, Ohio 129
Fort Pontchartrain du Détroit 8
Fort Wayne, Ind. 78, 111, 114
Fortier, Michel 351
40th Brigade New York Militia 194
40th Regiment of Infantry 54, 58
41st Regiment New York Militia 42
41st Regiment of Foot 64, 69, 160
41st Regiment Virginia Militia 304
42nd Regiment Maryland Militia 217, 220
42nd Regiment New York Militia 31
42nd Regiment of Infantry 43
45th Regiment Maryland Militia 230, 237
45th Regiment of Foot 237
45th Regiment of Infantry 196
48th Regiment Maryland Militia 228
49th Regiment Maryland Militia 216
49th Regiment of Foot 133, 160, 181
Forward, Oliver 176
Fosbenner, Daniel 285
Foster, Sir Augustus 10
Foster, Elisha 170
Foster, Jabez 19
Foster, Ralph 336
Foster, Ens. William 274
Foucher, Pierre 344, 349, 354
Four-Corners, New York 37
14th Regiment Mississippi Militia 320
14th Regiment of Infantry 24, 133
4th Brigade New York Militia 19
4th Division Ohio Militia 117
4th Maryland Cavalry District 239
Fourth Military District 211
4th Regiment Louisiana Militia 357
4th Regiment of Infantry 68, 74–5, 102, 197
4th Rifle Brigade 333
4th Rifle Regiment 25
Fowler, Jacob & Co. 159
Fox 308–9
Fox, Augustus 166
Fox, Daniel 169
Fox, Edward 316
Fox, George 169
Francis, Josiah 318
Frankfort, Ky. 313
Frankfort, Me. 58
Franklin, Capt. Jacob 260–1
Franklin, Stephen 167
Franklin, William 245
Franklin County, New York 38
Franklinton, Ohio 123
Fraser, Daniel 237
Fraser, Capt. QM Donald 205
Frasier, Maj. 162
frauds 147
Frazier, Charles 233
Frazier, Mary 231, 233
Frazier, Lt. Solomon 214, 258, 262
Fredericksburg, Va. 273
Fremont, Ohio 87, 117
French, David 52
French, Capt. John 51, 53
French Mills, New York 16, 26, 139, 142, 147; frauds at 147
Frenchman's Creek 177
Frenchtown, Md. 216
Frenchtown, Mich. 68, 86
Friar's Bay 55
*Friendship* 305
Frisby, Richard 279
Frost, John 216
Frye, Capt. Jonathan 60
Fulks, Lt. John 248
Fuller, Asa 179
Fuller, Capt. Horace 228
Fuller, Samuel 25
*Fulton* 337
Fulton, Robert 337
Fuquay, Joseph, Jr. 311
Furman, William 244–5

Gaines, Gen. Edmund 190, 207, 211, 323
Gallagher, William 142
Galloway, Maj. James 65
Galt, Capt. Peter 283
Gard, Lt. Ephraim 65
Gardiner, Eleanor 231
Gardiner, Henry 231
Gardner, QM Benjamin 130
Gardner, Robert 18
Garrard, Maj. James 93
Garrett, Capt. William 216
Garrow, Samuel 319
Garrow & Wilson 319
Gaynor, John 19
Gena, Capt. 270
*General Hunter* 71
*General Jackson* 319
*General Pike* 13
Genesee River 137, 161
Gentry, Reuben 308
Geohegan, Sailing Master John 227
*George* 294
George, Me. 58
George, New York 20–1, 29, 89, 132–3, 135–6, 141–3, 180
Georgetown, Ky. 68
Georgetown, Md. 263
Georgia 329
Gerrish Island, Me. 62
Gibson, Horatio 249
Gibson, John 249
Giffin, David 139
Gilbert, Capt. Jacob 116, 179
Gilbert, Marinus 24, 143, 184
Gilbert, Thomas 143
Gilder, Capt. Reuben 24
Giles, Jacob, Jr. 221
Gill, Whitford 18
Gillet, Lucas 29
Gilmore, John 319
Girod, Mayor Nicholas 357
Glasscock, Capt. George 244, 246
Glegg, Capt. John 69
Glengarry Light Infantry 64
Glover, Pvt. Elijah 120
Goddard, QM Maj. Hezekiah 51
Goddard, James 265
Godfroy, Maj. Gabriel 66, 77, 90, 92
Goff, Nathan 27, 148
Goldsborough, Howes 217
Gonzales, Don Ramon de Calmenero 357
Gonzales & Colmanero 357
Goodwin, Lt. Lyde 283
Gordon, Alexander 49
Gordon, Capt. James 273
Gordon, Lt.-Col. John 134
Gordon, Samuel 27, 148
Gordon, William 300
Gore, George 146
Gorsuch, Ens. John 283
Gorton, Sgt. Samuel 52
Gover, Pvt. Philip 236
Gover, Samuel 297
Grace, Samuel 293
Graham, Anthony 193
Grand Isle 49
Granger, Mr. 167
Grant, Capt. (Br.) 144
Grant, Vincent 168
Grant, William 166
Grape Isle, MI 81
Grason, Gov. William 256
Gratiot, Col. Charles 64, 82, 123
Gravelly Point, Lake Ontario 20–2
Graves, Lt. Joseph 194
Graves, William 216
Grawoss, Peter 209
Gray, Capt. Benjamin 229
Gray, Betty 258
Gray, George 209
Gray, James 258
Gray, Dr. John 258
Gray, Matthew 28
Gray, Samuel 28

Gray's Ferry, Penn. 209
Great Black Swamp 125
Green 41
Green, Capt. Jonas 283
Green, Col. Josias 286, 364
Greenbush, New York 11
Greene 41–2
Greene, Gen. Nathanael 126
Greene-Ville 126
Greenleaf Point hospital 277
Greenleaf's Point, Md. 272
Greenville, Ohio 126
Greenville Creek, Ohio 126
Greenwell, Lt. Samuel 239
Gresham, Thomas 300
Grieve, Col. Walter 149
Griffin, David 140
Griffin, Jonathan 204
Griffin, Robert 223
Griffing, C. 52
Griffing, David 39
Griffith, Adm. Edward 58
Grosh, John 293
Groton, Conn. 51
*Growler* 46
Grubb, Col. Curtis 210
Guest, John 220
Guest, Rebecca 220
*Gunboat No. 22* 333
*Gunboat No. 156* 332

Haile, John 305
Haines, Capt. Asa 174
Hale, David 326
Hales, James 251
Haliburton, Maj. William 103
Halifax, Nova Scotia 57
Hall, Gen. Amos 133, 160, 162, 165, 170, 173
Hall, Capt. Henry 196
Hall, Capt. John 65, 261
Hall, Jonathan 25
Hall, Richard 256
Hall, Roland 29
Hall, Washington 294
Halsey, Cornelius 200
Halsey, Frederick 199
Hambleton, Purser Samuel 209
Hamilton, Alexander 3
Hamilton, Maj. Archibald 266
Hamilton, Dr. Charles 214, 233–4, 243
Hamilton, Paul 12
Hamilton, Dr. Thomas 243–4
Hammond, John 180
Hammond, Capt. Rezin 261
Hampden, Me. 58–9
Hampstead Hill, Md.
Hampton, Gen. Wade 38, 47, 196
Hampton Roads, Va. 213
*Hancock* 58
Handford, Frederick 138
Hanger, Peter 8
Hanks, Lt. Porter 12, 63
Hanna, Capt. John 289
Hannibal, New York 186
Hansborough, A.H. 273
Hansborough, John 273
Harding, John 331
Hardy, Comm. Sir Thomas 50
Harmon, Anan 206
Harpers Ferry 258, 269
*Harriet* (schooner) 369
*Harriet* (sloop) 368
Harris, Col. John 155
Harris, John (Br.) 34
Harris, Sluman 170
Harris, Stephen 215
Harrison 111
Harrison, Gen. Benjamin 76
Harrison, Lt. Carlisle 83–4, 84
Harrison, Lt. Robert 144
Harrison, Gen. William 9, 63, 65, 75, 81, 87, 112, 114, 117, 123
Hart, Capt. 93
Hart, Eli 164
Hartcutt, Col. Joseph 15
Hauge, Spoko (Indian) 318
Havre de Grace, Md. 217
Haw, Joseph 115
Hawkins, Col. Benjamin 325
Hawley, David 168, 174
Hay, Charles 209
Hay, John 209
Hayden, Aaron 57
Hazen, Col. Moses 197
Heacock, Reuben 166
Heald, Daniel 29
Heald, Maj. Nathaniel 102, 112
Heard, Lt. Benedict 235
Hearsey, Solomon 154
Heath, Nathaniel 274
Heathsville, Va. 295
Helms, Michael 166
Henderson, Capt. William 246, 248, 251, 255
Henderson's Harbor, New York 136
Henley, David 316
Henley, Thomas 300
*Henrietta* 189
*Henry* 262
Henry, James 75
Hepbron, Col. Thomas 289
Hepbrontown, Md. 288
Herkimer, Maj. John 26
Herring Bay 296
Herring Creek 296
Hertick, Joseph 307
Hewitt, Benjamin 240
Hickey, Capt. Frederick 39
Hickman, Eliza 97
Hickman, Capt. Pascal 96–7
Hickory Island 63, 65
Higgins, Uriah 47
High Headed Jim (Indian) 318
*Highflyer* 216
Hight, QM Lt. George 141
Hildreath, Curtis 143
Hill, Ishmael 20, 34
Hindman, Col. John 116
His Majesty's Royal Artillery Drivers 133
Hitchcock, Reuben 143
Hoag, Samuel 139
Hodge, George 270
Hodge, Loring 141
Hodge, William 160
Hodson, William 296–7
Hogan, QM Maj. John 143–4, 147, 206
Hogan, Michael 23
Hogg, Samuel & Co. 218
Hoisington, Abishai 45
Hoisington, Orange 45
Hoit, Josiah 60
Holcomb, John, Esq. 32, 34
Holden, Capt. Lorton 167–8
Holden, Thomas 111
Holder, Capt. Caleb 79
Holliday, John 100
Hollinger, Mrs. 322
Hollinger, William 326
Hollingsworth 217
Hollingsworth, Levi 294
Hollingsworth, Samuel 293–4
Hollingsworth, Thomas 293–4
Hollister, Capt. Charles 190
Holmes, Maj. Andrew 64, 99–101
Holway, John 369
Hook, Josiah, Jr. 59
Hooke, Josiah 58, 61
Hooker, Samuel 20–1
Hooper, William 228, 261
Hope, William 223
Hopkins, Jesse 18
Hopkins, Gen. Samuel 110–11, 180
Hopkins, Gen. Timothy 160, 168, 173–4
Horton, Capt. James 284
Hosbrook, Capt. Daniel 125
Hoskins, Abel 203
House, Conrad 168, 174
Housefield, Ezra 21
Housefield, New York 21
Hovey, Ebenezer 136
Howard, Ens. Abraham 144
Howard, Capt. Benjamin 282
Howard, John 52
Howard, Capt. Lewis 63
Howard, Capt. William 156
Howe, Luther 356
Howell, Col. Gilbert 30
Hubbard, Eber 19
Hubbard, Matthew 206
Hubbell, Silas 193
Hudson, Sydney 251
Huggins, Reuben 155
Hughes, QM 127
Hughes, Samuel 217, 221
Hugunin, Peter 184
Hugunin, Capt. Robert 187
Hulings, William 354

Hull, Abraham 75
Hull, Gen. Amos, Esq. 33
Hull, Capt. David 118
Hull, Elias 31, 33–4
Hull, Jabez 163
Hull, Capt. William 160
Hull, Gen. William 12, 63–4, 68–70, 73, 102, 119, 124, 150, 174
Hull's Road 68
Humphreys, Capt. George 269–70
Humphreys, Lt. Reuben 144
Humphreys, Capt. Salusbury 9
Hungerford, Gen. John 244, 247, 251
Hungerford, Orville 19
Hunt, Henry 77, 85
Hunt, Dr. Simon 137
*Hunter* 158
Hunter, Pvt. Cyrus 119
Hunter, Col. Martin 133–4
Hunting Creek, Md. 298
Huntington, Ambrose 144
*Huntress* 305
Hurd, Reuben 155
Hurlbutt, Ralph 51
Huron River 117
Huson, Cornelius 21
Hyde, Elias 28

Île aux Noix 46
Illinois 102
import bans 8
*India Packet* 294
Indiana Territory 9, 63, 110
Indians: indemnity 325; petition to Alabama 326–7; recruitment 9, 156
Ireland, John 231, 243
Iroquois 24, 133
Irvine, U.N. 210
Isaac, Capt. (Indian) 318
Isle La Motte 49
*Islet* 257
Ives, Elisha 185
Izard, Gen. George 163, 193, 196

Jackson 319–20
Jackson, Gen. Andrew 325, 333, 337, 339–40, 350–56
Jackson, George 130
Jackson, John 41
Jackson, Maj. William 283
Janney, Elisha 278
Janney, Joseph 301, 303
Jarrett, Abraham 219, 221
Jarvis, John 215
*Java* 224, 276
Jeans, Elizabeth 215
Jeans, Joseph 215
Jefferson, Thomas 9
Jelly & Prior 336
Jenkins, QM Elisha 186
Jenkinson, Maj. Joseph 65
Jennings 87, 129
Jennings, Olivia 174
Jennings, Col. William 130
Jerome, Jean 91–2
Jerome, Medare 93
Jessup, Lt. Henry 155
Jett, Joseph 295
Jett, Capt. William 295–6
Johnson, Mayor Edward 291
Johnson, George 96
Johnson, Hickman 285
Johnson, Jeremiah 41
Johnson, Maj. John 154
Johnson, John J. 41, 42
Johnson, Nathan 185
Johnson, Col. Richard 77–8, 97–8, 138, 312
Johnson, Rinaldo & Anne 232
Johnson, Robert 308
Johnson, Ens. Seth 144
Johnson, Thomas 232
Johnston, John 99
Johnston, Stephen 112
Johnston, Susan 99
Jones, David 27
Jones, DeGarmo 66–7
Jones, Col. Elisha 18
Jones, Evan 354
Jones, Capt. H.D. (Br.) 346
Jones, James 229
Jones, Jonathan 128, 204
Jones, Nathaniel 183
Jones, Polly 326
Jones, Thomas 283
Jones, Lt. Thomas Ap. C. 332, 334
Jones, Col. Thomas L. 286
Jones, William 259
Jourdan, Barthélemy 348
Jourdan, Pvt. Celestin 351
Jourdan, Francis 351
Jourdan, Lt. Noel 351
Jourdan, Pierre 348

Kaine, Robert 172
Kalkman, Charles 295
Kaywood, Mr. 143
Keane, Maj.-Gen. John (Br.) 351
Keith, Robert (clerk)
Keith, Sgt. Robert 202
Keith, William 100
Kellar, Capt. William 111
Kellogg, Capt. Giles 26
Kellogg, Nathaniel, Jr. 34
Kellogg, Truman 170
Kelsey, Capt. Daniel 173
Kemper, Presley 76
Kendall, Capt. William 120
Kennedy, Lt. Edmund 214
Kennedy, Joshua 322–3
Kent Island 256
Kenton, Simon 96
Kenton, Ohio 87
Kentucky 310
Kentucky Light Dragoons 88
Ker, Dr. David 354
Kerr, Archibald 294
Kerr, Hon. John 358
Kerr, Pvt. Samuel 288
Kerr, Capt. William 133
Ketchum, Pvt. Zebulon 191
Kettletas, Sailing Master Samuel 46
Key, Francis, Esq. 237, 265, 279, 282
Key, Philip 238
Keyes, Perley 24
Keynau, John 263
Kilbourn, David 16
Kilgour, James 238
Kilgour, Capt. William 237
Killpatrick, William 218
Kindall, Peter 156
King, Amanda 169
King, Capt. Benjamin 262
King, Gideon 46
King, John 255
King, Nehemiah 206
Kingsbury, Col. Jacob 68
Kingston, Ont. 18, 132, 186, 191
Kinsale, Va. 224, 242, 251, 253
Kinzie, John 102
Kinzie & Forsyth 71, 102
Kirkpatrick, William 220
Kirks, Randall 296
Kitchen, Samuel 323
Kitchen, William 323
Kittery, Me. 62
*Kitty* 340
Knabb, Jacob 354
Knaggs, James 76
Knaggs, Josette 76
Knaggs, Peter 76
Knaggs, Capt. Whitmore 75
Knight, George 224
Knowles, Henry, Sr. 269
Knox, Gen. Henry 7
Knoxville, Tenn. 315

Labadie, Menard 123
Lacoste, Gen. Pierre 340, 345, 351
Lacroix, Maj. Hubert 75, 94, 98
*Lady of the Lake* 207
*Lady Washington* 20, 46
Laffite, Jean 332
Lafoy, Lambert 78, 85
Lake Borgne, La. 332, 358
Lake Champlain 14, 46
Lake Erie 205
Lake Gibson, Can. 132
Lake Huron 63
Lake Michigan 63
Lake Peoria 104
Lake Pontchartrain, La. 332, 353
Lambert, Pvt. James 354
Lancaster, Pa. 209
Landon, Charles 48
Lane, Wilt 193
Lanes, Capt. 192
Lanfant, Benjamin 92

Langeville, Francisco 349
Languille, Francis 350
Lanham, Capt. William 89
Lapoint, Pvt. Gabriel 119
Lapsley, John 307
Larche, Francis 338
La Ronde, Pierre 333
La Salle, Jacques 89
Latham, Pvt. Alden 52
Laughlin, William 260
Laughton, Maj. Pemberton 248
Lavergue, Hugues 347
Lavigne, Joseph 357
*Lawrence* 13, 209
Lawrence, Eleanor 38–9
Lawrence, John (sailor) 9
Lawrence, Capt. John 217
Lawrence, Robert 15
Lawrence, Dr. William 339
Lawrence, Maj. William 321
Lawrence, Zachariah 54–5
Lay, John, Jr. 165–6
Lay, Stephen 51
Layton, Lt. Charles 249, 302
Lea, Susanna 285
Leach, Elijah 166
Leach, Esther 166
Leamaster, James 110
Leamaster, Nancy 110
Learned, Capt. Benjamin 205
Leavenworth, Capt. 151
Leavenworth, Maj. Henry 153
Le Blanc, Pierre 138
L'Ecuyer, Philip 73–4
Ledgerwood, William 111
Lee, Edward 22
Lee, Isaac 91
Lee, Richard 24, 91
Lee, Silas 55
Leesburg, Va. 271
Lefebre, Joseph 343
Leighton, Samuel 62
Leland, Baldwin 254
Leland, Capt. Sherman 55–6
Lendy, P.S. 339
Lenfant, Benjamin 98
Lenox, James 19
Lenox, Robert 19
Leonard, Capt. Nathaniel 128, 166, 204
*Leopard* 9
Lernoult 67, 71
Le Roy, Herman 19
Levering, Capt. Aaron 236
Lewis, Abram 29
Lewis, Lt. Andrew 54, 58
Lewis, Curtis 320–1
Lewis, David 35
Lewis, Henry 20
Lewis, Reuben 150
Lewis, Thomas (Br.) 34–5
Lewis, William 251
Lewis, Col. William 88, 91, 96
Lewiston, New York 128, 134, 148, 154, 157, 161
Lexington, Ky. 311
Licking County, Ohio 120
Lilly, Lt. Asa 155
Lincolnville, Me. 60–1
Lindley, Rachel 141
Lindsay, Oliver 210
*Linnet* 47
Lionberger, Pvt. Peter 120
Little Prince (Indian) 318
Little River, Ala. 320
Little Salmon River 142
Little Sandy Pond, New York 189
Little Warrior (Indian) 318
Lively, Robert 223
*Liverpool Trader* 58
Livingston, Hon. Edward 338
Lockyer, Capt. Nicholas 333
Lolotte (slave) 346
Lomax, Maj. Mann 245
Long, Edward 116
Long, Col. Kennedy 244
Long Island, New York 40, 51–2
Loomis, Sailing Master Jarius 46
*Lord Nelson* 14
Loring, Samuel 126
Lott, Hendrick 40
Louisiana 331
*Louisiana* 349
Louisiana Light Horse Militia 354
Louisville, Ky. 307, 338
Louisville, New York 139
Lovejoy, Joshua 158
Lovering, Malachi 37
Lowe, James 268
Lowe, Maj. Jonathan 313
Lower Marlborough, Md. 298
Lower Sandusky, Ohio 117, 127
*Lucy* 58
Ludlow, Cornelius 40
Lunsford, John 248
Lyall, Alexander 34
Lynch, Gen. 120
Lynnhaven River 223
Lyon, Pvt. Alexander 236
Lyon, Lucius 138
Lytle, Capt. John 25–27, 28–9

Macarty Plantation 351
Macdonnel, Col. George 24
Macdonnell, Lt.-Col. George 24
Macdonough, Master Commandant Thomas 46
MacGhee, Lynn 326
MacGirt, Zacariah 326
Mack, Stephen 85
Mackall, Benjamin 231, 246
Mackall, James 260
Mackall, Capt. John 228–9
Mackall, Mid. Richard 224, 226
Mackinac 12, 63, 68, 101–2, 112
Mackinac Island 11, 63
Mackinaw City, Mich. 63
Mackintosh, Angus 103
Macomb, Gen. Alexander 191, 193, 199, 200
Macomb, Isabella 75
Macomb, John 162
Macomb, Sarah 81
Macomb, William 81, 92
Mad Dragon (Indian) 318
*Madison* 13
Madison 54
Madison Barracks 18
Madison, Maj. George 89
Madison, Pres. James 12, 68
Madison, Gen. William 273
Maglenen, Pvt. James 284
Magruder, Alexander 298
Magruder's Ferry and Warehouse, Md. 230, 232–5
*Maidstone* 216, 221
Maine, District of 10, 54
Maisonville, Capt. Alexis 88
Malcolm, Col. James (Br.) 234
Malcolm, Sir Pulteney (Br.) 266
Malden 12, 63, 65, 73–4, 86, 89, 94
Malden, Can. 161
Malheureux Island, La. 332
Malin, Pvt. Joseph 269–70
Mallory, Maj. Benajah 136, 179
Malone, New York 142, 144
Manchester, New York 134
Manley/Morley, Dr. 128, 204
Mann, Dr. James 151
Manwaring, Capt. Josiah 53
Marcus Hook, Pa. 211
*Maria Anne* 39
*Marlborough* 216
*Mars* 294
Marsh, Dr. 190
Marshall, Ann 211
Marsteller, QM Maj. Ferdinand 270
*Martin* 55
Martin, Daniel 9
Martin, John 211
Martin, William 46
Marvin, Dudley 34
*Mary* (Br. sloop) 60
*Mary* (privateer) 55
*Mary* (ship) 294
Maryland Sharp Shooters 282
Mason, Col. Jeremiah 52
Mason, Gen. John 277
Massey, Hart 24
Massicot, Capt. William 293
Mather, James 354
Matteson, Capt. Abraham 173
Matthews, Col. George 330
Matthews, Leonard 236
Matthews, William 281
Maumee Bay 88
Maumee River and Rapids 63, 68, 87, 117, 119
Maury, Jabez 57
May, Frederick 278

May, James, Esq. 75–6, 81–2, 92
May, Samuel 166
Mayer, Henry 249
Mayhew, Thaddeus 353, 356
McAlliston, Francis 29
McArthur 87, 122, 124
McArthur, Gen. Duncan 15, 66–8, 80–1, 98, 122
McBoy, Maj. Diego 320
McBride, Lapsely 96
McCalla, John 96
McCarty, Edward 355
McCarty, John 304
McCauly, Dr. John 191
McClain, John 56
McClanahan, Maj. Elijah 89
McClintock, Mid. Henry 223
McCloskey, Capt. James 64, 77, 80, 82, 85, 159
McClure, Gen. George 134–5, 148, 160
McCollum, Dr. Andrew 27
McComas, Pvt. Henry 282
McComb, QM William 73
McComb, William Gen. 18
McCormick, Alexander 271
McCoull, Neil 216
McCrea, John 146
McCutchen, James 110–11
McDonald, Hugh 289
McDonald, Col. John 69
McDonald, Col. William 282
McDonell, John 139
McDonough, Lt. Patrick 140
McDougall, George 92
McDougall, Col. Robert 64
McDuell, Capt. George 224
McFadden & Harris 368
McGawen, Capt. John 84
McGee, Leonard 318
McGillivray, Gen. Alexander 319
McHenry 265, 282, 290
McIlhenney, Alexander 193
McIntire, Rufus 184
McIntosh, Gen. John 319
McIntosh, William 318
McKnight, Calvin 24
McLain, John 56
McLean, Alney 311
McMahon, Col. John 163
McMillan, Arthur 146
McNair, Matthew 142, 184, 186
McNairy, Andrew 312
McNairy, Hon. John 315
McNeil, Joseph 353
McNiel, Charles 46
McNiff, Catherine 79
McPherson, Nancy 72
McWilliams, Capt. George 229
Mead, Gen. David 12, 13
Meads, Frances 268
Meads, James 268
Meads, William 268
Mechanical Volunteers 282
Meech, Judge Ezra 45
Meigs 76, 118, 123–4, 128
Meigs, Gen. Montgomery 65
Meigs, Phineas 53
Meigs, Gov. Return 112, 120, 126
*Melampus* 9
Melwood, Md. 270
Menard, Pierre 118
Menary, John 117
Mendenhall, William 125
*Menelaus* 278, 281
Merrill, Nathaniel 33–6
Merrill, Timothy 75
Metcalf, John 206
Mettez, Sgt. Theophilus 75
Miami 111–12, 114
Miami of Lake Erie 98
Miami of the Lake 72, 99, 118
Miami River 64, 123, 130
Michigan Legionary Corps 68
Michigan Territory 63
Michilimackinac 63, 67, 100
Middlebury, Vt. 47
Middleton, Capt. Arthur 242
Middleton, Sailing Master Joseph 257
Middleton, Capt. William 251–52
Middletown, Conn. 50
Militia 8, 13; New York, 199
Miller, Amos 120
Miller, Col. Charles 121, 130
Miller, Capt. James 262
Miller, Gen. James 68–9, 74–5, 90, 204
Miller, Col. John 68
Miller, Mary 120
Miller, Maj. Noah 60–1
Miller, Oliver 80
Miller, Lt. Samuel 226
Miller, Col. Thomas 194
Millward, Ens. James 289
Milne, Alexander 353
Milnor, Robert 210
Milton, Andrew 322
Mims 320, 322
Mims, David 320
Mims, Harriet 320
Mims, Samuel 317
Mims, Sarah 320
Miniton, John 294
Miskell, George 248
Missisquoi Bay 13
Mississippi River 316
Mississippi Territory 317
Missouri 307
Mitchell, Gen. David 324, 326
Mitchell, Col. George 183, 186
Mitchell, Hector 268
Mitchell, Obed & Sons 294
Mix, Sailing Master Mervine 207
Mobile Bay 318
Mobile Point, Ala. 319
Mobile River 318
Mohawk 133
*Mohawk* 186, 216, 223
Monday's Neck, Va. 223, 246
Moniac, David 319–20, 326
Moniac, Samuel 318, 325
Monmouth, Me. 152
Monroe, Frank 80
Monroe, Mich. 86, 97
Monroe, William 308
Montgomery, Lt. Andrew 339
Montgomery, James 245
Montgomery, Richard 283
Montgomery, QM William 357
*Montreal* 182, 189
Montréal, Can. 11, 138
Montresor, Capt. John (Br.) 157
Montreuil, Marie 345
Mooers, Gen. Benjamin 197–8
Moore, Allen 191, 193
Moore, QM Nimrod 192
Moore, QM Robinson 210
Moore, Capt. Samuel 23
Moore, Stephen 8
Moore, Thomas 305
Moore, Col. William 53
Morass, Ignace 80
Moraviantown, Can. 125
Moreau 199
Morgan, Benjamin 344, 349, 354
Morgan, Gen. David 339, 346, 356–7
Morgan, Gen. George 354
Morris, Capt. Charles 57–9
Morrison, Jesse 308
Morrison, Maj. John 155
Morrison, Lt.-Col. Joseph 138
Morrison, Thomas 205
Morristown, New Jersey 24
Morse, John 41
Morsel, William 303
Mullany, QM Col. James 197
Mullican, Mr. 269
Mundy Point, Va. 223, 242, 246, 251
Munger, Gen. Edmund 126
Murray, Capt. Elias 80
Murray, Dr. George, Esq. 216
Murray, Col. John 134
Murray, Thomas 287
Muscogee 318
Muse, Col. Lawrence 250, 300
Muse, Maj. Samuel 301
Myers, Capt. Mordecai 151
Myers, Moses & Son 215

*Nancy* 294
Napier, Benjamin 206
Napier, Joseph 206
Napoleon, Emperor 273, 282
Nash, Dr. Ira 308
Nashville, Tenn. 312, 315, 323
*Natchez* 338
Natchez, Miss. 336, 338
Navarre, Capt. Francis 91
Navarre, Isadore 123

Navarre, Peter 89
Navy Department 8
Navy Yard Rifles 262
Naylor, Capt. Joshua 230
Neal, Elizabeth 130
Neal, Pvt. Hosea 130
Neale, Christopher 303
Neale, Francis Lt. 229
Nevison, John 224
New Ireland 54
New London, Conn. 40, 50–1, 53
*New Orleans* 338
New Orleans, La. 316, 332; sufferers 340–3
New Utrecht, New York 43
New York City 38
New York Regiment 134
New York State Artillery 149
Newark 125, 132
Newark, Can. 14, 132, 134
Newark, New York 147
Newfane, New York 181
Newman, Col. Francis 239
Newport, Ky. 311
Newport, Rhode Is. 35
Newton, William 58
*Niagara* 13, 64, 100, 189, 209
Niagara 14, 67, 128, 133, 149, 151, 161, 181, 205, 315
Niagara, Can. (Newark) 134
Niagara Frontier claims 135
Niagara-on-the-Lake, Can. 14, 132, 181
Niagara River 132
Niagara Sufferers 177
Niantic River, Conn. 52
Nicholls, Caleb 199
Nichols, Col. Robert 12
*Nighthawk* 208
Nimmo, William 223, 257
19th Dragoons (Br.) 201
19th Regiment of Infantry 103, 123
95th Rifle Brigade 333
9th Regiment New York Militia 191
9th Regiment of Infantry 142, 151
Nixon, Artemas 47
Noel, Col. Jacob 120
Nomini Creek, Va. 244
Norfolk, Va. 9, 213, 215–16, 224, 257, 301
Norris, Capt. John 110
North Bay, New York 24
North Hero Island 49
North Point, Md. 214, 236, 281
North West Company 100–1
Northern Lt. Edmund 304
Northern Neck, Va. 242
Northport, Me. 54
Northum, Capt. Edward 255
Norton, James 158
Nostrand, Andrew 40
Nottingham, Md. 234, 265, 298
Nourse, Capt. Joseph (Br.) 260
Nuttrill, Sarah 232

O'Bannon, Presley 310
O'Brien, Frederick 286
Ogden, Capt. Peter 354
Ogden, Samuel 24
Ogden, Thomas 18
Ogdensburg 20, 24–5
O'Harra, Arthur 123
*Ohio* (storeship) 13
Ohio 114
Ohio River 120, 312, 316
Ojibwe 10
Old French Barracks 25
Oldham, Capt. Edward 216
Oldham, Sgt. Thomas 254
Oliver, William 111–12, 128, 302, 326
*Oliver Spear* 58
Olympian Springs, Ky. 312
102nd Regiment New York Militia 31
103rd Regiment of Foot 142
104th New Brunswick Regiment of Foot 132–3
109th Virginia Regiment 250
111th Regiment Virginia Militia 242
137th Regiment New York Militia 191
164th Regiment New York Militia 167, 173
O'Neal, William 257
*Oneida* 11, 13, 14, 30
Oneida 189
Oneida Circuit Court 188
O'Neill, Lt. John 217, 220
O'Neill, Matilda 217
O'Neill, Col. Richard 200
O'Niel, Col. 201
Onondaga 160
Ontario 183
Orr, James 295, 303
Orr & Greely 128
Ostrander, Lt. Philip 113
Oswegatchie River 24
Oswego, New York 21, 136, 182, 187–8
Oswego Falls 185–6, 189
Oswego River 182, 183
Otis, John 190
Ottawa 75, 125
Otter Creek, Vt. 46
Owen, Abel 48
Owing, Col. Thomas 312
Oyster Shell, Va. 247

*Packet* 294
Paddock, Col. Joseph 110
Painter, Sgt. Isaac 127
Pakenham, Gen. Sir Edward 340
Palmer, Judge John 202
Palmer, Col. Joseph 304, 304
Parish, Jasper 176
Parkenham, Maj.-Gen Sir Richard 351
Parker, Col. Alexander 242, 251
Parker, John 254
Parker, Peter 143
Parker, Capt. Sir Peter 256, 278, 280
Parker, Col. Richard 245–6, 251
Parkhill, Jacob 339
Parks, Elias 183
parole 12
Parran, Richard 229
Parris, Capt. Alexander 197
Parsons, Thomas 333
Partridge, Sarah 285
Pascal, Matthew 295
Passamaquoddy, Me. 55–7
Patapsco River 286
Patchen, Ralph 42–3
Patterson, Comm. Daniel 335, 346, 349, 356
Patterson, John 243
Patterson, William & Sons 294
Pattison, James 228, 231
Patuxent River 214
Payne, Jeremiah 110
Payne, Gen. John 88
Payson, Henry & Co. 294
Pearce, Lt. George 187
Pearl River, La. 335
Pearsall, Jacob 42
Pease, Enoch 182
Pease, Joseph 182
Pease, Willys 24
Peck, Ichabod 36, 37
Peck, John 263
Peck, Mary 36
Peckham, Lt. Paul 74–5
Peddie, Lt. John 333
Pellet, John 356
Penderghast, Sgt. 163
Pendleton, Joshua 56
*Penelope* 21, 187
Pennell, Lt. Stephen 289
Pennsylvania 209
Pennsylvania Militia 210
Penobscot, Me. 54, 59
Pensacola, Fla. 318, 332
Peoria, Ill. 104; claimants 105–9
Peregrine (slave) 280
Perkins, Capt. Ebenezer 58
Perkins, Joseph 58, 307
Perkins, Gen. Simon 87–8, 117, 122
Perry, Jeremiah 315
Perry, Comm. Oliver 13, 35, 159, 171, 209
Perry, Samuel 158, 320
Perrysburg, Ohio 68
*Perseverance* (cartel) 141
Peru, New York 30
Peter Sky (Indian) 160
Peters, Lt. George 74
Peters, Maj. John 26

Peters, Lt. William 155
Peters, William 118, 203
Peterson, Hannah 211
Peterson, Samuel 212
Petite Coquilles 332
Petteboug, Conn. 50
Phelps, Sylvester 48
Phelps & Landon 48
Phelps, New York 30
Philadelphia 211, 216
Phipps, Curtis 74
Piatt, John 128
Piatt, Capt. William 130
Piatt & Wallace 129
Pierce, Gad 136
Pierce, J. 323
Pierce, James 76
Pierce, Samuel 137
Pierce, William 323
Pierson, Capt. Silas 23
Pig Point, Md. 262
Pigeon Roost, Ind. 110
Pike, Pvt. Ignatius 240
Pike, Gen. Zebulon 17, 20, 44
Pinckney, Gen. Thomas 325
Pindell, Capt. Philip 258
Piney Point 225
Pinkney, Maj. William 282
Piqua, Ohio 112, 124
Piquet, Abbé François 24
pirates 332
Piscataqua, Me. 62
Piscataway, Md. 298
Pitcher, Lewis 56
Pitot, Judge James 355
Pitt, Capt. 251
Pittsburgh 12
Pitzer, Maj. Anthony 120
Place, Griffin 139
Plater, Pvt. George 239
Platt, Judge Charles 202
Platt, Levi 202
Platt, Nathaniel 198
Platt, William 197
Platt, Zephaniah, Sr. 198
Plattsburgh, New York 44, 143, 192, 194, 196–200; claimants 203
Plauché, Jean 351
Pleasure House, Va. 223, 257
Plumb, Samuel 42–3
Plummer, Gerard 303
Plummer, Gerome 303
Plunkett, Capt. James 262
Pogue, Col. Robert 125, 129
Point Albino, Can. 158
Point au Roche, New York 46
Point Peter, Ga. 330
Polhemus, QM Henry 155
Pollock, John 313
*Polly* 58
Polly, Capt. John 27
Pomeroy, Ralph 162
Pontchartrain du Détroit 8, 67
Pool, Asa 23
Popham, Capt. Stephen 182, 189
*Porcupine* 13
Portage River 119, 122, 159, 186
Porter, Augustus 158
Porter, Capt. David 269
Porter, Capt. Moses 8
Porter, Gen. Peter 133, 140, 158, 160, 174, 176
Portland, Me. 55
Portsmouth, Ohio 120
Posey, George 229
Posey, Capt. Thornton 131
Posner, Joseph 329
Posner, Sylvia 329
Potomac Flotilla 214
Potomoc Creek 273
Pottawatomi 75, 103, 112, 309
Potter, Herman 170, 176–7
Potter, Joseph 37
Powell, Cuthbert 278
Powell, Thomas 278
Prairie du Chien, Wisc. 125
Pratt, Joseph 193
Pratt, Samuel 166–7
Prentiss, Samuel 75
Prentiss, Pvt. Stephen 52–3
Prescott, Can. 28
Prescott, Col. William 140
*President* (cartel) 46, 265
Presqu'Ile, Penn. 12
Preval, Gallien 347
Prévost, Maj.-Gen. Sir George 134, 182, 199
Price, Ann 211
Price, Maj. Henry 126
Price, John 211
Prince, Pvt. Casper 283
*Prince Regent* 14, 189
*Princess Charlotte* 189
Principio Ironworks 221
Pring, Cdr. Daniel 47
Prior, Mr. 336
Pritchett, Capt. John 262
Proctor, Gen. Henry 69, 71, 85–6
Proctor, Capt. Richard 329
Provincial Artillery 134
Provincial Marine 14
Purkill, Jacob 340
Pursers 1
Put-in-Bay, Lake Erie 158
Putnam, Col. Rufus 114

Québec, Can. 14
Queenston, Can. 133, 134, 151, 156, 161; Heights 176
Queenstown, Md. 256
Quinn, Edward 156

Race, Andrew 118–19
Radford, Jenkin 9
Ragged Point, Va. 295
Raisin River 63, 68, 84, 90, 97–8, 119, 122
Rambo, Cpl. Peter 315
*Ramilies* 39
Ramsay, Capt. Robert (Br.) 245
Randal, Maj. Beale 285–6
Randall, James 215
Randolph, Peter 315
Randon, John 323
Randon, Peter 323
Raney, John 130
Ransom, Elias 178
Ransom, Lewis 204
Rapine, Daniel 272
Rappahannock River 300
Ray, Cornelius 19
Read, Lt. George 215
Red River 316
Ree, Capt. John 35
Reed, QM Duncan 66
Reed, Gen. Philip 42, 256, 280
Reed, Rufus, Esq. 11
Reed, William 12
Reeder, Richard 241
Reeder, William 241
Reeland, Joseph 98
Rees, Maj. James 197
refugees 123
Reid, Capt. Duncan 75, 78
Relf, Richard 344, 349, 354
Renick, Col. James 117
Renner, Daniel 274
Renner, Mary 274
Renner & Heath 274
Renshaw, Capt. James 46
Rescaneire, Peter 295
Reynolds, Joseph 229
Rhea, Capt. James 102, 112
Rial, Gen. Philip 150
Rice, William 59
Rich, Charles 193
Richard, the Rev. Gabriel 76
Richardson, James (Br.) 34
Richaud, John 57
Richelieu River 46, 196
Richmond Bath 329
Richmond Baths, Va. 329
Ricker, Sgt. Isaac 74
Riddle, Lt. David 151, 162
Ridgley, Lt. John 219
Rigden, James 141
Ringgold, Tench 274
Ritchie, Col. Archibald 300–01
Rivière aux Écorces 138
Robbins, Gurdon 50
Robert, Francis 91–2
Robert, Philip 44
Roberts, Benjamin 38
Roberts, Capt. Charles 12
Roberts, Maj. John 194
Roberts, William 38
Robertson, Edward 356
Robeson, Capt. William 64
Robinson, Daniel 78, 85
Robinson, Maj.-Gen. Frederick 199
Robinson, John 127
Robinson, Capt. John 64

Rock River 130, 308
Rockhill, Pvt. Joseph 239
Rodriguez, John 351
Rodriguez Canal 351
Rogers, Benjamin 19
Rogers, George 179
Rogers, Comm. John 290
Rogers, Maj. William 31
Rogers, Capt. William L. 225
Romayne, Maj. Benjamin 185
Romayne, Capt. James 183
Ronalds, Lt. Mason 144
Roosevelt, Lt. Thomas 180
Root, John 170
ropewalks 274, 289
*Rosanna* 294
Ross, Charles 330
Ross, John 330
Rose, John, Sr. 273
Ross, Maj.-Gen. Robert (Br.) 213, 258, 265–67, 270, 281; death 282
Ross, QM William 199
Rossel, Joseph 148
Roswell & Wait 191
Rouge River 63
Roughton, John 319
Roughton, William 319
Rouse's Point, New York 44
Rowe, Benjamin 311
Roy, Louis 308–9
Royal Artillery 346
*Royal George* 14
*Royal Oak* 266
Rudd, Theron 15
Ruland, Isaac 90
Russel, Ens. 269
Russell, Gilbert 317, 323
Russell, William, Esq. 27
Rutter, Capt. Solomon 214, 242

Sac 308–9
Sacket, Augustus 11, 21
Sackets Harbor 11, 14, 17, 19, 22, 44, 154, 186, 190–1, 199; claims, 17
Sackrider, Capt. John 191
Saddler, Ens. John 301
Sailley, Peter, Esq. 204
St. Amand, Maj. Aldre 357
St. Armand, Hilaire 345
St. Armand, Louis 345
St. Clair, Gen. Arthur 114
St. John, Ezra 149, 156, 166
St. John, Maj. Stephen 228, 246
St. Johns, New Brunswick 55
St. Joseph Island 12
St. Lawrence River 139
St. Leonard Creek 225; first battle 228; second battle 231; 289
St. Leonard's Creektown, Md. 225, 231, 232
St. Louis, Mo. 308, 334
St. Marie, Mich. 99
St. Marys 87, 129
St. Marys, Ga. 330
St. Mary's, Md. 236
St. Marys, Ohio 87, 100, 129–30
St. Regis, New York 142
*Salina* 11, 12
Salina, New York 11
Salisbury, Vt. 47
*Sally* 294
Salmon River 18, 139
Sampson, William 307
*San Domingo* 10, 222
Sandford, Daniel 23
Sands, Capt. Abraham 321
Sandusky Bay 87
Sandusky River 117
Sandwich, Can. 64–5, 68, 80
Sandy Creek, New York 189
Sandy Hook 40
Sandy Point, Va. 249
Sanford, Sen. Nathan 148
*Saratoga* 46
Sault Sainte Marie, Mich. 99, 215
Saunders, Mary 304
Schley, Maj. William 329
Schlosser 179
Schlosser, Capt. Joseph 179
Scholassie, New York 156
Schoultz & Voegeler 289
Schuyler, Lt. Abraham 144
Schuylkill River 209
*Scioto* 294
Scioto River 120
*Scorpion* 13, 214–15, 223, 263, 283
Scott, Col. Hercules 142, 146
Scott, Lt. James 270
Scott, John 27
Scott, William 126, 168, 174, 249
Scott, Gen. Winfield 141, 267
Scrivener, John 296
*Scudder* 295
Scudder, John 40
Seagrove, Lt. James (Br.) 281
Sears, Mary 219–20
2nd Brigade, 1st Division, Ohio Militia 126
2nd Brigade Pennsylvania Militia 210
2nd Canadian Regiment 199
2nd Independent Company of Foreigners 223
2nd Kentucky Militia 130
2nd Light Dragoons 197
2nd Regiment Essex Militia 88
2nd Regiment Kentucky Militia 130
2nd Regiment Lincoln Militia 181
2nd Regiment Louisiana Militia 351
2nd Regiment Maryland Militia 296
2nd Regiment Michigan Militia 83
2nd Regiment of Infantry 320
2nd Regiment of Leeds Militia 15, 16
2nd Regiment of Rifles 311
2nd Regiment Ohio Militia 68, 116–17, 120, 129
2nd Regiment Virginia Militia 330
2nd U.S. Artillery 141
Secord, James and Laura 133
Seely, Mr. 163
Selby, Jesse 230
Seminole 317
*Seneca* 14
Sergeant, Antoine 97, 123
Sergeant, Henry 23
Settle, QM William 304
17th Regiment Maryland Militia 230
17th Regiment of Infantry 68, 79, 112
7th Military District 330, 340, 347, 357
7th Regiment Kentucky Militia 129
7th Regiment of Artillery 149
7th Regiment of Infantry 130, 150
71st Regiment New York Militia 31, 35
Sevierville, Tenn. 315
Sewall, Clement 272
Sewall, Judge David 55
Sewall, Henry 267
Sewall, Maj. James 216
Sewall, Robert 267
Seymour, QM Maj. Henry 27
Shackelford, Capt. Charles 274
Shade, Lt. William 24
Shaker Prairie, Ind. 111
Sharp, David 171
Sharp, Peter 139
Shaver, Capt. Nicholas 121
Shaw, Basil 339
Shaw, Comm. John 334
Shaw, Jones 54
Shaw, Joshua 283
Shawnee 68, 112
Sheckley, John 9
Shelburne Bay 46
Shelby 71, 79, 84
Shelby, Gov. Issac 310
Sheldon, Capt. William 173
Shepard, Peletiah 206
Sherbrooke, Gen. Sir John 58
Sherwood, Capt. (Br.) 144
Shields, Thomas 333
Shinnick, Jacob 289
Shirden's Point, Md. 259
Shute, William 193
Sibley, Solomon, Esq. 79, 84
Sigemond, Arthur 327–8
Sigourney, Mid. James 223

Sills, Joseph 175
Simmance, John 327
Simmoice (Indian) 326
Simmons, Capt. Thomas 296–7
Simpkins, Cpl. Eli 283
Simpson, Maj. Richard 221
Sims, QM 127
Sinclair, Comm. Arthur 100
Sisson, Elisha 34
6th Maryland Cavalry District 283, 285
6th Regiment Baltimore Militia 282
6th Regiment Connecticut Militia 53
6th Regiment Maryland Cavalry District 283
6th Regiment Maryland Militia 283
6th Regiment of Infantry 144, 151, 196, 199
6th Regiment Virginia Militia 301
64th Regiment New York Militia 41
Sizemore, Arthur 326
Skinner, Alexander 243
Skinner, John 216, 222, 297
Skirver, William 281
Sky, Peter (Indian) 160
Slaughter, Francis 96
slaves 233, 238, 240, 245, 278, 280, 338, 345, 357
Slippery Hill, battle 256
Small, Col. Jacob 244
Smart, Robert 77, 79
Smith, Aaron 193, 193
Smith, Aaron, Jr. 193
Smith, Catherine 43
Smith, Francis 302
Smith, Henry 56
Smith, James 293, 311
Smith, John 259, 261
Smith, Pvt. John 123
Smith, John (deserter) 123
Smith, John L. 51, 180
Smith, Col. Melancton 197, 200, 202
Smith, Nathan 37
Smith, Neal 325
Smith, Paca 221
Smith, Lt. Col. Richard 19
Smith, Robert 75
Smith, Gen. Samuel 283, 285, 290
Smith, Samuel H. 278
Smith, Lt. Sidney 46
Smith, Thomas 43
Smith, Col. Thomas 317
Smith, Col. William 220
Smith, Zachary 349
Smith & Buchanan 294
Smithland, Ky. 313
Smoot, Benjamin 320
Smoot & Darling 320
Smyth, Gen. Alexander 175
Smyth, Richard 66, 77
Snelling, Capt. Josiah 75
Snow, Isaac 54
Snyder, John 290
Snyder, Gov. Simon 211
Sodus, New York 30
Sollers, Elisha 285
Sollers, Juliet 285
Sollers Point, Md. 285
Solo, Pierre 75
Solomon (slave) 280
Solomon, Purser Ezekiel 209
Solomons, Levi 161
Solomon's Town, Ohio 125, 130
Sothoron, Capt. James 236, 303
South Hero, Vt. 48
Southerlin, Mr. 275
Spalding, Erastus 138
Spalding, Francis 240
Spalding, QM Sgt. Thomas 239
Spanish East Florida 317
Sparrow, Stephen 166
*Speedwell* 265
Spencer, Capt. Robert 333
Spencer, Col. William 288
Spencer, William 231, 234
Spesutie Island 217
Spey, Capt. George 289
Spilsbury, Capt. Francis 183, 189
Spoko Hauge (Indian) 318
Sprague, Col. Anthony 137
Sprigg, Robert 336
Sprigg, Thomas 289
Spring Wells, MIich. 75, 77–8, 161
Stackpole, Capt. Hassard 216
Standiford, QM Daniel 48
Stansbury, Capt. Tobias 283, 285
Stansbury, William 285
*Statira* 216
Ste. Geneviéve, Mo. 307
Ste. Marie, Mich. 99
Steanburgh, Richard 45
Stephenson, Col. Mills 120
Sterett, Capt. James 283
Sterrett, Samuel 293
Steubenville, Ohio 336
Stevenson 116
Stewart, Capt. Charles 213
Stickney, Benjamin 112
Stiggins, George 322–23, 326
Stiles, George 291, 294
Stiles, John 291, 293, 303
Stockton, Capt. George 311
Stockton Station, Ky. 312
Stoddard, Robert 31
Stoddert, Benjamin 8, 278, 320
Stokes, William 219
Stone, Sgt. Bennet 239
Stone, George 229
Stone, Capt. Isaac 173
Stone, Col. Joel 16
Stoney Creek 132
Stony Point 18, 185
Strachan, John 9
Straughan, John 9
Stricker, Gen. John 282–3
Stuart, Gen. Philip 235–36, 257
Stubblefield, James 258, 269
Sturgeon's Creek, Can. 84
Sturgeon's Point, Lake Erie 158
*Success* 54
Sugar House Wharf, Md. 294
Sumner, Henry 294
Sumner, Pvt. Landy 310
Sumner, Capt. William 127
*Superior* 186, 189; anchor cable 190
Susquehanna River 217
Sutton, Col. David 65, 116
Sutton, Capt. Joseph 120–1
Suzare, Française 98
*Swallow* 295
Swann, Frances 298
Swann, William 298
Swanton, Jonathan 53
Swartout, QM Robert 23, 139, 142, 208
Swayze, Capt. Isaac 133
Sweet, Capt. William 75
Sweetland, Elizabeth 196
Swett, Daniel 56
Swift, Jonathan 278
Swift, Col. Joseph 39, 42–3, 139
Swift, Col. Philetus 30, 32, 35, 174
*Sylph* 13

Tallapoosa River 319
Tallassee Thicksico 318
Taney, Augustine 287
Taney, Col. Michael 225, 228, 246, 259–61
Tappahannock, Va. 299
Tarvin, Richard 324
Tate, David 320, 326
Taylor, Ephraim 29
Taylor, Henry 262
Taylor, QM James 69, 71, 115
Taylor, Jane 262
Taylor, Capt. John 64
Taylor, Philip 279
Taylor, QM Col. Richard 313, 355
Taylor, Capt. Robert 257
Taylor, Gen. Robert 215, 224
Taylor, Gen. Zachary 223
Tazewell, Littleton 224
*Teazer* 1
Tebbs, Capt. Foushee 304
Tecumseh (Indian) 9, 68, 87, 318
Teel, John 209
Teeters, Lt. John 116
*Telegraph* 295, 303
*Temperance* 295
*Tempest* 205
Templeman, Samuel 245
Tennessee 315, 317
Tennessee Militia 323

Tensaw Lake, Ala. 320
Tensaw River, Ala. 322
10th Military District 277
10th Regiment Kentucky Mounted Volunteers 311
10th Regiment of Infantry 48, 196
Terry, Enos 126
3rd Brigade Maryland Militia 282
3rd Division Maryland Militia 283
3rd Regiment Connecticut Militia 53
3rd Regiment Drafted Ohio Militia 121
3rd Regiment Louisiana Militia 351
3rd Regiment New York Militia 191
3rd Regiment of Infantry 116, 317
3rd Sub Legion 75
3rd U.S. Artillery 182, 186
13th Regiment of Infantry 143–5, 151, 196
30th Regiment Maryland Militia 221
31st Regiment Maryland Militia 228, 230
31st Regiment of Infantry 142
32nd Regiment of Infantry 101
33rd Regiment Connecticut Militia 52–3
33rd Regiment Maryland Militia 288
33rd Regiment of Infantry 196
34th Regiment of Infantry 55, 75, 196
36th Maryland Militia 230, 288
36th Regiment New York Militia 194
36th Regiment of Infantry 227, 238
37th Regiment Virginia Militia 223, 248, 254
39th Regiment Maryland Militia 244
39th Regiment New York Militia 31
Thom, Capt. John 330
Thomas, Capt. Arthur 124
Thomas, Charles 60–2
Thomas, Enos 130
Thomas, QM Col. James 172, 177, 196
Thomas, Gen. John 313, 355
Thomas, Joseph 205
Thomas, Gen. Philemon 331
Thomas, John & Co. 128
*Thomas Wilson* 295
Thomaston, Me. 54
Thompson, Elizabeth 244
Thompson, Mrs. George 245
Thompson, Col. John 210
Thompson, Jonah 278
Thompson, Richard 127
Thompson, Samuel 148
Thorn, James 21
Thornton, Dr. 294
Thornton, John 120
Thornton, John G. 56
Thorold, Ont. 132–3
Thorp House 25
Thrasher, N. 76
Thurber, Ezra 46
Tice, Elizabeth 140
Tice, Frederick 140
Tiernan, Michael 368
Tilghman, Capt. Matthew 289
Tilghman Island, Md. 296
Tillard, Capt. William 298
Tilliard, Col. Samuel 303
Tincombe, George 9
Tingey, Comm. Thomas 214, 263, 270, 294
Tippecanoe 9, 75
Tipton, Capt. John 110
Tiscom, Samuel 179
tobacco 226, 230–31, 237, 239, 252, 296–7; warehouses 298
Tobey, Capt. Charles 154, 205
Todd, Pvt. Bernard 283
Todd, Charles 266
Todd, Dr. John 93
Todd, Mary and children 283
Toledo, Ohio 99
Tombigbee River, Ala. 317
Tompkins, Gov. Daniel 11, 28, 30, 157
Tongue, James 296–8
*Tonnant* 265, 274
Toomy, Lt. Michael 315
Topp, John 315
Toronto, Can. (York) 10, 44
Torrence, William 80
Toulmin, Judge Harry 318, 322
Toulouse 320
Toussaint Island 29
Town Point, Md. 296–9
Townsend, John 172
Townsend, Col. Nathan 171
Townsend, Bronson & Co. 186
Towson, Gen. Nathaniel 267
Tracey's Landing, Md. 296–8
Tracy, Col. Freeman 53
Trainer, David, Sr. 211
Travers, Capt. Henry 254
Travers, Capt. John 228
Travers, Pvt. Thomas 227–8
Treasury Department 7
treaties: Fort Jackson 325; Fort Wayne 9; Ghent 306; Jay 24
Tredwell, Thomas 203
Trescott, Lemuel 55
Trimble, Dr. James 211
*Trimmer* 215
Trombly, Anthony 44
Trowbridge, Dr. Amasa 207–8
Truman, Edward 229
Trupeville, New York 36
Tryon, William 22
Tuckabatchee, Ala. 318
Tuckerman, Jacob 21
Tupper, Gen. Benjamin 65
Tupper, Col. Edward 87
Tupper, Percia 171
Tupper, Samuel 171
Turberville, Maj. John 252
Turkey Point 123, 216
Turner, Lt. Daniel 215
Turner, Pvt. Isaac 283
Turner, Samuel 232
Turrill, Hon. Joel 15
Tuttle, Dennis 184
Tuttle & Baker 184
12th Regiment Maryland Militia 239
12th Regiment of Infantry 177
20th Regiment Connecticut Militia 53
20th Regiment of Infantry 177
21st Regiment of Infantry 14, 152, 205
22nd Brigade New York Infantry 41
23rd Regiment New York Militia 25
23rd Regiment of Infantry 143, 199, 215
24th Brigade New York Militia 30
24th Regiment of Infantry 315
25th Regiment of Infantry 152, 156
26th Regiment of Infantry 80
27th New York Regiment 11
27th Regiment Maryland Militia 244
28th Regiment of Infantry 80, 83–4, 312
29th Regiment of Infantry 37, 196, 199, 203
Tyler, Isaac 156
Tyler, Pres. John 235
Tyson, Nathan 293

Ulmer, Col. Jacob 60
Ulmer, Philip 61–2
Underhill, William 192
Underwood, Hon. Joseph 311
U.S. Light Dragoons 142, 172, 198
U.S. Rifle Corps 24, 190
Upper Canada Militia 134
Upper Marlboro, Md. 258, 265, 298
Upper Marlborough Town, Md. 265, 298
Upper Sandusky, Ohio 87, 127
Urbana, Ohio 65, 122, 128
Utica, New York 23

Valentine, J. 293
Valentine, James 45

Van Brunt, George 43
Van Brunt, Rulif 40
Vance, Jacob 121
Vandenburgh, David 131
Van Hoevenberg, Dr. Henry 153
Van Horn, James 181
Van Horne, Maj. Thomas 68
Van Ness, Cornelius 13
Van Rensselaer, Col. Solomon 150
Van Rensselaer, Gen. Stephen 132, 156, 177
Vansicklin, John, Jr. 48
Van Vleek, Benjamin 16
Vaughan, William 23
Vaughn, Sailing Master William 14, 185
Vaughn, William C. 322
*Venture* 55
Vera Cruz 357
Vergennes, Vt. 46
*Vermont* 1, 44
*Vesuvius* 337
Viales, Lt. Louis 357
*Victory* 57–8
*Victory* (prize) 57
Vienna, Md. 305
*Vigilant* 214
Villard, Andrew 271
Villeré, Gabriel 333
Villeré, Gen. Jacques 333, 345–6
Vincennes, Ind. 68, 307
Vincent, Gen. John 85
Virginia Militia 215
Visscher, Sebastian 22
Vleek, Benjamin 16
Vose & Worthington 293
Vroman, Gabriel 29
Vroman, Peter 29

Wabash River 110, 114
Wadington, Joshua 19
Wadsworth, Col. Decius 271, 277
Wadsworth, Gen. Elijah 117
Wadsworth, Gen. William 151
Wafer, Thomas 34
Wagstaff, Samuel 128, 204
Wainwright, Capt. John 274
Wait, Edward 191
Waldoborough, Me. 61
Walker, Maj. James 229
Walker, Samuel 212
Wallace, George 128
Waller, Henry 278, 281
Walters, Lt. Aaron 197
Walters, Richard 294
Walworth, Reuben 203
War Department 7, 43
War Hawks 9
Ward, Capt. 184
Ward, Samuel 186
Ware, William 9
Warfield, Capt. David 236
Waring, William 300
Warren, Capt. Clark 183
Warren, Adm. Sir John 10, 213, 223, 299
Warren, Nathan 294
Warren, Stephen 157
Warren, Thomas 216
Warwick (slave) 357
Washington, George 249
Washington, William 272
Washington Bridge Co. 278
Washington City 211, 213, 231, 258, 262, 269; attack 270, 274; bridges 277; 290
Washington Hotel 278
Washington Navy Yard 263, 270
Waters, M.C. 61
Watertown, New York 143
Watson, Capt. Horace 186
Watson, QM John 319
Watson, Joseph 203
Watson, William Ens. 80
Watts, QM Richard 261
Wayne 102, 112
Wayne, Gen. Anthony 63, 68, 111, 126
Weatherford, John 326
Weatherford, William 317
Weaver, Lt. John 130
Webb, John 173
Webb, Joseph 173
Webster, Sailing Master John 231, 263
Weeks, George 44
Weir, Robert 301
Wellford, Dr. Horace 304
Wellington 24
Wells, Pvt. Daniel 282
Wells, Mary 114
Wells, Col. Samuel 68, 87, 112
Wells, Capt. William 102, 113
West, Richard 267
West Niagara, Can. 132
West Point 8, 63
Westphal, Lt. George 217
Wetmore, Collin 207
Whalen, Charles 139
Whann, Maj. Adam 238
Wheatley, William 240
Wheeler, George 58
Wheeler, Samuel 51, 57
Whipple, Russell 137
Whistler, Maj. John 71, 113
Whitaker, Seymour 170
White, Gardner 143
White Hall, New York 46
Whitman, Capt. John 40
Whitridge, Dr. Joshua 151, 191
Whitsett, Gen. William 310
Whittlesey, Elisha 193, 206
Wickham, William 35
Wightman, Capt. Asa 53
Wiley, Albert 44
Wiley, James 44
Wiley, Mary 44
Wiley, Oliver 44
Wiley, Stephen 44
Wilkinson, David 167, 175
Wilkinson, Jacob 119
Wilkinson, Gen. James 11, 16, 118, 139, 143, 168, 193, 202, 208
Wilkinson, John 174
Will, John 340
Willcocks, Col. Joseph 180
Willcocks, Lt-Col. Joseph 181
William (slave) 280
Williams, Henry 316
Williams, John 76
Williams, John R. 161
Williams, Lewis 84
Williams, William 221
Williamsburg, Va. 223
Williamson, James 216
Williamsville, New York 157, 174
Willis, Anthony 311
Willis, Maj. Perrin 36
Willson, David 287
Wilmer, William 279
Wilmot, Ens. John 236
Wilshorn, George 127
Wilson, Capt. Benjamin 286
Wilson, Capt. Henry 283
Wilson, John 61
Wilson, Luther 182
Wilson, Reuben 182
Wilson, New York 182
Wimp, Capt. James 116
Winchester 87, 128
Winchester, Gen. James 76, 86–7, 90, 112, 122, 315
Winchester, Ky. 313
Winder, Gen. William 258, 266, 269, 277
Wing, John 158
Winimac (Indian) 112
Winter, Elisha 30
Winteringer, Nathan 336
Witherell, Maj. James 75, 119
Withers, Thomas 310
Wolverton, Stephen 158
Wood, Maj. Eleazer 125
Wood, William 259
Woodburn, Capt. William 237
Woodland, Richard 264
Woodward, Col. Augustus 66
Woolsey, Capt. Melancthon 11, 14, 185, 189; claim, 196
Worrall, Gen. Isaac 211
Worthington, Dr. Charles 277
Worthington, Henry 294
Worthington, Gen. Thomas 112–13
Wright, Capt. Elijah 190
Wright, Lt. Joel 172
Wright, John 285
Wyandot 75, 89, 124
Wyandot, Ohio 117
Wynn, Edward 294
Wyvill, Sgt. Walter 296

Yates, Maj. Robert 251
Yeaton, QM Capt. Hopley 216
Yeo, Comm. Sir James 34, 182, 189
Yeocomico Creek, Md. 223, 242; landing 246
York, Can. 10, 44
York, Joseph 26
York, Lavinia 26
Young, Col. Guilford 37
Young, Lt. James 144
Young, Gen. Robert 303

www.ingramcontent.com/pod-product-compliance
Lightning Source LLC
LaVergne TN
LVHW060022210926
848481LV00013B/3763
* 9 7 8 1 4 7 6 6 5 8 5 9 9 *